Biomass, Capitalism, and Hegemony

Biomass, Capitalism, and Hegemony

A Rich and Powerful History

Benoit Daviron

BLOOMSBURY ACADEMIC
LONDON • NEW YORK • OXFORD • NEW DELHI • SYDNEY

BLOOMSBURY ACADEMIC
Bloomsbury Publishing Plc
50 Bedford Square, London, WC1B 3DP, UK
1385 Broadway, New York, NY 10018, USA
29 Earlsfort Terrace, Dublin 2, Ireland

BLOOMSBURY, BLOOMSBURY ACADEMIC and the
Diana logo are trademarks of Bloomsbury Publishing Plc

First published in 2020 in France as *Biomasse* by Éditions Quae
First published in Great Britain 2025

Copyright © Benoit Daviron, 2025

Benoit Daviron has asserted his right under the Copyright,
Designs and Patents Act, 1988, to be identified as Author of this work.

Cover design by Grace Ridge
Cover image: Castile and Leon. Spain. 16th century engraving
© PRISMA ARCHIVO via Alamy Stock Photo

This work is published open access subject to a Creative Commons Attribution-NonCommercial 4.0 International licence (CC BY-NC 4.0, https://creativecommons.org/licenses/by-nc/4.0/). You may re-use, distribute, reproduce, and adapt this work in any medium for non-commercial purposes, provided you give attribution to the copyright holder and the publishers, provide a link to the Creative Commons licence, and indicate if changes have been made.

Bloomsbury Publishing Plc does not have any control over, or responsibility for, any third-party websites referred to or in this book. All internet addresses given in this book were correct at the time of going to press. The author and publisher regret any inconvenience caused if addresses have changed or sites have ceased to exist, but can accept no responsibility for any such changes.

A catalogue record for this book is available from the British Library.

A catalog record for this book is available from the Library of Congress.

ISBN: HB: 978-1-3504-4324-2
       PB: 978-1-3504-4323-5
       ePDF: 978-1-3504-4326-6
       eBook: 978-1-3504-4325-9

Typeset by Integra Software Services Pvt. Ltd.
Printed and bound in Great Britain

To find out more about our authors and books visit www.bloomsbury.com and sign up for our newsletters.

Contents

List of figures	vii
List of tables	x
Acknowledgments	xiv
Introduction	1

Part 1 Where we see the United Provinces build wealth and power by trading distant biomass, 1580–1705

Introduction	21
1 The United Provinces: Territories, resources, and economic sectors	24
2 The Baltics and the North Sea: The first peripheries	31
3 Spices and companies: Trade with another world-economy, Asia	39
Conclusion	44

Part 2 Where we see England pull ahead of France by exploiting its territory and its colonies better, 1700–1846

Introduction	49
4 Mercantilism and the art of counting on your own forces	51
5 Mobilizing resources from the national territory	71
6 Distant biomass and social metabolism	86
Conclusion	99

Part 3 Where Great Britain, now a hegemon, mobilizes the world for its supply of biomass and prompts Europe to imitate her, 1815–1913

Introduction	103
7 A portrait of an English hegemon as a biomass importer	105
8 Overcoming "the tyranny of distance": Technical and institutional innovations	116
9 The golden age of frontiers	124
10 An intensive animal farming pole in Northwestern Europe	133

11 On free labor	138
12 And capital? Key for transport, negligible for agricultural production	154
Conclusion	159

Part 4 Where the rivalry between Germany, the United States, and others gives a key role to the chemical industry, 1865–1945

Introduction	163
13 Germany: On a quest for an industrialization not dependent on long-distance biomass trade	167
14 Imperialist strategies, the weapon of the weak: France and Japan	193
15 The United States: From the legendary frontier to resolution of the long farm crisis	208
Conclusion	227

Part 5 Where we see agriculture, under America's hegemony, become "modern," "conventional," and food-focused, 1945–72

Introduction	231
16 The American model	234
17 Uneven spread of the American model and the institutionalization of the Global North–South division	253
18 International agricultural trade: Limited, food-focused, and administered	278
Conclusion	288

Part 6 American hegemony: Season 2 globalization comes back

Introduction	291
19 The second age of American hegemony	293
20 Reorienting the world	301
21 The "oil-based model" of biomass production and consumption pursues its global conquest	317
22 The incomplete globalization of agricultural markets	336
Conclusion	356
General conclusion	358
Bibliography	365
Index	401

Figures

3.1	Ratio between sales price in Europe and purchase price in Asia for cloves and pepper, 1580–1800	41
5.1	Per capita energy consumption in Great Britain and Wales (cumulative curves), 1560–1815	82
6.1	Biomass imports by Great Britain, 1699–1815 (thousands of £)	87
6.2	British trade balance for wheat (in thousands of quarters)	94
7.1	England, value of biomass imports, 1814–1913	106
7.2	Origin of United Kingdom wheat imports, 1828–1912	111
8.1	Length of rail network in various countries, 1831–1911 (in km, logarithmic scale)	117
8.2	Monthly price of wheat in Liverpool, New York, and Chicago, 1800–1913	123
15.1	The conquest of the west, progress of rail networks in the United States from 1830 to 1890	210
15.2	Gross per capita agricultural production in the United States, 1869–1941 (in constant 1913 $)	215
15.3	Agricultural product exports and imports in the United States, 1869–1941 (in constant 1913 $)	216
16.1	United States and United Kingdom per capita energy consumption, 1830–1972 (gigajoules per capita)	236
16.2	United States, consumption of materials per person and by source, 1870–1973 (ton/person)	239
16.3	United States, per capita GDP and meat consumption, 1909–72	243
16.4	United States, agricultural production (in petajoules), cultivated land area (in millions of acres), and fertilizer consumption (in thousands of tons), 1870–1972	246
16.5	United States, labor productivity index, yields, fertilizer consumption per ha, and accumulated capacity of tractors, 1880–1975 (100 base year in 1935)	246
16.6	United States, balance of per capita biomass and fossil fuels trade (in tons), 1870–1972	251
17.1	Share of the richest 1 percent in national income for various OECD countries, 1905–73	256

17.2	Share of mineral resources in domestic material consumption in various "industrialized countries," 1900–72	257
17.3	Evolutions in yields and labor productivity in various countries, 1930–75 (in wheat ton equivalent)	260
17.4	Per capita GDP in France, Argentina, Ghana, and India, 1820–1980	265
19.1	United States' share of global wealth, 1950–2017	294
19.2	Constant price of oil in the United States, 1940–2018 (1967 dollars)	295
19.3	Growth in labor productivity and wages in the United States, 1948–2013	296
19.4	United States: Average annual income of individuals in the 99–100 and 0–90 percentiles, 1945–2014 ($1,000 of 2017)	298
19.5	Per capita energy consumption (GJ) and material consumption in the United States, 1945–2005	299
20.1	China's share in global income, 1950–2018	307
20.2	China: Consumption, investment, and exports as a % of GDP, 1978–2017	310
20.3	China, United States, and the rest of the world: Steel production, 1980–2017	311
20.4	China, United States, European Union: Energy trade balance (imports–exports) (in millions of oil equivalent tons)	312
20.5	Share of OECD in global income, 1950–2017	314
20.6	Share of various regions in global material consumption, 1950–2010 (in %)	315
20.7	Per capita material consumption, 1950–2010 (ton/year)	316
21.1	Nitrogen fertilizer consumption, 1961–2017 (in millions of tons of nutrients)	319
21.2	Quantity of pesticides used in agriculture in France and in Brazil, 1990–2017 (1,000 tons of active units)	320
21.3	Per capita consumption of pork meat (A) and chicken (B) (in kg/person/year)	329
21.3	*continued* Per capita consumption of corn (C) and soymeal (D) for animal feed (in kg/person/year)	330
22.1	Index of international biomass trade volumes, 1961–2017 (1961=100)	339
22.2	Relative rate of assistance (RRA) to agriculture in various countries, 1955–2010	340
22.3	Agricultural production support in the European Union, China, United States, and Brazil (PSE), in % of gross agricultural income, 1996–2016	341
22.4	Share of Europe and Asia in global biomass imports (intra-EU trade excluded), 1913–2017	342

22.5	Japan's share in global biomass imports	344
22.6	China: Ratio of net imports over consumption for wheat, rice, and corn (secondary cereals)	345
22.7	Volume of China's biomass imports, 1995–2017 (value in dollars deflated using the World Bank price index)	346
22.8	China, trade balance for biomass in value (exports–imports), 1995–2017 (in $ billions)	348
22.9	Share of Japan and of China in global biomass imports (intra-EU trade excluded), 1962–2015	348
22.10	Index of per capita agricultural production, 1961–2014 (100 = 1986–9)	349
22.11	Share of the United States, the European Union, and Cairns Group countries in global food exports (intra-EU and tropical products excluded), 1961–2016	350
22.12	Evolution of number of undernourished persons in the world according to the FAO, in 2009 and in 2013, in the annual report *The State of Food Insecurity in the World*	352
22.13	Index of the international price and of real national prices of cereals, monthly data 2000–18 (100 = January 2000)	353

Tables

1.1	Urbanization rate (in % of total population) of the United Provinces, 1525–1750	26
2.1	Total cereal imports, re-exports and net imports in Amsterdam, 1649–80 (in lasts; 1 last = approximately 2 tons)	32
4.1	Exports plus imports over GDP (%)	52
4.2	Colonies' share (in %) in total imports to England, 1663–1816	55
4.3	Colonies' share (in %) in total imports to France, 1716 and 1787	55
4.4	Trade of "exotic" products from England in the eighteenth century (in thousands of £)	56
4.5	Share of re-exports in total exports from England, 1663–1816 (in % of total exports)	57
4.6	Share of re-exported imported colonial products in France (in %)	58
4.7	Number of slaves transported in the Atlantic by ship nationality, 1519–1800 (in thousands)	61
4.8	Sugar production in the Atlantic region, 1456–1787 (in thousands of tons)	62
4.9	Population and production of French, English, Spanish, and Dutch colonies in the Caribbean, 1788	63
4.10	Net product of colonial goods from Saint-Domingue in France, 1788	63
4.11	Biomass imports in the English Caribbean sourced from English colonies in America, 1768–72 (in £)	69
5.1	Population of the United Provinces, England, and France, 1600–1800	72
5.2	Urban population of England, the United Provinces, and France (% of the total population)	73
5.3	Production of select agricultural products in England, 1600–1849	73
5.4	Urban, rural, and farm populations, 1670–1801 (million inhabitants)	75
5.5	Workforce employed in British agriculture, 1700–1850 (in thousands)	76
5.6	Number of inhabitants for 100 farmers, 1600–1800	81
5.7	Annual coal production in Great Britain and France (in millions of tons)	84
6.1	Composition (in %) of biomass imports by Great Britain, including imports from Ireland, 1699–1816	88
6.2	Composition (in %) of biomass imports by France, 1715–87	89
6.3	Annual average of British cereal trade, 1697–1801 (in thousands of quarters, 1 quarter = 12.7 kg)	93
6.4	Composition of trade in fibers and textiles, 1699–1846 (in thousands of £)	97

7.1	Composition of biomass imports into Great Britain, 1814–1913 (in % of the value of total biomass imports)	107
7.2	Calorific value (in billions of calories) of imports and share in consumption (in %) in the United Kingdom by product, average 1909–13	109
7.3	Average distance covered by different types of agricultural imports of the United Kingdom, 1831–1913 (in miles)	112
7.4	Share of the empire in United Kingdom biomass imports in 1854 and 1913 (as % of total import value)	113
8.1	Length of railroad used	117
8.2	Average transport costs for "developed countries," estimated by Paul Bairoch, and the price of wheat in Liverpool, 1830–1910	118
9.1	Change in cultivated land area, forest areas, and prairie areas between 1850 and 1920 (millions of ha, or 10,000 km^2)	126
9.2	Population densities, 1500–1800 (inhabitants per km^2)	128
9.3	Biomass exports by "continent," 1913 (in % of total world value)	130
10.1	Gross crop and animal production in value (millions of £) and in %	134
10.2	Origin and uses of cereals in the United Kingdom, 1909–13 (in thousands of tons)	134
10.3	United Kingdom: Imports of animal products (in £)	135
10.4	International trade in animal products and products intended for animal feed, 1911–12 (in millions of £)	136
10.5	Main indicators of Danish agriculture, 1870–1913 (in %)	136
10.6	Agricultural productivity index for various European countries (in millions of net calories per male farm worker), 1850–1910	136
11.1	Estimated flows of three types of forced labor, from the nineteenth century to early twentieth century	141
11.2	Market share (in %) of the United States, Brazil, Cuba, and São Tomé in cotton, cane sugar, and cocoa markets, 1790–1900	143
11.3	Destination of African slaves, 1776–1867 (in thousands)	144
12.1	Main destination countries and sectors of United Kingdom foreign investments in 1913 (in % of total)	156
12.2	Geographic and sectoral destination of United Kingdom's foreign investments, 1865–1914	157
I4.1	United Kingdom, Germany, United States: Population, GNP/capita, energy consumption/capita (gigajoules), share of coal in energy consumption, coal and steel production (millions of tons), 1870–1913	164
13.1	Global production of nitrogen fertilizers (in millions of nitrogen equivalent tons), 1860–1913	173
13.2	Quantity of nutrient supplements in German agriculture, 1878–1914 (in kg/ha)	174

13.3	Global output of centrifugal sugar (in thousands of tons)	178
13.4	Germany, consumption and imports of food products and animal feed, 1912–13 (in billions of calories)	180
14.1	Share of the empire in French metropolitan imports of agricultural products (in % of total imports for each product)	199
14.2	Composition of Japan's international trade in 1880 and 1930 (in thousands of yen)	202
14.3	Select agricultural performance indicators in Korea and Taiwan, 1915–39	204
14.4	Rice supply in Japan, 1912–38 (in thousands of *koku*)	205
14.5	Origin of Japanese imports of sugar, rice, and soybean, average for 1934–8 (in %)	205
14.6	Population (in thousands of inhabitants), surface area (in thousands of ha), and soy exports (in thousands of tons) in Manchuria, 1872–1940	207
14.7	Soy beans: Share of Manchuria in global exports and of Japan in global imports (in %)	207
15.1	US agricultural production 1800–1900	212
15.2	Developments in wheat harvesting in the nineteenth century	212
15.3	Yields and labor productivity for wheat, corn, and cotton, 1800–1914	213
15.4	Number of horses and mules, and number of tractors (in thousands), 1913–45	219
16.1	Internationalization rate (exports + imports/GDP) of the United States and the United Kingdom, 1890–1970 (in %)	238
16.2	Contribution of different "sources" to thermal energy supply in the United States, 1850–1973 (in British Thermal Units, BTU)	239
16.3	United States, share provided by biomass in various uses, and share of each of these uses in the total value of biomass consumed (in %), 1900 and 1975	240
16.4	United States, share of various foods in dietary protein intake, 1909–72 (in % of overall protein intake)	241
16.5	United States, consumption of cereals and oilseed meal for animal feed (in millions of tons), 1937–72	242
16.6	United States, shares of various fatty matter in dietary fat intake, 1909–72 (in % of overall fat intake)	242
16.7	United States, consumption of various food products per person 1889–1925	244
16.8	United States, percentage of farms producing the specified plant or animal product	247
16.9	Food system energy balance sheet of the United States in 1940 and in 1970	250
17.1	Annual growth rate in Western Europe and growth rate of wages in France, 1890–1973	255

17.2	Rate of internationalization (exports + imports)/GDP of various European countries and the EEC, 1913–70	258
17.3	Nominal and real rates of assistance to agriculture, 1955–72 (in %)	259
17.4	Energy balance of French agriculture, 1945 and 1975	261
17.5	Growth in GDP per worker in agriculture and in the rest of the economy (1957–68) and labor productivity in 1948 and 1968 of various OECD countries	262
17.6	Per capita material consumption in the main regions of the world (in tons) and as percentage of global total, 1950, 1960, and 1970	266
17.7	Nominal and real rates of assistance to agriculture, 1955–72	267
17.8	Interstate organizations of the global "North" and "South"	272
18.1	Share of biomass in global trade in goods and services (in %)	278
18.2	Share (in %) of various regions in global biomass exports (intra-EEC trade excluded), 1955 and 1972	281
18.3	The three postwar international complexes of food products	284
18.4	Global consumption of main textile fibers, 1929–73 (in thousands of tons, and as a % of global consumption of fibers)	286
18.5	Global consumption of natural and synthetic rubber, 1940–72 (in thousands of tons and % of total)	287
20.1	China, Japan, United Kingdom, United States, and Germany: Per capita GDP (in 1990 dollars) in 1820 and 1950	306
20.2	Distribution of global income by main world region, 1950–2017 (in %, three-year averages)	314
21.1	Nitrogen fertilizer consumption by main global region (in millions of tons)	318
21.2	The six large global agrochemical firms in 2015 and their recomposition	322
21.3	Fertilizer consumption per hectare of cultivated land, 2014–16 average (in kg/ha)	325
21.4	Consumption of various food products by urban and rural populations in China, 1985–2015 (in kg/person/year)	332
21.5	Population and consumption of various biomass in China, as % of global total, 1978–2018	333
21.6	Biofuel production, various countries, 1995–2017 (1,000)	334
21.7	Share of biofuels in consumption of products in various countries, 2015–17	334
22.1	Composition of USSR food imports (in millions of rubles)	337
22.2	Japan: Composition of biomass imports, 1962–2017 (in % of total imports)	343
22.3	China: Main biomass imports (as % of total biomass imports)	347
22.4	Share of China in % of global biomass imports (intra-EU trade excluded), 1995–2017	349

Acknowledgments

The debt I piled up during the decades of reading and reflection exposed in this book are numerous and diverse. Thanks to, above all, my wife, Laure Cordesse. For years, I have been benefiting from her advice, assistance and critical discussion. Without her, the writing of this book would not have been possible. She also drew the illustrations contained in the book at the opening of each part, giving it an aesthetic dimension sadly absent from the text, figures and countless tables.

I have profited greatly from the unwavering support and trust of Paule Moustier, the head of the Cirad research unit where I worked at the end of my career. Moreover, she found the adequate funding for the translation of the French version and an open access publication of the English version.

I also want to thank Yarri Kamara, translator of the French version. The process lasted several years and she stoically accepted the unstable timetables and changing contents.

I am very grateful to the Bloomsbury editorial team for their work and help.

Introduction

This book proposes a stroll through the history of the relationship between power, wealth, and biomass to explain the origins and characteristics of what may be termed "conventional" agriculture,[1] at a time when this model is being increasingly contested with calls for an "agro-ecological transition."

The book's journey starts from a simple (and quite classical) premise: the quest for wealth and power is an essential—if not the sole—engine of history. It is also an observable fact that there can be no accumulation of wealth and power without mobilization of (increasing quantities of) energy and matter. Using this premise and this observation, the book attempts to understand the role that biomass has played over history in supplying the energy and matter indispensable to wealth and power. In this book therefore the relationship with biomass refers both to how biomass is sourced and to how it is used. Agriculture evidently is a source of biomass, but it can also be a consumer of biomass.

I focus on the particular period in human history during which Europe and its North American extension showed great efficiency, with respect to other regions of the world, in the pursuit of wealth and power: that is, the period running from the seventeenth century to the early twenty-first century.

To undertake my analysis, I use the history of this period as presented by various authors inspired by Fernand Braudel: a sequence of phases during which successive hegemons reigned (the United Provinces, the United Kingdom, the United States), interspersed with phases of rivalry between potential successors of each respective hegemon. I attempt to account for the role of biomass—always vital, and yet also in constant regression—of its sources, and its uses under each hegemon. I also borrow from historical narratives proposed by authors interested in social metabolism, that is the flows of energy and matter that drive human societies. According to these narratives, the history of humanity experienced a radical break in the late eighteenth century when, under what is now commonly called the Industrial Revolution, the

---

[1] The use of the term "conventional" to qualify twentieth-century agriculture delegitimizes the desire one may have to break with this kind of agriculture, and also shrouds the fact that this model of farming is very recent. The term was coined in order to distinguish from "organic" farming. Had, for example, the term "chemical farming" been chosen instead, a different reaction would certainly have been elicited. As we will see, the two pillars of this "convention" are the specialization of agriculture on food production and, above all, its unprecedented dependence on products taken from underground, the main one being oil.

metabolism of Europe, and then progressively all of humanity, became increasingly dependent on resources taken from the underground, notably coal and oil.

My postulate therefore is that it is necessary to interrogate the relationship that hegemonic powers had with regard to biomass in order to analyze the logics that drove changes in agriculture.

Widening the food regime approach: Agriculture and the quest for power

The historical approach proposed by the food regime perspective serves as a major source of inspiration for this book. I have gratefully borrowed from this school the idea that it is possible to think about the transformations of agriculture in relation with the sequence of world hegemons.

In their foundational paper, Harriet Friedmann and Philip McMichael, the theorists of food regime, use the concept to characterize international exchange in food products based on different regimes of capital accumulation (Friedmann and McMichael, 1989). Taking inspiration from Michel Aglietta (Aglietta, 1976), they distinguish the extensive accumulation of the nineteenth century, based on incorporating increasing quantities of labor into wage work, from the intensive accumulation of the mid-twentieth century, founded on mass consumption. These two phases in the history of capitalism are marked by the successive hegemonies of the United Kingdom, followed by the United States. Two food regimes are thus described, and within each, agriculture plays a specific role in accumulation. In the first food regime, agriculture is subordinated to industrialization and provides cheap food products, and through rural migration, workers for industry. Under the second food regime, agriculture constitutes a market for products of industry (farm machinery, chemical inputs). The change in the nature of exchange of agricultural products over the two periods is a consequence of this transformation in the role of agriculture. In the nineteenth century, the United Kingdom imported massive quantities of cheap food products from new countries of European settlement, thus ruining its own agriculture. The United States, after the Second World War, achieved a state of permanent overproduction and exported its surpluses in the form of food aid to countries of the Third World.[2]

Use of the food regime concept and its definition have evolved since the 2000s, with some ambiguity and confusion. The question of international trade has lost prominence in favor of a wider and more abstract interrogation of the contribution of agriculture to capital accumulation. "Food regime analysis brings a structured perspective to the understanding of agriculture and food's role in capital accumulation across time and space," writes Philip McMichael in 2009 (McMichael, 2009: 140). This

---

[2] Each food regime also gives rise to two contradictory movements with regard to the "national question." The first regime saw the apogee of colonization of pre-capitalist societies by Europeans and the rise of the nation-state system. The second regime saw both the consolidation of nation-state system and its challenge by the transnationalization of the agricultural sector by agribusiness capital.

use of the food regime concept has led many authors (Giménez and Shattuck, 2011; Pechlaner and Otero, 2008; Burch and Lawrence, 2009; Pritchard, 1998), following McMichael (2005, 2009, 2013), to announce the advent of a third food regime, qualified as the corporate, or sometimes neoliberal, regime, whose organizing principles are the market, competition, and firms (McMichael, 2016: 649).[3]

This book tries to widen the food regime approach in two ways. Firstly, it does not attempt to explain history with sole reference to capitalism. No doubt capitalism—understood as the logic of "making money with money" espoused by a range of players—has been a driving force in History (with a capital H). No doubt also that it plays a decisive role today, and that large corporations wield a great amount of power. But, despite the permanent presence of this force (at least over the last four centuries), techniques and institutions have changed significantly. Sole reference to capitalism therefore is not sufficient to explain changes over time, and especially those brought about during the short twentieth century. How do you explain, by only referencing capitalism, why at some moments markets were organized mainly on a national basis and in other moments on a globalized basis? Similarly, how do you explain the similarities in the forms of organization and technologies in countries under "real socialist" systems and those under "real capitalist" systems?

Herein lies the interest of the concept of hegemony. Hegemony enables one to consider not only the question of wealth but also that of power, and to consider the quest for power as a driver just as forceful as the quest for wealth. Harriet Friedmann and Philip McMichael use the notion of hegemony, but in my view do not give enough importance to it as a fundamental aspect.

A whole strand of international political economy is built around the concept of international hegemony as formulated in the pioneering work of Immanuel Wallerstein (1974, 1983). Wallerstein takes up Fernand Braudel's central idea of a world-economy defined as a "an economically autonomous section of the planet able to provide for most of its own needs, a section to which its internal links and exchanges give a certain organic unity" (Braudel, 1979c: 12). A world-economy's space has three characteristics: it has limits, it has a dominant center (and a proliferation of other centers is a sign of its decline), and lastly it is clearly hierarchized.

Interested in capitalism from the sixteenth century on, and therefore in a world-economy that initially included Europe and Iberia-America, then later covered the whole globe, Wallerstein considers the world-economy under the successive hegemonies of the United Provinces (1625–72), the United Kingdom (1815–73), and the United States (1945–67). He is also interested in the periods of competition that separate each hegemonic period. These periods, which on average last thirty years, are marked by conflicts whose outcomes determine who the next hegemon is: the

---

[3] The culmination of this regime is the creation of a truly global agriculture, not in the sense of the corpus of agriculture in the world, but rather through a transnational space integrated through agricultural product markets. Under this regime, power lies with businesses and the Agreement on Agriculture established under the framework of the WTO in 1994 following Uruguay Round negotiations, as well as other free trade agreements such as NAFTA, represent the institutionalization of this state of affairs.

"Thirty Years War," 1610–48; the "Napoleonic Wars," 1792–1815; and the "European civil war," 1914–45 (Traverso, 2007). Giovanni Arrighi's analysis is particularly interesting as a complement to Immanuel Wallerstein's work, allowing us to address the two components of hegemony—wealth and power—without having to make one derivative of the other (Arrighi, 1994). Arrighi proposes that we consider capitalism, and what he calls territorialism, as two distinct, but potentially complementary, logics of power:

> Territorialist rulers identify power with the extent and populousness of their domains, and conceive of wealth/capital as a means or a by-product of the pursuit of territorial expansion. Capitalist rulers, in contrast, identify power with the extent of their command over scarce resources and consider territorial acquisitions as a means and a by-product of the accumulation of capital.
>
> (ibid.: 33)

This book covers both the transition periods between hegemonies and the actual periods of hegemony. Hegemonic transition periods are characterized by rivalry between the hegemon in decline and potential successors, as well as rivalry between those candidates: France and the United Kingdom in the eighteenth century, Germany and the United States in the late nineteenth century and early twentieth century, and perhaps China and India tomorrow. The periods of rivalry are marked by wars, but, as Michael Mann underscores, the social sciences, and especially economics, have difficulty integrating war in their analyses. This bias is manifest in Friedmann and McMichael's early papers, as well as in Michael Tracy's book on the history of agricultural policy in Europe (Tracy, 1986). These works cautiously avoid the two world wars even though their chronology runs from the late nineteenth century to the 1980s. This despite Charles Tilly's famous formula: "War makes states" (Tilly, 1985: 170). And even more! Wars are periods particularly propitious for technical and institutional innovations and their dissemination. These come about, in part to respond to the needs of war itself, and in part because wars transform incentive systems and constraints. Wars are also a time when property rights are redistributed.

The second widening of the food regime concept comes through interrogating the relationship between agriculture and hegemony. There can be no accumulation of wealth and power without the mobilization of energy and matter. It is indispensable therefore when thinking about the history of agriculture to link it to the need to access energy and matter, and hence to the role of biomass. Food is just one of the possible ways of utilizing biomass. For each possible use, agriculture is just one source of biomass among others, such as the forest and the sea (to which one must add organic waste from human activity).

The idea of centering an analysis on biomass is not a new one. I have adopted this approach in my previous research on fatty matter and in exchanges with fellow agronomists (Daviron et al., 2016; Daviron, 2014, 2016), drawing inspiration from English historian Antony Wrigley, and work by Fridolin Krausmann and Marina Fischer-Kowalski from the Vienna Institute of Social Ecology (Wrigley, 1988, 2010; Krausmann and Fischer-Kowalski, 2013, 2017).

Biomass—its sources, its position, and its utilization—plays an important role in analyses using the "social metabolism" approach. Social metabolism refers to the different flows of matter and energy that run through societies, and the origins and destinations of these flows (Fischer-Kowalski and Haberl, 2015).[4] Societies, like living organisms, consume resources and produce waste, hence the use of the term "metabolism" borrowed from biochemistry. Social metabolism analyses also attempt to assess, for a given territory, which resources are extracted, what part of these are consumed, and which resources are imported or exported. These analyses give rise to accounting similar to national accounts, the difference being that variables are measured in tons or in calories rather than in market value.[5]

The works of the Institute for Social Ecology which cover long periods (Krausmann and Fischer-Kowalski, 2013; Krausmann et al., 2016a), as well as those of historians of energy (Wrigley, 1988, 2004, 2010; Kander et al., 2014; Debeir et al., 2013), highlight the profound changes that the metabolism of human societies went through during the period that for Europe is referred to as the Industrial Revolution. Two metabolic regimes, or "specific fundamental pattern[s] of interaction between (human) society and natural systems" (Fischer-Kowalski and Haberl, 2007: 8), can thus be distinguished: the agrarian regime and the industrial regime. The passage from the former to the latter constitutes a "metabolic transition."[6]

A society with an agrarian metabolic regime is characterized by its dependence on biomass as the almost sole source of matter and energy. Biomass is therefore not just used as a source of food. It also provides households with combustibles, fibers and skins for clothing, a significant part of building materials, as well as with mechanical energy through animals. Biomass also plays an essential role in maintaining soil fertility. Lastly, biomass provides the main part of raw materials and thermal energy (charcoal) needed for most craft manufacturing: carpentry, glassmaking, iron-smithing, shoemaking, brewing, hat-making, etc.

By contrast, the particularity of a society with an industrial metabolic regime is that most of its resources come from exploiting matter that lies underground. This transformation is most evident in the field of energy. In a few decades for European countries, and in two centuries for the world as a whole, coal, and then oil and natural gas (and more marginally uranium) became practically the sole sources of mechanical and thermal energy. There was also a radical transformation in where materials were sourced from: products previously sourced from biomass were replaced by synthetic

---

[4] See Fischer-Kowalski (1998) for a history of the concept.
[5] These analyses have given rise to the material flow accounting (MFA) methodology, which is also sometimes called material and energy flow accounting (MEFA). Today most social metabolism analysts use this methodology.
[6] If we go much further back in history, another metabolic transition can be discerned: the passage from the metabolic regime of hunter-gatherer societies to the metabolic regime of agrarian societies. (For a political reading of this first transition see Scott, 2017.) Humanity has thus been through two metabolic transitions and today is confronted with the challenge of enacting a new transition in order to resolve multiple problems associated with the industrial metabolic regime (pollution of various sorts, global warming, resource depletion, etc.).

substitutes and mineral derivatives whose extraction and processes had now been enabled by availability of abundant energy. Thus, within an industrial metabolism, where the "industrial revolution" or "development" had occurred, biomass utilization became largely limited to providing food.

The concept of metabolic regime and the distinction between agrarian and industrial regimes provides us a first avenue for rethinking agriculture. In agrarian metabolic societies, agriculture was tasked with providing almost all energy and materials used. In this book, I have opted to use the term solar metabolic regime. This is a wider term than "agrarian," or the term "organic" used by Antony Wrigley (1988), and it gives consideration to the frequent use of wind and water bodies, which are indirect products of sunshine, as a source of energy within "solar" societies. It also avoids the ambiguity that the term "organic" has with regard to coal and oil.[7] In the same vein, I replaced "industrial regime" with the term mining metabolic regime, so as to underscore the importance of mineral resources, as does Wrigley (1988), as well as to mark the contrast with the previous regime (underground versus sky, night versus day). Furthermore, the term better highlights from the start the unsustainable nature of this regime. All mines, as we know, sooner or later are depleted through extraction.

Biomass and hegemony

This book presents a historical narrative of the transformations of agriculture based on an examination of sources and uses of biomass under each hegemon. The book, however, does not claim to, nor seek to propose a concept or a model that could account for the status and transformations of agriculture in all places of the world. In this sense, I am following the teaching of Karl Kautsky, who in his famed book *The Agrarian Question* stresses how it is important to not confuse "states" with "tendencies."[8]

In this book's analysis, tendencies in biomass sourcing and utilization are "set" by the hegemon and potentially influence all the territories in its world-economy. But the effects of these tendencies—the states that result—may radically differ from one territory to another due to the diversity of initial states and the type of resistance, or outright opposition, elicited.[9] This failure to differentiate between tendencies and states, and allowing the reader to think that the situation described prevails on the entire globe, in my view are the greatest weaknesses and ambiguities of a large part of work using the food regime concept, as well as analyses of the global food system (Rastoin and Ghersi, 2010).

---

[7] Organic chemistry, that is the chemistry of carbon, developed from the use of coal, and later of oil.
[8] Kautsky wrote: "The theorist must study the general tendencies of social evolution; the policymaker must take the specific state that they find as the point of departure. The tendencies in social evolution as well as in agricultural evolution, are essentially the same in all civilized countries, but the states that they have engendered are extremely different across countries, and even across different regions of the same country, due to differences in geography, climate, soil configuration, past history, as well as the power of the different social classes" (Kautsky, 1900: v).
[9] See Frödin (2013) on present-day India.

What is biomass?

Social metabolism analyses identify four types of material flows:

- Iron and non-iron metallic minerals
- Non-metallic minerals (essentially used in construction and in chemistry)
- Fossil fuels (coal, oil, natural gas, oil shale, etc.)
- Biomass

Biomass is the matter living organisms are composed of or produce. It is distinct from the three other materials due to the fact that it is constantly produced either in plant form (through the effect of sunshine), or in animal form (through the consumption of plant material and other animals), or through the breaking down of these two forms.*

Biomass possesses three attributes that are of interest in the context of the ecological crisis that today's human societies face.

Biomass is constantly generated, through the effect of an energy source that comes from the fusion of hydrogen far away from our planet. The waste from the production of this energy therefore does not encumber our environment, unlike nuclear energy, or of course, fossil energy. However, the quantity of biomass that is produced each year is limited by the quantity of sunshine and the state of ecosystems.

Many living organisms can produce useful materials or energy for man, using other living organisms or their products.

Waste produced by living organisms can play a role in the metabolism of other living organisms, and under some conditions (localization, density, or saturation), can be integrated into food cycles which, *in fine*, participate in the production of biomass used by humans.**

* Biomass is of a similar nature as living organisms. "Islands of order in a chaotic world" (Sieferle, 2001: 1), living organisms can only survive by importing free energy and exporting degraded energy (from entropy). They fall under the category that Ilya Prigogine calls dissipative structures (Prigogine and Stengers, 1979). A living organism may also be described as a relatively recent assemblage of carbon, enabled by solar energy recently arrived on earth, and temporarily stocked, awaiting death and decomposition through the action of other organisms.

**Fossil fuels derive from biomass from an ancient past that has been decomposed and concentrated in the form of carbon compounds.

Our narrative begins at the end of the sixteenth century with the hegemony of the United Provinces. Going back in time allows us to tackle the issue of biomass, and therefore of agriculture, in a solar metabolic regime, before the emergence of fossil fuels.[10] Authors employing the food regime concept tend to address history at a time (end of the nineteenth century) when the specialization of agriculture in food production was already well established, and write at a time when the mining metabolic

---

[10] Even if, as we shall see, the prosperity of the United Provinces was partially based on the utilization of peat.

regime has triumphed. As we shall see, biomass imports, including non-food biomass, were essential to life in the United Provinces at the height of their greatness. Within a solar metabolic regime, there is really no way for a given population in a given territory to become rich and powerful without importing large quantities of distant biomass.

The book's analysis of biomass sources and uses runs until the present day. Particular attention is given to the respective roles played by food and non-food biomass, to the modes of production of biomass, that is, the forms of ecosystem exploitation and forms of labor organization, and lastly to the technical and institutional mechanisms for mobilizing biomass, in particular, distant biomass.[11]

Colonizing living nature

To reflect on the different ways in which societies increase supply of biomass, I rely on the concept of the "colonization of nature" as proposed by Marina Fischer-Kowalski and her colleagues (Fischer-Kowalski and Haberl, 1993; Fischer- Kowalski and Weisz, 1999; Fischer-Kowalski and Erb, 2016). She defines the concept as the "intended and sustained transformation of natural systems by means of organized social interventions, for the purpose of improving (increasing) their utility."[12]

The colonization of nature therefore supposes technical means (tools) and institutions. Colonization has a strategic dimension as it is aimed at increasing the utility of natural systems for a class of actors. The concept is of interest because of its broad approach which enables reflection on the action of humans in long (even very long) history and at very different scales, from microscopic to macroscopic.

Agriculture is today the most widespread colonization of the living part of nature ("nature" here means every living being that is not human). Rolf Peter Sieferle defines agriculture as a "solar energy system controlled by humans: solar energy is stored photosynthetically by plants that are selected, bred and cultivated in such a way by humans that a large part of their biomass can be monopolized for their purposes" (Sieferle, 2001: 14). Colonizing interventions within the field of agriculture are thus plenty, and occur at multiple scales, as they can concern a whole region (an irrigation network for instance) or just a single gene (improved seeds for example).

---

[11] The term "mobilization" or the verb "mobilize" is given preference over more neutral terms like "utilization" or "consumption." Mobilization conveys the idea of something being rendered mobile. In our analysis, this is often the first challenge: how to move a resource or an individual from one place to another. The term also encompasses the idea of a finalized action, of means to put in place to reach the target end result.

[12] "In order to maintain their metabolism, societies transform natural systems in a way that tends to maximize their usefulness for social purposes. Natural ecosystems are replaced by agricultural ecosystems (meadows, fields) designed to produce as much usable biomass as possible, or are converted into built-up space. Animals are domesticated, genetic codes of species are altered to increase their resistance against pests or pesticides, or to produce pharmaceuticals. Such interactions between social and natural systems cannot be understood as metabolic exchanges of matter and energy. They are of a different character. After the Latin term for peasant 'colonna' we termed this mode of intervention into natural systems 'colonization' and defined it as the conundrum of social activities which deliberately change important parameters of natural systems and actively maintain them in a state different from the conditions that would prevail in the absence of such interventions" (Fischer-Kowalski and Haberl, 1998: 575).

But the colonization of living nature by humans is not just limited to agriculture. Older, and still relevant today, are extractivist practices which do not involve the "intended and sustained transformation of natural systems":[13] fishing, hunting, gathering, wood-collecting ... Far from being just a feature of prehistoric hunter-gatherer societies, biomass extraction in low anthropized environments has played very important roles in more recent history in the integration of entire territories into the world-economy (codfish for Canada, fur for Canada and Russia, leather for Argentina, rubber for the Amazon, etc.). It remains today the main means of obtaining fish (even if aquaculture is about to overtake fishing).

To increase its production of biomass, a population, living off agriculture or extractivism, or a combination of the two, has two possibilities: either expand the space that it exploits, as in a frontier economy, or increase exploitation of the space already used through intensification (Netting, 1993: 263).

A frontier may be defined as the process through which previously "uncultivated" lands (forests, pasture, shifting agriculture, etc.) are suddenly and briskly cultivated or through which exploitation of "natural" biomass (that is non-anthropogenic biomass) abruptly changes scale (and beneficiary). The distinction between agriculture and extractivism enables, in line with Daniel Geiger, the identification of two types of frontiers:

- agricultural frontiers—also settlement frontiers. These are associated with the mass migration of labor, and when possible, with labor that is relatively mobile as the frontier is by nature ephemeral: "Frontiers of settlement's most distinctive feature ... is that they are mobile and fleeting, often consuming large tracts of land along with the resident indigenous communities in their rapid advance" (Geiger, 2009: 33).
- frontiers of extraction, prospection and selective exploitation of natural resources. These frontiers do not need a large quantity of "migrants" but, like settlement frontiers, are mobile (Geiger, 2009: 33).

But a frontier is not just characterized by its ecological or demographic dimensions. It is also associated with very specific social and political configurations. Geiger writes "frontiers are areas remote from political centers which hold strategic significance or economic potentials for human exploitation and are contested by social formations of unequal power" (ibid.: 28). Frontiers are thus characterized by conflict and unregulated economic activity. Indigenous communities are considered outsiders to the political community, even when they belong to the same nation as the settlers (also see Rasmussen and Lund, 2018). Daniel Geiger adds:

> Here, at the state's remote ends, concerns for state—and nation-building [or empire-building]—outweigh considerations for political stability, biodiversity

[13] Very often, extraction is not limited to the harvest of a resource; it may have consequences on the environment of the resource in question or require prior intervention on its environment. An example among many others comes from the use of fire by North American Indians to promote grass growth in the underwood and thus attract game and make hunting easier (Cronon, 2011).

conservation, or for that matter, local communities' rights. At its margins, the state does not shun conflicts but accepts them as inevitable and even necessary. To national decision-makers ... violence and the loss of life in frontier conflicts over state-sanctioned development ... appear not as the lamentable breakdown of social order, but as the noble beginning of it.

(Geiger, 2009: 36)

Increasing biomass production through intensification involves increasing or reinforcing the colonization of ecosystems. According to Ester Boserup, the first mode of intensification consists in increasing the frequency of land cultivation: instead of several years of fallow under slash-and-burn agriculture, there is a shift to multiple harvests per year on the same farm plot (Boserup, 1965). The shortening of fallow times creates new needs in terms of tilling land, and changes in farming tools arise by consequence (from the digging stick, to the hoe and the plow). Shorter fallow also means that soil fertility increasingly depends on human labor and less on "natural" processes (the work of non-human living beings).

The introduction of non-indigenous species is another essential practice of intensification (Grigg, 1974). During the period covered in this book, exchanges in both directions between Eurasia and America—the Colombian exchange to use Alfred Crosby's formulation (Crosby, 1973, 1986)—were numerous and produced decisive effects. The impact of the adoption in Europe of the potato, corn, and the tomato are well known. The role that smallpox played as an exterminator of Amerindians is also of general notoriety. Less known are the roles played by a number of domesticated European species, in particular large herbivores, in the conquest's "success," or the role the sweet-potato played in farming for some Chinese regions.

The practices implemented to increase production by surface unit go well beyond reducing fallow intervals or introducing foreign species, as is well illustrated by Eric Mollard and Annie Walter's *Singular Agricultures* (Mollard and Walter, 2008). Three categories of practices can be distinguished, depending on whether they aim at reducing competition from other living beings (vegetal, animal, microscopic, or large), at increasing supply of nutrients or water (or more rarely to reduce the latter), or at selecting and then reproducing individuals presenting the most desirable traits or best adapted to environmental conditions. From this perspective, narratives presenting the history of global agriculture organized around a limited number of big agricultural revolutions (Mazoyer and Roudart, 1998) seem limited and impoverished, missing out on the variety and the multiplicity of agricultural techniques developed by humans to increase biomass production.

History shows us that intensification has always involved more work per surface unit, more time dedicated to work each day, and a fall in labor productivity. This observation is clearly demonstrated in the transition from hunter-gatherer societies to farming societies (Sahlins, 1976; Harris, 1977; Clark, 2007).[14] It is also evident if we compare over time and space different types of agricultures based on their degree of

---

[14] This transition is often associated with a deterioration in health status as sedentarization and animal domestication lead to increased vulnerability to parasites (Larsen, 2006; Mummert et al., 2011).

intensification (Bayliss-Smith, 1982; Netting, 1993). This historic "law" according to which intensification is accompanied by a fall in labor productivity has, however, been broken during the twentieth century. This represents a radical, and unprecedented, break with the past brought about by the "modernization" of agricultures since the Second World War: yields and labor productivity have since both increased at the same time. But this revolution was only possible through a massive injection of fossil fuels into the agricultural sector. If we reason in terms of total energy (and not just human labor), we have much less reason for astonishment: high-yield, high-labor-productivity "modern" agriculture presents a much lower energy yield than "traditional" agricultures (Bayliss-Smith, 1982; Netting, 1993: 123–46).

Mobilizing labor

The key exception of the post-1945 period aside, increasing biomass production, whether by extension of surfaces or by intensification, always involves more human labor, and therefore requires the resolution of two problems:

- First, that workers can undertake the necessary tasks for production at the right time and place.
- Second, that extra workers can be mobilized to increase production.

Chris and Charles Tilly identify three types of work incentives: coercion, compensation, and commitment (Tilly and Tilly, 1998: 74; Lucassen, 2004).

Coercion, with its threat to inflict physical harm, immediately evokes slavery. But slavery is far from being the only form of coerced labor. For a wage worker, the threat of unemployment may have very physical consequences (hunger, cold, illness, etc.). A credible threat of the use of violence is also strongly present in serfdom and various forms of indentured labor that were used in plantations, in particular in the Caribbean (Chapters 2 and 3). It is also often present in the management of family labor.

Compensation involves conditional gratification of the worker. It is not always monetary, but when it is, for it to be effective, it assumes the existence of a market for goods in a sufficiently developed form. Such is the thesis of Jan de Vries' concept of industrious (as opposed to the industrial) revolution. Thus, in seventeenth-century England, the development of a consumer goods markets resulted in a longer work day and in more time dedicated to the production of market goods (de Vries, 1994, 2008) (Chapter 2).

Commitment as a work incentive arises from solidarity that is felt with a group. The work of women and children within a family farm is supposed to be motivated by commitment. Commitment also, without a doubt, plays a role in the work of plantation company cadres stationed far away from their head office.

These three forms of incentives are not exclusive and are most often combined. Thus, coercion and compensation are clearly present in many types of wage work, as commitment and coercion are present in family or military labor.

Providing incentives for work well done is constrained by a major hurdle in the case of farm work arising from two challenges in assessing the quality of farm work (Hayami, 2003):

- Results of tasks are difficult to predict (lack of control over biological phenomena, climate risks, diversity in agro-ecological conditions) which makes it impossible to simply calculate a ratio of effort made to measured output.
- The spatial dispersion of activities makes surveillance complicated. Simply put, permanent surveillance of workers is probably indispensable, yet spatial dispersion makes this onerous.

This double constraint, in my view, is what gives family farming a competitive edge over salaried capitalistic farming, if one assumes equal access to product markets.

The issue of the incentives necessary to attract additional workers radically differs depending on whether labor is needed for intensification or for the extension of surfaces. From a certain perspective, mobilizing additional workers for intensification does not pose any problems, at least if we follow the logic of Boserup (1965). In effect, she argues that demography is the driving force of intensification. In contrast to Malthus for whom the capacity of food production for a given population linked to a given territory is inevitably limited by the law of decreasing returns—which imposes therefore an absolute limit for population growth—Boserup considers that the production capacity of a given territory can increase when its population grows through an increase in the quantity of labor available per surface unit, in other words, by intensification. Population growth hence precedes intensification, by creating both the need for and providing the labor necessary for intensification.

By contrast the issue of mobilizing additional workers is a central one for the expansion of frontiers. The frontier is by definition a space with very low population density, or inhabited by communities whose land the "pioneers" are going to grab. These communities, hostile or vilified, are not a source of easily mobilizable labor. Frontiers thus are by definition places of migration towards which labor is imported.

Migration towards settlement frontiers raises two main challenges: dealing with armed resistance from communities already living in the coveted land, and with the prohibitive cost of transport. William McNeill posits that these two challenges have long encouraged recourse to forms of forced labor: slave labor, indentured labor, and serfdom (McNeill, 1992: 22 onwards). The military power of communities living in the disputed territories was a main constraint for the expansion of frontiers in Eastern Europe, where the nomad communities of the steppes long prevented the settlement of isolated pioneers lacking protection. The nomads destroyed pioneer camps, and captured and sold camp occupants as slaves. This resulted in a second type of serfdom: protection for work on a feudal model. The military submission of the steppes, definitively achieved in the mid-nineteenth century, resolved this problem.

Until the mid-nineteenth century, the very high cost of transport meant that workers could not finance their travel by themselves. This is why in the Caribbean the first solution used was indentured labor, whereby plantation owners financed the journeys of indentured workers in exchange for obligatory work over several years. European indentured workers were later replaced by African slaves, whose journey was financed by ship-owners, and who were sold to plantation owners at destination.

When slavery was abolished, indentured workers, this time Asian, became once again the dominant form of labor for some decades.[15]

Labor shortages for long remained the main concern and a leitmotif in plantation owners' discourses. In the second half of the nineteenth century, a combination of vigorous population growth and radical transformations in communication and transport led to profound changes. European migrants moved *en masse* to the Americas, Oceania, South Africa, and Siberia, while Chinese and Indian migrants moved throughout Southeast Asia and Manchuria. "Free" labor henceforth become the new model.

Conquering distance

Taking into account demography, and more specifically the availability of workers, as William McNeill does, is not sufficient to understand why family farming rather than large-scale wage farming became the dominant model during the nineteenth century. For family farms to win out in the competition with large-scale farms, it was necessary that family farms were close to markets, that is that market transactions were possible at farm-gate or in the closest town. In other words, that distance was conquered.

Indeed, distance can act as a constraint. It makes impossible direct contact between producer and consumer, between banker and planter, between management at the trading company and its factories[16] … Observation, real-time monitoring, or immediate reaction are made impossible. Distant products were nonetheless sought out despite the distance, for their irreplaceable qualities, such as lead or salt, as well as simply for the distinction that remoteness conferred on them, for their exoticism (porcelain, silk, spices, for instance). Trade generates profit through difference, and distance is one source of difference.

For rural France of the yesteryear, indeed for most of humanity until the recent past, distance commenced beyond the market town which, according to Fernand Braudel (Braudel, 1979b, 1986), represented the first floor in the hierarchy of towns. For the peasant, the market town was the market place accessible within a day of walking (for a return trip). For distances beyond the market town, the intervention of traders was necessary.

When long distances involve several political entities, traders include on one side or the other of the chain, sometimes on both sides, foreigners or outsiders, who are not

---

[15] It should be noted, however, that forms of free labor were involved in biomass production for export to distant markets well before the nineteenth century. An emblematic example is the Canadian trapper, a Frenchman immersed in an Indian business acting as a trade intermediary for the sale of furs to Company trading posts. Similar figures are found in both East and West Europe, in America and in Siberia, as well as in different locations on the American continent, such as the *gaucho* in the Pampas, the *ranchero* in Mexico, and the buccaneer in the Caribbean (Curtin, 1990). The point these figures share in common is that of being "producers" in extractive pioneer frontiers (as opposed to settler frontiers). The extreme dispersion of resources in such contexts made the use of coercion totally impossible, freedom of movement of the worker being a *sine qua non* of the activity.

[16] Local stores of colonial companies.

a priori protected by the local laws. Philip Curtin's book *Cross-Cultural Trade in World History* (Curtin, 1984) addresses this topic. Traders with foreign status on both ends of the chain appears to have been the rule more often than the exception. Curtin also highlights the role that some communities—Chinese, Armenians, Jews—historically played in long-distance trade and how the communities were integrated into the "cultures" between which they organized trade. Many authors (Greif, 2002; Granoveter and many others) have pointed out the "functionality," related to the constraints of long-distance trade, of this integration of foreign communities. It allowed for the establishment of trust, but also sanction, and hence control. One can also consider the outsider status of traders as a quality making it easier for princes to govern them, and their isolation, as well as that of the market, from the rest of society as limiting the risk of disorder that a foreigner brings.

However, foreign status can present a very different face when the trader is in a position to resist constraints that the prince wants to impose, in other words, when the trader has means of constraint superior to those of the local prince. This configuration has existed at many points of history: notably in the distant past, with the Hanseatic League and with chartered companies and trading posts; in the more recent past, with banana multinationals in Central America; and today, with drug traffickers and companies operating under protection of private security forces in African countries and failed states.

Lastly, distance implies time, and time poses two challenges for trade: the need for credit and price-risks. The first constraint leads to strong imbrication of trade and financial activities. This fusion of roles is constant and as such often creates confusion over the identity of stakeholders: are they traders or bankers? Price-risks, for their part, in many cases lead traders to limit their activity to that of a commissary, never owning the product, but content to simply organize the product's movement and sale for the parties involved in production.

Alongside technical innovations, such as the railroad, two institutional innovations radically transformed the issue of distance in the nineteenth century. The first were standards and grades which enabled an "objective" definition of the quality of products. The second was the futures market (see Part 3) (Daviron, 2002; Daviron and Ponte, 2005; Daviron and Vagneron, 2008). These innovations would bring markets to the countryside and enable the victory of family agriculture.

About this book

This book draws from a wide variety of papers and books in history, historical sociology, anthropology, economics, and other disciplines. It does not give much consideration to the borders between disciplines, nor does it claim to offer new information, but rather just a new narrative, a new reading. I have also attempted as much as possible to provide quantitative data.[17]

---

[17] I must admit that I have a somewhat compulsive attachment to providing quantitative data. I see it as a conditionality for rigor. I hope that readers will bear with me.

The book has the ambition therefore of looking at agriculture differently and will do this by attempting to combine the four dimensions presented above: the different uses of biomass, the technical modalities for increasing biomass, the forms of mobilizing labor, and the spaces of exchange. Following the food regime analytical model, the book presents a long history of how different hegemons interacted with biomass from the sixteenth century on and tries to show that each hegemon can be associated with a clear pattern regarding biomass sourcing and utilization. With regard to biomass sourcing, I place special emphasis on the role of distant biomass and the technical and institutional methods employed for its mobilization, as well as on the methods of biomass production, that is, the techniques and forms of organizing labor. The issue of biomass utilization concerns mainly its role in the metabolism of societies as a source of matter and energy, and within this framework, the respective proportions of food and non-food usages.

The book is divided into six parts, organized chronologically, with periods that partially overlap.

Part 1 covers the United Provinces in the seventeenth century and focuses on the key role that distant biomass played in its trade regime and its metabolism.

Part 2 covers England and France during the eighteenth century and their race towards hegemony. Here I highlight the importance that national resources acquired, spurred on by mercantilist policies, and of two major transformations in the English social metabolism, which are commonly called the agricultural revolution and the Industrial Revolution. Part 2 also highlights the special role played by distant biomass. Increasingly sourced from plantations in islands subjected to exclusive colonial regimes, distant biomass would lose its metabolic significance (as a source of energy and matter) to become chiefly significant as a currency of exchange with the rest of Europe.

Part 3 examines the sources and uses of biomass of the United Kingdom in the nineteenth century when its position as world hegemon was established. This first phase of the mining metabolic regime, characterized by coal utilization, paradoxically led to an increase in the consumption of biomass. The enormous jump in the availability of mechanical energy created by the spread of the steam engine increased capacities for processing and transporting biomass. As the world's workshop, the United Kingdom imported biomass from the whole world to supply its factories. Moreover, from the second half of the nineteenth century, the country significantly opened up its food market. To satisfy these two types of demand, multiple frontiers were opened, ranging from Russia, to Argentina, and to Burma, to create a truly global biomass market within which the colonial territories only played a minor role.

Part 4 describes the period of the two world wars, during which rivalry for hegemonic succession pitted the United States against Germany. Both these countries would progressively diverge from the English model of the international division of labor and peaceful trade between biomass producing countries and industrial countries. Germany and the United States both recentered their economic space within their domestic territories. The former relied on the intensification of its agriculture and research on synthetic products that could substitute distant biomass. When the Nazis took power, research for biomass substitutes was supplemented by territorial expansion, with the ambition of acquiring territories to the East and building a large-scale economy that would rival America's. As for the United States, its status as a biomass exporter started to weaken from the first decade of the twentieth century due to the depletion of its frontier, and the acceleration of industrialization and urbanization. The 1930s crisis brought to light the increasingly critical state, in both ecological and economic terms, of a form of agriculture with a mining constitution. Overcoming the crisis would involve industrializing agriculture, in other words injecting fossil fuel energy in the form of tractors and farm machines, chemical pesticides, and fertilizers.

Part 5 of the book delves into the post-Second World War period up until the first oil shock. This period was marked by the triumph of oil, a second phase of the mining metabolic regime, and hegemonic dominance by the United States. Accumulation of wealth and power was now founded on Fordism: in contrast to the nineteenth century, the foundation was a domestically centered economy that was tightly administered, and in which increased production, thanks to Taylorism, found its markets through mass consumerism that was spurred on by the redistribution of income. This period saw wider deployment of two changes that had commenced in the preceding period:

- First, the generalization of chemical or mineral products as substitutes for non-food biomass, which led to the mono-specialization of agriculture in food production and imposed the conventional form of agriculture.
- Second, the industrialization of agriculture along with what this enabled in the form of a simultaneous increase in yields and labor productivity, which enabled a growing dependence on fossil fuels.

After metamorphosing the United States, this model of conventional agriculture presided over the "modernization" of agricultures, first in Europe and then, under the name Green Revolution, in Asia and in Latin America. It is this form of agriculture that made food self-sufficiency strategies, widely adopted across the world, viable. It also led to the drastic reduction of the share of the agricultural sector in national employment and gross national product (GNP). In this context, international trade of biomass became residual, essentially reduced to trading surpluses and deficits that threatened the stability of domestic markets.

Part 6 deals with the last four decades. The hegemony of the United States entered a new age with the victory of neoliberalism and the accelerated globalization of economies. This period has also been marked by the spread of the mining metabolic regime to the entire globe, excepting Africa. China is leading this movement, and through its steadfast commitment to both globalization and the mining metabolic system, has affirmed itself as a serious rival to the United States.

The role of biomass in the metabolism of this period has not seen any fundamental changes. The hold of the chemical sector on agriculture has strengthened a little more with increased quantities of chemical fertilizers and pesticides used in an increasing number of countries, in addition to the seed value chain being controlled by large corporations from the chemical sector. Biofuel production is the only real novelty in the utilization of agricultural products, but it is too early yet to understand whether this represents a real challenge to the centrality of food production.

Agricultural trade on the other hand has seen rapid acceleration, brought about both by the liberalization of agricultural policies and by Asian demand. Nonetheless, the so-called "food crisis" of 2007–8 demonstrated that agricultural markets are still far from being uniform on the global scale. As the new workshop of the world, China today seems hesitant to open its market significantly to biomass imports, including food imports, as England did in the first half of the nineteenth century. For the products for which China has already opened its borders, such as soybean, Chinese demand has generated a noted resurgence of the frontier dynamic, giving a foretaste of potential consequences of China becoming a high importer of biomass.

Part 1

Where we see the United Provinces build wealth and power by trading distant biomass, 1580–1705

Introduction

The United Provinces, led by Amsterdam, emerged in the late sixteenth century as an economic and military power which would dominate the European world-economy (that is, the economy whose center was Europe[1]) for a century. Their heyday came a few years after they gained independence from the Habsburg Holy Empire (Utrecht Treaty in 1579). Their expansionist power was thereafter deployed on several fronts. In the military domain, the Dutch, after liberating themselves from the Spanish, confiscated the Baltic[2] trade (in particular the grain trade) from the powerful Hanseatic League. They went on to win the monopoly of Asian spices in Europe from the Portuguese, to dominate the English in the White Sea for trade with Russia, and actively participate in setting up plantations in the Americas following their—temporary—conquest of northeastern Brazil. The United Provinces consolidated their commercial superiority by contesting all the European trade champions of the time.

Fernand Braudel explains "With Amsterdam the age of empire-building cities came to an end" (Braudel, 1984: 175). Amsterdam, in this view, was thus the final phase of domination by city-states (following Venice, Genoa, and Antwerp) before nation-states entered the scene. This vision is, however, contested by Jonathan Israel for whom the emergence of the United Provinces already represented a radical break, characterized by the unprecedented concentration of economic power within a territory (the United Provinces) and the establishment of a truly global warehouse (Amsterdam). The European world-economy was thus moving away from a multi-polar state, that is a world-economy with multiple centers, while both the Mediterranean and Hanseatic League cities weakened simultaneously (Israel, 1989).

In a solar metabolic society, any given economic entity can only become rich and powerful by mobilizing, that is by moving, large amounts of biomass. Biomass in effect is almost the sole source of energy and matter. The contrast between the narrowness of the Dutch hegemon's central territory and its remarkable capacity to mobilize biomass from distant territories that were on the periphery or outside their world-economy will be considered here as one of the defining characteristics of the historical period running from 1580 to 1705.

---

[1] The European world-economy did not end at the geographical limits of Europe. In the sixteenth century, it also included the North Sea, and a part of the Indian Ocean.

[2] The term "Baltic" is used to designate the sea itself, the surrounding territories that the sea gave access to, as well as territories further away, accessible thanks to fluvial networks.

Mobilizing biomass necessitated overcoming a major constraint that also characterized these societies: transport challenges. The challenges were particularly strong for land transportation for which the only available sources of mechanical energy were humans and animals, for whom it was also necessary most times to carry food, thus reducing the space available for transporting goods, if not completely eliminating it.[3] Access to water and the mastery of wind offered clear benefits.[4] Water offered surfaces that reduced friction (canals), currents that aided movement (rivers), and a space in which use of wind power could be optimized and obstacle-free movement was possible (seas and lakes). Proximity to water is thus a necessary condition for wealth and power in a solar metabolic regime. Rome and Constantinople had demonstrated this earlier, and after them Venice, Genoa, and Antwerp. The United Provinces excelled in maritime transport. Their excellence resulted from their remarkable mastery of the combination of wood-water-wind, characterized by what Lewis Mumford in *Technics and Civilization* calls the eotechnic phase (Mumford, 2016 [1934]: 110), materialized of course by sail ships, but also by canals and windmills.

Rome lived on tributes paid in kind by its subjects; Amsterdam on the other hand founded its rise to power on large-scale trading practices. Traders and bankers (capitalism) thus held a central position. The fact that the market was key did not mean, however, that coercion was excluded. This coercion, however, was externalized and, excepting a few rare cases, delegated to elites from the places of production (local nobility, for instance, as in Poland). Dutch traders limited their role to trade relations (products and credit) with these elites, who for their part were given the possibility to access new consumer goods.

Thanks to a successful combination of the art of transport and the art of trade, the United Provinces were able to import a very significant part of the biomass they consumed from distant territories. Their consumption, however, only used a part of the vast quantities of biomass that transited in the Provinces' warehouses. It was profits from the import–export trade that enabled a lifestyle, military power, and cultural influence beyond what the thin resources of their own territory could possibly offer.

In contrast to later hegemonies, the United Provinces established its power at a time when Europe was far from being the global economic power. In other words, the European world-economy did not cover the whole world. Other world-economies existed with their own logics, their own centers, their own peripheries—China, India,

---

[3] Von Thünen (1851) states "the transport of grain becomes impossible for the domain beyond fifty milles from the Town [1 mille = 7.5 km] because the cost of travel, food for the horses, and driver fees, absorb the full value of the load. Land cultivation therefore should be abandoned at fifty milles of distance, even in cases where grain cultivation does not engender any cost" (cited in Huriot, 1994: 19).

[4] A concrete illustration of the enormous advantages that maritime transport offered over land transport comes from two cases related by Glamann (1977: 220): in 1591, a Venetian attempting to buy wheat in Poland calculated the transport by road from Krakow to Venice would quadruple his purchase price (for a distance of around 1,000 km). At the same period, transporting wheat from Danzig to Amsterdam by sea only increased the price by 50% for a distance of 1,500 km.

Ottoman Empire, etc.—and the various world-economies exchanged with each other.[5] The United Provinces dominated trade between Europe and Asia and this trade was focused mainly on the spice trade. Spices were important not for the quantity of energy or matter they represented, but for their role as a currency of exchange within the European world-economy.

We will distinguish between trade with the internal periphery of the world-economy of the United Provinces from their trade with other world-economies (mainly Asia).

---

[5] This perspective would make André Gunder Frank jump! For Frank, the United Provinces was part of a world-economy centered on China, which covered the whole of Eurasia, a part of Africa, and the Americas colonized by the Europeans. From this perspective, the Dutch were simply the champions of the European peninsula (Frank, 1998). I will return to this issue in Part 6.

1

The United Provinces: Territories, resources, and economic sectors

Poor in resources, but rich in markets that encouraged the division of labor and specialization in both manufacturing and agriculture, and hence a boom in technics, the United Provinces buzzed with activity and functioned both as the warehouse and the workshop of seventeenth-century Europe.

Water, and more water!

The United Provinces, like Venice which had preceded it in the sequence of powers, were surrounded by water, and indeed practically built on water. The Provinces were situated on the Atlantic between the Baltic and Mediterranean seas from which they drew a bounty of resources while creating links between the two seas. The Provinces were also at the mouth of great rivers—the Rhine, the Maas, and the Schelde rivers—running from Germany, Belgium, and France respectively, and also close to the Weser River (which ends in Bremen) and the Elbe River (which ends in Hamburg). The abundance of rivers was supplemented by a vast network of canals which were used both for transport and for draining polders, land that had been conquered from the sea. Let us ponder this description of Holland by a visitor in the eighteenth century:

> In addition to these rivers, there's an infinite number of canals, capable of carrying large ships, that are possible to build in the low-lying and soft land without too much hardship. These canals are of great convenience for travelers and for transporting goods from one town to another. The barges which are used on these canals are pulled by horses, and they leave and arrive regularly at specific times. In winter, all the prairies are flooded and in spring they are dried using windmills, which throw the water in the canals.
>
> (Janiçon, 1729: 7)

Dykes were also omnipresent, and complemented the canals. They protected against the excesses of the North Sea and enabled farming of lands below the sea's normal level. These various technical devices—canals, windmills, and dykes—also represented situations of (or occasions for) learning in the field of collective action and institutional innovations which would serve as the foundations of the United Provinces' greatness.

Bunker and Ciccantell, echoing Arnold Toynbee's (1977) analysis of the emergence of the great civilizations of antiquity in terms of challenges and responses, write:

> The particular changes and opportunities that an environment, such as that of Holland, offers will, through ongoing interaction with the human population that work to modify and exploit it, mold the social construction of belief that provide the basis for social action.
>
> (Bunker and Ciccantell, 2005: 121)

This, perhaps is where one of the keys to the success of the Dutch model lies, possibly more significant than just geographical advantages.

The Dutch fleet

The Dutch had access to an extremely abundant navigable network, that moreover was situated at the crossroads of Mediterranean Europe and Northern Europe. They exploited this favorable position to the maximum, thanks to a highly efficient fleet, and became Europe's natural warehouse. They also leveraged their position to exploit resources, initially from their immediate periphery—both maritime (herring from the Baltic Sea) and land resources (German forests for instance) were involved—and later from territories increasingly more distant.

It is estimated that the fleet of the United Provinces in the mid-seventeenth century equaled the entire fleet of all other European countries. For Charles Wilson, the quantity and the quality of the United Provinces' trading fleet was the product of an "industrial" model of shipbuilding, that is, in his terms: highly mechanized (using for example saws powered by windmills), characterized by a profound division of labor, and based on standardized and repeated methods (Wilson, 1973). The fleet was also a result of the Dutch ability to procure all necessary products for building ships (wood for hulls and masts, hemp for ropes, linen for sails, iron for joints, pitch and tar for sealing, etc.) from distant locations ... an ability that itself was guaranteed by the efficiency of the fleet. A virtuous cycle of sorts! Thanks to this, in the mid-seventeenth century, costs of building a Dutch ship were significantly lower than costs for an English ship—£800 for a Dutch *fluyt* ship compared to £1,300 for its English equivalent (Özveren, 2000: 36).

The United Provinces therefore not only had impressive transport capacities but also very low costs, which allowed it to obtain a quasi-monopoly position over trade of heavy goods (wood, grain, salt, fish, raw flax and hemp, tar) as well as trade in precious products (silver, spices, fabric, and later sugar).

Precocious urbanization

With respect to European history, the United Provinces experienced remarkably precocious urbanization, only equaled in Flanders or on the Mediterranean coast. In 1675, 42 percent of the Provinces' population lived in towns. In the province of

Holland, the proportion was higher than 60 percent (Table 1.1) and Amsterdam had more than 200,000 inhabitants. During the same period, the urbanization rate in England was around 15 percent and that of France around 12 percent.

Table 1.1 Urbanization rate (in % of total population) of the United Provinces, 1525–1750

Period	Holland	Other provinces	Total United Provinces
1525	44	22	27
1675	61	27	42
1750	61	25	39

Source: de Vries and van der Woude, 1997: 61.

Flemish painting: Painting with biomass

Cultural excellence is one manifestation of hegemonic power. The golden age of the United Provinces was accompanied by a cultural effervescence that marked art history and continues to fascinate us today. Both the quantity and quality of art works were impressive. It is estimated that the Rubens atelier in Antwerp produced enough paintings signed by the hand of the great master (although not all were executed by him) to cover a football stadium. We should not be surprised that it was fifteenth-century Flanders that showed the path that would later be followed by Vermeer, Rembrandt, Frans Hals, Pieter de Hooch and company in the seventeenth century. Jan de Vries calculates that between 1580 and 1800, around 10 million paintings were produced throughout the Dutch territory, with an estimated 0.6 percent of adult men being painters.

The religious subjects that were dear to the Catholic Flemish were not favored as much by Dutch painters, who painted not just on commission, but also to sell their works in fairs, and even invented the first painting galleries. The practice of buying paintings became commonplace, even for relatively modest households. This artistic proliferation can be considered a sub-product of the boom in manufacturing and the increased material available as a result. A large part of materials used by modest artists were either recycled or artisanal products diverted for other uses (wood, sails, coloring for dyes …) and, in both cases, most materials transited through United Provinces' ports. The ports of Antwerp and later Amsterdam were the places where all these supplies congregated. They were also the meeting place for numerous dealers who exported the paintings throughout Europe. Dutch paintings often focused on the insides of homes and scenes from daily life, but they are nonetheless a testament to the openness of this country to the rest of the world, both outwardly (through representation of Chinese porcelain, geographical maps, Oriental carpets, etc.) as well as more intimately, that is intrinsically or physically, as they were composed of materials sourced from a wide range of geographies. Some dyes and mediums were mineral, such as clay, chalk, and various pigments, but it was biomass that provided the bulk of materials, and sometimes this biomass came from very far.

Painters used oak panels which came mainly from Baltic forests, through Danzig, and linen or hemp canvases from the plains of Silesia. They filled these in with the help of paintbrushes made from hair of gray squirrels, sable, or wolf (exported from Arkhangelsk on the White Sea), of paints composed from mineral pigments (precious lapis-lazuli from Hindu-Kush, azurite or "armenian stone," ochres and soils from all over Europe), plant matter (Toulouse pastels, or the indigo plant from India of course, and later the Caribbean, Brazil-wood red …), animal matter (vermillion,* scale insects from Languedoc scrublands, Mexican cochineal, Indian Kerrie lacca; or half-animal, half-plant (oak gall) or, already products of mineral chemistry (Montpellier green-grey, vermillion made from sulfur and mercury mainly in Germany, smalt, or "Saxony blue"). These dyes were diluted in eggs (certainly locally sourced), in terebinthinate from Venice (extracted from larch which did not grow in Venice, but simply transited there) or from Strasbourg (white fir tree) or Canadian balm (fir balm), and in oils from flax, poppyseeds (from the Baltics), or asp (lavender from France or Italy). Glues (from rabbit skin, bones, African arabic gum), rosin, birch bark, and other plant resins were mobilized to varnish the finished works. Upon these small canvas surfaces (Vermeer's *Lacemaker* only measures 21 x 24.5 cm) thus converged trade routes that crossed the entire world.

Sources: Brook, 2010; de Vries and van der Woude, 1997; Kirby *et al.*, 2010; de Patoul and van Schoute, 1994; Vermeylen, 2010.

* "Vermilio" means small worm in Italian, and it is the name given to the color extracted from the Kermes Vermilio or the Dyer's Kermes cochineal. Chemical vermillion, of the same color, was used from the Middle Ages on.

The large urban population found employment in the multiple professions related to the maritime trade (shipbuilding, loading and offloading of merchandise, goods registration and inspection, distribution, bagging, etc.). It also provided the labor needed for numerous manufacturing activities.

Flourishing manufacturing

In the fifteenth and sixteenth centuries, industrialization of the Spanish Netherlands (present-day Netherlands and Belgium) was concentrated in the south of the country in Flanders and Artois, and in the countryside.[1] The Dutch provinces were already experiencing spectacular growth in their agriculture, and their maritime and port sectors, but industrial production was limited to the local market and of poor quality. From 1560, religious persecution of Protestants in the south of the country and in

---

[1] All figures in this section are taken from de Vries and van der Woude (1997).

France provided towns in the north with a significant influx of qualified labor, while the insecurity created by the civil war in the countryside concentrated this wave of industrialization originating from the south in towns.

The province of Holland and its surroundings, in particular, benefited from this providential influx to spectacularly develop industry and its interior towns. Towns competed with each other to offer policies to attract migrant flows and become hosts to new industries: exonerations from various taxes, low-cost premises, and even goods recently confiscated from Catholic churches!

The towns tended to specialize in one specific product: textiles in Leiden and Haarlem, decorative pottery in Delft (the sector employed up to a quarter of Delft's active population in 1650), shipbuilding in the Zaan valley, and clay pipes in the town of Gouda. In 1730, an estimated 3,000 to 4,000 workers produced pipes for a total population of 18,000 inhabitants.[2] But some sectors were present everywhere, notably pottery, brasserie, biscuit-making, and distillery for the local market.

What is the link with flows of biomass? Well:

- From 1625 to 1700, the United Provinces, a country without forests and almost no trees, built between 400 and 500 ships per year, entirely in wood, in naval yards that employed around 10,000 people in just the province of Holland. These ships were sold in the Baltics, in the North Sea (70 percent of ships registered at the time in what is Oslo today), in England, and even in France.
- Three thousand people were employed in just Amsterdam to mix tobacco that arrived from the world over with locally produced tobacco for filling the pipes (made from Gouda clay) of all of Europe.
- In 1661, the United Provinces had sixty-six sugar refineries and in 1752 the figure had risen to 145. In 1752, the United Provinces imported £55 million of raw sugar, of which £50 million were refined in their territory, producing £45 million of refined sugar, two-thirds of which was destined for foreign markets. Revenues from just sugar refining were twice as important as revenues from all the cheese produced at the time, and comparable to tobacco industry revenues.
- The textile sector also prospered, particularly in the town of Leiden (which produced 40,000 pieces of bedsheets in 1590 and 100,000 in 1630), and the Dutch dominated the European market. Textile fibers used were wool (from Spain and England), linen (from Silesia and France), angora, cotton, silks, and camelhair. The more qualified tasks (dyeing and finishing) were undertaken in cities, but the sector also employed a lot of rural workers for more basic operations, often on a seasonal basis. England would soon forbid export of raw wool (in 1625) to protect its own weaving sector, but dyeing and finishing remained a Dutch activity until

---

[2] An average workshop, with a staff comprising the owner, his wife, his daughter, and an apprentice, at the time produced on average 1,000 to 1,500 pipes per day, which makes for 1 million pipes per day for the whole town! These pipes, very fragile and practically "single-use," were replaced frequently and domestic consumption was very high (cigarette paper was far from being perfected then), but a significant quantity of pipes was also exported.

1650. Dutch wool sheets dressed all the armies of Europe, and the most luxurious fabrics, in camelhair or angora goat hair, penetrated markets as far as the Levant.
- Other sectors also grew: the packaging sector (paper and clay pot packaging), ropes and sails for shipbuilding and maintenance, as well as salt refineries, tanneries, oil mills, soapmaking, and more. Paper production (from rags collected mainly in Germany), already strongly boosted by the packaging sector, experienced spectacular growth in the eighteenth century, thanks to a very dynamic printing sector: 781 printing presses existed in the territory from as early as 1660. In 1720, more than 200 paper mills were functioning in the regions of Zaan and Veluwe, some of them employing up to fifty workers.[3]

Clay-brick production, driven by the brisk-rate of urbanization and fire-control regulations that mandated building with bricks, was also integrated into the long-distance biomass trade. They were used as ballast in ships going to the Baltics, to Asia, and even later to Brazil, which would return loaded with all types of biomass. An estimated 50 million bricks per year arrived in Recife between 1641 and 1643, leaving their imprint on the physiognomy of its seafront still today, just as in many German and Baltic port towns.

Specialized farms integrated in the market economy

As we will see, the United Provinces imported massive quantities of cereals from the Baltic region. The resulting possibility to reduce land surfaces used for cereal production, the presence of large urban markets nearby, and the relative ease of "inland" transport thanks to a dense network of canals encouraged an intensification of agriculture around animal products (especially dairy products) and non-food crops: textile fibers (linen), dye plants, rapeseed, and tobacco. The size of herds increased, land that was previously left in fallow was cultivated, and temporary prairies (more productive than permanent prairies) were introduced. Many of the techniques that were used originated in nearby Flanders. These techniques had emerged in the Middle Ages during the golden age of Ghent, Bruges, and Antwerp (Slicher Van Bath, 1963: 71). For many aspects, Flanders had experienced some centuries earlier the developments that the United Provinces experienced in the sixteenth and seventeenth centuries. From the thirteenth century, several towns of Flanders (Ghent was then the second largest town after Paris in non-Mediterranean Western Europe) developed powerful textile industries. Food for these towns also in part came from cereal imports from the Baltics (Pomerania and Prussia) which arrived in particular in Bruges where there was a Hanseatic League factory (trading post) (Hybel, 2002). It is in Flanders that the use of legumes to improve soil fertility was "rediscovered"—a technique well known to the Romans (Shiel, 2006: 226). There was crop diversification: broad beans, vetch, turnip, rapeseed, woad, hops, and flax moved out of small specialized plots (*closières*),

---

[3] At the end of the eighteenth century, the United Provinces had twenty-eight book sellers for 100,000 inhabitants, compared to six for 100,000 in France or Belgium, and even fewer in Germany or Italy.

to be planted in open fields (Tits-Dieuaide, 1981). Marc Bloch offers the following perspective on this agricultural revolution:

> In a certain sense, the revolution in farming can be viewed as a conquest of ploughing through gardening techniques: borrowed products, borrowed techniques—weeding and intensive fertilizing—borrowed farming rules: an end of free-range grazing, and where necessary, the use of enclosures.
>
> (Bloch, 1952: 238)

Particular attention was given to the fertility of farmlands. Another Flemish technique that was adopted in the United Provinces involved the transfer of fertility from urban sources (De Graef, 2014). Towns in the United Provinces drew up contracts to collect urban waste—clay residues from brick production, ashes from soapmaking and more generally peat ash, which was particularly sought after—and deliver it to farmers. Several cases also attest to the use of human excrement, commonly referred to as "night soil," or "Dutch fertilizer" in the French literature. Dean Ferguson's claim that unlike Asians, "Europeans failed to develop markets for human manure until well into the late eighteenth century" (Ferguson, 2014: 384) is thus invalidated (van Driel, 2014).

Exploitation of peat resources

A solar metabolic regime? Not entirely, to be honest. Well before England started mining its coal, the United Provinces made large-scale use of a fossil source of energy: peat (De Decker, 2015). Along with the construction of canals, and the conquest of polders on the sea, the exploitation of peat resources features among the factors that contributed to making the United Provinces, and before them Flanders, a space profoundly shaped by man.

Peat replaced wood in the supply of thermic energy. The energy density of compressed and dried peat was in effect equal to that of wood. It was widely used for domestic heating and also provided the fuel for several heat-consuming manufacturing activities: ironworks, brewery, brickmaking, refineries, dyeing, etc.

Here as well, water transport played a decisive role (De Decker, 2015). Some canals were built specifically for transporting peat, especially for the peatlands up in the north.

Exploitation of peatlands in the north (Groningen) contributed to an expansion of cultivated lands: the areas where peat had been extracted were later drained using canals and pumps driven by windmills. Just like the famous polders, old peatlands gave birth to farmlands created by man.

According to de Zeeuw, during the seventeenth century, peat provided significantly more energy than windmills, which are seen as emblematic of Dutch inventiveness: 6,000 million calories on average per year compared to 45 million for mills (de Zeeuw, 1978: 20).

2

The Baltics and the North Sea: The first peripheries

The dominance of the United Provinces' fleet was particularly evident in the trade to and from the Baltics. "During the Middle Ages, the Baltic was a sort of America on Europe's doorstep," Fernand Braudel tells us (1984: 207). Sixty percent of the 400,000 passages through the Sound Straits between 1497 and 1660 were United Provinces' ships passing through. The Baltics and its numerous products (cereals, linen, hemp, peas, tar, wool, wood, ash, potash, tallow, furs, wax, etc.) played a key role in supplying the United Provinces with biomass, not only for food but also for manufacturing activities, of which the most important, as we have seen, was shipbuilding. Either in unprocessed form, or following processing, a large proportion of these products were re-exported and contributed to prosperity of trade with Southern Europe.

It is through trade, and hence exchange that the Dutch attracted these flows of biomass from the North. Which products crossed the Sound Straits in the opposite direction? In top position were Atlantic salt (salt is not a sea product, but a product of wind and sun!), manufactured goods—mainly fabrics (English wool and Northern linen manufactured in Holland), Mediterranean products (wine and olive oil) and later sugar and tropical products (sun, sun, and again sun), and finally precious metals from the Americas via Spain and Portugal.

Cereals

An essential element of social metabolism and trade

"Mother trade," *Modernegotie*, is the name that the Dutch gave to the cereal trade, a clear indication of the importance of this trade for the life of the country. The Dutch reached their heights of glory in the mid-seventeenth century. Baltic grain exports peaked at that moment. The United Provinces controlled 80 to 90 percent of those exports (van Tielhof, 2002: 73).

The Flemish, however, had already preceded the Dutch in procuring cereals from the Baltics (Hybel, 2002; Unger, 1999). But while Flemish purchases were limited to their own supply needs, in the early seventeenth century, Amsterdam was re-exporting half of the grain it imported. The city was the central market place for all European cereal markets including Mediterranean states (Spain and Italy) (Glamann, 1977: 223). They would, however, lose this dominant position later to the English (Table 2.1).

Table 2.1 Total cereal imports, re-exports and net imports in Amsterdam, 1649–80 (in lasts; 1 last = approximately 2 tons)

	1649	1667–8	1680
Total imports	112,091	63,829	64,535
Re-exports	46,049	1,864	8,394
Net imports	66,852	61,965	56,141

Source: De Vries, 1974: 172.

Nonetheless, cereal imports played a key role for the food security of the United Provinces and their precocious urbanization process. Available data on total imports and re-exports from Amsterdam suggest that in the mid-seventeenth century—the peak of the United Provinces' "food dependence," which would fall in later decades— cereal imports fed more than half of the 1 million inhabitants of the provinces of Holland, Utrecht, Friesland, and Groningen (de Vries, 1974: 172).

Organization of the trade

Trade in Baltic grain was a competitive trade undertaken by a large number of small firms that associated just a few individuals, most often from the same family. In 1612, the trade which was then experiencing rapid growth, was managed in the Amsterdam marketplace by sixty-two firms. Grain was purchased in the Baltic ports by agents working on commission, often for several different merchants. Given the distance and slow communications, these agents had great liberty of action and decision. In the late sixteenth century, a letter between the United Provinces and Danzig took from 11 to 51 days to arrive! (van Tielhof, 2002: 158). If faced with a sudden event (for example, a fall in prices) agents could not wait for instructions from Amsterdam to act. Relationships of trust between the merchant in Amsterdam and his agent in Danzig or Nerva were thus of key importance. Family ties therefore played an important role, as did belonging to the Mennonite religious minority, many of whom were exiled in Baltic towns and maintained strong ties with Mennonites of Holland.

During the two centuries in which the United Provinces controlled most of the Baltic grain trade, firms involved in this trade experienced two major developments.

First, over time, firms specialized in one single activity. Insurance was the first trade to emerge as a highly specialized profession. It was also the case with maritime transport in which most merchants participated actively at the end of the sixteenth century, owning ships or shares in ships.[1]

---

[1] For rye, the share of freight was around 15 percent of the sales price to the United Provinces and represented a third of the trading margin (difference between purchase price and sale price) (van Tielhof, 2002: 98). The desire to reduce this cost may have been instrumental in the progressive outsourcing of this activity.

Second, firms abandoned their role of merchants, of buying in the Baltics and selling in Amsterdam or Southern Europe (and vice versa), to take up the role of commissaries, organizing the movement and sale of goods on behalf of Baltic merchants, without ever owning the goods. The main advantage the commissary position presented was that it avoided price-risk, that is, the risks associated with short-term price fluctuations and more specifically the risk of having to sell at a price lower than the purchase price. The evolution of the Dutch merchant towards the profession of commissary could thus indicate that price-risks had risen with time (due to greater competition?) and it was necessary to transfer this risk higher up the chain towards merchants in the producer countries, or even towards the grain producers themselves.

Public authorities very rarely intervened to regulate the trade in cereals. Exceptionally, and with the aim of limiting rising prices, cereal exports were forbidden, sale of existing stocks was made obligatory, or a price ceiling was imposed. This very liberal policy environment nonetheless did see interventions from city authorities to protect the poor. Thus in Amsterdam, low-cost cereal stocks were distributed to bakeries in 1623, 1662, and 1698, years of cereal shortages (van Tielhof, 2002: 107, 109).

The second serfdom of Central Europe

At the other end of the chain, in the cereal producing regions (Poland, Pomerania, Prussia, etc.), the Baltic grain trade gave rise to an agriculture that was structurally very distinct from Western European agriculture. Growth in cereal exports was accompanied by the development of what is often called the second serfdom,[2] in other words, labor obligations imposed on the peasantry in large farms owned by the nobility. For Fernand Braudel:

> The great landowner was not a capitalist, but he was a tool and a collaborator in the service of capitalism in Amsterdam and elsewhere. He was part of the system. The mightiest landowner in Poland received advance payments from the merchant of Danzig [Gdansk] and through him from the Dutch merchant.
> (Braudel, 1983: 271)

This development affected all producer regions, that is all the territories fed by the rivers flowing into the Baltic Sea, from the Elbe River (whose port was Hamburg) to the Pregel River (whose port was Konigsberg, today's Kaliningrad). Within this territory, the basin of the Vistula River, which discharges into Danzig, played a pivotal role. Almost 80 percent of rye imported by Amsterdam during the sixteenth century and the first half of the seventeenth century came from this basin (Malowist, 1959: 184).

---

[2] The expression "second serfdom" is used by historians to designate the wave of subjugation that spread through central and Eastern Europe during the sixteenth and seventeenth centuries. According to Wallerstein, unlike medieval serfdom, the aim was not to render possible the lifestyle of a lord within a local economy, but to ensure a lord's participation in long-distance trade (Wallerstein, 1989: 87).

Indeed, it was the existence of navigable rivers with particularly large drainage basins which made possible the transport of large quantities of cereal to the sea.

The frontier to the east of the Elbe started in the twelfth century and advanced, progressively integrating new territories—up until Ukraine and Moldavia—with a similar mechanism that would be witnessed later in America. Migrants from the West (Flemish, German, Dutch, etc.) settled as peasants after land developments were undertaken by contractors. At the same time, the former Slavic nobility, monasteries, Teutonic Knights, and contractors established large domains with a workforce composed of the local Slavic population. As early as the thirteenth century these domains were living off grain exports towards Flanders and later towards Holland (Slicher Van Bath, 1963: 156).

The emergence in Central Europe of these vast domains using forced peasant labor (serfs) at a time when the peasantry in Western Europe was conquering greater rights and freedom has been widely commented, including by major authors such as Max Weber (Weber, 1927), Immanuel Wallerstein (Wallerstein, 1974), and Robert Brenner (Brenner, 1976). The strengthening of the economic and political position of the nobility in effect was associated with a diminishment in the power of towns and industries that could have existed in the region. This regression of capitalism saw the return of a feudal type of society and may explain the "under-development" of these societies in the nineteenth and early twentieth centuries. From this perspective, the development of the cereal export trade in Central Europe can be considered as a process of "development of underdevelopment" to use André Gunder Frank's expression relative to Latin America (Frank, 1966).

The chain of events, as described by Mariam Malowist with reference to Poland (Malowist, 1959, 2010), was as follows. Following a first phase during which local traders sold cereal from peasants and nobility to Dutch buyers, in a second phase the nobility bought the harvests from peasants and traded directly with Dutch merchants. An alliance between the Polish nobility and Dutch merchants thus resulted in the marginalization of local traders and bourgeoisie. Thus the weakening of Polish towns commenced. And it would continue, and was manifested in the prohibition on the peasantry migrating to towns. Rapid demographic decline of towns followed, as a continuous flow of rural migrants was a vital necessity, given high urban mortality rates (which exceeded birth rates). This decline weakened even further the peasantry, depriving them of the only market to which they could have direct access. At the same time, the nobility was also able to progressively increase work obligations on the local peasantry due to their divisions and resulting political weakness. The weakening of towns also contributed to maintaining peasant discipline as they could no longer seek refuge in towns (Carsten, 1947: 160). To conclude, the decline of towns, the impoverishment of the peasantry and a policy of openness to the import of manufactured goods led to the country's deindustrialization and opened up new markets for Dutch manufactures.

Forest products

Tree products have multiple functions in solar societies, the production of heat being the primary one.[3] But the United Provinces also used trees for three other functions:

- For lumber used in construction of buildings, ships, and machines (mills).
- For the side products of wood ashes or potash,[4] used in soapmaking as well as glassmaking.
- For tar, which is obtained through the slow combustion of wood, and pitch, obtained through distillation of tar, both of which are used for sealing ship hulls and extending the life of ropes, as well as being used in chemistry and medicine.

All these were vital products for the United Province economy. And yet the United Provinces had almost no forests or trees. Imports were thus indispensable. The extraction, or production, of tree products was characteristic of the frontier logic that governed the large forest tracts of Northern Europe (birch and poplar for potash, pine for tar). Tar production played an avant-garde role within these frontiers. Tar had a high weight value and could be transported in barrels that were relatively easy to handle. It was therefore supplied from the furthest regions of the frontier; whereas wood was supplied from the closest still existing forests.

> Small in volume but high in aggregate value was the trade in wood byproducts, carried via ports in the eastern Baltic, such as Danzig, Konigsberg and Riga. This consumed vast quantities of wood by the standards of the age: the Dutch annually imported twice as much wood again, in the form of ash, as grew in the entirety of Britain, and at its peak ash consumed around 17 times as much wood as the Republic's timber imports. Finland was the main supplier of tar and pitch, essential components of the shipping industry, a trade again that outstripped the demand for actual timber.
>
> (Warde, 2009: 3)

According to figures from Jan de Vries and Ad van der Woude covering the United Provinces' late period (1722–80), the share of tree products in total imports to the United Provinces from the Baltics was equivalent to that of grain, around 40 percent of the total volume and 30 percent of the total value (de Vries and van der Woude, 1997: 425).

---

[3] The production of domestic heat was an essential "function" expected from tree products. The availability of firewood, and its derivative charcoal, was also decisive for the growth of activities such as the steel industry and saltpeter production. Thus, one can practically assimilate iron and saltpeter with forest products. This explains why countries like Sweden or Russia were major iron producers until the eighteenth century.

[4] Potash is obtained by dissolving wood ashes in water, then drying the liquid and cooking the residue in an oven to eliminate organic compounds. Wood provides both the raw material (the ashes) and the energy needed for the process (heating and cooking).

The United Provinces' supply of products derived from trees came from two sources: the North Sea through Norway and its fjords which penetrated deeply inland, and the Baltics, within which Finland played a very particular role.[5]

In the sixteenth century, the Dutch controlled Norwegian wood, and Dutch ships were present in all the fjords located between Trondheim and Bergen. Wood was purchased as a standing crop on credit. It was transported in specialized ships which made several trips per year. In 1652, a third of ships departing from Amsterdam went towards Norway (de Vries and van der Woude, 1997: 423).[6] At the end of the sixteenth century, Holland also controlled the Baltic trade in tar. Its naval construction industry consumed a part of this tar, the rest was exported to England and France. At the time, tar came mainly from Prussian ports. In 1610, around 50 percent of Baltic tar was sent from such ports. But during the seventeenth century, Finland took the leading role in tar production in the Baltics and more widely in Europe (Kaukiainen, 1993: 343). From 1648 to 1715, tar exports from Finland, which at the time was a part of Sweden, were controlled under private monopoly bestowed by the crown and based in Stockholm (ibid.: 348). Later, during the second half of the eighteenth century, after Sweden adopted a navigation act similar to that of the English (see Part 2), merchants from Finland took control of the trade and transport of tar to final destination. Potash production appears to have commenced in Finland in 1672 with the creation of a factory in Revolax (Kunnas, 2007).

Fishing, not just for food

Many contemporaries consider that the true origin of the Dutch golden age lies in herring, but historians have put the importance of the fish in perspective. Nonetheless, it remains true that herrings and herring exports contributed greatly to Dutch development.[7]

The Christian calendar which proscribed meat for 135 days in the year (Fridays, Lent, the eve of holidays), but not fish, ensured European success for Dutch herring.[8] Herring is one of the fish types best suited for preserving; it could thus grace Christian tables which were far away from coasts and rivers, and deprived of fresh fish. The consumption of herring progressively became entrenched in the interior and eastern

---

[5] Some potash also came from the White Sea which gave access to Russian resources through the Arkhangelsk port.
[6] Some of the wood also came from Germany, and was floated down the Rhine.
[7] According to Richard Unger—who proffers this estimation to counter the idea that herring was a gold mine for Holland, but which in a way, rather validates the idea—during the 1630s, while fishing was beating records, the annual value of the catch in the United Provinces represented the equivalent of 30 tons of silver. During the same period, Spain received from its American colonies 140.5 tons of silver per year (Unger, 1980: 2550). United Provinces' herring may not have been a gold mine, but looking at these figures, it certainly looks like it was a small silver mine.
[8] Fortune for Dutch Protestants thanks to the rigors of the Catholic religion.

part of the continent from the fifteenth century on. By the end of that century, herring already occupied second place among all products imported into Danzig in Poland (Hoffmann, 2000: 144).

Hollanders and Zeelanders started fishing herring from the first half of the fourteenth century, in small boats that fished during the day and delivered fresh or slightly salted fish. The adoption of the *hering buss* which was much larger and a veritable floating factory, made it possible to gut and salt the fish immediately on board. Fishing could thus be extended to periods of five to eight weeks without returning to port. A fleet of more than 500 boats was now able to dredge the Dogger Bank on the English coasts. On these boats, fish were prepared and initially placed in barrels and once at port placed in new packaging (Unger, 1980).

Herring fishing was initially led by small boat owners, working in collaboration with brokers for funding and commission sales. The brokers progressively took control of the sector, and became owners and managers of boats. They mobilized urban capital keen for investment in order to incorporate port packaging activities, and remained owners of the product until its sale in the place of consumption (Unger, 1980: 258). Boat crews, including captains, hence became wage workers.

A college of commissionaires of large fisheries, *College van Commissarissen van de Groote Visscheri* was created in 1575. It distributed fishing licenses and organized ship convoys to ensure security. Above all, it fixed rules for the practice of fishing and for how the finished product was to be prepared (set times for gutting and salting, the type of salt to use, the materials that barrels should be made of, how different qualities should be graded, etc.) thus effectively regulating quality (de Vries and Van der Woude, 1997: 246). These rules were instrumental in enabling Dutch herring to acquire commodity, or raw material, status and became an important long-distance trade object.

Exports from the United Provinces towards the Baltics

The United Provinces has the historical particularity of having succeeded in obtaining the biomass needed for its economy and its metabolism not through force but through market exchange. Sourcing biomass for the Provinces meant selling goods that were desirable to communities, or at least the elites, in supplying territories.

In the sixteenth and seventeenth centuries, only a quarter of Dutch herring was consumed locally. The rest was exported. In 1640 for example, of the 20,000 lasts of herring fished (32,500 tons), 4,000 were sold on the local market, 4,000 in Hamburg, 4,000 in Cologne and in towns in Flanders and northern France, and 8,000 in Baltic ports. Herring was not only consumed in port towns but also carried inland on rivers. In the first half of the seventeenth century, no less than 11 percent of all Dutch herring destined for the Baltics arrived in Warsaw via the Vistula River (Unger, 1980: 263).

During the same period, herring and salt represented 45 percent of the value of goods exported by the United Provinces to the Baltics.⁹

The Baltics and the North Sea were also the locus of active trade in the textile sector. The United Provinces imported fibers (linen and raw hemp from the Baltics,¹⁰ and raw or processed wool from England) which were re-exported in the form of finished products. As suppliers as well as clients, Baltic states thus represented an important part of the United Provinces' textile industry.

Whale "fishing": Non-food fishing

The Dutch started to hunt whales in the early seventeenth century. Whales were initially captured for their oil (which comprises around 50 percent of a whale's weight) to be used in soapmaking, for lighting, and more marginally in leather working and paint production.

A whale "fishing" monopoly was conceded from 1614 to 1645 to a northern company, operating around Spitzbergen. In reality the company was a cartel which regulated competition and also set up facilities in Spitzbergen with the necessary equipment for processing whale lard to extract oil.

After 1645, the concession was taken away, and the number of companies, and therefore of boats, grew. During the last third of the seventeenth century, migration of whales obliged the Dutch to go further up north, and then at the beginning of the eighteenth century, to venture west of Greenland.

---

⁹ Fish catch and fish export volumes from the United Provinces, however, fell after 1650. Dutch fishing faced increased competition from fishing industries in Scandinavia, Scotland, and coastal Baltic countries. From 1661 to 1720, the Dutch still supplied 60 percent of Baltic herring imports. By the 1760s this had fallen to 10 percent. The Dutch lost their monopoly position, which they had enjoyed since the late sixteenth and early seventeenth century. Dutch fishing also faced the challenge of protectionist policies put in place by France from 1664, and England's subsidies to local fishing from 1726.

¹⁰ Until the last quarter of the sixteenth century, United Province trade with Russia was part of trade with the Baltics. It was mainly centered on the port of Narva, which handled a large share of hemp and linen exports from the Baltics, and practically all tallow, skin, and fur exports (Attman, 1981: 179). But Sweden took control of the Narva port in 1585, followed by Riga in 1621, and the White Sea and the Dvina River hence became the only maritime route available for Russians. The geography of exchange with Russia shifted again when Saint Petersburg was established in 1703. The Baltics then again became the shortest route for exporting Russian products, at a time when England was importing ever increasing quantities from Russia.

3

Spices and companies: Trade with another world-economy, Asia

Spices—especially pepper, but also nutmeg and cloves—hold a special position in European long-distance trade. For these products, the continent was marginal to Asia, in the sense that Europe did nothing more than divert a part of intra-Asian trade flows for its profit and always represented only a relatively limited market compared to regional markets. Chaunu states: "We can consider that 12 to 14% of Asian spice production was exported in the sixteenth century towards the Mediterranean and Western Europe" (Chaunu, 1969: 322). Although marginal, this trade had a long history: Ancient Rome, and later Venice, whose fortune was founded on spices, traded already with Asia for these products. The Portuguese explored the world in order to grab this lucrative trade away from the Venetians and Ottomans. They crossed the Cape of Good Hope, bringing with them a militarized logic that despite the numerous networks of traders that already existed, had been absent in the Indian Ocean until then (Tracy, 1990; Chaudhuri, 1985). Their network of forts, from Malacca to the Hormuz straits guaranteed their monopoly over trade towards Europe, which would later be taken from them by the Dutch, who in turn would lose out to the English.

European companies: Trade and violence

The spice trade as carried out directly by Europeans is the field, *par excellence*, in which the "company" model dominated[1] in the seventeenth and eighteenth centuries. The main characteristic of a chartered company was an exclusive right to trade accorded by a European "prince" between the territory of the "prince" and a distant territory. The first chartered companies appeared in the mid-sixteenth century with the establishment of the Muscovy Company in 1553. Two companies dominated trade with Asia: the Dutch East India Company (in Dutch, Vereenigde Oostindische Compagnie, VOC)

---

[1] The Portuguese were a partial exception. From 1506 to 1570 the spice trade was exclusively controlled by Casa de India, a royal establishment. This monopoly was later removed to the benefit of competing merchants. Administration of forts and trading posts, however, remained centralized under the Estado da India, an administrative organ of the Portuguese colonies in India which would survive until 1962.

and the English East India Company (EIC), created respectively in 1602[2] and 1600. The last companies disappeared in the mid-nineteenth century:[3] the VOC was dissolved as early as 1799, and the EIC in 1858.

The VOC, which held the United Provinces' monopoly on trade east of the Cape of Good Hope, was a vertically integrated company, with centralized management, whose capital was held by shareholders. It was constituted as a joint-stock company with a board of directors composed of representatives of different groups of shareholder merchants (eight representatives for Amsterdam, four for Zeeland, two for the Northern Provinces, and the one alternating between North or South Zeeland).

The VOC operated—selling and buying—in territories that were not under the authority of other European powers. The legal monopoly they held for supplying their country of origin depended on this. It was intended to compensate the costs of conquering and defending new sources of supply and new markets in territories that were potentially or effectively hostile. These costs took the concrete form of forts, trading posts, and armed ships. The VOC was active as much in war as in trade and their enemies were not just Asian or Arab princes and merchants, but also, or even more so, the companies of other European countries.

Chartered companies are considered as forefathers of the large bureaucratic firm, so well described by Chandler (Chandler, 1977). The VOC was by far the largest chartered company, with an estimated 46,000 "employees" (!) at the end of the seventeenth century, of which 28,000 Europeans, 10,000 free Asians (mainly military), and 8,000 unfree Asians and Africans (Lucassen, 2004: 15). Companies were also characterized by the wide autonomy that field agents in the forts and trading posts had in light of extremely slow communications. In the late sixteenth century, it took two years to exchange correspondence between Lisbon and Goa (Findlay and O'Rourke, 2007: 154), and five years for return correspondence between Spain and the Philippines (Chaunu, 1969: 277).

The spice trade differed from other trades by the lack of participation of Europeans in production until the late eighteenth century. Spice production remained the business of Asian peasants, traders, and princes. Europeans in most cases contented themselves with buying spices from their trading posts and then transporting them on their fleets to Europe.[4]

The quest for monopoly position over the European market, however, was more often explicit, with frequent use of violence and coercion to eliminate competitors. Thus, between 1605 and 1656, the VOC conquered the mythical spice islands of the

---

[2] The first Dutch expedition to reach the Indian peninsula took place in 1595. In the years that followed, trade was carried out in a decentralized manner along the Baltic trade model. However, it quickly became evident, after a quadrupling of purchase prices, that "free competition" was not well adapted to the spice trade (Masselman, 1961).

[3] On the English side, one can also cite the Hudson's Bay Company and the Royal African Company. Similar companies were created in France, Spain, Sweden, and Denmark. For France, one can cite the Compagnie des îles d'Amériques, the Compagnie de Chine, the Compagnie des Indes Orientales, as well as the Compagnie des Indes occidentales.

[4] There were, however, exceptions, such as, for the Dutch case, coffee or sugar production in Java, or very early on (1621) nutmeg on the Banda and Neira islands (van Welie, 2008: 78).

Moluccas previously under Portuguese control. The company allied with local sultans to destroy a part of the existing plantations on two Muslim islands which were the historical center of production and to concentrate production on four small islands that had already been evangelized (Bulbeck, 1998: 20). This is how the VOC gained a monopoly position over the supply of cloves from 1656 to 1770. Bolstered by this advantage, the company reduced volumes and raised clove prices on the European market.

The ratio between the sales prices of cloves in Europe and the purchase price in Asia, stood at around 7 to 1 at the end of the sixteenth century. The ratio started to fall during the first decades of the seventeenth century which were marked by competition between Portuguese, Dutch, and Arab traders, and reached a low point during the 1640s. After it eliminated its competitors, the VOC reversed this downward trend. It limited supply, from a peak of 300 tons to as low as 89 tons, which had the double effect of making prices rise in Europe and fall in Asia. The ratio between Europe and Asia prices rose sharply to around 14 to 1 (and occasionally higher) up until the late eighteenth century (Figure 3.1).

Trade in pepper, on the other hand, was never subject to such a monopoly over supply to Europe. The area where pepper was grown was much vaster, or rather became much vaster with time, making it impossible for one single company to have complete control over its export. Supply of pepper to Europe thus elicited strong competition from the late sixteenth century to the late eighteenth century, between Portuguese and Arabs first, and later between Dutch and English (and more marginally the French). Throughout this period, the ratio between prices in Europe and prices in Asia remained

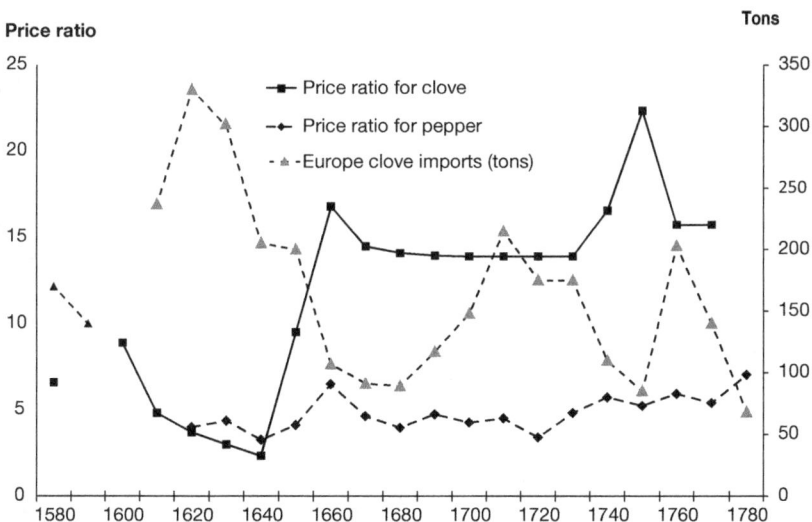

Figure 3.1 Ratio between sales price in Europe and purchase price in Asia for cloves and pepper, 1580–1800

Source: Bulbeck, 1998: 58 and 84.

stable, and appears low when compared to that of cloves. It remained low during the eighteenth century due to strategies that limited supply, and the practices of exclusivity contracts and administered prices by the VOC and EIC who faced falling demand (Bulbeck, 1998: 64).

From spices to slaves

The Banda archipelago is situated just south of the Moluccas islands. The Banda islands were the only place in the world in the sixteenth century where nutmeg grew. People traveled to the "Spice Islands" as were called the Moluccas at the time, specifically for nutmeg and cloves. When the Dutch arrived on the islands in 1599, they were already to a significant extent specialized in growing nutmeg for Javanese, Arab, Chinese, and Portuguese merchants (Jordan, 2016: 65).

Between 1602 and 1621, the Dutch tried to obtain an official monopoly over the nutmeg trade from the local chiefs and also chase the Portuguese and English from the archipelago through military means.

The inhabitants attempted armed resistance, and in 1621 the Dutch reacted with a "punitive" expedition, composed of Dutch soldiers, Japanese mercenaries, and Javanese slaves. This resulted in the massacre of the local populace (only 1,000 inhabitants of the islands' 15,000 inhabitants were spared) and the creation of sixty-eight plantations on the archipelago. These plantations were run by former VOC employees; the company therefore now had monopoly over nutmeg supply and control over its price. The company provided the planters with slaves and with rice to feed them. The slaves were bought in different Indian Ocean ports controlled by the Dutch. They were of diverse origins: "Gujerat, Malabar, Coromandel, Malay peninsula, Java, Borneo, the Chinese coasts, different locations in the Moluccas, Kai and Aru." To these were added "Spanish, Javanese and Makassar" prisoners (Loth, 1995: 23); 1,879 slaves were working in plantations on Banda in 1694 (Vink, 2003: 161).[5]

While this slave plantation episode is an exception in the United Provinces' Asian history, the Indian Ocean slave trade, dominated for two centuries by the Dutch, was for its part very dynamic (ibid.: 2003). Slaves came mainly from three regions: the East African coast and Madagascar, India, and Southeast Asia. Slavery as practiced by Europeans was superposed on preexisting forms of coerced labor. The Dutch bought slaves from native suppliers or obtained them in the fallouts of battles fought against local powers, of which they were many. The great majority of slaves had urban occupations. At the end of the seventeenth century, 57 percent of the population of Batavia (present-day Jakarta) were slaves (ibid.: 148).

In the [this] maritime network of colonial towns, slaves formed a unique element occupied with serving the Dutch inner circle: they worked on the docks, erected

---

[5] This type of organization was an exception in the United Provinces' Asian history, but it nonetheless prefigured the American history of slave plantations.

fortifications, tended to Company garden plots, functioned as artisans, and complemented the European households as domestic servants, concubines, or even as future wives. But they were almost never involved in commercial agriculture for the European market. In the Indian Ocean World, commercial production remained squarely in the hands of indigenous societies.

(van Welie, 2008: 78)

Conclusion

Wealth and power of a people and a political entity within a solar metabolic society depends on its capacity to mobilize biomass. The United Provinces, endowed with extremely limited territory and therefore limited biomass production, stood out for its remarkable capacity to mobilize biomass that was "external" to its territory and its time. It did this in three ways:

- Exploiting peat (biomass from the past)
- Fishing and whale hunting (marine biomass)
- Importing massive quantities of biomass (cereals, fibers, forest products) from coastal countries on the North and Baltic seas (biomass from other territories).

From an energy perspective, the United Provinces thus obtained a surplus of two types of energy: metabolic energy (cereals and fish) and thermal energy (peat, wood, whale oil). The Provinces used mechanical energy provided by wind, which enabled them to transport these products over long distances and, thanks to windmills, also to exploit peat resources and power machines.

While they took up some techniques developed by the Flemish, the United Provinces also distinguished themselves through the remarkable intensification and specialization of their agriculture. Contrary to the "metabolic rift" theory,[1] considered constitutive of urbanization within a capitalist structure by a whole range of authors (Moore, 2011; Foster, 1999; Schneider and McMichael, 2010), in the case of the United Provinces (and before them Flanders) there was apparently a positive relationship between town and country. Towns encouraged even further intensification of agriculture by providing both markets and fertility (through their supply of various forms of organic waste and ashes).[2] This dynamic was very largely founded on Baltic supplies on which the metabolism of towns was strongly dependent (in particular for cereals and wood). Upstream of the harmonious relationship that developed between

---

[1] According to Karl Marx, who was referring to work by Justus Liebig, the rural–urban transfer of nutrients occurs unidirectionally towards towns (Foster, 1999).

[2] The same positive relationship between town and country was found in the Japan of the Tokugawa, in particular around the capital Edo, whose population was estimated at 1 million inhabitants at the beginning of the eighteenth century. (On the agricultural use of urban waste in Asia, see Ferguson, 2014, for example.)

town and country within the Dutch territory, however, a permanent transfer of fertility operated—a one-way flow of nutrients from the Baltics to Holland. Between these two locations a metabolic rift effectively existed.

The historical particularity of the United Provinces is that they obtained a large part of their external biomass through trade and exchange. Their imports were financed through their commercial activities (transport, storage, and credit between Northern Europe and Southern Europe). These exchanges were partially based on their exports of manufactured goods (processed fish, fabrics, soaps, bricks, ships, etc.), but the bulk of finance came from re-exporting products from Southern Europe to the North (salt for example) or vice versa (cereals for example). The wealth of the United Provinces was thus to a large extent based solely on their capacity to organize trade from one end of Europe to another, to act as a supplier of what are today called "services" (finance, transport, storage, etc.). But from a metabolic perspective, the distinction between trade service activities and manufacturing activities, leading to the production of fabric, soaps, or glass, does not make much sense. In both cases, what is occurring is the transformation of available matter, either of its form and its composition (manufacturing), of its place (transport), or of its time (storage) through the implementation of human labor or other forms of energy.

Merchant trade activity, however, did not exclude use of coercion or force. The latter were indispensable for the correct functioning of the economy and the metabolism of the United Provinces. They were sometimes "sub-contracted" out as was the case in Poland for cereal production earmarked for the Dutch, in Brazil for sugar production, or in Spanish America for mining silver to be used for purchasing Asian spices. Force was also part of the means directly employed by the United Provinces to gain monopoly over fishing in the North Sea, or to acquire and then defend VOC trading posts in Asia.

The United Provinces would later be faced with the rise of two competitors, France and England, whose challenge was increasingly felt from the end of the seventeenth century. To reduce the power of the United Provinces, the two rivals implemented what would be called "mercantilism," highly proactive interventionist policies aimed at developing their own military capacity, as well as aiding expansion of biomass production and manufacturing activity within their own territories and in the colonies they acquired. The United Provinces thus lost the consumer markets they used to have in France and England. They also lost access to certain resources, such as English wool, and had to face increasing competition in various sectors (the textile sector). Both France and England would take advantage of the size of their territories, which were much larger than Dutch territories, and which expanded even further with their conquests in the New World, to cause the fall of the Dutch hegemon.

Part 2

Where we see England pull ahead of France by exploiting its territory and its colonies better, 1700–1846

Introduction

This second part of the book is focused on the period when Great Britain[1] and France contended to succeed the United Provinces. A long series of wars involving the three parties commenced in 1627. Distant territories (India, Canada, the "sugar islands") were the stage of several battles between France and Great Britain. France experienced a series of setbacks, culminating in the 1815 British victory at Waterloo.

It was a period during which biomass supply essentially was sourced from the national territory, which in Great Britain experienced intensified exploitation under the agricultural revolution. Distant biomass, produced mainly in the colonies, was managed and administered as a source of currency. Toward the end of this period, however, the growing needs of a booming manufacturing industry meant that Great Britain relied on massive importation of non-food biomass.

Competition between France and Great Britain played out decisively in the Atlantic space—within the ocean itself, in the Caribbean, and in North America, which were integrated as peripheries in the European world-economy, and from which the United Provinces were practically excluded. The Baltics stayed on the margins, just like the Mediterranean had in the earlier period. Trade in tropical products (sugar being the most important, but also coffee, indigo, tobacco, cotton, and rice) from European plantations, reliant on African labor and situated in the Americas (growing many crops that originated from Asia), was no longer organized on the chartered company model, but within a framework of colonial exclusivity which designated trade spaces reserved to "national enterprises." Like the United Provinces before them for spices, France and Great Britain re-exported the main part of their tropical production, which generated trade surpluses for both countries.

This double quest, for trade surpluses and self-sufficiency in biomass, led the two rivals to adopt very similar policies, which Adam Smith and his successors would later qualify as "mercantilist."

Asia still essentially lay outside of the European world-economy, even if the Dutch strengthened their hold over Java and if the English were commencing their colonization of India. Exchanges with Asia were a lot more limited than those with

---

[1] England, Great Britain, United Kingdom: I wrongly use these terms interchangeably as though they were synonyms, despite the distinct historical and geographical realities they represent. My use of the three should be understood as referring to the geographic zone that the English crown at the time considered as her metropole … and the "English" simply as the inhabitants of that zone!

the American colonies, and were increasingly focused on fabrics (cottons and silks) and tea. But Asia nonetheless cast a shadow: despite its low presence in the biomass trade, Asia influenced the way Europe exploited the American continent. The silver which financed Spanish colonization found its main market in China. A significant number of products from slave plantations served as substitutes to Asian imports: coffee, cotton, sugar, indigo, etc. Later on, English industries used a strategy of import substitution against Indian cottons to spur their own development.

The last part of this period was characterized by large-scale exploitation of Great Britain's underground and its coal. The invention of the steam engine at the beginning of the eighteenth century reinforced British wealth by increasing the availability of mechanical energy. The Industrial Revolution, associated with the use of coal, made importation of increasing quantities of biomass a necessity, initially in the form of non-food raw materials, and later increasingly in the form of food. The abrogation of the Corn Laws in 1846 denoted an official renouncement by Great Britain of its quest for territorial self-sufficiency in biomass, a self-sufficiency that in practice had long been chipped away.

4

Mercantilism and the art of counting on your own forces

Mercantilism refers to policies adopted by the princes of European nation-states aimed at putting trade, and more widely economic activity in their territories, at the service of their power. These princes at the international level sought to escape from the all-powerful Dutch, as well as to affirm their own power within the borders of their territories by unifying them to create a national market.

Wealth and power

According to Giovanni Arrighi, the emergence and adoption of mercantilism should be viewed as the solution embraced by European countries—England and France first and foremost—to counter the dominance of the United Provinces:

> All variants of mercantilism had one thing in common: they were more or less conscious attempts on the part of territorialist rulers to imitate the Dutch, to become themselves capitalist in orientation as the most effective way of attaining their own power objectives. The Dutch had demonstrated [...] that [...] the systematic accumulation of pecuniary surpluses could be a far more effective technique of political aggrandizement than the acquisition of territories and subjects. The more the Dutch succeeded in their endless accumulation of capital, and the more this accumulation was turned into ever-growing capabilities to shape and manipulate the European political system, the more European territorialist rulers were drawn into the Dutch path of development [...]. The creation of world-embracing commercial empires, the rerouting of commodity and money flows to entrepôts within one's own control and jurisdiction, the systematic accumulation of pecuniary surpluses in the balance of payments with other domains, were all expressions of this imitative predisposition of territorialist organizations. But mercantilism was not just the imitative response of territorialist rulers to the challenges posed by world-embracing Dutch capitalism.
>
> Equally important was the tendency to reaffirm or re-establish the territorialist principle of autarky in the new form of "national economy making," and to counterpose that principle to the Dutch principle of universal intermediation.

The central aspect of this tendency was the strengthening of "forward and backward linkages," in Albert Hirschman's sense, between the consumers and the producers of a given territorial domain – a strengthening which involved not just the establishment of intermediate (mainly "manufacturing") activities linking domestic primary production to domestic final consumption, but also the forcible "delinking" of producers and consumers from relationships of dependence on foreign (primarily Dutch) purchases and sales.

(Arrighi, 1994: 144–5)

For Adam Smith (1776) and his successors, these "mercantile policies" committed the grave error of confusing wealth with the accumulation of gold and silver (bullionism[1]), and favoring merchants above all else. In effect, mercantilism was based on the principle of a reciprocal stimulus effect between trade, or wealth, and power (summed up by the phrase "power and plenty"). Power enabled trade by making it possible to eliminate competition, and trade reinforced power by improving the finances of the prince (see Viner, 1948 for a discussion on the relationship between these two objectives).

In practice, mercantilist policies initially based the accumulation of wealth and power on a deliberate mobilization of resources from their own territories and from their colonies. External trade (imports plus exports) in 1790, despite strong expansion in preceding decades, represented only 20 percent of GDP for France and 24 percent for England, compared to 110 percent for the United Provinces (Table 4.1).

The goal of mercantilist policy was not just "managing" competition with other nations. Céline Spector, discussing Heckscher, notes that "Mercantilism appears to be a 'system of power' characterized by two fundamental goals: that of external power, seeking hegemony over other nations; and that of internal unification, which subordinates economic prosperity to the power of the state" (Spector, 2003: 293). The mercantilist period was characterized by the emergence of national systems for regulating the economy, which progressively replaced intervention by cities. According to Heckscher, the policy objectives of medieval towns could be summed up in five points (Heckscher and Shapiro, 1935: 128 and onwards):

- Guarantee an abundant supply of food products and agricultural raw materials for town dwellers. Interventions were thus clearly oriented in favor of the consumer.

Table 4.1 Exports plus imports over GDP (%)

	1720	1755	1790
United Provinces	82	84	110
United Kingdom	19	20	24
France	5.5	14	20

Source: O'Rourke et al., 2010: 106.

[1] Bullion refers to gold bricks.

- Reserve all economic activity of the town to its citizens.
- Exert control over "foreign" traders so that these were obliged to use local town traders as intermediaries. Foreign traders could thus be obliged to reside in a specific neighborhood.
- Attract as much traffic as possible to the town, for example by imposing transshipment on ships that passed by the town.
- Guarantee a minimum level of subsistence to citizens of the town by regulating competition, through for example, a system of guilds.

These rules, which discriminated systematically between citizens of a given town and "foreigners" from other towns, were dismantled by states, who then adopted them in improved versions at the level of the whole country to build a national economy.

A fundamental difference between France, and England and the United Provinces was that the former's territory was continental and immense. Land transportation, which was necessary but difficult as we saw within a solar metabolic system, strongly limited economic integration of the national territory. French kings undertook great investments in land infrastructure (roads and canals, including the Midi Canal) from the late seventeenth century and throughout the eighteenth century, but this was not enough to compensate for the advantage that being small and "insular" proffered to France's rivals. Fernand Braudel writes:

> The emergence of a national market was a battle against this omnipresent inertia, a battle which would eventually generate exchange and communications. But was the major source of inertia in the French case perhaps the very size of the country? The United Provinces and England—the former a small and the latter only a medium-sized country—had more compact nervous systems and were more easily unified. Distance was not such an obstacle for them.
>
> (Braudel, 1984: 315)

The construction of the French market, which involved on the one hand, establishing barriers at its borders, and on the other hand, eliminating internal obstacles, lagged behind the political unification of the country. In the eighteenth century when Great Britain already boasted a truly domestic market, exchanges across France were still encumbered by local custom duties and tolls. Jean Claude Toutain observed:

> The French space is a web of juxtaposed independent markets, as well as juxtaposed independent centers of production [...] Due to the extreme fragmentation of each region; to the tendency toward autarky in each province, each region, each commune, each household; to obstacles (prohibitions and customs duties) placed on trade of grain and other agricultural products, it may occur that some provinces experience surplus production and are reduced to destroying unsellable produce, while neighboring provinces suffer food shortages.
>
> (Toutain, 1961: 5)

The "exclusive (colonial)" regime, one of the mercantilist policy instruments, organized trade from the colonies along a principle that may be summed up as: any product exported from the colony must go to the metropole, and any product imported must come from the metropole, or at the least, be transported by a ship belonging to the metropole. The Navigation Acts were the best illustration of this principle for Great Britain. A series of Navigation Acts were promulgated in 1651, 1662, 1670, and 1673 respectively. The first act reserved the right to transport merchandise to Great Britain exclusively for English vessels when the merchandise originated from outside Europe, or for English vessels or vessels from the country of origin for merchandise originating from within Europe. The acts that followed stipulated that all merchandise going to the Americas had to first be offloaded and inspected on English territory, and that all tropical products (sugar, tobacco, cotton, ginger, indigo) exported from the English colonies pass through English territory before being re-exported. The acts were abolished in 1849, after 200 years of application. The Navigation Acts were supplemented by tax instruments which applied different rates of customs duty on products depending on their origin. Customs duties on sugar from the English colonies were thus three or four times lower than those on sugar from the French or Dutch colonies (Findlay and O'Rourke, 2007: 238). Measures were also adopted to foster domestic production. For example, England prohibited export of raw wool at the end of James I's reign (1625), while import of French and Dutch fabrics were subject to heavy taxation. A sliding scale of import tax and export subsidies was also implemented for cereals (the Corn Laws) so as to support national production and stabilize domestic prices.

Splendor and decadence of the colonial supply chain

During the eighteenth century, external supplies to England and France increasingly were limited to imports from their colonies.

In 1772, 63 percent of imports into England came from its colonies (Table 4.2). These colonial supplies originated from three regions:

- Neighboring Ireland.[2] During this period, Ireland really came to be used as a supplier of biomass.
- American territories (the Caribbean and North America). Exports continued growing as they had in the seventeenth century.
- Asia. To a lesser extent than the other regions, and with greater diversity of origins, as it involved products that were centralized by the East Indian Company.

We were not able to find a similarly exhaustive overview of French external trade. The 1789 publication by Ambroise-Marie Arnould, deputy director for trade balance, is one of the rare sources available. He compares the situation in 1717 with that of 1787. Like England, France saw the share of its imports in its colonies rise significantly.

---

[2] Ireland which was conquered progressively by England between the twelfth and fifteenth century, did not become an English colony until 1800 when it was integrated into the United Kingdom. During the course of the seventeenth century, a significant part of the Irish population was massacred by Cromwell, and a settler colony (with English and Scottish settlers) was established, which would to a great extent feed Great Britain during the eighteenth century.

Table 4.2 Colonies' share (in %) in total imports to England, 1663–1816

	1663–9	1699–1701	1772–4	1814–16
Colonies' share in total imports	25	39	63	52
Ireland	1	7	11	10
Americas	12	18	37	26
Asia	12	13	15	16

Sources: Davis, 1954, 1962, 1979.

Table 4.3 Colonies' share (in %) in total imports to France, 1716 and 1787

	1716	1787
Colonies' share in total imports	25	42
Asia	7	6
Africa	1	1
Americas	17	35

Sources: Arnould, 1791, t. 3. Arnould's data includes monetary products of diverse origins in the 1787 imports.

Colonial products imported by France came almost exclusively from its American territories, and the last trade posts it still had in Asia (Table 4.3) The share of colonial imports rose from 25 percent in 1716 to 42 percent in 1787, of which 35 percent originated from the American colonies.

American independence in 1776 signaled the start of England's colonial decline. With its new status of a sovereign nation, the United States took on the role of key supplier to England, thanks to English imports of American cotton. France's colonial supply chain system collapsed around the same period, beleaguered by repeated defeats at the hands of the English in India and Canada, by the French Revolution, and the Napoleonic period. The slave revolt in Saint-Domingue, the most productive of the Caribbean islands, and later the island's independence, in addition to repeated occupation of French colonies by enemy countries (the first of which, England) led to sharp falls in colonial imports. Official French statistics (*Les Statistiques de la France*) published in 1838, report 9 million francs' worth of imports from the colonies for the year 1810, over a total import value of 339 million francs, in other words just 3 percent of imports. The same source reports that for the year 1822, the first successive year with data, imports from the colonies stood at 48 million francs over total imports of 426 million francs (11 percent), and in 1836, the figures were 68 million francs over 905 million francs (7 percent) (Ministre des Travaux Publics, 1838: 6, 10, and 14). Supplies from the colonies thus rose slightly following the restitution of some territories obtained through the 1814 Treaty of Paris, but they were still far from pre-French Revolution levels.

Colonial products, first and foremost, a source of currency

In the competitive race between the United Provinces, England, and France, the importance of products from the Atlantic plantations resided in the fact that the main part of these products were re-exported from the metropole. Their contribution in terms of matter or energy was not significant, but their role in generating currency was crucial. Currency made it possible to obtain other goods which were truly important for the economy and metabolism of the three countries, and also funded the (mercenary) wars that they undertook. The exclusivity principle effectively reserved European supply of plantation products to the colonial powers. The sizable share of re-exports reveals the structural role that colonial territories—and trading posts—played in the French and English economy and metabolism.

Of all plantation products, only two were significantly consumed within England: sugar and dyes, indispensable for its booming textile industry. For tobacco, coffee, and rice, the value of re-exports exceeded that of imports (Table 4.4).

Ralph Davis speaks of a "commercial revolution" when describing the transformation in the composition of English exports between the Civil War (1642) and the beginning of the eighteenth century. Wool fabrics (generally undyed), which until then made up the great majority of English exports (80 percent), after 1700 made up less than half of total exports as a result of the growth in re-exports of exotic products (Davis, 1962). These products, which included textiles, cottons, and silks from India, in 1700 represented 31 percent of the value of goods sold overseas by

Table 4.4 Trade of "exotic" products from England in the eighteenth century (in thousands of £)

		1699–1701	1722–4	1752–4	1772–4
Imports	Sugar	630	928	1 302	2 364
	Tobacco	249	263	560	519
	Coffee	27	127	53	436
	Rice	5	52	167	340
	Dyes	226	318	386	506
	Total	**1,137**	**1,688**	**2,468**	**4,165**
Re-exports	Sugar	287	211	110	429
	Tobacco	421	387	953	904
	Coffee	2	151	84	873
	Rice	4	53	206	363
	Dyes	85	83	112	211
	Total	**799**	**885**	**1,465**	**2,780**

Source: Davis, 1962.

England, and rose to 37 percent in 1772–4, before falling to 27 percent in 1815 (Davis, 1979: 31) (Table 4.5).

Fabrics were a dominant product in English re-exports until the last quarter of the eighteenth century. For the most part these were Asian calicos and silks, but there were also linens made in Ireland whose re-export was encouraged by subsidies. In the late eighteenth century, however, the re-export of textiles practically ceased, as they were sacrificed for the development of England's own textile industry. Re-exports thereon mainly involved sugar, tobacco, and coffee. The two latter products had re-export values that were higher than their import value.

Re-exports in France, represented a third of all exports just before the French Revolution (1787–9) (Besnier and Meignen, 1978). Jean Tarrade affirms: "The main element in the favorable metropolitan trade balance was the re-export of colonial products abroad, generating a surplus which gave the illusion of a prospering economy despite the economic difficulties of final period of the Ancien Régime" (Tarrade, 1972: 749). Similarly, Jean-Antoine Chaptal laments the disappearance of this source of income thirty years after the French Revolution:

> In the past, sugar was the most significant article among those that France supplied abroad: its colonies produced much more than needed for domestic consumption and the surplus was exchanged, with benefit, for products from the north. It is with a true feeling of pain that I submit to the eyes of the reader, the state of sugar imported from our colonies in 1788.
>
> (Chaptal, 1819: 491)

Table 4.5 Share of re-exports in total exports from England, 1663–1816 (in % of total exports)

	1699–1701	1772–4	1814–16
Re-exports	31	37	27
Fabrics	10	10	1
Silk	1	1	0
Dyes	1	1	3
Sugar	4	3	4
Pepper	1	1	–
Tobacco	6	6	1
Coffee	–	6	5
Tea	–	2	1
Rice	–	2	–
Rum	–	1	1

Sources: Davis, 1954, 1962, 1979.

Table 4.6 Share of re-exported imported colonial products in France (in %)

	1775–7	1785–9
Cocoa	48	64
Coffee	85	89
Cotton	–	37
Indigo	53	60
Sugar	75	69

Source: Tarrade, 1972: 753.

But this pain blinded Chaptal. It was not sugar (to which of course he owes the appearance of his name in the Larousse dictionary of common nouns![3]), but coffee that was at the top of the list of French exports before the Revolution. Coffee became commonplace in the 1780s thanks to a sharp rise in production in Saint-Domingue. In 1788, it represented half the value of re-exports, compared to 40 percent for sugar. It should be noted that almost 89 percent of imported coffee was re-exported, compared to "only" 69 percent of sugar. Cotton was the only product for which more than half of the imported quantity was used within the metropole (Table 4.6).

A permanent transfer of wealth thus took place from the colonies towards the metropoles. For both France and England, the balance of trade between metropole and colonies had a high deficit (metropoles imported a lot more than they exported). In 1772, England imported from its colonies one and a half times more than it exported to them. For France, this ratio reached two and half in 1787! But this apparent deficit, in reality was a surplus, as one comment from a trade officer shows: "As for trade with the islands, 42 million worth of merchandise was sent there and 136 million [of merchandise] was taken, that's 94 million in profits" (Besnier and Meignen, 1978: 589). Knowing that more than half of the products would have been re-exported for a neat profit, it's not just 94 million of profit, but much more that would contribute to the surplus in the French trade balance.

Slave plantations, the productive part of mercantilism

European conquests (Portuguese, Dutch, English, and French) in the Indian Ocean were most often limited to trading posts. This was not the case in the Atlantic where conquests took the form of wide-scale territorial expansion in both the islands and along the American coast. This development was the continuation of a process of conquest that had manifested itself in Europe, in the Spanish Reconquista, the British

---

[3] The French term "*chaptalisation*" refers to the process of adding sugar to grape must in order to increase the final alcohol content of wine after fermentation.

colonization of the Celtic fringe, and the movement of Germanic peoples toward the east.

A particular type of territory developed on the Atlantic facade of the Americas:[4] the plantation economy specialized in exotic products (sugar, coffee, cocoa, indigo, etc.). Philip Curtin proffers six traits to characterize the territories that participated in what he calls the Atlantic plantation complex (Curtin, 1990):

- The bulk of the workforce are mobilized through physical coercion.
- The population reproduction rate is less than 1. A continuous supply of new arrivals (slave or free) is thus required.
- The agricultural enterprise is organized as a large-scale system, employing from fifty to several hundreds workers.
- While capitalist, the plantation also has many feudal traits: plantation owners, for instance, wielded jurisdictional and police powers.
- Production from the plantations is specialized and intended for distant markets: a large share of food must be imported.
- Political control over the territory (or the system) is exerted from another continent and another type of society.

More than the surface area, the number of workers, or the invested capital, what first and foremost defined the plantation as an economic organization was the existence of a management hierarchy. At the top of this hierarchy was the plantation owner, owner of the land and equipment, an entrepreneur who, in certain periods and certain places, wielded the power of a sovereign. Under the plantation owner's authority were several layers of supervision. In Chandler's view, plantations were thus one of the first cases of an enterprise employing salaried managers (Chandler, 1977). Of such managers, the overseer played a central role:

> It was this agent who, in great measure determined the success or failure of planting operations on the larger estates devoted to the production of staple agricultural products. To the overseer were entrusted the welfare and supervision of Negroes; the care of land, stock and farm implements, the planting, cultivation, and harvesting of both staple and subsistence crops, and many other responsibilities associated with management of commercial agricultural enterprise.
> (Scarborough, 1966: xi)

Work surveillance was an essential activity in plantation life. The gang system, so often represented on engravings (and later in photos) by lines of farm workers with hoes carrying out the same gesture rhythmically, is the emblematic illustration of this, showing an intricate division of tasks intended to facilitate supervision (Mintz, 1986: 48–52). As Fogel (1989: 25) notes:

---

[4] From Rio de Janeiro to Virginia.

Sugar planters led the way in still another major technological innovation—the development of a new industrial labor discipline. [...] The industrial discipline, so difficult to bring about in the factories of free England and free New England, was achieved on sugar plantations more than a century earlier.

From indentured labor to slaves

The history of plantations is linked to mass migration, both forced and voluntary. A product of frontiers, plantations were established in territories that were sparsely populated or that had been depopulated through the violence and disease associated with European colonization. But the importance of using migrant labor must also be considered from the angle of work discipline. Discipline was more easily imposed on workers for whom the strangeness of the local context made it difficult, if not impossible, to escape and survive outside of the plantation.

The form of work referred to as "indentured labor" predates the transatlantic trade in the British Caribbean (West Indies). It was essentially characterized by a contract between a European worker and the plantation owner (or an association of plantation owners) which obliged the former to work for several years (most often four or five) for the latter in exchange for the cost of travel to the colony.

Indentured labor disappeared from plantations with the establishment of the slave trade. For Richard Pares, the replacement of indentured Europeans with Black slaves was based on simple economic logic. A slave cost more than an indentured laborer in the immediate term—£20 to £25 compared to £5 to £10 at the turn of the seventeenth and eighteenth centuries—but the cost of food and clothing was lower, the slave was purchased for life and any future children belonged to the plantation owner (Pares, 1970: 19). It has to be pointed out, however, that the terrible mortality rate in plantations made it necessary to have a continuous supply of new slaves just to maintain a constant labor force. For proof: the population of the Caribbean stood at less than 1 million in 1750 despite the arrival of more than 2 million Europeans and Africans in the two preceding centuries (McNeill, 1992: 26).[5]

From the early sixteenth century to the late eighteenth century, in total almost 8 million African slaves were sold in the Americas. The Portuguese were the first to partake in the slave trade; they were quickly copied by the Dutch, the French, and above all the British, who would profit greatly from this lucrative trade (Table 4.7).

---

[5] The replacement of tobacco production by sugar production is also often put forward as an explanation for why European indentured labor was substituted by African slaves. Sugarcane farming was better suited for less qualified and less motivated (to use a euphemism) workers. However, the idea that specific constraints of some plants determine how agricultural production is organized loses all credibility when the vast variability in forms of labor organization for the same plant over space and time is considered. For example, tobacco, which was grown on small and medium-sized farms using indentured workers in the island plantations, was later grown in Virginia and Maryland in large slave plantations. Similarly, a significant part of sugar production, from the cane to the finished product, or indigo production, relied on slaves who were highly specialized in certain tasks.

Table 4.7 Number of slaves transported in the Atlantic by ship nationality, 1519–1800 (in thousands)

	Portuguese	British	French	Dutch	Spanish	United States	Other	Period total
1519–1600	264.1	2.0	0	0	0	0	0	266.1
1601–1650	493.5	23	0	41	0	0	0	503.5
1651–1675	53.7	115.2	5.9	64.8	0	0	0.2	239.8
1676–1700	161.1	243.3	34.1	56.1	0	0	15.4	510.0
1701–1725	347.3	380.9	106.3	65.5	11.0	0	16.7	958.6
1726–1750	405.6	490.5	253.9	109.2	44.5	0	7.6	1,311.3
1751–1775	472.9	859.1	321.5	148.0	1	89.1	13.4	1,905.2
1776–1800	626.2	741.3	419.5	40.8	8.6	54.3	30.4	1,921.1
Country total, 1519–1800	2,824.4	2,855.3	1,141.2	525.4	65.1	143.4	83.7	7,615.6

Source: Eltis, 2001.

The spatial dynamics of the plantation economy: Follow the sugar!

The main organizational characteristics of the large plantation developed in the Mediterranean with sugarcane growing (Solow, 1987; Galloway, 1989). The development of sugarcane in the Mediterranean region came about under the "green revolution" that Muslim expansion instigated (Watson, 1974). The West came into contact with the crop thanks to the crusades. Cyprus inaugurated the slave plantation model through an astute combination of the spirit of conquest from the crusades, of slave practices that had survived in the Mediterranean[6] since antiquity, and of the capitalist rationality of Italian merchants (Curtin, 1990). Slave labor initially was taken from north of the Black Sea, but the capture of Constantinople by the Turks in 1453 and Portuguese exploration in the Gulf of Benin led to the progressive introduction of African labor.

The shift towards the Atlantic hence started. The territories involved, in rough chronological order, were: the Atlantic islands (Madeira, the Canary Islands, São Tomé), Brazil (Bahia, Rio, São Paolo), the Caribbean (Table 4.8), and later and to a lesser extent, the Gulf coast of Mexico and the south of present-day United States. Changes in the geography of sugarcane production, the main crop in the Atlantic complex, illustrate the spatial dynamic.

Things started in the Atlantic with the (re)discovery of Madeira by Portuguese navigators in 1422. It is then that, according to Alfred Crosby, the Portuguese gained knowledge of the winds that would enable them to cross the ocean in both directions

---

[6] James Belich notes that the sugar plantation, built on an Asian plant and grown in American lands with African labor, may historically be considered the first globalized enterprise (Belich, 2009: 22).

Table 4.8 Sugar production in the Atlantic region, 1456–1787 (in thousands of tons)

	Cyprus	Madeira	São Tomé	Brazil	British Caribbean	French Caribbean	Other Caribbean
1456	0.8	0.1	–	–	–	–	–
1500	0.4	2.5	–	–	–	–	–
1580	–	0.5	2.2	2.3	–	–	–
1700	–	–	–	20	22	10	5
1760	–	–	–	28	71	81	20
1787	–	–	–	19	106	125	26

Source: Maddison, 2001: 60.

(Crosby, 1986). Sugarcane farming was established on the island around 1455 with capital from Genoa and sales mainly to a Flemish market. Much further south, São Tomé, from 1500 onwards, innovated and adopted systematic use of African slaves.

And then sugarcane production moved to the Americas. By the end of the sixteenth century, northern Brazil, under Portuguese tutelage, occupied a dominant position in the sugar market, while all the characteristic elements of the slave plantation were being put in place in the New World. In 1630, the United Provinces' West Indies Company gained a foothold in Brazil's Nord-Est. It would remain present there until 1647.

The "sugar revolution" (Higman, 2000) did not reach the Caribbean until after 1640 when the Dutch, expelled from northern Brazil, migrated towards the Caribbean, from where they would soon be chased again, this time by the French and the English. Both the English and French initially perceived the Caribbean islands as settlement colonies based on European indentured workers, that were also to serve as a launching pad for the conquest of parts of the Spanish empire.

Barbados was the first island to convert to sugarcane farming. The pinnacle of sugar production in the late eighteenth century, after strong growth over the century, was located in Saint-Domingue and Jamaica. The British Caribbean by then produced around 100,000 tons of sugar—of which half in Jamaica—and the French Caribbean around 125,000 tons—of which two-thirds in Saint-Domingue (Table 4.8).

Just before the 1789 French Revolution, Saint-Domingue represented the pearl of the French Empire and was also the most prosperous island in all the Caribbean. More than a third of slaves and production in terms of value of the region were concentrated on the island (Table 4.9) which at the time hosted 34,000 Whites and 309,000 slaves. Saint-Domingue did not only produce sugar (Table 4.10); coffee farming was also a key activity. At the end of the 1780s, the island provided half of the coffee consumed in Europe and significant quantities of indigo too (Di Fulvio, 1947).

Colonization as extraction: The methodical depletion of new territories

> In each period of this history [of the Caribbean] we see the same causes produce the same effects. The clearing of new land, combined with the freedom of trade,

Table 4.9 Population and production of French, English, Spanish, and Dutch colonies in the Caribbean, 1788

	Population		Production (in millions of Francs)
	White	Black	
Saint-Domingue*	34,500	308,000	135
Martinique	12,500	83,000	26
Guadeloupe	14,600	89,500	23
Other	3,800	33,000	13
French colonies total	**65,400**	**513,500**	**197**
Jamaica	18,700	195,000	45
Barbados	1,000	50,000	10
Grenada	3,800	46,000	15
Antigua	3,500	27,000	11
Saint Christopher	1,800	26,000	8
English colonies total	**32,800**	**380,000**	**99**
Cuba	170,000	30,000	14
Puerto-Rico	75,000	6,000	3
Santo Domingo	22,000	4,000	1
Spanish colonies total	**267,000**	**40,000**	**18**
Saint Eustache	6,000	8,500	20
Curaçao	12,000	3,000	10
Dutch colonies total	**18,000**	**12,000**	**30**
European colonies in the Caribbean total	**383,200**	**945,500**	**344**

Source: Avalle, 1798.

*From the mid-seventeenth century, France and Spain divided the island of Hispaniola between them: to the west was Saint-Domingue, which at independence changed its name to Haiti, to the east Santo Domingo, present-day Dominican Republic.

Table 4.10 Net product of colonial goods from Saint-Domingue in France, 1788

	Net product	
	In millions of Francs	In % of total
Sugar	79	58
Coffee	33	24
Indigo	13	9
Cotton	9	7
Other	3	2
Total	136	100

Source: Avalle, 1798.

give a sudden impetus to settlement and activity; land is cultivated by free owners, and a general but rustic prosperity prevails. Then follows a period of more organized agriculture, during which large farms are created, teams of slaves replace the groups of free men, and the rudimentary collective is transformed into a productive enterprise. But fertility falls; production costs rise; slave labor, always expensive, becomes more expensive due to the increasing challenges to ensure upkeep; new areas of settlement are occupied, new production capacities are created; the former colonies, incapable of withstanding the ruinous competition, even with the aid of bans, after a period of suffering and difficulty, fall to a secondary position, in which capital, the economy, and accumulated skills, compensate for or mask the resources they have lost.

(Merivale, 1861: 86)

Just as is the fate of a mineral resource, the fertility of the soils in the sugar islands was systematically depleted. Expansion in the plantation economy was driven not only by a frontier dynamic but also by an extractive dynamic. The spaces conquered by plantations generally experienced a decline in production after a few decades because of declining soil fertility and rising pressure from pests. Maintaining the same production volumes thus required the colonization of new spaces. In the Caribbean, the extractive dynamic is discernible in the sequence of leading sugar islands and their gradual displacement from the east towards the west—from Barbados to Cuba—which by geographical coincidence meant establishing production in increasingly bigger islands.

In the newly colonized islands, sugar expansion benefited from forests which had become particularly dense following the wiping out of indigenous populations. François Ruf aptly coined the term "forest rent" to describe this windfall that all frontiers in humid tropical zones benefited from: abundant wood resources, and thus abundant thermic energy, nutrient rich soils, combined with an absence of parasites and weeds (Ruf, 1995).

However, deforestation occurred extremely rapidly, and clearing land for farming was the main cause. In the case of sugarcane, the need for firewood for sugar factories was an additional contributing factor. Other factors also drove forest destruction:

- The introduction of large mammals (cows, pigs, and goats).
- The aesthetic aspirations of planters, and the drive to sanitize the countryside and eliminate the "miasmas"[7] of the forest.
- The quest for recognition of property rights, as on the island of Montserrat in 1665, under incitement of the local authorities (Grove, 1995: 65).

All the forest in Barbados was thus destroyed in about forty years.

Environmental problems hence started to proliferate: catastrophic erosion in sloped regions, leaching of soils, loss of biodiversity, and rising prevalence of weeds and parasites.

---

[7] The miasma theory was an epidemiological theory that today has been discredited, which blamed diseases such as cholera, chlamydia, the Black Death, and malaria (which in Italian literally means bad air) on miasma, a noxious form of "bad air."

John McNeill, in a remarkable exercise of environmental history (McNeill, 2010), shows how the destruction of insular forest ecosystems and their replacement with the plantation ecosystem encouraged the spread of yellow fever and malaria imported from Africa with the slaves. He also shows how these two diseases, which became endemic in the Caribbean region in the eighteenth century, played a decisive role in confrontations between European powers, bestowing a certain advantage on Spanish Creole populations with respect to military forces arriving directly from Europe. McNeill rightly points out the cruel irony in the fact that diseases imported with African slaves, who themselves had partial resistance unlike European workers, contributed all the more to promoting slavery (ibid.: 46).

In the islands where forest cover disappeared, and with it the possibility of planting new lands, the depletion of the soils very quickly resulted in reduced production and lower labor productivity. Between 1771 and 1773, the slave population in Barbados increased by 30 percent while sugar production fell by 20 percent (Pares, 1970: 41).

Thus, the apparent abundance of resources that Europeans found on the American islands, leaving aside continental America, led them to radically change their methods of agriculture. As Galloway notes in his history of sugar:

> The initial reaction of the first sugar cane planters to this abundance of resources was to abandon the conservationist practices that were hallmarks of the industry in the Old World. There were no need to spend capital on irrigation systems, no need to build terraces, no need to manure in a land where clearing new fields was less effort than striving to maintain the fertility of the old. In the absence of comment of manuring, sixteenth descriptions of sugar cane cultivation in America stand in marked contrast to the close attention the medieval Andalusian writers gave the subject.
>
> (Galloway, 1989: 63)

Observations by Herman Merivale and the works of Richard Grove[8] resonate with Christophe Bonneuil and Thomas Fressoz' criticism of today's concept of Anthropocene (Bonneuil and Fressoz, 2013). The latter two authors highlight how environmental protest and demands existed very early on in the history of the modern world, contrary to the dominant idea that considers awareness of environmental destruction a recent phenomenon enabled only by new scientific discoveries (Grove, 1995).

---

[8] Richard Grove shows how the profoundly disruptive effects of European colonization on the environment of tropical islands (deforestation, biodiversity loss, changes in rainfall patterns, erosion, etc.) did not go unnoticed by the settlers (Grove, 1995). These changes gave rise to a precursory form of environmentalism promoted by naturalists—mainly doctors and administrators of botanical gardens—and resulted in various attempts at action intended to limit environmental destruction, in particular to fight against deforestation. He also shows the extent to which the authorities, from the outset of the colonization of the Americas and up until at least the mid-nineteenth century, were open to proposals from scientists in a context of great uncertainty over the long-term viability of sugar islands (ibid.: 33).

The commercialization of plantation products

The organization of the commercialization of plantation products between the early seventeenth century and late eighteenth century experienced developments similar to those seen in the Baltics grain trade, with the transformation of buyer/seller merchants into commissaries (Pares, 1970).

At the beginning of the colonization of the Americas by the English and the French, in the early seventeenth century, trade was frequently handled by companies (Providence Company, Virginia Company, Bermuda Company, Compagnie des îles d'Amérique, Compagnie de Saint Louis, etc.) which effectively had financed the setting up of the colony. Benefiting from monopolies, these companies collected exotic products and supplied in return consumer goods and equipment that the plantations required.

However, the system of sales on commission[9] became the dominant system for commercialization from the eighteenth century onwards. Under this system, the plantation owner remained the owner of the product up until the point of sale in a European country, thus taking upon himself all risks inherent to the operation. The transportation of the product from the plantation to the European market and its sale in an auction market were organized by a representative—or a commission factor—who never owned the products.[10] On the auction markets, buyers made bids for distinct lots, which were described in a catalogue sent by the seller's broker. Buyers could also, before the transaction, access the lots stored in warehouses (Reese, 1972).[11]

The representative was the metropolitan agent of the colonial plantation owner. He acted both as his dealer and his banker. He purchased goods that the plantation owner needed and sold goods on behalf of the plantation owner. Providing loans to plantation owners was another key activity of representatives. In all, the representative was more than just an agent of the plantation owner on the "European market." He handled:

- Transport of the product by contracting transporters.
- Storage of the product by taking engagements with warehouse owners in the destination countries.
- Insurance and payment of taxes and port duties.
- Quality grading of the product.
- Relations with the broker in charge of the sale.

In some cases, the representative also handled the purchase of new slaves for the plantation, the procurement of consumer equipment and goods for the plantation

---

[9] Sales on commission were organized by an intermediary who never owned the product, but took a commission on its sale.
[10] However, buying/selling was not always replaced by commission selling. According to Pares (1970), direct purchase from plantations remained the norm in Saint-Domingue up until the end of the eighteenth century, while in Virginia both systems alternated over time.
[11] When Saint-Domingue was in its golden age, French auction markets were the most important ones, first the Bordeaux market and later Le Havre's (Rees, 1972). The slave revolt which would give birth to Haiti, the Napoleonic wars, and the Continental blockade changed things. London became the center of commerce, thanks to wide availability of warehouses and easy access to cheap credit.

owner, and even served as guardian to plantation owners' children while these schooled in England. The representative may also have kept the plantation's books.

The commission sales system first took shape in Barbados; it was also on this island that the first large plantations, belonging most often to English aristocrats, were established. K-G Davis says this about these kinds of plantation owners:

> Though they might be debtors, they were still men of substance, men whose promissory bills might be expected to command acceptance, men whose estates were such that they did not feel the same urgency as their lesser brethren to turn their crops immediately to account, men, in short, who could forbear returns long enough to send their products to the best accessible market, however distant it might be. The commission system was in origin the method of disposal for the sugar produced by the large, intensively cultivated, highly capitalized estate.
>
> (Davis, 1952: 101)

Other factors also appear to have encouraged the adoption of a commission sales system:

- The reduction in return trade[12] due in part to the substitution of European indentured workers by African slaves, who had little to no demand for goods from the metropole, as well as to the increasing capacity of the "temperate" American colonies (New England and the Middle and Lower South) to satisfy plantation demand. The almost total decline of return trade made managing price-risks more complicated for merchants. This may explain why "classic" merchants continued operating in Saint-Domingue, as this island had almost no suppliers from North America (excepting Louisiana).
- The need for large plantations to be able to finance the purchase of large quantities of slaves in the metropole through letters of credit, which required putting merchandise in consignment as a guarantee.
- The absenteeism of plantation owners, who living in Europe, in particular in England, preferred sales to take place in Europe where they could monitor them.
- The desire to sidestep merchants who were abusing their monopoly, or at least oligopoly, position, which they enjoyed due to exclusivity rules; in the early 1650s, sugar which sold at £3 in Barbados was resold for £12 in London (Davis, 1952: 103).

Supplying plantations and the North American English colonies

Plantations in the Atlantic complex could not meet their own needs in terms of biomass, whether for food or for raw materials (wood in particular). An efficient system for exporting agricultural biomass to the plantations developed in North America, which later in the nineteenth century became a main supplier of Europe.

---

[12] The term "return trade" refers to flows of European products sent to the American colonies.

Sugar policies: Mercantilism illustrated

Intervention by the metropoles in sugar policy were frequent and extremely unpredictable. In France, as in the other countries, sugar was one of the most highly regulated products, and taxation was the favored instrument to influence sugar production. The book *Histoire de la législation des sucres* written by the bureau chief at the Ministry of Finance, E. Boizard, and by industrial engineer, H. Tardieu dedicates 412 pages to regulation for the sole period 1664–1891 (Boizard and Tardieu, 1891)! In France, regulation started in 1664 when Colbert created a tax of "15 *livres* per quintal" on refined sugar. This tax, however, was reduced to 4 *livres* for sugar coming from French colonies. In 1665 in response to pressure from French refineries, "the duties on sugar were changed to 22 livres and 10 sous per quintal while duty on brown sugar from Brazil was maintained at 15 livres and that on raw sugar from French colonies at 4 livres per quintal" (Boizard and Tardieu, 1891: 4). After that, things got more complex. In 1681, sugar refineries obtained a ban on re-export of raw sugar. In response, the colonies complained of the excessive power of metropolitan refineries and were soon allowed to refine sugar themselves. But then the commercial marine, for whom the shift from raw sugar to refined sugar had resulted in lower volumes to transport, obtained a ban on new refinery plants "at origin."

This sequence of measures in 1684 led to the adoption of a decree attempting to satisfy the competing interests. The re-export of raw sugar was once more authorized. But in order to "indemnify" private refineries for their lost privilege, an export bonus on refined sugar was implemented. This bonus was designed to compensate taxes paid on raw sugar. Its rate was initially set at 9 livres 15 sous per quintal, corresponding to the import duty of 225 pounds of raw sugar which were considered necessary for obtaining one quintal of refined sugar (ibid.: 6).

This apparently technical measure is essential for understanding what followed next, because in reality the bonus acted as an export subsidy. The rate of conversion of raw sugar into refined sugar used to set the export bonus in reality deliberately underestimated the efficiency of the refining process. Refineries did not need 225 pounds of raw sugar, but only around 170 to 180 pounds to produce 100 refined pounds. The "compensation" received when refined sugar was exported was thus significantly higher than the tax previously paid on the raw sugar. This support for exports was very effective, and at the eve of the Revolution, France was re-exporting 80 percent of the sugar imported from its colonies (Chaptal, 1819).

Richard Bean estimated that food imports into the English Caribbean represented about 500 calories per inhabitant in the eighteenth century (Bean, 1977: 586). This corresponds to about a quarter of the ratio estimated by Allen for Europe in the mid-eighteenth century (Allen, 2005: 115). The rest of the calories came from local production such as yams that were grown by slaves in the plots that were granted to them—their "living quarters." When food products, however, are divided into those intended for consumption by slaves and those intended for consumption by Whites, it appears that imports made up a much larger share of food consumed by Whites (practically 100 percent), but also that imports played an increasingly larger role in food consumed by slaves, growing from an average of 140 calories per person per day in 1680 to 500 in 1815 (ibid.: 587). The role of imports is even more striking in protein intake, in the form of pork products or dried and salted beef initially, and later also increasingly cod fish, and other fish either dried, salted, or marinated.

A very immediate consequence of deforestation was that wood, necessary for building, for making sugar barrels, and for producing sugar itself (obtained by boiling cane juice) quickly became a key import to the islands along with food products.

The role of continental North America for supplying both food products and wood was an indispensable one. In 1805, North America provided all the wood, 98 percent of rice and dried fish, 92 percent of flour, 72 percent of grains (cereals and legumes), and between 78 and 92 percent of live animals to the English Caribbean (Edwards, 1819: 70).

At the end of the eighteenth century, a division of labor within the English colonies of continental North America to supply the Caribbean was entrenched. New England specialized in animal products. Cereal exports (including rice) came from the mideast and south, which also supplied all the wood, reflecting the dynamism of frontiers at work. Cereals represented 40 percent of exports from the colonies towards the Caribbean, and fish, meats, and wood were all about equal at 15 percent of the total (Table 4.11).

The situation in the French Caribbean is less well documented. Lacking colonies on the continent, except for distant Canada and precarious Louisiana,[13] biomass imports for the French islands came from English colonies and later the United States in disregard of the colonial exclusivity principle. Such trade was considered "interloper trade,"[14] and authorities tried to combat it, refusing to register it. Hilliard d'Auberteuil,

Table 4.11 Biomass imports in the English Caribbean sourced from English colonies in America, 1768–72 (in £)

	New England	Middle Colonies	South	Total
Fish/whales	115,170	–	–	115,170
Meat and animals	89,118	16,692	–	105,810
Rice	–	–	55,961	55,961
Grain	15,764	178,962	80,152	274,878
Wood	57,769	18,845	31,815	108,429
Other	247	6,191	13,153	19,591

Sources: McCusker et al., 1985, cited in Findlay and O'Rourke, 2007: 235.

[13] Louisiana was ceded by France to Spain in 1762. It returned to French rule in 1800, and then was sold by Napoleon to the United States in 1803.
[14] Trade that flouted the colonial exclusivity rules.

an observer at the time, writing about Saint-Domingue in the late eighteenth century, noted that trade with English colonies provided "wood for lumber, planks, oak staves, rice, flours, grains, fruits of all types; oils for burning, sperm oil candles, wax, and tallow; iron products, hardware, butter, cured meats, dried and cured fish; in sum all those things necessary for the sustenance and maintenance of men" (Hilliard d'Aubertueil, 1776: 295). These same products were imported into the English Caribbean; however, d'Aubertueil's book cites almost no quantities. The only figure he provides is for flour: according to him for an annual consumption of 90,000 barrels of flour, less than 40,000 were provided by French traders (ibid.: 297).

5

Mobilizing resources from the national territory

The agricultural revolution and the Industrial Revolution (understood as the intensive exploitation of underground coal) have in common a dynamic of increasing productivity of the national territory, that is, of increasing the wealth that each unit of surface area—arpen, square foot, square inch, rood, furlong, acre, perch—of the national space can produce.

The English agricultural revolution: A history of productivity

The concept of "agricultural revolution" was born at the end of the nineteenth century, introduced by a series of authors (Toynbee, Ernle) who tried to show how after a long period of immobility, English agriculture underwent sudden transformations between 1750 and 1850. Today most historians agree that the process was a long one, a very long one even (beginning for some as early as the thirteenth century) with advancement and regression, and that most of the techniques implemented under the "revolution" were techniques known for centuries by the Dutch, the Flemish, and even by the Romans.[1] For Paul Bairoch: "Put briefly, the onset of the agricultural revolution consisted in the accelerated application, in sparsely populated territories, of agricultural techniques that had been gradually developed in regions confronted with the problem of a high-density population" (Bairoch, 1973: 460). Le Roy Ladurie similarly states: "From the 1650–1700s, the English had a stroke of genius: they introduced Flemish methods, invented by and for smallholding, in large-scale farms" (Le Roy Ladurie, 1975: 416).

Demographic growth and urbanization

There may be considerable debate, but historians agree on the fact that Great Britain's demographic trajectory experienced a turning point during the seventeenth century. The English population, which had practically stagnated during the second half of the sixteenth century, grew by 14 percent between 1700 and 1750 and by 50 percent between 1750 and 1800 (Table 5.1). This growth was all the more remarkable given that,

---

[1] Observations by Virgil and other authors from antiquity were collected and published by someone named Crescentius in 1240 under the title *Ruralium Commodorum libri duodecim* (Shiel, 1991: 54).

Table 5.1 Population of the United Provinces, England, and France, 1600-1800

		1600	1650	1700	1750	1800
Population (in thousands)	United Provinces	1,500	1,875	1,900	1,925	2,100
	England	4,110	4,980	5,060	5,770	8,660
	France	19,000	*18,000	21,500	24,500	29,100
			1650-1600	1700-1650	1750-1700	1800-1750
Growth in %	United Provinces		25	1	1	9
	England		21	2	14	50
	France		-5	19	14	19

Sources: Wrigley, 1985; Le Roy Ladurie, 1975: 361.
*Le Roy Ladurie's data does not include Corsica and Lorraine.

during the eighteenth century, the former hegemonic power, the United Provinces, experienced weak population growth.

France had 20 million inhabitants at the end of the seventeenth century. Its population then fell to 18-19 million around 1717, to rise again to 27 million in 1789, of which 1 million can be credited to the incorporation of the territories Lorraine and Corsica (Le Roy Ladurie, 1975: 370). Of these 27 million, 22 million were rural, including 18 million peasants, a proportion that for long remained stable. Le Roy Ladurie notes:

> Only an agricultural revolution would have permitted a number of farmers in relative decline to feed a number of non-farmers, of city dwellers, etc. in relative expansion, yet this technological revolution of the countryside did not, or barely occurred.
>
> (ibid.: 371)

The size of the French territory[2] and its low population density may have been a handicap for market organization, but it was a sizable advantage in terms of availability of mobilizable biomass. This clear advantage, however, contributed to the technology backwardness of the country with respect to its competitors who were less well endowed.

The rise in the English population by contrast was accompanied by very rapid urbanization. Between 1600 and 1800 the percentage of the population living in towns jumped from 8 percent to 28 percent. During the same period, urbanization in the United Provinces barely grew—just from 29 percent to 33 percent—and even regressed from 1700 (from a peak of 39 percent), a sign of the economic decline of the country.

---

[2] It should be noted that France's surface area expanded from 44 million ha in 1600 to 50 million ha in 1700, and to 53 million ha in 1789. England's surface area was 13 million ha.

In 1700, London became Europe's biggest city. It alone accounted for 11 percent (or 550,000 inhabitants) of the English population, and would maintain this share throughout the century that followed (Table 5.2). It was the growth of towns other than London that drove English urbanization in the eighteenth century, in particular the new industrial towns such as Birmingham, Manchester, and Leeds, and port towns such as Liverpool and Hull, which overtook ancient medieval towns such as Norwich and York.

Biomass production: Food versus non-food

English population growth was enabled by growth in biomass production. As we will see below, even if the use of fossil fuels started very early on in English history, and very early on became important, the socio-ecological metabolism of England until the end of the eighteenth century remained largely dependent on biomass produced within its own territory.

Growth was particularly strong in food production. Between the early seventeenth and early nineteenth century, wheat and oat production quadrupled, while production of barley, milk, and beef tripled. By contrast, wool production only doubled (Table 5.3).

Farmland area increased greatly between the early eighteenth century and mid-nineteenth century from 21 to 30.6 million acres (Allen, 2008b: 104). The share of farmland in the total surface area of the country thus rose from 55 percent to 82 percent. This development occurred to the detriment of forests, coppices, and rangelands whose surface area fell from 16 to 8 million acres between 1700 and 1800. The potential in wood production, and in particular wood for supplying thermal energy (directly

Table 5.2 Urban population of England, the United Provinces, and France (% of the total population)*

	1600	1650	1700	1750	1800
England	8	14	17	21	28
United Provinces	29	37	39	35	33
France	9	–	11	10	11

Source: Wrigley, 1985.

*Wrigley considers people living in towns with more than 5,000 inhabitants as urban.

Table 5.3 Production of select agricultural products in England, 1600–1849

	Cereals (millions of bushels)			Animal products (millions)		
	Wheat	Barley	Oats	Milk (gallons)	Beef (pounds)	Wool (pounds)
Avg. 1600–1649	18	16	13	170	56	33
Avg. 1800–1849	72	47	48	497	151	59

Source: Apostolides, Broadberry et al., 2008: 42 and 44.

or in the form of charcoal), was thus greatly reduced. This shift coincided with the development of underground coal production; coal became the primary source of thermal energy, and thus freed up lands for agriculture that had previously been used for energy-wood production.

Moreover, an increasing share of cultivated land was dedicated to food production (at the expense of non-food crops). It was this land that benefited from the technical changes included under the term "agricultural revolution" (Clark, 1999). This was particularly the case in the early nineteenth century. The share of pastureland, which had increased at the beginning of the eighteenth century, started to fall in the next century. Wool production thus stagnated or even fell. Likewise, increasingly smaller quantities of plowed land were dedicated to growing plant fiber crops (flax, hemp) and dye plants. These crops had occupied 400,000 hectares at the beginning of the eighteenth century—or almost 10 percent of arable land; by the mid-nineteenth century they occupied an area ten times smaller (Overton and Campbell, 1996: 276). The English Industrial Revolution thus occurred against a background of lower non-food biomass production, and dependence on imports (cotton) or biomass from the past (coal).

More nitrogen for greater yields

An incontestable feat of English agriculture after 1600 was the achievement of a sustained increase in yields. Cereal yields increased twofold (wheat, barley), or even threefold (oats) between 1600 and 1800 (Wrigley, 2010: 79).

From an agronomic point of view, at the heart of this "agricultural revolution" lay the increase in the quantities of nitrogen provided to the soils or improved recycling in farms (Shiel, 1991; Allen, 2008a). At first, English farmers adopted periodical cropping of pastureland every 20 years (convertible husbandry). The blurring of the distinction between cropped lands and permanent prairies allowed farmers to benefit from nitrogen accumulated during the non-cropped years. But it was the replacement of fallow with planting legumes that proved decisive (Ambrosoli, 1997). This innovation initiated the gradual perfecting of the Norfolk four-course system (wheat, turnip, barley, and clover) considered as a game-changer (Mazoyer and Roudart, 1998). Planting turnips and legumes prevented nitrogen leaching, and enabled increases in the size of herds which could be kept in stables, thus greatly increasing the quantity of manure available and its use for fertilizing farmland.

Summing up the characteristics of the agricultural revolution, Thompson writes:

> The concept of the mixed farm, the spearhead of this revolution, was essentially a concept of a self-sufficient productive unit [...]. Fundamentally the production cycle of the mixed farm was, then, a closed circuit, and this was its whole beauty and symmetry. It produced for sale wheat, barley, meat, and some wool; the roots, clovers or other rotation grasses, and perhaps pulses, as well as the hay which it also grew, were consumed on the spot and furnished the richer and more abundant supplies of manure from which the larger cereal yields came, as well as supported the livestock production and the horsepower which worked the farm.
> (Thompson, 1968: 64)

Nonetheless, farms were not fully self-sufficient. In one of the few papers addressing the use of urban and manufacturing waste in English agriculture, Liam Brunt draws mainly on Arthur Young's 1760 survey of farms in 200 villages, which noted usage of twenty-one different types of fertilizers originating from outside the farm, both organic (by-products of brasseries, ashes, oilseed cakes, algae, bones, urban waste) and mineral (lime, chalk, marl, salt, sea sand). These transfers had two objectives: to provide the soil with nitrogen and to control soil acidity, a key factor for soil fertility. Brunt shows that in 62 percent of villages surveyed, farmers used external fertilizers: liming with a wide range of materials, was the most frequent practice. In conclusion, he estimates that between 1700 and 1840 wheat yields were almost 20 percent higher than they would have been without these practices.

A mysterious increase in labor productivity

If population growth is a reflection of rising yields, urbanization necessarily implies considerable increase in farm labor productivity (production per worker).

Anthony Wrigley develops an analysis along these lines, taking into account not just growth in urban populations but also the reduction in the share of farmers in the rural population[3] (Table 5.4). According to his calculations, the number of British fed by a single farmer doubled between 1600 and 1800, from 1.43 to 2.76.

Other more sophisticated analyses have confirmed Wrigley's results. Apostolides and colleagues show for instance that labor productivity, which was falling at the beginning of the seventeenth century, increased between 0.4 to 0.7 percent per year, at different periods between 1650 and 1850 (Apostolides et al., 2008: 41).

The simultaneous rise in yields and labor productivity in England between the seventeenth and eighteenth century is in contradiction with Ester Boserup's hypothesis

Table 5.4 Urban, rural, and farm populations, 1670–1801 (million inhabitants)

	Total Population	Urban Population	Rural Population	% rural population in agriculture	Farm population	Total population for 100 farmers
1600	4.11	0.34	3.77	76	2.87	143
1700	5.06	0.85	4.21	66	2.78	182
1750	5.77	1.22	4.55	58	2.64	219
1800	8.66	2.38	6.28	50	3.14	248

Source: Wrigley, 1985: 700.

---

[3] Wrigley also assumes an absence of external trade in food products and stable food rations over the period. In reality, England was a net exporter of food products at the beginning of the period, but later became a net importer. The food ration most likely also increased over the period. These two phenomena should be taken into account, as one tends to temper, and the other to boost, the rise in productivity.

according to which these two parameters can only evolve in opposing directions (Boserup, 1965). This paradox thus calls for explanation.

Changes in the composition of farm labor workforce is a first explanation. According to Robert Allen's data (Table 5.5), adults, and among these men, increasingly made up a larger part of the workforce: 71 percent of adults, of which 39 percent men in 1700 compared to 90 percent of adults, of which 65 percent men in 1850. For farming methods that involved many physically demanding tasks, this trend could have resulted in improving productivity per individual. The gains in energy productivity, however, were probably lower.

Another decisive factor for the rise in productivity was without doubt the increasing use of horses in English agriculture. Farm production requires vast quantities of mechanical energy for tilling soil, and transporting harvests and farm inputs. Draft animals (oxen and horses in Europe) were an alternative to human labor, and horses had the specific advantage of being able to generate greater mechanical energy per unit of time. By reducing the time necessary for a task, horses enabled a significant increase in labor productivity.

Horses started to replace oxen in English agriculture from the Middle Ages. At the beginning of the twelfth century there were already twice as many horses as oxen (300,000 compared to 170,000). The headcount rose to 1.12 million at the beginning of the nineteenth century (Apostolides et al., 2008), while the farm population was only growing by 10 percent (note that the size—and therefore power—of horses also increased significantly). If one considers that one horse provided the equivalent of labor by five men, then with seven horses for nineteen male adults in English agriculture in 1811, each human hour of labor would have been supplemented by 3.5 equivalent human hours provided by horses (Wrigley, 1988, 1991).

Other possible explanations of the paradox are proposed in academic literature. Authors point to the fact that medieval fallow systems created seasonal underemployment, which disappeared when the Norfolk four-course system (planting different crops at different times, and larger herds) emerged. Additionally, the number of religious holidays when no one worked, fell significantly: working days rose from 250 in the late fifteenth century to 307 days annually in the late eighteenth century (de Vries, 2008: 89). Others also highlight the increasingly significant role that trades external to the farm world played (ironsmiths, craftspeople, transporters) for production in the farm sector, but which was not accounted as farm work. De Vries

Table 5.5 Workforce employed in British agriculture, 1700–1850 (in thousands)

	1700	1800	1850
Men	612	643	985
Women	488	411	395
Children	453	351	144
Total	1,553	1,405	1,524

Source: Allen, 2008b: 105.

insists on the role of the increased division of labor, which implied that everyone dedicated more hours of work to the task that they mastered best: there may have been proportionally fewer farmers in the active population, but these farmers dedicated a greater part of their time to farm production, and less time to producing tools or clothes,[4] for example, tasks which became the domain of other specialized workers. But, as Adam Smith has taught us, division of labor is determined by the size of the market. And the market in effect grew specifically during the eighteenth century in response to new consumer desires, if we accept Jan de Vries proposition, that then gripped the English populace.[5] In short, hourly productivity appears to have increased, and this rise can be explained by the increased use of animal labor as well as increased specialization of workers. However, this rise was doubtless lower than the rise in the productivity of farm workers. Other factors therefore have a role in this apparent miracle, notably the increased working hours of each farmer, and the division of labor involving non-farmers in farm production.

Jan de Vries' thesis is presented as an alternative to Marxist analyses which attribute the proletarization of the people, and in particular of the rural populace, to processes of expropriation. In my view, the two interpretations complement each other. In both periods, incentives to work, and to work harder, arose from pressure on (direct and indirect) income and threats to ways of life (unemployment, privatization of the commons and public goods, etc.), as well as from a profusion of desirable consumer goods. It cannot escape our notice how in today's world consumer desire is vigorously encouraged and legitimized by the cult of growth.

Enclosures and the development of capitalist farms

Changes in English agriculture did not just occur in the field of agronomy. Rural societies were radically transformed by two key events of this period: the rise of a capitalist class of farmers at the expense of the peasantry, and the rise of enclosures in a process of organized privatization of collective lands (and the materialization of plot boundaries).

The vanishing of peasants from English agriculture is a well-established phenomenon. The peasantry was replaced by the emblematic trio of landowner, capitalist farmer and farm wage worker. By the end of the eighteenth century, the peasantry had practically disappeared. By then, in a lot of counties capitalist farmers farmed 90 percent of the land. In 1831, there were fourteen times more farm wage workers than peasants (Overton, 1996).

As for enclosures, these put an end to collective management of open fields and commons practiced by medieval villages. From now on, the farmer, renting lands fully owned by a large landowner, took decisions alone (on crop rotation patterns, on the use

---

[4] From the eighteenth century, England underwent a process of "agriculturalization of the peasant" which Alavi and Shanin have explored, and which benefited agricultural productivity at the expense of the peasant tradition of self-sufficiency (Alavi and Shanin, 1988: XXXI).
[5] The specialization that a market economy enabled in turn enabled a rise in productivity that Ester Boserup had not considered, for her analysis does not consider trade.

Agricultural revolution, industrial revolution, industrious revolution

The concept of an industrious revolution was developed by Jan de Vries (1994, 2008).* It is of interest to us for the light it sheds on how production and consumption of market goods developed, including that of biomass of course.

The theory was developed to elucidate a paradox: how can you explain that falling daily wages, measured in terms of purchasing power of cereals, witnessed between 1430 and 1550, and which did not significantly rebound before 1840, were accompanied by a rise in the quantity of goods households owned?

Jan de Vries argues that the long eighteenth century (1680–1840) saw people in Northwestern Europe and in New England increase participation in the labor market significantly prior to the Industrial Revolution. During this long century, the consumption of market goods (estimated from inventories in wills, or from net imports of exotic products) rose rapidly, in contrast to salaries which stagnated. Jan de Vries proposes as an explanation the fact that households developed other activities to procure monetary income. They therefore worked more, by reducing their leisure time** and time dedicated to non-market domestic activities. This market insertion took various forms: wage work, home-based manufacturing (the putting-out system), specialization of farms on market crops, and lastly, petty trading activities. Historians record a rise in the number of days worked annually. The increase in monetary income-generating activities in particular drew in participation from women and children. Between 1775 and 1830, their contribution to English working-class households grew from 25 percent to 40 percent (Horrell and Humphreys, 1995).

De Vries argues that this insertion into the labor market resulted from strong incitements to consume elicited in households by the arrival of new products on the market: exotic products (cottons, porcelain, alcohol, tobacco, sugar, coffee, …), manufactured goods, lighting, and paintings. These products were expensive but nonetheless affordable for those willing to work more. De Vries suggests that a similar trend, a second industrious revolution, occurred after 1950. The family ideal of the working husband and the stay-at-home wife, which reigned from 1850 to 1950, was then replaced by a household with two working adults, better able to satisfy new consumer aspirations.

* De Vries did not invent the term "industrious revolution" (de Vries, 2008). The term originates from Akira Hayami (2001) who used it in his analysis of the development of Japanese agriculture under the Tokugawa regime (Part 4).

** The number of hours worked grew from 2,600 to 3,100 hours in Holland between 1574 and 1680, and from 2,700 to 3,300 hours in London between 1750 and 1830.

of the plot, etc.). The use of enclosures spread from the sixteenth century to the early nineteenth century. They initially arose "spontaneously," put in place by lords wishing to develop wool production, but were later officialized by "acts" of parliament from the eighteenth century onwards. Overton (1996: 148) estimates that 2 percent of English lands were enclosed in the sixteenth century, an additional 24 percent in the seventeenth century, another 13 percent in the eighteenth century, and 11 percent in the nineteenth century.

France: The agricultural revolution that (almost) did not happen

Analysis of the French situation is complicated by the absence of historical work concerning exchanges between agriculture and the rest of the economy, external markets included, during the Ancien Regime. James L. Goldsmith in his very critical paper reproaches French historians for having neglected this subject and having focused on, in a perspective he terms Ricardo-Malthusian inherited from agricultural geography, the constraints of the environment, hence producing an essentially static vision of French agriculture under the Ancien Regime (Goldsmith, 1984). Was there an agricultural revolution in France in the eighteenth century? The question has elicited considerable research and intense debate. Voltaire himself, and he was not alone, in the eighteenth century pointed out the contrast between the proliferation of writing calling for an agricultural revolution (or proposing the direction to take) and the markedly sluggish rate of transformations that French agriculture actually underwent (Morineau, 1968).

Yet, as we have seen, the French population grew during the eighteenth century—from 20 to 30 million inhabitants—at a rate close to that of England's, and despite several episodes of shortages, there was no wide-scale famine after 1693, nor mass importation of food products. Agricultural production, or at least food production, thus must have risen. For Le Roy Ladurie, "real or deflated growth in agricultural production appears to have been around a minimum of 25 percent, and more likely 40 percent (maximum), for the whole period running from the 1700–1709 decade until the 1780–1789 decade" (Le Roy Ladurie, 1975: 395).

The extension of cultivated surfaces was the first factor contributing to growth. France's farmland area grew from 35 to 43 million hectares between 1700 and 1789. This growth can be partially attributed to the expansion of the French territory (Toutain, 1961) arising from the incorporation of Corsica and Lorraine, but it was mainly a result of land clearing undertaken in Brittany, Burgundy, Languedoc, and Provence. The share of farmland in France thus rose from 70 percent to 80 percent during this period.[6] Farmland area per capita therefore remained practically unchanged, despite demographic growth. What about technical changes? All historians agree that there were great regional disparities in agriculture, its resources, and its development during the eighteenth century. Poussou writes: "If there was a French agricultural revolution in the eighteenth century, it only covered a part of the kingdom, certainly not its entirety" (Poussou, 1999: 279). As such, it is impossible to establish the same kind of analysis for France as it is for England: there is both a lack of sources and great disparities in local situations.

In Morvan for example: "Until the end of the eighteenth century, in the mountain regions, the pastureland economy combined with semi-extensive farming of rye maintained its traditional aspect" (Poitrineau, 1965: 321, cited by Poussou, 1999: 278). By contrast, corn farming around Toulouse or tree-cropping in Provence, and of course in the areas neighboring Paris and its market, matched performances in

---

[6] A 1770 royal decree exempted newly cultivated lands from taxation.

England. In large farms in Ile-de-France, the amount of land in fallow fell from a third of tillable land to a quarter (Moriceau, 1994: 38), and sometimes even less. In Caux country, cereal yields rose by 40 percent between 1720 and 1789, with the adoption of clover in lieu of fallowing, the planting of vetch or peas to serve as green fertilizer, and the development of animal husbandry and therefore increased availability of manure. The Parisian market encouraged the development of viticulture in the Paris periphery and Normandy's specialization in animal farming. Alsatian agriculture, for its part, was boosted by the introduction of new crops—potatoes, flax and hemp, rapeseed and poppy, madder, tobacco, and saffron.

According to Toutain and Le Roy Ladurie, a long period of immobility preceded the significant technical changes that came after 1750 (Toutain, 1961; Le Roy Ladurie, 1975[7]). For Morineau, by contrast, there were no developments meriting the label "agricultural revolution" before 1840; however, numerous marginal changes continuously marked the period. He states:

> Progress [in corn, potato, buckwheat, etc.] always occurred in response to a subsistence crisis, a shortage. The 1740 food shortage, more precisely from 1737–1741, catalyzed potato farming not just in Lorraine, but also in North Brittany [...] just as the shortage of 1693–1694 had led to the development of corn farming in Aquitaine. [...]. In the end, the introduction of new crops coincides with regressions in standard of living and nutritional deprivations, and contributes to maintaining such regression [...]. Progress has thus obeyed a sort of logic of poverty, which has ceaselessly pushed towards a quest for less noble food for survival and we should regard with the same pity hawkers of Arrée Mounts gobbling black wheat pancakes, the "poor people" fed on "polenta and wild fledglings" of backward Aquitaine where corn is king, and the crammed potato-eaters depicted by Van Gogh in Dutch Brabant.
>
> (Morineau, 1968: 70–1)

In France, like in England, a series of edicts issued from 1767 onwards limited communal management of lands and initiated a process comparable to that set off by English enclosures, albeit of much smaller magnitude and with different consequences from those on the other side of the Channel. Marc Bloch speaks of the "fight for agrarian individualism" with regard to this development (Bloch, 1930). Thus commenced the dismantlement of the commons and abolition of collective uses of individually owned land, such as through enforced crop rotation or free-range pastureland (which made access to community herds, or even herds from neighboring communities, obligatory, thus in effect prohibiting enclosure). When labor productivity in agriculture is

---

[7] "Overall, from the fourteenth to the early eighteenth century, and until 1750, we were in the presence of what, to paraphrase C. Lévi-Strauss, could be called a cold economy: agricultural production, without doubt was shaken by fluctuations, sometimes huge ones, but it was not over the very long term, animated by a sustained movement of growth [...]. Veritable growth only occurred, a little bit all over France, but very timidly, after 1750" (Le Roy Ladurie, 1975: 395).

Table 5.6 Number of inhabitants for 100 farmers, 1600–1800

	1600	1700	1750	1801
England	143	182	219	243
France	145	158	163	170

Source: Wrigley, 1985: 720.

compared, however, there is no doubt about how far "behind" France lagged with respect to England. The productivity index developed by Anthony Wrigley (total population to farm population) is once more very insightful. At the starting line in 1600, France was at the same level as England in terms of the number of inhabitants fed by each farmer, with 145 inhabitants for 100 farmers compared to England's 143 inhabitants. Two centuries later France was outpaced by a stretch: only 170 inhabitants for 100 farmers compared to 243 in 1801 (Table 5.6)!

I cannot resist the pleasure of also pointing out the difference between French and English agriculture with regard to draft animals. The gap in the supply of mechanical energy alone can explain the difference in productivity.[8] Drawing again from Wrigley's analysis, each man work hour in France was supplemented only by two animal work hours, compared to 3.5 in England.[9]

The English Industrial Revolution, the first large-scale use of fossil fuels

Coal has been used in England for centuries. There are traces of coal exploitation dating from the Roman Empire. Significant usage of coal occurred in the Middle Ages, as is evidenced in the number of written accounts complaining of the nuisance generated by its smoke (Sieferle, 2001). The demographic collapse of the fourteenth century and the reforestation that resulted, however, led to coal temporarily being abandoned.

---

[8] France in 1800 was still using a lot more oxen than horses. If we suppose, as does Wrigley, that three oxen provide the work of two horses, then French agriculture benefited from the equivalent of 1.87 million horses for 4.5 million adult men (compared to 700,000 horses for 1 million men in England, with horses doing the work of five men).

[9] In a recent analysis of the energy provided by draft animals, Kander and Warde (2011) affirm: "We demonstrate that at the end of the Napoleonic period, and in contrast to what has been supposed, the amount of energy from draught animals per worker in agriculture was not high in England and Wales in comparison to France, regardless of how we measure it (pure numbers or taking size into account). [...] high English labour productivity in agriculture was [thus] not a consequence of peculiarly high availability of draught power, either in 1815 or in 1913" (Kander and Warde, 2011: 5). However, Kander and Warde's analysis is based on an estimation of the number of draft animals in France double that estimated by Wrigley, without any explanation proffered or discussion on how the estimation was made.

In the mid-sixteenth century coal usage resumed, but wood continued to provide most thermal energy while mechanical energy was provided by animals and by humans themselves (Figure 5.1). Coal really made its comeback from the mid-seventeenth century when shortages of firewood—the wood needed to make charcoal—occurred again.[10] By the end of the seventeenth century, coal already accounted for almost half of Great Britain's energy consumption, and its use had already enabled the doubling of the quantity of energy consumed per capita (Warde, 2007).

Coal mining started initially in mines close to the coast or rivers. Its use was first domestic and later spread to certain manufacturing activities for which replacing coal made from wood with coal sourced from the underground did not affect the quality of finished products (through direct contact with sulfurous and other coal residues). This was the case of salt refining (6 tons of coal to "manufacture" 1 ton of salt) and soapmaking. During the eighteenth century, solutions were found for brickmaking, glassmaking, brewing, and dyeing. Coal usage became the norm despite the complaints that its acrid smoke elicited.

A second phase of growth in coal consumption started around 1760 with a clear acceleration from 1830 onwards. Its use as a replacement of charcoal in cast iron and

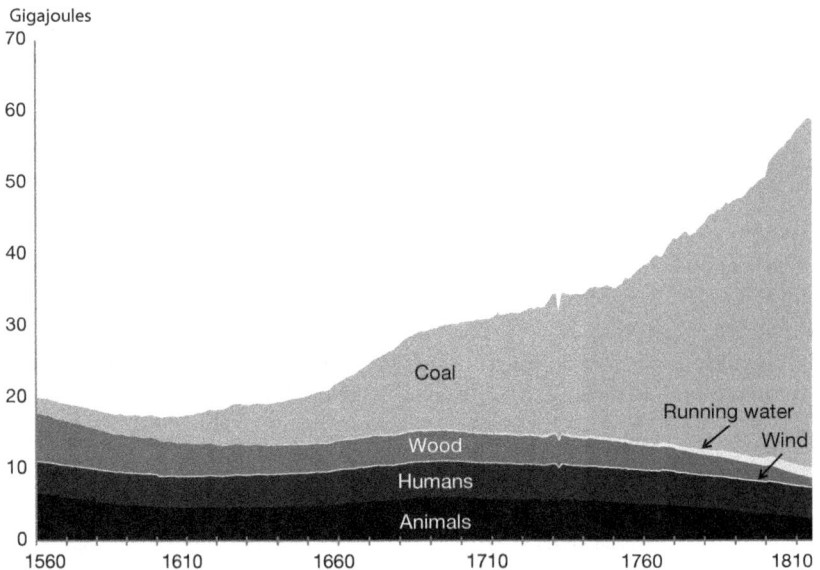

Figure 5.1 Per capita energy consumption* in Great Britain and Wales (cumulative curves), 1560–1815

Source: based on Warde, 2007.

*This is energy consumed and not energy supplied in the form of work. The difference can be significant: in the case of humans and animals, a good part of energy consumed is used for base metabolism; and in the case of coal, efficiency of the first steam engines was extremely low.

[10] The price of wood rose twice as fast as the general price index during the second half of the seventeenth century.

steel production was the primary cause of this acceleration. Until the mid-eighteenth century, cast iron and steel production were intimately linked to the availability of charcoal, and thus to that of forest resources. There was thus significant production in countries such as Sweden and Russia, but production in England had stagnated (Sieferle, 2001: 112). In 1750, 43 percent of iron used in England was imported from Sweden despite very high import taxes. The development of the process for making coke—coal rid of its impurities—changed the state of affairs considerably within the space of a few decades. Comparing cast iron production in Russia and Great Britain shows how fast the change was: Great Britain produced half the amount of cast iron that Russia did in 1788, as much as Russia at the end of that century, and double Russia's amount in 1815 (Mitchell, 1975: 391)! By then the Industrial Revolution was in full swing.

William McNeill emphasizes the fundamental role that the numerous wars England waged played in the development of the iron industry. He writes:

> Both the absolute volume of production and the mix of products that came from British factories and forges, 1793–1815, was profoundly affected by government expenditures for war purposes. In particular, government demand created a precocious iron industry, with a capacity in excess of peacetime needs, as the postwar depression 1816–20 showed. But it also created the condition for future growth by giving British ironmasters extraordinary incentives for finding new uses for the cheaper product their new, large-scale furnaces were able to turn out. Military demands on the British economy thus went far to shape the subsequent phases of the industrial revolution, allowing the improvement of steam engines and making such critical innovations as the iron railway and iron ships possible at a time and under conditions which simply would not have existed without the wartime impetus to iron production. To dismiss this feature of British economic history as "abnormal" surely betrays a remarkable bias that seems to be widespread among economic historians.
>
> (McNeill, 1982: 211–12)

I could not have put it better myself!

One cannot exaggerate the extent of the changes in societal metabolism caused by the use of coal. The energy yield of a miner, even if mining remained lightly mechanized until quite late,[11] is overwhelmingly higher than anything that can be obtained through agriculture, fishery, or forestry. Ralph Peter Sieferle estimates that a miner produces 2,500 times more energy than they consume in one day (Sieferle, 2001: 136). To put this in context, recall that the remarkable calculations undertaken by Tim Bayliss-Smith estimate the energy yield of slash-and-burn agriculture in Papua New Guinea

---

[11] The quantity produced by a miner only rose very little during the eighteenth and nineteenth centuries. According to Wrigley (1988: 77) it grew from 120–200 tons per year in 1700 to 250–300 tons in 1800.

at 14 (14 joules produced for each joule consumed) and that of a large English farm in the early nineteenth century at 40 if one considers just human labor, falling back to 14 if energy provided by horsepower is included (Bayliss-Smith, 1982: 32 and 53)!

We can get an idea of the significance of coal by estimating the forest area that coal use substituted. Coal consumption in 1700 in Great Britain was estimated at 2.2 million tons. The quantity of forest land necessary to permanently produce the energy equivalent in wood is estimated at between 8,000 and 10,000 square kilometers, in other words, almost 10 percent of the country's surface area. The 15 million tons of coal consumed in 1800 were thus equivalent to what a forest of 44,000 square kilometers, that is a third of the country's surface, would produce (Krausmann et al., 2008).

Coal was not only a formidable substitute to wood for providing thermal energy. The challenges of extracting and transporting coal propelled man towards a whole series of innovations and investments.

The steam engine was first used to pump water that infiltrated coal mines, a problem that occurred with the mining of increasingly deeper veins (Daumas, 1968). Initially, use of the steam engine far from the immediate vicinity of mines was not possible due to its very low efficiency and the large quantities of coal it required. It was only after the mid-eighteenth century, with the improvements made by Watt, that the steam engine could be used by other industries, but it was not used in transport until the beginning of the nineteenth century. And of course, the transport of coal itself, given its mass, was the greatest challenge of all.[12] Wrigley notes that in 1800 the total weight of cotton imported (23,000 tons of the raw material so essential to the country's industry) was equivalent to the annual production of just 150 coal miners, that is 0.5 percent of all the coal produced in the same year (Wrigley, 1987: 87). Coal initially was transported on water, thanks to the construction of canals. The first rails were laid to transport coal on horse-pulled trolleys to waterways. These were followed by the first coal locomotives whose initial low efficiency restricted their operations to the vicinity of the mine (the locomotive had first and foremost to carry the quantity coal necessary to return to the mine). The range of operation progressively expanded as efficiency was improved, to result in the end with a rail network that covered the entire country.

Table 5.7 Annual coal production in Great Britain and France (in millions of tons)

	1781–5	1801–5	1811–15
Great Britain	7.55	12.9	16.5
France	0.21	0.84	0.88

Sources: Block, 1860, for France and Pollard, 1980, for Great Britain.

The data for France corresponds respectively to the years 1787, 1802 and 1815.

---

[12] It is estimated that before the development of railroads, land transportation of coal doubled its cost every 2 miles (Nef, 1932).

The introduction of the steam engine in textile production was another factor that gave England a decisive advantage. The first machines were used for carding and spinning in the 1770s and 1780s, and then adapted to weaving in the early nineteenth century.

The goal of this chapter being to compare the two rivals that were France and Great Britain, one is obliged to note that France was not seduced by the new developments. Let us let the figures do the talking!

With a population that was three to four times greater (around 20 million inhabitants for 5 million in Great Britain), France produced (and consumed) in 1815, twenty times less coal, even if its production quadrupled in thirty years. The train of the Industrial Revolution had not yet passed (Table 5.7). David Bruce Young suggests that the abundant supply of wood in France, and therefore combustibles for industry, partially explains this superb disregard for fossil fuels (Young, 1976).

6

Distant biomass and social metabolism

In the eighteenth century, the Americas, previously conquered by the Spanish and the Portuguese, became the battlefield where France and Great Britain clashed, and where according to Fernand Braudel, the United Provinces lost their footing. At stake in this rivalry, was the exploitation of the immense biomass resources of the New World, where land and seas abounded in wood, in fish, and in furs, products which were starting to become scarce in Europe. Europeans exploited these apparently unlimited resources using a logic of frontiers and extraction, systematically depleting resources in one location and moving on to seek the next location. Throughout the period, the Americas kept their promises, but that did not stop Europeans from rivaling each other to ensure they grabbed the best next locations.

Great Britain imported increasing amounts of biomass at the end of the eighteenth century. According to Davis' estimations, net imports (re-exports subtracted) of biomass, which represented in value the equivalent of 11 percent of British agricultural, fish, and forest production in 1770, by 1804–6 had already risen to 48 percent, and then to 60 percent in 1814–16 (Davis, 1979: 51). The French situation, less well documented,[1] was also marked by strong growth in trade, but biomass almost certainly counted for a much lower share, given the resources that France had available within its own territory and its limited level of industrial development.

My analysis of the composition of biomass imports distinguishes between three types of biomass: non-food biomass, European food biomass, and exotic food biomass.

Non-food biomass covers textile fibers, dyes, fatty matter (the share of this used in food production remained minimal until the nineteenth century, Daviron, 2014), leathers, skins and furs, and lastly wood. These biomass products provided the bulk of raw materials needed for craft and manufacturing in a solar metabolic regime and in the first phase (the English phase, Part 3) of the mining metabolic regime.

European food biomass designates all food products that could be obtained from agriculture in European countries. The range of these products widened thanks to the Colombian exchange, the term coined by William Crosby to designate transatlantic migrations of plants, animals, and germs after the "discovery" of America (Crosby,

---

[1] As indicated in the introduction, the economic history of England has been subject to greater study than that of France. This is even more true for external trade. The type of work undertaken by Elizabeth Schumpeter (1961) and Ralph Davis (1954, 1962) on English trade has no equivalent on the other side of the channel.

1973). In Europe, this involved the arrival of corn, potato, and various types of vegetables (tomato, squash, etc.). The spread of these products occurred at very different rates in different regions. By the end of the eighteenth century, they held a significant position in European diets (potatoes for England and Ireland, corn in southwest France and northern Italy).[2] However, they appear neither in England's nor France's external trade data. Only six "products" with a long European history are considered: wine, wheat, rice, meat, butter, and cheese.

Lastly, exotic food biomass covers all the products from long-distance trade, particularly sought after for their strangeness or for the "distinction" that they conferred on their consumers: spices, sugar, coffee, cocoa, tea, rum, and tobacco. This category of products is unique due to the contrast between their marginal significance for metabolism and their great economic significance. Exotic biomass products, which for long were unknown in Europe and then later the reserve of a tiny elite, were superfluous and above all reserved to trade. In domestic trade, exotic products played a great role in the "industrious revolution" which would serve as a powerful engine for the intensification of human labor. In re-exportations, they were in large part exported towards countries without any colonies who thus participated in financing colonial powers.

The first three quarters of the eighteenth century in Great Britain were marked by rapid growth in "exotic" food biomass imports (Figure 6.1 and Table 6.1). The share of these products in total biomass imports peaked during the 1770s. They represented then a little less than half of total biomass imports. Exotic food biomass imports were

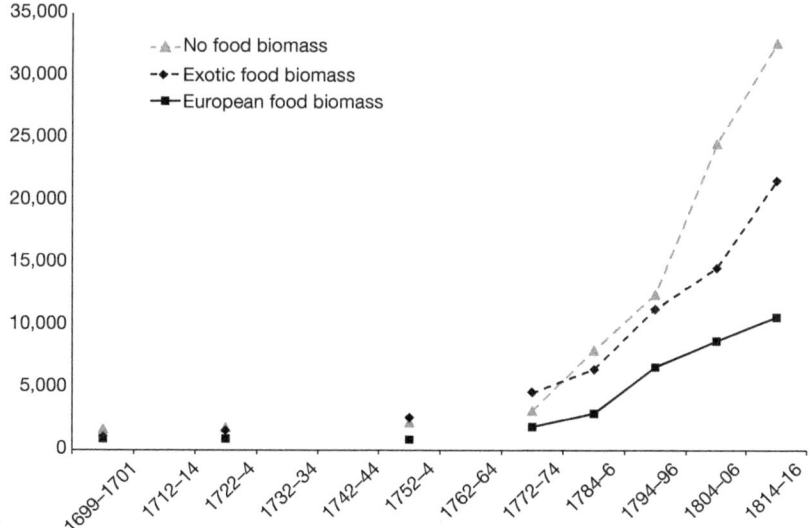

Figure 6.1 Biomass imports by Great Britain, 1699–1815 (thousands of £)

Sources: adapted from Davis, 1962, 1979.

[2] The spread of these crops explains a good part of the rebound in European population growth during the second part of the century.

Table 6.1 Composition (in %) of biomass imports by Great Britain, including imports from Ireland, 1699–1816

	1699–1701	1772–4	1814–16
Exotic food biomass	29	47	34
Sugar	18	24	17
Tea	0	9	7
Coffee	1	5	4
Spices	3	2	2
Rum	0	2	2
Tobacco	7	5	1
European food biomass	25	20	16
Wine	15	4	4
Wheat	0	4	5
Rice	0	4	0
Meat, butter, cheese	10	8	7
Non-food biomass	47	33	51
Total fibers, of which:	28	20	28
Cotton	1	1	13
Silk	10	8	4
Wool	6	1	6
Linen and hemp	5	5	4
Threads	6	5	1
Total dyes	6	5	7
Leather and skins	2	2	5
Total fatty matter	6	3	5
Wood	4	3	6

Sources: adapted from Davis, 1962, 1979.

primarily composed of sugar. Sugar was already the most imported product at the beginning of the eighteenth century, ahead of wine, and in 1770 it alone represented almost a quarter of Great Britain's biomass imports. Three other exotic products also had a place on the podium: tea, whose imports from China grew explosively in the eighteenth century, tobacco which declined throughout the century, and coffee.

In the decades that followed, however, despite continued strong growth in absolute values, exotic food biomass was overtaken by the sharp increase in non-food biomass imports, driven by the Industrial Revolution: the latter increased tenfold between 1770 and 1815. Of remark in this increase is the emergence of cotton at the end of the eighteenth century: in three decades, cotton established itself as a vital resource for the British economy. Cotton imports by volume increased fifteenfold between 1780 and 1815.

Analyses dealing with France are much scarcer. In *Histoire du Commerce de la France*, Émile Levasseur (1911) provides some data taken from work by Ambroise Arnould (1791) which I have presented in Table 6.2.[3] The data helps us, at least for the year 1787, approximatively divide biomass imports into different categories.

In 1787, the category non-food biomass—the sum of the sub-categories "wood," "matters," and "beasts of burden" in imports from Europe, of imports from India and China, presumably consisting respectively of cotton and silk, and of cotton imports from America—accounted for 40 percent of French biomass imports. Exotic food

Table 6.2 Composition (in %) of biomass imports by France, 1715–87

Imports from Europe	1715	1787
Wood, metals, tar, fats (land coal, tallow)	9	7
Matters: wool, wax, feathers, etc. (silk, cotton, hemp, leather, oils)	18	20
Edibles	18	11
Drinks	1	2
Drugs	4	4
Spices	3	2
Livestock	4	3
Beasts of burden	0	1
Tobacco leaves	8	3
Europe total	65	53
Imports from the colonies and trading posts		
India and China	10	7
Americas, including fisheries of which:	25	40
Sugar and coffee	–	28
Cotton	–	5
Colonies total	35	47

Sources: Levasseur, 1911: 518, based on Arnould, 1791.

---

[3] The categories that I proudly proposed earlier are completely ignored by Ambroise Arnould (1791). We note with delight the category "beasts of burden," which are distinguished from "livestock," the same way we would distinguish today between a tractor and a chicken.

biomass—the sum of the sub-categories "drugs," "spices," "leaf tobacco," and "sugar and coffee"—accounted for 37 percent. Lastly, "European" food biomass imports—composed of the categories "edibles," "drinks," "livestock," and remaining imports from America with cotton, sugar, and coffee subtracted, presumably mainly codfish—were estimated at 23 percent of total biomass imports.

Exotic food biomass: Combining biomass, pleasure, and industrious revolution

Not all exotic products were re-exported. A proportion was intended for domestic consumption. How should we view this domestic consumption of exotic food biomass, as opposed to re-exports, at the end of the eighteenth century and early nineteenth century?

Sugar played a key role as a sweetener in the adoption and spread throughout Europe of three exotic but bitter drinks: tea, coffee, and chocolate. Sugar also has in common with these three products, and with tobacco, psychotropic properties, that is, it acts on the central nervous system.[4] As Robert Lustig has persistently highlighted, sugar does not simply provide calories or taste (in the manner of spices) to the human body, it also acts directly on the hormonal system (Lustig, 2013). While there is no visible effect on immediate behavior or on physiology—unlike caffeine, nicotine, or alcohol—like any addictive product, sugar is also characterized by diminishing effects over time for any given dose, thus inciting higher consumption.

Sugar deserves special attention due to the important position it held in trade, as well as for the diversity of uses it was put to. Sidney Mintz distinguishes five functions that sugar historically filled in England even before contributing in any significant way to the calorie intake of Europeans: for medicines, for spicing, for decoration, for sweetening, and for preserving.[5] It was only at the end of the eighteenth century that sugar changed its status to become truly a food product. It would consequently lose its role as a marker of social distinction (tea would be subject to the same fate).

One should not, however, overestimate the contribution of sugar to English diets, as do Wallerstein (1974: 43) or Pomeranz (2000) who affirm that from the eighteenth century, sugar constituted an essential component of European nutrition. Sieferle calculates that despite an increase in average consumption per English person of 1–10 kilograms per year between 1700 and 1800, sugar calories only contributed 4 percent of dietary needs (Sieferle, 2001: 97). As for France, per capita consumption of sugar was still limited to 1 kilogram per person per year at the end of the eighteenth century.

---

[4] Sydney Mintz refers to these products as "drug foods" (Mintz, 1986: 99).
[5] For France, the practice of wine "chaptalization," adding sugar to wine to increase the alcohol content, and of course molasses distilling in New England, should be added.

The codfish rush

Control of codfish fishing in the waters of the North Atlantic was a significant battlefield in the contest between France and England in the seventeenth and eighteenth centuries. Codfish was found in the Baltic and Barents seas. Hanseatic League merchants traded the fish from the thirteenth century on and quickly depleted stocks. The Basque undertook repeated fishing expeditions to Iceland, and later to Newfoundland and the southern part of Labrador where they discovered enormous stocks of codfish before 1490. The fabulous codfish banks of Newfoundland, and later New England, were considered as trophies of the New World. These fish stocks abounding in waters that were not very deep, available to anyone who made an effort to present a little bit of bait, seemed inexhaustible to Europeans. Codfish are big fish with voracious appetites that make them easy to catch; they are also easy to preserve, tasty, and have exceptional nutritional qualities. Codfish banks were systematically exploited in an extractive logic, as were other fish species present, as well as sea birds and their chicks: "An early seventeenth-century complaint about planter fishermen by migratory interests accustomed to using Baccalieu Island (today a provincial seabird reserve) suggests no shortage of cod but rather a perceived shortage of petrels, puffins and murres to use as bait" (Pope, 2008: 142).

The French, and to a lesser extent the Spanish Basques, dominated the sector in the early sixteenth century (the English were constrained by limited salt supplies), but by the end of that century the French and English reigned exclusively, with the catch roughly shared equally between the two. The English fleet eliminated Spanish and Portuguese ships through military means, in wars between England and Spain during this century. The peace treaty signed in 1604 authorized the English to sell codfish on Spanish markets, thus extorting a share of Spain's riches from the New World (and obtaining salt in the process).

At the beginning of the seventeenth century, the fish-rich waters of New England (Cape Cod is aptly named) were discovered and explored through expeditions undertaken by both England and France, and then later claimed by John Cabot for the English. Small colonies grew around the seasonal salting facilities, and hosted around 100,000 people at the end of the century. The combined catch of the French and English during the seventeenth century was estimated to average 47,000 tons per year. A triangular trade with New England as the departure point was quickly established following the direction of dominant winds: ships left Boston loaded with codfish, which they sold mostly in Bilbao, Spain (to buy salt, wine, and oil), then they went towards the Caribbean plantations to sell lower-quality codfish to be fed to slaves, and to obtain spices, tobacco, and rum (later, they would export molasses towards New England for local distilling).

During the eighteenth century, the French, who had settled mostly in New France (Quebec) and in Newfoundland, were obliged to concede these territories under the treaties of Utrecht (1713) and Paris (1763) following their military defeats. The French, however, held on to Saint-Pierre-and-Miquelon, a territory insignificant in size but which permitted access, albeit limited, to fishing zones.

Colonial products (sugar, tobacco, and tea) must also be considered as significant agents of the "industrious revolution," motivating Europeans to work harder so as to earn more money to satisfy new desires. The desires may not have been entirely new—as consumption of tea, coffee, and strong liquors (by-product of sugar) spread, the consumption of wine and beer apparently fell in France and England (Muldrew, 2011)—but they were now felt by wider swathes of the populace.

European food biomass: The birth of the English deficit

England

English imports of "European" food biomass in terms of value remained stable, or in some cases even fell, during the first half of the eighteenth century. This was mainly due to a fall in wine imports, a product that could actually be categorized as exotic in the English case. From 1750, however, European food imports grew at an accelerated rate, and this growth was based on a new mix of products. Imports now focused on very ordinary consumer products, such as wheat, meat, and butter. England, which had until then been self-sufficient, and in some cases even enjoyed surpluses, now embarked on a period of food deficiency, and this deficit became decidedly more entrenched over the course of the nineteenth century.

We will limit ourselves here to the cereal market. With the improving performance of agriculture, cereal markets regularly had surpluses, which peaked around 1750. Exports were also encouraged by an export subsidy mechanism, which was associated with a very mercantilist obligation to use English boats for transportation (van Tielhof, 2002: 111). Thus, between 1730 and 1760, cereal exports from England significantly exceeded exports from the Baltics. Half of these exports consisted in barley for distilleries, particularly in Holland (Ormrod, 2003: 210). This single export flow would last until the nineteenth century, and English barley played a significant role in Europe's supply chains. Wheat exports from England, by contrast, only represented 1 percent of bread consumption of Europeans in 1750. This is not insignificant but certainly not sufficient to consider Great Britain the breadbasket of Europe (Moore, 2010: 394).[6]

In any event, this state of affairs would not last long. By the last two decades of the eighteenth century, Great Britain became a net importer of all cereals except barley; and from 1800, even of barley (Table 6.3 and Figure 6.2).

Imports of oats were a particularly significant component of the cereal deficit. At the beginning of the eighteenth century, a light deficit in the oats trade appeared, and it grew strongly from 1760 on. Oats at the time were still the main food cereal for 90 percent of Scottish and a third of English (Thomas, 1985: 139). It was also a basic

---

[6] As for wheat exports, these peaked at 950,000 quarters, that is around 237,000 tons in 1750. Assuming an average consumption of bread estimated for this period at 208 kg/year/inhabitant (Allen, 2005: 115) and a rate of conversion of wheat to bread of 0.99 to 1.05 (Guerreau, 1988), exports from Great Britain can be estimated to have fed between 1.1 and 1.2 million people, thus 1 percent of the European population estimated at 120 million inhabitants at the time.

Table 6.3 Annual average of British cereal trade, 1697–1801 (in thousands of quarters, 1 quarter = 12.7 kg)

	1697–31			1732–66			1767–1801			1801–15		
	Export	Import	Balance	Export	Import	Balance	Export	Import	Balance	Export	Import	Balance
Wheat	106	4	102	310	9	331	90	310	−220	81	714	633
Barley	220	1	219	302	1	300	77	58	19	27	78	51
Oats	6	13	−6	11	31	−20	22	439	−417	22	1,045	1,023
Total	332	17	314	622	41	611	189	806	−618	130	1,837	1,707

Sources: adapted from Skene Keith (1802) for 1697–1801, and Mitchell (1962: 96) for 1801–15.

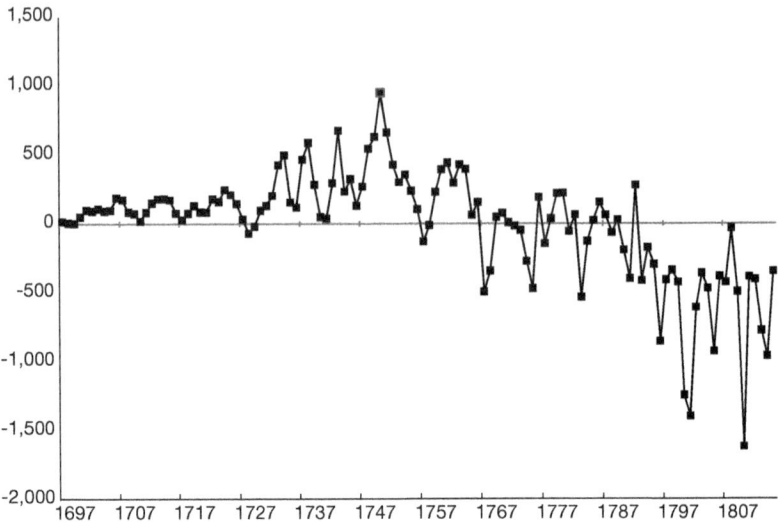

Figure 6.2 British trade balance for wheat (in thousands of quarters)
Source: adapted from Mitchell, 1975.

food for draft horses when these were required to carry out intense tasks. From this latter usage, oats can also be considered non-food biomass, and changes in demand for oats can be analyzed against the background of the Industrial Revolution. Human consumption of oats in Britain's Celtic fringe was far from negligible; however, it was its use as horse-feed, which intensified due to urbanization and industrialization of the economy, that gave rise to a level of demand that clearly exceeded the country's production capacity.

The role played by the quite particular colony of Ireland in supplying Great Britain in the late eighteenth century merits comment. Ireland provided between 70 and 90 percent of British oats imports, and from 1770 on, Great Britain adopted several laws to subsidize Irish cereals intended for its market. Following the elimination of import barriers in the English market, Ireland also started supplying increasing quantities of animal products: between 1760 and 1800, beef exports to England increased by a factor of 4, those of pork by 7, and those of butter by 6 (Thomas, 1982: 334).

Apart from Ireland, Great Britain's main sources of cereals were the Baltics—cereals from the Vistula basin were increasingly targeted at the British market—and for animal products, the North Sea region (Holland, Friesland, Holstein) (Peet, 1972).

France

The previously cited French politician, Chaptal (1756–1832) had this to say about the French situation:

> France has the considerable advantage of being both agricultural and industrial: except for cotton, it is products from its own soil that supply almost all the raw

materials necessary for its industry. The fate of agriculture and that of factories thus are naturally linked, and their prosperity seems inseparable. France is one of few privileged countries that can, to put it thus, be self-sufficient: agriculture abundantly supplies what is needed for the subsistence of its numerous inhabitants, and its manufacturing provides for the consumption of all that the luxury of the rich or the needs of the poor may require.

(Chaptal, 1819: 137–9)

Research by Toutain on the century before Chaptal's seems to confirm this assessment of auspicious self-sufficiency:

Statistical data is missing. But most writers of the time (1700–1780) concur in considering trade in cereals as being very limited: the intendants of the survey undertaken in the 1690s, Beausobre, Expilly, de Fresne, and Herbin, estimate that cereal imports and exports were close to just 1% of consumption.

(Toutain, 1961: 88)

Growing luxury consumption for the rich or growing demand from the poor? Toutain estimates that net exports of wine, which amounted to 14 percent of wine production in the 1710s, only represented 8 percent in the 1780s (Toutain, 1961: 124).

Distant non-food biomass in the Industrial Revolution

The textile industry was a key sector in the English Industrial Revolution. It was also the key driver of rising biomass imports from the late eighteenth century. Purchases of cotton, which were negligible at the beginning of the 1770s, grew rapidly in the decades that followed. From this perspective, the Industrial Revolution, as it occurred, would not have been possible without access to biomass resources from the American continent.

The Asian textiles trade took on increasing significance for the operations of the East India Company over the eighteenth century. Cotton fabrics had qualities that wool, silk, and linen fabrics did not. They were a great success because they were lighter, and easier to dye and to wash. The British textile industry, feeling threatened, demanded protective measures. As a result, Great Britain throughout the entire eighteenth century implemented an import substitution policy aimed at replacing purchases of Indian and Chinese cotton and silk fabrics with domestic production (O'Brien, 1982: 11).[7]

In 1701 import of printed, dyed, or painted cotton was banned, then in 1721, to rein in the development of local dyeing of imported white calicos, the sale and purchase of such cottons was also prohibited (see O'Brien et al., 1991 for a detailed description). Support was also given to the spinning and weaving of silks from imported raw silk: in

---

[7] The wool industry was very early on supported by embargos on exports of raw wool. The first such embargo was in implemented in 1336.

Tree products: The substance of the Royal Navy

Great Britain with its modest-sized territory and growing population, lacked wood, and this is visible in its international trade balance. The country imported large quantities of ships, lumber, tar, pitch, and charcoal.

From 1686 on, half of the ships that sailed between New and Old England were owned by Americans, and probably built in America. This state of affairs was a precursor to that of 1774 when, given the extraordinary boom in North American shipbuilding, a third of English-owned ships were built in America (Davis, 1962: 66; Özveren, 2000: 38, 47).* However, English shipbuilding had not entirely died out, and in particular ships for the powerful navy continued to be built in England. In 1750, wood accounted for half of the volume of merchandise offloaded in the port of London (Thomas, 1982: 333). As such, Great Britain was largely dependent on the exterior for the existence of its navy. Tar and pitch (as well as hemp and linen) for caulking, ropes and sails were imported from the Baltics or from America. Charcoal was another significant import as in 1788, two-thirds of cast iron production still depended on it. Three-quarters of the charcoal consumed was imported from Sweden or Russia (Thomas, 1985: 736).

* For the year 1786–7, Great Britain's fleet, excluding ships situated in the colonies, had a total carrying capacity of 882,000 tons, France's 729,000 tons, and Holland's 397,000 tons (Özveren, 2000: 48).

1776 silk imports were banned, and imports of silk threads were taxed at more than 50 percent. Legal imports of cottons and silks were henceforth supposed to only serve the lucrative re-export market.

Despite the presence of smuggled fabrics from the United Provinces, where imports of Asian fabrics remained unconstrained, the policy did enable the development of an industry processing cotton fibers. The industry initially produced fustian, a fabric made from linen and cotton, the only fabric allowed until 1774 when manufacture of 100 percent cotton fabric would be authorized once more.

At the beginning of the eighteenth century, imports of fabrics were 50 percent higher than those of fibers (among which, silk fiber was the most important product) but they were more than offset (doubly offset) by wool exports and re-export of a significant share of fabrics imported from Asia (Table 6.4). The state of affairs in the late eighteenth century had not changed much: quantities had grown significantly, but the English still exported twice as much (wool fabrics) as they imported (Asian fabrics). The trade balance in fabrics thus remained positive. On the other hand, imports of fibers—cotton fibers in particular—grew significantly and the "textile trade balance"—fibers and fabrics—in 1784–6 was negative despite the continued re-export trade.[8]

In the decades that followed, with the English cotton industry taking off, the textile trade balance once again was in a surplus position. The use of cotton fibers grew by

[8] The deficit, however, is partially fictional, as £1,081 million of linen fabrics from Ireland and £890,000 of cotton from the Caribbean counted as imports.

Table 6.4 Composition of trade in fibers and textiles, 1699–1846 (in thousands of £)

	1699–1701	1772–84	1784–6	1814–16
Imports				
Linen fabrics	903	1,246	1,753**	2,111*
Cotton and silk fabrics from Asia	575	779	1,344	515
Threads	232	424	–	–
Cotton	44	132	1,817***	11,306
Silk	346	751	1,218	4,002
Wool	200	102	268	5,408
Linen and hemp	194	481	939	3,468
Other fibers	–	–	438	449
Exports				
Cotton fabrics	20	221	797	16,529
Wool fabrics	3,045	4,186	3,882	8,626
Silk fabrics	80	189	412	617
Linen fabrics	–	740	743	1,675
Cotton thread	–	–	–	2,465
Wool thread	–	–	–	96
Re-exports				
Cotton and silk fabrics	490	1,202	395	433
Linen fabrics	182	322	182	20
Silk	63	70	92	316
Cotton	–	–	36	933
Wool	–	–	26	89
Balance	1,386	3,015	1,212	4,540

Sources: Davis, 1962, 1979.

*of which 1,998 from Ireland;

**of which 1,081 from Ireland;

***of which 890 from the Caribbean.

7 percent per year on average between 1770 and 1815, the year when the volume of cotton imports overtook the volume of domestic production of wool, which had for long been such an emblematic English product.

This growth in the cotton industry, which had initially been supplied by Mediterranean cotton, was encouraged by the development of cotton plantations, first in the Caribbean slave plantations, actively supported in the English colonies by spinners and the Board of Trade, and later in Brazil, and finally from the end of the 1790s in southern United States (we will discuss this in the following section) (Edwards, 1967: 75–106).

Various technical innovations enabled reductions in production costs for both spinning and weaving—even before the steam engine became a widespread source of mechanical energy—and English cotton fabrics conquered the domestic market, and very quickly also export markets (Riello, 2009: 211–37). In 1815, overseas sales of cotton fabrics represented 60 percent of the output of the English cotton industry and 42 percent of total British exports.

The less-studied sector of leather and skins, the third largest employer in Great Britain according to the 1841 census, also imported significant amounts of raw materials from the late eighteenth century on. The share of imported skins in the production of tanned leather grew from 5 percent in 1750 to 20 percent in 1800 and to 40 percent in 1850 (Wrigley, 2006: 63). Skins were a stable product that could be preserved for long periods and during travel over long distances, and were one of the rare products that made use of the cattle herds of the steppes of Central Asia and, above all, the herds that prospered extraordinarily in the neo-European countries (Argentina, Texas, and South Africa) (Crosby, 1973, 1986).

Similarly, Great Britain imported increasing quantities of tallow—or its by-products such as candles—from Ukraine and Western Siberia. Transported by river to Saint Petersburg or Archangel, tallow allowed one to concentrate the solar radiation of several hundred hectares in a few kilograms of matter.

Conclusion

The United Provinces built their power and wealth by mobilizing external biomass from outside their territory. Two centuries later it was Great Britain's turn to transcend the limits of organic societies and to establish, at the beginning of the nineteenth century, its hegemonic position in international trade and relations, relying on the mobilization, and combination, of three types of resources:

- Biomass from domestic agricultural production, and more specifically food biomass.
- Coal, the fossil resource that Sieferle calls the "subterranean forest."
- Biomass sourced from its colonies.

Nevertheless, from a metabolic perspective, unlike the United Provinces, Great Britain founded its rise essentially on resources sourced from its own territory, except at the very end of the period. The adoption of Dutch agricultural techniques in a territory that was ten times less densely populated is what enabled this feat. Like the Dutch, the English turned to their underground from which they extracted coal, greatly superior to peat in energy content. We recall that coal consumption grew quickly from the beginning of the seventeenth century, and after a pause, accelerated once more after the mid-eighteenth century; 80 percent of energy consumed in England in 1815 was already being provided by coal. It was thus during this period of rivalry that the country experienced the transition that moved it from a solar metabolic regime towards a mining metabolic regime.

France trailed behind in both agriculture and industry (that is, the use of fossil fuels). For Fernand Braudel, France was a victim of its considerable land mass which slowed down internal trade, and perhaps through the advantages that large size conferred for a solar metabolism, made the need for the innovations which transformed England less urgent.

Under the mercantilist policy environment put in place by the two rivals, biomass imports essentially were sourced from newly acquired territories in the Americas under a colonial exclusivity principle. Unlike the Dutch who only controlled trade, the French and English organized the whole production chain. They set up plantations with the aim of replacing Asian trade posts with American colonies as a supply source, in a logic that was a sort of "import substitution."

The "sugar islands" constituted a mechanism for transferring biomass and wealth to European metropoles through the assembly of resources external to the territory of these metropoles:

- American lands where (after a brief episode of indentured labor) African workers dressed in Indian cottons, and fed on Newfoundland codfish and Louisiana rice labored.
- Products transported on ships manufactured with American wood.
- The very essence of the crops (tea, coffee, sugar, rice, indigo, cotton), which are plants that Europeans sought out from the world over, very often from Asia, to acclimatize them in the plantations.

Nothing was extracted from the European powers, who contented themselves with providing some capital and a handful of squires transformed into planters. Exports from the colonies represented a net transfer of matter and energy to the metropole, without any returns to the colonies; a radical example of ecologically unequal exchange (Hornborg, 1998).

To truly understand the social metabolism of these metropoles, a distinction should be made between biomass imported from the colonies, which was for the most part re-exported, and products intended to supply energy and matter to the metropoles. The former (sugar, coffee, indigo, etc.), like spices for the United Provinces in the past, played a role of exchange currency. The latter, mainly non-food products, were earmarked for the manufacturing sector (wood, cotton, etc.). From the last quarter of the eighteenth century, a growing share of British biomass imports were of this latter category. After processing by the manufacturing sector, products based on non-food biomass themselves were in part re-exported, and they would with time come to dominate exports (in particular, fabrics: the value of cotton fabric exports overtook those of wool fabrics in 1802). From this perspective, the British model at the end of the period is not radically different from the United Provinces' model. To increase their exports, very quickly the two powers came to physically depend on what they imported, given the few local resources they had, and therefore limited surpluses that could be sent out of their territories.

Food product imports intended for domestic consumption progressively took on greater significance. As the next part will show, it was only after 1840 that Great Britain, followed by the other Western European countries, experienced a dramatic rise in its imports of food products and that a truly global food market was born.

The loss of their best American colonies by both England and France constituted a decisive turning point for the dismantling of mercantilist policies and colonial exclusivity, and the move towards opening markets. The United States became independent in 1776, as did Saint-Domingue in 1804, after ten years of unrest and war, to become Haiti. The elimination in 1813 of the trade monopoly that the East India Company enjoyed also contributed to opening international trade up to competition. After the Napoleonic wars, England embarked on a century of "free trade" well before the emblematic abrogation of the Corn Laws in 1846, which would simply officialize the movement.

Part 3

Where Great Britain, now a hegemon, mobilizes the world for its supply of biomass and prompts Europe to imitate her, 1815–1913

Introduction

After defeating the French at Waterloo in 1815, Great Britain became the undisputed hegemon and would remain so for about a century. Europe entered a period termed by Karl Polanyi the "hundred-year peace" (Polanyi, 1983 [1944]), that could be considered relatively peaceful, if we abstract from revolutionary insurrections (1830 and 1848), battles for independence (Greece, Italy, Poland, and Hungary), which were quickly contained, and the brief wars between Prussia and Austria, and later France. It was the era in which philosophers announced the advent of the positive state and the age of science, and the replacement of soldiers by scientists and industrialists.

Hegemony by the English was linked to the expansion of their Industrial Revolution, the rapid growth in international trade encouraged by free trade policies and the adoption of the gold standard, and to political liberalism, of which the abolition of slavery was emblematic. The age of English hegemony also coincided with the independence of the Iberian colonies on the American continent, and in contrast, a new wave of European colonization in Africa, Asia, and the Pacific. However, the eighteenth-century colonial exclusivity principle was abandoned in favor of creating a truly unified global market.

Great Britain, the biggest maritime power at the time, in the mid-nineteenth century favored a biomass supply chain that was resolutely opened towards the exterior. The abolition in 1846 of the Corn Laws, which protected the cereal market, signaled the end of mercantilism, and officialized the turnabout towards free trade policy, and above all towards free importation of biomass, including food products. The abolition effectively acknowledged a growing trend of biomass importation already well entrenched since the end of the eighteenth century. Imports then had mainly involved non-food biomass as raw materials for a booming industrial sector, but there were also some European food products, provided mainly by the Irish colony.

Now English biomass demand, and to a lesser extent that of other European countries, sought out supplies from across the whole world, including—and above all—from sovereign and quasi-sovereign states such as the dominions (Canada, Australia, and New Zealand). A series of technical innovations (the telegraph and the undersea cable in telecommunications, and the railroad and steamship in transport), institutional innovations (standards, and futures markets) made it possible to obtain a supply of biomass cheaply, even when this biomass was very heavy or very distant. The "tyranny of distance" which governed the solar metabolic regime had been vanquished.

Biomass demand during this period gave rise to a proliferation of new frontiers, as the railroad enabled the commercial exploitation of the interior of continents, difficult until then. The bulk of agricultural expansion occurred in North and South America, in Russia, in Southeast Asia, and to a lesser extent in Oceania.[1] With the exception of India, colonies played just a minor role in supplying biomass. A truly international division of labor was hence put in place between Europe, which was chiefly an exporter of manufactured goods, and the rest of the world, as exporters of raw biomass.

The period also, paradoxically, saw the decline of large production units in agricultural production for long-distance trade and the victory of market-oriented family farming, at a time when opposite trends were occurring in manufacturing, with wage work becoming the norm.

---

[1] Oceania refers to the region situated between the Indian Ocean and South America: it was mainly Australia and New Zealand that exported biomass.

7

A portrait of an English hegemon as a biomass importer

In the introduction we presented two contrasting metabolic regimes, the solar and the mining regimes. England's regime was a hybrid. Its hegemonic power was rooted in its exploitation of underground coal, but also in its remarkable use of biomass. The replacement of solar resources by mineral resources took place especially in terms of energy: for thermal energy, coal replaced wood; for mechanical energy, the steam engine replaced wind, waterways, draft animals, and humans. By contrast, raw materials remained essentially of organic matter, even if the volumes consumed rose vertiginously thanks to the abundance of thermal and mechanical energy available, and thanks also to a game of substitution of biomass products that took place on a global scale: American cotton and Australian wool replaced English wool; palm oil, tallow, and corn replaced barley, and so on.

Rising consumption of biomass was in large part fueled through imports. The dismantling of protectionist regulations inherited from mercantilism, subject of intense debate, provided the framework for the official opening of the English market to foreign biomass. History has retained the 1846 abolition of the Corn Laws as the key turning point in this movement.

Dynamics and composition of biomass imports

We saw previously that from the late eighteenth century, Great Britain started importing increasing amounts of biomass. This trend would continue until 1913. There were two distinct phases in the trajectory of biomass imports: before and after the adoption of a free trade policy. Before free trade was officialized, rapid growth in imports of non-food biomass products was pulled by industrial development. After 1846, disproportionate growth was seen in the "European food products" category. In 100 years (1815–1913), the value of such imports grew by a factor of 8, and for the sole period of 1846 to 1913 by a factor of 7.

Imported volumes for all biomass products increased overall; however, growth was initially concentrated in non-food biomass, a continuation of the eighteenth-century trend, while later growth involved mainly European food biomass. Exotic food products gradually diminished in significance, displaced by raw materials from farm and forest between the 1800s decade and the 1840s (Figure 7.1). Between 1813 and 1846, the share of exotic food products in total biomass imports fell from 33 percent to 18 percent, while that of raw materials grew from 51 percent to 64 percent. Textile fibers alone represented 36 percent of imports, and dyes 7 percent. From this, we can clearly see the role of the textile sector in English industrial growth, as well as the decisive role that the capture of external biomass played in this growth.

Due to the rise in food imports, after 1846 the share of non-food products started to fall even while the volumes imported continued to rise.[1] Two raw materials that had played an instrumental role in earlier long-distance biomass trade practically disappeared from United Kingdom imports: silk and dyes. In the mid-nineteenth century these two products alone accounted for 13 percent of biomass imports. By 1913, they counted for nothing (Table 7.1). By contrast, the exponential rise in imports of natural rubber, a radically new product whose use was closely linked to the automobile, contributed to the rebound in the share of non-food biomass between 1900 and 1913.

Imports of basic food products thus took off significantly in the mid-nineteenth century. Between the mid-nineteenth century and 1913, European food products went from accounting for a fifth of biomass imports to a half. Wheat was by far the most important such product: from 1840 on it became the leading European food product

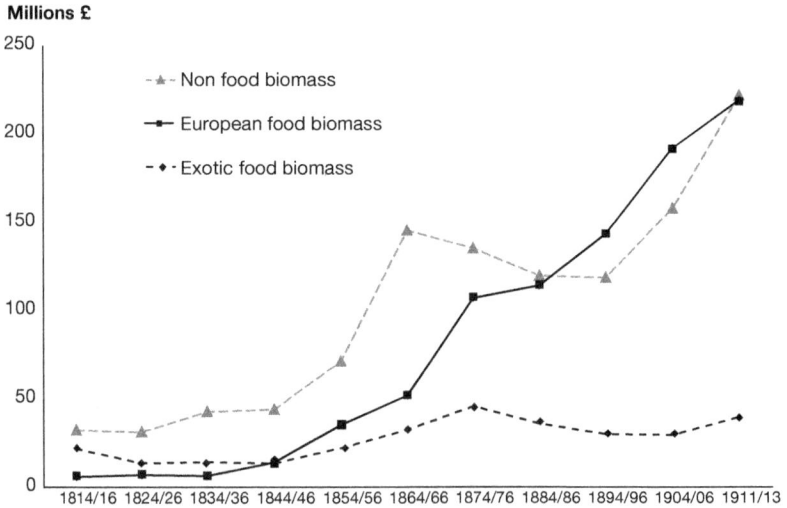

Figure 7.1 England, value of biomass imports, 1814–1913

Sources: Davis, 1962, 1979.

---

[1] Their falling value during the second half of the nineteenth century should not deceive the reader. The fall was linked to price fluctuations of textile fibers: prices rose sharply during the War of Secession, before falling heavily in the decades that followed during the Long Depression at the end of the nineteenth century (1873–96).

Table 7.1 Composition of biomass imports into Great Britain, 1814–1913 (in % of the value of total biomass imports)

	1814–16	1844–6	1911–13
Exotic food biomass	33	18	7
Unrefined sugar (cane)	17	11	2
Tea	7	4	3
Coffee	4	1	1
Spices	2	1	0
Rum	2	1	0
Tobacco	1	1	1
European food biomass	16	18	47
Wine	4	3	1
Cereals and flours	5	9	17
Alcohol	0	1	0
Animal products	7	3	21
Refined sugar (beet)		0	3
Fruits and vegetables		2	4
Fish			1
Non-food biomass	51	64	46
Total fibers	28	36	26
Cotton	13	16	15
Silk	4	6	0
Wool	6	8	7
Linen	4	3	1
Hemp		1	1
Jute and other fibers	1	1	2
Dyes	7	7	0
Leather and skins	5	3	3
Fatty matters	5	6	6
Wood	6	9	6
Rubber			4

Sources: adapted from Davis, 1962, 1979.

imported by Great Britain, thus replacing wine, a historical imported product for obvious agro-climatic reasons. Later on, animal products (meat, butter, cheese, eggs) would also experience a sharp rise, and between 1843 and 1913, their share in biomass imports jumped from 3 percent to 21 percent.

The share of exotic food products in biomass imports fell continuously. Raw cane sugar imports stagnated, explaining a large part of the falling share. The period in question saw the development in continental Europe of sugar production from beet, a lot of which was exported to the United Kingdom (Part 4). Hence, sugar lost its status as a purely exotic product, becoming partially European.

Imports: Vital for food supply and decisive for industrialization[2]

Fifty-eight percent of food calories consumed in the United Kingdom over the period 1909 to 1913 were imported (Table 7.2).[3] The share of imports in consumption varies from a low of 16 percent for vegetables to a high of 100 percent for sugar and cocoa. Lying between the two extremes, are high ratios such as 89 percent for fruit and 79 percent for cereals.

No similarly satisfactory summary of the situation of non-food biomass imports is available. And yet textile fibers offer a spectacular illustration of dependence on imports. Imported fibers in the mid-nineteenth century already represented 90 percent of fibers available (domestic production + imports). This share climbed to 97 percent by the eve of the First World War. While wool production, the last vestige of local fiber production stagnated, imports tripled. Describing the rise of Europe, Eric Jones speaks of the "import" of "ghost acreage," the farmland necessary for the production of all the biomass that was imported (Jones, 1981). To produce 265,000 tons of fibers (240,000 tons of cotton and 25,000 tons of wool) which Great Britain imported during the first half of the 1840s, the country would have had to dedicate 14 million hectares of farmland, that is a surface area slightly larger than the entire country (13 million ha).[4]

---

[2] What role was played at the time by biomass imports in the English metabolism and its economic growth? Food products were a source of energy, consumed locally, while non-food products were a source of matter, in part re-exported after processing that consumed coal, and human labor—that is, food imports. Thus, a significant part of non-food biomass imports barely made any contribution to the metabolism, but played an essential role in the economic dynamism of the country. To assess the importance of biomass imports, I will therefore compare food imports with consumption, but non-food imports with available product—that is, the sum of domestic production and imports.

[3] This calculation for food products was undertaken by the British authorities when the country experienced supply chain difficulties during the First World War. The Board of Trade thus calculated the respective shares of local production and import for main groups of products, and converted all the quantities into calories to obtain a general perspective.

[4] This calculation is based on an estimated surface area of 55 ha to produce at the time one ton of wool (the only fiber comparable to cotton for manufacturing, and adapted to the English climate) (Hornborg, 2006: 76), and a total output of 265,000 tons of wool. In actual fact, the surface area that was used overseas was a lot smaller because the production of one ton of cotton required less land than the production of one ton of wool: 5 ha as opposed to 55 ha. At the beginning of the 1840s, British cotton imports thus involved the cultivation of about 1.15 million ha in the south of the United States (American historical statistics report cotton yields of 210 kg/ha on average at the beginning of the nineteenth century).

Table 7.2 Calorific value (in billions of calories) of imports and share in consumption (in %) in the United Kingdom by product, average 1909–13

	Calorific value of imports	Share in consumption
Cereals	14,007	79
Meat	3,521	40
Poultry, eggs	236	49
Fish	139	27
Dairy products	3,538	43
Fruits	909	85
Vegetables*	753	16
Sugar and cocoa	6,633	100
Total	29,731	58

Source: Board of Trade, 1917: appendix 1.

*Including potatoes.

I will leave it to the attentive reader to calculate the surface area necessary for the 200,000 tons of wool and 939,000 tons of cotton imported in 1911–13!

Despite coal having replaced wood in supplying energy, wood remained irreplaceable as a raw material and its consumption continued to rise. The entire rise in consumption was satisfied through imports. Between 1850 and 1913, consumption of wood and wood pulp almost quadrupled. This rise was all the more remarkable, given the fact that wood by then was no longer being used for shipbuilding or road infrastructures, activities that in the past had consumed a lot of wood. New uses of wood developed, such as for railroad tracks, mines, electrical and telegraph lines, numerous forms of packaging needed in the transport sector, furniture, and lastly paper production. The share of imports in available wood grew from 53 percent to 87 percent between 1850 and 1913 (Iriarte-Goñi and Ayuda, 2012; see also Chew, 1992).

Double globalization: Geographically and politically globalized supply chains

Throughout the eighteenth century, the colonial exclusivity principle limited the colonies, especially the Atlantic colonies,[5] to a role of biomass suppliers. From 1815, however, supply chains underwent a globalization on two levels, spatial and political. Biomass was sourced from increasingly distant places and sovereign nations (the

---

[5] Ireland included.

Americas gradually became independent) or quasi-sovereign states (the dominions) played a growing role in supply.

An initial phase of political opening up encouraged European and Mediterranean supply. Until the mid-nineteenth century, the majority of heavy-weight products, whether food or non-food (cereals and wine for the former, wood, linen, hemp, and fatty matters for the latter) were imported by the United Kingdom from the Europe region (Mediterranean, Baltics, North Sea). Great Britain's main sources of cereals were the Baltics—cereals from the Vistula basin were increasingly targeted at the British market—and for animal products, the North Sea region (Holland, Friesland, Holstein) (Peet, 1972). Cotton and sugar[6] were the only bulky products imported in large quantities from outside of Europe. They represented the "heaviest" or "bulkiest" demonstration of Europe's opening towards the Atlantic that had commenced more than three centuries hence.

However, during the latter half of the nineteenth century, the geography of United Kingdom imports was revolutionized. In a few decades, the whole planet was put to work supplying the United Kingdom in biomass, including in low weight-value biomass (wool) and perishable biomass (meat).

The origin of wheat imports to the United Kingdom illustrates this development well. At the beginning of the nineteenth century, and until the 1830s, wheat imports came mostly from Prussia[7] and Russia (Figure 7.2). The United States then entered the supply chain and became, by far, the leading supplier by the end of the 1870s. For about thirty years, the United States controlled 50 to 60 percent of English supply. At the turn of the century, additional suppliers emerged—India, Argentina, Canada, Australia—and Russia reemerged. Four continents now competed to feed wheat to the United Kingdom: Oceania, America, Asia, and Europe.

The same developments can be observed for most products. We will limit ourselves to the case of wool, a non-food product. In the early nineteenth century, Prussia was the leading supplier, along with Spain, followed by Russia and Turkey. But distant Australia, India, Argentina, and South Africa soon entered the scene and gradually sidelined the European suppliers. By the start of the First World War, the resolutely global supply chain had been simplified: Australia, New Zealand, and South Africa now supplied three-quarters of English wool imports.

Richard Peet's work gives us an overview of the shift towards globalized English supply, which implied increasingly remote suppliers (Peet, 1969: 295) (Table 7.3). His calculations show that the average distance imported products covered to arrive in the United Kingdom continuously rose, going from 2,928 miles in 1830 (as the crow flies, the equivalent of London–Istanbul) to 9,460 miles in 1913 (London–Rangoon)!

---

[6] Equal volumes of sugar and cotton were imported around 1850: roughly 300,000 tons. The volume of tea imported was ten times less.
[7] Wheat sometimes was grown in Poland but left from Prussian or Russian ports. In any case, it was European.

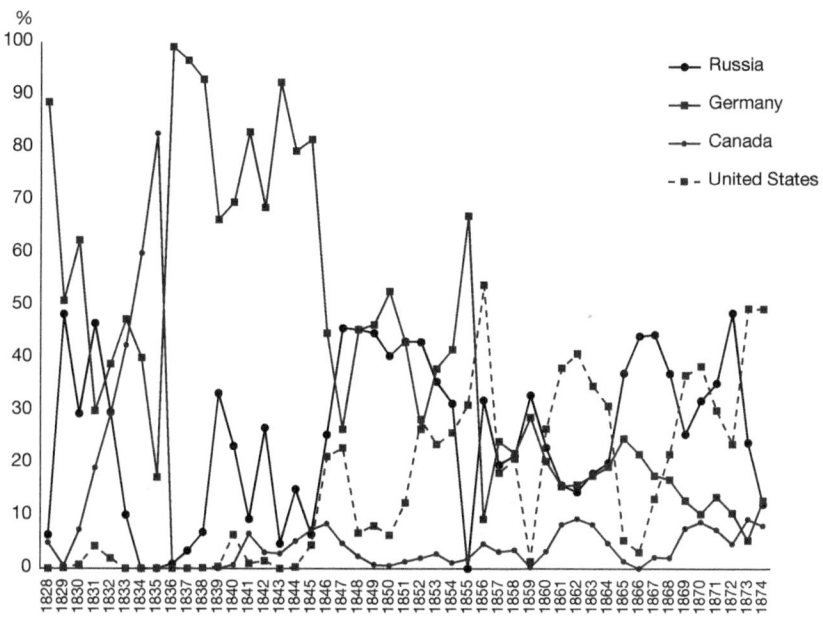
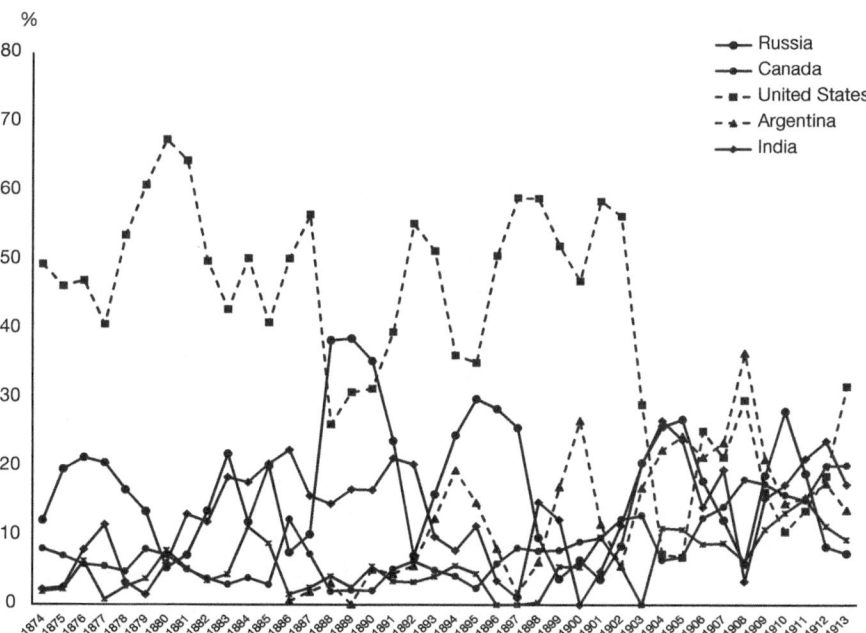

Figure 7.2 Origin of United Kingdom wheat imports, 1828–1912

Source: adapted from Mitchell, 1962.

Table 7.3 Average distance covered by different types of agricultural imports of the United Kingdom, 1831–1913 (in miles)

	1831–5	1856–60	1871–5	1891–5	1909–13
Fruits and vegetables	–	521	861	1,850	3,025
Live animals	–	1,014	1,400	5,680	7,241
Butter, cheese, eggs	422	853	2,156	2,590	5,020
Secondary cereals	1,384	3,266	3,910	5,213	7,771
Linen (fiber and seeds)	2,446	5,229	4,457	6,565	6,275
Meat and tallow	3,218	4,666	6,018	8,125	10,056
Wheat and flour	3,910	3,492	6,758	8,286	9,574
Wool and skins	3,749	14,207	16,090	17,715	17,538
Average weighted distance	2,928	5,873	6,919	8,125	9,460

Source: Peet, 1969: 295.

A minor role of empire in supplying the metropole

The nineteenth century of historians (1815–1914) is the century *par excellence* of English imperialism. Those one hundred years saw the United Kingdom take possession of, or reinforce its control over, a great number of distant territories. The British Empire, on which the sun never set, in 1913 covered 394 million individuals, or nine times the population of the metropole, and stretched over 32 million square kilometers (Etemad, 2000: 185, 231). Nonetheless, throughout this nineteenth century, the empire only played a minor role in the United Kingdom's foreign trade. In 1913, the empire accounted for only 25 percent of metropolitan imports and 37 percent of exports, with just minor fluctuations in the preceding fifty years.

The pattern for biomass supply was not very different (Saul, 1960). The empire's participation was just lightly felt during the latter half of the nineteenth century: only a third of biomass imports were sourced from the empire in 1913, and in 1854 it was just 27 percent (as a reminder it was 63 percent in 1772!) (Table 7.4).

European supply of food biomass was the reason for the slight increase in the early twentieth century. Imports from the empire grew particularly for wheat (which came, in order of importance, from Canada, India, and Australia) and for dairy products (from Canada and New Zealand). By contrast, the role of empire tended to decline for exotic food biomass, despite the remarkable breakthrough of India and Ceylon in the tea market, which made up for the lost position of the Caribbean colonies in the coffee, and especially sugar markets. Finally, while the global share of the empire in non-food biomass remained stable, contrasting trajectories for different products were hidden: a strong fall for wood (Canada was overtaken by Scandinavia), a rise in oilseeds (again India), and a de facto monopoly for jute (a new fiber exclusively produced in Bengal).

In sum, at the eve of the First World War, the empire was a main supplier for some products: jute (100 percent of the supply), tea (87 percent), cheese (82 percent), wool

Table 7.4 Share of the empire in United Kingdom biomass imports in 1854 and 1913 (as % of total import value)

	1854	1913
Biomass Total	27	33
Exotic food biomass	**43**	**41**
Tea	1	87
Coffee	76	19
Cocoa	55	51
Spices	94	72
Raw sugar	65	9
Tobacco	0	1
European food biomass	**5**	**28**
Wheat and wheat flour	2	47
Rice	93	60
Other cereals (corn, barley, oats, etc.)	3	9
Meat	1	25
Butter	2	19
Cheese	0	82
Non-food biomass	**35**	**35**
Wood	55	16
Cotton	8	3
Wool	71	80
Jute	–	99
Skins	33	42
Oilseeds	27	53
Rubber	11	57
Indigo	96	87

Source: Schlote, 1976: 164–5.

(80 percent), rubber (57 percent), oilseeds (53 percent), and wheat (48 percent). By contrast, it only supplied a minor share of English imports of meat (only 25 percent), butter (19 percent), cereals for animal feed (9 percent), sugar (9 percent), coffee (19 percent), cotton (3 percent), and wood (16 percent). Great Britain thus depended strongly on "the rest of the world" for the latter range of products.

The empire itself was vast and highly differentiated. There were three distinct categories of territories.

The self-governing colonies of Canada, Australia, New Zealand, Newfoundland, and South Africa were referred to as dominions after the Imperial Conference of 1907. These dominions were in fact English colonies of European settlement (with large white majorities, excepting South Africa) and enjoyed great autonomy in economic policy (expenditure, taxation, custom duties, etc.). Their foreign and defense policies, however, were directed by the metropole. These countries were very active suppliers of biomass to meet English demand. They were behind the moderate rise in the empire's share in English imports, supplying roughly one-third of England's imperial imports in 1860, but more than half in 1913 (Schlote, 1976).

The old eighteenth-century colonies, and in particular the Caribbean colonies, gradually disappeared from the list of England's suppliers. Newly conquered territories (Malaysia, Burma, Africa) contributed modestly to supplying Britain (rice from Burma, rubber from Malaysia). In a certain sense, the United Kingdom undertook its new territorial conquests half-heartedly (hence the expression "reluctant empire"), most often to protect commercial interests elsewhere (gaining control of the Cape at the tip of Africa, for example, aimed at protecting the trade route with India) or to prevent the advancement of other colonial powers (Coquery-Vidrovitch, 1970).

Lastly, India was a special case: even though the English were present early on with trading posts, colonial governance over the full territory was not established until the nineteenth century. As we have seen, India occupied a significant position in British imports.[8] The Indian continent was at the time a major exporter of basic biomass products (cereals and oilseeds), despite its high population density (much higher than densities in the dominions[9]).

The idea that after 1880 imperialist ambitions were reinforced was, and is still, hotly debated. Under Lenin's thesis, "imperialism, the highest stage of capitalism" was aimed at responding to the growing difficulties and contradictions of capitalism.[10] The British Empire in the nineteenth century was, however, very different from what it had been in the eighteenth century. The (moderate) rise in trade within the empire did not result in any way from policies comparable to eighteenth-century mercantilism. The project to make the empire a favored space for trade protected from the rest of the world, was not concretized until the 1930s even though it was discussed from the beginning of that century (Part 4).

Conversely, English political influence outside of the formal empire was powerful. This was especially true in its main supplier territories. John Gallagher and Ronald Robinson consider that focusing only on formal possessions—"those colonies colored

---

[8] India and Ceylon were administered by the East Indian Company until 1857, the year when the English crown got involved, following attempts by the Company to colonize the interior of the subcontinent which had sparked off the Sepoy mutiny.

[9] For Mike Davis, the English "were eating the bread of Indians," which appears to be corroborated by the terrible famines experienced at the end of the century (Davis, 2002).

[10] The "highest stage of capitalism" is characterized by: concentration of the production of capital, and therefore the creation of monopoly; the fusion of bank and industrial capital in the form of financial capital; the preponderance of export of capital over export of goods; the internationalization of monopolies aimed at dividing the world; and the political sharing out of the world, as the culmination of the preceding processes.

red on the map"—ignores the submerged part of the iceberg (Gallagher and Robinson, 1953: 1). The free trade imperialism of the nineteenth century was reflected in a logic of multiform and permanent expansion (migration, investment, trade) which sometimes took the shape of empire when security could not be guaranteed and it was easy to exert force:

> The type of political lien between the expanding economy and its formal or informal dependencies, as might be expected, has been flexible. In practice it has tended to vary with the economic value of the territory, the strength of its political structure, the readiness of its rulers to collaborate with British commercial or strategic purposes, the ability of the native society to undergo economic change without external control, the extent to which domestic and foreign political situations permitted British intervention, and, finally, how far European rivals allowed British policy a free hand.
>
> (Gallagher and Robinson, 1953: 7)

In sum, England expanded its control informally as much as possible, and formally only when necessary.

This policy of informal empire was particularly manifest in Latin America. When, in 1810, the English fleet provided assistance to the King of Portugal to flee to Brazil, England negotiated in return lower custom duties for its products than those paid by Portuguese products in order to penetrate the Brazilian market (Gallagher and Robinson, 1953: 8)! As early as 1824, George Canning, then foreign affairs minister, declared: "Spanish America is free and if we do not mismanage our affairs sadly she is *English*." And it was through the signing of trade treaties that England recognized the newly independent states of Argentina, Mexico, and Colombia.

8

Overcoming "the tyranny of distance": Technical and institutional innovations

Globalization of English biomass supply chains was only possible on condition that goods could be moved around profitably. This implied purchasing goods while at distance, that is, being able to communicate with the country of origin, and transporting goods in suitable conditions at an acceptable cost. Over the course of the nineteenth century the obstacles posed by distance were gradually overcome. The creation of international standards, the setting up of futures markets and the invention of the undersea cable—the telegraph—made it feasible to buy products without seeing them. And then coal enabled rail transportation, shipping on fast steamships, and for perishable products, refrigerated containers. These innovations in overcoming the tyranny of distance[1] had impacts not just in Great Britain, but in the world as a whole.

The steam engine revolution

The steam engine opened up a new era in land, river and sea transportation.

Railroads

Railroads are of interest to us above all for their impact outside of Europe. The railroad finally permitted access to the interior of entire continents for which no previous convenient access had existed in the absence of navigable rivers.

The development of railroads commenced in England and in Europe in the 1830s, but it quickly spread to the United States, and then Russia and Canada, and finally South America and Australia from the 1860s.

The train truly reshaped geography, not in England where it had been in invented, but in the United States. Until then, urban centers in the United States had been trade ports turned towards England. Henceforth new towns sprung up in the interior, drawing their industrial wealth from their location at strategic rail

---

[1] *The Tyranny of Distance* is the title of a book by Geoffrey Blainey in which he underscores the decisive role that distance played in Australian history, both distance from Europe and distance within the national territory (Blainey, 1966).

crossroads, where minerals, farm products from the plains, and immigrant labor came together. The American rail developed at full steam, and overtook the English rail for length by 1841. In 1913, it was longer than all the rail networks of all other countries in the graph combined (420,000 compared to 349,000 km, Figure 8.1, Table 8.1) (Cottrell, 1970).

Table 8.1 Length of railroad used

	Total		For 10,000 inhabitants	Per 100 km²
	1851	1913	1913	1913
Great Britain	10,656	32,259	7.8	14
France	3,010	50,933	12.9	12.9
Germany	6,053	62,734	9.4	11.6
United States	14,519	420,137	43.5	5.4
Canada	256	47,165	61.3	0.27
Australia	37	31,773	65.0	0.41
Argentina	0	31,451	41.9	1.07
Brazil	0	22,287	9.3	0.27
Russia	499	70,295	4.2	0.32

Source: INSEE, 1952: 485–7.

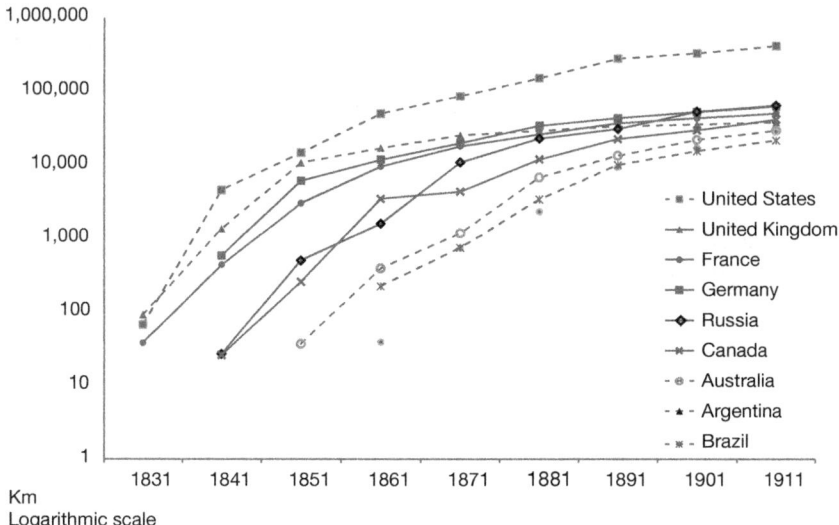

Figure 8.1 Length of rail network in various countries, 1831–1911 (in km, logarithmic scale)

Source: INSEE, 1952: 485–7.

The steamship

The steamship was perfected during the 1810s, and first used for transportation on rivers. The United States, which had a large river network and went through an intensive phase of canal construction between 1815 and 1843 (Fishlow, 2000), was an early adopter of the steamship. Steam replaced sails in this country, first on rivers, then on lakes and in coastal navigation, and finally in the open seas. The steamship was also very successful in territories endowed with many rivers and where the railroad arrived tardily. It played a key role for colonial enterprises in Africa and Asia. Steam-powered ships were also a prerequisite to make the use of large canals feasible, and in particular the Suez Canal which opened in 1869 and greatly reduced the time needed for transport between England and India (Fletcher, 1958).

But the main use of steamships was on the sea: the first steamships were introduced into the United Kingdom fleet in the early 1830s. During an initial phase, their number and overall tonnage progressed in parallel with those of sailships. But after 1865, the tonnage carried by the sail marine started falling, and steam-driven fleets dominated tonnage from 1885 (Mitchell, 1975: 618–23). In effect, steamships initially were the ship of choice only for short or medium distances, for which the necessary load of combustibles remained reasonable. Over longer distances, sailships maintained their dominant position for some decades. Thus, for the longest route, that between Europe and California, sailships remained predominant until the First World War.

Transportation times and costs

Table 8.2, taking data from Paul Bairoch (1989), presents changes over time in average transport costs, and compares the cost of continental transport (per ton and per kilometer) to the cost of maritime transport (for crossing the North Atlantic). The most radical change engendered by the steam engine was increased feasibility of moving heavy freight inland. But, overall, all transport costs experienced a very rapid shift in scale.

Table 8.2 Average transport costs for "developed countries," estimated by Paul Bairoch, and the price of wheat in Liverpool, 1830–1910

	1830	1850	1880	1910
Land transport (dollar/ton/100 km)				
Road	6.2	5.0	4.0	3.6
River and canal	1.0	0.7	0.4	0.2
Train	–	1.5	1.1	0.8
Transatlantic maritime transport	9.5	9.0	8.5	3.3
Price of wheat in Liverpool (dollars/ton)	70	45	49	43

Sources: Bairoch, 1989: 56; Jacks, 2006 for the price of wheat.

The new transport techniques also provided the solution to the labor problem, the Achilles heel of the New World. The forms of forced labor (slavery and indentured labor) which provided seventeenth- and eighteenth-century plantations with workers whose "employers" had paid the cost of their transportation, had no reason for continuing. The nineteenth-century frontier mobilized free labor which abounded thanks to the falling costs of transport. The cost and duration of the voyage proceeded to fall so much, that after 1880 seasonal migration from Europe and Asia even occurred. Young men called "golondrinas" (swallows) or "birds of passage" migrated towards a frontier for one or two seasons to then return to their country of birth awaiting the next opportunity (Nugent, 1989: 398).

Telecommunications

Distance posed challenges not just for the movement of goods but also for the transmission of information. Until the nineteenth century, transport of information was no different from that of men, whether by messenger or mail. Human speed thus determined the speed of information. Commenting on the results of an analysis of the time needed for letters sent to Venice between the late fifteenth century and the eighteenth century, Fernand Braudel noted: "with horses, coaches, ships and runners, it was the general rule to cover at most 100 kilometers in 24 hours. Higher speeds were very infrequent and a great luxury" (Braudel, 1981: 424).

The invention of refrigerators and the meat trade

The perishability of meat for long restricted its trade over long distances to a few products processed through salting, smoking or drying, and to live animals. In the nineteenth century, several innovations, linked to the names Liebig and Appert, started being applied to facilitate intercontinental transport of processed meats (meat extract, meat meal, jars and tins of corned beef). Live animals also supplied the English market, shipped over from the United States, later Argentina (350,000 heads in 1894), New Zealand, and Australia. It was coal that enabled the transportation of fresh meat, either refrigerated or frozen. The steam engine provided the mechanical energy needed for the compression–decompression of refrigerant gases, thus transforming coal into cold. The first cargo of frozen meat crossed the Atlantic in 105 days in 1876 (Rouen–Buenos Aires) on *Le Frigorifique*, the first ship equipped with compressors. The banning of live animal imports (1,900 heads) for health reasons in 1900 encouraged the new innovation. In 1913, England imported 42 percent of its meat, of which 56 percent consisted in frozen or refrigerated beef and mutton, originating from, in order of importance, Argentina, Australia, and New Zealand. (The remaining English imports consisted mainly in bacon and ham from North America and Northwest Europe) (Crossley and Greenhill, 1977; Perren, 1978).

Progress in transportation of humans in the nineteenth century not surprisingly impacted the transportation of information. Transmission times on all routes fell greatly, and by 1860 were on average a third of what they were in 1820. The longest delivery time was now only a month and a half, and was for communication with Sydney, while information from Batavia only took a month to arrive in London. The increasing reliability of means of transport also considerably reduced variability in communication times (Kaukiainen, 2001).

The invention of the telegraph freed information from the constraints of the movement of a messenger. The semaphore (or the optical telegraph) developed during the French Revolution already represented a major technical breakthrough. But it was created for the state service, and its use was thus reserved to the state. The electrical telegraph was "invented" at the end of the 1830s, both in England and in the United States. The first truly operational lines were installed in 1842 and the Morse code language, invented in 1856 in the United States, became the international standard (Wenzlhuemer, 2013: 72). The quantities of information communicable by unit of time and the distances covered rose continuously from then on. Instantaneous (or almost instantaneous) long-distance communication was now possible, and information circulated throughout the globe independently of humans, indeed much faster than them.

Telegraph development was intimately tied to railroad development. The telegraph was indispensable in the United States for the organization and safety of rail traffic, while the embankments along rail tracks were an ideal place for installing telegraph lines (Chandler, 1977: 195 and 89).

The telegraph very quickly also crossed seas. The first undersea cable was laid in 1851, running between France and England. The thorny problem of how to isolate the wires was resolved thanks to the use of gutta percha, a type of rubber extracted from various Southeast Asian tree species (Tully, 2009). From then, undersea cables quickly linked all the big economic centers together, as well as linking metropoles with their colonies. In 1865, a cable was laid in the Persian Gulf to connect the United Kingdom to India, and in 1866, after several trials, another cable was laid in the Atlantic. The "network" was supplemented by a transpacific cable that was laid at the turn of the twentieth century (see the map at the beginning of this section).

The invention of "raw materials": Standards and futures markets

The last leg of the fight against the "tyranny of distance" consisted in the creation of a specific category of goods: "raw materials" or "primary commodities," which were clearly distinct from manufactured products. Two institutional innovations shaped the formation this category in the mid-nineteenth century. The first was the creation of systems for standards and grading to be able to assess the quality of products in an objective and consensual manner, and the second was the invention of futures markets.[2]

---

[2] The two institutions emerged in Chicago for cereals sold in the English market, and their application spread very quickly to other products, initially in the large market centers of the United States (New Orleans for cotton, New York for coffee) and of Europe (London for cocoa, Le Havre and Hamburg for coffee, etc.).

Standards and grades

The standardization of raw materials "means making uniform among buyers and sellers, and from place to place and time to time, the quality specifications of grades" (Thomsen, 1951: 76). The uniformization of quality criteria was built on a series of agreements between the major traders of a given raw material on:

- The list of measurable attributes: size, color, etc.
- The way to measure these attributes
- A classification into different classes, that is, the definition of border values for the attributes.

The standardization of agricultural products for long-distance trade was initially undertaken by traders and their business associations in the late nineteenth century and early twentieth century.[3] Standardization was a means for them to resolve two considerable hurdles that large distances posed for market transactions. First, standardization provided operators, even when separated by thousands of kilometers (but communicating instantaneously thanks to the telegraph and undersea cables), a common vocabulary on which to base their negotiations. Secondly, it enabled the substitutability of consignments across time, a necessary condition for the creation of futures markets. Indeed, the desire to create futures markets was one of the driving forces for standardization of agricultural products in long-distance trade (cocoa, rubber, etc.).

Futures markets and hedging

During the latter half of the nineteenth century, new communication technologies encouraged synchronized prices across the globe. The combined use of long-distance communication and standards enabled the sale of consignments of products well before they left the region of production. Standards allowed buyers to know exactly what they would receive, while telecommunications allowed them to conclude a contract on the basis of a price common to both places. It was the existence of such "future contracts" that enabled the creation of futures markets. A merchant could now sell a "future contract" without possessing the product, with the hope of buying the product more cheaply than the price (of resale) stipulated in the contract in the time gap until delivery. These contracts could even change hands several times in the intervening period. This process based on future contracts ultimately was organized within commodities exchanges. Futures contracts that were sold and bought in these exchanges stipulated a grade, a volume, and a delivery date. They could be sold and bought independently of all operations on the real market (the physical market).

The last step in the construction of a modern commodities market was the invention of the hedging operation. Hedging used futures contracts as insurance

---

[3] In a fascinating and detailed history of the standardization of cereals in Chicago, William Cronon skillfully relates the forces that led to the emergence of standards and the major transformations they brought about around 1855 (Cronon, 1991).

against the risk of price fluctuations.[4] Concretely, it involved the purchase (or the sale) of a futures contract simultaneously with a real sale (or purchase) of the product. Hedging enabled operators who wished to buy a physical product and conserve it for a period before selling—under the same form or in a semi-processed form—to protect themselves against price fluctuations (in this case, a price fall). Because fluctuations on futures markets were correlated to fluctuations on markets for "real products," undertaking the reverse operations on futures markets enabled operators to minimize losses linked to price fluctuations on the physical market.

The spread of the practice of hedging transformed the organization of trade in agricultural products. Protected against price fluctuations, traders gradually abandoned their previous status of commissaries (Part 2), and were now able to actually purchase the product from the producer and hold on to the product at length even in the absence of a monopoly position. The location of the market transaction, previously very distant from the farm producer, was suddenly brought to the next town, or even to the gate of their farm. We will see later how this development contributed to the later triumph of the "small family farm."

The formation of global markets and prices

> Yet in 1914, one could rightly speak of the world's agriculture as a system of communicating vessels. Farm produce was loaded or unloaded in all the important ports of the world, and the size of the crops in distant lands was reflected in prices in all those ports and frequently in prices in exporting as well as importing countries.
> (Brandt, 1945: 21)

Technical and institutional innovations which had made it possible to minimize or overcome constraints imposed by distance, gave rise to truly global markets for agricultural commodities, and this led to a convergence in prices between places separated by great distance, and their relative stabilization in the early twentieth century. This convergence was reflected in a rise in prices in exporting regions and a fall in prices in importing regions. Thus, the first consequence of the victory over distance in the United Kingdom was the falling biomass prices, and this for all categories— exotic food, European food, and non-food biomass.

An initial period of falling prices was experienced from the early nineteenth century. Douglas North notes a series of price falls for imports into England during the first half of the nineteenth century (North, 1958: 544). This was followed by a second wave of falling prices in the last quarter of the century. This is precisely what characterized what is commonly referred to as the "Long Depression," and in long-wave cycle analyses, the descending phase of the Kondratiev cycle.[5] In the United Kingdom, the price of wheat

---

[4] Hedging appears to have been first used by Chicago cereal traders, and later by New York exporters in the third quarter of the nineteenth century (Rothstein, 1983).
[5] Nikolaï Kondratiev was an early twentieth-century Russian economist who showed the existence of waves of rises and falls over the long term (40 to 60 years) in price fluctuations.

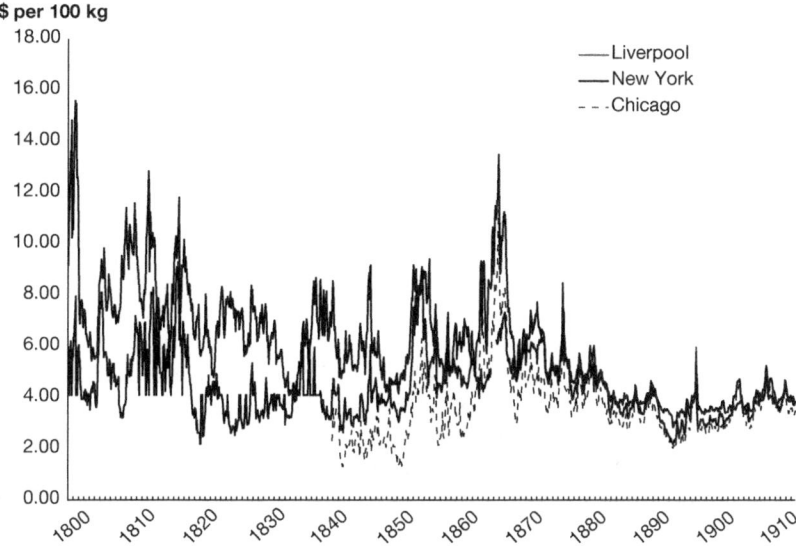

Figure 8.2 Monthly price of wheat in Liverpool, New York, and Chicago, 1800–1913
Source: adapted from Jacks, 2006.

fell by around 35 percent between 1870 and 1913, and that of barley by 25 percent (O'Rourke, 1997).

O'Rourke and Williamson show how this broad movement of falling prices was accompanied by a net convergence of prices on both sides of the Atlantic. The price of wheat in Liverpool, which had been 58 percent higher than the Chicago price in 1870, was only 18 percent higher in 1895 and 16 percent higher in 1913. The bacon market experienced a similar trend. In 1880, bacon prices in Liverpool were twice those in Cincinnati. In 1913, they were only 18 percent higher (O'Rourke and Williamson, 1999: 45–50). The same convergence of prices between the United States and the United Kingdom was found for cotton, wool, and other products; same thing for the English and Swedish markets, for the Danish and American markets, and many others.

A last trend is worth noting: greater price stability (Figure 8.2). The shift towards stabilization of prices was spectacular. It was particularly notable in Liverpool. At the beginning of the nineteenth century, the price of wheat could double in a few months, or conversely be halved or more. This variability reduced considerably before the First World War, with fluctuations of less than 25 percent and a period of remarkable stability between 1897 and 1907.

What explains this trend towards stabilization? The widening of the geographical space of trade probably played a role, but it certainly was not the only factor. The institutional innovations that we have just discussed also encouraged stability. Standardization which offered the possibility to substitute product origins, and therefore increased the number of suppliers, and the deployment of futures markets and telegraphs through the impacts these had on information and on the coverage of storage costs, were also powerful factors in price stabilization.

9

The golden age of frontiers

The history of humanity is filled with frontiers and pioneers; take for example the slow descent of Han China towards the south. The United Provinces founded their power on the mobilization of maritime and land frontiers, with perhaps the specificity, according to Jason Moore, of using the market and thus giving rise to commodity frontiers, frontiers whose production was dedicated to the market and not self-consumption (Moore, 2000). It is the nineteenth century, however, that can truly be considered the golden age of frontiers due to the scale at which frontier dynamics occurred, and frontiers' role in supplying biomass to Europe. No continent outside Europe was spared. Even Africa, which without doubt was the least involved, was affected, mainly in its northern and southern extremities, but also more locally in Senegambia and Nigeria for example.

For Jürgen Osterhammel, two simultaneous dynamics situated at opposing poles of global biomass markets drove the great migrations of the nineteenth century: the advancement of frontiers and the acceleration of urbanization. The frontier constitutes the extreme opposite of the city in expansion. Towns and frontiers were the main destination of the great migrations and both offered the same hope (at least in the eyes of migrants) of social permeability and malleability: "Those who *have* nothing but are *capable* of something can achieve it here" (Osterhammel, 2014: 322).

Walter Nugent argues that the rapid advancement of frontiers and the wave of imperialism between 1870 and 1914 shared the same origin and were both reflections of the pinnacle of Europe's expansionist power and civilizing mission (Nugent, 1989). Economic and demographic growth bolstered Europe:

> The frontiers people and the empire-builders—all Europeans or European-Americans sharing the same trans-Atlantic economy, technology, and migration pool, all migrants, all in some way expanders—differed less in who they themselves were than in whom they met.
>
> (ibid.: 398)

The particularity lay not in the cropping (or *"mise en valeur"*—development—as the French called it in their colonies) of empty lands, but in the establishment of exclusive property rights over land, which in extreme cases resulted in enclosures within livestock herding zones. Exclusive property rights replaced rights of "usage" which had covered only the products of labor (through wild harvesting or cultivation) on lands, which most often had shared commons status (Richards, 2002).

The "*mise en valeur*" of "empty" lands: Steppes, forests, and deltas

The frontiers that would feed Europe developed mainly on three major types of biomes: forests, steppes (this generically designates both steppes themselves, and prairies and savannah), and deltas.

The figures on deforestation are very eloquent. Between 1750 and 1850, 1.8 million square kilometers of forest were cut in temperate latitudes, and 0.7 million square kilometers of tropical forest. These already astounding figures were outdone in the decades that followed: in just 70 years, between 1850 and 1920, respectively 1.35 million and 1.52 million square kilometers were cut (Williams, 2006).[1] It is estimated that this represented approximately 10 percent of the total forest area that existed in the mid-eighteenth century.

The destruction of steppes, while less spectacular than that of forests, was strongly linked to the advancement of nineteenth-century frontiers: the steppes north of the Black Sea, the plains in North America, the Pampas in Argentina, and the *veld* in South Africa. To these one can add certain savannahs in the Sahel. According to John McNeill, the global surface area of steppes that were farmed (as pastureland) between 1850 and 1910 was much higher than that of forests put to the same use: 8 million square kilometers compared to 3 (McNeill, 2000: 213).

The third natural habitat devoured by advancing frontiers was the large deltas of Southeast Asia (Irrawaddy in Burma, Chao Phraya in Siam-Thailand, Mekong in Cochin China-Vietnam), although there are no figures on the extent of the destruction. Deltas represent modest surfaces, but their productivity meant that they played a key role in feeding their regions, as well as producing exports, in particular rice. We will see this in the case of Burma.

A comparative look at the dynamics of frontiers shows that North America saw the most spectacular increase in cultivated land area. In a bit more than a century before 1910, the region became the first region in terms of cultivated land area (Table 9.1).

Intra- and intercontinental migrations

Walter Nugent (1989), like Walter Webb (1964) and many others, confines the frontier dynamic to countries that were destinations for European emigration, the countries that Alfred Crosby (1986) calls neo-European: North America and the southern tip of Latin America, South Africa, Australia, and New Zealand. But contrary to the legend that has been created and maintained by scholars from these neo-Europeans lands, the mass migrations that characterized the nineteenth century also had other origins and other destinations.

This is particularly the case with Russia, whose frontier had the specificity of being internal to the country, or in territories only recently conquered and that were contiguous to the country (the Caucuses). During the course of the nineteenth century, the European population of Russia gradually settled across Asian territories, Siberia included.

---

[1] For an overview of forest destruction, see Williams (2006: Chapters 10 and 11), and for in-depth details of various local situations, see Dean (1997), and Tucker and Richards (1983).

Table 9.1 Change in cultivated land area, forest areas, and prairie areas between 1850 and 1920 (millions of ha, or 10,000 km^2)*

	Increase in cultivated surface areas between 1850 and 1920		Change in forest surface area between 1850 and 1920	Change in prairie surface areas between 1850 and 1920
	In millions of ha	In % of cultivated surface area in 1850		
North America	129	258	−27	−103
Australia/New Zealand	13	217	−6	−8
Southeast Asia	14	200	−5	−9
Latin America	27	150	−52	25
Russia	84	89	−80	−4
North Africa	16	59	−7	−8
Sub-Saharan Africa	31	54	−61	30
South Asia	27	38	−28	1
China	20	27	−17	−3
Europe	15	11	−5	−11

Source: Richards, 1990: 164.

*This data, which aggregate prairie lands and pasture lands, do not allow one to measure the scale of the transformations that occurred on steppes (in their different forms), and more specifically, the transformation of regions occupied by nomadic herders into pasturelands farmed by European-style livestock farmers.

Lastly, there was Asia, with migratory flows mainly originating from India or China, and which in actuality exceeded European migrations (Lewis, 1978: 181–8). These flows fed two frontiers, in northeast Asia (Manchuria in particular) and in Southeast Asia. Both these regions contributed to supplying biomass to Europe.

It is a complicated task to provide a quantitative overview of the great migrations of the nineteenth century. Adam McKeown proposes an analysis of three large migratory flows between 1846 and 1940:

- the flow from Europe towards the Americas, mainly the United States, of 55 to 58 million people.
- the flow from India and China towards Southeast Asia, the Indian Ocean rim, and the South Pacific, estimated at 48 to 52 million people.
- the flow from northern regions of China and Russia towards Manchuria, Siberia, Central Asia, and Japan, estimated at 46 to 51 million people.

According to this analysis, from the mid-nineteenth century until the Second World War, international migration was divided into three main flows, each roughly equivalent (of more or less 50 million people), and Europeans only represented a third of all migrants.

McKeown's data, however, has the inconvenience for our own analysis of including the interwar period during which long-distance migration underwent major shifts[2] (Ferrie and Hatton, 2013).

This description of migratory flows also has the shortcoming of not accounting for intracontinental—or even infranational—migrations, which in some places played a very significant role, both in Africa and India. This is also the case for nineteenth-century Russia, where internal migrations towards Siberia and the Caucuses are estimated at around 10 million people (McNeill, 1992).

Destruction of indigenous peoples

We are as a nation engaged in a race war in which the indigenous people carry the tremendous anathema of their disappearance, written in the name of civilization. Let us then morally destroy this race, annihilate their resources and their political organizations, eliminate their tribal order, and if need be, divide their families. Broken and dispersed, they will end up embracing civilization.

These were the words of Julio Argentino Roca (1843–1914), twice president of Argentina between 1880 and 1904.[3]

Frederick Jackson Turner in the nineteenth century (1893) or Walter P. Webb later in 1964, naively presented the American frontier as a conquest of virgin lands, of the wild. This idea is obviously mistaken. Excepting for a few very rare cases, humans had colonized all places on earth, long before the pioneers. The characteristic of the frontiers did not lie in conquering an empty territory but in changing the modalities under which these lands were used, which could involve emptying them, wholly or partially, of preexisting occupants. That in particular was the case in the Americas, where in the early nineteenth century, the average population density was extremely low compared to densities in Europe (outside Russia), India, or China (Table 9.2). But, as William McNeill underscores: "Thus the 'empty' frontier Turner spoke of

---

[2] Neo-European countries adopted increasingly restrictive immigration measures from the early twentieth century, while intra-Asian migrations by contrast accelerated considerably, which explains why the cumulated total migration figures for the 1846–1940 period show three flows of equivalent size. In actuality, between the mid-nineteenth century and the First World War, the European flow towards the Americas was considerably and permanently higher than the other two flows. The European flow is even greater if migration towards Australia and New Zealand are included (around 4 million). The opposite trend occurred after the First World War. According to Gregg Huff and Giovanni Caggiano, over the period of 1886–1910, 5.9 million European migrants arrived in the United States each decade, compared to 3.6 million for Burma, Malaysia, and Thailand combined. But after the First World War, the proportions were inverted. Between 1911 and 1929, 3.2 million migrants arrived in the United States each decade, compared to 6.8 million in the three Southeast Asian countries. For the 1930–1939 decade, the figures were 0.7 million and 4.8 million respectively (Huff and Caggiano, 2007: 261).

[3] https://es.wikiquote.org/wiki/Julio_Argentino_Roca (accessed August 16, 2024).

Table 9.2 Population densities, 1500–1800 (inhabitants per km²)

	India	China	Europe (without Russia)	Americas
1500	23	25	14	2
1800	42	80	29	0.6

Source: Sieferle, 2001: 96.

arose from the destruction of Amerindian populations by infections imported from the Old World, sporadically reinforced by resort to armed force" (McNeill, 1992: 18). Despite their small numbers, the arrival of Europeans led to the collapse of the region's previous inhabitants.[4]

The arms that Europeans and neo-Europeans possessed in the nineteenth century gave them an advantage over other peoples in the world, equivalent to the advantage that germs bestowed them in the sixteenth century during the conquest of the Americas. A second phase of conquest in the Great Plains of the Americas thus opened up: in the United States, as famously portrayed in its cinema, and in Argentina (the "conquest of the desert" led by General Julio Argentino Roca against the Mapuche). In actuality, there was a sizable population in the Americas' Great Plains in 1800, but the abundance of space and the introduction of horses meant this populace was largely nomadic. They would gradually be enclosed in ever smaller reserves, and the population reduced to a quarter of its size during the course of the nineteenth century.

Outside of the Americas, the elimination of local communities often occurred within a much shorter time span and concomitantly with the settling of European and Asian migrants. Disease and war also played an important role, for example in Oceania. In New Zealand, between 1842 and 1900, the Maori and White populations changed respectively from 80,000 to 40,000 and from 2,000 to 700,000. In Australia, between 1788 and 1900, the Indigenous population fell from 750,000 to 95,000, while the White population grew from 1,000 to 3,774,000 (Caldwell et al., 2001: 3).

Several genocides occurred: Tasmania Aboriginals, Herero in the German South-West Africa colony (present-day Namibia), and the Yaki in California (Madley, 2004). Conflict with the pioneers arriving to colonize the land was inevitable. Local communities quickly found themselves on a weak footing in their resistance, and very early on there were public authorities that made the annihilation of these communities their goal. The doctrines of *terra nullius* (that is land on which nothing exists) in Australia or *vacuum domicilium* (empty home) in the United States encouraged such a project. Sven Lindqvist (1999) relates and analyses such massacres in his book

---

[4] The estimation of the population in the Americas and how it changed has been subject to much study and debate. Russel Thornton estimates it at 72 million in 1492 and at 4 million at the end of the nineteenth century (Thornton, 1987). But the major population collapse occurred during the first two centuries of colonization. By the end of the seventeenth century, 90 percent of the Amerindian population had disappeared. Historians agree in considering the importation of European diseases (smallpox, measles, etc.) as the leading cause of mortality, followed by overworking and wars (Crosby, 1973; McNeill, 1989).

Exterminate All the Brutes: One Man's Odyssey into the Heart of Darkness and the Origins of European Genocide.[5]

The period was also marked by extermination of those whom Jürgen Osterhammel (2014: 330) called "transfrontier," communities who had blended in with the local environment beyond the frontier, sometimes genetically mixing with local communities, and escaping colonial administration control: *gauchos* in Argentina and southern Brazil, the *métis* in Canada, *buccaneers* in the Caribbean, *vaqueros* in Mexico, *llaneros* in Venezuela, bushrangers in Australia, or *griquas* in South Africa (Curtin, 1990: 88).

Diversity in local situations: Beyond settler states

In Anglo-Saxon literature,[6] settler states (or societies or countries) refers to Anglophone countries with majority populations of European origin: the United States, Canada, Australia, New Zealand, and South Africa. This group is composed of one sovereign nation (the United States, which gained independence in the late eighteenth century) and of four English colonies, which over the course of the long nineteenth century acquired the special political status of dominion, giving them their own government (representative of European colonizers), sovereignty over domestic policy, finance, and trade. The five countries received around 80 percent (71 percent for just North America) of migrants that left Europe between 1820 and 1913 (Ferrie and Hatton, 2013: 4). They share many historical, political, and economic similarities. James Belich's book *Replenishing the Earth: The Settler Revolution and the Rise of the Anglo-World, 1783–1939* (Belich, 2009) proposes the thesis that these frontier communities of European migrants are the foundation of the rise of the Anglo-world.

These settler states are often presented as the main suppliers of biomass to Europe in the nineteenth century (Friedmann and McMichael, 1989). However, their significance may not have been so great, at least for the years preceding the First World War (Table 9.3). By then, the whole world was involved in responding to European biomass demand. According to the figures in the table, countries of Anglo-Saxon immigration (assimilated to North America and Oceania combined) represented only a quarter of world biomass exports measured in value, specifically 21 percent for food biomass (exotic and temperate combined) and 32 percent for non-food biomass. Latin America at the time alone exported more food biomass than all Anglo-Saxon migration countries.

The case of settler states is presented in greater depth later (see Chapter 15) with an analysis of the emblematic United States; here we will focus on three other, and quite contrasting, frontier terrains: Argentina, Russia, and Burma.

---

[5] Let us recall also that not all Indigenous communities were hunter-gatherers. The Zulu of South Africa were a sedentary community based on crop farming and livestock, with a centralized monarchical administration. Most of these communities were not completely exterminated, but were partially transformed into a labor reservoir.

[6] For a long history of the European settler colonies and for an overview of recent ongoing debates, see Lloyd and Metzer (2013).

Table 9.3 Biomass exports by "continent," 1913 (in % of total world value)

	Food biomass	Non-food biomass	Biomass total
United States and Canada	17	25	20
United Kingdom and Ireland	3	2	2
Other European	33	29	31
Oceania	4	7	5
Latin America	22	10	17
Africa	5	9	7
Asia	16	18	17

Source: adapted from Lamartine Yates, 1959.

Argentina, a non-Anglo-saxon, neo-European country

European history in Argentina started with Spanish colonization in the sixteenth century. While the colony remained sparsely populated for 300 years, it had a high population of livestock. Argentina is a very neat example of the "ecological imperialism" of Europeans: a population of horses, sheep, and cattle introduced in 1516 multiplied in the immense spaces of the pampa "in a manner similar to smallpox virus in the salubrious environment of Indian bodies" (Crosby, 1973: 84). According to some early eighteenth-century voyagers, some horse herds were so large that when they crossed your path, you had to wait for a day or two before being able to pass (ibid.).

These herds were the livelihood of *gauchos*, a typical example of European and indigenous mixed communities. The *gauchos* kept cattle, either for ranches belonging to large landholders or, illegally, for themselves, and from these they drew hides, fats (tallow), and salted beef for export towards Europe (1 million cow hides were exported each year at the end of the eighteenth century) or towards the slave plantations (Slatta, 1992). They also played a role as conscripts in defending against incursions by Indians. But they lived on "the margins" of urban communities and the elite, and they were swept away by the advancing frontier.

From 1820, a boom in wool exports displaced cattle products and dealt a first blow to the extractivist logic of their ranching model. In 1880, with the ending of the "desert war," the large-scale farming of the Pampas commenced and a massive wave of European immigration arrived. Contrary to the United States, land in Argentina was already controlled by large landowners. Land clearing was thus organized in the form of "associations": the migrants, as tenant farmers, cleared and prepared the pampa land (breaking the soil of prairies requires a lot of work), sowed wheat (for a few years), then left the land, which by then was enclosed and planted with alfalfa for feeding an English race of cows, and advanced once more with the frontier (Adelman, 1994).

The main exported products in 1913 were cereals (wheat for 19 percent of total Argentine exports and corn for 16 percent), frozen meat (13 percent), wool (12 percent), flaxseeds (9 percent), and skins (8 percent) (Tena-Junguito and Willebald, 2013: 46).

Biomass exports ensured prosperity for Argentina of a level it would never regain. In the early twentieth century, its GDP per capita stood at the same level as Canada's or the Netherlands'. With trams, public lighting, and opera houses, Buenos Aires was then a town that had nothing to envy of European capitals. It was not just chance that the whole world danced the tango.

Russia, a Eurasian frontier

"But in what do you see the special characteristics of the Russian laborer?" said Metrov; "in his biological characteristics, so to speak, or in the condition in which he is placed?" Levin saw that there was an idea underlying this question with which he did not agree. But he went on explaining his own idea that the Russian laborer has a quite special view of the land, different from that of other people; and to support this proposition he made haste to add that in his opinion this attitude of the Russian peasant was due to the consciousness of his vocation to people vast unoccupied expanses in the East.

(Tolstoy, *Anna Karenina*, part 7, chapter 3)

The history of Russia is a long history of frontiers, moving from west eastwards, and of exploiting the resources from these, in part to serve distant markets. Frontiers for long had advanced along the Boreal forest, where for several centuries fur-hunting had been undertaken, leading Russian trappers ever further eastwards, through Siberia and up until California. The Urals were crossed in 1580, the Pacific reached in 1617 and California in the nineteenth century. At the same time, there were advancing frontiers to the south and southeast, from the poor soils of original forest regions towards the rich black soils of the steppe, and then south of the Oka River, in the vast Eurasian steppe extending from Hungary to Mongolia, crossing through Siberia and northern Central Asia. Progressive control of these zones was made possible through a succession of wars won against the Ottoman Empire, which at the end of the eighteenth century gave Russia control of the whole northern coast of the Black Sea, west of the Don River, and the environs of the Azov sea (Richards, 2003: 517 and following). Odessa, which had been insignificant at the beginning of the century, in 1850 became Russia's leading port for exporting cereals. Situated on the Black Sea, the town had the great advantage of having a port that could function throughout the year, unlike Baltic ports or those on the White Sea which remained paralyzed by ice for several months a year. Odessa also gave access to the Mediterranean, and to the enormous catchment area of the Dnieper, that crossed Russia, Ukraine, and Belarus (Kagarlitsky, 2008).

Agricultural colonization of the steppe from the late eighteenth century was carried out by populations from Central Russia, northern Ukraine, and more marginally, from Germany. The number of peasants present on the Russian steppe grew from fewer than 50,000 in 1719 to 5 million in 1897 (Moon, 2005: 153). Moreover, between 1897 and 1916, more than 5 million Russian peasants also settled in Siberia, in Kazakhstan, in the Far East, and in the Northern Caucus (Gammer, 2005: 495).[7]

---

[7] The number of European Russian migrants going to Siberia grew from an annual average of 35,000 in the 1880s to 96,000 in the 1890s and a peak of 759,000 in 1908 (Osterhammel, 2014: 364).

Half of the wheat production at the end of the nineteenth century was exported, as the "wheat belt" progressed south-eastwards with land cultivation expanding to the Northern Caucuses and regions of the Lower Volga, and beyond toward west of Siberia (Falkus, 1966: 423). The nature and destination of exports also changed. Durum wheat exported towards Italy and France tended to replace soft wheat targeted at the English market.

Burma, a Southeast Asian delta

The frontier in the Irrawaddy delta commenced with English colonization in the early 1850s. Cultivated surfaces there grew from 0.9 million acres in 1855 to 8 million in 1914. Rice exports grew from 310,000 tons in 1862–3 to 2.4 million tons per year for the period 1902–11, in other words, as much as the entire quantity of cereal exports from Canada (Owen, 1971: 87). These exploits were the fruits of labor of migrants from the dry regions in northern Burma, as well as a large number of migrants from India. The Indians also worked in construction or in the ports, as well as money-lenders and traders. In all, about 4.2 million Indians are estimated to have migrated towards Burma between 1880 and 1910; there was, however, a significant return rate (Huff and Caggiano, 2008: 260). During the 1901–10 decade, Burma was the primary destination for Indian migrants, with three-quarters of them going there.

Burmese rice, which was initially targeted at the English market (re-export, distilleries, starch manufacture, animal feed), diversified its European markets until 1914. The rest of Burmese rice—1.3 million out of 2.4 million tons exported over the period 1902–11 (Coclanis, 1993: 1068)—also contributed, but indirectly, to supplying the English with biomass, as it was used to feed Tamil Indian migrants who worked in the tea plantations in Ceylon, and in sugarcane and later rubber plantations in Malaysia (Latham, 1988: 91).

For Michel Adas, rice plantations without doubt represented the type of "*mise en valeur*" that was least harmful for the environment. While high grasses and pockets of tropical forest that had earlier covered the delta were all eliminated by the early twentieth century, mangroves, partial protection against the sea, were for the most part maintained, and the natural environment underwent relatively little transformation. Over the longer term, however, dykes and other mechanisms posed challenges for soil fertility of the natural habitat, preventing the seasonal floods full of natural fertilizer from reaching the soils (Adas 2009).

10

An intensive animal farming pole in Northwestern Europe

Crop-based biomass flowed liberally from the whole world towards England. Animal-based food products, and meat in particular, on the other hand, traveled with less ease, at least until refrigerated ships emerged. A part of European agriculture exploited its proximity to the hegemon to capture a share of the flow by specializing in animal farming based on imported livestock feed. Farmers in Northwest Europe (Denmark, Holland, Belgium, and northwest France) thus reproduced, but on a grander scale, the strategy of specializing in animal production that had initially been adopted by English farmers after the abolition of the Corn Laws.

Repositioning of English agriculture on animal production using imported biomass

Faced with competition from imported biomass, English agriculture, whose output remained stable in value, gradually turned to animal farming. In 1846, the year in which the Corn Laws were abolished, the value of animal production represented 42 percent of the total agricultural output; in 1913, it represented 75 percent. This growth was mainly generated by cattle farming, which was the least exposed to competition from imports, before freezing meat became possible. Sheep herds by contrast suffered from the loss in competitiveness of English wool (Table 10.1).

This animal production increasingly depended on animal feed bought on the market, of which a growing share was imported. Analysis of data provided by T.B. Wood (1917) on the sources and uses of cereals in the United Kingdom prior to the First World War leaves little doubt as to the scale of this process (Table 10.2):

- Fifty-four percent of cereals consumed in the country were used for animal feed. While a significant share of these cereals were oats used for feeding draft horses, which was nothing new, when oats are excluded, animals still account for 43 percent of total consumption.
- The share of imports varies widely between various cereals for animal feed: they represented only a quarter for oats, but doubtless almost 100 percent for other cereals. This was clearly the case for corn. It is not possible to make the same certain assertion for wheat and barley from Wood's data. It is plausible, however,

Table 10.1 Gross crop and animal production in value (millions of £) and in %

	1846		1867–9		1911–13	
	Value	%	Value	%	Value	%
Crop production	127	58	104	45	56	25
Animal production	91	42	125	55	165	75
Total	218	100	229	100	222	100

Source: Perren, 1978: 4 and 6.

Table 10.2 Origin and uses of cereals in the United Kingdom, 1909–13 (in thousands of tons)

	Origin			Use				
	Local	Imported	Total	Seeds	Animal feed	Breweries & distilleries	Other industries	Human food
Wheat	1,584	5,671	7,255	130	2,500	–	125	4,500
Barley	1,522	1,061	2,583	120	978	1,435	–	50
Oats	3,004	899	3,903	200	3,503	–	–	200
Corn	–	2,068	2,068	–	1,683	233	100	50
Rice	–	303	303	–	52	70	41	140
Rye	50	44	94	10	84	–	–	–
Total	6,160	10,046	16,206	460	8,800	1,738	266	4,940

Source: adapted from Wood, 1917.

to consider that the full local production of those two cereals went above all to the production of bread and alcohols for the English market, and that therefore animal farming relied on imports.

The United Kingdom's dependence on international supply of meat was thus much higher than estimations based only on meat imports imply.

Animal farming in Northwestern Europe: An offshoot of crop biomass flows from frontier economies

England's specialization in animal farming did not prevent the country from also increasing its imports of animal products: a sharp rise in consumption resulted in quadrupling of the value of imports between 1872 and 1913. The development of refrigeration processes enabled a part of this growth, particularly for meat, but here I will focus on other animal products: butter, the leading animal food product that was imported, and bacon, the second most imported product. In 1913, 65 percent of butter, 89 percent of cheese, 75 percent of bacon, and 69 percent of ham were imported (Table 10.3). Around these products an export-oriented animal farming pole, based on imported plant biomass, emerged in northwest continental Europe.

Denmark was the country where the development of animal farming using imported feed was the most spectacular (Table 10.4). In 1913, Denmark was the world's leading exporter of butter, and the second largest exporter of pork after the United States. The country, which had traditionally exported cereals produced in the large estates of Jutland, from 1870 saw a radical shift in the composition of its agricultural production. The share of cereals and tubers fell sharply while those of dairy products and pork products (especially bacon) spiked (Table 10.5).

Like Argentina, Denmark prospered by occupying a position of agro-exporter in the international division of labor that prevailed under the English hegemony (Table 10.6). In 1913, its per capita gross domestic product (GDP) stood at 80 percent of that of England.

The number of pigs in Denmark grew from 300,000 to 2.5 million between 1816 and 1913, and that of cattle from 1.1 million to 2.4 million. The human population for its part grew from 1.6 million to 2.8 million. In 1913, there was thus almost one pig and one cow for each Danish inhabitant. During the same period, butter exports rose

Table 10.3 United Kingdom: Imports of animal products (in £)

	1872–4	1892–4	1911–13
Meat			
Live cattle	3,112	7,833	–
Live sheep	1,702	804	1,720
Live pigs			
Beef	487	5,525	13,603
Mutton/lamb	–	4,049	9,720
Ham and bacon	5,445	11,038	18,386
Other	1,041	845	7,393
Share of imports in total meat consumption	14%	32%	42%
Other animal products			
Cheese	3,858	5,350	7,196
Butter	7,344	12,724	24,345
Eggs	2,184	3,818	8,650
Lard	1,193	2,595	4,792
All animal products	26,369	54,120	95,508

Sources: Statistical Abstract of United Kingdom, various years.

Table 10.4 International trade in animal products and products intended for animal feed, 1911–12 (in millions of £)

	Net exports of animal products	Net imports of animal feed products	Balance
Denmark	21.93	−6.59	15.34
Holland	6.64	−8.93	−2.29
Ireland	23.52	−5.01	18.51
Sweden	3.12	−0.47	2.65

Source: Shanahan, 1920: 34.

Table 10.5 Main indicators of Danish agriculture, 1870–1913 (in %)

	1870–2	1911–13
Composition of agricultural production		
Cereals and tubers	30	2
Milk and dairy	18	38
Pork and live pigs	11	25
Other animal products	36	31
Share of agricultural products in total exports	88	87
Share of agriculture in GDP	50	30
Share of agriculture in employment	51	39

Source: Henriksen, 2009: 139–44.

Table 10.6 Agricultural productivity index for various European countries (in millions of net calories per male farm worker), 1850–1910

	1850	1880	1910
Denmark	15.0	27.4	39.8
United Kingdom	17.3	19.2	24.1

Source: Bairoch, 1999: 136.

from 2,000 to 95,000 tons, egg exports from 8,000 to 23 million, and pork exports from 2,000 to 188,000 tons.

The strength of Danish agriculture resulted from a social revolution which saw the peasantry win out over the Jutland large cereal producers (Servolin, 1985). Small Danish livestock farmers blocked the introduction of protective measures against the invasion of "foreign" cereals. They thus secured access to cheap animal feed to develop their animal production. They also gained force thanks to a dense network of cooperatives for the production and sale of butter: in 1903, 81 percent of milk passed through cooperatives (Henriksen, 2009: 129). These cooperatives played an important role in standardizing the quality of exported butter. They quickly adopted the steam engine for skimming milk (Teives Henriques and Sharp, 2014). They also facilitated the purchase of cattle feed in winter thus allowing Danish farmers to produce butter throughout the year (Henriksen and O'Rourke, 2005).

Dairy production and pork farming were closely linked: whey from milk, which cooperatives gave back to farmers, was used to feed pigs and produce bacon at competitive prices.

Changes in domestic consumption occurred as a result of this economic orientation: Danes may have exported butter, but they consumed margarine, made from imported oilseeds from which meal was made to use in animal feed. They also imported "lower grade animal foodstuffs, e.g., American bacon, Siberian butter, etc., partly for home consumption, to replace high-grade goods of the same kinds exported" (Shanahan, 1920: 24).

11

On free labor

Agricultural biomass production for long-distance trade towards Europe, in accordance with Immanuel Wallerstein's (1974: chapter 2) thesis on the organization of labor within the European world-economy, was for several centuries undertaken through forced labor: slavery in the Americas, serfdom in the East (Russia, Prussia, etc.) (Parts 1 and 2). In the nineteenth century, however, large holdings founded on forced labor came to be replaced by market-oriented family farming, even in the colonies, with the exception of the relative success of large plantations using wage labor in Asia. Paradoxically,[1] it was not the English model of large capitalist farms employing wage workers that emerged, even if this was the model used in the contemporaneous transformation of the manufacturing sector, which saw the generalization of large production plants relying on wage labor and bureaucracy (Chandler, 1977).

English public opinion called for the abolition of slavery in various parts of the world, and English public institutions, including the military, concretized such calls. The power of the hegemon was clearly manifest in the process that led to the emergence of agriculture based on free labor.[2] The synchronicity of the process of labor emancipation and the elimination of forced labor—serfdom or slavery—across countries mean that interpretations focused on changes of government or the action of remarkable individuals are unsatisfactory. For Stanley Engerman (1996), the only factor capable of explaining this synchronicity is the development of capitalism (I would add "industrial" capitalism). It is not a matter of economic determinism as proposed by Eric Williams (1968) for whom slavery, after having played an essential role in the birth of capitalism in England, disappeared when it was no longer profitable. Works that came after Williams' show that slavery was still profitable, and that the bourgeoisie was

---

[1] And despite many "prophecies": see Kautsky, 1900 for example.
[2] The title of this section "On free labor" is perhaps not fully accurate, or shall we say, too hasty a declaration. The line between "free labor" and "non-free labor" is a moving one. Many societies may distinguish between the two, but the way in which they are defined in each country varies widely. There is a continuum between different forms of labor, and the role that coercion plays in each. For Alessandro Stanziani, Central European "serfdom" or the indentured labor that served as a substitute for slave labor in the nineteenth century is simply a radicalized form of house-servant status. Such status in effect involved marked dissymmetry between the rights of the employer and those of the employee: for example, breach of contract by the employee was penalized, while the employer was at total liberty to fire a house-servant. Yet in the Anglo-Saxon world, house-servants (a very significant share of the population until the mid-nineteenth century) were considered as free workers, because they were hired of their free will through a contract (Stanziani, 2013).

not politically in a position to impose abolition. In the end, the conflict between forced labor and capitalism appears to have been mainly ideological: modes of forced labor are irreconcilable with the importance that capitalist ideologies places on the freedom of enterprise and freedom to succeed (or fail) through one's own effort.

Opponents of slavery defended the principle of free labor. Plantations were not challenged because they were large capital-intensive production units. Rather, opponents called for slave labor to be replaced by wage work (Cooper, 1977; Roberts and Miers, 1988). A succession of unforeseen obstacles, however, prevented this transformation from taking place:

- First, former slaves once freed showed no desire to remain on the plantations; and the system of "indentured workers," now from Asia, made a comeback, but only temporarily.
- Stiff competition gradually emerged from new regions of production which continued to use slave labor successfully, and some even the slave trade, until the early twentieth century.
- Above all, both in America and Europe, market-oriented family farming emerged strongly, and technical and institutional innovations of the nineteenth century (Chapter 8) now gave these farmers access to distant markets.

Citizen activism and legislative developments in England

Opposition to slavery emerged from the eighteenth century and lasted until the 1920s. Initially, opposition targeted the plantations that Europeans had established in the Americas[3]—mainly in the Caribbean, in the southern United States, and on the Brazilian coast. Later, as territorial conquest of Africa progressed, African or Arab slave plantations that existed prior to colonization,[4] such as those in the Niger delta or in Zanzibar, became targets, and lastly, attention turned to the exploitation of "natives" (Miers and Roberts, 1988).

The antislavery movement may be considered as a transnational advocacy network, equivalent to those that exist today on human rights issues or environmental protection activism. At the heart of the network were the Quakers (and other Protestant groups like the Methodists and the Unionists) who drew on hundreds of local chapters that were networked together, to amplify inquiries, witness accounts, information campaigns, and petitions (Keck and Kikkink, 1998). England's national legislature was a particular active terrain of the opposition to slavery. The English state's commitment to the fight against slavery was decisive for the movement. Participation by English ships in the slave trade was prohibited in 1807, and later in 1833 slavery was abolished in all English colonies, excepting India.

---

[3] To this list one must add the Indian Ocean "sugar islands" like Reunion and Mauritius, and African Atlantic islands like São Tomé. We will return to the latter case.
[4] Plantations which were often set up in reaction to the prohibition of the slave trade, and which gave rise to what Anglo-Saxon historians call the "legitimate commerce" (Law, 1995).

The English state, with its considerable naval power, also intervened to interrupt slave trading on the West African coast. England, moreover, used its diplomacy to influence policies of other countries involved in slavery, and worked to obtain the signing of treaties with other European powers present on the West African coasts (France, Spain, and Portugal), and later with various African authorities (Miers, 1975).

Abolition and emancipation

1783: Abolition of slavery by the Massachusetts Supreme Court.
1794: French emancipation.
1803: Guadeloupe retaken by the French who reinstate slavery.
1808: Prohibition of the slave trade by the English.
1815: Slavery reinstated in all sugar islands under French control. The Vienna Congress, under English pressure, declares slavery immoral.
1823: Abolition of slavery in Chile.
1829: Abolition of slavery in Mexico.
1833: British Emancipation Act abolishes slavery in the British colonies.
1838: End of the apprenticeship system.*
1848: Abolition of slavery in French territories.
1843: Abolition of the legal status of slave in India.
1851: Abolition of slavery in Colombia.
1853: Abolition of slavery in Argentina.
1861: Emancipation Manifesto for serfs in the Russian Empire.
1863: Abraham Lincoln proclaims the emancipation of slaves in the Confederate States.
1863: Abolition of slavery in Dutch colonies.
1871: Rio Branco law in Brazil: children born of slaves are free from birth but maintain a status of *ingenuo* (a slave status) until the age of 21.
1884–5: The Berlin Conference prohibits slavery and the slave trade in the Congo basin.
1886: Abolition in Cuba.
1888: Abolition in Brazil.
1889: Conference in Brussels between France, the United Kingdom, Germany, and Belgium on "harmonization" of colonial policies. Promotion of "free labor."
1897: Abolition of slavery in Zanzibar (English protectorate since 1890).

*A system of apprenticeship, an eight-year transition period for slaves to learn to manage freedom, was part of the abolition of slavery in the English colonies. The system obliged slaves to remain on the plantations, but they had the right to work for their own account or for another employer for a quarter of their time, and plantation owners were obliged to pay a small wage. The system was abandoned in 1838, and in the years that followed, huge numbers of former slaves left plantations to set themselves up as farmers where land was still available.

In the colonies, slave revolts, and particularly the early victory in Saint-Domingue that resulted in Haiti's independence, of course had a significant impact on progress in abolition.

Return of indentured labor in the islands

The role of European indentured workers in the initial phase of establishment of Caribbean plantations was presented in Part 2 of this book. Having been profitably replaced by slavery for more than a century, indentured labor made a comeback with the abolitions. However, nineteenth-century indentured workers were Asian, mainly Indian, and they headed towards sugar plantations in European colonies, the Caribbean, Mascarenes (Mauritius and La Réunion), and southern Africa in particular. Indentured labor was openly considered a solution for replacing former slave labor (Northrup, 1995). This new migratory flow reproduced the same practices as seen with seventeenth-century European indentured workers.

The earliest departures for Mauritius (English colony) took place in 1829, even before slavery was abolished (Tinker, 1993: 69). French colonies also adopted indentured labor, from 1849 in Reunion Islands, and from 1852 in the Caribbean.

As the majority of indentured workers came from India, flows were controlled by the English colonial administration, thus penalizing plantation owners in the French colonies, who were often refused access to this labor source.[5] Indentured labor, however, was a poor palliative to the abolition of slavery. The workforce size mobilized was comparable to that of the late period in the slave trade, when it was already being obstructed by the English (Table 11.1). In effect, very early on, measures restricting the departure of indentured workers were put in place. Countries of origin were worried about availability of workers at home, as well as about the type of treatment

Table 11.1 Estimated flows of three types of forced labor, from the nineteenth century to early twentieth century

Status	Origin and destination	Period	In thousands
Slaves	Africa towards America(s)	1821–67	1,757
Indentured workers			
	India	1838–1922	1,334
	China	1852–1907	330
	Japan	1868–1923	83
	Africa	1834–67	91
Total indentured workers		1834–1923	1,839
Convicts	From United Kingdom to Australia	1788–1868	162

Source: Engerman, 1986.

---

[5] Here we have an explanation for the strong growth in sugar production in Mauritius, while production in the Reunion Islands and the French Caribbean floundered.

that migrants would be subjected to—both the working conditions on the plantations and the process of recruitment itself, which frequently resembled kidnapping (blackbirding)—and eventually banned the practice.

> ### Slavery and citizen activism in the nineteenth century—the birth of consumer activism
>
> Alongside legislation, which evolved slowly, various "non-state" initiatives and product-specific campaigns were launched, conceived either as a way of exerting pressure for laws to change, or as providing alternatives to the legislative route.
>
> Boycott campaigns were aimed at changing laws. The first calls for boycott took place in the late eighteenth century and targeted sugar production (Sussman, 2000); they were new boycott campaigns in the early twentieth century against cocoa from São Tomé.
>
> The movement for "free produce" on the other hand was conceived as an alternative to legislative measures. It was launched around 1820. Its initiators opened shops in the United States and in England selling products (fabric, shoes, soap, ice, sugar) that were guaranteed to be slave-labor free. According to Glickman,
>
>> free produce activists were also the first to affirm that consumers—rather than land owners or the productive classes—were representative citizens and the moral heart of the Republic. By considering consumers as agents for moral and economic change, by using the term 'consumer' in a positive sense, and by conceptualizing the notion of 'consumer conscience' they laid the foundation of the modern consumer movement [...]. Free produce activists did not impute any morality or immorality to the market itself: the market was a power that could be used for good or for bad.
>> (Glickman, 2004: 218)

Success of later abolitions: Four examples

The prohibition of the slave trade (1808) and the abolition of slavery in England were far from signifying the immediate end of all slave plantations. On the contrary, a new phase in the history of slave plantations opened up, named by historians the "second enslavement," reminiscent of the more common formula of second serfdom (Tomich and Zeuske, 2008; Boatcă, 2013). The second enslavement period ran from 1780 to 1888, the year slavery was abolished in Brazil. It occurred in a context of declining island or coastal plantation colonies and emerging new territories that were vaster, and therefore more productive. It was accompanied by the adoption of new technologies, like the steam engine for preliminary post-harvest processing on farms (sugar mills) or for transportation (railroad), including inside plantations themselves. The first half of the nineteenth century was the period during which the greatest number of slaves were mobilized to produce quantities of biomass for long-distance trade, significantly higher than eighteenth-century volumes (Tomich, 1991: 299).

For several products (cotton, coffee, and sugar, which together represented a third of British biomass imports in 1815), the second enslavement meant the quasi-monopolization of export supply by one single territory (either sovereign—United States and Brazil—or colonial—Cuba) founded on spectacular growth in production. These latter-day slave plantation regions shared the distinctive feature (perhaps the most important feature with regard to international trade in biomass) of maintaining for the most part their dominant market position despite the abandonment of slavery—a sort of successful "transition," to use a term that is dear today (Table 11.2).

If slavery persisted and prospered it was because initially the prohibition of the slave trade was very relative. The number of slaves that were victims of the trade had fallen only modestly at the turn of the nineteenth century: from 1.7 million between 1776 and 1800 to 1.5 million between 1801 and 1825 and 1.4 million between 1826 and 1850 (Table 11.3). Only after 1850 did the numbers really start to fall, with "only" 180,000 people traded between 1851 and 1867, the year in which the trade definitively ended (Eltis, 2001). The nineteenth-century transatlantic trade targeted mainly Iberian America. Between 1800 and 1850, 62 percent of slaves went towards Brazil and 20 percent towards the Spanish Caribbean, mainly Cuba. Moreover, continental countries like Brazil and the United States redeployed already present slave labor within their own borders, from regions in decline towards new regions of production (from Nordeste towards Rio de Janeiro, and then São Paolo, and from the Old South towards the Deep South).

Table 11.2 Market share (in %) of the United States, Brazil, Cuba, and São Tomé in cotton, cane sugar, and cocoa markets, 1790–1900

Market share	Around 1790	Around 1840	Around 1860	Around 1880	Around 1900
United States in British cotton imports	1	79	75	74	78
Brazil in global coffee exports	0	24 (1830)	55	41	76
Cuba in global cane sugar exports	5	21	33	41 (1871–2)	33 (1894–5)*
São Tomé in global cocoa exports	0	0	1	2	14

Sources: United States' share in 1790, see Edwards, 1967: 250–1; from 1840 to 1900, see Mitchell, 1962: 180–1; Brazil's share in 1790, see Topik and Clarence-Smith, 2003;** in 1830, see Daviron, 1994; 1860, 1880, and 1900, see Topik and Clarence-Smith, 2003; Cuba's share in 1790, see Prinsen-Geerligs, 1912: 11; for the American territories, see Galloway, 1989: 212; for Java, 1840, 1860, 1880, and 1900, see Moreno Fraginals, 1978; São Tomé's share, see Clarence-Smith, 2000;

*The years 1894–5 were chosen as these were the last years before production collapsed due to the battles for independence and invasion by the United States. In the 1920s, Cuba returned to the market share it had enjoyed prior to these events.

**The data available for 1790 is very partial. Saint-Domingue is missing although prior to its slave insurrection it produced at least two-thirds of coffee exports. See Laborie (1798, appendix: 82) on Saint-Domingue exports.

Table 11.3 Destination of African slaves, 1776–1867 (in thousands)

	1776–1800	1801–25	1826–50	1851–67
United States	24	73	0	0.3
Brazil	569	806	962	6
Spanish Caribbean	57	269	297	152
Total	1,735	1,458	1,398	177

Source: Eltis, 2001: 46.

In the aftermath of its independence, the United States exported very little cotton. Over the period of 1786–90, its share in British imports was estimated at 0.2 percent (compared to 8 percent for Brazil, 71 percent for the British Caribbean, 20 percent for Mediterranean countries, and 1 percent for the distant Dutch Indies) (Ellison, 1886: 86). But by 1801, the United States exported as much as all the British Caribbean countries combined, and fifty years later was supplying three-quarters of British imports (Riello, 2013: 203). A whole society, whose splendor and violence would be abundantly portrayed in literature and cinema, grew up around cotton.

The history of plantations in the southern United States went through the same main phases described earlier for the Caribbean sugar islands. In the seventeenth century, the initial workforce, in plantations that at the time focused on tobacco in Virginia and Maryland, was composed of European indentured workers whose conditions were very close to slave conditions (sale possible at any moment, separations from family, corporal punishment, etc.). Use of African slaves came later, but was reserved for crops with a high level of profitability (tobacco, rice, and indigo) which was not the case for cotton before the late eighteenth century.

In 1793, Eli Whitney developed the mechanical cotton gin, which is said to have multiplied labor productivity by a factor of fifty, and was thus the catalyst for the cotton farming boom in the southern United States. It should be noted, in reference to the theory of induced innovation, that this innovation came at a time when demand for cotton, driven by the growth of the British textile industry, was particularly high, thus driving up prices. The arrival of planters who had been chased from Saint-Domingue may also have encouraged the development of cotton farming. Production grew through the planting of new lands ever more westwards, following the classic frontier logic, and saw declining production in former cotton regions. At the eve of the War of Secession, cotton farming stretched from the Atlantic coast (the Carolinas) to east of Texas, with the two densest zones being along the Mississippi and in Alabama.

It was indeed the persistence and the thriving of slavery that made possible the spectacular increase in land area planted with cotton. The slave population in the American South grew from 657,000 to 3,950,000 between 1790 and 1860, although their proportion within the total population remained more or less stable, at around one-third (Kolchin, 2009: 53). The key specificity of the United States lies in the fact that the rise of the slave population in the South after 1807 was no longer driven by the transatlantic slave trade, but much more by demographic growth. The advancing frontier was based on internal migration: 855,000 slaves were displaced from Maryland, Virginia, and South Carolina towards Alabama, Mississippi, Louisiana, and Texas (Fogel and Engerman, 1995: 47).

At the end of the War of Secession, former slaves, hostile to any form of work reminiscent of former slave plantations, mostly rejected the wage-worker status that planters tried to promote. Moreover, the abandonment of all ambitions for agrarian reform strongly limited the possibilities for owner–operator farming. The percentage of Black families in the South that owned land (through purchase of farm plots) did rise from 2 percent in 1870 to 21 percent in 1890 (Kolchin, 1998), but in 1910 was still at just 24 percent. The vast majority of former landowning planters put in place systems of sharecropping, whose principal characteristic was that they gave greater autonomy to the worker by putting an end to collective work (Danbom, 1995). After a brief period of the share wage system, whereby the planter provided the sharecropper with a house, draft animals, and in some cases seeds, and then kept a share of the harvest (initially five-sixths or seven-eighths, later three-quarters), the share rental system was adopted, which transferred the operating costs to the sharecropper for an equal division of the harvest.

The shift from large plantation to smallholder farming was also aided by the gradual movement of growing areas more westwards, a movement which saw the emergence of the small white farmer in the cotton sector.

This passage from large plantation to small units, with farmers as either owners or tenants, did not weaken the dominant position of the United States, which in 1900 still supplied 78 percent of English cotton imports.

In 1830, Brazil was already the world's leading coffee producer, providing a quarter of global production; in 1860 Brazil's share rose to 55 percent. Until 1870, the heart of coffee growing in Brazil was located in the state of Rio. When Rio coffee farms started declining, the frontier moved towards the state of São Paolo, where in the space of 30 years, coffee production increased twentyfold on a cultivated (former forest) land area equivalent in size to France (Daviron, 1993). During the period of growth of São Paolo's coffee production, labor issues were dealt with in two very distinct phases, interspersed by a period of stagnation.

Until 1850, coffee farming developed using slave labor, and took advantage of the considerable supply provided by the transatlantic trade. When the slave trade slowed, the coffee region for some years still had a supply of slaves coming from declining sugar and cotton regions in the north of the country. But this supply gradually dwindled away, and coffee farms felt the pinch of the shortage of workers. In the early 1870s, slaves, whose price had risen continuously, represented a half of the capital held by *fazendas* (Mauro, 1979). From 1873, the absolute headcount of slaves started to fall.

The *fazendeiros* were faced with the urgent need to find new sources of labor, even though there had already been earlier attempts to "import" European labor from the late 1840s. In 1847, Nicolau Vergueiroe, was the first *fazendeiro* to obtain a loan from the São Paolo provincial authorities to cover the costs of transporting several hundred German emigrants. Ten years later, sixty *fazendas* hosted settlement colony communities, mostly German, but also some Swiss, Spaniards, and Italians. However, the experiment did not last long. The emigrants were responsible for the upkeep and harvesting of the coffee plots; they were allocated plots for planting food, and shared half of their gains with the owner. But they started out highly indebted to the *fazendeiro* who employed them, having to reimburse the costs of the voyage, and their upkeep during their first year in Brazil. This debt tied the emigrants to the planter who had brought them over for a long duration, creating for the planter a captive workforce. Resembling a system of semi-slavery, the contract system led to numerous labor conflicts, and the Prussian and Swiss governments prohibited this form of recruitment from 1857 (Dean, 1976).

A new system to generate mass immigration flows towards coffee farms was not put in place until the boom years that preceded the abolition of slavery. During these years the *fazendeiros* ended up making concessions to appease European émigrés. In 1887, one year before slavery was abolished, they created the Society for Immigration Promotion, which, using subsidies from the state of São Paolo, covered the full costs of emigrant travel. They built an Immigration Hotel in São Paolo to welcome immigrants and provide them with some orientation at arrival. Farm workers, under the system called *colonato*, received remuneration in three parts:

- A fixed income for every 1,000 coffee plants for the upkeep of the land and to prepare for harvest.
- Income for each day worked for pruning, fertilizing, etc.
- An income proportional to the harvest.

Families of the farm laborers also had plots to grow food or had the right to grow food between the rows of coffee bushes (Holloway, 1978).

The policy was a resounding success: the number of immigrants grew from 9,000 in 1886 to 32,000 in 1887 and to 92,000 in 1888, the last representing for one single year almost the equivalent of the number of slavers present in the state. For twenty years, São Paolo's coffee sector would thus benefit from a continuous inflow of labor, with a total of more than a million arrivals, the large majority from Italy. Brazil was the only tropical Latin American country to thus benefit from a part of the European emigration flows of the late nineteenth century. In 1900, the country supplied 76 percent of global coffee exports.

During this same period, Cuba dominated the sugar market. Absent from the sugar market in the late eighteenth century, Cuba took advantage of the difficulties experienced by the French and British Caribbean countries in sugar production—the Saint-Domingue slave revolt, depleted soil fertility, and then the abolition of slavery in the English colonies.

Cuban sugar production also benefited very directly from the arrival of Saint-Domingue planters, and after abolition, of planters from the British Caribbean, sometimes along with their slaves (Curry-Machado and Bosma, 2012: 243). Cuban plantations thus had a continuous inflow of slaves until late into the century, making it, after Brazil, the main destination for the dwindling transatlantic trade. Despite the signing of an Anglo-Spanish treaty in 1817, supposed to put an end to the trade, 573,000 slaves arrived on the island during the next fifty years; some of these were even Blacks kidnapped on neighboring islands where slavery had been abolished.

These were the conditions under which Cuban sugar production took off. Bolstered by the advancing frontier which moved from west to east, sugar production grew from 14,000 to 720,000 tons between 1790 and the late 1860s, and at its peak accounted for 40 percent of world exports,[6] whose volumes had during the period grown by a factor of seven.

Cuban plantations combined slavery traditions with the modernity of the Industrial Revolution. Steam engines and "scientific methods" imported in part from the new European production of beet sugar were introduced in the *ingenios* and *centrales* (sugar mills). Railroad lines within plantations enabled enormous extension of the surface areas feeding each factory. During the course of the nineteenth century, the optimal size of factories thus increased tenfold (Tomich, 1991: 307). It was also in Cuba where, in 1837, the first railroad of Latin America was built, to carry sugar production to the Havana port for export. In 1860, more than 1,200 kilometers of railroad were operational. Another sign of modernity, from 1867 an undersea cable linked Cuba to Florida.

At the beginning of the 1870s, labor became the key constraint limiting the continued expansion of sugar production. It was already very difficult to obtain African slave labor. Between 1847 and 1874, 125,000 Chinese indentured workers were recruited to live and work in the same conditions as slaves. The planters faced a complex equation. They of course had to obtain cheap and docile workers and ensure that their expenses to travel to Cuba were covered, but without falling into a system of indentureship which had been decried as disguised slavery. And above all, the "racial balance" was not to be compromised, that is the predominance of Whites. The Saint-Domingue slave revolt was still on everyone's minds and its memory was sharpened in Cuba during the 1868–78 insurrection in which slave and Chinese populations participated.

In his book *Los Brazos Necessarios*, Imilcy Balbao Navarro presents a detailed account of the debates that took place during 1870–80 on the labor shortages induced by the end of the slave trade and the planned abolition of slavery (Navarro, 2000). A new agreement was signed in 1878 between Spain and China for the recruitment of coolies, a project to import labor from the Tonkinese or Philippine colonies, seeking out "free" labor in Liberia (a US colony), recruitment of Indians from Central America, creation of the *Junta Protectora de Immigracion* (1882)—these schemes show how Cuban elites continuously vacillated between employing servile labor and employing a colonial workforce, if possible from Spanish colonies, who would grow sugarcane in family farms.

The solution that ended up being adopted fell between the two systems. A combination of settlers—190,000 Canarian and Spanish migrants, driven from their land by collapsing agricultural prices, arrived in Cuba between 1886 and 1895—and seasonal Jamaican and Haitian workers, recruited for harvests through subsidized immigration societies.

São Tomé, a small island off the coast of Gabon, for its part, never attained a monopolistic position in the cocoa market. Its global market share peaked at 18 percent

---

[6] There was significant Indian and Chinese sugar production, part of which was traded on the markets, during the nineteenth century, which is not accounted for in this figure.

in 1905, which, however, is a considerable feat given the small size of the island. The São Tomé case, however, has the sad distinction of holding the record for longevity of its slave plantations system. The first slave plantations emerged in São Tomé a few years after 1500, and persisted on the island practically unchanged until the early years of the twentieth century. Being located so close to the African continent, São Tomé escaped control of the English marine and thus had access to a continuous supply of slaves.

Auguste Chevalier's 1908 description of the conditions of São Tomé's workforce (*services*) is instructive:

> Native traffickers, who are sort of caravan chiefs, bring long lines of natives from the most remote districts of Angola, apparently even from Kassai and Katanga situated in independent Congo, who have been recruited only God knows how [...]. The caravans normally arrive on the Angolan coast loaded with rubber. Once [the rubber is] sold, the chief proposes to some of the intermediaries to leave a number of the men and women with them in return for remuneration, as for lack of loads of merchandise to carry to the interior, they are no longer useful to him. A contract is drawn up in the presence of an officer of the colonial administration under whose terms the *serviçae* (or more precisely the chief who brought them) rents their services for a duration of five years to the intermediary who acts as the representative of the planter in San-Thomé. The renter hands over the agreed sum to the caravan chief [...] The natives thus engaged are loaded by the administration on a ferry boat of the *Empreza nacionale* that goes to San-Thomé.
>
> (Chevalier, 1908)

Given the living conditions in São Tomé, a five-year contract practically covered the life expectancy of the *serviçaes*. Their annual mortality rate on the São Tomé island stood at 10 percent at the beginning of the century. The colony was obliged to "import" 5,000 to 6,000 workers each year just to keep the workforce level. On Principé island, things were even worse, with an annual mortality rate of 21 percent. In 1900, for a population of 3,607 *serviçaes*, there were 586 new arrivals but 867 deaths!

Pressure from English cocoa buyers,[7] notably from the big chocolate firms, of which the three leading ones—Cadbury, Fry, and Rowntree—had the specificity of being owned by Quakers, ended up inciting change in the labor mobilization system (Satre, 2005; Duffy, 1967).

The planters, keen to show their good will, softened work conditions a bit and established some social services on the *roças*, including spectacular hospitals (see Mantero, 1910 for a plea on behalf of planters). In the years that followed, wage workers from Cape Verde gradually came to represent the majority in the workforce. In any case, São Tomé soon came to be marginalized on the cocoa market, as production became principally an affair of small family farms with the extremely rapid rise of "native production" of cocoa in Ghana. By 1928, São Tomé only accounted for 3 percent of global cocoa exports (Daviron, 2002: 166).

---

[7] Almost half the supply of chocolate factories came from São Tomé.

Abolition of serfdom in Eastern Europe

A vestige of the feudal period, serfdom was a component of the tripartite order in societies with the estate system, that is, formal hierarchies that divided the population into social groups holding different legal statuses. Within these societies, serfs were peasants (they had land that they could use) tied to an estate and to a lord. Serfs had to submit to the lord's judicial and penal authority, fulfill obligatory work duties for the lord, pay various types of taxes to the lord, undertake infrastructure works, and even serve as soldiers.

The status of serfs in Europe deteriorated quite clearly as one moved from west to east of the continent, with the Elbe representing a demarcation line (Blum, 1978). In Western Europe, despite some obligations remaining in place until the eighteenth century (in France until the Revolution), most constraints linked to serfdom had gradually disappeared, and labor obligations were often replaced by taxes, in-kind or in cash (in France it was the cens). East of the Elbe, by contrast, serfdom persisted until the mid-nineteenth century, locally reinvigorated in the seventeenth century by long-distance trade opportunities. Russia constituted its own world of serfdom with its own rules and customs. There a serf could be legally bought, sold, exchanged, or given away by their owner, even when the land was not being sold. A lord could also rent his serfs to an industrialist. Peter the First at the beginning of the eighteenth century created a status of "state peasant." These serfs, former free peasants descended from communities that had migrated to the empire's frontiers in Siberia, and from non-Slavic communities from the Volga basin, were thus considered property of the state and not of a lord (Blum, 1978: 43). Living on land belonging to the state and controlled by bureaucrats, these serfs enjoyed a certain amount of autonomy and did not have labor obligations, but they lived under the permanent threat of "their" lands being conceded to a lord. They could also be administratively posted to work in factories or mines belonging to the state. In 1858, state serfs outnumbered "private" serfs: 27.4 million compared to 22.8 million.

In the century preceding the emancipations, conditions of serfdom worsened. Stronger constraints were placed on mobility. New peasant populations were subjected to serfdom. At the end of the eighteenth century, the word "slave" (*Leibigenschaft*) came to replace the expression "hereditary subjection" (*Erbuntertänigkeit*) in the German-speaking regions (ibid.: 39), while the number of days of obligatory labor due was increased by a factor of 1.5 or 2.[8] For Jerome Blum, this hardening in the exploitative mobilization of peasant labor was a reaction of the nobility to interventions by the central powers (absolute monarchs), kings, or emperors, who sought to affirm their control over territories by eroding the power of lords (ibid.: 138).

---

[8] In northeastern Germany, 156 days per year were due (compared to 14 days in the southwest), and almost 300 days were due near Hanover. In Poland, a serf household with a full allotment of land, had to provide two workers and a draft animal four to six days per week; in Prussia, two men and four horses, six days per week; in Russia the obligation could be as high as six to seven days during harvest period.

The wave of emancipation started truly with the French Revolution and ended in 1864 in the Danube principalities, after having swept through Prussia in 1807 (following the defeat at Jena), Austria in 1848, and Russia in 1861. Reforms coincided with the arrival of new monarchs in power (in Denmark, Bavaria, and Russia). But they were also the result of a context that was favorable to the peasantry: a fear of a repeat of the French Revolution, the destabilization caused by Napoleon's occupations, independence movements seeking wide support (Poland, Hungary, and Romania), and peasant rebellions (Russia during the second quarter of the nineteenth century).

Emancipation processes differed across countries, but were all very gradual. In Russia, well before the 1861 reform which officially abolished serfdom, half of the peasants living on private estates already held a status other than peasant, "state peasant," or "urban peasant." Among these, only half had labor service obligations (Engerman, 1996). Gradual and lengthy: in Prussia, the 1850 decree, which finalized the emancipation of serfs, came after thirty-three laws adopted between 1807 and 1849—that is, a little more than a law each year. The Russian bill of February 19, 1861 was 466 pages long. The reforms focused on two main issues: the elimination of labor obligations and restrictions on freedom, and the question of land tenure.

Freeing serfs from their obligations first involved allowing them freedom of movement (domestic passports) and allowing them to exercise professions previously prohibited, for example in Denmark, trade and cattle-fattening. Land tenure issues were addressed in different ways in various countries. As a general rule, the nobility was always obliged, whether with or without financial compensation, to allocate to former serfs at least a part of the lands that the serfs had farmed for them before emancipation. The former serfs sometimes had to rent their land (a lease of fifty years in Denmark) or had to give a part of their land to the nobility (a third in Prussia, a fifth in the black lands of Russia). Russia and Prussia had the least generous terms of emancipation. In Russia, land ownership was attributed to the peasant community which was supposed to redistribute it periodically or to divide it out definitively. State peasants became tenants on the lands that they were farming in 1866, and later a new law in 1886 made them owners in exchange for payment to the state over forty-five years.

Eastern European countries and Russia thus saw the emergence of a new population of free peasants, working for themselves or to pay taxes (and for the rent-to-own acquisition of their land). Alongside the peasantry, large farm holdings of lords persisted with a wage workforce.

The wage-labor plantation: Success in Asia, failure in Africa

The last quarter of the nineteenth century saw a marked rise in Southern and Southeast Asia of a plantation economy where land ownership was held by Europeans who employed wage labor. The rise in the output of these plantations was spectacular. New products stimulated this growth: tea, rubber, and later, oil palms. Indonesia initiated the movement after the Dutch colony was opened to foreign capital. Sugar prospered in Java, while Sumatra, particularly the region of Deli, was subjected to intense land clearing to prepare for all types of plantation crops. The Malaysian peninsula and—much more modestly—Ceylon hosted prospering rubber plantations after the First World War. Lastly, tea plantations remained the quasi-monopoly of India and Ceylon.

Proximity to large reservoirs of poor people, in India, China, and Java, was the first factor that contributed to the Asian dynamic. Colonial policies also intervened actively to ensure a supply of cheap and disciplined wage workers to plantations: laws were passed criminalizing breach of contract by coolies (Asian wage farmworkers) in southwest India in 1865, and in Sumatra in 1880.

Europeans colonized Africa at the very end of the nineteenth century, with the ambition of creating wage-labor plantations based on the existing model in Asia. However, on the eve of the First World War, after thirty years of unfruitful attempts, and frequent recourse to coercion to mobilize natives to work on the plantations, results remained thin on the ground. The output of European plantations in 1913 represented less than 17 percent of the value of agricultural and forestry exports from European colonies in Africa. Cocoa from São Tomé alone contributed 11 of the 17 percent. Besides that, cocoa from Cameroon and sisal from German East Africa were the only products to exceed the 1 percent level (Daviron, 2010). Products already exported under the legitimate trade[9] before colonization (Nigerian oil palm, Gambian and Senegalese peanuts) still represented more than half the value of exports (around 52 percent). Lastly, the value of cocoa exports from Ghana, a very recent crop there but grown exclusively on African farms, equaled the entire range of exports from European plantations. The productivity of European plantations in colonial Africa was thus very low. Moreover, the plantation system was shaken by various scandals (slave-grown cocoa in São Tomé, "red rubber" from the independent state of Congo, etc.) which led to condemnation of the systematic use of force in labor recruitment.

Hugh Tinker compares the performance of plantations in Africa in 1913 against those of plantations in Asia, where production soared, thanks in part to the abundant supply of coolies from India and China. That year, exports to England represented 105 million francs for tea from Ceylon, almost 200 million for tea from India, and 280 million francs for natural rubber from Malaysia and Ceylon. All African plantations combined, those of São Tomé included, totaled only 65 million francs of exports (Tinker, 1993)!

Forced labor, two historical scandals

Various forms of forced labor were used as an alternative to slavery. Forced labor involved coercing "free" individuals to work for the colonizers (whether private firms or the administration), but without ownership of human beings. Special legislation made forced labor possible, based on racial categorizations. In effect, the history of humanity is "infested" with myriad examples of forced labor. It was a regular practice in colonial France in the interwar period. However, two

---

[9] The expression "legitimate trade" is used by historians to designate trade in agricultural and forest products that was put in place by African elites from 1808, to compensate the loss of income resulting from the prohibition of the slave trade (Law, 1995).

emblematic cases scandalized public opinion and contributed to changing the "native policies" of European colonial powers.

The publication of the novel *Max Havelaar* in 1860 (Multatuli, 1860) that recounted the forced labor farming system (*cultuurstelsel*) set up in Java by the governor-general of the island, J. van den Bosch, in 1830 and that remained in place until 1870, elicited a wave of emotion. The slave system in Java had been replaced by a forced labor system through an obligation to pay taxes in the form of tropical products or to work on plantations which were initially owned by the Dutch treasury, and later privatized (Fasseur, 1991).

This scandal set the stage for the "red rubber" scandal thirty years later. A lucrative forced labor system had also been implemented in Congo, benefiting the Belgian king, Leopold II: its purpose was to harvest wild rubber in the "Independent State of Congo," his personal property (Hochschild, 1998). "Natives" were extorted through taxes that had to be paid in the form of rubber and labor with penalties for non-payment including mutilation, death, destruction of villages, or execution of family hostages.* A low estimate of deaths caused stands at 6 million between 1885 and 1908. A long campaign against this genocidal policy was spurred in Europe and the United States, and this resulted in the "independent state of Congo" being transformed in 1908 into a colony of the Belgian state.

* In the Times of November 18, 1895, the American missionary Murphy wrote: "The rubber question is accountable for most of the horrors perpetrated in the Congo. It has reduced the people to a state of utter despair. Each town in the district is forced to bring a certain quantity to the headquarters of the Commissary every Sunday. It is collected by force; the soldiers drive the people into the bush, if they will not go they are shot down, their left hands being cut off and taken as trophies to the Commissary" (Doyle, 1909: 56).

Victory of market-oriented family farming

Between the late nineteenth century and 1914, family farms replaced plantations in the market for tropical products. In the space of a few decades, agricultural production for long-distance trade came to be supplied mainly from market-oriented family farms, and this held for both independent nations, as for the majority of colonies. Small Ghanaian cocoa farmers overtook the large *roças* of São Tomé. The output of Malay peasants cultivating jungle rubber exceeded that of European rubber plantations (Byerlee, 2014). The expansion of peasant coffee farmers in Colombia led to a crisis of the Brazilian *fazenda* (Daviron, 2002). It was a radical shift. In its "pure" form, the plantation tended to deny the existence of the family: "family life" on plantations was limited to nights, meals were prepared and taken in a collective kitchen, and children were tended in nurseries.

Market-oriented family farming also became the dominant model in continental Europe during the same period. Peasant agriculture, with its origins in the Middle Ages, could have disappeared during the modernization process of European societies. Indeed, in eighteenth-century England, where like in the rest of Western Europe peasant agriculture had dominated, a capitalist form of agriculture emerged whose output essentially targeted rapidly expanding urban markets. But contrary to forecasts (Kautsky, 1900), this model did not conquer the rest of Europe, and the existing peasantry, through significant transformations, particularly the privatization of the commons, was able to respond to market demand. Finally, in the United States (Part 4) where there had been no tradition of peasant agriculture to block the creation of capitalist farm enterprises, family farming prospered and its output was sold on distant markets (Friedmann, 1978).

Between 1850 and 1914, with the exception of the Southeast Asian plantations, agrarian capitalism failed to dominate the markets (Koning, 1994). In effect, the family farm presents an incontestable advantage over the wage-based enterprise with regard to the problem of labor surveillance, which is a particularly thorny issue for agriculture. Family farming proposes effective means of control, gratification, and sanction (including physical coercion), thus making labor surveillance much easier and much cheaper.

The superior performance of peasant forms of agriculture, based on their effectiveness compared to large wage-based units, nonetheless, supposes the existence of open competition in accessing agricultural product consumers. This is what occurred in the nineteenth century: the creation of product standards and futures markets brought smallholders closer to the market, making it possible to undertake market transactions in remote countryside regions, even for products targeting distant markets (Daviron, 2002; Daviron and Ponte, 2005: 2–11). Capitalist agriculture, which had deep pockets and could take on the cost of credit and of risk, lost its position as exclusive supplier of distant markets.

Last but not least, the relative competitiveness of the family farm also resulted from public intervention to promote or to protect such entities motivated by purely political reasons. This was the case in France, where elites threatened by the urban working classes during the Commune sought out allies in the peasantry, by protecting it from international competition (Gervais et al., 1978). It was also the case in the United States, where family farming was encouraged because it was considered better suited for achieving rapid colonization of the Great Plains in a context of potential competition from Canada (Friedmann, 1978).

12

And capital? Key for transport, negligible for agricultural production

"The late nineteenth century saw international capital flows larger in scale than anything seen before or since," write O'Rourke and Williamson in 1999[1] (O'Rourke and Williamson, 1999: 207). The United Kingdom played a central role in this. Already, at the time, the City, in London, was where the majority of financial transactions were undertaken. The gold standard, which fixed exchange rates, made international investments secure. England was above all the main source of foreign investment flows. These represented the equivalent of 35 percent of national savings at the end of the 1860s and early 1870s, 47 percent at the end of the 1880s, and 53 percent in the years running up to the First World War (O'Rourke and Williamson, 1999: 208)—the equivalent then of 10 percent of the country's GNP.

Most of these investments were in the form of loans to governments or acquisition of shares, and especially bonds[2] sold in the City's financial market. In 1913, bonds and shares represented 79 percent of English capital invested in Latin America, and 85 percent of capital invested in Australia and the United States.

But, the financial markets, in the nineteenth century as today, were not a calm sea. Crises, panics, bankruptcies, and other herd phenomena were regular occurrences during the period, without, however, deflecting the overall trend of rising volumes, which greatly accelerated just before the First World War.[3] From an annual average of £21 million during the 1900–4 period, external investment flows grew to 110 million per year between 1905 and 1909, and to 185 between 1910 and 1913 (Feis, 1930: 11).

The share of national income that was generated by these external investments rose from 4 percent in 1880 to 7 percent in 1903, and to 10 percent in 1913. The English

---

[1] And yet they were writing during a period of intense globalization and financialization. As we will see, using these terms in reference to the nineteenth century is not an exaggeration. However, I am not interested here in knowing whether the fluctuations of the last twenty years have beaten this record.
[2] A loan to a public or private entity without holding shares in its capital.
[3] The amounts invested fluctuated greatly: there was a strong contraction during the second half of the 1870s, followed by a renewed rise during the 1880s, and then a decline from 1890 to 1905 (for several diverse reasons: the 1893 panic that ensued after half of US rail companies went bankrupt, the Argentinian government's default, disappointing output of South African mines, the Boer War, etc.).

economy, during this phase and in accordance with Giovanni Arrighi's (1994) theory on the financialization of hegemons in decline, then took a very particular position within the global economy, ever more distant from its earlier role as the workshop of the world. Exports of goods produced in the United Kingdom (£487 million in 1912) amounted to less than half of foreign exchange earnings (£1,004 million). A significant share of export revenues still came from re-exports, but especially from "invisible exports"—that is, income from foreign investments (£185 million), income from the fleet (£100 million), and income from diverse financial services (insurance, credit, brokerage) and commercial services the United Kingdom provided to other countries (£55 million) (Crammond, 1914: 799).

The geography of English foreign investment follows the same trajectory as that of its biomass imports. Until the 1870s, investments focused on continental Europe. They were mainly targeted at government finance, initially in Spain, Portugal, and Greece ("precocious and disappointing" investments according to Herbert Feis (1930)), and later Germany, Austria, Scandinavian countries, Russia, and even Turkey. But it was also the period of the first investments in railroad construction: in France for example, the first rail line, Paris–Rouen, was built in 1843, partially with English capital.

In the decades that followed, the development of French and German finance and industry "expelled" English capital from the European market. Investments from the United Kingdom then turned towards India, a few African regions, and above all towards the neo-European countries, then later after 1905 towards Japan, Russia, and China.

I will rely on two sources to gain a picture of the geographic distribution of invested capital: Herbert Feis (1930), and Lance Davis and Robert Huttenback (1985). Feis' data (Table 12.1) gives an overview of the assets held abroad by English citizens in 1913, while Davis and Huttenback's data shows cumulative investment over the period 1865–1914 (Table 12.2). The difference between the two is explained mainly by reinvestments made locally or asset liquidation.

Feis' data shows that neo-European countries, both dominions and independent states, attracted 63 percent of English investments. The United States received the lion's share (20 percent), followed by Canada (14 percent), the Australia–New Zealand pair (11 percent), South Africa (10 percent), and Argentina (8 percent).[4] Aside from the aforementioned dominions (accounting for 35 percent of investments), the other investments flowing towards the empire went almost entirely to India (10 percent); all the other colonies combined made up just 1 percent of investments. In total, the Empire received 46 percent of investments. This figure is significantly higher than Davis and Huttenback's 39 percent; the discrepancy can be explained by the fact that most investment in the empire occurred later, encouraged from 1900 by the Colonial Stocks Act.

---

[4] In Argentina, English capital played an even more significant role than in the dominions: in 1913, 48 percent of capital present in Argentina was held by foreigners. Foreign investment represented 70 percent of Argentina's gross capital formation between 1870 and 1910 (Taylor, 1992).

Table 12.1 Main destination countries and sectors of United Kingdom foreign investments in 1913 (in % of total)

Destination countries (in % of total)		Sectors (in % of total)	
Total empire, of which:	47.3	**Total loans to governments, of which:**	25.8
Canada	13.7	Empire	17.9
Australia and New Zealand	11.1	Others	7.9
South Africa	9.8	**Total railroad, of which:**	**40.7**
India	10.1	Empire	11.8
Other colonies	1	United States	16.4
Total outside empire, of which	**52.7**	**Mines**	7.2
United States	20.1	**Industrial and commercial firms**	4.1
Argentina	8.5	**Rubber plantations**	1.1
Brazil	3.9	**Tea and coffee plantations**	0.6
Other Latin American countries	7.7	**Others**	16.6
Russia	2.9		
Other European countries	2.9		
Egypt	1.2		
China	1.2		
Japan	1.7		
Rest of world	4.2		

Source: adapted from Feis, 1930: 23 and 27.

Feis' data also shows that the biggest share of English capital was held in railroads (41 percent). National and municipal governments received 30 percent of investments in the form of loans, which were also used to finance transport infrastructure (roads, ports, railroads) and urban facilities, but their share of investments fell over time. Finally, in third position was mining (7 percent).

Agricultural finance, and more widely the financing of biomass production only held a marginal position in English foreign investments. In 1913 they were only significant in the plantation sectors of rubber (Malaysia), tea (India and Ceylon), and coffee (Kenya), totaling 1.7 percent of investments. Investments in large US ranches (in Texas, Arkansas, and Dakota) were liquidated even before the First World War. It is to be noted that investments in commodities (mining and agriculture) were relatively more significant in the colonies (excepting India and the dominions), compared to investments in local government and transport infrastructure, which were poorly financed, following a logic of production enclaves controlled directly by investors.

Table 12.2 Geographic and sectoral destination of United Kingdom's foreign investments, 1865–1914

		Total	"Foreign"	Dominions	India	Other colonies
Total	Millions of £	3,163	1,938	872	239	114
	%	100	100	100	100	100
Government	Millions of £	1,318	656	502	130	30
	%	42	34	58	54	26
Transport	Millions of £	1,199	904	203	77	15
	%	38	47	23	32	13
Agriculture and mining	Millions of £	227	123	60	13	31
	%	6	6	7	5	27

Source: adapted from Davis and Huttenback, 1985.

All things considered, English capital investment in agricultural production overseas, of which the plantation constituted the archetype, while it has impressed the imagination and literature (as well as tropical agricultural research institutes), was much more of an exception rather than the rule. The spectacular development in production capacities which enabled the response to European demand was self-financed. This phenomenon is to be connected with the victory of market-oriented family farms over large agricultural production units, which was accompanied by a shift towards techniques that were significantly less capital-intensive. The trajectory of tropical product production is an eloquent demonstration of this (Huff, 2007).

The contrast between cocoa growing in São Tomé and that in Ghana, which eliminated the former from the market, is edifying. Cocoa cultivation in São Tomé was clearly conceived as a heavy industry similar to European mining or steel industries—huge buildings, rail tracks, irrigation systems, impressive facilities for fermentation and drying, and living quarters for workers, which made the countryside resemble *coron* mining villages.[5] Here the logic was taken to its extreme. In sharp contrast, Ghanaian cocoa production, when it conquered the market had as its only equipment a machete, a wooden crate, banana leaves for fermentation, and a mat for drying.[6]

The shift from large plantation to smallholder farming thus resulted in a dramatic decapitalization of tropical agricultural production. Smallholder tropical production in coffee, in cocoa, and in rubber was undertaken without capital except for the tree plant. Furthermore, launching production did not require access to credit, despite the fact that, because the crops were tree-based, there was a waiting period before the first

---

[5] Groups of identical houses built for miners in northern France and southern Belgium.
[6] European rubber plantations, in Malaysia, Indonesia or Vietnam, and the jungle rubber of smallholders, which overtook the former in 1930, present the same type of contrast.

harvest of the cultivated plants was possible. In effect, smallholders regularly planted food crops alongside their young cash crops. As Hla Myint points out, the crops earmarked for long-distance trade were able to be produced easily and rapidly by smallholder farmers because no radical change in methods of subsistence agriculture was required (Myint, 1966: 36).

> Except for land, smallholder production required very few durable capital goods. Circulating capital, or "subsistence funds", composed essentially of food items and consumer goods necessary for the upkeep of the farmers until harvest, constituted the main capital needs [...] When its expansion commenced, smallholder production for export was self-financed.
>
> (ibid.: 34)

The shift from the plantation to the smallholder farm also resulted in a process of vertical disintegration. Certain processing operations carried out prior to exporting (cotton ginning, hulling of coffee cherries) were now undertaken outside of the farm unit. This gave rise to local markets for "intermediate" products—such as cotton seeds, parchment coffee, rubber cup lumps or slabs—which were sold by smallholder producers. For the rubber sector, large-scale businesses emerged. These bought the rubber, processed it, and transported it to the export port, packaging it in suitable forms for international trade. These businesses had access to foreign capital.

If, to low capital requirements, we add an abundance of land and frequent episodes of chronic "under-employment," that is a lifestyle in which a significant part of one's existence was dedicated to many other activities than agriculture; thus, it is easy to understand how agricultural production in many countries or colonies, in West Africa, Southeast Asia, and Central America, experienced a spike in output when traders entered the scene, as buyers of their production but also, and above all, as sellers of new objects of desire (Drake, 1972: 956). We also understand that the growth in production for export was able to occur without threatening the food security of these communities, contrary to the predictions of proponents of the theory of colonial opposition between "cash crops" and "food crops."

François Ruf supplements this interpretation by adding the concepts of forest rent and tree capital to explain the spatial dynamics of cocoa production on the global level (Ruf, 1995) and the sequence in leading cocoa-producing countries since the nineteenth century. He posits that tropical forest situated on a frontier offers a double rent: an absolute rent linked to its null price, and a differential rent generated by the ecosystem services provided by the forest,[7] which are no longer generated where cocoa farming has been introduced a long time ago. Smallholder farmers differ from "industrial plantations" in their greater know-how of how to benefit from the differential rent.

---

[7] For François Ruf, the forest provides eight ecosystem services which benefit new smallholder cocoa farms: pest control, soil fertility, erosion protection, water retention both in the soil and in plants, protection against disease and parasites, wind protection, provision of food and other forest nutriments, and rainfall regulation (Ruf, 1995: 7).

Conclusion

There remains not a single rock without a flag; not a single empty spot on maps; not a single region outside trade duties and outside laws; not a single tribe whose affairs are not in some administrative file and do not depend, through the curse of writing, on various distant humanists sat in their offices.
(Paul Valéry, *Regards sur le monde actuel* [Views on the Current World], 1931)

Nineteenth-century Great Britain organized a transfer of biomass drawn from the entire globe to its benefit. It replicated the logic of the United Provinces on a larger scale. The revolution that the combination of coal and steam engine represented in terms of availability of mechanical energy permitted Britain to reshape the whole planet to its whim. Under its hegemony, the world was divided into countries producing biomass, and industrialized countries processing this biomass, and in some cases then re-exporting it in the form of manufactured goods. The dramatic increase in energy availability boosted the capacity for transforming biomass into manufactured goods, which enabled Britain to become the workshop of the world, and also made it possible to overcome the constraints of transport associated with a solar metabolic regime. Thus, this first phase of the mining metabolic regime for the hegemon and its imitators (Western Europe) was associated with a dramatic increase in demand for biomass imports, and for those tasked with supplying biomass, with a period of vigorous growth and prosperity (at least for the elites) founded on the exploitation of biological resources that had accumulated over centuries of low population density existence.

This upscaling had drastic consequences for innumerable communities across the globe as now the biomass necessary for supplying the hegemon was extracted from inland, within the hearts of continents. From 1913, there was hardly a place on earth, except perhaps in Africa and in some islands of Southeast Asia, that was not likely to be called on to supply Europe.

Europe's colonial conquests, which peaked during this period, contributed little to the biomass supply chain, which was essentially catered to by sovereign nations (or quasi-sovereign in the case of the dominions) of the Americas, Oceania (Australia and New Zealand), and even Europe (Russia, Denmark, and the Netherlands).

The groundwork for the shift towards specialization and organizational differentiation, which in the twentieth century would appear so natural, was laid in this period. The first factor concerned the use of violence. With the disappearance of the "Companies" and slave plantations, use of violence was, at least by law, forbidden for private enterprises, and reserved only for state institutions.[1]

Similarly, cultivation, collection, processing, transport, trading, and retail became activities handled by distinct economic units (family farms, local traders and processors, international dealers, shipping companies, etc.). In short, global biomass value chains went through a process of vertical disintegration. The English hegemony amplified the logic that prevailed under the Dutch hegemony by even greater recourse to the market, which now governed the mobilization of resources and of labor.

The free movement of capital, goods, and people was also a distinguishing feature of the period. Colonial exclusivity rules faded away in the early nineteenth century. European capital, chiefly English and French capital, now found investment opportunities on all continents, in particular in railroads, including in countries outside of their empires. The trend was clearly that of creating a truly global biomass market, with local prices fluctuating in unison. Lastly, this period was also characterized by mass migration, not just of Europeans but also of Asians, towards two main, and contrasting, poles: rapidly expanding industrialized towns, and frontiers.

From the last quarter of the nineteenth century, two countries who *a priori* were destined to occupy opposing positions in the division of labor promoted by the English hegemon, deviated from the trajectory expected of them. These were Germany and the United States. The former, although experiencing a veritable population boom and accelerated industrialization, limited its biomass imports by combining remarkable agricultural growth with a strategy of substituting non-food biomass with chemical products. The latter, all while remaining a key supplier of biomass to the United Kingdom and Europe, industrialized and gradually became a continent-country capable of producing everything it consumed and consuming everything it produced.

These two countries would soon emerge as potential candidates to succeed the United Kingdom as the global hegemon. Their inevitable rivalry, which is the subject of the next part, would lead to a profound recomposition of sources and uses of biomass.

---

[1] In accordance with Max Weber's definition of the state as the holder of the monopoly of the legitimate use of physical force within a given territory (Weber, 1963 [1919]: 22).

Part 4

Where the rivalry between Germany, the United States, and others gives a key role to the chemical industry, 1865–1945

Introduction

What an extraordinary episode in the economic progress of man that age was which came to an end in August 1914! The greater part of the population, it is true, worked hard and lived at a low standard of comfort, yet were, to all appearances, reasonably contented with this lot. But escape was possible, for any man of capacity or character at all exceeding the average, into the middle and upper classes, for whom life offered, at a low cost and with the least trouble, conveniences, comforts, and amenities beyond the compass of the richest and most powerful monarchs of other ages. The inhabitant of London could order by telephone, sipping his morning tea in bed, the various products of the whole earth, in such quantity as he might see fit, and reasonably expect their early delivery upon his doorstep [...] He could secure forthwith, if he wished it, cheap and comfortable means of transit to any country or climate without passport or other formality, [...] and could then proceed abroad to foreign quarters, without knowledge of their religion, language, or customs [...]. But, most important of all, he regarded this state of affairs as normal, certain, and permanent [...] The projects and politics of militarism and imperialism, of racial and cultural rivalries, of monopolies, restrictions, and exclusion, which were to play the serpent to this paradise, were little more than the amusements of his daily newspaper, and appeared to exercise almost no influence at all on the ordinary course of social and economic life, the internationalisation of which was nearly complete in practice.

(Keynes, 1920: 11)

The First World War signaled the end of the English hegemony, and for Europe the end of the "hundred-year peace" (Polanyi, 1983 [1944]). Twenty years of international political and economic instability ensued, followed by a new world war. In all, thirty years of conflict, which led some authors to call the 1913–45 period the second Thirty Year War, in reference to the war that had ravaged Europe from 1618 to 1648.

The spread of the Industrial Revolution in continental Europe and in the neo-European countries eroded the United Kingdom's hegemonic standing from the late nineteenth century on. Two countries quickly emerged as main contenders: Germany and the United States. Two countries whose rise to power was fed by their political, economic, and territorial construction. Germany was the product of the 1871 union of a large number of autonomous political entities with differing statuses, to which were added the regions of Alsace and Lorraine. The United States for their part unified only in 1865 at the end of the War of Secession, and did not finish the colonization of their full territory until 1897.

The waning of the English hegemon was manifested in the modest—although still real—growth of its economic indicators, but above all by the gap that grew between its indicators and those of its competitors. To take just one example: annual English energy consumption grew from 89 to 142 gigajoules per capita between 1870 and 1913 (+59 percent), while in the United States it grew from 70 to 199 (+184 percent) and in Germany from 18 to 97 (+438 percent) in the same period!

We saw previously how, in the nineteenth century, England's hegemony was accompanied by a structural and severe biomass deficit, compensated by a considerable surplus of manufactured goods (of which some of the key ones, such as textiles, were produced from imported biomass) and of coal. But hegemony does not necessarily mean that countries adopt the same strategy. Alexander Gerschenkron showed how the transformation of the international context engendered through the emergence of the leader makes it impossible for others to replicate their trajectory

Table I4.1 United Kingdom, Germany, United States: Population, GNP/capita, energy consumption/capita (gigajoules), share of coal in energy consumption, coal and steel production (millions of tons), 1870–1913

1870	United Kingdom	Germany	United States
Population	31 million	39 million	40 million
GNP/capita	$3,191	$1,821	$2,445
Energy consumption/capita	89 GJ	18 GJ	70 GJ
Share of coal	92%	28%	16%
Coal production	160	74	103
Steel production	2.4	0.9	2.6
1913			
Population	45 million	65 million	98 million
GNP/capita	$4,921	$3,648	$5,301
Energy consumption/capita	142 GJ	97 GJ	199 GJ
Share of coal	95%	89%	50%
Coal production	276	234	234
Steel production	6.1	13.7	13.7

Sources: Maddison, 2001 (population and GNP/capita); Kander et al., 2014 (energy consumption/capita and share of coal in the United Kingdom and Germany); Gierlinger and Krausmann, 2012 (energy consumption/capita and share of coal in the United States); Crammond, 1914: 783 (coal and steel production).

(Gerschenkron, 1962). In the case of the English hegemon, replication was even less probable, given that the hegemony was based on an international division of labor, and its stability came from the specialization of partner countries in complementary activities, especially for biomass production and export.

In the mid-nineteenth century, Germany (or rather Prussia, as Germany did not yet exist) and the United States both supplied biomass to the United Kingdom, mainly fibers (wool for the former, cotton for the latter) and cereals. Both these countries however, experienced sustained growth of their manufacturing sectors during the second half of that century, and played a pioneering role in what is commonly called the second industrial revolution (electricity, internal combustion engine, and chemistry). But neither of the two followed the United Kingdom's trajectory. They also experienced very rapid growth in fossil fuel consumption and production (coal and later oil for the United States), and like the United Kingdom were net exporters of fossil fuels.

While Germany had a deficit in biomass, it limited this deficit considerably by adopting an import substitution strategy. The strategy had two main components:

- Reduce the use of non-food biomass by replacing them with synthetic products derived from coal. This gave birth to the powerful German chemical industry. The leitmotif was, replace all forms of biomass with coal!
- Increase food biomass output thanks to a rise in use of mineral fertilizer through the development of beetroot and potato farming.

Both components involved intensifying exploitation of the domestic territory and more specifically its underground—both shallow and deep. Intensification was presented as the only option, given Germany's lack of colonies (even though colonies played only a minor role in Britain's biomass supply chain) or neo-German overseas countries. This strategy was strongly supported by diverse stakeholders, ranging from Junkers to the big chemical industry firms. It was also supported by a protectionist policy which was a part of the power strategy of this new country playing catchup. The course of the strategy would run into two world wars, which resulted in even stronger intensification of the utilization of the national territory, as well as increased planning.

The quest for new territories that could supply biomass was one of the goals pursued during the Second World War. For the Nazis, the First World War had shown that the sole resources of the German territory, even when exploited as efficiently as possible— the case particularly for coal—could not suffice. It also provided a warning of the great vulnerability of relying on supplies from abroad. The lesson that was retained was that the United States, a territory of continental dimensions, was without contest the true rival and also the model to be imitated (Tooze, 2006: xxiv). The ambition to conquer, empty, and then colonize regions situated to the east of Germany was the logical conclusion of this line of reasoning. The war against France and the United Kingdom was a necessary condition to realize ambitions for eastward expansion, and not an end in and of itself; that is, territorial conquest of these countries was not the goal. We know that Germany lost the war; however, its strategy of intensified exploitation of the domestic territory, and that of substituting non-food biomass with synthetic products persisted beyond the defeat.

As for the United States, a supplier of biomass to Great Britain and the rest of Europe, at the end of the nineteenth century, the country was the product of a combination of two distinct processes, both of which, however, depended on the advancing frontier for their expansion, and even their sustainability:

- In the South, the late and large-scale expansion of slave plantations, mainly dedicated to cotton farming, was an exact replica of the economic system that had prevailed in the English and French Caribbean colonies in the eighteenth century.
- The legendary movement westwards, a process specific to the nineteenth century, the dramatic rise in neo-European family farming, specialized in food biomass production and was founded on the mass immigration of the latter half of the nineteenth century.

The United States' position as a biomass supplier progressively dwindled at the turn of the twentieth century. Exports declined while imports rose, and from the 1920s, the United States started running a deficit in biomass: the end of the American frontier, competition from new frontiers in "younger" countries (like Argentina and Australia), and strong growth in domestic demand—fueled by rising populations, urbanization, and industrialization—all combined to diminish the competitiveness of US agriculture. During the 1930s, a combination of economic and ecological constraints plunged farmers into a deep crisis.

It was also during the 1930s that a new model of agriculture gradually emerged (using tractors, chemical fertilizers and pesticides, and improved seeds). This was the model of "conventional agriculture" which would provide the foundations for a new phase of agricultural prosperity, but not before the Second World War. A partial copy of rival Germany and its intensification strategy, the model also relied on very active state intervention, both for the design and promotion of new techniques, and for market regulation.

This part of the book includes a chapter that delves into the other smaller contenders to turn the lens on imperial strategy, and specifically the French and Japanese imperial strategies. Addressing these countries and their imperial strategies allows us to clarify the role of imperialism and colonies. Contrary to how these are presented retrospectively, they played a relatively marginal role, including during the Second World War, and the imperial strategy was mainly one of second-tier powers, adopted during their rise or their decline, playing too late a game already played in the eighteenth century.

13

Germany: On a quest for an industrialization not dependent on long-distance biomass trade

From the second half of the nineteenth century, Germany (or rather the entities that would soon form Germany) was incredibly dynamic. It experienced concomitant demographic, agricultural, and industrial revolutions. Between 1870 and 1913, its population grew from 39 to 65 million inhabitants, and at the same time per capita GNP and energy consumption increased by a factor of two and five respectively. Steel production grew fifteenfold, and was by 1913 double the output of the United Kingdom.

In this context of rapid industrialization, Germany's biomass imports grew, especially for non-food biomass. At the same time, there was also rapid intensification in German food production (in calories per hectare) thanks to increased fertilization and the growth of tuber farming.

The construction of the nation-state and Germany's protection policy: Under the stewardship of Junkers

Germany's trade policy was an instrument in its competition with England, just like French and English mercantilism had been against the United Provinces. It was a sign of the process of German state construction. It was also a means of this construction, alongside wars (against Denmark in 1848 and 1864, Austria in 1866, France in 1870, etc.).

The unification of Germany as a nation-state was a gradual process guided by Prussia which orchestrated the union of various principalities and autonomous cities (including Hamburg, with its many ties to England), born from the disintegration of the German Holy Roman Empire, and presided over the separation from Austria. The defeat suffered at the hands of Napoleon's troops can be considered as the starting point of the unification–separation process. The establishment of a customs union[1] in 1834 between various principalities (the *Zollverein*) and the crushing victory of Prussia over Austria (1866) which confirmed Prussian leadership, were two decisive milestones.

---

[1] A customs union is an agreement between several countries to eliminate trade barriers between themselves and adopt the same customs tariffs for third countries. By contrast, in a free trade zone, the customs tariffs applied to third countries are decided by each country.

The German Empire was finally created in 1871, following defeat of the French, whose declaration of war had enabled Prussia to rally the diverse German states politically and militarily (and to capture the mineral resources of Alsace and Lorraine).

Germany east of the Elbe and the Junkers

"These Prussians, in their boastful audacity, coarse pretension, and vulgar self-sufficiency, are the Yankees of Europe, and, if they have a success, will be unendurable" (Charles Lever, 1866 letter, in Downey, 1906).

The history of agriculture and the agricultural policy of "Germany" were influenced greatly by developments in its eastern regions, more specifically the regions east of the Elbe River: Pomerania, Brandenburg, Silesia, and of course Prussia. These regions can be considered as part of the frontier of Eastern Europe. They were conquered in the thirteenth and fifteenth centuries by Teutonic knights and, from the sixteenth century, formed part of the cereal supply chain for Western Europe, producing cereals in large estates using servile labor, under the control of Junkers, the aristocrat owners and managers of these estates.

Serfdom was formally abolished in 1807 after the humiliating Prussian defeat at Jena. Peasants could now own land but had to concede to or buy back from the lords between a half and a third of their farmland to gain ownership. A reform in the 1820s resulted in the redistribution of village commons, of which four-fifths were captured by the Junkers. The "liberation" of peasants thus occurred alongside a notable reduction in farmland available to them due to enclosures. Moreover, Junkers maintained their hereditary judicial authority until the revolutionary crisis of 1848–9, and policing prerogatives until 1870. East of the Elbe, the abolition of serfdom strengthened the landed nobility and their production capacity. In 1907, estates of more than 100 hectares accounted for more 40 percent of farmland in this region, compared to just 8 percent in the other regions of Germany. Junkers also occupied a dominant position in the Prussian bureaucracy and army. Given the weight of Prussia within German government (the title of emperor was reserved for the king of Prussia, and his prime minister held the title of chancellor), Junkers preserved their decisive influence in defining German agricultural policy until the First World War.

Sources: Davis Bowman, 1993; Gerschenkron, 1966.

Customs policy, which was a key part of Germany's nation-building, went through different phases. In the first phase, the policy was directly tied to the interests of the powerful Junkers and to Germany's role as a biomass supplying country under the English hegemony. Unlike the industrialists, the Junkers, alongside traders from towns in the north, remained favorable to free trade as long as they remained the preferred suppliers of cereals and wool to the United Kingdom.[2] The abolition of

---

[2] Adepts of the economic liberalism of physiocrats and Adam Smith, Junkers had long been producers of cereals for long-distance trade and had developed wool sales to England. The size of sheep herds had doubled between 1816 and 1840, when a third of Germany's wool production was exported. At the beginning of the 1840s, Germany was a net exporter of cereals and wool, and was the United Kingdom's leading supplier of these two products.

internal customs barriers in Prussia, in 1818, came along with low external custom duties. This free trade orientation remained in place several decades, including under the *Zollverein*.

In effect, following England, from the mid-nineteenth century, continental European countries adopted free trade policies, starting first with the "small" countries (Netherlands, Denmark, Portugal, Switzerland, Belgium, etc.), followed by the "big" countries like France, which in 1860 signed what was referred to as the Cobden-Chevalier Treaty with the United Kingdom which abolished customs duties on raw materials and the majority of food products between the two countries. This treaty was followed by many others involving a greater number of European countries, making free trade and the most-favored nation clause[3] the norm of European trade policies. The *Zollverein* was a part of this.

But the free trade policies of continental European countries were short-lived (Bairoch, 1993: 39), and their end was prefigured in the response in 1879 to the general crisis of agricultural markets following a dramatic rise in production from frontiers, and a fall in transport costs. In 1892, under minister Jules Méline, France reneged on the Cobden–Chevalier Treaty and re-established customs duties at levels close to those prior to 1860. The collapse of the whole network of agreements guaranteeing freedom of trade between European countries ensued. The United States, for its part, raised customs duties in 1890 with the new McKinley rate. The free trade policy that had been typical under the English hegemony was increasingly challenged during the closing years of the nineteenth century.

Germany followed the trend. In the early 1840s, Germany was still a net exporter of cereals and wool, and for both these products the leading supplier of the United Kingdom.[4] But competition from neo-European countries in the Americas and Oceania inexorably marginalized Germany: the German share of the English cereal market fell from 26 percent to 3 percent between 1856 and 1875, while that of the United States grew from 18 to 60 percent. The Junkers switched sides in 1878 and disavowed their historical alliance with merchants to join forces with industrialists,[5] and with them lobby for policy that protected the domestic market (Kindleberger, 1975: 478). The 1879 adoption of highly protective customs tariffs for cereals, beet sugar, and steel earned Bismarck's Germany the title of "Empire of rye and steel."

Industrialists abandoned the alliance in 1890, and Germany opened up to trade with the Austro-Hungarian Empire and Russia, in 1892 and 1894 respectively (Torp, 2010: 411). The Junkers, however, did not abandon their protectionist crusade, for which they sought out other sources of support, this time among the peasantry. The

---

[3] The most-favored nation clause, common in many trade treaties, specifies that signatory countries commit to according to all any privileges—reduced custom tariff for instance—that they accord to any other party among them.
[4] The abolition of the Corn Laws is sometimes interpreted as an attempt to maintain continental Europe, and above all Prussia, in a role of biomass exporters thus containing the region's industrial development.
[5] Industrialists created their own association for the promotion of protectionism in 1876 called the Central Association of German Industrialists (Centralverband Deutscher Industrieller). The Junkers intervened mainly through their association, the Association for the Reform of Taxes and the Economy (Vereinigung der Steuer-und Wirtschaftsreformer) created in the same year (Torp, 2010: 405).

1893 establishment of the Agrarian League (*Bund der Landwirte*), which included representatives of the peasantry, represented a new configuration as the peasantry was mainly specialized in animal products. In 1902, after years of campaigning, the Agrarian League obtained a new customs tariff favorable to agriculture.[6] It provided animal products equal protection to main farm crops (Webb, 1982: 323).[7]

The giants of organic chemistry and eliminating non-food uses of biomass

Invention of synthetic dyes and the birth of the German chemical industry

Given the importance of dyeing in the value of finished fabrics, access to dye products was essential for the textile industry of any country, as the seventeenth-century United Provinces had made clear. Until the early nineteenth century, dealers in dyes "were heavily dependent on animal and vegetable substances produced in limited localities. Even his 'chemicals' were largely organic, especially his alkaline salts such as potash, and his acids such as sour milk and vinegar" (Fairlie, 1965: 500). The inventiveness of humans in making dyes appears to have been limitless. Some raw materials were produced in specialized farms, such as indigo farms in the Caribbean slave plantations (Siguret, 1968); others were collected through gathering (galls, lichen, various woods or insect secretions such as Indian lacquer) (Llano, 1948; Melillo, 2013).

Like spices, dye products early on became a key item in long-distance trade as the variety and quality of dyeing was an essential factor in the value of a fabric. There was strong competition between local and exotic raw materials in the seventeenth and eighteenth centuries: for the color blue, indigo from the Americas (Guatemala, Saint-Domingue) competed with Languedoc pastel; for the color red, the Mexican cochineal was pitted against Languedoc kermes and European madder: for the color yellow, quercitron from America against dyers reseda, etc. (Nieto-Galan, 2001: 12–22).

At the end of the nineteenth century, the cards were re-dealt. Between 1879 and 1913, the value of natural dye imports into the United Kingdom fell from £6.7 million to £1.2 million, and the share of dyes in biomass imports collapsed from 7 percent to 0.25 percent.[8] The change was correlated with a rise in synthetic dye imports, which in the same period grew from 0 to £3 million, and for which Germany held almost a monopoly as supplier.

In the realm of dyes (and we will see later, also for sugar), Germany was the source of radical change in the origins of biomass supplies for the United Kingdom, all the more radical as it was not based on a new crop, but on the development of synthetic

---

[6] For many historians, the protectionist concessions in favor of farmers were reward for their vote in the Reichstag for the highly interventionist military naval construction strategy and colonial expansion policy of the Kaiser, both very expensive (Macmillan, 2013).

[7] The Junkers were not left out, however: export subsidies for rye and oats were also put in place. Sugar also benefited from such subsidies.

[8] The United Kingdom itself did not have any dye plants or insects, with the exception of reseda (Fairlie, 1965).

coal-derivative products. This transformation of the dye market in the late nineteenth century prefigured the vast movement of substitution of natural products by synthetic products which would be a distinctive feature of the entire twentieth century, and would gradually eliminate almost all non-food uses of biomass.

The development of synthetic dyes also laid the foundations of large firms specialized in organic chemistry and pharmaceuticals, many of which were German, and which today are still implementing substitution strategies. Lastly, the dye sector heralded the advent of "industrialization of invention" to use Meyer-Thurow's (1982) expression for what today is called "research and development" (Pickering, 2005).

Paradoxically, it was black coal that provided the synthetic colors and dyes. Or rather, it was a by-product of coal (of its gasification which revolutionized lighting): tar, which was just as black! Coal tar, rich in numerous aromatic compounds, served as the raw material for the development of a large part of organic chemistry. A whole field of research developed during the nineteenth century around tar, both to determine its composition and to separate its various compounds: naphthalene, anthracene, benzene, toluene, etc. Fractional distillation made it possible to obtain a large number of molecules. From these, a specific industrial field developed, carbon chemistry, which became the source of several biomass substituting products.

The first synthetic colors were obtained from aniline, a molecule initially extracted from indigo by distillation (in 1826), and later from coal tar (in 1835). In 1856, oxidization of aniline gave rise to the first synthetic dye: mauveine, of a purple color. In 1859, fuchsia red or magenta red was developed in France. Aniline was later used as a base to produce a yellow color in Manchester in 1864 (Bensaude-Vincent and Stengers, 2001). In the years that followed, all new colors were created in Germany (Hohenberg, 1967: 28). In 1869, alizarin, the dye principle in madder, was produced synthetically from a coal tar distillate. It was obtained in a Berlin institute working for a firm that had a bright future ahead of it: the Badische Anilin und Soda Fabrick (BASF). This firm gave structure to ongoing experimental work and invested heavily in research for new colors, "programmed synthesis" to use Bensaude-Vincent and Stengers' (2001) expression. Thirty years of research finally resulted in 1897 in a synthetic indigo dye that could be commercialized!

In Germany, synthetic dyes catered for more than half of the market for dyes from 1890. By 1913, this share had reached 86 percent. In other European countries and the United States, synthetic dyes also came to dominate, though slightly later. In 1913, they accounted for three-quarters of dye imports by the United Kingdom, and 90 percent of these were supplied from Germany (Stokes, 1994: 16). That year, total production of the three leading English firms was estimated at 4,000 tons compared to 140,000 tons for the German giants, and a global total of over 160,000 tons (Morris and Travis, 1992: 20). German synthetic dyes, of which 80 percent were exported, also dominated the American market (which was their leading destination) and were sold as far as China, India, and Japan.

The German organic chemistry industry developed thanks to synthetic dyes, and would play a very particular role in the history of the country. At the beginning of the twentieth century, the main firms were BASF, and Bayer and Hoechst (today Sanofi after several mergers), followed by Weiler-Ter-Meer, AGFA (Aktiengesellschaft für

Anilinfabrikation), Cassella, Kalle, and Griesheim Elektron. In 1906, Bayer, BASF, and AGFA united to create a "common interest group," *Interessen Gemeinschaft* in German, that was called the "little IG."

Growth of Germany's chemical industry benefited from particularly advanced scientific and industrial research capacity. Germany amassed several Nobel Prizes in chemistry: Emil Fischer (1902), Adolf von Baeyer (1905), Eduard Büchner (1907), Otto Wallach (1909), Richard Willstätter (1915), and Fritz Haber (1918).

The biggest firms integrated production of upstream products (soda, chlorite, sulfuric acid) and diversified their activity by increasing the range of products synthesized—textile fibers, explosives, pharmaceutical products—and these products transformed material life. There was no more need to go and seek raw materials in some distant country, as the resources from Germany's soil, the first of which coal, provided both energy and matter.[9] The ambition was to produce everything necessary for Germans to house themselves, heat themselves, clothe themselves, and move around, everything that until then had been provided by biomass. The only exception was food.

We will see, however, in the section that follows on fertilizers, that food was not completely left aside. "Substitution was the mantra of German chemistry" Esther Leslie tells us (Leslie, 2005: 10).

Fertilizers and plant nutrients: The revolution in ammonia synthesis

> Great Britain robs other countries of the conditions necessary for their fertility. It has dug the battle fields of Leipzig, Waterloo and Crimea to extract bones [...] Like a vampire, it has latched on to Europe's throat, one could even say onto the world's throat, sucking its best blood, without being compelled by imperious need, and without any lasting utility for the country.
>
> (Liebig, 1862: 150)

Unlike the frontier economies, Europe did not exploit the fertility of its soils with an mining logic, but from the nineteenth century it did mobilize increasing amounts of mineral resources to maintain its soil fertility. Agricultural chemistry emerged in the early nineteenth century. Justus Liebig gave the industry a real boost mid-century. His 1840 book, *Organic Chemistry in its Application to Agriculture and Physiology* (Liebig, 1840), translated into several languages, presented state of the art knowledge on the role played by mineral elements in plant nutrition.

Before 1914, nitrogen in the form of fertilizer was the nutrient of most strategic interest and around which long-distance trade developed, as it had for biomass.

Two natural deposits of nitrates were exploited during the nineteenth century: the Guano islands off the coast of Peru, and sodium nitrate mines in the north of

---

[9] Until 1880, Germany imported coal tar from England, but after that, thanks to the development of coke ovens which made it possible to recuperate tar, the country ran a surplus and the flow of trade was inverted (Hohenberg, 1967: 39).

what would become Chile in 1879. The two deposits existed thanks to highly specific conditions that could not be found in Europe: an absolutely dry climate, and therefore no rain to leach out nitrogen, and in case of Guano, the presence of large banks of anchovies, and birds which ate these, their droppings accumulating "since time immemorial" on the rocks.

The first significant importation of guano started in 1841 towards the United Kingdom (Clark and Foster, 2009: 317), which was to become a hub for guano trade. In 1854, guano accounted for 74 percent of exports from Peru (Hunt, 1973: 38) and brought to Lima two decades of prosperity. But the stock was limited and production fell quickly. At the end of the 1910s, guano only contributed 1.5 percent of nitrogen supplied by fertilizers (Smil, 2001: 43).

Peruvian guano's contribution to European soil fertility had lasted only forty years. Ten years after guano extraction commenced, nitrate mines were launched in southern Peru, in Bolivia, and in northern Chile, the latter country acquiring the entire mining region following the Pacific War (1879). Germany quickly became the primary importer, and sodium nitrate, the primary fertilizer, in terms of value, used in the country, mainly to the benefit of sugar beet farmers (Melillo, 2012: 105).

A third source of nitrogen played an important role (Table 13.1) prior to the First World War both for the United Kingdom and for Germany: ammonium sulfate, a by-product of coal distillation during the fabrication process of town gas or coke used in the steel industry (Smil, 2001: 51). From the 1860s, ovens were equipped with apparatus to "capture" unoxidized ammonia and to "fix" it in the form of ammonium sulfate (Smil, 2001: 50). Production in Germany grew very rapidly in the early twentieth century and exceeded British production in 1911 (Institut International de l'Agriculture, 1914: 27).

In 1908 there was a dramatic development in the nitrogen market when Fritz Haber and Carl Bosh invented a technique for obtaining synthetic ammonia from atmospheric nitrogen in a laboratory at the BASF factory. The famed "Haber–Bosch" procedure required large amounts of energy (both high pressure and high temperatures were needed) (Travis, 2015), but coal provided an abundant supply. The first factory opened its doors in September 1913, a few months before the First World War broke out. Ammonia production in Germany grew from 800 tons (in nitrogen equivalent)

Table 13.1 Global production of nitrogen fertilizers (in millions of nitrogen equivalent tons), 1860–1913

	1860	1890	1913
Nitrate (Chile–Peru)	10	130	410
Guano	70	20	10
Coke oven gas (ammonium sulfate)	0	0	270
Others	0	0	40
Total	80	150	730

Source: Smil, 2001: 240.

Table 13.2 Quantity of nutrient supplements in German agriculture, 1878–1914 (in kg/ha)

	1878–80	1911–14
Nitrogen	14	33
Manure	0.7	6.4
Artificial fertilizer	14.7	39.4
Total		
Phosphate	12	28
Manure	1.6	18.9
Artificial fertilizer	13.6	47.9
Total		
Potash	11	26
Manure	0.8	16.7
Artificial fertilizer	11.8	42.7
Total		

Source: Grant, 2009.

in 1913 to 96,000 tons in 1918 (Smil, 2001: 242), which was more than what Chilean nitrates and ammonium sulfate from gas factories and coke plants provided in 1913.

It was a decisive turning point. With the Haber–Bosch process, any country that had a supply of fossil fuels could now inject as much nitrogen as it wanted into its soils (and therefore into its agriculture) without depending on a local transfer of biomass (animal-farms-to-crop-farms, town-to-countryside, forest-to-crops), or on a limited and distant physical stock. This laid the foundations for many major transformations in how biomass was used in the twentieth century: spectacular growth in agricultural yields, disintegration of crop and animal farming, the end of exploitation of urban waste, and the advent of national food self-sufficiency.

Increasing production within the domestic territory, 1870–1913

The German agricultural revolution

Between 1850 and 1910, Germans tripled both agricultural output and labor productivity in agriculture. During the same period, English agricultural output grew by only 2 percent and agricultural labor productivity by 30 percent (Table 13.2).

Potato and beet farming were the major drivers of this growth. Their contribution to plant calories grew from 18 percent to 34 percent between 1850 and 1913, and they accounted for two-thirds of the increase in available calories per inhabitant. Focus on these crops was a way of intensifying land use: from 1909 to 1913 yields were estimated at 23.8 billion calories per hectare for sugar beet and 9.6 for potato, compared to 5.1 and 6.5 billion calories per hectare for rye and wheat respectively (Eltzbacher, 1914: 106). Their low protein yields were compensated by their use—or the use of the waste from processing them into sugar or alcohol—in animal feed. Pig herds grew from 7 to 26 million between 1873 and 1913, and cattle herds from 16 to 21 million (Mitchell, 1992: 337).[10] In 1913, animal feed absorbed 31 million tons of potatoes for a harvest of 52 million tons (Eltzbacher, 1914: 41). The animal farm sector depended also on significant quantities of imported foods.

The internal combustion engine: French theory, German practice

Anyone who has ever filled a car tank knows that there are two types of internal combustion engines: the gasoline engine and the diesel engine. Both these engines were designed and made functional to a sufficient degree of reliability between 1870 and 1913. In both cases, Frenchmen can be considered to have been the original inspiration for the inventions: Alphonse Beau de Rochas for the gasoline engine, and Sadi Carnot for the diesel engine. However, the practical application was undertaken by Germans.

Alphonse Beau de Rochas was the first to file a patent describing the "theoretical" functioning of a four-stroke engine (intake, compression, power, and exhaust, with spark ignition starting the combustion process) without, however, using it himself to make an engine. The credit for that goes to Nikolaus Otto, a German engineer, who developed the four-stroke engine with gas compression in 1876 using coal gas as a combustible. The engine was later perfected by two of his former employees, Gottlieb Daimler and Wilhelm Maybach, using petrol gasoline (which is 1600 times more energy dense than coal gas), introducing water cooling, and producing the first four-cylinder engine. Wilhelm Maybach went on to found the firm Mercedes, whose first model reached a record speed of 64 km/h.

Rudolf Diesel, on the other hand, directly influenced by his thermodynamics classes, sought to design an engine that would closely follow what was called the "Carnot" cycle. The key idea here involved relying on increasing pressure to obtain a sufficiently high temperature in a cylinder to provoke spontaneous combustion of fuel. Rudolf Diesel exposed the idea in 1893 in a book, but did not put it into practice to make a functional engine until four years later, thanks to financing from Heinrich von Buz, the managing director of the first German mechanical engineering firm, and Friedrich Alfred Krupp, inheritor of the famous foundries. Nearly another ten years would be needed to obtain engines that were really stable, but less time was necessary for the development of new applications: 1903, the engine was used for the first time on a ship, 1904 for electricity production to run Kiev tramways, 1904 in a submarine; 1911 in the first transatlantic ship; 1913 in the first locomotive; and 1924 in the first truck.

During the period of gestation and gradual improvement of the engines, there were significant developments in two variables, which would revolutionize

---

[10] The number of sheep fell from 19 million in 1883 to 8 million in 1907 (Perkins, 1981: 78) due to competition from foreign wool.

> transport, and more widely the supply of kinetic energy: the yield when converting chemical energy from fuel to mechanical energy; and the ratio of weight to power. The yield of the very first gasoline engines was only 4 percent; this grew to 20 percent at the beginning of the twentieth century, and 25 percent for diesel engines at the same time.
>
> Improvement in the weight/power ratio, an essential criterion for land transport, was even more dramatic. According to Vaclav Smil's estimations, the ratio fell from 900 g/watt for humans or animals (the only source of mobile mechanical energy in solar metabolic regimes) and for the first stationary steam engines, to 200 g/W for the first locomotives, then 45 g/W for the first Daimler/Maybach engine, 8.5 g/W for the first Mercedes car, and 5 g/W for the Ford T that was put on the market in 1907!
>
> By then, all the pieces were in place for motor vehicles (motorcycles, cars, buses, trucks, and tractors) as well as motor pumps and generators, to radically transform the world, even in its most remote locations.
>
> Source: Smil, 2010.

Root and tuber crops, which dominated the German agricultural revolution, profoundly modified the technical physiognomy of agriculture: new farm machines were taken up (harrow sowers, steam plows, etc.), the practice of fallow was abandoned thanks to fertilizer use and frequent weeding, and the size of livestock herds grew. They also generated many other changes in the size of farms, and labor organization. To grow one hectare of beetroot required three times as much work as growing cereals. This work, which was highly seasonal and not aligned with the harvest period, led to an increase in agricultural wage work, and in particular in seasonal migrants.[11] Large farm units of more than 1,000 hectares, with internal sugar processing plants and distilleries emerged. Little by little these distilleries became independent (in the form of holdings or cooperatives) and opened up to small producers, which enabled the growing of beet even in small plots.

According to Perkins,

> the rapid expansion of the area devoted to rootcrops from the 1850s had profound effects upon agriculture as a whole and upon agrarian society in Germany. It was in fact the basis of the modernization of agriculture, in that it acted to transform the archaic field systems, techniques and technology of cultivation, and initiated the development of scientific plant breeding and protection as well as the usage of artificial fertilizers.
>
> (Perkins, 1981: 108)

---

[11] Beetroot harvesting led to seasonal migration of peasants from eastern Germany and Poland, and later from Russia and elsewhere, many of whom were women, towards central Germany: their numbers grew from 17,000 in 1890 to 433,000 in 1914.

The intensification of German agriculture also involved increasing yields of the main crops grown. Yields of all cereals practically doubled (from 10 to 20 quintals per hectare on average), with the exception of rye, and quintupled for potato between 1848 and 1913 (from 25 to 121 q/ha). Beetroot yields grew by a factor of 2.3 (from 109 to 249 q/ha) between 1880 and 1913.[12] This growth in yields was of course a sign of increased fertilizer use. Based on Grant's (2009) calculations, nutrient supplements (nitrogen, phosphorous, potassium) increased three- or fourfold between 1878 and 1914. The growing availability of manure, linked to the rise in animal herds, contributed to this fertilization. Increased amounts of manure were particularly decisive for nitrogen supplements: manure provided 85 percent of these, compared to 58 percent for phosphates and 60 percent for potash.

But the real novelty of the period was the introduction of "artificial" fertilizers, in various forms. This development was particularly precocious in Germany. According to Paul Bairoch, in 1913 the fertilizing content of chemical fertilizers consumed totaled 204,000 tons in the United Kingdom, compared to 1,277,000 in Germany (Bairoch, 1999: 90). Different sources of fertilizers had widely differing contents of three main nutrients—nitrogen, phosphorous, and potassium.

As mentioned, for nitrogen, Germany was the main importer of sodium nitrate from Chile and soon thereafter invented synthetic nitrogen.

The only source of potassium-based fertilizer (including for international trade) at the time was potassium salts from Stassfurt in Germany (Institut International de l'Agriculture, 1914: 16) Half of this production was used in German agriculture, whose consumption per hectare multiplied twentyfold between 1880 and 1910.

Lastly, phosphorous was obtained from two main sources:

- The first involved extraction from a sedimentary mineral, lime phosphate, which when treated with sulfuric acid yields superphosphate which is easily assimilated. This source was supplied mainly by the United States (half of global production), and Tunisia (one-third) (Institut International de l'Agriculture, 1914: 14).
- The second source was dephosphorization slags (or Thomas slags) from steelmaking: the Thomas process, developed in England in 1879, enabled the use of iron ores rich in phosphorous (such as minette from Lorraine, a region under German control after the 1870 war) and yielded a residue, the slag, which, once ground, provided soil with phosphorous and lime.

In 1912, Germany was an importer of mineral phosphate, but a very large exporter of superphosphate and Thomas slags.

The never-ending sugar rent

Drug food? Sugar holds a special status among food products. Trade in sugar, like that of alcohol, salt, and tobacco, has always been highly regulated, protected, and

---

[12] The sugar yield from beet increased exponentially between 1876 and 1915, going from 8.8 to 15.7 percent, a 78 percent improvement.

taxed. The eighteenth-century arsenal of regulations for the cane sugar market gave way to a similar arsenal for beet sugar in the nineteenth century. Sugar thus traversed the "liberal interval" of the nineteenth century unscathed. The development of sugar production on the European continent was a harbinger, a century early, of a food biomass supply strategy that would prevail during the short twentieth century (1914–91, see Hobsbawm, 2003): import substitution in a context of strong international rivalries, heavy state intervention, and international regulation (Part 5).

The first attempts to produce sugar from beet started in the late eighteenth century in Silesia, where the Prussian king financed the construction of the first sugar factory for someone named Achard. German production, however, did not really take off until 1870. By the first two years of the twentieth century, production reached 2 million tons. Germany was at the time the leading producer of sugar and its share in global production reached 22 percent.[13]

Austria-Hungary, Russia, Belgium, and Holland followed suit. Thus, the production of beet sugar grew rapidly and continuously throughout the second half of the nineteenth century, while cane sugar production was handicapped by the abolition of slavery in old European colonies, before Asian plantations entered the scene.[14] The global output of beet sugar outstripped that of cane sugar from 1880 until the First World War (Table 13.3).

At the very beginning of the twentieth century, Germany exported almost 60 percent of its sugar output, two-thirds of which went to the English market where European beet sugar had essentially replaced sugar from the colonies. In 1846, the United Kingdom, in addition to abolishing the Corn Laws, had reduced taxes on sugar that had been in place since 1651, and later in 1874 eliminated them altogether, both for colonial sugars and "foreign sugars" (Galloway, 1989: 133).

State support was multiform and decisive for this shift. Direct aid for cultivation and import taxes enabled conquest of the domestic market, and soon after, an export subsidy (restitution) system was adopted by Germany, and later by Austria, and then in retaliation, by France in 1884. The war of subsidies between European beet

Table 13.3 Global output of centrifugal sugar (in thousands of tons)

	1852–3	1875	1882–3	1900–1	1913–14
Cane sugar	1,269	1,923	1,917	3,563	7,683
Beet sugar	202	1,329	2,114	6,090	9,035

Sources: Prinsen-Geerligs, 1912, for 1852; INSEE, 1952, for 1875; International Sugar Council, 1963, for the other years.

---

[13] In France, production started a bit earlier, thanks in part to deliberate policy under the First Empire, but the country was quickly outstripped by Germany.

[14] After slavery was abolished in the English and French colonies, cane sugar production experienced a first resurgence in Cuba, and then a second, and more remarkable, resurgence when cane cultivation was intensified in Java.

sugar-producing countries soon gave rise to "sugar diplomacy" aimed at regulating the use of subsidies, a foretaste of "commodity diplomacy" that would flourish during the twentieth century. A first convention was signed in Paris in 1864, but it was only in 1901 that a veritable agreement was reached and ratified by all the large sugar-producing countries and the United Kingdom, the main importer (Kingsman and Gafner, 2000: 54). The "Brussels Convention" which entered into force in 1903, was a remarkable demonstration of English hegemonic power (Pigman, 1997), as it was founded mainly on the possibility it gave to importing countries (that is, the United Kingdom) to refuse (or strongly tax) sugars that had benefited from subsidies during production or commercialization—that is, sugar from beetroot (Richardson, 2009: 55).

Germany's food supply chain in 1913

A detailed analysis of the performance of German agriculture, published during the First World War by the English Board of Agriculture (Middleton, 1916) with the aim of assessing anticipated success of the blockade, provides in-depth insight into Germany's food balance. In particular, for 1912–13, there is an estimation of human and animal consumption in calories that moreover distinguishes between local and imported products. We therefore have a unique snapshot of Germany's food consumption and the weight of imports just prior to the war (Table 13.4).

Middleton calculated that imports only represented roughly 10 percent of calorie intake for human food, and 11 percent for animal feed. This is far removed from figures for the same period in the United Kingdom, where 58 percent of food calories consumed were imported. The contribution from the exterior was, however, much higher for the oilseed sector: vegetable oils for human consumption (92 percent were imported), and seedcakes for animals (98 percent). The German situation, moreover, was similar to that of France and other European countries. At the beginning of the twentieth century, oilseeds were incontestably the biomass category for which Europe had extreme dependence on imports from distant territories.

The estimates highlight significant consumption of potatoes, pork, and dairy products in Germany. These three products together equaled the contribution of cereals in human calorie consumption. The figures also indicate the importance of animal farming in German agriculture: animals consumed twice as many calories as humans. This reflects the dynamic specialization in animal products present in many Northwestern European countries (Part 3). In Germany, two-thirds of imported calories went to feeding animals.

The "Second Thirty Year War": Autarky, nutrition, and territorial conquest

The First World War brought globalization to a brutal end. For Europe, it also put a stop to the illusion that merchants and industrialists had definitively replaced armies in managing world affairs. It brought a new form of war, total war (Shaw, 1988; van

Table 13.4 Germany, consumption and imports of food products and animal feed, 1912–13 (in billions of calories)

	Human food			Animal feed		
	Consumption	Imports	% imports /consump.	Total consump.	Imports	% imports /consump.
Cereals	32,873	3,716	11	72,459	15,031	21
Pulses	1,346	821	61	4,040	140	3
Potato	10,358	276	3	18,065	0	0
Sugar (beet)	4,689	−2,344	−50	–	–	–
Other roots and tubers	1,621	92	6	20,742	99	0
Vegetable oils	1,683	1,553	92	–	–	–
Oilseed cakes	–	–	–	4,204	4,133	98
Hay	–	–	–	55,711	0	0
Fruits	2,025	639	31	–	–	–
Honey	56	6	11	–	–	–
Cocoa	273	273	100	–	–	–
Alcoholic drinks	4,251	477	11	–	–	–
Bovine (meat and fat)	2,968	496	17	–	–	–
Pork (meat and fat)	10,398	1,134	11	–	–	–
Sheep, goats, horses, etc.	396	168	42	–	–	–
Poultry and game	490	168	34	–	–	–
Fish	490	346	71	–	–	–
Dairy products	12,633	597	5	–	–	–
Eggs	607	245	40	–	–	–
Total	87,157	8,663	10	175,221	19,403	11

Source: from Middleton, 1916: 73.

Creveld, 1998; Kaldor, 1999). This involved the mobilization of all sectors of society by the state, direct mobilization in military apparatus, as well as mobilization in the national productive apparatus. The war involved a generalized violence which targeted not just troops and military equipment but also civilians and economic activity. Thus, one of the innovations of the First World War was the sub-marine war undertaken by Germany and its extension to commercial ships, which was a response to the "prolonged blockade" imposed by the Allies from March 1915.

Total war indisputably legitimated state intervention to decide on the allocation of resources and priorities for production. State intervention proved itself to be highly effective, in particular during the Second World War. The "superior interest of the nation" (superior to individual liberties, as well as to property rights) made the war a period of experimentation and accelerated learning on how to administer things and govern peoples. It was an occasion for creating new institutions, which, like planning, would outlive the war, and which would be enduringly shaped by the circumstances of their creation, both in terms of their goals and their rules of functioning.

Total war also contributed very strongly to legitimizing the goal of national self-sufficiency. From the First World War, European countries started to suffer the economic and social costs of too strong a dependence on long-distance trade, or simply on trade with other countries now turned enemy states. Self-sufficiency became an important goal for all economic sectors, the first of which being the raw materials sector. Developing the synthetic chemistry sector was an essential pillar of this strategy. But Europeans learned with the two wars that there was a category of biomass for which there were no chemical substitutes: food biomass (Offer, 1989: 23).

Lastly, total war, and in particular that of the Second World War, laid the conditions for social reform: "Total war is at its very best a two-way process, in which the state coerces the population but the population endorses its own coercion and thereby improves its position in and influence on the state" (Shaw, 1988: 51). The practice (or preparation) of war and policies related to well-being—warfare and welfare—tend to converge. This is what happened in Nazi Germany. It was also the case in the United Kingdom, in France, and in the United States. The establishment of welfare states, based on solid and lasting compromises between the state and various sectors of society, was a result in large part of the two wars. Thomas Piketty and Emmanuel Saez underscore the very particular role of the Second World War in the implementation of a new, more egalitarian, model of income distribution in Europe and the United States (Piketty et al., 2001; Piketty, 2003).

Germany was one of the countries where the concept of total war, mobilization of all parts of society and destruction of adversaries, was implemented with particular acuity. During the First World War, the Prussian government undertook wide-scale planning aimed at securing supplies for the arms industry. Such planning would later serve as a model for the young Bolshevik regime in the USSR (Sapir, 1990: 25). Hitler's rise to power gave a new impetus to mobilization of wide society for war purposes. The key objectives of economic policy at the time were to generate financial resources and construct the industrial apparatus necessary for Germany's rearmament. In 1933, while the job creation program was allocated 1 billion Reichsmarks, the secret rearmament plan was allocated 35 billion Reichsmarks over eight years (Tooze, 2008: 180). The adoption in 1936 of the "four-year plan" (*Vierjahresplan*), spearheaded by Goering and tasked with preparing the German army and economy for war within four years, further reinforced this mobilization. Germany's entry into the war in 1939 broke the last political limits on military spending which reached 44 percent of national income in 1940, and rose to 76 percent in 1943.

The First World War: Scientific management of unanticipated shortages

From 1914 the Allies implemented a blockade against Germany. Recourse to distant biomass (and to fertilizing minerals, in particular nitrates from Chile) was henceforth no longer possible. Moreover, former trade partners like Russia were now enemies and stopped supplying Germany. In any case, Germany itself experienced production difficulties linked to its own state of war. To complete the picture, transportation, in particular rail transportation, was disrupted and re-affected to meet military priorities, such that even domestic output moved around with difficulty. To put it simply, total war did not create favorable conditions for biomass imports.

Production, for its part, suffered from the mass enrolment of men and horses into the army: in 1918, 11 million out of 67 million Germans were enrolled in the army. Agriculture lost roughly 60 percent of its workforce (Offer, 1989: 27). The sector also faced the challenges of a shortage of imported inputs, the confiscation of nitrates by the army, and the transformation of farmlands into battlefields, or more simply, collateral damage to harvests.

The functioning of supply chains may be difficult in times of war, but on the other hand, needs and demand increase dramatically. First there was the necessity of feeding sufficient quantities of food to troops in order to maintain their fighting force, and also to additional workers recruited in industrial sectors linked to the war effort. The military industry also competed with other sectors of the economy for certain types of biomass (fatty matter, leather, fabrics) and inputs (nitrates). Horses, which were still present in significant numbers on the 1914–18 war fronts, also had to be fed—by an agricultural sector that could no longer count on these animals.

Despite the optimistic forecasts by German authorities (see box below), prices started to rise after the first few months of the war. The first rationing measures were established by municipal authorities until May 1916 when the War Food Bureau (Kriegsernährungsamt—KEA) was created within the Ministry of War. This new institution, according to Avner Offer, operated a de facto "nationalization of the food distribution system" (Offer, 1989: 28). The regulatory state became trader and manager. An individual calorie ration was fixed nationally. All households were registered at a neighborhood shop from which they were to procure their ration.[15] Rations were initially set at 1,985 calories (and not the 3,000-calorie ration considered optimal by experts) and were lowered to 1,100 calories in July 1917, to rise again to 1,619 calories in November 1918.

Must one conclude that Germans were famished during the First World War? Despite the postwar analyses by both Germans and non-Germans (for example

---

[15] State intervention in the food sector did not end there. It is estimated that in March 1917, f governmental organizations worked in the food sector, and that between 1914 and 1918 in total, 892 laws, proclamations, and decrees relating to food were promulgated by the German imperial government (McKinnon Wood, 1918).

Starling, 1920), Avner Offer does not think so. Relying on consumption surveys, he shows that the low point in the spring of 1917 only lowered food consumption to 85 percent of the norm fixed by nutritionists, and thereafter food consumption rose (Offer, 1989: 50 and following). He explains the gap between the ration stipulated by the government and real consumption by the size of the black market (providing +40 to 50 percent of the ration), as well as supplementary distribution of food by municipalities and large firms in canteens.

The interwar period: Quest for food self-sufficiency and promotion of the peasantry

The quest for self-sufficiency in biomass, or more precisely the management of biomass supply, was a constant concern for governments in interwar Germany, albeit for different motivations. The shortages experienced during the First World War convinced German leaders of the need to rationalize and intensify domestic agricultural production. The balance of payments difficulties experienced from 1920 to 1930 in any case prevented reliance on imports. Germany lost its colonies in 1919, thus losing "secure" access to certain products, in particular fatty matter. In addition, German industry, including the arms industry on which the Treaty of Versailles had imposed reconversion, saw an opportunity in the modernization of agriculture. The Nazis' rise to power bolstered the ambition for self-sufficiency. The Nazis considered that food shortages had played a significant role in Germany's defeat. For them, this is what allowed Jews and communists to undermine the country from the interior. A repeat scenario had to be avoided.

"Nutrition, first and foremost at the service of war"*

Management of shortages would in large part be based on nutrition, a new scientific discipline, largely founded on German research. The first appliance that could measure the metabolism of living beings was developed by Carl Voit and Max von Pettenkofer. Their student, Max Rubner, in 1883 introduced the concept of calories in nutrition, determined the calorie content of various foods, proved that the law of energy conservation applied to living beings, and that fats and carbohydrates were interchangeable in nutrition based on their energy content (Todhunter, 1959: 11). Rubner was a promoter of "rational nutrition"** which proposed nutritional guidelines for families, prisons, and barracks.

Nutritional analyses undertaken after the war broke out used the work of these pioneers. The Eltzbacher Commission, *Die deutsche Volksernährung und der englische Aushungerungsplan* [Feeding Germans and the English plan to starve us] (Eltzbacher, 1914) laid our dietary norms for the whole nation. The commission's analysis used Voit and Rubner's calculations to estimate calorie and protein needs based on the age and sex of individuals. The requirements of an adult male were estimated at 3,000 calories and 80g of proteins per day. The requirements for the whole population were then compared to the food supply that was available in 1912–13.*** The estimated 92.9 g of protein and 3,642 calories (of which 25.7 g of protein and 715 calories were imported) available per inhabitant exceeded the requirements of an adult male, and even more so the average requirements of the whole population, given the lower needs estimated for women and children.

The consumption surplus in total was estimated at 59 percent for calories and 44 percent for proteins. Thus, even without imports, supply of calories maintained a surplus, with the exception for a slight deficit in proteins (3 percent). To resolve this deficit, the commission recommended a series of measures that were quite close to those prominent in contemporary debates on food security policies: ban the export of food and the use of bread-making cereals for alcohol production, reduce waste, encourage consumers to favor plant-based products, and promote techniques for conserving fruits and vegetables.

*The title is inspired by the title of a 1976 pamphlet by the prominent French geographer Yves Lacoste: *La géographie, ça sert, d'abord, à faire la guerre* [Geography is first and foremost at the service of war].

**In a book published in 1913, Rubner using an assessment of the price of calories consumed demonstrated the irrationality of sandwiches, which were fashionable in Berlin at the time.

***These are the figures that we used in Table 13.4.

German agricultural production was highly insufficient for two categories of products: fatty matter and animal feed (Table 13.4). In 1933, domestic production supplied only 53 percent of fatty matter consumed. The 90 percent self-sufficiency for milk, butter, cheese, and pork is deceptive because a significant part of domestic production of animal products depended on imported feed (25 percent for dairy products) (Perkins, 1990: 510). The plant protein deficit was estimated at 15 percent of needs (Strauss, 1941: 375). Cereal self-sufficiency was relatively easy, and already achieved before the Nazis rose to power, but later endangered by the shift from rye to wheat consumption. At the same time, increasing quantities of rye were used in animal feed.

In the short term, food security was achieved through agreements with continental European countries, particularly in Southeastern Europe[16] and with the USSR. Through these agreements, Germany bought agricultural products at a price higher than world price, and in exchange exported industrial goods (fertilizer, machines, and arms). At the end of the 1930s, half of Bulgaria's foreign trade was with Germany. Under this system, Bulgaria developed its sunflower, soybean, and textile fiber production.

But the long-term security of food supply was above all achieved through renewed intensification of domestic farming ("internal colonization"). According to Suzanne Heim, German research in agronomy, for example, did not need to protect itself from

[16] See Hirschman (1945) for an analysis of how trade policies were used as an instrument for Germany's power during the interwar period.

political interference of the Nazi party, but on the contrary, benefited from their full support (Heim, 2008: 195).[17] Research was an essential piece of the scientific foundation necessary for the "battle for agricultural production" launched in 1934, as well as for the 1936 Four-Year Plan (ibid.: 7). Three main priorities were set: variety improvement, rationalization and mechanization of production, and lastly organization of rationing. From 1936, agricultural research received more funding than other "hard science" research sectors (ibid.: 9).

Fertilizer use increased significantly in this period and resulted in an increase in yields (between +9 percent and +16 percent between 1932 and 1939). Nitrogen consumption grew from 210,000 to 633,000 tons between 1913 and 1938, and potash consumption from 536,000 to 1,156,000 tons. Consumption of phosphates, which were imported, remained stable (Strauss, 1941: 382). However, agriculture was constrained by the scarcity of labor. With growth in industrial jobs, the farming population fell by 18 percent between 1935 and 1938, and yet the crops that were most grown—potatoes, beetroot, and corn—were labor-intensive.

Another means of reaching self-sufficiency is to modify consumption. Nazi government policy in effect promoted products that could be produced domestically: more bread and potatoes, less fatty matter, milk, fruits, and vegetables. In 1937, Germans were already on a precocious war diet, consuming 15 percent fewer calories than in 1932 (Strauss, 1941: 367).

During the Nazi period, agricultural policy focused on self-sufficiency went hand-in-hand with a "cult" around the German peasantry, presented as the foundation of the nation, the race, as well as the political base of the regime. In 1933, 29 percent of the active population, in other words 9.3 million people, worked in agriculture. The State Hereditary Farm law (Reichserbhofgesetz) which was passed in 1933 was emblematic of the "blood and soil" (*Blut und Boden*) ideology ardently promoted by Richard Wallther Darre, agriculture minister from 1933 to 1942 and member of the SS. It created a legal category specifically for farmers of pure race from medium-sized farms, who were the only ones to hold the honorific title of "peasant." Their farms could not be seized, nor used as collateral, nor sold and had to be passed on to a single male inheritor. Moreover, debts of these farms were covered by a state organ, and reimbursement funded through proportional fees based on the value of the farm (Tooze, 2006: 184).

Direct administration of agricultural markets worked towards two objectives: self-sufficiency and defense of the peasantry. The establishment of the Reich Food Organization (*Reichnährstand*—RNS) in 1933 put an end to the free functioning of markets. The RNS, in Adam Tooze's opinion, became the biggest economic organization in Germany at the time. All foreign trade, as well as domestic trading

---

[17] Several research institutes and experimental farms were created from the early 1920s (for milk in Kiel and Weihenstepha, for improvement of animal races in Tschechnitz and Grub, for cereals in Berlin, etc.) (Heim, 2008: 4). From 1928, the Kaiser Wilhelm Society (Kaiser-Wilhelm-Gesellschaft), the main research organization funded by the state and private sector, established a large number of specialized institutes, some of which during the Second World War opened offices in occupied territories.

circuits of agricultural products, were now controlled by the state. Prices were set, with seasonal and regional variations, for each transaction from producer to consumer. A controller was designated in each one of the 50,000 villages of the country. The RNS alone employed 20,000 people. It more or less directly administered 25 percent of the country's GDP and 40 percent of the active population (agriculture, and upstream and downstream activities), and thus had a grip on food expenditure, in other words, half of the expenditure of households. In 1937, a vast stockpiling program was established: a stockpile of cereals equivalent to one year of bread supply was constituted.

Nonetheless, in 1938 the agriculture minister himself recognized that self-sufficiency was not possible. The military conquest of new territories was then touted as indispensable.

Second World War: Intensification of the nutritional government and colonial expansion

The struggle for hegemony in the world is decided for Europe by the possession of Russian territory; it makes Europe the place in the world most secure from blockade [...] The Slavic peoples on the other hand are not destined for their own life [...] The Russian territory is our India and, just as the English rule India with a handful of people, so will we govern this our colonial territory. We will supply the Ukrainians with headscarves, glass chains as jewelry, and whatever else colonial peoples like [...] My goals are not immoderate; basically, these are all areas where Germans (Germanen) were previously settled. The German Volk is to grow into this territory.

(Hitler, September 17,1941, cited in Zimmerer, 2008: 95)

Even before the First World War, nationalists had decried the "injustice" of Germany's geopolitical situation. While the country had some colonies[18] in Africa and the Pacific Ocean, it did not have an equivalent of the English dominions, which as the destination countries of the majority of English migrants, and mainly populated by English, were veritable resurgences of the United Kingdom overseas. These extensions of the United Kingdom were prodigious sources of raw material, as well as indefectible allies during times of war. Germany did not have any settler colonies,[19] and worse still, its numerous nineteenth-century emigrants had been lost to the motherland. Settled in the United States, Brazil, or Argentina, the emigrants had not founded any political entity linked to Germany.

---

[18] Which Germany lost in the Treaty of Versailles.

[19] With the exception of Southwest Africa (present-day Namibia) and unfruitful attempts in Tanganyika.

For Hitler's Germany, this handicap was to blame for the 1918 defeat, and it could be redressed by conquering a new "vital space" or *Lebensraum*. The mobilization of the entire German economy would not suffice to establish a power capable of rivaling England, and even less the United States, which possessed a vast territory emptied of past occupants. Conquest, second component of the total war that the Nazis waged, implied not the destruction of the economic apparatus of conquered countries, but rather destruction of the people themselves, and their replacement by pioneers from a booming German populace.

> Nazi Germany was not seeking to turn back the clock. It was simply refusing to accept that the distribution of land, resources and population, which had resulted from the Imperial wars of the eighteenth and nineteenth centuries, should be accepted as final. It was refusing to accept that Germany's place in the world was that of a medium-sized workshop economy, entirely dependent on imported food.
>
> (Tooze, 2006: 169)

The issue of feeding Germans became all the more crucial during the war waged by Germany as the population to feed grew in size. German campaigns across Europe, and especially on the Russian front, emptied the country of workers at a time when the arms industry needed ever more. Germany thus had to recruit many foreign workers, prisoners of war, or workers that had been captured and coerced (in 1944, 8 million foreign workers were present on German soil, that is 20 percent of its manual workers). Getting supplies to distant troops was also a problem as troops did not always find enough food to requisition where they were.

Nutritionally, German citizens with full rights did not experience shortages comparable to those they suffered during the First World War. Support for domestic agricultural production through the mobilization of foreign workers was a priority (these workers are estimated to have contributed 20 percent of food production), and agricultural output in conquered territories was requisitioned. A highly sophisticated system of rations was put in place on August 27, 1939, a few days before the invasion of Poland. It was characterized by differentiation to the extreme of the populace, and by flexibility. Different rations were set for a large number of categories of Germans, which increased even more as the war progressed. In the end, sixteen different rations existed. Germans citizens with full rights were distinguished as "normal citizens," military, manual workers, night workers, nursing mothers, the sick, the elderly, children, and even dogs. The first products to be rationed were bacon, butter, sugar, meat, tea, oil, and milk, each of which had a ration card. The weekly ration allowed to a "normal" German in August 1939 was composed of 700 grams of meat, 350 grams of fat, 280 grams of sugar, 110 grams of jam, 63 grams of coffee, 150 grams of cereal products (*Nährmittel*), and 60 grams of dairy products. In practice, for a significant part of the working class (42 percent), this ration was an improvement in their diets (Gerhard, 2015: 66).

Lebensraum and the Nazi project of division of labor to ensure biomass supplies for the Third Reich

Having noted in 1938 its incapacity to feed itself off its own land, Nazi Germany developed a precise vision of the division of labor within the empire that it aimed to build in Europe. To rival the British Empire, Germany's design was for a Roman-style empire, with requisition of local resources as tributes.

The initial project relied on the constitution of *Lebensraum* (a vital space) constituted of three concentric zones: the Reich, that is the territory controlled by the state; the *Volksboden*, or the "ethnic territory" with Germanic people, and the *Kulturboden* (the "zone of Germanic culture").

The first circle (Reich) covered Germany (with its 1937 borders), Denmark, Holland, Belgium, Northwest France, Austria, Czechoslovakia, Poland (excluding the zones occupied by the USSR), and the Baltic countries. Within this circle, some countries had an industrial vocation: Austria and Czechoslovakia, who moreover had the advantage of being relatively shielded from aerial bombing, would be supplied in the same way as German regions. Belgium and the neighboring regions of France, the industrial basins along the Ruhr and Saar rivers, by contrast, were to aim to achieve food self-sufficiency, given the quality of their agriculture. The other countries in the first circle were to play an essential role in supplying the Reich. Their food sectors were closely managed, put under the control of the German ministry of agriculture, either in their preexisting state, as was the case with Danish and Dutch producer cooperatives, or after confiscation and restructuring. The planned contributions included dairy products for Holland and Denmark, animal products for Moravia and Estonia, and so on.

The second circle of biomass supply was composed of two regions with very different resources: four Danube countries (Bulgaria, Romania, Hungary, and Yugoslavia) versus Norway. The Danube countries were traditionally exporters of cereals, oilseeds, and in more modest quantities animal products. Norway was targeted for its herring, codfish oil, wood pulp, and nitrogen fertilizers, thanks to hydroelectric factories.

A General Plan for the East (Generalplan Ost) proposed that German emigrants settle the lands to the east (Ostraum, the equivalent of the American Far West). The plans for the colonization of Eastern Europe became increasingly ambitious as German troops advanced. Initially limited to Poland, plans ended up integrating vast portions of the USSR, the Urals sometimes being evoked as the ultimate limit.

Sources: Brandt, 1945, 1953; Gerhard, 2009.

Specific rations were set for foreign workers by nationality, for Jews, and from November 1943, also for the mentally ill, and many other categories. Each German was registered at a shop. Those who had been labeled as Jewish could only get their provisions from designated shops during restricted opening hours. Nutritional science was once again called on, in particular to determine what foreign workers should eat.

Many studies were carried out by the Institute of Work Physiology. The goal was to identify the optimal calorie intake needed to maximize physical performance. One of the sinister conclusions was that it was of apparent greater utility to provide 3,000 calories to one single worker rather than 1,500 calories to two workers (Gerhard, 2015: Chapter 5).

Rations were adjusted every four weeks, and there were special rations for celebrations and holidays. The adjustments tended towards a reduction in ration sizes as the war progressed. In April 1940 and again in the summer of 1941, the meat ration was cut by half. In February 1943, the bread ration was reduced to 300 g. Despite these reductions, Germans with full rights were adequately fed until the last year of war. Between 1939 and 1944, rations only fell from 2,400 to 2,000 calories. It was only after 1945, with the loss of a part of the conquered territories and the bombing of the country's infrastructure, that the food situation degenerated considerably (Brandt, 1945).

During the first weeks of 1941, in contradiction with the pressing need for workers, the Ministry of Food and the Wehrmacht agreed to roll out the Hunger Plan whose ambition was to starve 30 million inhabitants of the USSR (even before the SS' project to exterminate Jews was established). Requisitioning farm produce in regions that had been conquered in the USSR thus had a double objective: in the short term ensure food for Germany at a time when obtaining foreign supplies was difficult, and in the long term to empty the region of its undesirable population through famine, thus enabling colonization by German farmers.

Biomass for non-food uses: Still more synthetic products

Research to develop synthetic products from coal was a major component of the quest for self-sufficiency, in both Germany and other countries aiming for self-sufficiency.

The "Four-Year Plan" adopted in 1936 by the Nazi government in preparation for the war greatly accelerated this, and enormous sums of public funds were injected into relaunching the manufacture of synthetic products. After the arms industry, synthetics were the second priority of the plan. The production of coal gasoline[20] was the favored sector by far, and alone attracted a quarter of "investments for autarchy" (Scherner, 2008: 870). This was followed by substitutes for three types of non-food biomass: nitrogen fertilizers, rubbers, and textile fibers, which would all have brilliant futures.

The Haber–Bosch process for the synthesis of ammonia was utilized from 1914 to supply factories making explosives. In 1916, while the Battle of Verdun waged, the German government supported construction of a new plant for ammonia synthesis by

---

[20] The production of fuel from coal started during the First World War and continued throughout the 1920s under an alliance between IC Farben and Standard Oil of New Jersey. In 1931, a production capacity of 100,000 tons was reached. In 1933, IG Farben signed an agreement with the Nazi government to triple production through coal hydrogenation. In 1944, annual production rose to 4 million tons.

BASF. In that year, synthetic ammonia already represented 45 percent of Germany's nitrogen production, and all of it was earmarked for the manufacture of explosives. The Haber–Bosch process indisputably helped Germany maintain its military capacity until November 1918. Production by then had reached around 100,000 tons, and this would increase by a factor of eight over the next two decades to peak at 845,000 tons in 1928. Output fell during the production crisis, but later doubled under the Four-Year Plan, and from 1939 exceeded the 1-million-ton mark (Smil, 2001: 242).

With the emergence of motorized warfare, rubber became a highly strategic raw material on which the rapid movement of troops depended. All competing powers during the new "Thirty Year War" were aware of the necessity of ensuring reliable supply of rubber, in a context where almost all natural rubber was geographically concentrated in very distant English, Dutch, and French colonies in Southeast Asia.[21] Prior to the Second World War, three countries endeavored to find substitutes for natural rubber: the United States (Herbert and Bisio, 1985), the USSR, and of course Germany. In Germany, Bayer managed to produce synthetic rubber as early as the First World War, but the process, uncompetitive with respect to natural rubber in peacetime, was abandoned. Production thus halted, but research continued. IG Farben, a firm which was a conglomerate of the main Germany chemical industries (BASF, Bayer, Agfa, etc.) established in 1925 under Carl Bosch's leadership, registered several patents between 1925 and 1933 (Borkin and Welsh, 1943: 190). Research was undertaken in close collaboration with the American company Standard Oil, and this collaboration continued until the United States joined the war against Germany. Various types of synthetic elastomers were developed, but IG Farben's favorite was "Buna," whose production was relaunched under the Four-Year Plan. It was produced in three factories, one of which was located in the Auschwitz-Monowitz labor camp, causing the camp to be bombed by the Allies (Hayes, 2000). The plan for the development of synthetic rubber production was an outright success. In 1943, despite the higher volumes consumed with respect to the prewar period, Germany achieved self-sufficiency in rubber.

Textile fibers were the third type of non-food biomass for which an ambitious strategy for autarky was successfully deployed. At the beginning of the 1930s, Germany, like other industrialized nations of Europe, imported almost all the textile fibers it used. This was obviously the case for cotton and silk, but it was also true for 95 percent of wool, despite a glorious but now distant past of Prussian sheep herding. Production of rayon was launched, but remained quite limited, accounting for barely 5 percent of total textile fiber consumption. By 1943, the figure had jumped to 43 percent of total fiber consumption which had remained stable in volume (Scherner, 2008: 872)!

---

[21] Aside from the supply chain risks linked to the war, rubber-importing countries may have also felt threatened by attempts to establish a natural rubber cartel under the Stevenson Plan in the 1920s and 1930s, and later by the international agreement signed in 1934.

Textile fibers occupied a special place in the German economy. In early 1930s, wool and cotton alone represented 20 percent of total imports in value, and the textile industry was the leading employer of the country (19 percent of industrial jobs in 1934). There was thus little room for maneuver. During the March 1934 balance of payments crisis, the Nazi government banned purchase of fibers from abroad, and this quickly led to shortages. In July 1934, the National Textile Fiber Program (Nationales Fasertoffprogramm) was launched. It started by prohibiting increases in capacity of spinning plants, and reduced weekly working hours to thirty-six hours in these factories. The program also set very ambitious targets for rayon production and encouraged the firms already in the sector—that is VGF (Vereinigte Glanzstoffabriken) and IG Farben—to increase their productive apparatus. To put pressure on these giants, the state created incentives for the establishment of new rayon factories funded by spinners on a voluntary basis; various public policy instruments were used to encourage their participation (tax exemptions, guaranteed loans, grace periods for reimbursement, etc.) in exchange for strict state control of these firms (Scherner, 2008).

Artificial fibers conquer the textile fiber market

The first artificial fibers were all derived from organic matter, mainly cellulose sourced from wood pulp. The first method, using nitrocellulose, was developed in 1884 and from 1892, scaled up industrially in Besançon by Hilaire de Chardonnet. The new product was named rayon. The aim then was to produce an "artificial silk" that could replace natural silk, at a time when French production of the latter experienced several difficulties. In the years that followed, three other methods using cellulose were invented, thus putting on the market four different kinds of rayon, of which viscose would soon become the most produced.

Rayon production only reach significant levels during the late 1920s, and especially during the 1930s. Its share in global production of textile fibers thus grew from 0.5 percent in 1921 to 3 percent in 1930 and 13 percent in 1940 (FAO, 1947: 173)!

Rayon was used in two forms: continuous fiber rayon (like silk), and short fiber rayon (also called stale fiber) which was then spun either mixed with cotton, or pure as a substitute to cotton. Wood, which was relatively abundant especially after coal had replaced it as the main combustible, now enabled the elimination of, or at least the reduction in, imports of two textile fibers (silk and cotton) which had weighed heavily in the balance of trade of many countries. Developing rayon production was a key element in autarky strategies deployed in Japan, Germany, Italy as well as in the United States where tensions with Japan threatened access to silk. These four countries produced 25 percent, 20 percent, 19 percent, and 14 percent respectively of global rayon output over the period 1935-9 (Zimmerman, 1951: 368).

Various trials were also carried out in the 1930s to produce textile fibers from animal proteins (milk casein, egg albumen, feather keratin) and plant protein (soy, peanut, corn). These trials contributed to the development of what was then called chemurgy, research for new bio-sourced materials that would provide wider opportunities for surplus agricultural production, a strategy that in many aspects resonates with today's bio-economy (Finlay, 2003).

Most of the trials would fail. They did not stand up to competition from truly synthetic fibers, that is, fibers produced from coal, and soon from petrol. Nylon was first obtained in 1938 after ten years of research in the Du Pont de Nemours laboratory in the United States. The initial goal once again was to find a substitute for silk. Commercial production started in 1939 and grew exponentially during the war, when nylon was used for many military purposes such as in parachutes and tires. The textile fiber market would progressively become almost totally dissociated from the biomass market.

In addition to these grand schemes for developing non-food biomass substitutes, mention should also be made of the attempts to develop synthetic food products. Saccharine, produced from coal tar and supported by lower consumer taxes (with respect to sugar), was relatively successful: consumption grew from 14,000 tons to 22,350 tons between 1933 and 1939 (Perkins, 1990: 508). Jonathan Littell in the novel *The Kindly Ones* (2006) also mentions a margarine derived from coal, but no scientific reference can be found on this.

14

Imperialist strategies, the weapon of the weak: France and Japan

European colonial expansion of the nineteenth century involved only a late, even very late, and very brief mobilization of colonies in biomass supply chains. We saw in Part 3 that empire held just a minor position in British imports, and did not benefit from any special treatment within English trade policy. This tendency was one of the essential characteristics of the British hegemony. A few protective measures were adopted during the First World War, but it was not until the 1930s that the United Kingdom really challenged, and one could say grudgingly so, its attachment to free trade and globalized supply chains. In 1931, the UK adopted the Abnormal Importation Act, and in 1932 the Import Duties Act, both of which raised customs duties, and also introduced preferential treatment for products sourced from the empire. The Ottawa Conference, which from July 1932 brought together representatives of all entities of the empire (dominions, colonies, and protectorates), confirmed the turnabout in English trade policy.[1] The new policy would profoundly modify the United Kingdom's trade flows. The share of empire in total imports into the United Kingdom grew from 30 percent in 1929 to 42 percent in 1938 (League of Nations, 1939: 35).

Unlike England, France and Japan openly asserted their ambitions for imperial autonomy through the creation of an exclusive trade space between the metropole and colonies. These deliberate colonial policies involved the establishment of trade barriers against the rest of the world ("foreign"), as well as active support for biomass production in the colonies.

The *mise en valeur* of French colonies

France's growth during the nineteenth century seems sluggish compared to Germany's. Its population growth is a clear example. Between 1850 and 1913, France's population grew from 36 to 41 million inhabitants only, while the populations of its English

---

[1] The policy confirmed duty exemptions on products from the empire and established imperial preferential treatment measures for products that had remained duty free. Import quotas were also established in 1933 for mutton, and frozen or refrigerated beef. They were extended to pork by the new Agricultural Marketing Act (de Bromhead et al., 2017: 7–12).

neighbor grew from 27 to 45 million, and its German neighbor from 34 to 65 million inhabitants (Maddison, 2001)! Its per capita energy consumption in 1913 stood at only 60 percent of that of Germany, and per capita coal consumption at half (Kander et al., 2014). France was clearly a power running out of steam, both in European competition, and on a global scale.

In the nineteenth century, France copied British trade policy, albeit half-heartedly. The country adopted a free trade policy in 1860, only to start contravening it from 1892 and return to protecting its agriculture. But its imports of agricultural products, which had grown sevenfold between 1850 and 1910, represented no less than 35 percent of its own production in 1910 (Toutain, 1961). Unlike England, France, however, remained a biomass exporter (16 percent of its production) and most of its biomass imports were non-food products: mainly textile fibers (41 percent of biomass imports) and fatty matter (14 percent) to be used in lighting, soapmaking, and manufacturing.

During this period of globalization only a minor share of France's trade was with its colonies. Its supply chain for fatty matter in 1913 is a good illustration: three distant continents ensured supply—Asia, America, and Africa (Daviron, 2014). India for long remained the leading distant supplier of plant fatty matter (43 percent of French imports at the end of the century). It supplied a wide variety of oilseeds: peanuts, flax, mustard, sesame, and copra. The French trading post in Pondicherry and its numerous Marseille merchants (working for the soap industry) played a key role in this trade. Argentina and the United States supplied animal fatty matter: tallow and lard. Lastly, West Africa supplied peanuts (Senegambia) and palm oil (Niger delta). This African trade had started before European colonization under the legitimate trade. From 1880 and with the construction of the rail, peanuts from Senegal took on increasing importance in the French supply chain. Despite this, however, in 1913 all French colonies combined still only supplied 25 percent of oilseed imports.

It was not until 1930 that France, turning its back on globalization, progressively opted for an imperial autarky strategy and attempted to obtain from the empire most, if not all, the products it had to import. This strategy would prevail until the end of the 1950s when France had to import large quantities of capital goods (in $) for its reconstruction efforts, and thus gave preference to raw material imports from its empire, which it could purchase in francs.

At the same time, the rule that colonies had to have budgetary autonomy was gradually relaxed, and several infrastructure investments realized, in accordance with earlier appeals by Albert Sarraut for a *"mise en valeur,"* or development, of French colonies (Sarraut, 1923). These developments were mostly visible after the Second World War when the Investment Fund for Economic and Social Development (Fonds d'Investissement pour le Développement Economique et Social—FIDES) was created in 1946.

The signing of the Treaty of Rome in 1957, under which France chose Europe over its colonies, rang the death knell for the imperial economic strategy. This chapter will thus address colonial policy well beyond 1945, up until 1957, in order to highlight certain continuities.

Trade policy

Trade measures that gave preference to colonial products over "foreign" products were implemented. Several ad hoc measures were put in place, product by product, to administer the imperial space of production and trade. Coffee is an excellent illustration of the creativity in policymaking to regulate trade. For fatty matter, a law was passed in 1933 regulating import of oilseeds and setting custom duties for certain fatty matter of foreign origin (Marseille, 1984: 285), in response to the collapsing price of peanuts which threatened the whole economy of West Africa, and of Senegal in particular. The law was supplemented by the implementation in 1934 of quotas for foreign imports of oilseeds.

The four phases of imperial policy for coffee

From 1929 to 1939, policy clearly aimed to promote colonial coffee production, which was protected from falling world prices and competition from "foreign" coffees. The standard customs duty on coffee, from which colonial coffees had already been exempted since 1913, was increased to finance a support fund for the coffee sector. Lastly, in November 1932, the entry of "foreign" coffees was subjected to quotas.

From 1939 to 1948, during the war and in the immediate postwar period, avoiding shortages became the key priority. Exporting colonial coffee outside the empire was banned, and the French market was supplied practically exclusively by its colonies. Coffee consumption was rationed, and deliveries of coffee, as well as of coffee substitutes (barley and chicory), to roasters were subjected to quotas. The rare imports of foreign coffees in the immediate postwar period were negotiated on a state-by-state basis.

The years 1948 to 1954 saw a return to greater trade freedom. Import taxes were eliminated, foreign coffee could enter freely into France, and exports of colonial coffee outside of the empire were authorized. These measures of market opening were mostly a result of rising world coffee prices which reduced the need for colonial protection.

But from 1955 to 1958 protective measures made a comeback. A 20 percent tax on foreign coffee financed an equalization fund for colonial coffee. Coffee producers in the colonies benefited from export subsidies for exports to the "dollar zone." In 1955, a National Fund for the Price Regularization of Overseas Products (Fonds National de Régularisation des Cours des Produits d'Outre-mer) was created, and minimum export ratios were set for the colonies (Côte d'Ivoire: one ton for every four tons going to France; Madagascar: one ton for every five; Cameroon and Guinea: one for six). The year 1956 saw the birth of stabilization funds in Côte d'Ivoire, Cameroon, Guinea, and French Equatorial Africa. Finally, in 1958 import quotas on coffee from the "franc zone" were established, with a guaranteed price 30 percent higher than global prices.

Source: Daviron, 1993.

Mobilization of "native agriculture"

The shock of the First World War, and the failure of plantations in French Africa led to debates in colonial circles on the role that, what was then called "native agriculture" could play (Denys, 1918). The colonial administration little by little resigned itself to the fact that it would be African farmers who supplied the metropole (Daviron, 2010). Nonetheless, there was no question of giving up the governance of the new form of agriculture.

A wide panoply of measures was experimented to reach the targets set by the metropole. Studying a product such as cotton shows the extent to which the years between 1905 and 1920 were a period of intense experimentation. Promotion of cotton farming began with the creation of the Colonial Cotton Association (Association Cotonnière Coloniale—ACC) "founded in 1903, by members of the General Syndicate of the French Cotton Industry (Syndicat Général de l'Industrie Cotonnière Française) in order to free our industry, both from the economic servitude imposed by the obligation to purchase all of its raw material from foreign countries, and from the fear it felt of being one day deprived of this raw material" (Lavit, 1937: 311). Before 1913, the association's activities were very limited—crop experiments and setting up ginning factories (nineteen in total in all the colonies)—but real collaboration with the colonial government to promote cotton farming was bolstered when the war broke out.

Five instruments were generally used to mobilize native agriculture:

- Support: establishment of experimental farms, setting up technical advice, and seed distribution.
- Constraint: this was the means often used to encourage the uptake of cotton farming, and involved either an obligation to plant cotton or a prohibition from uprooting cotton, along with promoting mono-cropping to facilitate surveillance work.
- Taxation: creating an obligation to pay taxes, either by head or by family, and therefore making it necessary to earn cash, was widely used to incentivize adoption of "cash crops" (to use the colonial term) which could be sold.
- Population displacement and organization of internal migration towards development projects: the Office of Niger is a good example. The Office whose goal was the development of cotton and cereal production in irrigated zones, is an illustration of the "native colonization" policy that led to the displacement of significant parts of the population, for example Mossi from Upper Volta moved towards the interior Niger delta (van Beusekom, 1997).
- Cooperatives: the creation of farmer "associations" was a means for the colonial administration to structure various activities: dissemination of agricultural techniques, cereal storage, construction of rural infrastructure. "Native prudential societies" (*sociétés indigènes de prévoyance*) were thus set up in the 1920s in the French African colonies (Chauveau, 1994).

It should be noted, however, that the colonial administration had very few resources for government. There were two levels of "distance" in how colonial governance was exercised: the first level was geographic distance (the colonies were literally "*outre-mer*," overseas), the second level was linked to the shortage of human resources. The colonial administration did not have the means to be close to those it was supposed to govern. Thus, the promotion of "tradition," of "African culture," and of "local chiefs" was aimed at stabilizing colonial societies and fostering local aides for governance. Sara Berry ironically describes this form of colonization as "hegemony on a shoestring" (Berry, 1992).

Organization of value chains

Under the autarky strategy, a whole range of organizations specialized in single-product value chains (or *filières*) sprung up, generally under the initiative of three types of actors:

- Initiatives from French industrialists who sought to secure supply chains for their factories and thereby promote increased production of specific products by the empire. Cotton was the textbook example. The Colonial Cotton Association (ACC in its French acronym) was created in 1903, copying the model of the British Cotton Growing Association, with the aim of promoting the development of cotton farming in the French colonies, thus ending dependence on American cotton. The first ACC president was Robert Esnault-Pelterie, president of the General Syndicate of the French Cotton Industry.
- Initiatives by the public sector seeking to guarantee supply chains to France for military purposes, and therefore once again aimed at stimulating production within the empire. This was the case for tropical wood needed for manufacturing helixes of war planes. Research was set up from the First World War to test different species of wood.
- Initiatives by French planters with plantations in the colonies concerned about protecting their ventures from competition from other production zones. Rubber was the best example of this. A French Rubber Institut (Institut Français de Caoutchouc—IFC) was created in 1936,[2] steered by the Union of Rubber Planters of Indochina (Union des Planteurs de Caoutchouc de l'Indochine—UPCI). Its first president, Philippe Langlois-Berthelot, was also president of the Rivaud Group's Society of Plantations of Indochina, which was the biggest conglomerate at the time. The Rubber Institute was part of a mechanism that complemented the international agreement signed in 1934 to regulate production and trade of natural rubber to stabilize global prices.

The various initiatives converged during the Second World War, a period during which the Vichy government promoted corporatist policies. Those years were marked by the establishment of numerous institutions which would persist after the end of the war (Daviron, 2016). Indeed, the postwar years amplified the trend of organization by value chain, by articulating private economic interests with the states around "colonial

---

[2] The IFC started its research activities in the promises of the Collège de France, and then in 1939 bought a building situated on 42 Scheffer Street, Paris, where the French agricultural research institute CIRAD is headquartered today.

products," and all the more so now that considerable public funds were mobilized (through plans and the FIDES fund). This enabled infrastructure projects and land development efforts, and bolstered operational research which (also) targeted native producers, all still in liaison with agricultural firms. The logic of territorial specialization in one product dominated the management of metropolitan supply chains (cotton from French Sudan; coffee from Côte d'Ivoire and Madagascar, peanuts from Senegal, bananas from Guinea, rubber from Indochina, copra from Oceania, etc.) This strategy reinforced the articulation between applied agronomic research structured by product, and offices providing support and marketing which were also specialized by product. The promotion of cotton, which like coffee and cocoa had the specificity of being farmed by African producers, was reorganized. Two distinct but closely linked entities were created to replace the Cotton Union of the French Empire (Union Cotonnière de l'Empire Français): the Institute for Research on Cotton and Textiles (Institut de Recherche sur le Coton et Textiles) in 1946, and the French Company of Textiles (Compagnie Française des Textiles) in 1949. Finally, in 1958 the French Institute for Coffee and Cocoa (Institut Français du Café et du Cacao) was founded, dedicated to promoting these crops in the colonies.

Mission accomplished!

The imperial autarky strategy implemented by France can be considered a success. Between 1913 and 1938, the share of the empire in food imports into the metropole rose from 29 percent to 71 percent, while on an international level, the share of colonial territories (grossly estimated by summing exports from Africa, Asia, and Oceania) rose only from 26 percent to 34 percent of global exports.

By 1938, colonial autarky was practically achieved for food biomass. It was consolidated in 1958. Progress was particularly remarkable for coffee, cocoa, and fruits (Table 14.1).

Oilseeds were a special case, because they changed category over the period to become essentially food products, and among them, peanuts (50 percent of oilseeds) and palm oil were mainly supplied by African colonies. Flax whose usage remained exclusively non-food, was still sourced from Argentina.

Cotton, on the other hand, despite being a darling of colonial policy, was an outright failure. In effect, tropical wood excepted, and to a lesser extent also rubber (plantations in Southeast Asia suffered political instability), non-food biomass was the weak point in the quest for autarky.

The general success of the autarky strategy was mainly a result of native agriculture—with the exception of rubber. Measures to support and stabilize prices encouraged growth in colonial production much more than technical assistance to producers. Christophe Bonneuil who closely studied the work undertaken by French agronomists argues that they focused too much on their experimental stations relying on seed and variety improvements as instruments of change (Bonneuil, 1999). Seeds are a good example of what Bruno Latour (1995) terms immutable mobiles (things which travel with their characteristics). Thanks to seeds, the "black peasants" of distant places were supposed to be "mobilized" and connected to "calculation rooms" of the colonial administration!

Table 14.1 Share of the empire in French metropolitan imports of agricultural products (in % of total imports for each product)

	1913	1929	1938	1958
Wines	57	84	97	71
Cereals	12	29	80	78
Dessert fruits	17	14	49	72
Coffee	2	4	43	76
Cocoa	2	56	88	85
Oilseeds	25	25	54	78
Sugar	100	16	78	94
Cotton	0.1	2	3.6	18
Silk and silk floss	0.2	3	2	0
Wool	3.2	3	5	1
Skins	11	17	16	15
Wood	4.5	11	28	40
Rubber	14	9	25	31

Source: adapted from Marseille, 1984: 55.

Japan and the "Greater East Asia co-prosperity sphere"

The United States was what Japan sought to be.

(Barnhart, 2013: 50)

Japan emerged as a major global player at the end of the nineteenth century. To counteract inequitable trade agreements imposed by Western powers, Japan rapidly developed its military capacity which allowed it, at the turn of the century, and within a ten-year interval, to defeat Chinese and Russian armies, thus acquiring an empire. Contrary to European powers whose overseas expansion was mainly based on opportunities and uncoordinated initiatives, Japan's advance was a result of a strategy aimed at countering the threat that these same European powers represented (Peattie, 1988: 218).

The forced opening of Japan

In 1853, the threat took on a very concrete form: the arrival of an American military fleet demanding that Japan open up to trade with the West. This came after more than two centuries of deliberate isolation, a period referred to as Tokugawa, or Edo, the old name for the capital city Tokyo.

Tokugawa Japan had many aspects of a feudal society. Two hundred lords (*daimyo*) controlled its territory between then and collected rent in rice, which they used to pay the samurais they managed. They themselves swore allegiance to the Tokugawa *shogun* who was based in Edo (which already had 1 million inhabitants in the early eighteenth century!). Between 1635 and 1853 the country stood out for its almost total voluntary reclusion. Japanese did not have the right to leave Japan, nor foreigners to enter, and the rare trade that took place was done on the artificial island of Dejima, in the Nagasaki bay, with access authorized only to a few Dutch and Chinese traders.[3]

Japan therefore, unlike Europe did not build its growth on external resources, but on intensive labor technologies, which substituted for increasingly scarce natural resources. Japanese agriculture was based on farms that were one to two hectares in dimension, with twice-a-year harvests achieved through intensive and qualified labor, essentially carried out by the household: irrigation networks, drainage, transplanting, etc. (Francks, 2016: 64). Farmland, moreover, benefited from considerable quantities of fertilizers: night soil brought from the city, soymeal and fish meal (quantities were much higher than in Europe at the time: 2.5 tons per hectare during the second half of the nineteenth century) (Sugihara, 2003).[4]

Akira Hayami also shows population growth occurred concomitantly with a reduction in the number of draft animals in agriculture, these being replaced by additional human labor (Hayami, 2001). To designate this intensification, Hayami coined the concept of "industrious revolution," which, as we saw earlier, was taken up by Jan de Vries to characterize changes in England and the United Provinces during the eighteenth century. Despite its feudal organization, Japan was rich in markets and trade activities. According to Penelope Francks, practically all households, including rural ones, were involved in market exchanges. A wholesale market, which some consider as being the first futures market, existed in Osaka for rice sold by the lords. The behavior of prices in the different regions shows that the market for rice was an integrated one at the national level. Monetization was also advanced during the Tokugawa era, and even included financial instruments like bills of exchange (Francks, 2016: 42). From the eighteenth century, manufacturing activities also developed among the peasantry, and new networks of traders collected products from them: threads, fabric, pottery, *sake*, paper, salt, indigo, wood objects, and so on. Small factories were also established; these employed young girls from peasant families, signing contracts directly with their parents. As in England and the United Provinces in the eighteenth century (Part 3), Japan also experienced a revolution in consumption (sugar, *sake*, tobacco, and tea) which pushed households to engage in market-based activities. GDP per capita is estimated to have grown by around 40 percent during the Tokugawa era.

Westerners thus were not gate-crashing on a sleeping beauty in a castle in the mid-nineteenth century. The forced economic opening, and the new industrial

---

[3] Restrictions imposed on trade in 1630 put an end to the active participation of Japan in intra-Asian trade, which had mainly consisted in silver exports towards China and imports of silks and guns, as well as cottons from India.

[4] In actuality, fish meal involved mobilizing biomass from outside the Japanese territory (Gruber, 2014: 412). Marine resources generally played an important role in supplying Japan with biomass, as had been the case for the United Provinces in their ascent.

path taken by Japan following the restoration of Meiji imperial power in 1868, was built on a foundation of preexisting dynamics. Kenneth Pomeranz (2000) and, above all, Kaoru Sugihara (2013) show how East Asia took a different path towards industrialization from that taken by Western Europe, a path that was labor-intensive. Industrialization was not preceded in Asia, as it had been in England, by an increase in agricultural labor productivity, which then provided both the necessary capital and workforce. Technologies imported from Europe were adapted to the Japanese context. Industrialization relied on labor that was cheaper than in Europe or the United States.[5] Under Asia's "forced free exchange," its industrialization was also driven by exports of cheap consumer goods (textiles in particular) to low-income Asian markets, including China and India. These exports played as important a role in Japan's industrialization as did the domestic market.

The labor-intensive industrialization of Meiji era Japan also maintained its rural base. The urban population only represented 18 percent of the population in 1920 and 38 percent in 1940 (compared to 65 percent in the United Kingdom as early as 1870) (Sugihara, 2013: 36).

The evolution of external trade between 1880 and 1930 shows the transformations that Japan's economy underwent after the country opened up. At the end of the nineteenth century, Japan exported above all biomass, mainly silk and tea, two historical long-distance trade products from Asia. There were also, in much lower quantities, exports of sea products (kelp and sardines), mineral products (coal and copper), and pottery. Cotton and wool threads, as well as fabrics accounted for most imports. Fifty years later, silk still led in exports, but it was followed closely by cotton fabrics, and rayon fabrics had already emerged in fourth place. As for imports, in 1930 these were dominated by raw materials, and among these biomass products (cotton, sugar, rice, soybeans and soymeal, wood, and wheat) and fossil fuels in the forms of petrol and coal (Table 14.2). Japan's economic and military security was dependent on the supply of these imported products; and its colonial policy was designed to secure such supply.

Colonization of Hokkaido island: A dress rehearsal

Even before its colonial expansion phase, Japan had experienced territorial expansion through its colonization of the large northern island, Hokkaido. This colonization started timidly under the Tokugawa era, and gained momentum during the Meiji period. Colonization of Hokkaido satisfied three objectives:

- Affirming Japanese sovereignty over the island, which had been recognized by Russia in 1867.
- Providing the nation with natural resources it needed.

---

[5] For Kaoru Sugihara, the considerable gap between labor costs in Japan and Western countries in the late nineteenth century can be explained partly by lower fossil fuel (coal) usage and partly by the fact that there were many more emigration opportunities for Europeans than there were for Japanese, given the restrictions imposed on Asian migrants in North America and Australia.

Table 14.2 Composition of Japan's international trade in 1880 and 1930 (in thousands of yen)

1880				1930			
Exports		Imports		Exports		Imports	
Raw silk	8,607	Cotton thread	7,700	Raw silk	416,647	Cotton	369,261
Tea	7,498	Wool fabric	5,792	Cotton fabric	316,993	Sugar	169.873
Silk waste	1,291	Cotton fabric	5,523	Silk fabric	79,343	Rice	167,785
Kelp	697	Kerosene	1,400	Rayon fabric	34,934	Petrol	83,629
Sardines	648	Iron products	1,079	Pottery	27,171	Soymeal	58,960
Pottery	475	Rice	434	Sugar	26,735	Soybean	54,153
Copper	474	Cotton	171	Coal	26,200	Lumber	53,058
Coal	460	Rails	163	Flour	22,704	Wheat	41,509
				Cotton thread	15,032	Coal	36,890
Total	28,396		36,626		1,871,176		2,005,399

Source: Yasuba, 1996: 546.

- Providing "employment" for former samurai, the *shizoku* who had been made redundant as the Meiji restoration had stripped them of their historical privileges. Later it became a case of finding employment for communities impoverished by the 1873 privatization of land ownership and tax reforms, which meant taxes were now due in cash.

For Sideny Xu Lu, colonization of Hokkaido gave form to the Meiji regime's ambitions to create settler colonies. It was during this period that Japanese government discourse on the necessity of its surplus population emigrating towards territories presented as empty or underpopulated emerged (Lu, 2016: 251). The Hokkaido Development Agency (Kairakushi) managed all the financial and political affairs of the island from 1869 to 1882. In 1874, the agency created a settler soldiers program initially targeted at the *shizoku*, which later opened up to other willing migrants. In 1880, funding of the agency accounted for 7 percent of Japanese state expenditure.[6]

An American expert, Horace Capron, between 1871 and 1875 shared his experience of implementing resettlement schemes for Native American communities, following the conquest of Texas, with the agency, in order to "find a best way to utilize the

---

[6] In 1899, 7,337 households, or around 40,000 people, were settled under this program (Hirano, 2015: 199). They received land, seeds, and a three-year supply of rice and vegetables.

resources of Eso [Hokkaïdo] for the material enrichment and elevation of imperial Japan" (Hirano, 2015: 200).

In 1872, Japan promulgated a land law which declared Hokkaido *terra nullius*, that is "land without master" (無主の地) (ibid.: 197) as the United Kingdom had done earlier in many of its colonies (Lindqvist, 2007). The development agency was disbanded in 1886 and a more "liberal" strategy was adopted for Hokkaido's colonization. Private capital investment was now encouraged to create large-scale farms along the American model. The island, sometimes presented as the America of Japan (Lu, 2016: 262), went through a phase of rapid land grabbing. Land ownership quickly came to be concentrated in the hands of a few Tokyo residents while migrants were now hired as wage workers. According to Robert Calvet, the colonization of Hokkaido is estimated to have enabled an increase in Japan's farm area by 3 million hectares, which effectively doubled available land. In 1900, 600,000 Japanese emigrated to the island, and in 1913 its population had reached 1.8 million inhabitants. In the space of a few decades, the tragically banal scenario was played out once again: the indigenous population of hunter-gatherers, the Ainu, were practically wiped out through disease and exclusion from their hunting and fishing grounds.[7]

Taiwan and Korea: The first victories over China

The Sino-Japanese War of 1894 resulted in the occupation of Taiwan by Japan, and in Korean independence. In the years that followed, Korea would be subject to increasing Japanese influence and then finally annexed in 1910 (under the name Chosen). Through this acquisition of two colonies, Japan attained a status of colonial power—meaning that it was a "civilized" nation of the same standing as France, England, or Germany (Myers and Peattie, 1984).

In both cases, colonization also involved the settlement of migrants. At the end of the 1930s, 16 to 17 percent of farmland in the two countries was farmed by Japanese. The introduction of a land registry had enabled the confiscation of lands that were not claimed, as well as lands belonging to the Yi dynasty in Korea. Two agrarian reforms with opposing thrusts were also implemented. In Taiwan reforms favored mainly small landowners, whose numbers increased. In Korea on the other hand, property was concentrated and small landowners were transformed into farmers for large owners.

Taiwan and Korea also played an important role in supplying Japan with rice during the interwar period. The "rice riots" of 1918 give birth to the Program for Rice Development (Sanmai Zoshoku Keikaku) aimed at achieving self-sufficiency for Japan's empire (Hayami, 1988: 36). Improved seeds were distributed (Japonica rice in Korea, Hora Mai rice in Taiwan), and irrigation and fertilizer use were promoted, with notable effects on yields (Table 14.3).

---

[7] The Japanese administration undertook to "reform" the way of life of the Ainu, prohibiting use of their language, making school obligatory, and restricting them to farming on plots provided by the government. In 1899, a law for the protection of Ainu was passed, but it only covered those who were farmers.

Table 14.3 Select agricultural performance indicators in Korea and Taiwan, 1915–39

	1915–19	1925–9	1935–9
Rice yields (kg/ha)			
Korea	1,384	1,553	2,084
Taiwan	1,413	1,642	2,052
Sugarcane yields (kg/ha)			
Taiwan	30,973	49,919	70,332
Variance in fertilizer consumption (base 100 in 1915–19)			
Korea	100	457	1,129
Taiwan	100	167	315

Source: Lee, 2010: 28.

Japan, which imported rice from Indochina and Burma at the beginning of the twentieth century, increasingly obtained its rice from its own colonies. The share of imports in Japanese rice supplies grew from 2 to 19 percent between 1912 and 1938, the year when all imported rice was sourced from the colonies (Ericson, 2015: 345). These colonies exported roughly half of their harvests to Japan (in 1943, this peaked at 64 percent in Korea) (Table 14.4).

In Taiwan, sugarcane was also a key product for Japan's biomass supply chain. Between 1903 and 1940, sugar production of the island jumped from 30,000 to 1.1 million tons. Sugarcane here was not grown in large plantations, but on small family farms under contract for factories owned by Japanese capital (Table 14.5).

Manchuria: Rail imperialism and frontiers

Manchuria, a region in northeastern China, bordering Korea, Mongolia, and Russia, remained a vast pastoral land until the mid-nineteenth century. The Qing dynasty (1644–1912), whose distant origins were linked to the region, had always restricted Chinese migration, reserving to Manchurians the exploitation of furs, pearls, and other extractive resources.

The rivalry for the control of Manchuria is a remarkable example of "rail imperialism," which was a common trend in the nineteenth century, mainly under English impetus, and continued to play out in the early twentieth century. Investment in railroads, which as previously indicated were the main destination for English capital during their hegemony, offered both an opportunity to generate value with one's capital and the possibility to control and profit from the territories that the rail would pass through. In Manchuria, two powers competed fiercely for control of the railroad: Russia and Japan (Chou, 1971).

The Russians arrived first. As early as 1860, they signed a treaty with China, which opened the port of Newchwang to the Russians. At the same time, Manchuria gradually

Table 14.4 Rice supply in Japan, 1912–38 (in thousands of *koku*)*

	1912	1930	1938
Japanese production	51,711	59,557	52,820
Imports from			
Korea	246	5,167	10,149
Taiwan	652	2,185	4,970
Others	211	1,248	151
% imports/consumption	2	13	19
Share of colonies in imports	81	85	99

Source: Lee, 2010: 20.

*The *koku* (石) is a traditional Japanese unit of measure of volume that continued to be used for some cases. In 1891, Japan adopted the international system of units, and redefined the *koku* as precisely: one *koku* = 240,100 / 1, 331 = 180.39 liters (source: https://fr.wikipedia.org/wiki/Koku, accessed August 16, 2024).

Table 14.5 Origin of Japanese imports of sugar, rice, and soybean, average for 1934–8 (in %)

	Sugar	**Rice**	**Soybean**
Taiwan	86	31	–
Korea	–	67	21
Manchuria	–	–	79
Other countries	14 (Indonesia)	2	–
Total in 1000 t.	1016	2024	825

Source: Sharron, 1957: 86.

opened up to colonization by the Chinese population (Han). Japan's victory over China in 1894–5 strengthened somewhat the Sino-Russian alliance. Between 1897 and 1903, Russia built the Chinese Eastern Railway which crossed Manchuria to link up with the Trans-Siberian (in Chita), with Vladivostok to the east, and Port Arthur, the base of the Russian military fleet (Liaodong Peninsula, Dalian), to the south.

In 1905, Japan won the war against Russia. Its aim in this war was to establish its hold over Manchuria and to conserve control over Korea. For Russia the defeat meant losing the Harbin–Port Arthur line to the Japanese company "Southern Manchurian Railways." Russia also lost Port Arthur which was renamed Ryojun by the Japanese who took control of the entire Liaodong Peninsula where they founded three new ports: Antung, Tatungkow, and Dairen (Dalian in Chinese). The last became the leading economic pole of Japan in the region, and soon China's second biggest port after Shanghai.

It was against this background that the soybean became an economic engine. Soy accounted for 81 percent of exports from the region in 1899, and still for 60 percent in 1929. Soybeans had long been grown in northeastern China. The beans were used in various forms as food, its oils for both food and non-food purposes (lighting, lubrication, waterproofing), and soymeal as a fertilizer as far as the southeast of the country for sugarcane farming (Shaw, 1911: 9). Soymeal was exported towards Japan from the late nineteenth century, but it was exports of soybean towards Europe from 1908, out of Vladivostok and Dairen (Wolff, 2000: 246), which gave a real boost to production. Volumes exported grew by 11 percent each year between 1907 and 1929 as the frontier advanced, driven by mass immigration, mostly composed of Chinese. The Manchurian population grew from 4 million in 1872 to 20 million in 1914, and 31 million in 1930. Cultivated surface areas grew in similar proportions. But the frontier was exhausted around 1930, and exports of soybeans and soy oil peaked in 1931 (at 3.1 and 0.2 million tons respectively) and those of soymeal in 1927 (2.2 million tons), and then drastically fell (Table 14.6).

A full-fledged international soy market thus existed from the first decade of the twentieth century. Manchuria then was practically the sole producer and remained so until the Second World War. Initially the reserve of Japan, the soy market gradually shifted towards Europe (Table 14.7). During the interwar period, the main importers, alongside Japan, were Germany, Great Britain, Denmark, and the Netherlands (Prodöhl, 2013: 466). In these countries, soybeans were sold for oil (for making margarine), and above all for soymeal which supplied animal farms, whose importance we discussed earlier. In the early 1930s, 40 to 50 percent of soybean produced in Manchuria was exported towards Germany (Landy, 1938: 18). The autarky strategy and "neighborhood imperialism," however, strongly reduced the share going to Germany from 1933 on.

The "rail imperialism" phase ended for Manchuria in 1931.[8] Japanese troops invaded the region and established an independent state under the name of the "Great Manchu State (Manchukuo) of China." Aixinjueluo Puyi, the last emperor of the Qing dynasty, in 1934 became emperor of Manchukuo.

Taking power over Manchuria was aimed at securing Japanese supply chains. Japanese military elite had discovered, along with the rest of the world, the logic of total war. Germany's defeat in 1918 had demonstrated the necessity to ensure Japan's economic autonomy, which implied developing a "modern" industrial apparatus, as well as ensuring reliable supply of raw materials to the country (Barnhart, 2013). Japan's handicap, with respect to European powers, and even more with respect to the United States, was its lack of mineral resources. The country's leaders very quickly judged it necessary to take control of new territories, that is, of parts of China. The creation

---

[8] On September 18, 1931, a section of the railway belonging to the Japanese company South Manchuria Railways was destroyed near Mukden (Shenyang today). This event, referred to as the "Mukden Incident" (or the Manchuria Incident), served as a pretext for the Japanese invasion. Readers of Tintin will remember images of the attack presented in the book *The Blue Lotus*. Likewise, for more details on the incredible story of Manchukuo, watch Bernardo Bertolucci's film *The Last Emperor* (France, Hong Kong, Italy, Great Britain, 1987).

Table 14.6 Population (in thousands of inhabitants), surface area (in thousands of ha), and soy exports (in thousands of tons) in Manchuria, 1872–1940

	1872	1914	1930	1940
Population	4,454	19,652	31,300	38,400
Surface area	1,752	9,501	12,576	15,251
Soybean exports				
Beans	82	672	2,473	2,390
Meal	44	805	1,673	960
Oil	3	49	149	63

Source: Eckstein et al., 1974: 248 and 263.

Table 14.7 Soy beans: Share of Manchuria in global exports and of Japan in global imports (in %)

	1909–13	1924–8	1934–6
Manchuria's share in global exports	89	90	91
Japan's share in global exports	39	37	33

Source: Institut International de l'Agriculture, 1939: 74 and 76.

of Manchukuo was a first step.[9] It came along with massive Japanese investment, including in the mining and industrial sectors.[10] Japan's annual growth rate reached 7 percent between 1936 and 1944, and the share of agriculture in GDP fell to 29 percent in 1941.

The new invasion of China in 1937 was the second step. But Japan was too ambitious! That invasion ended up triggering the Pacific War, which resulted in the imposition of an embargo by the United States and the Netherlands on petrol exports towards Japan. Japan thus decided to take control of Southeast Asia in order to access the resources it needed to continue its war in China. After having entered Indochina with the agreement of the Vichy government, Japan attempted to reinforce its position by destroying the American fleet at Pearl Harbor, and then invaded the Philippines, Malaysia, Indonesia, and Burma. The end of the story is known to all.

---

[9] The ambition was to create a multi-ethnic society, starting with a considerable influx of Japanese immigrants, which would seal the pan-Asian alliance against Western expansionism. This gave rise to the concept of New Order in East Asia in 1938 (Japan, Manchukuo, Korea, Taiwan, and Northern China), then in 1940 the concept of the Great East Asian co-Prosperity Sphere, which included Southeast and Southern Asia, and aimed at building a grand alliance against the West, a self-sufficient alliance led by Japan, in which colonies did not benefit from any of the autonomy that the dominions had within the British Empire (Lee, 2010).

[10] For Prasenjit Duara, keeping Manchukouo as an independent—but militarily and economically dominated—state prefigured the form of imperialism that the United States and USSR would deploy after the Second World War (Duara, 2006).

15

The United States: From the legendary frontier to resolution of the long farm crisis

Frontiers are constitutive of the United States. The frontier dynamic was manifest right from the colonial period, especially in the south within the slave plantation model. It would resurge during the Civil War (or the War of Secession as the French tend to refer to it). Four essential laws were voted in 1862, in the absence of representatives from the southern states: the law establishing the United States Department of Agriculture, in other words a ministry of agriculture, the Morill Act, the Homestead Act, and the Pacific Railroad Act. These acts gave impetus to, and provided the framework for the colonization of the Midwest by "pioneers" who had arrived from Europe. The biomass exporting potential of the country got a new boost, and later Hollywood cinema would have a limitless subject matter to exploit.

A generation later, the United States reached the end of the reserve of "virgin" lands, at a time when the country had urbanized and industrialized, and new exporting countries had emerged onto the global market. These developments, taken together, gradually reduced the United States' capacity to export biomass. From 1920, the country even became a net importer of biomass, and its farming sector faced a double crisis—economic and ecological. The state intervention response was proportional to the severity of the crisis, and it would give rise to a new model of agricultural growth whose wellspring lay in the utilization of oil.

The lure of the frontier, until 1897

In the nineteenth century, the United States was the neo-European settler state *par excellence*. The continental territory, constituted in 1867, occupied a surface area of 9.8 million square kilometers, as much land as Europe to West of the Urals (10.2 million km^2). Its population grew from 4 to 32 million between the time the republic was created and when the civil war broke out. By 1914, the population had reached 99 million (USDC 1976: 8). Between 1820 and 1870, 6 million Europeans immigrated to the United States, and another 23 million between 1870 and 1920.

The US territory was constituted over the course of the nineteenth century, at a slow pace prior to 1870, and then accelerating as the Great Plains were colonized and native inhabitants brushed aside by military might as European migrants advanced.

The development of farming in this country-continent is a classic case study of the frontier dynamic: land that was formerly prairie and forest was farmed, turning the United States into a country with large biomass surpluses.

The steam engine and the advancing railroad were essential elements in this "conquest" and enabled the surplus to be exported towards Europe (Figure 15.1). According to Fred Cottrell:

> It was in the United States that steam had a chance to show the outlines of a pattern of civilization based on large surpluses from sources other than food and sail. The early coastal settlements and the plantations of the south, being parcel of the English system, developed few railroads, and such as there were served British trade. But with the westward movement a new kind of civilization began to emerge. The American "age of steel" was an outgrowth of the use of cheap transportation, furnished by steam, in the canals, and the Ohio River, plus the development of railroads.
>
> (Cottrell, 1970: 118)

Throughout the whole nineteenth century and until 1914, US agricultural growth was driven by long-distance trade, and the country was a major global supplier of agricultural products. The United States' contribution to Europe's biomass supply, however, had two distinct phases.

Until the 1860s, the colonies that were later to become the United States, were a component within the larger Atlantic plantation complex (Curtin, 1990). This phase preceded the Industrial Revolution. English colonies established on the continent were a direct part of the complex, as they produced products such as tobacco (Virginia), rice, indigo (South Carolina), cotton (mainly in the Sea Islands), and sugar (Louisiana) on slave plantations. Some colonies, such as New England also participated indirectly in the complex by providing food products (flour and meat), wood, and horses to the southern slave plantations and the English Caribbean. The dramatic expansion of cotton farming, the most prosperous activity of late-phase slavery, prolonged the lifespan of this system beyond independence and beyond abolition of the slave trade. In 1835, cotton accounted for two-thirds of total US exports, and maintained such significant proportions until the 1861 Civil War.

From 1860, exports of food products from the northern and Midwest states increased. They peaked between 1878 and 1900. In 1897, when the advancing frontier reached its end, cereals accounted for 32 percent of biomass exports, of which 8 percent for corn and 20 percent for wheat (grain and flour), and 21 percent for animal products, of which 12 percent for just pork products (bacon, ham, and lard) (Bureau of the Census, 1902: 202–6). The prominence of pig farm products, and in particular of lard, was closely linked to corn farming. Pigs in the Midwest were in many senses a form of condensed corn (Taylor, 1932: 92). Cincinnati became the world capital of deli meats.

Cotton did not disappear from US exports during this second phase. It is true that after the Civil War, cotton's share in biomass exports fell to around 20–30 percent, but it would then remain at that level until the First World War, which in reality meant

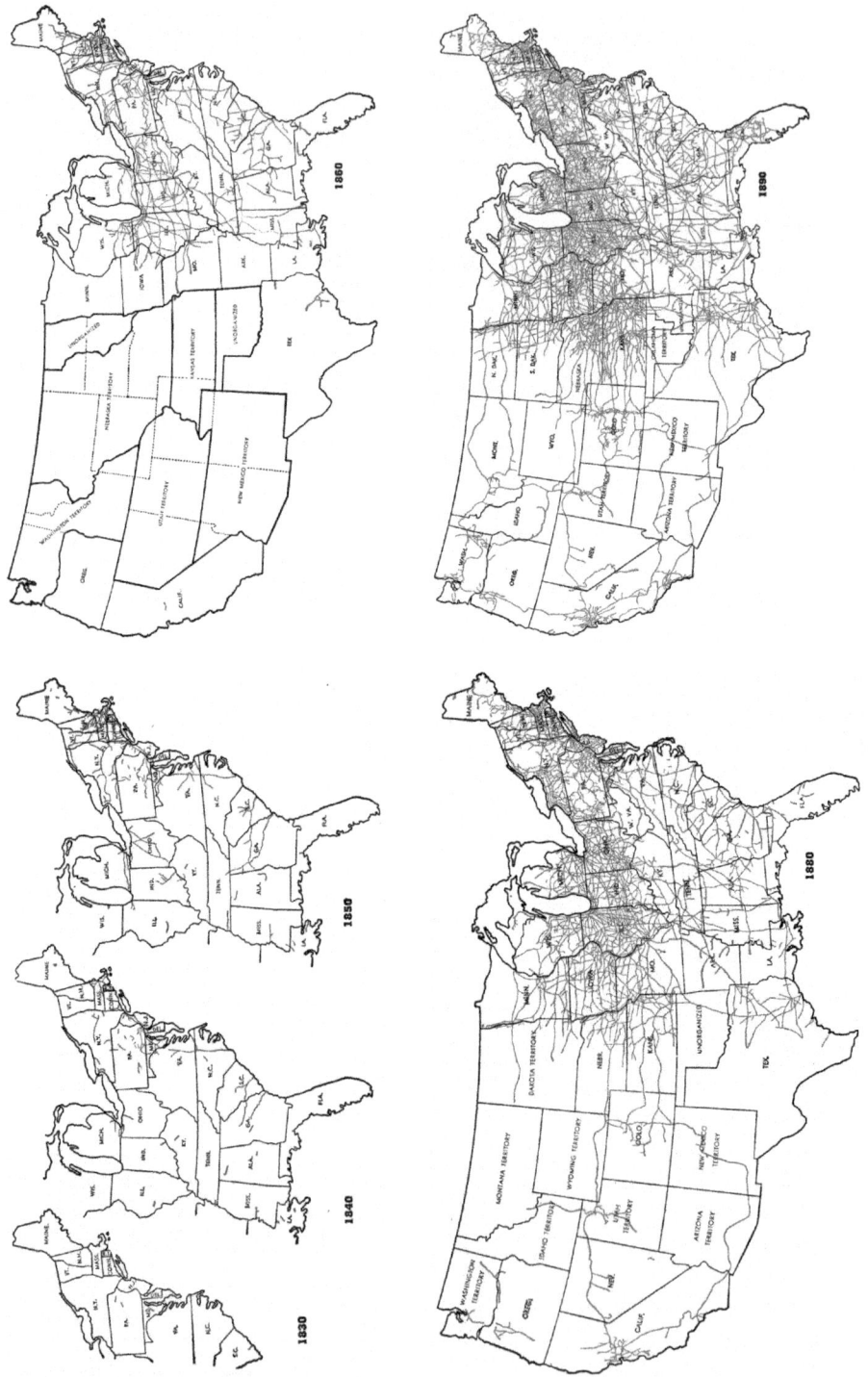

Figure 15.1 The conquest of the west, progress of rail networks in the United States from 1830 to 1890

Source: adapted from "Maps showing the progressive development of US Rail Roads, 1830–1950" (http://www.cprr.org/, accessed September 19, 2024).

there was a considerable increase in production. Several factors contributed to the revival of cotton farming, which was now based on sharecropping: the opening up of new regions to cotton farming (Texas and Arkansas), at the expense of other crops usually grown in monocrop "small white" farms (Danbom, 1995: 126).

Between 1850 and 1900, cotton crop acreage grew by a factor of three and the number of farms by a factor of four (Table 15.1). The American frontier was a process that involved grabbing land and establishing individual property rights. From the first laws in 1785 to the 1862 Homestead Act,[1] the legislative framework evolved, progressively reducing the minimum size of allotments and their prices so as to favor the establishment of family farms, and to regularize the status of pioneers who lacked land titles. The importance of this legislative framework, however, was not preponderant because in reality, of the 500 million acres of public land distributed between 1860 and 1900, only 80 million were distributed under the Homestead Act—100 million hectares were auctioned off and the rest attributed to state governments and rail companies in exchange for investment. In many other cases, land was sold to speculators who then sold it on to farmers or ranchers.

In 1900, at the height of the colonization process, the agriculture of American pioneers was characterized by labor productivity much higher than in their European countries of origin. Paul Bairoch estimated that productivity stood at 41 million net calories per male farm worker in the United States, compared to 25 million in Germany, 21 million in the United Kingdom, and 17 million in France (Bairoch, 1999: 136). The high fertility of "virgin" land was one factor, but there was also the systematic use of horses as draft animals, instead of oxen as was the continental European practice. Use of horses was facilitated by the abundance of land available for growing oats, indispensable for feeding horses (15 million hectares of oats in 1900 compared to 21 million for wheat). We saw earlier with England the significant productivity gains linked to using horses.

The productivity gap also resulted from a continuous process of mechanization that was made possible by the generalized use of horses, and made necessary by the chronic shortages of labor that characterized the frontier economy. Table 15.2 gives an idea of the gradual mechanization of harvesting, an operation that is particularly labor-intensive over a short period of time: the work day with a horse-drawn combine harvester with four horses was fifty times more productive than harvesting with a sickle.

During the entire first half of the nineteenth century, production grew proportionally to the quantity of additional land and labor, without any gains in yields nor in productivity. Mechanization did not really take off until after 1850 and the Civil War which sent men to the front, and therefore created incentives for replacing human

---

[1] The Homestead Act, promulgated during the Civil War, allowed any individual over the age of twenty-one, or head of family holding American citizenship or intending to obtain it, who could justify that they had occupied a plot of land for five years, to claim it as private property, and this for up to 65 hectares, by paying $10. If the family had lived on the land at least six months, it could also, without any wait period, purchase the land at the relatively low price of $1.25 per acre ($3 per hectare).

Table 15.1 US agricultural production 1800–1900

	1800	1850	1870	1900
Cultivated land area (millions ha)[a]	–	118	164	340
Number of farms (in thousands)[b]	335	1,449	2,660	5,737
Active agricultural population (in thousands)[b]	1,140	4,902	6,850	10,912
Gross agricultural production (millions of 1910–14 dollars)[b]	333	1,442	2,479	5,740

Sources: [a] Carter et al., 2006; [b] Towne and Rasmussen, 1960: 266–7.

Table 15.2 Developments in wheat harvesting in the nineteenth century

	Date of emergence	Area harvested per day (ha)
Sickle		0.1 to 0.2
Harvest cradle	Late eighteenth	0.4
Reaper	1834	0.6 to 1
Harvester	1850	1.2 to 1.6
2-horse combine harvester	1873	3.2
4-horse combine harvester	1881	7.3

Source: Hayami and Ruttan, 1985: 80.

labor with animal labor provided by horses and mules, and to increase the types of equipment harnessed to such (Rasmussen, 1962; Danbom, 1995: 111–12). This was an ideal situation for John Deere, who had just developed in 1837 the cast steel plow for prairie land: by 1857, his factory was producing 10,000 plows a year. McCormick introduced the harvester in 1850, and by 1860 there were harness machines for all the steps of wheat farming. The shortage of cowboys also explains the success of barbed wire fencing, invented in 1874 (Razac, 2000: 12).

Mechanization of harnessed equipment experienced a brief period of gigantism. Between 1870 and 1910, several immense cereal farm projects in California and the Dakotas, called "wheat bonanza farms" (Briggs, 1932), used harvesters pulled by forty horses or more. None of these large farms lasted long, and they are mainly significant as new proof that wage-labor farms were less competitive than market-oriented family farms (Friedmann, 1978).

It is difficult to assess how the performance of the agricultural sector as a whole evolved. A retrospective study by the USDA (Cooper, Barton et al., 1947) gave very optimistic estimates of increases in labor productivity for corn, wheat, and cotton, showing rises starting in the early nineteenth century, but stagnation during the last few decades preceding the First World War (Table 15.3). Estimated yields for their part remained clearly stable through the period, which is fully coherent with the logic of frontier economies. The exception for cotton is due to the early rarefication of new

Table 15.3 Yields and labor productivity for wheat, corn, and cotton, 1800–1914

	1800	1840	1880	1900	1910–14
Wheat					
Yield (bushels/acre)*	15	15	13	14	14
Productivity (bushels/hour)	0.27	0.42	0.65	0.92	0.94
Corn					
Yield (bushels*/acre)	25	25	26	26	26
Productivity (bushels/hour)	0.29	0.36	0.55	0.68	0.74
Cotton					
Yield (pounds/acre)	154	154	196	198	210
Productivity (bale/hour)	0.8	1.1	1.6	1.7	1.7

Sources: adapted from Cooper et al., 1947: 3; Rasmussen, 1962, for 1910–14.

*A bushel equals roughly 35 or 36 liters. Imperial bushel = 36.368 l, US bushel = 35.239 l.

spaces that could be colonized, and thus forced recourse to fertilizers, guano, and phosphates (Earle, 1992), which in turn, explains the robustness of yields.[2]

Fossil-fuel driven agricultural growth: Genesis of the model through policy support

The long American farm crisis

The United States is the typical example of the logic of mining soils that was so constitutive of the frontier economy. European migrants, both large planters and small peasants, adopted a form of itinerant agriculture, as had Native Americans before them (Cronon, 2011), leaving depleted lands after a few years to return to forest or become thin pastureland, and move on to plant new land (Cunfer, 2004: 561).

The problem of soil depletion was an old one in the south on the cotton and tobacco plantations producing for Europe:

> In the upland areas from Virginia to Georgia the expansion of cotton and tobacco left behind an ever-widening circle of lands suffering from soil exhaustion. Year after year the old lands were depleted until it was no longer profitable to farm

---

[2] Towne and Rasmussen, who base their analysis on the value of all agricultural production, and not individual products, note increases only after 1850: 25 percent between 1850 and 1870, and 45 percent between 1870 and 1900 (Towne and Rasmussen, 1960). They find that yields also rose, although more modestly. The relatively good yields for cotton is one explanation, in addition to the shift towards products with higher value added thanks to the growth of urban markets.

them. By 1850 a large proportion of Virginia and Maryland east of the Blue Ridge was a waste of old fields and abandoned lands covered with underbrush and young cedars.

(Gray and Thompson, 1933, cited by Towne and Rasmussen, 1960: 258)

The same pattern was repeated region after region, and crop after crop, as the frontier advanced, to the great despair of Justus Liebig.[3]

The instructive family history of Thir (Theyren, Austria 1884, Finley, Kansas 1937)

This is the sad story of George Thir, who left northeastern Austria and arrived in Kansas in 1884 aged 19.

Theyren, his Austrian home village, had practiced agriculture for centuries alongside considerable animal farming, which ensured sustainable maintenance of soil fertility (Krausmann, 2004). Population density in the village was high (forty-two inhabitants/km^2) and the average size of farms small. A three-year crop rotation system was still being used. Forests counted for a third of land area in the commune. These were considered part of the commons and served as pasture, thus allowing a transfer of fertility towards the cultivated fields. In Finley county, in Kansas, where the Thir family settled, population density stood at two inhabitants per square kilometer and the farm they established measured 65 hectares. Thirty-five years later, in 1915, their farm measured 259 hectares. In Theyren, in Austria, cereal yields stood at about 820 kilograms per hectare, which along with the animal products, provided a yield of 2.9 GJ per hectare and energy equivalent of 9 GJ per farm worker. In the new farm in Thir, in Kansas, cereal yields in 1895 reached 1,270 kilograms per hectare, energy yield 4.6 GJ and energy production per farm worker 168 GJ, almost twenty times greater than in Austria! The first harvest in effect benefited from the new planting effect of prairie land which had accumulated nutrients over millennia. However, in the absence of livestock, the stock of nutrients was not renewed. According to the authors, only 27 percent of the nitrogen exported was restituted. The situation therefore quickly deteriorated. On average in Finley county, yields fell from 1,687 kilograms per hectare to 1,244 in 1915, 736 in 1935 and to less than 400 kilograms at the end of the 1930s. That is two times less that what the Thir family obtained in Austria in the mid-nineteenth century (Cunfer and Krausmann, 2009)!

---

[3] "The effects produced by this wasteful farming are perhaps nowhere more evident than in America. There, the first settlers who came to New York State, to Pennsylvania, Virginia, Maryland, etc. found vast stretches of land which, after ploughing and sowing just once gave them for several consecutive years a series of harvests of grain and tobacco, without any need for the farmer to think of restituting to the soil what the harvests had taken from it. We know now what happened to these so fertile lands. In less than two generations, these productive plains were transformed into real deserts, and in many districts they were in such a poor state that even if they lay in fallow for a whole century, they would still not be able to yield a decent harvest of cereals" (Liebig, 1862: 168).

Th comparison with Austria in the box shows how the disintegration of crop and animal farming that prevailed in North America contributed to lower soil fertility. For Jeremy Adelman (1994), the institutional and economic logic of the frontier brought with it an opposition between crop farming and animal farming. Ranchers, who settled before farmers, wanted to maintain open spaces without fences or roads, and above all without disgruntled farmers upset about their harvests being destroyed by animals. They did not produce any fodder, convinced that the natural prairie provided sufficiently. In 1916, land areas growing fodder accounted for just 150,000 acres compared to 9 million acres for wheat. Crop farmers for their part, did not see the benefit of troubling themselves with a herd of animals, which implied significant investments to acquire cattle, and required large land areas and long delays before any income was generated.

The mining of soil fertility was based on the illusion of the availability of unlimited quantities of "virgin" lands. The hard reality of a finite world, or at least a finite continent, however, made itself evident from 1896, the year when Frederick Jackson Turner announced the end of the American frontier (Turner, 1986 [1893]).[4] All the available data (cultivated land areas, production, etc.) confirmed that Americans now lived in a finite world. The invasion of the Philippines (1898), Central American escapades, and lunar expeditions that followed were but pale imitations of the conquest of the Far West.

The effects on agriculture were felt immediately: labor productivity, land areas, and harvests stagnated from 1900 on.[5] Given the rate of population growth, per capita production fell sharply from this date on (Figure 15.2)—by 20 percent in constant

Figure 15.2 Gross per capita agricultural production in the United States, 1869–1941 (in constant 1913 $)

Source: Lipsey, 1963.

[4] Turner's essay is above all known for claiming that the pioneer spirit played a foundational role in American democracy. This thesis has been widely contested (see notably McNeill, 1992).
[5] The growth rate of agricultural production fell by 2.5 percent per year between 1869 and 1904, to reach 0.6 percent for the 1905 to 1940 period. Per capita production (measured in constant dollars) fell by a third between 1900 and the 1930s.

dollars between the end of the nineteenth century and the 1920s. But prices rose sufficiently during the first years of the twentieth century so that the first two decades of the century were a period of prosperity in terms of farm incomes, and for many observers, constituted the golden age of American agriculture (Danbom, 1995: 162–7).

The difficulties US agriculture faced resulted at first in a spike in imports. Domestic consumption, in effect, had grown strongly driven by a rising population, rapid urbanization, and accompanying industrialization. From this point of view, the United States was confronted with the same equation that Europeans had faced in the nineteenth century, where economic growth was closely linked to biomass imports. Imported products included both exotic food products, like coffee and cocoa, as well as sugar and vegetable oils (copra, etc.), and rubber.

On the other hand, until the 1920s the value of exports (wheat, lard, corn, cotton, etc.) did not fall and even grew robustly during the First World War. But after that a long downward slide began until 1941, bringing with it a biomass trade deficit that would grow ever deeper with time (Figure 15.3).

In European markets, American agriculture had to compete against products from territories with younger frontiers—like Argentina, Canada, or Australia in the wheat market, and various colonies in fatty matter markets—who had been stimulated by the price increases during the First World War. The market difficulties that lard faced, as recounted by Alonzo E. Taylor, were a good illustration of this competition:

> It is no longer possible to produce palatable animal fat by means of the "corn-hog combination" with less expenditure of land and human labor than in any other way. The vegetable oils have entered into the picture. We recognize that corn is the most efficient plant in the Temperate Zone in fixing the energy of the sun's rays and

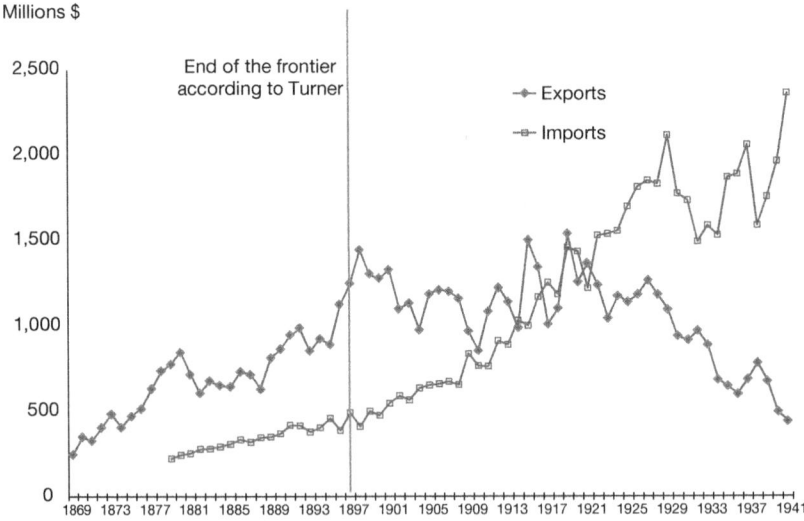

Figure 15.3 Agricultural product exports and imports in the United States, 1869–1941 (in constant 1913 $)

Source: Lipsey, 1963.

that the hog is the most efficient animal for converting the sun-energy of corn into fat; but these circumstances lose much of their importance when we recall that the tropical sun produces fats and oils directly at a lower cost than the sun in the Temperate Zone and that a one-stage production of fats and oils from sunshine is inherently cheaper than a two-stage production involving domesticated animals.

(Taylor, 1932: 7)

Rising production in new territories, combined with the slowing down of European imports due to autarky policies adopted there,[6] in the 1920s led to a fall in international prices which turned into an outright crash after 1929. Net agricultural income was divided by three in the space of just three years, falling from $6.1 to $2 billion (Carter et al., 2006)! The demonstration of the material limits of the mining agricultural growth model took a dramatic turn from the 1930s with the Dust Bowl phenomenon. The term was a literal description of an American Midwest ravaged by terrible sand storms. Deprived of all organic matter, arable soil had turned light and dry, easily carried away by the wind. At a time when no more new land was available, it became fully clear that the outright plunder of resource richness had led American agriculture to a dead-end. Millions of farmers lost their farms without any possibilities of settling further west.[7] John Steinbeck's novels and Dorothea Lange's photographs presented the plight of these farmers to the whole world.

How agriculture became a state-organized and funded sector

During the entire period of the advancing frontier, state intervention in agricultural markets was minimal, despite the action of organizations like the Grange, or the electoral successes of the agrarian People's Party (or the Populist Party) in the 1890s, who protested against the excess levies by intermediaries and railroad companies. The first series of measures, aimed at regulating markets and controlling prices, were adopted during the First World War. In effect, difficulties in importing cereals from Argentina or India led English demand for cereals to shift towards North American production. Prices doubled between summer 1916 and summer 1917. On August 10, 1917, the Food Control Act founded an agency to control the price of food products and fuels. The future president, Herbert Hoover, was designated as the "boss" of Food Administration.

---

[6] To add further confusion to the state of agricultural markets, there was also a profound shift in American demand due to a decrease in human food calorie consumption (thanks to heating, and less physical work) (Wolman, 1929). Additionally, organic resources were increasingly substituted by mineral resources (the combustion engine led to the disappearance of horses from towns and farms), and the first synthetic products (dyes, fibers) emerged.

[7] This phenomenon was not unique to the United States. Russia had experienced the same problem earlier, as shown by this description of drought on the steppes in 1892: "The dry autumn …, the snowless winter and, finally, the dry spring turned the top layer of … earth partly into a dry dust, [and] partly into a fine-grained, crumbly, powder, which, with the onset of strong storms in April, lost their hold, and were raised up in whole clouds, concealing the sun's rays and turning day into night. Witnesses unanimously testified that the phenomenon had such a dreadful and frightening character that everyone expected 'the end of the world'" (Zemyatchenskii, 1894, cited by Moon, 2005: 158).

But as soon as the war ended, a new problem of overproduction and falling prices dominated American public debate.[8] The McNary-Haugen Bill to establish public procurement of surpluses was debated several times between 1924 and 1928. In 1929, the Federal Farm Bureau was created, with the primary task of financing purchase and storage activities by cooperatives in order to shore up prices.

Lastly, against a background of a profound crisis, Roosevelt adopted as soon as he arrived in power in 1933 the first Agriculture Adjustment Act, which introduced the concept of income parity between the industrial sector and the agricultural sector (Backman, 1938). For the Secretary of State for Agriculture under the New Deal, Henry Wallace, falling prices and the ecological crisis were two strongly interlinked problems (Wallace, 1934). He thus ardently pushed for a set-aside land policy, to both reduce production and stop soil degradation. Stabilization of agricultural prices could, and should also, contribute to the preservation of resources (Ciriacy-Wantrup, 1946: 412–52).

Measures to support prices and control production quantities were put in place for "basic" products: corn, wheat, cotton, tobacco, pigs, milk, and rice. The aim was to increase farmers' incomes, and therefore through administrative means, balance supply and demand for agricultural products on the domestic market, using production and consumption forecasts.

Several provisions concerning farm debt were put in place from 1933 and the Credit Commodity Corporation (CCC) was created to provide seasonal loans that could be paid back either in cash or in kind (with farm produce) in the event that prices fell below a certain threshold. In addition to the CCC, also created were the Farm Credit Administration (which bought up loans of indebted farmers from banks and transformed them into longer-term loans at lower rates), the Farms Security Administration (which provided loans to farmers who did not have sufficient collateral for commercial banks), the Resettlement Administration (which bought and withdrew from production land that was highly degraded, and resettled the owners of such lands in regions with more favorable conditions), and lastly, the Agriculture Adjustment Administration. The latter institution worked to directly control volumes produced by limiting the land area under cultivation by setting aside a portion of land in each farm. The set-aside land was imposed as a prerequisite to benefit from the guaranteed income offered by the CCC. A grant was provided to compensate the lost income from the set-aside; from 1936, soil preservation measures had to be implemented to access this grant.

The three components of a new fossil fuel technical-based model

Mechanical: The tractor replaced the horse, and electricity, humans

Agricultural production benefited from a new source of kinetic energy in the form of the steam engine. At first it was used to pull cables to which were attached plows, and

---

[8] American agriculture faced challenges less from overproduction, but more from competition from new producer countries that had emerged from the beginning of the century. The emergence of some of these countries received a boost during the First World War. However, interpreting the source of the problem as being overproduction legitimized state intervention to purchase surpluses.

then in the late nineteenth century, it was used especially for moving four-wheeled machines. Five thousand such machines were produced in 1900, but they were extremely heavy and guzzled combustibles (wood or coal), and thus had low uptake. The first trials on machines powered by internal combustion engines were undertaken in 1901, but the weight problem persisted. The first model still weighed 10 tons. The name "tractor" was coined in 1906. In 1909, thirty companies had offerings of these heavy internal combustion engine "tractors," in total producing about 2,000 tractors a year (Cochrane, 1979: 109). That's the history in a nutshell!

But things really got to a start in 1913, year in which the Bull, the first tractor with a spark ignition engine, small and easy to maneuver, was put on the market. The Fordson, sold by Ford from 1917, then became the first "tractor of the masses" (Olmstead and Rhode, 2001: 668). Growth in number of tractors was very rapid in the decades that followed. By 1945, there were 2.5 million tractors.

The number of horses and mules on farms followed a similar but opposite trajectory. They fell from 26 million in 1913 to 11 million in 1945 (Table 15.4). But substitution was not total. For several decades, the two sources of mechanical energy existed side-by-side on farms. Their capacities, however, were far from comparable: in 1945, the available tractor park generated more than 63 million horsepower of energy.[9] Agriculture therefore had at its disposal (if we include the 12 million horses still in use) three times more mechanical energy than in 1913. These figures start sketching out how energy yields of farming activity would fall over time (Part 5).

In addition to the rising numbers of tractors, there was an increase in the ways that tractors were used, and the transformations they brought about. Several innovations widened the range of services provided by tractors. Initially they had been used mainly for plowing, but soon tractors were also used for threshing, harvesting, and transporting. The combine harvester, first horse-drawn and later automated, completed the mechanization of the harvest process, combining cutting and threshing. Machines drawn by five or six horses had from the beginning of the century enabled mechanization of corn harvesting (and even earlier, binders to make sheaves). In the late 1920s, the upgrade in power fostered the production of machines made to be latched onto tractors. The cost of mechanized harvesting was estimated to be half that of manual harvesting (Bogue, 1983: 19–20). By 1938, half of the US wheat crop was

Table 15.4 Number of horses and mules, and number of tractors (in thousands), 1913–45

	1913–1915	1929–1931	1945
Horses and mules	26,120	19,112	11,950
Number of tractors	19	914	2,354
Power (in horsepower)	18	21,804	63,600

Sources: USDA, Agricultural Statistics, different years for the number of horses and tractors; Hayami and Ruttan, 1985, for the power of tractors.

[9] It should be noted that, in 1913, on average tractors were less powerful than horses. It was therefore a leap of faith to persevere!

harvested by combine harvester (Olmstead and Rhode, 2000: 707), and 35 percent of the corn harvest in Iowa and 43 percent in Illinois was mechanized. The Second World War and the labor shortages that resulted encouraged further mechanization and motorization, which accelerated even more for cereals and spread to new crops. This was particularly the case for cotton. International Harvester developed a machine that reduced labor time from 125 to 25 hours per acre (Cochrane, 1979: 126).

The expansion of the electricity grid provided a new source of energy even in rural areas in the late 1930s. In 1935, when only 11 percent of farms had electricity, the Roosevelt administration established the Rural Electrification Administration, which offered subsidized loans to businesses and to local electricity cooperatives. The scheme was a resounding success, and at the end of the Second World War, 86 percent of farms were electrified (Grigg, 1992: 50). With electricity came lighting and radio, revolutions in the daily lives of farmers.[10] Milking cows, which was a highly labor-intensive task benefited greatly from electricity access: milking machines, of which the first models had been commercialized at the beginning of the century, now spread very quickly. And their numbers doubled between 1940 and 1945.

Chemical: Nitrogen and pesticides

Before the First World War, the organic chemistry industry in the United States did not count for much. Dyes were the key sector in the peacetime chemical industry, but domestic production (3,000 tons) did not even cover an eighth of consumption. The United States were also very far behind Germany in terms of chemistry being taught at university level, and even more in industrial research. The country was then, by far, the leading client of Germany's chemical industry.

Dye production in the United States suffered from an absence of protection, due to pressure from the textile industry for access to German dyes which were much cheaper. German businesses, for their part, protected themselves first by filing patents in the United States, where they were granted without any obligation to use them, thus allowing the firms to continue selling dyes made in Germany without fear of competition. Bayer thus invested in a factory in New York State in 1905, but did not produce any dyes there until 1909.

In 1914, the outbreak of war in Europe, along with the blockade against Germany by Great Britain, underscored not only the dependence of the textile industry on dyes, but also the close links between dye manufacturing and munition manufacturing, both of which relied on the same intermediate products derived from coal.

Chemical firms present on American soil then engaged in a race for German technologies. Until the United States entered the war, German firms invested in American factories for dye production, as well as production of medicines. DuPont,[11] formerly specialized in dynamite production, hired a certain Mr. Livinstein, of German

---

[10] For an enthusiastic historical account of these developments, see Joris Ivens' documentary "Power and the Land" (1940) available on YouTube: https://www.youtube.com/watch?v=-KVwWAJBJUA (accessed August 16, 2024).
[11] Its full name was "E.I. du Pont de Nemours and Company."

origin, who before the war had managed German firms based in England (abandoned after the conflict broke out), and thus obtained a slice of German know-how. The American firm Cyanamid, at the outbreak of hostilities, rushed to buy from Germany equipment necessary for ammonia production before their export was prohibited. German subsidiaries or their staff were also integrated into American firms (some BASF staff moved to DuPont).

But a great part of technological transfer resulted from action by the American administration. In 1917, when the United States entered the war, patents held by German citizens were suspended, and in October of that year, the act regarding trade with enemies created the Office of Alien Property Custodian (APC) to manage the property of foreigners, and businesses held by persons of enemy nationality. The APC soon took possession of the patents and resold these to American firms, so as to cut the ties linking the American chemical industry to Germany (Wilkins, 2000: 300); 4,500 chemical patents held by the Germans were thus seized and sold by APC, including in 1919 after the armistice, at very low prices to the Chemical Foundation, property of American chemical industrialists under the leadership of DuPont.[12]

After the war, everything accelerated. Dye production now benefited from protection from imports. German firms were thus obliged to negotiate cooperation agreements with American firms, offering a transfer of technologies in exchange for access to the market. The United States also recruited many German chemists keen to leave their crisis-stricken country, and set up industrial laboratories (DuPont was the first to do so in 1921). American dye production thus increased tenfold between 1914 and 1922 (Hugill and Bachmann, 2005: 180), by which time it covered 93 percent of domestic consumption.

Prosperity of the American chemical industry was further boosted in the years that followed by two very favorable factors: access to cheap petroleum as a raw material, and the development of an automobile industry, hungry for new materials (paints, additives for rubber for tires, antifreeze for refrigerants, additives for gasoline).

Nitrogen

American agriculture, from the late nineteenth century, and even earlier in cotton plantations, experienced increasing difficulties linked to poor soil fertility. The end of the frontier meant that there was no other choice for those who wanted to continue farming, but to import the nutrients that their soils lacked. Guano, as mentioned earlier, was one of the products used in plantations in the US south from 1840 on. Its consumption peaked at 194,000 tons in 1855. The rapid depletion of guano deposits led to a reduction in imports which fluctuated at around 30,000 tons per year throughout

---

[12] The expropriation of German patents would be confirmed in 1919 by an article in the Treaty of Versailles on intellectual property rights. Despite the legal action that German firms took in courts after the war, they were never able to recuperate their seized assets (factories or patents) nor did they receive compensation (Wilkins, 2000). Moreover, under the reparations imposed by the Treaty of Versailles, the Allies took possession of half of the stock of dyes in Germany at the time of the armistice and claimed a quarter of the dye produced over the next five years (Steen, 2000: 329).

the first decade of the twentieth century. Nitrates from Chile then stepped in, as had also been the case in Europe. In 1913, the United States was the second largest importer after Germany (Gini et al., 1921: 228).

Alongside guano and nitrate imports, American farming also benefited from nitrate fertilizers produced from waste from slaughterhouses, fisheries, and oilseed processing plants. The steel industry additionally provided ammonium sulfate (170,000 tons in 1913), and several firms developed methods for fixing atmospheric nitrogen, either through the electric arc technique, or using cyanimide, both of which used great quantities of electricity (a plant was built for this in 1910 near the Niagara Falls).

The war, once again, shook things up. When the war broke out, there was a rush for nitrate imports from Chile. Imported volumes doubled between 1913 and 1916, making the United States Chile's biggest buyer by far. But this distant supply source was not sufficient. In 1916, the US Congress passed the National Defense Act which provided a legal framework to prepare America's entry into the war. Section 124 of this act, titled "Nitrate supply" gave the president full powers to develop through any possible means nitrate production necessary for the manufacture of munitions and fertilizer. Timothy Johnson, for this reason, calls the National Defense Act "one of the most important pieces of agricultural legislation in the nation's history" (Johnson, 2016: 211). The concrete results, however, were disappointing. Two factory projects were launched, financed respectively for $22 and $12 million. The first, based on the cyanimide procedure, involved the construction of a dam on the Tennessee River, which was finished just before armistice. The second, the Haber project, was handicapped by the incapacity of American chemists to replicate the Haber–Bosch procedure.

But it was out of the question to give up: in 1919, the Fixed Nitrogen Research Laboratory (FNLR) was established, initially within the War Secretariat, but later in 1921 transferred to the United States Department of Agriculture (USDA). The laboratory would later become the Division of Chemistry under the USDA. Mastery by the United States of the technique of nitrogen fixing would finally be achieved within this laboratory. Benefiting from access to patents and manufacturing secrets taken from German factories during the war, the laboratory soon focused all its efforts on the Haber–Bosch procedure. The know-how was then transferred to various firms in the American chemical industry, including the General Chemical Company, which, after having failed during the war, became the leading ammonia producer in the United States until the Second World War, thanks to this transfer of technology. Two factories produced synthetic ammonia in 1924; by 1932 the number had grown to eleven. The Second World War and its endless demand for explosives relaunched ammonia production, and six new factories were built, many of which belonged directly to the government. At the end of the war, the state controlled 60 percent of synthetic ammonia production in the country (Mehring et al., 1957: 12–13),[13] with synthetic nitrogen production experiencing spectacular growth between the end of the First and Second World Wars: from 700 tons in 1922, to 103,000 tons in 1932, 438,000

---

[13] These factories were transferred to the private sector after the war for symbolic sums.

tons in 1941, and 1 million in 1945! In 1945, 95 percent of nitrogen contained in nitrate fertilizers was of chemical origin, and 80 percent was produced through the Haber-Bosch procedure.

Pesticides

The development of organic pesticides and their widespread uptake in farming constitutes the last innovation clearly linked to fossil energies. The chemical industry once again played a key role in developing and disseminating these new inputs.

Before synthetic pesticides were developed, plant extracts were used to protect crops: nicotine, rotenone, and pyrethrum (Perkins, 1982). Mineral substances—petrol or sulfur—were also used for their effects on pests. In the late nineteenth century, new products from mineral chemistry were put on the market: lead arsenate, Paris green (initially a pigment), Bordeaux mixture, and calcium arsenate, whose efficacy against the boll weevil (that ravaged cotton plants) was established in 1917, and met with great success in the United States until the Second World War.

As Edmund Russell (2001) has shown, insecticides from organic synthesis were a direct by-product of the First World War. The concentration of men on war fronts, and their infestation with parasitic insects, coupled with the understanding that was simultaneously gained about their role in spreading diseases such as typhoid, which decimated troops, gave rise to the total war approach being transposed to the fight against insects. Organic chemistry, whose development was strongly driven by the war and its demand for explosives and combat gases, provided new molecules which would substitute the mineral compounds that had been used as insecticides until then. The most illustrious example of these new molecules was without a doubt paradichlorobenzene (against moths), which was initially a by-product from the manufacture of picric acid used in the production of explosives. Paradichlorobenzene was available in large quantities and tested by American entomologists in 1916 and 1917, and then quickly put on the market (Russell, 2001).

But the real star was DDT (dichloro-diphenyl-trichloroethane). Synthetized for the first time in 1874 in Germany, and developed in 1938 by the chemist Mueller of the Swiss firm Geigy (Mueller would receive the Nobel prize in medicine in 1948), as protection for wool (Perkins, 1982), DDT quickly proved itself to be a very effective insecticide that was both cheap and (apparently) inoffensive for humans. From 1942, DDT was used by the Swiss army to treat refugees against fleas. Passed on to American officials, DDT was tested by the USDA from 1942, in its quest for substitutes to rotenone and pyrethrum whose importation had stopped. DDT production was initially reserved for the army. It was widely used during the war to protect military and civilian personnel from mosquitoes that were carriers of malaria, and from the carriers of typhoid. After the war, it was used in agriculture, forestry, and gardening.

Uptake of pesticides made it possible to abandon crop rotation, to plant seeds closer, and to apply fertilizers without attracting more insects. Faced with the miraculous efficacy of these new instruments for controlling harmful insects, other methods were pushed to the margins.

Biological: the soybean–hybrid corn pair

Two major biological innovations were the last components in the "technological package" described thus far. These were soybean and hybrid corn. Both these "plants" did not exist in the United States at the beginning of the twentieth century. Soybean was an exotic plant in the true sense, introduced from Asia (see preceding chapter). Hybrid corn was an invention, a creation. But both resulted from a long-term public strategy.

The improvement of varieties was one of the foundations of state intervention in the agricultural sector.[14] From 1835, the US Patent Office, in charge of registering patents, launched the creation of a world collection of varieties. Henry Ellsworth, director of the Office from 1836 to 1849 considered the introduction and dissemination of exotic plants as important as the protection of mechanical inventions and obtained from Congress funds for collecting and disseminating seeds and plants, as well as agricultural statistics. At the same time, the navy undertook exploration missions in the field of botany. Thus, the Perry naval expedition, famous for forcing Japanese ports to open up to the West, also brought back large quantities of Asian seeds and plants.

The imported exotic plants were disseminated widely across the country. During the twenty years that followed the creation of the collection, 2.5 million packets of seeds were sent to famers, leading Jack Kloppenburg to conclude that: "There is no question that the Patent Office program of plant introduction resulted in substantial infusions of foreign germplasm into the American gene pool prior to the Civil War" (Kloppenburg, 2005: 56). In 1862, year of the Homestead Act, the agricultural division of the US Patent Office became the United States Department of Agriculture (USDA), that is the American ministry for agriculture (Danbom, 1995: 112).[15] The USDA took over and expanded the collection and dissemination of information and plants. In 1892, it established a section on the introduction of seeds and plants, responsible for coordinating all exploration and introduction activities. Over the course of twenty-five years, it organized forty-eight expeditions the world over.[16]

In addition to introducing exotic plants, a public experiment facility was established that made it possible to do tests on the plants, and more widely, to improve crop techniques. From 1862 (once again), the Morrill Land Grand Act attributed land to universities in exchange for them setting up agricultural experiments. In 1887, the Hatch Experiment Statin Act provided each state with an experimental station. This was the USDA formula—agriculture colleges and experimental stations—which developed the knowledge and techniques of the new American agriculture. Lastly in 1914, the Smith Lever Act founded an extension system that was halfway between an agricultural university and a research station.

The development of soybean crop was a direct outcome of this type of organization. The Oriental Agricultural Exploration Expedition, undertaken from 1929 to

---

[14] See Jack Kloppenburg's (2005) excellent book on this subject—a lot of the historical information presented in this section is taken from there.
[15] We can understand better through this history why the idea that genes could be patented became common so easily.
[16] The USDA would continue sending seeds out until 1924.

1931, enabled samples of 4,500 different varieties in China, Japan, and Korea to be collected and tested in the United States (Prodöhl, 2013: 476). The USDA and the experimental stations carried out the selection: Illinois State University played a key role in improving varieties and mechanizing soybean farming.[17] Soybean's key advantage then was its capacity to fix nitrogen.

Soybean was first planted in the early 1930s. The crop then occupied 1 percent of cultivated land. The development of the soybean crop was encouraged by the restrictions imposed on other crops under the Agriculture Adjustment Act and by programs for soil conservation. Soybeans then were mainly used as a green fertilizer or as fodder. Only 40 percent of the planted crop was harvested as beans at the end of the 1930s.

Then the war came and changed things, once again! Ninety percent of soy planted was soon used for its bean, as improved refining techniques (by German chemists) had enabled unpleasant odors to be removed from soy oil, which was now used to produce margarine and other products for human consumption (Fornari, 1979: 246). The crop thus experienced renewed expansion, which responded to the US deficit in fatty matter and the difficulties it experienced procuring supplies from the Philippines and Indonesia. In 1941, soybean was added to the list of crops benefiting from price support.

But that was not all! The secret weapon for soybean, decisive in the crop's expansion, was the efficiency of soymeal in animal nutrition. Soymeal was boosted by USDA research on the best suited rations for milk and pork meat production, and research on methods for crushing soybean. In the case of pork, the success of soymeal, rich in proteins, was linked directly to shifts in demand. From the 1930s, pig farming was no longer considered as a process to produce fatty matter in the form of lard as previously exposed, but chiefly as a process to produce meat. Protein-rich animal feed based on the corn–soybean combination was much better adapted for that than the previous diet based (almost) exclusively on corn.

The development of hybrid corn can be considered both as a product of public action in the field of improved varieties research, and as the first stage in the dramatic growth that was to come for seed companies.

The gains in yields enabled by hybridization, that is the crossing of two distinct lines of a same species, were understood as early as the nineteenth century, Charles Darwin himself having made a demonstration of the process (Bogue, 1983: 10). Research on hybrid varieties was systematized in the early twentieth century, with the rediscovery in 1900 of Mendel's laws, which fueled a real enthusiasm for hybridization techniques. These techniques no longer just limited themselves to selecting the "best" within a spontaneous diversity, but actually oriented, or in some cases, created diversity to achieve varietal improvement. This presented the use of "foreign" plants under a new light. The goal was no longer to acclimatize, or adapt, strategic exotic plants to

---

[17] In 1924, planting an acre required thirteen hours of human labor, twenty-nine hours of horse labor and three-quarters of an hour of tractor labor. In 1929, the first two values had fallen respectively to 4.2 and 2.4 hours (Dies, 1942: 36).

American conditions, but to introduce the characteristic of interest in an exotic plant into a local variety. It was no longer plants that were useful, but specifically some of their genes. Varietal improvement thus became gradually an affair for professionals from which farmers were excluded. Hybrid varieties of cross-pollinating plants like corn, whose descendants were attributed characteristics unpredictably, presented the additional advantage of "biologically" preventing farmers from using their own production as seeds, and thus obligating them to buy seeds each year. Hybrids thus opened up a seeds market that firms could engage in, undertaking research with the assurance their efforts would be remunerated.

For corn, it all started in 1908 when G.H. Shull, a researcher at the Carnegie Institute, produced a pure line, and then a hybrid through simple crossing. He was the one to give the name heterosis to the additional vigor that hybrids demonstrated. In 1918, the Connecticut experimental station produced the first double hybrid—that is a crossing of two hybrids originating from four "pure" lines—which made it possible to significantly increase the quantity of seeds produced. The double hybrid had yields that were 20 percent higher than those obtained through free pollination.

The dissemination of hybrids within the Corn Belt and the Midwest meant the development of new varieties adapted to the rigors of the climate. Henry C. Wallace, then Secretary for Agriculture, organized the selection of varieties in a collaborative framework between the federal level and the local level. He had as advisors his son, Henry A. Wallace, future Secretary for Agriculture, and later vice-president under Roosevelt, and chose a scientist favorable to double hybrids and private investment to direct the research program. The same Henry A. Wallace quickly grabbed the opportunity and created his own firm, Hi-Bred Seed Company, which later became Pioneer Hi-Bred International Inc., and commercialized the first hybrid corn in 1925. By 1938 in Iowa, more than half of corn acreage was planted with hybrid seeds. Nationwide, the percentage of corn acreage grown with hybrid seeds rose from 2.5 percent in 1935 to 25 percent in 1943.

There is debate among scholars as to why hybrids were so successful. For Richard Sutch, the enthusiasm of American farmers had more to do with infomercial campaigns by seed companies and the USDA than with immediate economic gains. He estimates that in Iowa yields for hybrids were between just 7 and 9 percent higher than those of seeds from free pollination (gains were higher, and by up to 100 percent, in drought periods when average yields fell) (Sutch, 2008: 10). David Danbom affirms that the set-aside land policy created a real obsession with increasing yields among farmers, as it was the only way to increase production, and therefore pushed them towards improved varieties, which for corn involved hybrids (Danbom, 1995: 235).

Conclusion

This period of rivalry was played out in two places, with the same two protagonists, the state and the chemical industry, working hand-in-hand. Their actions on the biomass market were complementary; the state administered the use and sourcing of biomass, while chemistry supplied substitutes.

State management of food supply chains, improvised in 1914–18, and refined during the Second World War, overall enabled the civilian population (with the exception of undesirable groups, and those in asylums and concentration camps who were deliberately starved) to survive in a context of resource shortages resulting from two wars in succession. The state management of agricultural markets also enabled American farmers to get through the overproduction crisis of the 1930s. States emerging from the "Thirty Year War" consolidated in their role as high priests of domestic food self-sufficiency. They would continue to play this regalian role until the beginning of the twenty-first century, giving wings, in countries that were nonetheless part of the "capitalist West" to plans, to ministries of planning, and to multiple interventions in agricultural produce markets.

> Indeed, the Third Reich can claim to have initiated the hybrid system of private ownership and state management that continues to prevail in European agriculture to this day.
>
> (Tooze, 2008: 176)

The dramatic rise of the chemical industry, prodigal child of coal and war, and soon fueled by petrol, was the decisive event of this period. The development of synthetic products, to substitute biomass, prepared the ground for agriculture's future specialization in food production. The synthesis of ammonia from atmospheric nitrogen made it possible to envisage addressing the problem of soil fertility without recourse to biomass transfers or imports of distant nitrates, and to imagine a solution for American agriculture's fertility crisis. But, during the period under study in this Part, ammonia was used above all to feed war machines with explosives.[1] The spread

---

[1] In 1920, the chief of the Bureau of Plant Industry at the USDA, W.A. Taylor, still wrote "the use of fertilizer will be an incidental and supplemental rather than a fundamental factor in the production of most staple crops. ... their place must always be subordinate to the use of animal and green manures in staple crop production." What foresight!

of the internal combustion engine, for tractors and personal vehicles, eliminated the use of biomass as a source of mechanical energy by eliminating horses in the space of a few decades from both country and town, along with the oat fields that were dedicated to them.

Germany may have claimed to be America's match, nonetheless the latter represented the model that Germany tried to emulate—a country-continent with the necessary resources for its own growth within its own territory. The year 1914 signaled the end of the first era of globalization, and for international trade the end of the key role it had played in the conquest of wealth and power.

Its vast territory, filled with a variety of resources, unscathed by the collective suicides ravaging Europe, became the core asset of the United States. The country had an abundance of farm and forest land, of coal, of mineral resources, and of oil—the guest star!—essential in the new "motorized war." They could, unconstrained, develop a chemical industrial complex based on their own resources, and on the scientific and technical potential of a defeated Germany, obtained thanks to a German "brain drain," but also thanks to the expropriation of patents and companies.

The transformations that the agricultural world went through after the Second World War were driven by techniques that in some cases had been developed as early as 1910, but whose uptake had been limited by the low farm incomes that prevailed until 1939 (Cochrane, 1979: 125): improved seeds and races, in particular hybrids (corn), mineral fertilizers, chemical pesticides, motorization and mechanization, and the uncoupling of crop farming and animal farming. The logic that drove these transformations was the product of a "hybridization" between American and European logics. The process of motorization and mechanization was an integral part of American farming history, which from the nineteenth century was characterized by labor shortages. The use of mineral fertilizers pursued the mining logic that had characterized frontier economies, but was based on German technology that had been developed to address the problem of limited farm land. Lastly, the shift towards industrial feed for cattle was an extension of the very American separation of animal production from plant production (cattle rearing in large extensive ranches, and grain in family farms along the Corn Belt), combined with the model of enclosed herding developed in Northwestern Europe.[2]

It was this hybrid model, precisely thanks to its hybrid nature, that would go on to conquer the world, under the name of conventional agriculture, as we will see in Part 5.

---

[2] During the interwar period, imports of soybean from Manchuria by Denmark, Germany, and the Netherlands grew sharply. Soymeal quickly gained prominence in animal feed: in Germany for example it accounted for 19 percent of meal used in animal feed in 1926, and 39 percent in 1928.

Part 5

Where we see agriculture, under America's hegemony, become "modern," "conventional," and food-focused, 1945–72

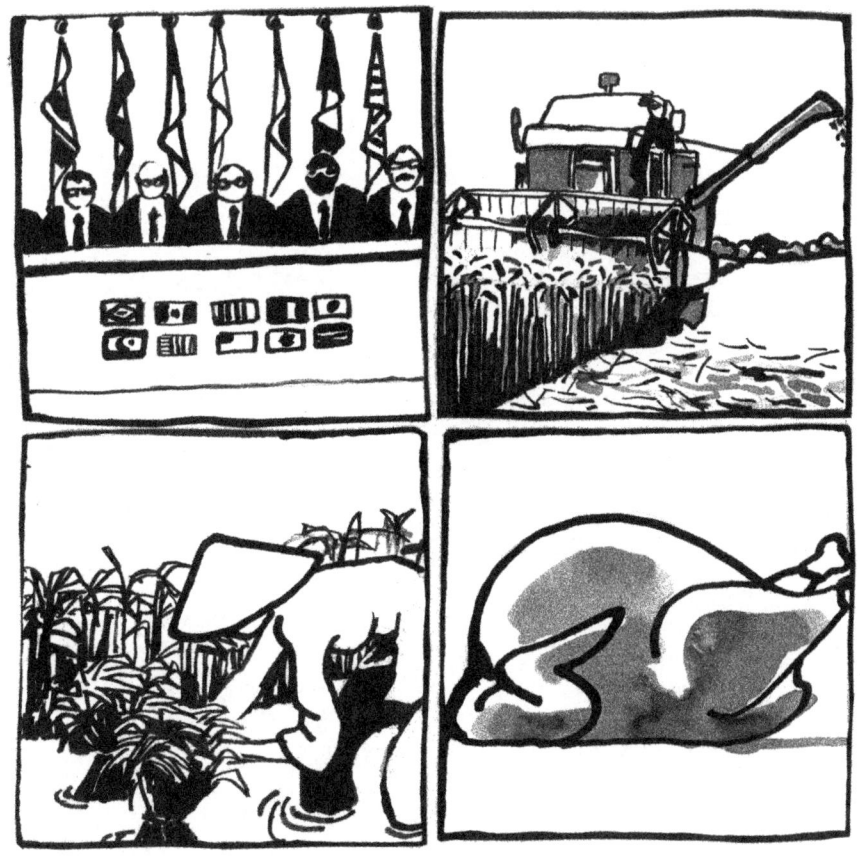

Introduction

In Part 5 we will cover the period from the end of the Second World War to the early 1970s. This period saw American hegemony enjoy its first apogee, and with this triumph came a dramatic deployment of a second phase of the mining metabolic regime, that was based on oil and natural gas. The year 1972 closes the period. This date may seem a bit premature to some readers, but that year signals the end of an economic logic that had dominated the postwar period: the end of cheap energy started to shake the Fordist conviction that growth could be sustained within a national economy that was inward-looking, that growth would be generated by wages that rose as fast as labor productivity. This conviction, which became an illusion, continued to prevail in certain countries for some years before crumbling in the face of rising energy prices, globalization, the triumph of neoliberal policies, and the "revolt of the elite" (Lasch, 1996).

During this period, state action was at the heart of regulation and dissemination of the mining metabolism. Governments were omnipresent and acted at various levels through a panoply of new institutions and organizations. This state of affairs was first and foremost an outcome of the second "Thirty Year War" as presented in the previous chapter, during which states acquired strong legitimacy, and showed great effectiveness in mobilizing national resources. It was also a result of the great Depression of the 1930s, which for long was perceived as a clear demonstration of the incapacity of markets to regulate the economy and guarantee full employment of "factors" (land, labor, and capital), much less the well-being of the people. It was also the result of communists coming to power, in Russia in 1917, then in various Central European and Asian countries after the Second World War. It was lastly also the result of decolonization, which conferred to young states a leading role in realizing the ambitions of independence in the field of economy.

At the end of the Second World War, the world found itself with fragmented markets (national or regional[1]), which were isolated—or relatively isolated—from each other. A good part of state intervention was focused on building and maintaining national economies that were inward-looking, and on generating, as much as possible, their own means for sustained growth. That was the goal of the New Deal in the United States, as well as of Europe's reconstruction policies, and of what would be called "development" for countries in Latin America and newly independent states in Asia and Africa.

---

[1] Or imperial, for a few European powers, particularly France until 1957.

All these countries, implicitly or explicitly, shared the same slogan: "the economy in one country" (Didry and Wagner, 1999: 30).[2]

The agricultural sector was a favorite for state intervention, and a target for ambitions of self-focus and self-sufficiency. On the consumption side, the development of synthetic products derived from fossil fuels, presented in Part 4 in relation to Germany's metabolic transformation, grew to new heights, and within a few decades, non-food uses of agricultural products faded away to practically nothing. Only two non-food agricultural products resisted, and not without difficulty: cotton and rubber. In economic discourse, the concept of agrifood—and of the agrifood sector—became a self-evident fact. On the production side, it was the golden age for the wide dissemination of German and American innovations that had emerged since the First World War, and the advent of what I have called in this book "chemical farming" with its remarkable performances resulting from the injection of (increasing quantities of) fossil fuels in the sector. Agriculture, historically an input for all the rest of the economy, both as a source of energy and a raw material, found itself in a subordinate position, as a client of chemical and mechanical industries. The emergence of an omnipresent agrifood industry increasingly distanced agriculture from the final consumer, while at the same time imposing its ever-growing demands. States were the drivers of the processes of agricultural modernization: developing agronomic research focused on improving varieties, deploying land tenure policies that encouraged bigger farms, or on the opposite end, land redistribution (agrarian reforms), intervening in "modern" input markets (improved seeds, tractors, fertilizers, and pesticides) to encourage their uptake, and lastly intervening in product markets with the goal of supporting and stabilizing prices.

The reduction in uses of agricultural biomass, combined with the chemical intensification of production, made self-sufficiency possible, and soon led to the production of surpluses. This problem of American agriculture, and later of European agriculture, quickly became a structural one, and all the more inextricable as the agricultural sector had become an irreplaceable client for a whole range of industries. The quest for new markets, including foreign markets, became a permanent concern for public policy, even if this quest contradicted goals of self-reliance.

During the period, the United States was not only a hegemon but also a model, the ideal that all other countries (including Communist countries) wanted to emulate. Far from a logic of an international division of labor that had characterized the English hegemony during the nineteenth century, this period was dominated by a logic of replication (Friedmann, 1993; McMichael, 1996), in which international trade was subordinated to full employment of "factors," of which the key factor was labor.[3]

---

[2] With this expression, Didry and Wagner make an obvious reference to the policy of "socialism in one country" defended by Stalin, and adopted by the USSR from 1925, contrary to Trotsky's point of view.

[3] In reality, a large number of countries were vitally dependent on imports of oil to replicate the model that the United States represented. The United States, moreover, itself became an oil importer from the 1960s. But given the extremely low price of oil until 1972, these imports did not represent a constraint. For a former imperial power, like France, oil supplies were secured through the close control maintained through the "Françafrique" system in a number of oil-rich former colonies.

But despite countries wishing to imitate the United States, the American model did not spread to the rest of the world homogenously, either as far as the economic model as a whole was concerned, or specifically for agriculture. East–West, North–South, are terms normally associated with bridge games. These terms also came to classify countries according to their ability to replicate the American model. The analysis here will be centered on capitalism, and so will not cover the Soviet bloc. Great attention, however, will be given to the North–South axis to structure the analysis.

The North–South axis is articulated around the omnipresent and polysemous concept of "development." Under the label of "developing countries," an international alliance demanding new rules of international economic relations emerged, and the group constituted the target for aid distributed through a whole new institutional apparatus (the aid industry) by countries that were now defined as "developed." The study of the replication of the American model will be undertaken using this analytical perspective.

16

The American model

After the Second World War, the United States was the uncontested hegemon of the capitalist world-economy. The US economy was by far the most prosperous on all indicators (see Chase-Dunn et al., 2005; Webb and Krasner, 1989; Maddison, 2001, for example): in 1944, the United States alone accounted for 35 percent of global GDP, and still for 25 percent in 1955. That year, American GDP was three times that of the USSR, eight times that of Germany or the United Kingdom, and the United States accounted for almost a third of international trade and controlled 42 percent of global currency reserves. Their military prowess was uncontested since their simultaneous victory over Germany and Japan. Lastly, the United States held increasing cultural sway across the world. The American way of life conquered the world thanks to the country's cinema and music.

The United States had at its disposal a whole architecture of international organizations created during, or just after the war, and covering the fields of diplomacy (UN, OAS, etc.), military cooperation (NATO, ANZUS), as well as specific issues (FAO for food and agriculture, WHO for health, GATT for trade, IMF and the World Bank for finance and loans, and the OECD for economic policy).

There was, however, a nuance. The United States may well have been the hegemon within the capitalist world-economy, but this was not the same as being hegemon of the whole world. Outside of the capitalist world-economy, lay a vast exterior, which at the time was labeled the East. However, contrary to earlier hegemonic configurations, this exterior did not have any existence prior to the emergence of the capitalist world-economy. The East was a product of the partitioning of the world during the two world wars and the immediate postwar years. Despite being situated outside of the capitalist world-economy, the East exerted nonetheless decisive influence on the latter through the military competition it imposed. The short twentieth century, which for Eric Hobsbawm (2003) lasted from 1914 to 1991, viewed from the perspective of the United States was characterized by total war. As soon as the Second World War ended, the Cold War developed, and sometimes outright war broke out, as in Korea (1951–3) and Vietnam (1955–75). The permanent rivalry with the East, war, or the possibility of total destruction, reinforced and legitimized American leadership over the capitalist world-economy.

A new phase in the mining metabolic regime

The United States embodied a second phase of the mining metabolic regime, consisting of a prodigious increase in the flow of energy and matter drawn from the underground, compared to what occurred in the United Kingdom in the nineteenth century.

Even before it started exploiting its fossil fuel resources, the United States was a land of abundance, underpopulated with respect to Europe, giving inhabitants and arriving migrants an illusion of inexhaustible resources. The frontier did not lay the foundations of the country's political institutions, as Frederick J. Turner (1986 [1893]) likes to think, but it did profoundly influence the American way of life. Energy overconsumption was the main manifestation of this influence. In the mid-nineteenth century, firewood consumption was estimated at around 199 gigajoules (GJ) per capita per year, compared to between 15 and 50 in Western and Northern Europe. More than half of the wood came from land clearing linked to the advancing frontier (O'Connor and Cleveland, 2014: 7963).[1] After the American Civil War, abundant wood biomass was supplemented by coal. The United States then shifted from a solar metabolic regime towards an mining metabolic regime. In 1914, per capita energy consumption was twice as high in the United States as it was in the United Kingdom: around 300 GJ per inhabitant per year.[2]

After the 1930s, recovery from the crisis was founded on the industrial collective of "oil + car + chemistry + electricity." Coal consumption diminished while oil and natural gas consumption rose. This characteristic of the American mining metabolic regime had heavy political, social, and military implications as Timothy Mitchell (2013) explains. The decade of the glorious sixties was characterized by a new leap in energy consumption, which rose to 450 GJ per capita (Figure 16.1).

Consumption of matter, for its part, more than doubled between 1932 and 1970, rising from 13 to 29 tons per capita per year (in other words, 80 kg per day) This high consumption resulted in large part from the birth of "suburbia" (Mumford, 2011), that is, suburban townships that brought with them rising individual urban housing, construction of infrastructure (highways), and a dramatic rise in the number of cars (600 per 1,000 inhabitants in 1973 compared to just 165 in 1945). The share of mineral resources in the consumption of matter grew from 20 percent in 1870 to 75 percent in the early 1960s, and to 80 percent in 1970 (Gierlinger and Krausmann, 2012).

---

[1] Firewood was mainly used for heating, but in the mid-nineteenth century, steam engines already accounted for 6 percent of consumption. Wood later came to represent up to 90 percent of combustibles used for trains.

[2] Until the 1930s crisis, the US mining metabolic regime, from an energy perspective, was based on coal exploitation. Per capita coal consumption reached a peak of 5.6 tons in 1920 (Gierlinger and Krausmann, 2012: 368), that is 50 percent higher than the peak reached in the United Kingdom.

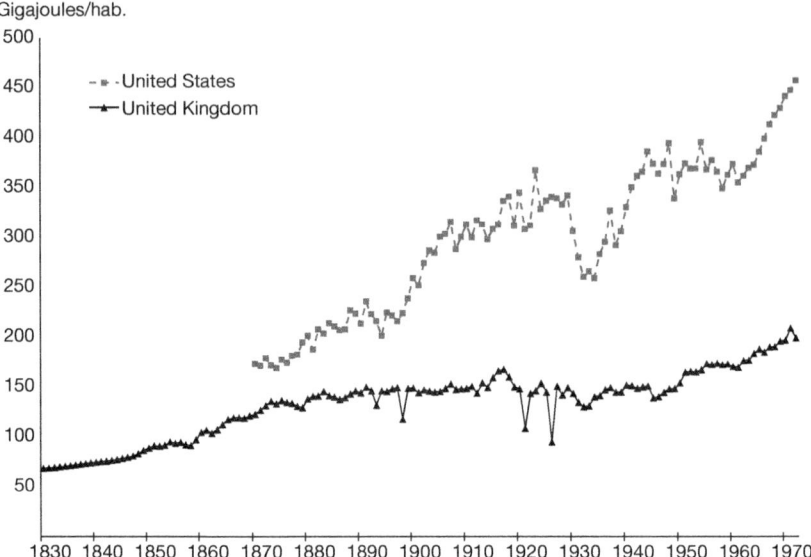

Figure 16.1 United States and United Kingdom per capita energy consumption, 1830–1972 (gigajoules per capita)

Sources: adapted from Gierlinger and Krausmann, 2012 and Krausmann et al., 2008.

Fordism and growth focused on the domestic space

The theory of regulation[3] distinguishes between several periods in the history of development of capitalism, depending on the institutions and specific norms that guarantee the regular accumulation of capital. The concept of Fordism occupies a central place in the theory. The expression "Fordism" is borrowed from Antonio Gramsci, and designates a regime of intensive accumulation,[4] founded on the continuous growth of labor productivity and centered on mass consumerism. Fordism is the combination of three characteristics (Boyer, 1995: 371):

- Organization of labor founded on principles of Taylorism: tasks broken down into smaller tasks, mechanization, and strict separation of design operations from execution.
- Lasting increases in wages based on the distribution of productivity gains (for Henry Ford, the workers of his factories were his future clients).

---

[3] This school of economic policy, which originated in France and of which Michel Aglietta and Robert Boyer were the main inspiration, excelled in describing the economies of countries called "developed" after the Second World War (Aglietta, 1976; Boyer, 1986, 2015).

[4] The dominant accumulation regime in the nineteenth century can be qualified as extensive, in the sense that it was based on the incorporation of increasing quantities of labor, of sectors, and of new territories.

– A dynamic of adjustment between production and consumption mainly occurring within the domestic market, and in which the state, through expenditure, played an essential stabilizing role.

The three characteristics are closely linked. It was gains in labor productivity that made possible increasing wages, and these increased wages created permanent new demand within the domestic market, thus avoiding an overproduction crisis without having to seek recourse in foreign markets. The imbrication between these elements led Pierre-Noel Giraud to characterize Fordism as an "inward-looking social democracy" (Giraud, 1996).

Free trade was therefore not the "dominant" ambition for trade policies of the period under study. The role of free trade has been wrongly emphasized by a great number of authors (Kindleberger, 1973, 1981; Krasner, 1976; Lindert and Williamson, 2001), who argue that the rapid growth of OECD countries in the 1950s and 1960s was due to the relaunch of globalization.

John G. Ruggie was one of the first to contest this "truth." He proposed the term "embedded liberalism," rather than free trade, to characterize the postwar trade regime influenced by the American hegemony (Ruggie, 1982, 1998). It was an international, a multilateral regime—which was a shift from the nationalism and economic bilateralism of the 1930s—but which permitted internal interventionism, a fundamental contrast with the British policy of the gold standard and free trade of the nineteenth century. The failure of negotiations during the conference on trade and employment, and the signing of the GATT treaty were a direct consequence of this "embedded liberalism." The GATT treaty, which was the only outcome of this negotiation, had non-discrimination as its first and main rule. It enshrined multilateralism, but not necessarily the abandonment of protectionism.

In this context, foreign trade played a very limited role compared to its role in the English economy during the nineteenth century. Table 16.1 presents the changes in foreign trade to GDP ratios in the United States and the United Kingdom. It shows how low this ratio was for the United States as a hegemon (1950), compared to the ratio for the United Kingdom when it was the hegemon (1880): 9 percent for the former versus 59 percent for the latter! During the entire period of uncontested hegemony, this ratio in America remained lower than it had been prior to the First World War.

Thus, internationalization or globalization of the global economy was not relaunched after the Second World War. The second Thirty Year War (1914–45) was not an intermission, temporarily suspending a long wave of globalization. The economic model embodied by the American hegemon was a domestic economic model in which foreign flows (both of goods and capital) played a subordinate role in economic policy, which had as its primary goal ensuring full employment.[5] André Grjebine rightly speaks of neo-mercantilism with regard to this policy (Grjebine, 1980).

---

[5] This vision of international trade was perfectly coherent with Keynesian economics, for which, as Gunnar Myrdal points out, "the welfare state is nationalist." According to Fred Block, "Implicit in the views of Keynes and his co-thinkers was the conception of a 'national capitalism' in which state intervention and planning would be used to maintain full employment of labor and industrial capacity. Even if certain goods might more cheaply be produced abroad, the beneficial employment effects of producing them domestically would justify restricting imports" (Block, 1977: 8).

Table 16.1 Internationalization rate (exports + imports/GDP) of the United States and the United Kingdom, 1890–1970 (in %)

	1880	1913	1920	1938	1950	1960	1970
United States							
Deutsch/Eckstein*	13.9	13.6	11.3	7.8	8.6	8.1	–
Webb/Krasner	13	12	12	–	9.8	9.5	11.2
United Kingdom							
Deutsch/Eckstein	59	59.3	49.1	28.3	48	40	–
Webb/Krasner	49	52	38	–	51.3	43.9	46.1

Sources: Deutsch and Eckstein, 1961; Webb and Krasner, 1989.

*The paper by Karl Deutsch and Alexander Eckstein (1961) from which the data comes, had a title that is revealing of its times: "National industrialization and the declining share of the international economic sector, 1890–1959."

Biomass use: The triumph of agrifood

Non-food uses of both agricultural and non-agricultural biomass declined steadily or disappeared outright, with the exception of a few products such as rubber and cotton. It was during this period that the terms "agricultural product" and "food product" became practically synonymous. The concept of agrifood came to constitute the main way to frame discussion about agricultural issues. It was also during this period that giant firms specialized in processing and distributing food products emerged, some of which would go on to cover the whole globe with their disposable cans.

The end of non-food uses of biomass

Between 1900 and 1950, per capita biomass consumption fell, in opposition to the rise in uses of other types of material. It fell from 10 to 6 tons per person per year (Figure 16.2), and then stagnated in the decades that followed (Gierlinger and Krausmann, 2012). This fall was entirely due to the reduction, or the outright disappearance, of non-food uses of biomass.

Biomass use fell the most in the field of energy. Two organic sources of energy were practically abandoned: wood for thermic energy, and draft animals for mechanical energy.

In the early nineteenth century, forest reserves in the United States markedly outstripped those in England. Coal use therefore started later in the United States, but progressed quickly when it did. In 1850, wood still represented 90 percent of thermal energy consumption, but this fell to 21 percent in 1900, to 7 percent in 1925, and to 3 percent in 1950 (Table 16.2). Firewood consumption per person fell by a factor of three between 1850 and 1900, and again by three between 1900 and 1950 (Schurr et al., 1960: 48).

Biomass for feeding draft animals (horses and mules in the United States), another essential use of biomass, disappeared during the course of the twentieth century. In

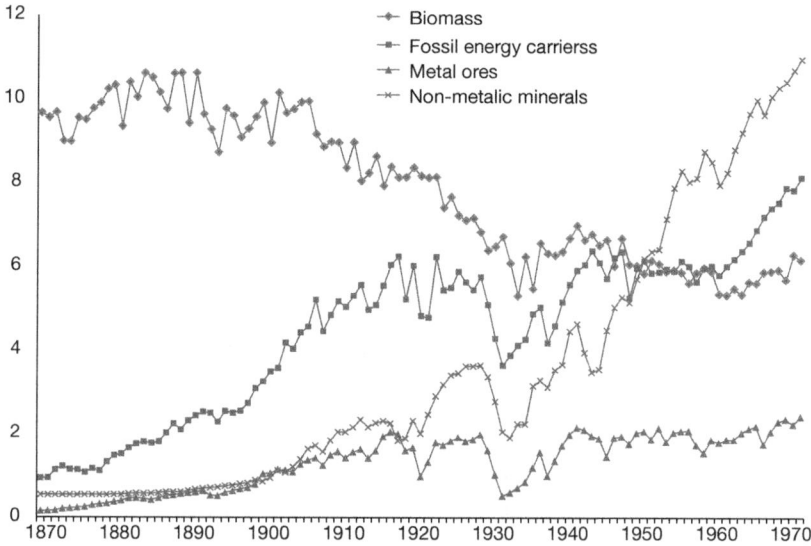

Figure 16.2 United States, consumption of materials per person and by source, 1870–1973 (ton/person)

Source: adapted from Gierlinger and Krausmann, 2012.

Table 16.2 Contribution of different "sources" to thermal energy supply in the United States, 1850–1973 (in British Thermal Units, BTU)

	1850	1875	1900	1925	1950	1975
Wood	138	2,872	2,015	1,533	1,067	341
Coal	219	1,440	6,841	14,706	12,913	14,362
Oil and gas	–	11	481	5,471	19,458	50,083

Sources: adapted from Schurr et al., 1960: 47, for 1850–1950, and Spencer, 1980, for 1975.

1850, animals still provided 1.5 times more work than all inanimate sources of energy (wood, coal, water, wind) combined, and in 1870, the same quantity (Dewhurst, 1947: 1116). In 1900, food for draft animals, still represented, in energy terms, more energy than oil, and only two times less than firewood. In value it represented 36 percent of all energy consumption (human food excluded). The emergence of the internal combustion engine led to a sharp fall in the number of horses and mules used in farms from a peak of 26 million in 1920 to 3 million in 1960[6] (USDA, 1962). But use of draft animals for transportation had been reduced even earlier: from 3 million heads in 1910, they fell to 2 million in 1920 and to just 380,000 in 1925 (Olmstead and Rhode, 2001: 670). The decline of draft animals "freed up" vast quantities of agricultural land.

---

[6] They were no longer included in USDA censuses after 1960.

In 1920, 95 million acres, or a quarter of total cultivated land area, as much as corn acreage, and 1.5 times the wheat acreage, had been dedicated to feeding draft animals.

Moreover, biomass was often displaced by the development of synthetic products, derived from coal, and increasingly from oil. The United States proved to be particularly effective in implementing the substitution logic imported from Germany. Between 1939 and 1950, production of the American chemical industry quadrupled.

Between 1900 and 1973, annual consumption of organic textile fibers fell from 12 to 8 kilograms per person, and only cotton consumption remained stable. Consumption of leather and skins fell from 6 to 2 kilograms, consumption of oilseeds for non-food uses (cotton, flax) fell from 11 to 4 kilograms. Wood consumption for its part fell only from 792 to 515 kilograms. The relative buoyancy in wood consumption can be partially explained by its use in construction of family homes, and especially by a new market for wood in the paper-making industry. Use of wood for paper rose very dramatically during the twentieth century: from 3,000 kilograms per person in 1900 to 200 kilograms in 1973 (Kelly and Matos, 2013).

In total, between 1900 and 1975, the share of biomass in energy consumption, measured in value, fell from 58 percent to 1.5 percent. Its role in material consumption for the manufacture of "physical-structures" fell from 84 percent to 46 percent. At the same time, the share of food in biomass consumption, measured in value, grew from 56 percent to 82 percent. Human food became the dominant use of biomass, and the almost exclusive market for agricultural production (Table 16.3).

The remarkable expansion of animal protein consumption

Donald Paarlberg, an economic advisor in the USDA who continued to hold positions of influence under Eisenhower's two terms, in 1954 wrote:

> We come now to the one type of adjustment which many, including myself, hold in high regard. It is a shift in the composition of the diet, toward more livestock products. Does this type of shift provide an opportunity during the years ahead to keep our agricultural resources largely in use, to consume the production of these

Table 16.3 United States, share provided by biomass in various uses, and share of each of these uses in the total value of biomass consumed (in %), 1900 and 1975

	Share provided by biomass in supply		Share of total biomass consumed assigned to each use	
	1900	1975	1900	1975
Energy (feeding horses, firewood)	58	1.5	13	1
Physical-structures*	84	46	31	17
Food	100	100	56	82

Source: adapted from Spencer, 1980: 62–3.

*In other words, all non-food consumer goods (furniture, clothing, buildings, road, vehicles, household appliances, etc.) whether durable or non-durable.

resources, and to do this without sharply depressing farm prices and incomes? I believe it does, if we can make the needful changes. Livestock condense about 7 pounds of dry matter in the form of grain and other feed to about 1 pound of dry matter in the form of meat, milk, and eggs. The other 6 pounds are used for heat and energy or are wasted and cannot be recovered by man. Thus, far more agricultural resources are needed to provide a diet which contains a high percentage of livestock products. Increasing and decreasing livestock numbers is the time-honored method of adjusting the food supply to changing needs. The amount of flexibility provided by this system is tremendous.

(Paarlberg, 1954: 49)

Whatever was the effectiveness of agriculture policy, in the 1950s and 1960s consumption evolved in such a way that these expectations were largely met. Between 1950 and 1972, US beef consumption (in carcass equivalents) grew from 65 to 115 kilograms per person, chicken from 21 to 41 kilograms, and turkey from 4 to 9 kilograms. It was during this period that animal products, the first of which meat, became America's primary source of protein. In 1970, meat alone provided 40 percent of proteins, compared to just 18 percent from cereals and 5 percent from pulses (or fabaceous plants). The transformation in diets from the early twentieth century onwards was a spectacular one. In the 1910s, cereals were still the first source of proteins, accounting for 37 percent of protein intake compared to 30 percent for meat (Table 16.4). It should be underscored that there was a substitution effect here—cereals were replaced by animal products—as daily protein intake per person for the period remained unchanged at 96 g.

The sharp growth in animal product consumption led to a very significant increase in the use of cereals and oilseed meal in animal feed. In the space of thirty years, animal consumption of cereals increased by 75 percent, and that of seed meal increased fourfold (Table 16.5)!

The use of cereals to feed animals intended to later feed humans—excluding therefore oats to feed horses—was already widespread before the Second World War. The corn–pig pair in effect played a key role in the Great Plains of the Midwest with the emergence of the Corn Belt after the American Civil War. Then, the targeted animal product was not meat, but lard. But from the end of the Second World War, what was sought from animals was above all protein production (meat). Dairy products experienced the same rise, as butter (fat) gradually lost ground to cheeses and

Table 16.4 United States, share of various foods in dietary protein intake, 1909–72 (in % of overall protein intake)

	Meat	Dairy products	Eggs	Pulses	Cereals
1909–19	30	14	5	5	37
1930–9	29	19	6	6	30
1970–2	40	22	6	5	18

Source: Gerrior et al., 2004.

Table 16.5 United States, consumption of cereals and oilseed meal for animal feed (in millions of tons), 1937–72

	1937–41	1945–7	1965–7	1970–2
Cereals	85	98	126	148
Seed meal	4	6	13	16

Sources: USDA, Feed Situation, various years.

Table 16.6 United States, shares of various fatty matter in dietary fat intake, 1909–72 (in % of overall fat intake)

	Butter	Lard and tallow	Margarine	Vegetable oils
1909–19	35	30	30	5
1930–9	32	27	28	13
1970–2	8	7	49	35

Source: Gerrior et al., 2004.

yogurts (protein). This transformation of the role of animal products in human diets was reflected in the evolution of the composition of fats used in human food. At the beginning of the twentieth century, butter, lard, and tallow represented two-thirds of fats consumed; in the early 1970s these represented only 15 percent (Table 16.6).

In short, animals became factories producing protein, which, given the context of saturated calorie demand, was certainly the best way to guarantee a market for animal products while conserving, and even increasing, their capacity to absorb plant production surpluses.

The decisive role that animal feed thereon played as a consumer of American agricultural output, in particular of its cereal crop, cannot be overstressed. In 1972, 85 percent of US cereal production went to feeding animals, representing a massive market that had exceeded all hopes.

Contrary to what is often today presented as obvious, growth in incomes had not always resulted in an automatic rise in consumption of animal protein, at least not in the United States, and therefore was not always accompanied by an opportune growth in the markets for cereal and oilseed crops. Before the Second World War, income growth did not bring about a rise in meat consumption (Figure 16.3).

Analysts at the time highlighted, moreover, that GDP growth was correlated with a fall in consumption of food products. Many reports published in the interwar years (Wolman, 1929; Mixed Committee of the League of Nations on the relation of nutrition to health, 1937) mentioned that one of the causes of the surplus situation in agricultural markets was the recent trend of falling cereal consumption. This trend seemed to prevail in all Western European, as well as North American countries. Between 1910 and 1936, per capita wheat consumption was estimated to have fallen by 5 percent in Western Europe, and by 13 percent in the United States (Bennet,

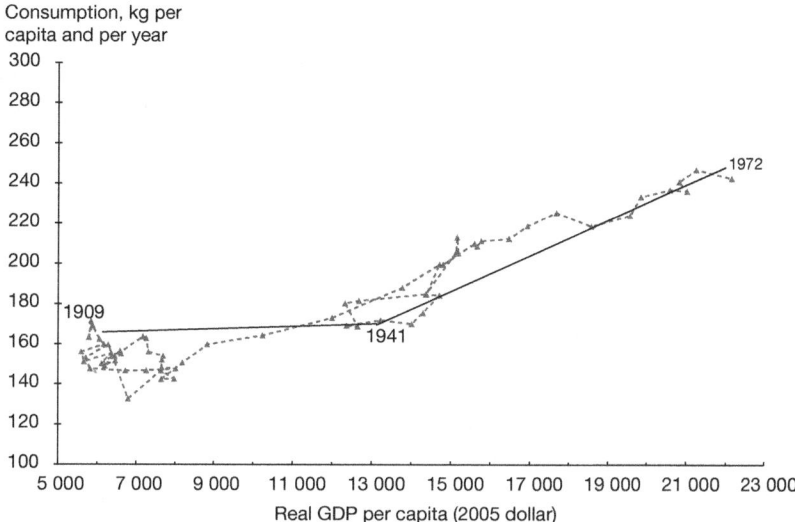

Figure 16.3 United States, per capita GDP and meat consumption, 1909–72

Sources: USDA, Feed Situation, various years; Maddison, 2001.

1936, cited by Altschul and Strauss, 1937). The trend at the time was interpreted as being a sign of reduced calorie needs, linked in part to changes in working conditions (motorization and mechanization of previously manual activities, shortened working hours, office work, etc.) and in part to the spread of indoor heating. The phenomenon was particularly pronounced in the United States. The quantity of calories per person provided by consumption of wheat and corn fell by half between 1889 and 1925. The falling cereal consumption was countered by a rapid rise in sugar consumption, but not in meat consumption as we saw previously (Table 16.7).[7]

Increasing animal protein consumption, and of meat in particular, after the war was thus considered a solution to overproduction problems that had plagued the United States throughout the whole interwar period and returned menacingly as soon as peace was re-established. As we saw, Don Paarlberg, made no secret of this intention. His position reflected a common view that saw overproduction as *the* main problem in agriculture, and animal farming as a solution to this problem.[8] It was therefore necessary to create markets, and increasing meat consumption, which today appears to

---

[7] For the League of Nations, this observation held for all countries: "No clear trend in total meat consumption can be discerned on the basis of the available statistical material" (Mixed Committee of the League of Nations on the relation of nutrition to health, 1937: 110).

[8] The same idea is repeated, for example, by Walter Wilcox, a key postwar agricultural economist, who wrote "Each dollar spent in the grocery store for choice beef, at 1953 average prices, purchased the equivalent of 29 pounds of feed grains. On the other hand, a dollar spent in the grocery store for either eggs or poultry purchased the equivalent of only 11 pounds of feed grains ... an increase of $1 to $2 in per capita expenditures for these 5 livestock products would absorb all excess output in most years" (Wilcox, 1954: 512).

Table 16.7 United States, consumption of various food products per person 1889–1925

	Wheat (calories per day)	Corn (calories per day)	Meat and lard (pounds per year)	Sugar (calories per day)
1889	1,537	531	143	242
1925	895	102	144	542

Source: Wolman, 1929.

us as organized wastage, was at the time perceived as an astute solution to this problem. The idea, which had circulated since the 1930s, had already been defended in the report by the Economic Committee on the agricultural crisis published in 1931.[9] In 1949 again, the president of the American Farm Bureau Federation, the main agricultural trade union, declared before Congress, "We are interested in trying to develop policies and programs which will avoid burdensome surpluses in feed grains by encouraging the translation of increased feed production into greater livestock production," and highlighted that "it takes seven times as many acres to feed a people on livestock products as it takes if people eat grain" (cited by Winders and Nibert, 2004: 80).

Publicity campaigns were thus organized for the general public, mainly by the American Meat Association which had been established at the beginning of the century by Chicago meat industrialists. Given the figures cited, it was not necessary to do much more. State intervention did not play a great role in driving the change in consumer habits; as we will see, it focused rather on industrializing animal farming.

The advent of chemical farming

In the space of three decades, innovations conceived in Europe (enclosed herding, chemical fertilizers, and pesticides) and those conceived in America (mechanization and motorization, hybrid seeds) conquered the whole of the US territory. The model that transformed American agriculture was itself a hybrid. It included solutions, proposed at varying periods and in different places, to constraints that were also diverse: competition from imported cereals had led to the invention of intensive livestock herding by the Danes; a shortage of land had led Germans to turn to fertilizers; a lack of manpower had turned Americans to mechanization, etc. In 1960, 95 percent of corn acreage was planted with hybrid seeds, 95 percent of wheat was harvested with combine harvesters, and 97 percent of farms had electricity. The number of tractors stabilized around the 5 million mark, but even if their numbers stopped rising, their power continued to grow prodigiously (Olmstead and Rhode, 2000).

---

[9] "The value of increasing the consumption of animal products with a view to absorbing the excess agricultural production should not be overlooked. Though the individual demand is inelastic, as we have seen, in the case of a large number of agricultural products, the consumption of animal products per head of the population can be greatly increased, especially among workmen and employees when wage conditions improve" (Economic Committee, 1931: 57).

This "modernization" of American agriculture was greatly facilitated by active state intervention in markets to guarantee farm incomes, and thus the capacity of farmers to invest and repay loans. Public procurement, direct assistance, and export grants were the norm then. Instability in agricultural production was to be "exported," or externalized as we would say today, towards the national budget or to international markets.

Yet another agricultural revolution

The spread and uptake of innovations in the realm of energy, chemistry, and biology that occurred in the early twentieth century, accelerated in the years following the end of the Second World War.

Mechanization boomed: the number of tractors (already 2.3 million in 1945) peaked in the mid-1960s at around 5 million. The number then fell slightly, but the installed capacity of tractors more than tripled between 1945 and 1972. Combine harvesters and corn-pickers proliferated, and in the late 1950s their numbers peaked (at 1 and 0.8 million respectively), to then later fall as their sizes increased. In 1945, 365,000 farms had milking machines; by 1955 this had risen to a peak of 712,000 farms.

Between 1945 and 1972, fertilizer consumption rose: from 600,000 to 8 million tons for nitrogen; from 1.4 to 4.8 million tons for phosphate; and from 700,000 to 4.3 million tons for potash. The share of hybrids in corn production reached 100 percent of corn acreage from the early 1960s (it had already doubled to reach 60 percent of acreage during the war). Soybean acreage, which stood at 10 million acres in 1945, reached 45 million acres in 1972.

The effects of the spread of these innovations were instant. Production growth, which until 1910 had been linked to increasing acreage (thanks to the frontier), had stagnated along with total acreage until 1945. The increased use of nitrogen fertilizers and improved seeds adapted to such fertilizers, enabled rising output in the postwar decades, despite total acreage no longer increasing. Production more than doubled between 1945 and 1980, mirroring perfectly the rise in the quantity of fertilizers used (Figure 16.4).

Even more spectacular was the growth in agricultural labor productivity between 1935 and 1975: it increased almost tenfold, while yields "only" doubled during the same period. Agronomists may not like to hear it, but the main effects of the industrial modernization of agriculture did not arise from performances from the soil, but rather from improved labor performance (Figure 16.5).

"Modernization" of agriculture also involved farms becoming strongly specialized in just a limited number of products. In 1910, American farms were highly interdisciplinary, almost systematically combining crop farming with animal farming (Table 16.8). This changed drastically during the period under study, which ended with the majority of farms specializing in just one product, whether animal or plant-based. At the same time, vast "animal protein factories" developed, copying the model of "animal fat factories" (butter and bacon), based on the uncoupling of crop and animal farming and the purchase of cereals and oilseed proteins, as had been developed in Northwestern Europe in the late nineteenth century.

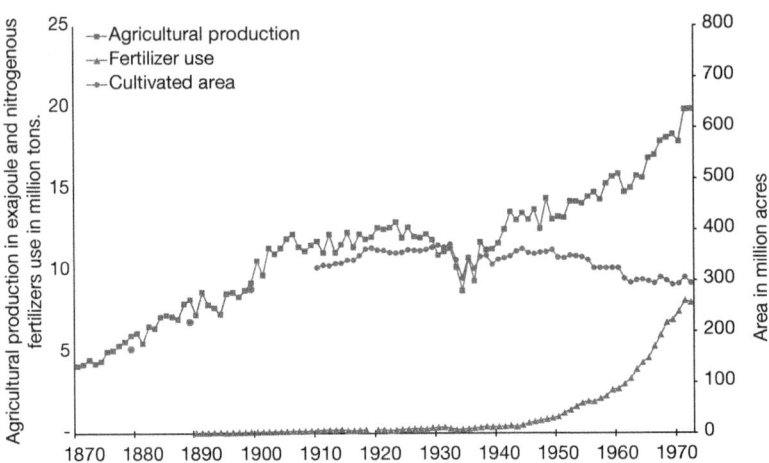

Figure 16.4 United States, agricultural production (in petajoules), cultivated land area (in millions of acres), and fertilizer consumption (in thousands of tons), 1870–1972

Sources: adapted from ISDC, 1976; USDA, Feed Situation, various years; Gierlinger and Krausmann, 2012.

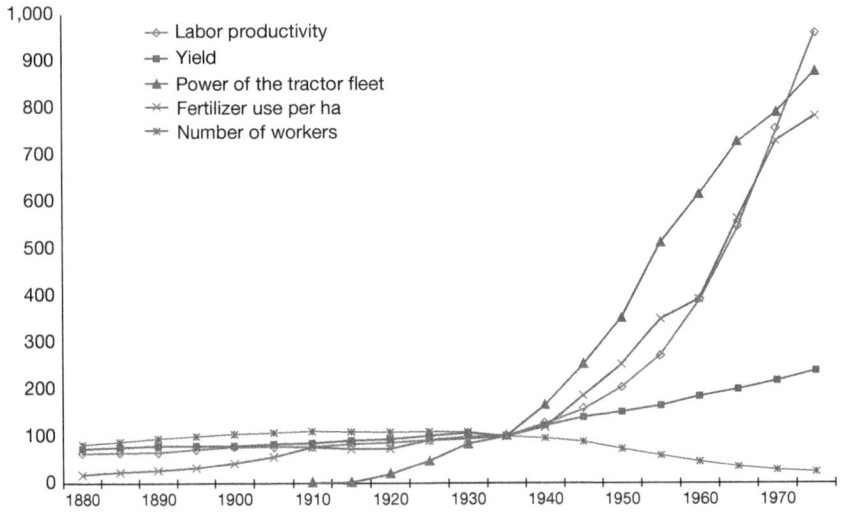

Figure 16.5 United States, labor productivity index, yields, fertilizer consumption per ha, and accumulated capacity of tractors, 1880–1975 (100 base year in 1935)

Source: adapted from Hayami and Ruttan, 1985.

Table 16.8 United States, percentage of farms producing the specified plant or animal product

	1910	1974
Poultry	88	13
Dairy cows	81	17
Horses	74	15
Pigs	68	20
Corn	76	43
Orchards	48	4

Sources: Olmstead and Rhode, 2001: 725 and USDC, 1977.

Specialization of farms in animal farming shook up farming methods and agriculture's relation to animals: what are sometimes called CAFO, for "concentrated animal feeding operations," emerged and flourished. The term is not quite accurate, but calling the method concentration camps for animal fattening is probably too shocking!

Transformations were most dramatic in broiler chicken farming. Poultry production in the United States was the terrain for a series of innovations that had no precedents in European animal farming. Until the 1930s, as mentioned previously, almost all farmyards kept at least a few chickens. They were kept to lay eggs, and their meat was just an adjunct product (what were eaten were "reformed" chickens that no longer laid enough eggs, or young "chicks," excess males, consumed young during spring). The chickens kept were of races selected for their egg production capacities and their meat was wiry and tough. In 1935, Americans consumed just 300 g per person per year. The Second World War, during which chicken meat, unlike other meats, was not rationed, opened up new perspectives for the sector. Production of broiler chickens tripled between 1940 and 1945.

During those years, and during the 1950s, there was "progress" on all fronts: in genetics, nutrition, veterinary care, and poultry coops and equipment (Martinez, 1999: 5). Vitamins (B12) and antibiotics were introduced into chicken feed as growth accelerators; the antibiotics also helped control illness, thus making it possible to raise poultry in confined spaces with very high densities per square foot. Vaccination through drinking water was developed. Food rations, which were very energy dense, were rich in fatty matter that could easily turn rancid; this problem was resolved by the systematic addition of antioxidants. Conveyor belts to automatize feeding were introduced in the early 1940s, and later other automatic equipment for ventilation, drinking water supply, and cleaning.

There was active encouragement to find genetic improvements for the quality and quantity of meat produced by each chicken. A program called "The Chicken of Tomorrow," sponsored by a large supermarket chain, in close collaboration with the USDA Cooperative Extension Service for the state of Delaware, was launched in 1945. The extension service organized several promotional events, such as for example an auction market that served to identify the attributes that consumers desired, and a competition for race selectors, whose annual event of pride was the Delaware Chicken Festival (on this topic, see Horowitz, 2006: 111–14).

All these efforts were rewarded by a sharp improvement in the conversion yields of food to meat: they fell from 5 kilograms to 2 kilograms of corn-equivalent for 1 kilograms of chicken between 1940 to 1972. Likewise, the amount of time necessary to produce 1 kilograms of meat was divided by five between the late 1940s and the late 1950s, and then once more by two during the next decade. Total production of broiler chickens increased tenfold between 1945 and 1972, and per capita consumption reached 16 kilograms per year in 1972 (Kim and Curry, 1993).

As production required high investments, particularly for poultry buildings, chicken farming quickly became a concentrated sector, and in 1974, 90 percent of poultry farms had more than 60,000 chicken, and 70 percent had even more than 100,000 (Lasley, 1983: 10). Despite an extreme rationalization of labor, along a Taylorist model, and chain production comparable to that of the automobile industry, the slaughter and cutting phases remained labor-intensive. Production therefore delocalized towards the southern states (Georgia, North Carolina, Arkansas, Alabama, and Mississippi) where labor was abundant and cheap (female and African American). The share of these states in national production grew from 27 percent in 1950 to 60 percent in 1965 (Reimund et al., 1981: 8).

The process of industrialization was initially based on a division of labor between hatching, feed supply, fattening, slaughter, and commercialization, but very quickly systems of contract farming between poultry feed suppliers and chicken producers were set up. The feed suppliers financed a part of the buildings if the farmer used their feed regime. The share of production produced under contract by feed suppliers was already 88 percent as early as 1955. In a second phase, feed suppliers bought up hatcheries, and later, slaughter and cutting firms. However, they very rarely engaged directly in the actual animal farming phase, the least predictable step of all.

More generally, while there was an increasing decoupling of the animal and plant production sectors, these sectors became more closely linked to the manufacturing sector which provided their inputs. The share of expenditure on inputs and on fixed capital depreciation grew from 35 percent of gross agricultural income in 1929 to 62 percent in 1972 (Carter et al., 2006: 226). Agriculture, now consuming increasing amounts of inputs, became a sector that drove whole sections of the economy: supporting and structuring the sector meant supporting the chemical industry, the pharmaceutical industry, the metal industry, the banking sector, etc., in an effort to ensure optimal growth within an inward-looking domestic economy.

Let us focus one instant on how this system belonged to a specific time in history and in particular on how it coupled agricultural growth with industrial growth. In the preceding century, the English hegemon had depended on the rest of the world for most of its biomass supply. Domestic agriculture and industry in England therefore followed inverse trajectories. Liquidation of agriculture at the time even appeared to be a necessary condition for the development of industry. Under the "Fordist growth" model of the postwar period, development of agriculture and of industry by contrast were complementary (Kenney et al., 1989 for the United States, and Allaire, 1995 for

And American agriculture became an energy sink ...

The energy yield of agriculture is the ratio of the total quantity of energy used in production, in all forms except solar energy, and the quantity of calories, food, or other, that is produced. Analysis of energy yields sheds light on the transformations that agriculture and food underwent during the transition from the solar metabolic regime to the mining metabolic regime. Under the first regime, agriculture was the main source of energy for human societies; under the second regime it became a big energy consumer. Between 1910 and 1970, energy consumption of American agriculture increased five times faster than agricultural production (Cleveland, 1995). In effect, it was only under such conditions that chemical farming was able to achieve its remarkable performances in labor productivity and yields from the land. Gerald Stanhill noted about the 1970s:

> If the energy/labour ratio of maize production is compared with that of other manufacturing industries in the USA, the values for the most recent period show that this subsystem of agriculture falls into the same category—i.e., Level One—the highest level of energy labor intensities of all US manufacturing industries. This highest category—corresponding to 1,500 kWh per work-hour or more—is made up very largely of the chemical, paper, and petroleum industries.
>
> (Stanhill, 1984b: 124)

By 1963, the energy yield of agriculture was already as low as 0.9. To produce one calorie, agriculture consumed 0.01 calories in the form of labor, and 1.14 in the form of fossil fuels and electricity. The replacement of human labor by fossil fuels was therefore occurring at the considerable rate of twenty-one times more fossil energy used than human labor spared. In 1970, the energy yield fell to 0.8 (Hamilton et al., 2013).

Agriculture was obviously not the only energy-consuming activity in food production. Processing, distribution, and household food-related activities also required high amounts of energy. An estimation of the energy balance sheet of the food system undertaken just after the first oil shock showed that, between 1940 and 1970, energy consumption of all segments of the food system rose much faster than the energy available in the form of food. The energy yield of the entire food system fell from 23 percent to 11 percent between the two dates. In 1970, almost nine calories of fossil energy were needed to provide a single food calorie to an eater (Steinhart and Steinhart, 1974)!

France). Rising wages in industry and services guaranteed the development of markets for agricultural products. Similarly, the continuous "modernization" of agriculture, that is substituting capital for labor, provided growing markets for some branches of industry (chemistry and mechanical industries in particular).

In both models, however, agriculture was a reservoir of labor, and its modernization, thanks to rising labor productivity, liberated this labor for industry, which was still

Table 16.9 Food system energy balance sheet of the United States in 1940 and in 1970

	1940		1970	
	10^{15} BTU*	%	10^{15} BTU	%
Energy consumed by the "food system"				
Agriculture	0.5	19	2.1	24
Processing	0.6	22	1.2	14
Packaging	0.2	7	0.8	9
Transport	0.3	11	1.3	15
Wholesale/retail distribution	0.5	19	1.2	14
Restaurants and households	0.6	22	2.0	23
Total	2.7	100	8.6	100
Food energy available for eaters	0.6		1.0	

Source: Steinhart and Steinhart, 1974.

*BTU—British Thermal Unit, an Anglo-Saxon energy unit defined as the quantity of heat necessary to raise the temperature of an English pound of water by 1°F at constant pressure of 1 atmosphere. It is equivalent to roughly 254 to 255 calories, 1,054 to 1060 joules, or 0.293 to 0.294 KW.

labor-intensive. Between 1935 and 1974, the number of hours worked in agriculture fell by 70 percent. This fall was due to the almost complete disappearance of seasonal wage work, and the drastic reduction in the number of farms (especially smaller farms), which fell from 6.8 to 2.3 million. The workforce of sharecroppers in particular was affected. African American farms which had produced cotton after the dismantling of Southern plantations almost all disappeared (Harris and Macheski, 1992: 319). The American rural world emptied out: the number of Americans living on a farm fell threefold between 1940 and 1970, and the mass rural exodus was accompanied by a sharp fall in birth rates. The rural birth rate converged with the urban rate, in line with the reduced need for arms to work.

Thus, market-oriented "family" agriculture in reality was transformed into individual farming, that no longer even employed both members of the traditional farming couple (see Nicourt, 2013, on the same phenomenon in France).

Market regulation and resurgence of exports to manage surpluses

The wars and the 1929 crisis led to the conviction that only price stability could guarantee the effectiveness of agriculture. The policy of price support conceived in the 1930s was thus maintained for its main aspects, with just a few adjustments aimed at helping facilitate exports and avoid overproduction.

The 1965 Food and Agriculture Act lowered the guaranteed price to the level of global prices to facilitate exports. This measure was accompanied by direct financial assistance to farmers (deficiency payment) to compensate the difference between the guaranteed price and an "objective" price (target price) calculated for each crop on the basis of production costs. In exchange, farmers, once again had to commit to a land set-aside scheme. Fighting overproduction and managing surpluses firmly remained a priority for agricultural policy.

But the market regulation policy aimed at stabilizing prices had been put in place in the 1930s, at a time when foreign trade was very limited. New tools were needed to render the policy compatible with increased participation in international commerce. In effect, with the spread of techniques that successfully bolstered production, the price support policy based on public procurement quickly resulted in the accumulation of public stocks held by the Commodity Credit Corporation. By the end of the Korean War (1953), overproduction and surpluses were once again key topics in policy debates.

In addition to promoting domestic consumption of meat, it quickly became necessary to also export. Food aid and "concessional" sales (subsidized exports) were to play a decisive role in this (Friedmann, 1982: 190). In 1948–9, during the Marshall Plan, 60 percent of international "sales" were funded by foreign aid programs. In 1954, the Agricultural Trade and Development Act on food aid, also called the Public Law 480,[10] was voted in. It helped to officialize this policy approach, which became known as "Food

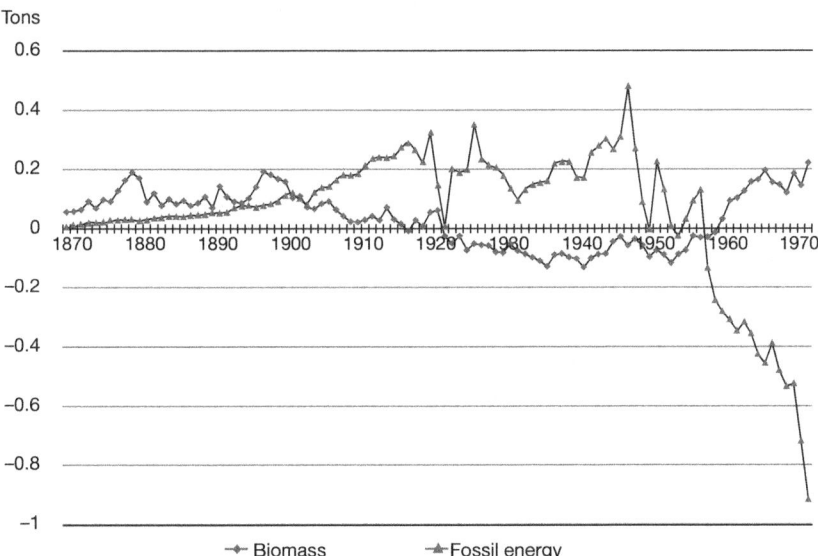

Figure 16.6 United States, balance of per capita biomass and fossil fuels trade (in tons), 1870–1972

Source: adapted from Gierlinger and Krausmann, 2012.

---

[10] The US had already had practice with implementing an ambitious food aid policy after the First World War. Under the leadership of Herbert Hoover, future US president, the American Relief Administration provided wheat to all the former European belligerents, regardless of which side they had fought on (Cullather, 2010: 22).

for Peace," and which accounted for between 30 and 40 percent of exports during the late 1950s, and between 20 and 30 percent during the 1960s (Hopkins and Puchala, 1980).[11]

Whatever geopolitical interests lay behind the provision of food aid, a strong US presence on international "grain" markets was an explicit component of policy aimed at managing surpluses and stabilizing the domestic market. Henry Wallace, Secretary for Agriculture under Roosevelt, in the 1930s declared: "Farmers are to be given the centralizing power of the Federal Government so they could dump enough of their surplus abroad to raise prices in the domestic market" (Wallace, 1934: 148). The postwar administrations applied this recommendation on a grand scale. Thanks to these support measures, in 1960, after forty years of deficits, the United States once again became a net exporter of biomass (Figure 16.6).

Allow us to point out that the balance of external trade in fossil fuels followed an exactly synchronous but opposite trajectory: the emergence of a biomass surplus coincided with the emergence of a deficit in fossil fuels, and their variations were mirror reflections of each other. The United States thus adopted a strategy that contrasted with the former English hegemon which had been a big net biomass importer, but a net coal exporter. In 1972, the United States imported 20 percent of the fossil fuels it consumed. Given the very low price of oil, these imports did not significantly affect its trade balance. On the hand, they increasingly affected the American social metabolism. It is on this front that the limits of the inward-looking American model were evident.

---

[11] The system involved mainly two products, wheat and soy oil, and went on to cover almost 70 percent of American wheat exports, in other words almost 30 percent of global exports (Friedmann, 1982: 271).

17

Uneven spread of the American model and the institutionalization of the Global North–South division

In the decades that followed the end of the Second World War, two groups of countries emerged, mirror images of each other. History had presaged neither the internal unity of the groups, nor their separation into two groups.[1]

The partition, in part, resulted from the uneven spread of the American model in the name of "reconstruction," "development," or "modernization" (see McMichael, 1996, on the concept of development project). Results from replicating the American model depended highly on what place each country had held in the international division of labor instituted during the English hegemonic phase. Adopting an inward-looking model was much easier for industrial countries, the "center," than for biomass-exporting countries, the "periphery" of the era of English hegemony.

But the partition was also the outcome of diplomatic maneuvering. In the postwar years, a series of conferences, diplomatic events, and international organizations were established, which would go on to institutionalize the division–vision of the world, reinforcing convergence of economic policies within each of the two groups and divergence between the groups. The dichotomy between the Global North and South, between developed and developing countries, etc., is of particular relevance for analyzing the postwar period in history; it holds little relevance, however, for the period that followed, and even less for the preceding periods.

Catching up with the center

Adoption of the American model

The US government played a very active role in the uptake of the American model by countries that had suffered great destruction during the Second World War, resulting

---

[1] Many texts link this division of the world to European colonial history. However, neither dates of colonization, nor duration of colonization, nor even the fact of having been colonized or not, are decisive in whether a country belongs to one group or the other. The United States were colonized from the end of the sixteenth century until 1776, Argentina from 1516 to 1816, Australia from 1788 to 1900, Ghana from 1902 to 1957, Haiti from 1492 to 1804, Finland from the Middle Ages to 1914, Thailand never, Côte d'Ivoire from 1920 to 1960, Ireland from 1494 to 1921, and so on. Which of these should belong to the Global North or to the Global South?

in serious balance of payments difficulties, and which were geopolitically situated on the front line of either side of the Socialist bloc. The top two of these were Germany and Japan.

The US brought with it the "religion of growth." The "politics of productivity," to use Charles Maier's expression, was based on an American vision of how they had regained prosperity following the trauma of the 1930s Depression.

The idea was that growth and productivity enabled resolution of both internal conflicts (on income distribution, on the respective roles of large firms, trade unions, and public administration in setting policies, etc.), and international ones. Prioritizing the quest for productivity, in other words, also enabled the settling of nagging problems (Maier, 1987: 128). This hypothesis was confirmed during the Second World War, a period that demonstrated to the United States that prosperity could be attained without any major redistribution of economic power, all while legitimizing state interventionism and planning.

American intervention in countries situated in the center first occurred under the form of direct administration of defeated countries: in West Germany until 1949, and in Japan until 1952. In Germany, the Morgenthau Plan, which had aimed to deprive Germany of all industrial sectors and turn it into an agricultural country, was very quickly abandoned in favor of rebuilding the whole economy, industry included, of the only country seen as capable of blocking Soviet expansion. Similarly, in Japan, rising social contestation forced the American administration to abandon its drive to eliminate all the institutions from the imperial era, and roll out support to economic growth.

In the Allied countries, active promotion by the United States of the "American model" did not occur through direct administration of the country in question, but through conditions tied to American loans. Through these loans, the United States exerted strong influence on the economic policies adopted in the immediate postwar period, for instance in France (Wall, 1991: chapters 2 and 6).[2] France was very dependent on American financial support for its imports of consumer goods, which were in short supply, as well as for undertaking the investments required for reconstruction and "modernization." The Monnet Plan made explicit reference to American funding for its implementation. The first loan agreements signed between Léon Blum and American Secretary of State Byrnes in 1946, like the 1948 Marshall Plan, came with conditionalities that were as specific and as diverse as opening up the French market to American cinema, or policies to stabilize exchange rates.[3]

---

[2] To official funding, one must add funding that was more or less hidden and that originated from the US administration, as well as from private entities (unions, foundations, and so on), which enabled the emergence of organizations perceived as being more favorable to the American model than to the rival Soviet model. The support provided for the establishment of the French union, Workers Force (Force Ouvrière), born from the scission of CGT (Confédération Générale du Travail) is one of the best illustrations of this.

[3] Pure imitation, without any prior intervention, also cannot be neglected in a context of international rivalry. According to Kenneth Waltz, father of "neo-realist" theory, imitation of the strongest is without doubt the best strategy for other countries to adopt: "In any competitive system the winners are imitated by the losers, or they continue to lose" (Waltz, 1999: 695). It is possible thus to see replication, without any subordination or cooperation: countries of "real socialism" thus chased the American model with the sole ambition of appropriating it for themselves, or surpassing it.

The "Trente Glorieuses"

The three decades that followed the end of the Second World War, baptized the "Trente Glorieuses" (Glorious Thirty Years) by Jean Fourastié, for Europe were a period of exceptional growth, unprecedented in its history (Fourastié, 1979). Between 1950 and 1973, Western Europe's GDP grew by 4.6 percent per year, much faster than during the interwar years, but also much faster than during the nineteenth century and Europe's first globalization.[4]

The Trente Glorieuses period differed greatly from the nineteenth century because of the very rapid increases in labor productivity—increases that explain why "regulationist" economists speak of intensive growth, as these productivity gains were redistributed in the form of increased wages (Table 17.1). Europe chose to adopt the Fordist model, and growth in purchasing power absorbed growth in production output in the domestic market.

Like in the United States, the postwar period differed from the prewar period in how incomes were redistributed: Figure 17.1 shows how fast the share of the richest 1 percent fell (on average from 20 to 10 percent of national income) to a level where it remained stable for the next thirty years of prosperity.

The case of the "Japanese miracle" was even more spectacular. Japan's GDP grew at a rate of 9 percent per year during the 1950s, 10 percent in the early 1960s, and 13 percent from the late 1960s until the 1973 oil shock! The average wage increased by a factor of three between the mid-1950s and 1973. The number of automobiles in circulation grew from 48,000 to 14 million between 1950 and 1973 (Allen, 1981: 268).

Japanese growth, moreover, was greatly bolstered by the war in Korea from the 1950s on. The war, which the Japanese Prime minister called "a gift from the gods" (Henshall, 1999: 191), gave Japan a role as a crucial supplier of the American army. Sales to the military brought in a third of Japan's foreign exchange earnings during the three years of war. Thanks to this stimulus, by 1953 industrial production had rebounded to its prewar level. The Korean War also accelerated the signing of a peace treaty between Japan and forty-eight countries, putting an end to direct administration by the Americans, which was replaced simply by American military bases.

Table 17.1 Annual growth rate in Western Europe and growth rate of wages in France, 1890–1973

	Overall rate	Rate per hour worked	Wages in France
1890–1913	2.6	1.6	0.4
1913–50	1.4	1.9	1.3
1950–73	4.6	4.7	3.6

Sources: Crafts and Toniolo, 1996: 2; Boyer, 1979, for French wages.

---

[4] Although it was often forgotten later, Eastern Europe initially had similarly impressive performances, with 4.9 percent annual growth between 1950 and 1973, and even record growth in Bulgaria and Romania (of 6 percent and 5.9 percent respectively) (Wakeman, 2003).

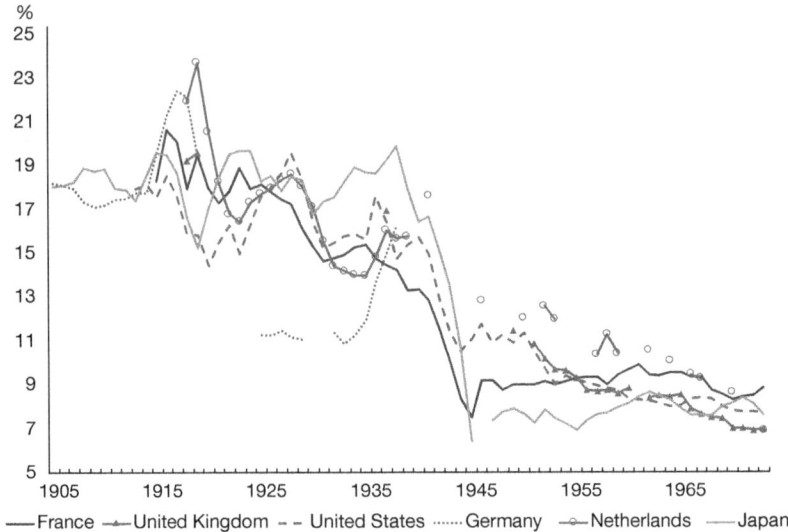

Figure 17.1 Share of the richest 1 percent in national income for various OECD countries, 1905–73

Source: adapted from Atkinson and Piketty, 2007.

However, the Japanese and European miracles have little that is miraculous when analyzed through the prism of material flow accounting; the "glory" for rebuilding these ruined countries goes mainly to an unprecedented mobilization of various minerals and of (imported) oil. The share of mineral matter in total material consumption (Figure 17.2) exceeded the peak that it had reached during the interwar period, and in a massive carbon dioxide cloud, latched on to growth with its teeth (excavators and drills).

The Western European countries, however, did not fully adopt the American model of an inward-looking economy. Economic growth in Europe was accompanied by a process of trade integration, of which the most accomplished form was the European Economic Community (EEC), which brought together West Germany, Belgium, France, Italy, Luxembourg, and the Netherlands. The first negotiations aimed at economic integration in Europe were carried out under the auspices of the Organization for European Economic Cooperation (OEEC) and pushed by the United States. However, very quickly the ambition to build a supranational organization was contested by the United Kingdom, Sweden, and Switzerland, and another avenue was sought by figures like Jean Monnet.

The Coal and Steel Economic Community, created in 1951, under French and German leadership, but including also Italy, the Netherlands, Belgium, and Luxembourg, was a first step. The goal was to create a common market for coal and steel through a higher authority that could impose decisions on national governments (Urwin, 2014: 67). The EEC was then created in 1957 based on the principle of a customs union, with the adoption of a common tariff for all countries, the elimination of all obstacles to trade between them, and the establishment of a supranational

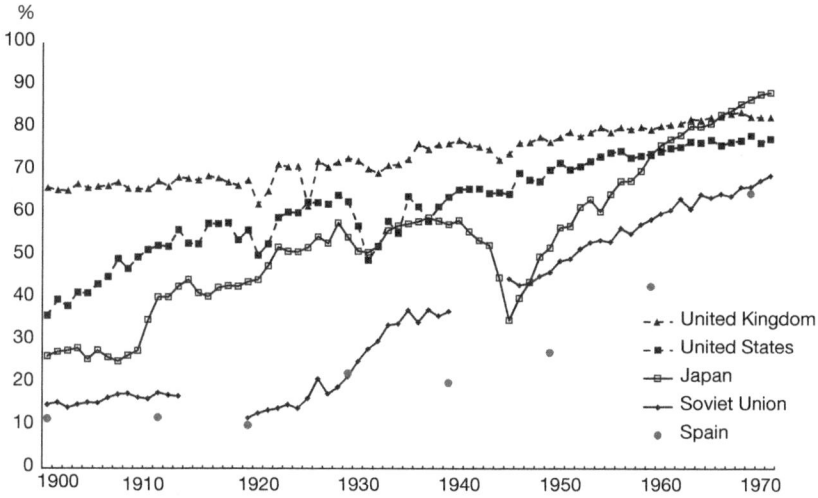

Figure 17.2 Share of mineral resources in domestic material consumption in various "industrialized countries," 1900–72

Sources: Krausmann et al., 2016b; Infante-Amate et al., 2015, for Spain.

authority, the European Commission, responsible for leading international trade negotiations. From then on, firms in the six member states openly competed with each other, but also benefited from a vast market, protected behind trade barriers (the Common Market), allowing them to make the most of economies of scale. For each of its member states, the EEC created the conditions for growth focused on a wider but protected space—one could speak of region-focused growth.

Growth in the share of intra-community trade in EEC countries' trade was a clear demonstration of this new focus. In 1957, 28 percent of total imports by EEC countries and 32 percent of their exports were intra-community exchanges (Bank for International Settlements, 1960: 110). By 1972, these ratios had reached 51 percent and 49 percent respectively (Eurostat, 1973: 10 and 11).

The regional focus is even more clearly evident in the ratio of foreign trade over GDP, if only extra-community trade is considered as foreign. This ratio stood at 20 percent in 1960 and 19 percent in 1970 (Table 17.2). It was, thus, for 1960s Europe, much lower than it had been for European countries during the years preceding the First World War (between 59 percent and 29 percent), and, moreover, the trend was towards further reduction. What in fact was not globalization, but Europeanization.

Protection of the agricultural sector

There are several excellent books on the history of OECD country agricultural policies and on the Common Agricultural Policy (CAP) of European countries (Bureau and Thoyer, 2014 on the CAP, and Sheingate, 2001 for a comparative analysis of the United States, France, and Japan). Generally, the interventionist policies for agricultural

Table 17.2 Rate of internationalization (exports + imports)/GDP of various European countries and the EEC, 1913–70

	Around 1913	Around 1938	1960	1970
United Kingdom	59	28	42	42
Germany[a]	42	15	36	35
France	42	21	27	31
Italy	29	17	25	30
EEC 6 without intra-trade	–	–	20	19

Sources: for 1913 and 1938, see Deutsch and Eckstein, 1961; for 1960 and 1970, see World Bank data for the United Kingdom, France, Italy, and the Netherlands; for Germany, see Deutsch and Eckstein, 1961; for the EEC 6, see Mitchell, 1992 for GDP, and Eurostat, 2008 for trade without intra-trade. [a] West Germany for 1960 and 1970.

markets that were adopted during the 1930s Depression years, and reinforced during the war were preserved to pander to farmers, who were well represented and still constituted an important voting demographic.

The CAP was the reproduction, at a regional level, of an inward-looking strategy, and one of the best practical applications of a food self-sufficiency policy. The Treaty of Rome, signed in 1957, explicitly stated this objective. In practice, the CAP consisted of the implementation of a mechanism of variable levies on imports and subsidies for exports, thus enabling a perfect disconnect between domestic producer prices and international prices, and maintaining the former at a higher level. Under pressure from Northern European countries (the Netherlands, Belgium, and Germany)—and the United States—the market for oleo-proteins, including soybean and therefore cattle feed, remained open to imports.

The Australian economist Kym Anderson undertook an immense task of data compilation to measure and compare the support accorded to agriculture in a very large number of countries in the fifty years that followed the war (Anderson, 2009, and Anderson and Nelgen, 2013 for updated data). He thus calculated what he respectively called the nominal rate and the relative rate of assistance to agriculture. The nominal rate is supposed to account for the differential in income generated by agriculture for all public interventions—grants or levies—targeting specific products (excluding therefore direct income aid granted without any production requirements). The relative rate takes into account protection provided to other sectors of the economy, "subtracting" this from support provided to agriculture (thus, if domestic fertilizer production is protected, farmers will pay more for their fertilizer, and this protection will result in a loss of income for them). Table 17.3 presents the value of these rates in the mid-1950s and early 1970s for France, West Germany, the UK, and Japan. The rates are all positive, even if, with the exception of Japan, when protection in the industrial sector is considered, the rate tends to fall. Moreover, except in the UK, protection of the agricultural sector rose between the two dates.

Table 17.3 Nominal and real rates of assistance to agriculture, 1955–72 (in %)

	1955–7		1970–2	
	Nominal rate	Relative rate	Nominal rate	Relative rate
France	33	20	63	53
Germany	48	43	82	79
United Kingdom	57	36	29	11
Japan	31	35	57	65

Sources: Anderson and Nelgen, 2013. Data: http://microdata.worldbank.org/index.php/catalog/388/get_microdata (accessed August 16, 2024).

For France, the Treaty of Rome entailed abandoning its strategy of imperial autarky. French colonies, on the eve of their independence, thus lost the preferential and protected access they used to have to the French market. The case of the Senegalese peanut kicked out of the French market by the American soybean sums up well the shift that occurred. France also experienced clear Europeanization of its agricultural trade.[5] Growth in the latter was pushed almost exclusively by trade with other EEC countries, while trade with the rest of the world followed a downward trajectory. Between 1961 and 1972, the rate of internationalization of French agriculture (sum of imports and exports over agricultural GDP) grew from 7 to 23 percent for trade with other EEC countries, while it fell from 32 to 25 percent for trade with the rest of the world (author's calculations based on INSEE data from various years). These figures clearly show the swing from empire towards Europe that the Treaty of Rome brought about.

Agricultural modernization: Synchronous developments

Several national narratives exist of how each country modernized its agriculture. In France, modernization is said to have been driven by enlightened figures such as Pisani, Batisse, and the Catholic Agricultural Youth group (Jeunesses Agricoles Catholiques) (Alphandéry et al., 1989; Gervais et al., 1978; Muller, 1984).

In reality, what is remarkable is the simultaneity and the similarity of the developments that occurred in various so-called "developed" countries. What we actually have is a case of replication of a hegemonic model, with but minor variations. All OECD countries during this period experienced increases in their yields, and above all in labor productivity in agriculture, and saw their numbers of farm workers decline sharply.

As we saw in the preceding chapter, some of the characteristics of "chemical farming" which spread in the United States from the 1930s, were already present in late-nineteenth-century Europe. Some regions, or even entire countries, at the time were already specialized in animal production using imported feed, while others focused

---

[5] And not full-blown internationalization as has often been claimed (Marloie, 1984).

solely on plant production thanks to mineral fertilizers (sourced either synthetically or from underground). After the Second World War, these developments continued and to them were added two "technical packets" which were more directly tied to the United States: the pairing of mechanization–motorization and "animal protein factories" (Grigg, 1992; Bairoch, 1999; Federico, 2005).

Without a doubt, the best comprehensive overviews of all the transformations that agriculture in what are called "developed" countries underwent after the Second World War are those that Yujiro Hayami and Vernon Ruttan produced over their long careers (Hayami, 1971; Ruttan, 1977; Hayami and Ruttan, 1985). Fathers of the theory of induced innovation, Hayami and Ruttan tasked themselves with comparing historical trends in factor productivity (land, and above all labor), and analyzing this productivity in function of the availability and the relative prices of factors.

Figure 17.3 which summarizes an essential part of their results, presents the trajectory of yields and labor productivity between 1930 and 1975 for six countries: Japan, Germany, Denmark, France, the United Kingdom, and the United States. The vertical axis shows yields, and the horizontal axis labor productivity. The two variables are measured in tons of wheat (in other words, in energy value) and are five-year averages.[6] The figure uses a logarithmic scale, which makes it easier to see when trajectories shift. The slope between two dates gives an indication of the evolution of

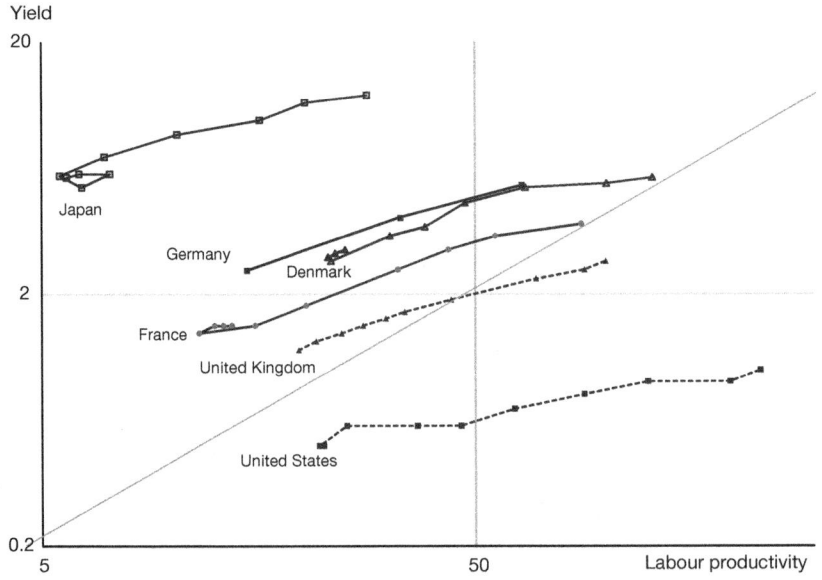

Figure 17.3 Evolutions in yields and labor productivity in various countries, 1930–75 (in wheat ton equivalent)

Sources: adapted from Hayami and Ruttan, 1985; Ruttan, 1978 for Germany.

---

[6] The method used to calculate the indicators is described in Hayami (1971).

Energy yields: A taboo subject in French agriculture debates?

There is very little literature available on the evolution of energy yields in French agriculture during its modernization phase, so little that one wonders if the subject is not a taboo one for discussion and for agronomists.

Work published by Jean-Paul Deléage and his colleagues in 1979 is one of the few exceptions to have tackled the issue. Deléage in a few figures summarizes the extent of the transformations that took place in thirty years. Measured in energy, production increased by a factor of almost three, ... and labor productivity by a factor of nine! With such figures, one should speak of a revolution, even if it was a "silent" one (Debatisse, 1963). Silent as the revolution may have been, it was not free of charge: fossil fuel consumption also increased by a factor of nine. The result is that the energy yield ratio collapsed, falling from 2.3 to 0.7. Overall agriculture, rather than providing energy, was consuming it very liberally.

Table 17.4 Energy balance of French agriculture, 1945 and 1975

	1945	1975
Energy inputs (in petajoules)		
Human labor	11.5	3.5
Fossil fuels	55.4	665.5
Total	78	688
Energy outputs (in petajoules)		
Plant	170.2	393.6
Animal	50.0	91.4
Total	183.0	485.0
Labor productivity per farm worker (in gigajoules)	27.9	242.9
Energy yield	2.3	0.7

Source: Deléage et al., 1979 cited in Stanhill, 1984b: 116.

yield with respect to changes in labor productivity. When the slope is weaker than the diagonal, labor productivity growth is higher than growth in yields, when it is stronger, the opposite holds.

European performance fell in between that of land-scarce Japan and that of land-abundant United States: land yield was higher than the United States' and lower than Japan's. Labor productivity, by contrast, was lower than the United States' but higher than Japan's.

The acceleration after the war and the parallel trajectories of European countries in terms of energy productivity—of both land and labor—are striking. The differences at point of departure persist at the end, but the growth trajectories are the same in all cases: labor productivity growth is more rapid than growth in yields. Therefore, certain national specificities aside, the same trends shaped by policy and markets are observed.

In all of the countries, the growth in labor productivity is remarkable (Table 17.5). This growth reflects the scale of the shift towards mechanization-motorization. When measured in energy produced per worker, labor productivity in many European countries grew threefold between the 1940s and the early 1970s, that is in just a little more than twenty years. Even more striking, growth in labor productivity of the active population is higher than that of other sectors of the economy—up to 2.5 times more in the UK. The glorious thirty were glorious above all in the field of agriculture.

One of the consequences of this productivity growth was, logically, a drastic reduction in agricultural employment. In Western Europe, the absolute size of the agricultural active population, which had remained stable since the late nineteenth century, fell sharply, from 44 to 24 million between 1950 and 1970, and its share in the total active population from 30 to 15 percent (Bairoch, 1999: 38). Once again, there was nothing magic behind this: progress, modernization, development, and so on, are just other names for the injection of oil into the agricultural sector. While labor (both human and animal) was disappearing, it was being replaced by a much larger quantity of energy (see box).

Table 17.5 Growth in GDP per worker in agriculture and in the rest of the economy (1957–68) and labor productivity in 1948 and 1968 of various OECD countries

	Agricultural labor productivity (millions of net calories per worker)		GDP growth per worker, 1957–68 (%)	
	1948–52	1968–72	In agriculture	In other sectors
Germany	32	107	6.9	4.8
Denmark	59	146	6.1	3.0
France	22	64	6.5	4.2
Italy	9	31	7.8	4.9
Netherlands	28	63	6.4	3.9
United Kingdom	37	85	6.0	2.4
United States	95	184	5.5	2.4

Sources: Johnson, 1973: 67, for GDP growth rate; Bairoch, 1999: 148, for productivity.

René Dumont's (1949) lessons from American agriculture

René Dumont was the first candidate for the French presidency (in 1974) from an ecological party. He was an activist pushing for the modernization of French agriculture in the immediate postwar period, and a stern opponent of what he called agricultural Malthusianism, that is, measures aimed at restricting supply as a way to keep prices and incomes high. He, on the contrary, pleaded for the need to simultaneously increase yields and labor productivity, through the use of fertilizers and tractors, or the cultivation of natural prairie land (Dumont, 1946).

As a lecturer at the National Agronomy Institute of Paris (Institut National Agronomique de Paris), he participated in the "secret drafting of a report on the French agricultural problem" during the war, which took up the conclusions of the International Food Conference held in Hot Springs (United States) in 1943 (Alphandéry et al., 1989: 144).

When the war ended, he became an advisor at the Commissariat of Planning for Modernization and Equipment, and actively contributed to the agricultural component of the Monnet Plan which affirmed that "an agriculture that is suitably guided and powerfully equipped, that combines the character of Northwestern European agricultures which developed thanks to the equipping of family farms, with in some regions, mechanization of large intensive cultivations could contribute effectively to the economic wealth of this country, all while ensuring the prosperity of the rural world" (First report of the Commission for Rural Modernization [Commission de modernisation rurale] 1946, cited by Alphandéry et al., 1989: 149).

It was in this capacity that Dumont in 1946 went on a mission to the United States, and it was this trip that would form the basis a few years later of his book *Les leçons de l'agriculture américaine* [Lessons from American Agriculture] (Dumont, 1949). In the book he underscored the differences in the labor productivity of an American farmer, a Tonkinese peasant, and a French peasant, showing the first to be fifty times higher than the second, and 3.5 higher than the third. He observed thus that "the staple food of the modest classes [corn] practically no longer requires any work: a capital event in the history of humanity" (ibid.: 328) but also that "of the 1,600 million quintals of cereal produced in the United States, only 10 percent are used directly for human consumption," and added that "this share seems to me one of the best indicators of the quality of nutrition; nutrition quality increases when higher proportions of grain are fed to cattle" (ibid.: 335).

René Dumont's mission was followed, between 1950 and 1959, by a series of sixty-eight "productivity missions" dedicated to the study of American agriculture (Brunier, 2012: 108). These missions supported the roll out of French agricultural modernization policy, agriculture having been considered since the launch of the Marshall Plan as a key basic sector, on the same level as energy and transport.

"Under-development" in the periphery

Industrialization through import substitution policies

For countries of the periphery, countries whose insertion into the global economy during nineteenth-century globalization occurred through the export of raw materials (mainly biomass) and import of manufactured goods, transitioning towards domestically centered growth, as existed in the United States and Europe, meant achieving accelerated industrialization. Most of these countries therefore made industrialization a priority in their economic policy choices. Sometimes presented as a strategic choice of elites faced with falling terms of trade,[7] accelerated industrialization was also the only possible response of these countries who were faced with the shutting off of their historical markets and the dismantling of the division of international labor that had prevailed until 1914. The strategies would take the form of policies that were called "import substitution industrialization (ISI)," deliberate industrialization policies based on strong protection of domestic markets and financed through taxing exports of raw materials. Latin American countries adopted ISI from 1945,[8] and were soon followed by former colonies as these gained their independence.

Regarding the theory on declining prices of raw materials, ISI policies had easier success in the immediate postwar period, precisely because raw materials were at a high price, bolstered by European reconstruction efforts and later the war in Korea. But after 1953, the situation turned about, product by product, and a long period of falling prices generated growing balance of payments difficulties for raw-material-exporting countries.

Several observers at the time accused import substitution industrialization policies of being the structural cause of the balance of payments deficits. For these analysts, after an initial phase during which substitution is easy, such as in light industry (textile, shoes, etc.), industrialization has to overcome increasing hurdles. Imports of industrial goods do not decrease because consumer goods imports are replaced by imports of semi-finished goods, spare parts, and machines. In addition, small population sizes, as well as the unequal distribution of wealth mean small markets which make it difficult

---

[7] In the field of international trade, "terms of trade" refers to the ratio between the price of goods imported and that of goods exported. Falling terms of trade means that the price of goods that are imported has risen with respect to that of goods exported.
[8] Before the Second World War, Latin American countries were identified, and identified themselves, as "raw material exporters," in relation with the place they occupied in the international division of labor engendered by globalization processes under the English hegemon in the nineteenth century. Thus, in a study on the global economy published by the League of Nations in 1938, these countries were included in the same group of "primary producer countries," along with Australia, Canada, New Zealand, Hungary, Romania, and Yugoslavia (Arndt, 1973: 18). After the Second World War, the Economic Commission for Latin America proposed a new vision of the global economy which focused on the hierarchized nature of this economy that distinguished between countries of the center, exporters of manufactured goods, and peripheral countries, raw material exporters (Prebisch, 1949). Under this vision, periphery countries in the long run would inevitably get poorer, at least in relative terms, under the effects of an international trade environment in which the price of products they exported (raw materials) tended to fall, compared to the value of what they imported. This was the thesis of falling terms of trade.

to benefit from economies of scale in manufacturing, which leads to high production costs and makes it impossible to export industrial goods (Furtado, 1970; Hirschman, 1968; Cardoso and Faletto, 1979).

The trajectory of GDP in Argentina, a rich country under the first globalization, which moreover played a crucial role in postwar trade negotiations, is a good illustration of this phenomenon. Thanks to impressive growth in its agricultural exports, Argentina's GDP per capita had caught up with that of France at the end of the nineteenth century, and just before the First World War had even slightly exceeded France's. The 1930s Depression ended this upward trajectory. Argentina lost ground during the decades that followed, except for the period of the Second World War. In 1980, its per capita GDP only represented 60 percent of France's.

Figure 17.4 also shows the trajectories in per capita GDP for India and Ghana. Despite the very imperfect nature of GDP as an indicator of the status of a country, we can see here the extreme heterogeneity of the group of countries called "developing." Their only point in common in reality is balance of payments difficulties; it is senseless to invent other technical, political, institutional, or cultural similarities.

Difficulties with industrialization slowed replication of the mining metabolic regime and of America's material voracity. Per capita material consumption of the countries called "developing" rose little after the Second World War, and particularly during the 1960s, and in any case much slower than in countries, capitalist or socialist, called "developed." Despite the demographic explosion experienced in Asia, Africa, and Latin America, the distribution of global material consumption remained practically unchanged (Table 17.6). In 1950, the share of the OECD and the USSR in global consumption stood respectively at 46 percent and 16 percent. In 1970, they

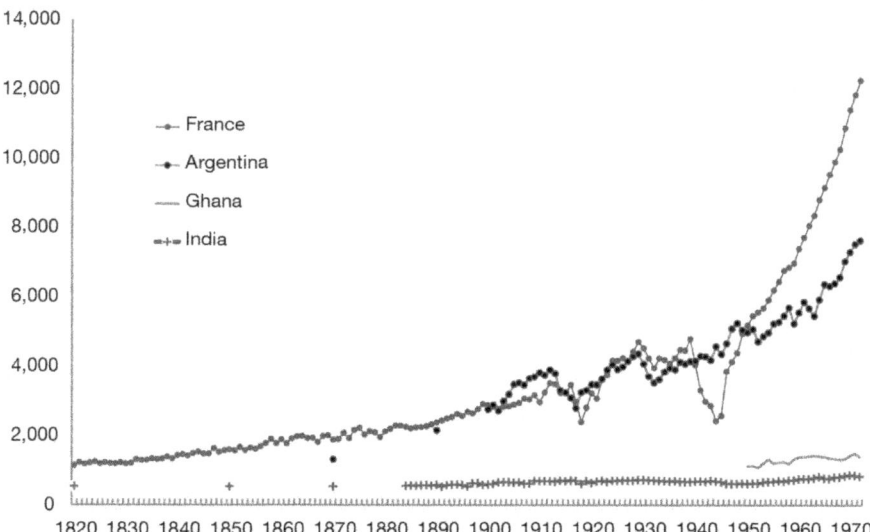

Figure 17.4 Per capita GDP in France, Argentina, Ghana, and India, 1820–1980

Source: adapted from Maddison, 2001.

Table 17.6 Per capita material consumption in the main regions of the world (in tons) and as percentage of global total, 1950, 1960, and 1970

	1950		1960		1970	
	Per capita	% of global total	Per capita	% of global total	Per capita	% of global total
OECD	9.7	46	12.1	43	15.9	45
USSR	8.1	16	10.8	17	14.4	17
Asia (Japan excluded)	2	20	2.9	22	2.9	20
Middle East & North Africa	1.8	1	3.6	2	3.4	2
Latin America	8.3	11	8.5	10	8.8	9
Africa	4.8	7	5.9	7	6.1	6

Source: adapted from Schaffartzik et al., 2014.

stood at 45 percent and 17 percent. This data appeared to corroborate those who at the time saw the division of the world between a rich North and a poor South as a structural feature of the global economy. The decades that followed, however, would challenge that view (Part 6).

Taxed agriculture

Under import substitution industrialization policies, what were called "developing" countries instituted a strict division between the domestic market and the international market for agricultural products. In agricultural markets, stabilization funds, marketing boards, and other agencies responsible for commercialization, in association with tariff policies, ensured that domestic prices were disconnected from swings in international prices.

An important difference, which however does not negate the inward-focus of growth strategies of the day, lay in the relations between agriculture and industry. Import substitution policies, a sort of "Fordism for the poor," everywhere were accompanied by changes in the terms of trade between agriculture and the rest of the economy, changes which were unfavorable to the former. The industrialization of countries that had previously specialized in biomass exports, as well as the construction of state apparatus for newly independent nations, could rely only on taxing agriculture to raise funds. Explicit or implicit taxation (in particular through overvalued exchange rates) was thus the norm for many developing countries until the 1970s, and sometimes even until the adoption of structural adjustment programs in the 1980s (Bates, 1984; World Bank, 1986; Krueger et al., 1991).

Price stabilization policies also became another instrument for taxing the agriculture sector, and these policies organized the transfer of resources towards the industrial sector. Export product prices were thus set much lower than international prices, the difference being kept by the state (Krueger, 1992). Capturing this difference was the main function of price stabilization funds and marketing boards in sub-Saharan Africa following independence.

The policy of low agricultural prices also extended to products intended for urban consumers, with the aim of securing political support and keeping wages low to support industrialization. The "discount sales" of American food products facilitated these policies aimed at low prices for agricultural products. In the early 1960s, American aid accounted for 55 percent of total cereal imports of developing countries, and this proportion rose to between 80 and 100 percent for countries such as Taiwan, India, Iran, Pakistan, Egypt, Korea, and Tunisia (Hopkins and Puchala, 1980). These "free" imports, resold at low prices by beneficiary states, made it possible to contain domestic prices of food products, as well as to fund the state's budget.

Estimations by Kym Anderson of the rate of assistance for agriculture during the periods of 1955–7 and 1970–2 show very clearly the contrast between policies implemented in the "North" and those in the "South" (Table 17.7). In what are considered "developing" countries, the rates were always negative, no matter the region, and always positive in the "developed" countries. In other words, "developing" countries taxed their agriculture, and "developed" countries protected it. If one considers also protection provided for the industrial sector—high, or even very high, for the former countries, and relatively weak for the latter—by calculating relative rates, the gap between the types of countries grows even wider.

There was, however, among those considered "developing" countries, a clear tendency to tax products intended for export much higher than products intended for the domestic market, or even to protect the latter (Krueger, 1992). This was the case in Asia (Timmer, 2009: 28). Taxation of agricultural products through price was also partially compensated in many countries by the availability of subsidies for inputs (fertilizer, pesticides, electricity for irrigation, etc.). As Robert Bates highlights for the African case, support through subsidies rather than prices provided government with a means for implementing clientelist politics, of which they made great use (Bates, 1983).

Table 17.7 Nominal and real rates of assistance to agriculture, 1955–72

	1955–7		1970–2	
	Nominal rate	Relative rate	Nominal rate	Relative rate
Africa	−14	−37	−13	−24
Developing Asia	−27	−55	−19	−42
Latin America	−18	−25	−13	−24
OECD	+18	+10	+30	+24

Sources: Anderson and Nelgen, 2013; data accessible on this webpage: http://microdata.world-bank.org/index.php/catalog/388/get_microdata (accessed August 16, 2024).

Agrarian reforms and the Green Revolution

Agrarian reforms and the "family farming" model

Market-oriented family farming was part of the standard production system that prevailed in the capitalist world under the American hegemony. Americans viewed family farms as one of the pillars of American democracy. Large landowners, the first of which the German Junkers, by contrast, embodied its worst enemies.

After the Second World War, the US administration sent USDA officials (from the Foreign Agricultural Service) to the countries that had lost the war to promote and structure agrarian reforms as a component of the demilitarization process of those societies. In Germany, the territories previously dominated by Junkers were under Soviet control, and therefore agrarian reform was not a priority issue for US policy there. In Japan, however, when MacArthur took over the country's administration, 70 percent of farmers were sharecroppers who ceded roughly half of their harvest to landowners. Here, the Americans were able to give free rein to their "democracy project."

A first bill tabled on December 4, 1945 (only four months after Hiroshima!) by Japanese authorities (Takigawa, 1972) was rejected by the Supreme Commander of Allied Powers (SCAP) who requested instead a bill

> [to] remove economic obstacles to the revival and strengthening of democratic tendencies, establish respect for the dignity of men, and destroy the economic bondage which has enslaved the Japanese farmer to centuries of feudal oppression. [...] The purpose of this order is to exterminate those pernicious ills which have long blighted the agrarian structure of the land where almost half the population is engaged in husbandry.
>
> (SCAP, 1945, cited by Kawagoe, 1999: 28)

A new law was passed in October 1946 limiting the land that a landowner farmer could keep to 3 hectares and to 1 hectare for absentee landowners, and making it compulsory for rent to be paid in monetary amounts, which were capped at 25 percent of harvest value. Owners who had their land confiscated received compensation in the form of treasury bonds with a 3.6 percent interest rate to be paid over thirty years. The farmers purchasing land could pay the state immediately or over a thirty-year period. During the passing of the bill, MacArthur declared:

> the Land Reform Bill is one of the most important milestones yet reached by Japan in the creation of an economically stable and politically democratic society [...] There can be no firmer foundation for a sound and moderate democracy and no firmer bulwark against the pressure of an extreme philosophy.
>
> (cited by Kawagoe, 1999: 29)

The landscape of Japanese agriculture was greatly transformed through the legislation: the percentage of farmers renting their land fell from 48 percent in 1941 to 9 percent in 1955.

Thereafter the fight against Communism became the driver and the goal of agrarian reform policies. In October 1950, President Truman declared:

> We know that the people of Asia have problems of social injustice to solve …. They want their farmers to own their own land and to enjoy the fruits of their toil. That is one of our great national principles, also […] this is the basis of our agriculture, and has strongly influenced our form of government.
>
> (cited by Gittinger, 1961: 197)

Within the United Nations system, the United States stepped up its commitment to agrarian reform, to counter the collectivist positions of the Soviet bloc. The United States thus promoted a very ambitious vision of agrarian reform within the UN, through their representative to the UN Economic and Social Council in 1951,[9] as well as through the Food and Agriculture Organization (FAO), where they affirmed, once more in 1951, that the FAO could only achieve its main goals if a large percentage of farmers in the world owned their land.

In Taiwan, American support to agrarian reform was the continuation of their commitment to the nationalist government of China before Mao came to power. The agrarian reform program was one of the first outputs of the Sino-American Joint Commission on Rural Reconstruction established in 1948. The reform, initiated in continental China, was implemented in Taiwan after 1949. Farm rents were reduced by more than a third, and land owned by the state was redistributed, as was privately owned land. When the reform was fully implemented, during the course of 1953, it had reduced the share of land worked by tenant farmers or sharecroppers from 39 percent to 15 percent (Gittinger, 1961: 291).

In October 1950 a mission undertaken on the request of Truman to the Philippines, a former US colony, to propose American technical and financial assistance, put the focus on agrarian reform. The mission was followed by the formulation of an action plan by an expert who had previously been involved in the Japanese agrarian reform: the plan proposed large-scale redistribution. Despite support from the then American ambassador, the plan was never implemented.

Ten years later, in Latin America, the Alliance for Progress, an ambitious aid program for the sub-continent, was initiated in 1961 by Kennedy for fear that Fidel Castro's ascension to power in Cuba would have a domino effect, and put agrarian reform back on the agenda. The Punta del Este Charter, founding document of the Alliance for Progress, proclaimed that all countries of the continent agreed:

---

[9] Reform was presented as "compris[ing] improvement in all the social and economic institutions surrounding farms," and included "redistribution or consolidation of holdings […] security of tenure […] improvement of title […] reform of the tax system […] and establishment of cooperative societies for common purchase, marketing, and credit" (Isador Lubin cited by Gittinger, 1961: 196).

To encourage, in accordance with the characteristics of each country, programs of comprehensive agrarian reform leading to the effective transformation, where required, of unjust structures and systems of land tenure and use, with a view to replacing latifundia and dwarf holdings by an equitable system of land tenure so that, with the help of timely and adequate credit, technical assistance and facilities for the marketing and distribution of products, the land will become for the man who works it the basis of his economic stability, the foundation of his increasing welfare, and the guarantee of his freedom and dignity.

Under the Alliance for Progress, many agrarian reform programs were undertaken in Latin America, and some of the guideline documents reiterated the charter's proclamation. This was the case in Venezuela, Costa Rica, Honduras, and Peru (Delahaye, 2003). Agrarian reforms were far from being a novelty in the region. There was already a long history of such reform, with highly variable, and often very limited, results depending on the country (de Janvry, 1981: chapter 6; Rudel and Hernandez, 2017).

Lastly, the promotion of family farming also took the form of state programs for agrarian colonization, supported by the World Bank, like in Indonesia (transmigration program) or in Brazil (in the Amazon, viewed as being a "land without men[10] for men without land"). In both cases, the displacement of landless communities was a welcome alternative to less palatable agrarian reform for the authoritarian regimes in power.

The green revolutions

Intensifying production, that is, increasing yields, was viewed as a necessity by the United States in order to avoid famine, and more generally reduce food insecurity in what were called "developing" countries. It was also a way of improving livelihoods of small-scale producers without having to engage in large-scale agrarian reform, which was often considered too complicated to implement, given local political economies. Moreover, focusing on yields was a conservative alternative that respected private property, an indisputable American value.

In his book *The Hungry World: America's Cold War Battle against Poverty in Asia*, Nick Cullather analyses the process by which the agrarian issue first came to be reframed as a food security issue, which in turn was reframed as an issue of yields (Cullather, 2010: 56). In 1968, the term "Green Revolution," coined by William Gaud, director of the US Agency for International Development (USAID[11]), contrary to what one may be tempted to think today, was neither a reference to ecology nor to Islam, but rather a term coined in opposition to the red revolutions, which were considered as carrying out reckless expropriations.

The "Green Revolution" project was born during the Second World War, following a visit by Henry Wallace, then US vice-president, to Mexico in 1943. Initially it consisted

---

[10] "Without men": the myth of virgin land and pioneers still prevailed.
[11] The American aid agency, USAID, was founded in 1961 as part of the Alliance for Progress. USAID was the leading funder of international research centers in the mid-1960s; it was replaced by the World Bank in later years.

of a Rockefeller Foundation program focused on improving wheat varieties. A few years later, Cimmyt (the International Maize and Wheat Improvement Center) was created; it was the pioneer in the realm of "international" agronomic research centers.

As Deborah Fitzgerald explains, the Rockefeller Foundation, without explicitly attempting to export the American farming model, promoted techniques that had emerged in an American context: large family farms that were capital-intensive rather than labor-intensive, producing for the market, integrated into a network of private and public institutions guaranteeing the farms' effectiveness. In Mexico, the foundation obtained good results only from farms that shared these characteristics, most of them located in the northern part of the country (Fitzgerald, 1986).

In 1960, the International Rice Research Institute (IRRI) was established in the Philippines with funding from the Rockefeller and Ford Foundations. In 1966, the institute developed a new variety of rice, IR8, which became very famous; IR8, a "miracle rice," was a short-straw variety that ensured that added fertilizers went to the rice grain rather than the straw.

These varieties proved their effectiveness in India, then the country most exposed to famine, under its self-sufficiency policy implemented in the mid-1960s by the minister of agriculture, Chidambaram Subramaniam. In the mid-1960s, most Indian imports of cereals were composed of American food aid. This gave the United States all the latitude to convince India to adopt a self-sufficiency strategy. There are divergent views on what motivated the United States. For Hoda and Gulati (2013), the Indo-Pakistani war led America to reduce aid to both countries. Ahlberg (2007) emphasizes doubts that Americans had about their capacity to continue satisfying India's growing needs. Varshney (1989) on the other hand sees above all an Indian decision to put an end to two decades of unsuccessful attempts at land reform and developing cooperatives, by turning towards a technological solution, a decision which also happened to reinforce American policy. In effect, in 1965, the Johnson administration adopted the "short tether" policy, eliminating all long-term commitments on food aid volumes to be delivered (these were now to be decided on a monthly basis). The Indian government thus started to support the Green Revolution, and also opened up the agrochemical sector to foreign investment (Union Carbide Corporation, which would rise to tragic fame in Bhopal in 1984, opened its first factory in India in 1969). With Cimmyt wheat seeds and Irri[12] rice, wheat production grew from 10 to 25 million tons between 1966 and 1973, and rice production from 30 to 44 million tons. During the same period, wheat imports fell from 7 to 2 million tons, and rice imports from 1 million to 300,000 tons.

---

[12] A high-yield variety, "ideal variety" capable of transforming in the most efficient way possible water, sunshine, and chemical inputs, in particular nitrogen, into food (calories) (Cullather, 2004: 239). Thus, the varieties of rice developed by Irri had to be short-straw to not waste resources in the form of non-food products, dark green to better absorb light, rigid to enable mechanization of harvesting, growable in all parts of tropical Asia, and resistant to parasites and disease. Such varieties implied significant changes in the way rice is grown, which was one of the goals of the American promoters, who saw improved seeds as a vector of modernization. IR8 was presented as doing for rice farming what the Ford T had done for the automobile.

The institutionalization of the North–South divide

After the Second World War, while the American model spread at differentiated speeds, a geopolitical polarization along a North–South axis took shape, formalized, organized, and reinforced by the creation of international organizations and clubs of countries (Table 17.8).

Table 17.8 Interstate organizations of the global "North" and "South"

	North	South
1948	OEEC (Organization for European Economic Cooperation) brought together 16 Western European countries, with the US and Canada as observers.	
1949	NATO (North Atlantic Treaty Organization)	
1951	ECSC (Economic Community for Steel and Coal): France, Italy, West Germany, and Benelux	
	ANZUS (Australia, New Zealand, United States Security Treaty)	
1955		Bandung Conference, bringing together 29 African and Asian countries
1957	EEC (European Economic Community): West Germany, Belgium, France, Italy, Luxembourg, Netherlands	
1959	DAG (Development Assistance Group)	
1960	EFTA (European Free Trade Association): United Kingdom, Portugal, Denmark, Norway, Switzerland, Austria, Sweden	OPEC (Organization of Petrol Exporting Countries)
1961	Transformation of the OEEC into the OECD (Organization for Economic Cooperation and Development) with the US and Canada becoming members, and DAG became DAC (Development Aid Committee)	Non-Aligned Conference in Belgrade
1963	Yaoundé Convention, EEC-ACP (Africa, Caribbean, and Pacific), bringing together former French and Belgian colonies from these regions: founded European aid and established a preferential trade regime.	
1964	UNCTAD (United Nations Conference on Trade and Development)	
	DAC (Development Aid Committee),	
	Japan becomes an OECD member	
1968	Finland joins the OECD	
	Adoption of the Generalized System of Preferences (GSP) by UNCTAD	
1971	Australia joins the OECD	
1973	New Zealand joins the OECD	Restriction of oil exports by OPEC
1973	The UK, Ireland, and Denmark join the EEC	

The idea that the United States, Western Europe, Australia, New Zealand, and Japan formed a homogenous group of countries sharing the same interests and objectives was not in any way self-evident in the 1930s, and even less, of course, during the Second World War. The terms "developed countries" or "industrialized countries," invented to create that union, only really came into use, and forcefully so, after 1945. Similarly, the concepts of "developing countries," of "Third World," or of the Global "South" have not always existed. They are also postwar inventions that emerged from a highly particular configuration of international relations at the time.

At the end of the period under study, membership in the OECD,[13] or in the Group of 77, was the most objective marker of one's status as a "developed country" or a "developing country" respectively. These organizations, which brought together countries with very different economic performances, were built over nearly thirty years of diplomatic maneuvering, and one was a reaction to the other. Under the Cold War, American hegemony was contested by both the Soviet bloc and countries of the "Third World." NATO was created in response to the former contestation, the OECD in response to the latter.

The OECD is thus a legacy of the Cold War, and with it, the category of "developed countries." It was born from the recomposition of an organization created in the immediate postwar period, the Organization for European Economic Cooperation (OEEC) established in 1948 to manage funds from the Marshall Plan, formally called the "European Recovery Program." In effect, one of the conditions of the Marshall Plan was that there be cooperation between European countries, given the joint plan for their reconstruction. When it became clear that in the Cold War context, the USSR and its satellites could not participate in an initiative that was clearly at the service of the United States, the OEEC was founded through initiatives from France and the United Kingdom. It brought together sixteen countries, as well as the United States and Canada who had formal status as observers—very influential observers as far as the United States was concerned.[14]

Despite failing to concretize the economic and political integration of Western Europe as was America's ambition, the OEEC was maintained when the Marshall Plan ended in 1952, as an instrument for economic cooperation to complement NATO.[15] In 1961, the OEEC became the OECD, with the United States and Canada now as full members.

---

[13] The OECD is a very curious international organization. It is rarely under the spotlight in the news, and has not been the target of mass protest movements as have been the WTO, the World Bank, and the IMF. And yet, the OECD plays a crucial role in the design, homogenization, one could even say standardization, of policies of its member states. Contrary to many other organizations, the OECD does not have any financial or legal resources. According to Matthieu Leimgruber and Matthias Schmelzer, the OECD can be defined as both "a 'forum organization' providing a framework in which member countries exchanged views, negotiated common initiatives and agreements, and collectively legitimated their policies, and a 'service organization' which itself conducted services important to member countries such as the collection, standardization, and dissemination of information and data" (Leimgruber and Schmelzer, 2017: 24).

[14] The German occupied zone initially also had observer status, but later became an associate member.

[15] René Sergent, a senior French official, who was Secretary-General of the OEEC between 1955 and 1960, was previously deputy Secretary-General of NATO.

The shift from OEEC to OECD was aimed at overcoming divisions within Western Europe, and above all at establishing common positions to counter the influence of the USSR in former European colonies, and to defend these positions jointly at the United Nations where the United States and its European allies had become a minority. Matthieu Leimgruber and Matthias Schmelzer define the OECD as the "identity-generating Club of the West," whose double mission was to support global growth by coordinating Keynesian style policies, and to organize official development aid under the framework of the DAC (Leimgruber and Schmelzer, 2017: 46).[16]

What is a developing country?

The extreme heterogeneity of the countries that are grouped together under the terms "underdeveloped countries," "developing," or "the (Global) South" calls for an interrogation of the substance of these terms. When and how were they imposed, and for what reasons?

These terms were used, along with the term Group of 77, to constitute a vast tri-continental alliance defending common positions in trade negotiations. In actuality, using trade positions to distinguish a particular group had already been done after the First World War, when the expression "backward countries" was used in international conferences to refer to territories just recently industrialized (mainly in Latin America and Asia) who were viewed as a potential threat to the "old industrialized countries." Establishing global standards to counter this threat was part of Woodrow Wilson's global pacification project. The establishment of the International Labour Organization (ILO), under the framework of the Versailles Treaty in 1919, was aligned to this ambition. The ILO's founding text affirms: "the failure of any nation to adopt humane conditions of labour is an obstacle in the way of other nations which desire to improve the conditions in their own countries."*

But the emergence of the category "developing countries" was associated mainly with another type of logic, the logic of aid, a direct legacy of European powers' colonial policies. "Development," that is, the ambition to change, from the outside, a local situation deemed unsatisfactory, or in other words a project in social engineering, initially did not target societies, but resources that were considered insufficiently employed. This vision of development was close to Keynesianism and its focus was on the under-employment of factors, in particular of labor. The term "development," which is to be linked with "*mise en valeur*" of French colonies, was very early on officially used to define one of the objectives of English colonial policy.

Antony Anghie attributes a decisive role to the system of mandates put in place after the First World War by the League of Nations in the expansion of colonial "developmentalism" (Anghie, 2002: 515). The Pact of the League of Nations, another product of the Versailles Treaty, specified that "development" was the goal of the

---

[16] The Development and Assistance Group (DAG) was created at the request of the American administration in 1959, and was a precursor to the creation of the OECD. Re-baptized a year later as the Development Aid Committee (DAC), it established development aid as one of the identifying attributes of what were called "developed" countries.

system of mandates. Henceforth associated with the pursuit of "well-being" and the "protection" of native populations, development involved formulating a science of colonial administration capable of directing, documenting, and comparing progress based on the accumulation of detailed knowledge of the territories concerned. This vision gradually penetrated policies of European metropoles who were confronted with increased native social contestation. The 1929 English Colonial Development Act attests to this, as does, for the French side, the establishment in 1946 of the Economic and Social Investment and Development Fund (FIDES) (Cooper, 1996).

Contrary to some claims (Escobar, 1995; Rist, 1996; Rahnema and Bawtree, 1997), Harry Truman did not invent "development," but his 1949 speech about "underdeveloped regions," which he defined by low levels of capital and knowledge, heralded a foundational period in the immediate postwar years for a whole battery of organizations and funding which held in common a vision of underdevelopment as being a deficit in "something" (institutions, infrastructure, physical capital, human capital, social capital, technical and scientific knowledge, etc.), which "developed" countries supposedly had, and the latter had the moral duty to help the "underdeveloped" benefit from these.

This conception led to a revival in the 1960s of some of the apparatus of colonial administration in the form of aid mechanisms, which in France were termed as "cooperation." It was during this period that the newly created EEC transformed the protection that French colonies enjoyed into "development aid," and that the United States launched the Alliance for Progress, with the creation of the USAID, keen to avoid contagion of other Latin American countries by the Cuban Revolution. It was also at this time (1960) that the International Development Association (IDA) was created within the World Bank, with the mission of distributing grants and concessional loans to the poorest countries.

Within the context of the first UNCTAD conference, one can also interpret the institutionalization of aid as compensation by "developed" countries for their refusal to compromise on GATT rules. In the end, the alliance of countries of the Group of 77, with their initially almost opposed histories and demands, were met with in an undifferentiated response to their "inaptitude to prosperity," in the form of aid (thus remaining in the hands of "developed" countries).

In 1986, the Group of 77 was replaced, especially on agricultural issues, by the Cairns Group composed of "developed" countries (Australia, New Zealand, and Canada), "underdeveloped" countries (Brazil, Argentina, Thailand, etc.), and even one country from the East (Hungary). Henceforth, the distinction between "developed" and "developing" no longer held relevance for trade negotiations. Today a "developing country" is merely a country that receives aid, and all that accompanies such aid (advice, expertise, conditions, agreements, ...).

The term "backward country" made a comeback with the Second World War, but the reference to labor norms disappeared. Thus Rosenstein-Rodan in his article "The international development of economically backward areas" distinguished between five economically backward regions: the "Far East," that is India and China, "the colonial empires, in particular in Africa," the "Caribbean zones," the "Middle East," and Eastern and Southeastern Europe (Rosenstein-Rodan, 1944: 159). Latin America thus was not a backward region.

Development aid held such importance in the OECD's identity because it represented the response to demands concerning the rules of international trade by the group of countries collectively referred to as "developing countries": in short the leitmotiv of the OECD at the time was "aid, not trade."

Given the extreme heterogeneity of situations, the creation of a "developing country" group in the arena of global economic negotiations did not happen spontaneously. Such a grouping came into existence mainly with the goal of changing GATT rules that governed trade policies.[17]

In 1956, an amendment introduced the first distinction between GATT "contracting parties" by mentioning countries "which can only support low standards of living and are in the early stages of development." The expression "first stages of development" did not apply only to countries "which have just started their economic development, but also to contracting parties the economies of which are undergoing a process of industrialization to correct an excessive dependence on primary production" (Evans, 1968: 81).

The July 1962 Conference on the Problems of Economic Development organized in Cairo was the first joint initiative of countries from the three continents (Africa, Asia, and Latin America). Its final resolution called for the launch of a grand conference on "international trade, trade in primary products, and the economic relations between developing and developed countries." In August 1962, a UN Economic and Social Council resolution[18] called for a UN conference on trade and development which was to address two priority themes: access to global markets for developing countries, and price stabilization of basic products. In December 1962, the UN General Assembly decided that the conference would be held in 1964.

The first United Nations Conference on Trade and Development (UNCTAD) was thus prepared under the leadership of Raul Prebisch, former Secretary-General of the Economic Commission for Latin America, where import substitution policies had been conceived. The replacement of the "center and periphery" dichotomy in discourse by "developed and underdeveloped" then created the possibility of establishing a grand alliance between Latin American countries and former European colonies, while the focus on balance of payments problems made it possible to unite countries with very different levels of wealth and industrialization. Two groups of countries with clearly distinct profiles came together on this occasion:

– The countries of Latin America (Brazil, Argentina, etc.) and Asia (India, etc.) who had engaged import substitution industrialization policies and who faced the problem of rising imports of capital goods.
– African countries with very low levels of industrialization who faced the problem of closed European markets and, for former French colonies, the dismantling of imperial preferential treatment.

---

[17] Alongside initiatives aimed at defining a distinct position in a Cold War context (the Bandung Conference, and the Non-Aligned Conference).
[18] Sponsored by India, Yugoslavia, Brazil, Ethiopia, and Senegal.

UNCTAD presented an opportunity to institutionalize alliances. Four distinct negotiation groups emerged in the conference: OECD countries, European socialist countries, China, and a group of "developing" countries, the Group of 77. Under UNCTAD, "developing countries" were not identified as countries needing "aid" from developed countries, but as countries demanding specific rights: the right to establish agreements between raw-material-exporting countries to shore up international prices, and the right to special access to "developed country" markets.[19] These two demands openly went against the principles that had been adopted in the postwar period for the governance of international trade (the Havana Charter and GATT): principles which limited the establishment of agreements on specific products to temporary management of crises of overproduction, as well as the most-favored nation principle.

The idea that the OECD grouped together all "developed countries" and represented them emerged reinforced from the first UNCTAD conference (Hongler, 2017). The OECD countries, initially disorganized in front of this new unity of "developing countries," strengthened their conviction that it was necessary that "developed" countries adopt common positions, and that membership of the OECD was now no longer just a positioning with regard to Socialist bloc countries but also with regard to "Third World" countries.[20] This perception would also play an important role in Australia and New Zealand later joining the organization (Carroll, 2017).[21]

---

[19] This demand led to the creation in 1968 of the generalized system of preferences (GSP) principle within UNCTAD. The GSP was validated as part of GATT in 1971. Each member of the OECD had its own GSP through which it bestowed preferential customs rates on products of its choice to "developing" countries of its choice. Newly industrialized countries were the biggest beneficiaries of this system (see Part 6).

[20] From this viewpoint, it is interesting to observe that Finland, Australia, and New Zealand were admitted as participants to the DAC discussions on UNCTAD, well before being afforded full membership to the OECD (Hongler, 2017: 148).

[21] Australia, however, shared a certain number of demands expressed by "developing" countries in the framework of UNCTAD, and therefore under GATT too, in particular concerning the liberalization of agricultural trade. New Zealand, for its part, in 1963 signed the Call of Developing Countries to the UN Secretary-General. Both countries nevertheless ended up heeding the siren call of the OECD, which with their joining stabilized its membership for the next twenty years.

18

International agricultural trade: Limited, food-focused, and administered

As early as 1973, David Gale Johnson's book *World Agriculture in Disarray* offered a perfect diagnosis. Global trade in agricultural products in the postwar period was first and foremost determined by state policies, in particular those of industrialized countries, which drastically reduced such trade and generated a geography of flows that was not linked to production costs (Johnson, 1973).

The slowed growth that prevailed in the international biomass trade after the First World War continued after the Second. The share of biomass in international trade in goods and services fell from 50 percent in 1913 to 17 percent in 1972 (Table 18.1). The decline was particularly marked for non-food biomass, whose share in global trade fell from 21 percent in 1913 to 3 percent in 1972 (food biomass fell from 29 to 14 percent), due in part to protection and self-sufficiency policies, and in part to the rise of synthetic substitutes.

Very weak and very tolerant multilateral regulation for "developed countries"

During this period, in which states played a key role in the regulation and the use of biomass output, few international rules constrained their action. Yet it was also during this period that several international organizations with such ambition were created: the FAO, GATT, UNCTAD, etc.

The initial ambition of the FAO, as defined by the Hot Springs Conference in 1943, was to facilitate the transfer of food products from regions with calorie surpluses

Table 18.1 Share of biomass in global trade in goods and services (in %)

	1913	1929	1937	1953	1966	1972
Food biomass	29	26	25	26	17	14
Non-food biomass	21	20	19	14	5	3

Sources: Lamartines Yates, 1959; FAO, various years.

towards regions with deficits, as food crises or famines were not to be considered as local problems, but rather as the expression of a global disequilibrium whose solution was to be found in international cooperation (Jachertz and Nützenadel, 2011: 102). The war had already given birth to international cooperation mechanisms around food, such as the Combined Food Board, the United Nations Relief and Rehabilitation Administration (UNRAA), and the International Emergency Food Council.

The ambition to regulate, or even to organize, international trade, however, was quickly deflated by divergences between English and American authorities. For the English, who were strongly influenced by J.M. Keynes, the goal was to return to free trade as had prevailed prior to the First World War through global regulation of stocks to guarantee a basic level of stability of international prices, considered a necessary condition for free trade.[1] The Americans, who were strongly engaged in administering their own agricultural markets, excluded the possibility of free trade for this sector. They went so far as to conceive a system for planning agricultural production at the global level, and wanted strict regulation of international trade which was considered simply a residual trade (Daviron and Voituriez, 2003).

The first director general of the FAO, Boyd Orr, following the English vision, envisaged the creation of a World Food Board responsible for establishing a global food reserve and funding the supply of agriculture surpluses to the neediest countries. But the commission responsible for finalizing the FAO's mandate did not subscribe to the idea, and the FAO was dispossessed of the field of agricultural market regulation (Daviron and Voituriez, 2006).[2] One of the rare interventions of the FAO in this field was in 1954: when the United States passed legislation on international food aid, the FAO defined a set of rules on the utilization of surpluses so as to prevent food aid being used as a disguised export subsidy. Thereafter, with the exception of managing food aid in the immediate postwar period, the action of the FAO was limited to providing technical assistance to "developing" countries. The history of the FAO is a reflection of the immobility resulting from the dissensions between the English and American positions described earlier.

But independently of the contrarian winds that rocked its cradle, the FAO also harbored within it a structural incoherence. The FAO presented its main ambition as being to fight hunger in the world—and reaffirmed this each time there was a hike in international prices. The final declaration of the Hot Springs Conference thus affirmed: "The first cause of hunger and malnutrition is poverty. It is useless to produce more food unless men and nations provide the markets to absorb it." The priority accorded to food, proclaimed during the FAO's creation, was confirmed in the 1970s with the creation of the Committee on World Food Security (CFS) and the World Food Council, and once again in 2008, when the CFS was reformed and opened up to "civil

---

[1] For Keynes, the instability of markets in the interwar period was the cause of rising protectionism, and therefore needed to be addressed directly if one wished a return to free trade. Public policies of stockpiling and free trade were viewed as complementary at the time; which is not at all the case today with the WTO.

[2] This area of action would itself fade away with the failure of the negotiations that were supposed to lead to the creation of the International Trade Organization.

society." Nonetheless, the FAO's activities and performance indicators were profoundly agrarian and productionist: in short, good agricultural yields would automatically guarantee satisfactory levels of food for all. Despite the presence of both the terms "food" and "agriculture" in the organization's name, the equation agriculture equals food was taken for granted. The specialization of agriculture in food production likely had something to do with this conception of things, as it led one to consider that agricultural problems were food problems, and the inverse. Yet, while agriculture was increasingly reduced to food, food was far from being limited to agriculture, and in fact the consumer was ever more distanced from agriculture.

The GATT, which was the only international regulation governing global trade after the Second World War, established a negotiated form of protectionism implemented under a multilateral framework, based on the subordination of external trade to domestic stability. This principle of subordination was clearly illustrated in the field of agriculture: the agricultural rules of 1947 resulted from the lessons drawn from the farm crisis of the 1930s. American and European leaders emerged from the crisis convinced that overproduction was inevitable and insensitive to lower prices. Supporting farm incomes therefore called for very active intervention from states.

A series of derogations established under GATT gave agriculture a different status from industry (Daviron and Voituriez, 2003). The following were thus authorized:

- Quantitative restrictions on imports of a product when domestic production of the product in question was subject to certain restrictions or to domestic measures aimed at stabilization or price support.
- Agricultural export subsidies, on condition that market shares remained equitable (but the term "equitable" was difficult to define).
- Other mechanisms aimed at protecting agriculture, such as variable levies on imports and domestic subsidies.

The exceptional status of agriculture was confirmed in 1955 when the United States was attributed a waiver allowing them to limit volumes of beef imports. In short, from the perspective of international law, each country could implement the policy of its choice and employ all the instruments, or almost all, necessary to protect agricultural employment and income (Hopkins and Puchala, 1980; Cohn, 1993). "Developed" countries took great advantage of these provisions to protect their agriculture.

And it was this state of affairs that countries from the ex-periphery, now grouped under the G77, contested in the late 1960s, given how it dwindled their agricultural markets. Raul Prebisch, who was considered the G77 spokesperson, clearly stated that the opening up of agricultural markets of European and North American countries was the key topic for the UNCTAD negotiations. He wrote:

> The restrictive measures applied to imports by the industrial countries cover the whole vast range of primary items except for those which, by their nature, cannot be produced domestically in these countries. In western Europe, cereals and meats, milk products, vegetable fats and oils, sugar and other foodstuffs are thus well-protected by fixed or flexible tariffs and import quotas. Thanks to

this protection, it is possible to pay domestic producers, as stated above, prices much higher than those prevailing on the international market, or to grant them substantial subsidies. While the effects on consumption vary, depending on the nature of the measures adopted, all these measures serve to stimulate increased domestic production at the expense of imports, which have thus dropped to a level where they are merely residual.

(Prebisch, 1964: 23)

But the demands of the G77 would not be met, and it was not until the Uruguay Round of GATT in 1986 that the issue was seriously addressed.

The protection of agriculture by "developed" countries, alongside its almost systematic taxation in "developing" countries, engendered a sharp recomposition of the geography of biomass exports (Table 18.2). The share of all "developing" countries in global biomass exports fell from 46 percent in 1955 to 34 percent in 1972. All three continents—Africa, Asia, and Latin America—regressed. By contrast, Europe, both West and East, and the United States gained market shares, while the former dominions maintained their former levels.

Establishing agreements around specific products was another issue the G77 fought for. Their ambition differed considerable from that of the immediate postwar period, when agreements were perceived as exceptional and temporary measures for managing disequilibrium situations to enable the sectors in crisis to adjust. Henceforth, the goal was to set up permanent mechanisms to shore up prices. Until the surprise blow to oil markets dealt in the 1970s by the Organization of Petroleum Exporting Countries (OPEC), negotiations on product agreements undertaken through UNCTAD achieved just one single agreement, on cocoa.

Table 18.2 Share (in %) of various regions in global biomass exports (intra-EEC trade excluded), 1955 and 1972

	1955	1972
Latin America	17	13
Africa	10	7
Asia	19	13
Total "developing countries"	**46**	**34**
Western Europe	21	25
United States	12	17
Canada, Australia, and New Zealand	13	14
Total "developed countries"	**47**	**56**
Eastern Europe	7	9

Source: UNCTAD, 1976.

International trade: Residual and administered

We have seen the key role that states played in managing biomass supply and utilization. In almost all countries now, state agencies controlled volumes of biomass that entered and left the country. This state of affairs—very unique in history—enables one to consider countries as units on the international market. After the Second World War, the long-distance trade became a truly international trade, that is, trade taking place between different nations.

National prices, which still fluctuated in unison in the late 1920s (Zapoleon, 1931), started acting independently after the Second World War. Stabilization policies that were implemented from the Second World War disconnected domestic prices from world prices. This was their fundamental difference from the protectionist measures that emerged in the late nineteenth century, which had limited themselves to taxing foreign trade. International markets henceforth functioned like sluices:[3] the prices varied constantly, but they put two spaces—an exporting country and an importing country—where prices were stable, in relation to one another. Thus, at any given moment, prices could vary greatly between countries. Gale Johnson shows that, in 1968, producer prices were in the range of $4 per quintal (Argentina) to $14 or more (Finland, Japan, Switzerland) for wheat, $6 per quintal in Thailand to more than $30 in Japan for rice, $30 per quintal in Argentina to $130 in the USSR for beef, and $100 per quintal in Australia to $280 in Switzerland for butter (Johnson, 1973: 56).

With the exception of specifically tropical or subtropical products (coffee, cocoa, tea, natural rubber, and cotton), "international" markets for agricultural products became the residual spaces of domestic markets. Only deficits and surpluses were traded internationally, and thus volumes with respect to global production or consumption were low. It was as if, on these non-tropical markets, each country was exporting its production instability towards the international market. Given the low volumes of trade, the high variability in export supply and in import demand had potentially significant repercussions on prices.

The control that exporting countries now had on global stocks, however, enabled them to partially contain the instability of international prices. By accumulating stocks as part of their price support policies in their domestic markets, states were also able to act on the stability of international prices.

In effect, as McCalla (1966) underscored, the market power of an actor was based much more on their capacity to stockpile than on the market share they controlled.[4] Almost all of the international markets at the time could be assimilated to exporting state oligopolies, and the issue of regulating these markets became a question of

---

[3] However, contrary to the functioning of a sluice, prices in the buffer zone could reach much higher, or lower, levels than the price extremes of the countries concerned.
[4] In the case of agricultural products, given that it is practically impossible to control all the productive apparatus (given the atomization of producers, unpredictable weather, delays in production response, etc.), a producer country without stockpiles, nor the capacity to stockpile, is limited to exporting what they produce. From this perspective, the elasticity of their export supply at any given instance can be considered to be zero. That country thus can influence neither prices, nor volumes traded on the international market.

coordinating between the members of each oligopoly, and their export and stockpiling policies. The 1953–64 decade, after the Korean War, saw the establishment of a number of cooperation mechanisms within such oligopolies: the FAO's Consultative Subcommittee on Surplus Disposal, international agreements on wheat, the Food Aid Convention, and regulation on dairy products under GATT. These institutions mostly based themselves on a solidly constructed hierarchy between countries, and on the existence of an uncontested leader taking on the role of residual supplier.[5] The coffee market, although it was tropical and therefore non-residual, saw the establishment of international agreements based on the same logic of coordinating export and stockpiling policies, and the central role of residual exporter was played by Brazil (Daviron, 1993). This logic of cooperation and cartelization on international markets got a renewed boost when the G77 and UNCTAD were established, and the agreement on cocoa was concluded.

Despite the predominance of self-sufficiency ambitions for biomass, some zones of international trade in agricultural products continued to exist. I will adopt the term of "international complexes" used by Harriet Friedmann (1991, 1992) to distinguish between and describe the different logics that underlay these trades, and to briefly present the array of national policies and international organizations that determined and regulated trade in these agricultural products. The description of four complexes (Table 18.3) allows us to illustrate how this system of complexes worked:

- The food aid complex: the logic here was one of overproduction. The complex was initially mainly centered on wheat and on the United States' concessional sale policy. The United States saw aid as a market for their surpluses, while recipient countries, where state offices were responsible for distributing the food aid, saw it as a tool to keep wages low to favor industrialization. It was partially regulated internationally by the International Wheat Agreement and the FAO Consultative Subcommittee on Surplus Disposal. During the 1960s, the complex developed, integrating new products (soybean, powdered milk), new suppliers (the EEC), and new international organizations (the World Food Program) and the Food Aid Convention.
- The livestock complex. This initially consisted of flows of animal feed (corn and soybean) towards Western Europe and Japan. Germany, and especially the Netherlands, who historically had depended on foreign trade for animal feed for their livestock sectors, imposed a "chink" in the EEC common market protection so as to maintain these imports. This "chink" would be institutionalized under GATT during the Kennedy Round negotiations. The United States also played a key role here in export supply and in price formation by controlling the main part of global stocks of corn and soybean. From the 1960s, this complex also involved dairy products and beef, whose exports were supported by European refunds, and were soon to be governed by two agreements concluded under GATT, which set minimum export prices.

[5] This strategy of residual supplier (who adjusts their export volumes to guarantee price stability) was carried out by the dominant country(ies): the US–Canada duopoly for wheat (McCalla, 1966); the United States for corn (Bredahl and Green, 1983), soybean (Bertrand et al., 1985), and rice (Benz and Mendez, 1994); Brazil for cocoa, Ghana, in its own way, for cocoa; and the India–Sri Lanka duopoly for tea.

Table 18.3 The three postwar international complexes of food products

	Food aid complex (wheat, oil, powder milk)	Livestock complex—animal feed (wheat, corn, oilseeds, cereal substitutes) and animal products	Tropical food complex	
			Drink stimulants (coffee, cocoa, tea)	Sugar
Domestic policies for … Import demand	Public agencies with monopoly of trade in recipient countries	"Chink" in European protection for oilseeds and cereal substitutes. Japan's 1961 Agricultural Law		Import quotas in the EEC (ACP), the US (Caribbean and Philippines) and the USSR (Cuba)
Export supply	American food aid, and later European aid	American (and Canadian) international price stabilization policy for "grain" (wheat, corn, soybean)	Government agencies controlling exports and stockpiles in "developing" countries	Government agencies controlling exports and stockpiles in "developing" countries
International rules and agreements	International wheat agreement. FAO Subcommittee on Surplus Disposal. Food Aid Convention. World Food Programme	PAC agreement during GATT Kennedy Round. GATT agreement on certain dairy products (minimum price). GATT agreement on beef (minimum price)	UNCTAD. International coffee agreement. International cocoa agreement	International sugar agreement

Source: Daviron, 2008.

- The exotic drug foods complex, which was a legacy of colonialist Europe's eighteenth-century long-distance trade. The complex involved coffee, cocoa, tea, and cane sugar. The last, facing competition in Europe from beet sugar, continued to play an important role in supplying the United Kingdom and the United States. Exports of these products were strictly controlled by state offices, which existed in practically all producer countries. For coffee and cocoa, exports were also coordinated internationally through interstate agreements. Trade in cane sugar, for its part, was administered by four bilateral agreements[6] which set import quotas at guaranteed prices, in addition to the International Agreement on Sugar.
- And lastly, a fourth logic prevailed through the persistence of trade in two non-food products, natural rubber and cotton. It was impossible to substitute these two products with synthetic matter for some uses (natural rubber for plane tires, for example). For both products, the main exporting countries, Malaysia and the United States respectively, played an essential role in determining trade volumes and international price formation via the effects of their stockpiling policies. This unilateral action was complemented by the existence, for cotton, of an international agreement—the International Cotton Advisory Committee, based in Washington on USDA premises—and for rubber, an association of exporter countries.

The difficult survival of fibers and natural rubber

In the introduction to this chapter, it was stated that, after the Second World War among non-food agricultural products, only cotton and rubber resisted replacement by substitutes drawn from underground resources. Nonetheless, even the story of these surviving products illustrates how strongly non-food usage of biomass was challenged by competing alternatives, as both cotton and rubber's shares in global consumption fell drastically.

Societies with solar metabolic regimes used a wide variety of textile fibers, some of them of most surprising origin: broom in the Midi region of France, glycine in Japan, in addition to feathers, animal hairs, and cocoons of all sorts. We saw how cotton, which for long played an essential role in Asia, grew to prominence in the European market from the late nineteenth century, replacing linen and hemp to triumph alongside wool. The dominance of cotton and wool would be short-lived. Already, by this time, the chemical industry was working to develop new fibers, and soon "invented" rayon from wood cellulose. Rayon consumption spiked in the 1930s. Then the first truly synthetic fibers appeared, not based on cellulose, but on coal and petroleum. This was the grand development of the postwar textile fiber market (Table 18.4). At the end of the 1920s, cotton accounted for 82 percent and wool for 14 percent of textile fibers consumed. By the early 1970s, the two

---

[6] The sugar protocol between the EEC and ACP countries, the British Commonwealth Sugar Agreement, the USSR/Cuba Delivery Agreement, and lastly the US Sugar Act, which organized US imports from the Philippines and various Caribbean island states.

Table 18.4 Global consumption of main textile fibers,* 1929–73 (in thousands of tons, and as a % of global consumption of fibers)

	1929–33	1939–43	1949–53	1959–63	1969–73
Cotton	5,576	6,111	7,705	10,197	12,540
	82%	74%	75%	67%	54%
Wool	942	988	1,118	1,484	1,521
	14%	12%	11%	10%	7%
Cellulose-based synthetics	237	1,164	1,285	2,730	3,533
	3%	14%	13%	18%	15%
Non-cellulose-based synthetics	–	8	101	899	5,700
	–	0%	1%	6%	24%
Total	6,812	8,309	10,209	15,310	23,294

Sources: for the periods 1929–33 and 1939–49, see Blau, 1946: 188; for 1949–53 and 1959–63, for cotton see International Cotton Advisory Committee data; figures for wool and synthetic fibers were produced from USDA data (USDA 1970); lastly, for the 1969–73 period, see the International Cotton Advisory Committee, 1993.

*Silk, which throughout the twentieth century never accounted for more than 0.8 percent of global consumption of textile fibers, is not included in the table.

accounted respectively for just 52 percent and 7 percent of consumption compared to 15 percent for cellulose synthetic fibers, and 24 percent for non-cellulose synthetic fibers.

The glory days of natural rubber were even briefer than those of cotton. Rubber consumption on a large scale was closely linked to the development of the automobile and the associated tire industry. Natural rubber was initially obtained from tapping "sub-spontaneous" natural rubber trees in the Amazon, then other plants and liana in Africa. From 1910, it was grown in colonial plantations, first European-owned, and later peasant-owned, in Asia (Barlow, 1986). Under the latent war environment of the 1930s, chemists in Germany, the USSR, and the United States worked frantically to develop a synthetic elastomer. By the end of the Second World War, Nazi Germany was self-sufficient in synthetic elastomer. The United States, cut off from Southeast Asia by Japanese invasion, focused intensely on both a vigorous rubber recycling program, and synthetic rubber production in factories funded and owned by the state, but managed by chemical firms. Production jumped from 1,750 tons in 1939 to 820,000 tons in 1945! Production declined in the immediate postwar period as trade with Southeast Asia resumed, but grew again from the early 1950s. Henceforth, thanks to wartime investments, the competitiveness of synthetic rubber was well established. Production also developed in Europe during the same period, including in Germany, where following the industry's dismantlement by the victorious Allies, the industry was relaunched after 1951. In 1972, only a third of all rubber consumed was of plant origin (Table 18.5).

These two examples illustrate well the ineluctable sidelining of non-food uses of biomass, even for the two products that best resisted, and whose consumption rose prodigiously: in 1970 the consumption of just synthetic fibers was higher than that of cotton in 1930!

Table 18.5 Global consumption of natural and synthetic rubber, 1940–72 (in thousands of tons and % of total)

	1940–2	**1948–50**	**1960–2**	**1970–2**
Natural	1,038	1,521	2,183	3,150
	93%	75%	46%	34%
Synthetic	76	503*	2,533	6,186
	7%	25%	54%	66%
Total	1,114	2,024	4,716	9,336

Sources: 1940–2 and 1948–50: United States Department of Commerce; United States Department of Commerce, National Production Authority, 1952; 1960–72 and 1970–2: International Rubber Study Group, various years.

*USSR's production excluded.

Conclusion

In 1945 and for a few decades thereafter, the United States, victorious in two world conflicts, dominated the capitalist world militarily and economically. In many aspects, their hegemony was even more pronounced than England's had been in the nineteenth century. It was expressed through the creation of a series of international organizations aimed at "governing" the behavior of states and interstate relations. And above all, the United States exerted an intellectual and cultural force of attraction, still in effect today, through new means of communication and expression (Debray, 2017).

Until the 1970s, the United States were shaped by a logic of inward-looking growth founded on expanding mass consumerism enabled by the redistribution of productivity gains through wages.

Oil became the foundation of wealth and power. It was the main provider of thermal energy and, indirectly, mechanical energy. It also enabled the exploitation of prodigious quantities of mineral resources. Oil was also at the source of the formidable growth experienced in agricultural production. The—temporary—lifting of all constraints on social metabolism gave birth to Kenneth Galbraith's "affluent societies" (Galbraith, 1958). Affluence, however, did not guarantee smooth-sailing capital accumulation—quite the contrary. The extreme division of labor and the omnipresence of market relations made the emergence of imbalances between production and consumption highly probable.

The problem of affluence is flagrant in the case of biomass. While biomass had been a limiting factor in the accumulation of wealth and power under the solar metabolic regime, now its excessive availability became cumbersome. Biomass truly took the shape of what Georges Bataille, writing at the beginning of the oil prosperity period, called the "accursed share" haunting human societies. It was necessary to make biomass disappear. Food aid, promotion of meat consumption, and "hidden calories" were some of the avenues explored to this end. The model spread to the whole world, and in particular to Asia under its Green Revolution.

A series of events contributed to accelerating intensification of production in the 1970s. The specter of shortages, then the emergence of new markets internationally, and lastly the contraction of demand in the 1980s destabilized the postwar regulation mechanisms, which ended up being abandoned, without, however, the chemical farming model being truly challenged.

The partitioning of the world into "developed–developing" was the product, and the distinctive mark, of this period. It arose from differentiated capacities of countries of the former periphery and those of the former center to replicate the American model.

Part 6

American hegemony: Season 2 globalization comes back

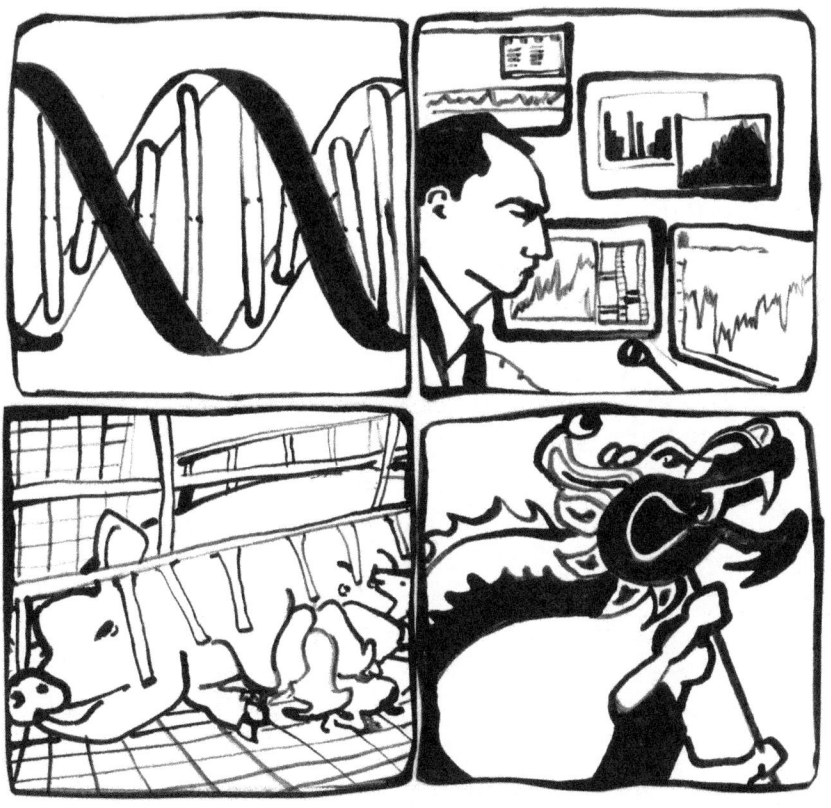

Introduction

The turn of the twenty-first century in many aspects resembles the turn of the twentieth century. The world seems to have returned to its pre-1914 trajectory, experiencing a similar vitality in international exchange of goods and capital, and a similar exuberance in financial markets, albeit on a grander scale.

The "American model" of accumulation of wealth and power born during the interwar period, under which economic growth found both its resources and its markets within the domestic space, was torn asunder in the 1970s. The Keynesian policies of OECD countries, as well as the import substitution industrialization strategies of developing countries, were abandoned in the name of the quest for competitiveness, in other words, policies aimed at optimizing integration in a vast global market. To use Philip McMichael's (1996) expressions, the "development project" was abandoned for the "globalization project," which breathed new life into American hegemony, now converted to neoliberalism.

The reasons for this transformation have been the subject of several analyses;[1] detailing these is well beyond the scope of this book. The successive oil shocks (1973-4 and 1979-81) dealt the final blow to domestic-focused growth, which had already been undermined by a long period of reversals.

The dismantling of protection mechanisms for domestic markets started at the end of the Second World War. It progressed, decade after decade, with the trade negotiation rounds under GATT, to which an increasing number of countries signed up. It was accompanied by the gradual abandonment of mechanisms for derogations, such as various agreements on "voluntary export restraints." The system of bilateral or multilateral multifiber agreements, which from 1957 had placed caps on textile exports from developing countries, was thus eliminated in 2005. This dismantling facilitated international trade and increased interconnection between domestic markets, especially between OECD countries until the 1970s. The capacity of each country to regulate its domestic economy, obviously, was weakened as a consequence.

East Asia benefited from this opening up, and Asian emergence accelerated the rhythm of internationalization of the global economy. Japan, with an industrialization model significantly more export-oriented than that of other OECD countries, was at the forefront of this movement. It was soon followed by the "newly industrialized

---

[1] Analysis of this shift is one of the foundations of the theory of regulation (Boyer, 1986).

countries" (NICs) which included the "four dragons" (South Korea, Taiwan, Hong Kong, and Singapore), whose status as "developing countries" gave them preferential access to "developed country" markets.

Lastly, an unforeseen event provided the final push for the swing towards this new model of growth: the collapse of the Berlin Wall, which resulted in former socialist countries being reintegrated into the capitalist global economy in the space of a few years.

China proved itself capable of fully exploiting the new configuration, by adopting a strategy of export-based industrial growth, like other East Asian countries before it had done. Within a few years, China emerged as champion of the mining metabolic regime. Its growth was so rapid that it raised the question of whether China would be the world's next hegemon, and led the United States to consider the country as their new main rival.

Nonetheless, for the moment China has not proposed a new metabolic regime, nor even a new phase in the mining metabolic regime. Fossil fuels still reign. The risks that the accumulation and proliferation of fossil fuel waste present gave rise to contestation, which led to the adoption of the Sustainable Development Goals (SDGs), and the signing of the Paris Agreement in 2015. But international consensus does not always lead to action. Presently, the mining metabolic regime may have increasingly fewer believers, but its number of practitioners is still rising.

During the period covered in Part 6 (the 1970s on), the notable exception of biofuels aside, sources and uses of biomass continued on the path that had been traced in the preceding period. Chemical farming, almost exclusively focused on food production, and increasingly turned towards animal products (see also the section "The advent of chemical farming" in Chapter 16) continued to be the norm. What changed was the scale; and this changed exponentially, both in terms of number of countries involved, as in terms of volumes produced and consumed. The only break that occurred was with regard to the market: there was an almost generalized abandonment of self-sufficiency strategies and an explosive growth in trade.

Part 6 starts with a chapter on the transformations that occurred in the American hegemon. Thereafter particular attention is given to China, whose emergence is recounted in Chapter 20. China also appears in dedicated sections in the last two chapters that respectively deal with the model of oil-based consumption and biomass production, and the globalization of agricultural markets.

19

The second age of American hegemony

The decline of the "American empire"

When can one consider that the American hegemony started truly to weaken? Was it just a recent phenomenon?

These questions agitated many minds during the 1970s and 1980s, given the abandoning of the dollar's convertibility to gold, the first oil shock, demands from Third World countries for a new economic world order, the resurgence of Europe and Japan, and the American defeat in Vietnam. For Immanuel Wallerstein (Wallerstein et al., 2013), the hegemonic period started to come to a close in the early 1970s. Robert Keohane, in his book *After Hegemony*, published in 1984, considered America's decline as already consummated, as his book discussed the conditions for stable international relations in a post-hegemonic world.

Yet, during the 1980s, the winds shifted. The debt crises, which started in 1982 and affected several countries in Latin America, Africa, and Asia, made it possible to rein in "developing countries," putting an end to demands from the Global South. In 1989, the fall of the Berlin Wall, followed by the collapse of the Soviet bloc, appeared to crown the victory of the United States, and signal the advent of a unipolar world. Lastly, September 11, 2001 designated a new enemy against which the "war on terrorism" was launched, reinvigorating alliances under American leadership. On September 13, 2001 the French newspaper *Le Monde* published an editorial written by its editor-in-chief titled "Nous sommes tous Américains" [We are all Americans].

This chain of events opened a pathway for what could be considered a resurgence of imperialist ambition (Maier, 2009). Openly defended by the proponents of the "Project for the New American Century" (Arrighi, 2007: 175–89), these ambitions were concretized in the invasion of Iraq. It was this invasion, which ended up being a military disaster, and the ensuing chaotic entanglement in Afghanistan, that for a large part led to the deterioration of America's image from the 2000s, and to the tone of discourse changing once again. As the United States chalked up military setbacks, their share of global production of manufactures was overtaken by China's share. The decline of the American hegemony was once again announced, despite the overwhelming predominance of American cultural references, American supremacy in the field of information and communications technologies, and the emergence of the new giant firms, the GAFAs, capable of imposing their will across the world.

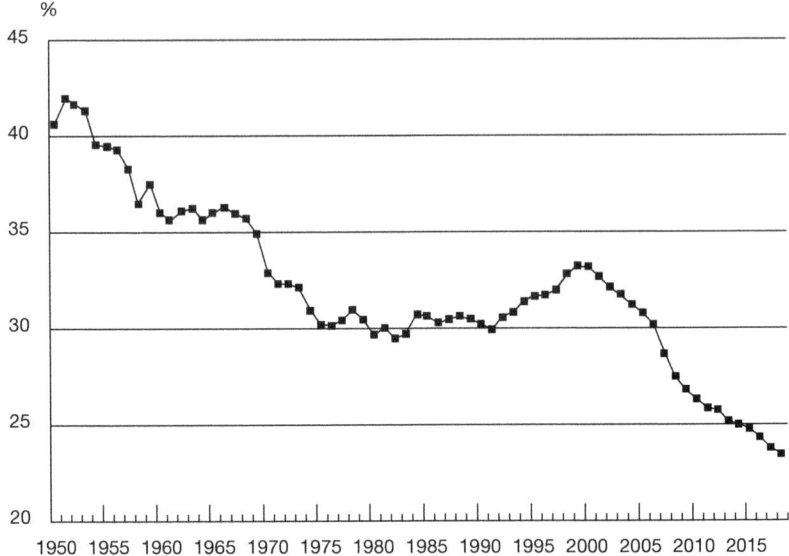

Figure 19.1 United States' share of global wealth, 1950–2017

Source: data from the World Inequalities Database, https://wid.world/ (accessed August 16, 2024).

Beyond the changes in how American power was perceived, the US share in global wealth, in sharp decline in the 1950s and 1960s due to reconstruction in Europe and Japan, had stabilized at around 30 percent in the 1970s, and even rose after the collapse of the Soviet Union (Figure 19.1). Only after the 2008 financial crisis did the United States' share fall under the symbolic threshold of 30 percent, and this time the cause was related to the rise of China.

The triumph of the neoliberal project

The vigor of the American economy between 1973 and 2008 in reality dissimulated a profound shift in the logic of production and distribution of wealth within the country. The first oil shock of 1973, which occurred alongside growing competition from Europe and Japan, was for the United States the catalyst for changing its growth model. In effect, the inward-looking domestic economy founded on an mining metabolism had one weakness: oil imports. It seemed that everything could be produced and consumed at home, but it was necessary to have access to oil, and none of the industrialized countries had sufficient oil resources to meet their needs. Even the United States, the original promoters of the model, became net oil importers as from 1947, and of fossil fuels as a whole from 1953. In 1973, a quarter of US consumption of oil and natural gas was imported (Gierlinger and Krausmann, 2012).

The successive increases in the price of oil under OPEC's action—the constant price, that is without inflation, of the barrel quadrupled between 1973 and 1981 (Figure 19.2)—made this weakness of the inward-looking social democracy model blaringly

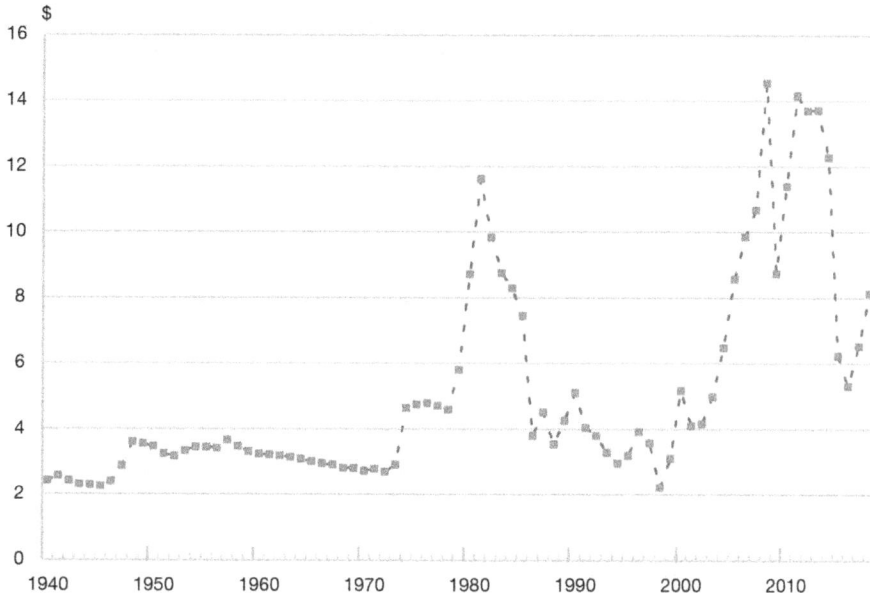

Figure 19.2 Constant price of oil in the United States, 1940–2018 (1967 dollars)

Sources: adapted from US Energy Information Administration, current price of oil, https://www.eia.gov/opendata/ and US Department of Labor, consumer price index, https://www.minneapolisfed.org/about-us/monetary-policy/inflation-calculator/consumer-price-index-1800- (both accessed on August 16, 2024).

clear. The United States became conscious of its extreme dependency on external supplies for energy. The only way to pay for oil imports was to increase exports, and the only way to increase exports was to seek international competitiveness at all cost.

Breaking with the postwar growth model focused on one's own domestic space, the internationalization of economies was now the order of the day.

In the United States, the ratio between trade and GDP, which had been stable at around 7 percent since the end of the war and during the 1960s, climbed to 13 percent in 1975, 17 percent in 1980, 20 percent in 2000, and 24 percent in 2008, but fell to 21 percent in 2018, after the financial crisis.[1]

Keynesian policies lost their effectiveness in this new context. When demand stimulus policies were applied in response to rising unemployment, they invariably resulted in a rise in imports. Stimulus created no, or few, jobs, and widened the trade deficit, already under pressure from oil imports.

Demand-side policies, through which governments seek to achieve full employment of factors by playing on consumption, gave way to supply-side policies, whose primary goal was to strengthen the competitiveness of a few national champions, by promoting technological innovation and through "labor market reform," that is, reducing the cost of wages and "flexibilizing" labor conditions.

---

[1] https://data.worldbank.org/country/united-states (accessed August 16, 2024).

There is no better illustration of the break in growth model that such policies entailed than the comparison of the evolution of the growth rates of labor productivity and hourly wages in the United States (Figure 19.3). Until 1973, productivity and wages grew together. This synchronous growth was part of the Fordist recipe, it was what made it possible to permanently ensure new markets within the domestic economy and full employment of factors. That fortuitous link was broken in 1973.

For a whole swathe of the population, economic growth now no longer meant income growth. And with that any possibility of managing growth within the confines of the domestic space disappeared. The constraint of international competitiveness, initially just a short-term necessity, became a central characteristic of the new economic regime. And competition was not only sought in international trade, it became the norm everywhere.

Beyond the change in direction of economic policy, the triumph of neoliberalism also brought about a new conception of the place and role that markets played, a conception that over the years rose to dominance. Several books and papers have been written on this topic. Examples, with very different takes, include Brown (2007), and Dardot and Laval (2009). Under neoliberalism, competition became the only means of managing and governing human beings, in the wide sense intended by Michel Foucault's "Conduct of Conduct." The liberalism of the nineteenth century and the neoliberalism of the twenty-first century differed in two ways:

- For the former, the market emerged spontaneously, from the natural propensity of humans to trade finding an outlet for expression, and the role of the state

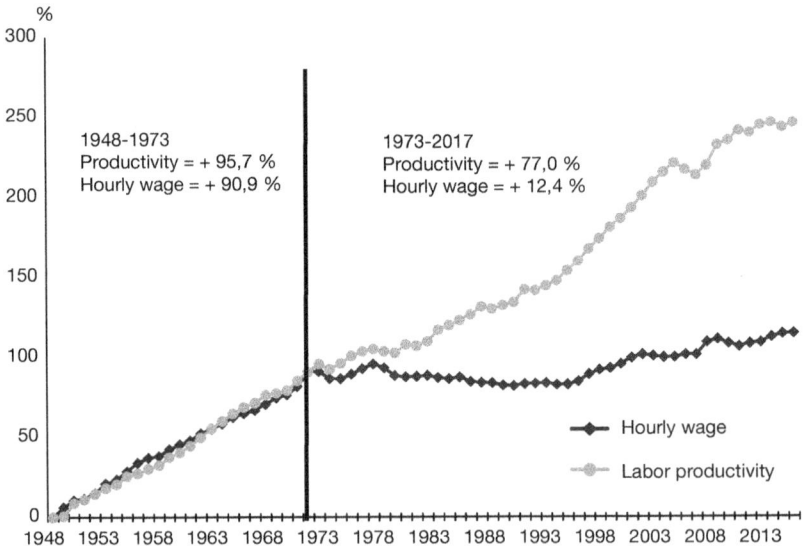

Figure 19.3 Growth in labor productivity and wages in the United States, 1948–2013

Sources: adapted from Bivens et al., 2014; updated data from the site https://www.epi.org/productivity-pay-gap/ (accessed August 16, 2024).

was to abstain from constraining the market. For the latter, market exchanges were a product of history, and the existence of markets could require very active intervention from states: sometimes heavy oversight was required, such as for example audit and certification procedures, for the market to be free.
- For the former, the market was first and foremost a means of exchange, and therefore a means for cooperation through the division of labor. For the latter, what was sought from the market was first and foremost competition, and here once again state intervention could be primordial. The state had the task of making everyone accept the virtues of competition (although the state was not alone in playing this role; consider the space sport occupies in the media today, for instance), and of helping to ensure that everyone has the possibility to participate in the competition.

A last characteristic of this new era was the development of the financial sphere and its osmotic relations with the sphere of government. If we follow Giovanni Arrighi's theory, the financialization of the economy was a confirmation of the decline of the American hegemony; this phenomenon was also present during the declines of the Dutch and English hegemons in the past. Capital favors liquidity and mobility, turning away from productive activities to focus solely on trade of paper: stocks, futures, currency, etc. (Arrighi, 1994: 6). The extreme mobility of capital and the homogeneity of points of view of global leaders helped discipline even more economic policy, which came to be characterized, with reference to "trickle-down theory," by efforts to reduce the tax burden on the highest incomes (Saez and Zucman, 2019).

As the work by Thomas Piketty and colleagues[2] teaches us, a consequence—and a symptom—of the phasing out of the Fordist regime was the rise of intra-national inequality. GDP growth between 1940 and 1973 had involved a rise in average incomes of the vast majority of the population and stagnating incomes of the richest. But after 1973 growth benefited exclusively the richest percentiles, and incomes of the rest of the population embarked on a long a period of stagnation. We can see this in Figure 19.4, which compares the evolution in average annual incomes in thousands of constant 2017 dollars of the 99–100 decile (the richest 1 percent) on the left scale, and of the 0–90 decile (the poorest 90 percent) on the right scale. Between 1945 and 1973, income of the richest 1 percent grew by a factor of 1.5, and that of the poorest 90 percent by a factor of 2.1. Between 1973 and 2014, average incomes of the two groups grew respectively by a factor of 2.7 and 1.5, that is, a complete inversion with respect to the preceding period in how benefits from growth were distributed.

The soaring cost of oil imports, on the other hand, did not present any real challenge to the mining metabolic regime and its logic of methodically depleting resources. The double constraint of the rising cost of energy and of competitiveness, nonetheless, from the early 1980s provided an incentive to achieve better energy yields (the case for the automobile), and resulted in a stabilization of the level of per capita consumption both of energy and of materials.

---

[2] The work of the World Inequality Laboratory, https://wid.world/fr/world-inequality-lab-fr/

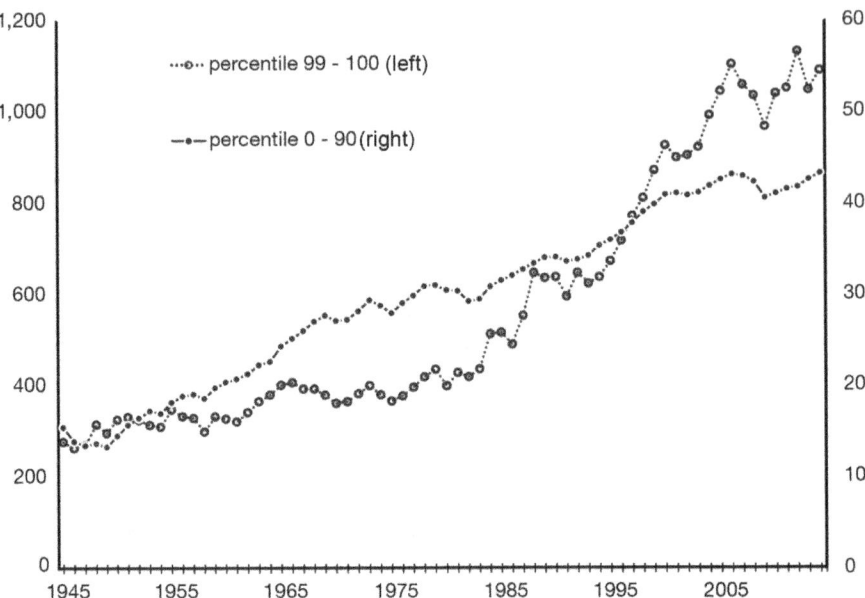

Figure 19.4 United States: Average annual income of individuals in the 99–100 and 0–90 percentiles, 1945–2014 ($1,000 of 2017)

Source: World Inequality Database, https://wid.world/fr/donnees/ (accessed August 16, 2024).

Per capita energy consumption peaked at 485 GJ per inhabitant in 1979, to then fall to around 420 in the early 2000s, of which 72 percent came from fossil fuels, compared to 78 percent in 1973 (the fall being mainly due to progress in electricity supply from nuclear power). Material consumption, for its part, "stabilized" in the mid-2000s at around 27 tons per inhabitant (Figure 19.5), of which 80 percent were mineral resources, compared to 79 percent in 1973.

Neoliberalism makes the world go round

The United States was not the only country to experience transformations in its growth model. The model represented a new hegemonic norm, characterized by a combination of the mining metabolic regime and neoliberalism, which during the 1980s and 1990s spread to a large part of the globe.[3] The UK played a pioneering role, thanks in particular to Margaret Thatcher's election and her slogan *There Is No*

---

[3] In other OECD countries, dependence on energy imports was even higher than in the United States. In 1972, the share of imports in fossil fuel consumption (coal, oil, and gas) reached 56 percent in the United Kingdom, 70 percent in Austria (Krausmann et al., 2008), and 92 percent in Japan (Krausmann et al., 2011)!

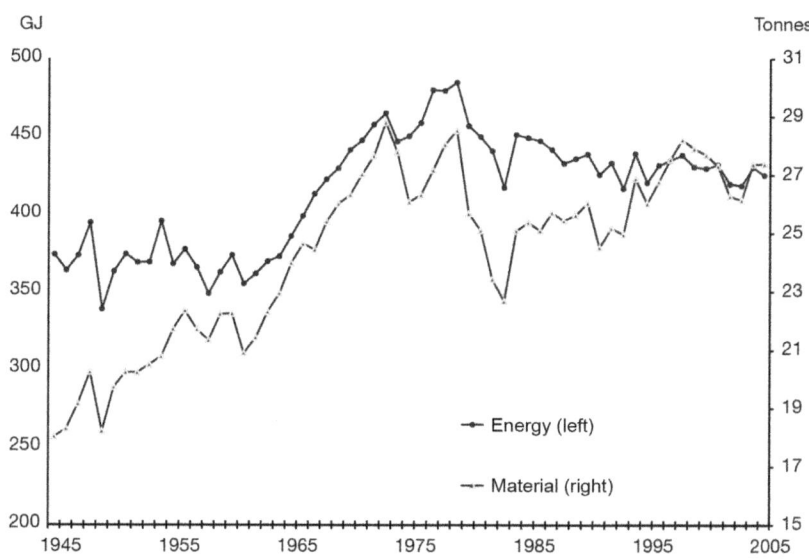

Figure 19.5 Per capita energy consumption (GJ) and material consumption in the United States, 1945–2005

Source: Gierlinger and Krausmann, 2012.

Alternative (TINA) which became the credo of neoliberal policies. Closely mirroring developments in the United States, inequality rose sharply in the UK.

Social protection systems and stabilization mechanisms for domestic markets that had been put in place during the "second Thirty-Year War," the reconstruction period, or as part of developmentalist ambitions, were gradually or, depending on the country, abruptly dismantled.

In continental Western Europe, the process is still ongoing through successive reforms under the framework of European integration, which is often reduced to the creation of a giant market and the promotion of pure competition. The relative endurance of social protection systems has slowed down rising inequality here compared to the United States or the United Kingdom.

With the fall of the Berlin Wall in 1989, the "transition" as it was called then—with significantly more precise and defined intent than today—occurred much faster for Eastern Europe and the ex-USSR. In Russia, a few years of privatization and liberalization gave a part of the Soviet nomenklatura a chance to transform itself into an oligarchy controlling the main part of the country's wealth. Russians, like Americans, today give 45 percent of their income to the richest 10 percent. In France, the richest 10 percent hold 33 percent of income, the same level as the poorest 50 percent.

In "developing countries" the debt crisis put an end to import substitution policies and opened the way for the spread of neoliberal policies. In actuality, "development" strategies had started to diverge from the mid-1960s, with the adoption of export-oriented industrialization strategies by East Asian countries, and even further in the

1970s with the influx of oil rents. Paradoxically, and despite these divergences, the 1970s also represented the "golden age of the Third World," the zenith of global "North–South" dialogue, in large part thanks to a balance of power favorable to raw material exporters. In the 1980s, with the effects of the monetarist policy adopted by the United States (interest rate hikes, recession, and the start of the debt crisis), the balance of power reversed and a new illusion of similitude appeared: "developing" countries now were those countries that were indebted, crippled by financial crises, on whom the IMF imposed the same reform "package." With the aim of rebalancing both state budgets and trade balances, these countries implemented policies of liberalization and deregulation of all sorts, which later came to be designated by the term "Washington consensus" (Williamson, 2009).

20

Reorienting the world

The title of this chapter is borrowed from Andre Gunder Frank who as early as 1998, in his book *Re-Orient: Global Economy in the Asian Age* called attention to the new emergence of Asia in the last decades of the twentieth century.

Until this point, there has been little mention of Asia in this book. It is certainly a mistake. Not because the book has the ambition to present a history of sources and uses of biomass in the whole world, but rather because several developments, strategies, and turnabouts in European and neo-European countries resulted from interactions with Asia. In many ways until at least the early nineteenth century, Europe chased after Asia, or at least after its products; in other words, during the greatest part of Europe's written history.

East Asia constitutes a very particular region. For Giovanni Arrighi and his colleagues (2003a), the unity of the East Asian region arises from the long-lasting interactions and interdependencies that have existed there. Their analysis was a continuation of Janet Abu-Lughod's (1991) analysis, in which she considered that from the thirteenth century, Eurasia augmented by the southern coast of the Mediterranean and the western coast of the Red Sea, constituted a world-economy, in which East Asia, with China as the center, was one of the eight sub-systems of trade.

Andre Gunder Frank is even more radical. For him, the Sinocentric world is not just limited to East Asia, or even Asia, but covers the whole Eurasian region, parts of Africa and the Americas after its colonization by Europe:[1]

> The world economy continued to be dominated by Asians [...] until about 1800. Europe's relative and absolute marginality in the world economy continued, despite Europe's new relations with the Americas, which it used also to increase its relations with Asia. Indeed, it was little more than its new and continued access

---

[1] In the introduction to the book *Re-Orient: Global Economy in the Asian Age*, Gunder Frank writes: "The implications of this book are that the 'Rise' of East Asia need come as no surprise just because it does not fit into the Western scheme of things. This book suggests a rather different scheme of things instead, into which the contemporary and possible future events in East Asia, and maybe also elsewhere in Asia, can and do fit. This is a global economic development scheme of things, in which Asia, and especially East Asia, was already dominant and remained so until—in historical terms— very recently, that is less than two centuries ago. Only then, for reasons to be explored below, did Asian economies lose their positions of predominance in the world economy, while that position came to be occupied by the West—apparently only temporarily" (Frank, 1998: 7).

to American money that permitted Europe to broaden, though hardly to deepen, its participation in the world market. Productive and commercial economic activities, and population growth based on the same, also continued to expand faster and more in Asia until at least 1750.

(Frank, 1998: 53)

He adds:

> In the structure of the world economy, four major regions maintained built-in deficits of commodity trade: the Americas, Japan, Africa, and Europe. The first two balanced their deficit by producing silver money for export. Africa exported gold money and slaves. In economic terms, these three regions produced "commodities" for which there was a demand elsewhere in the world economy. The fourth deficitary region, Europe, was hardly able to produce anything of its own for export with which to balance its perpetual trade deficit. Europe managed to do so primarily by "managing" the exports of the three other deficitary regions, from Africa to the Americas, from the Americas to Asia, and from Asia to Africa and the Americas. The Europeans also participated to some extent in trade within Asia, especially between Japan and elsewhere. This intra-Asian "country trade" was marginal for Asia but nonetheless vital for Europe, which earned more from it than from its own trade with Asia.

(Frank, 1998: 126–7)

The peripheral position of Europe, as we know, changed dramatically from the eighteenth century, and for nearly two centuries the winds shifted for East Asia. As Kenneth Pomeranz reminds us:

> Somebody writing at any point between roughly 1860 and 1960, then, might have doubted that East Asian experiences contained any particularly useful lessons, either positive or negative. Instead, they might have lumped almost all of the region into a broader "third world", which had experienced only limited development.

(Pomeranz, 2012: S142)

It is also true that as late as 1960, only Japan and tiny Hong Kong had a per capita income higher than that of Senegal. Today, however, everyone is aware that for decades something has been going on in that group of countries situated in the eastern Eurasian fringe.

The return of East Asia, like the flight of wild geese[2]

After the Second World War, Japan was the first to make the headlines (once again). American and European newspapers of the 1970s were full of narratives of Japan's economic prowess, and shops were full of Japanese electronic goods. Japan's cars

---

[2] The pattern of industrial production in East Asia—places of production succeeded each other, as did the various things produced in any given country—inspired the Japanese economist Kaname Akamatsu to compare the model with the "flight of wild geese (*gankō keitai*)" as early as 1937 (Akamatsu, 1962).

invaded our cities, its four-wheel drives and all-terrain motorcycles the countryside, and its tourist buses the Eiffel Tower. Attention then shifted towards the newly industrialized countries (NICs), first the four dragons (Taiwan, South Korea, Hong Kong, and Singapore), then Indonesia, Malaysia, and Thailand. Textile products, and then electronics once again, were the flagship products. And then finally China, the giant sometimes considered to be sleeping (Peyrefitte, 1973), reared its head.[3] There is no doubt that this was not a case of a string of fortuitous national success stories, but rather the rise of an entire region, East Asia.

Much has been written about the central role of the state in the Asian successes, and some authors have formulated a theory of the "developmental state" in Asia (Johnson, 1982; Wade, 1990). They show how the international economic context in which these countries industrialized had little to do with that which England faced in the eighteenth and nineteenth centuries; the Asian countries had to take on an already industrialized Europe and North America. The constraint of competitiveness and the market opportunities generated by this environment required proactive policy from the state to achieve industrialization.

But even more, as Kaoru Sugihara notes:

The key to the East Asian success was that the region was able to respond to the growth of resource-intensive and capital-intensive industries across the Atlantic resulting from the "great divergence", by creating a resource-saving and labour-intensive path to industrialization.

(Sugihara, 2003: 95)

Lastly, another dimension of the East Asian success story, which would have heavy consequences for the global economy, was its early adoption, including by the "developing" countries of the region, of export-oriented industrialization strategies.

Japan was the first to go down this path, opting for this avenue as, just like the United Provinces of the seventeenth century, the country had very few natural resources. It was thus obliged to import resources, and to be able to do that, it had to export manufactured goods. Japan's colonial conquests presented earlier were supposed to address this resource weakness, but in the 1930s, Japan was nonetheless dependent on British Malaysia for rubber, Australia for iron ore, India for cast iron, Canada for aluminum, Australia and Canada for zinc, and the United States and Indonesia for oil (Sugihara, 2003: 102). After the Second World War, Japan's "miraculous" growth was once again based on the mobilization of distant mineral resources (which had low value per unit weight), and this time at an unprecedented scale, as Stephen Bunker and Pol Ciccantell show. Japan was the cause of a record rise in the number

---

[3] The fact that East Asia was included in the category "emerging countries" prevented an understanding of the specificity and the importance that these countries were acquiring on the global level. "Emerging countries" was used to refer to countries that occupied very different positions in the global economy. For instance, Brazil and Russia, also included in this category, were on a trajectory of reprimarization of their economies in response to formidable growth in Chinese demand, and were thus once again returning to periphery status.

of ton-kilometers that global trade moved around. The figures for oil, iron ore, coal, and bauxite transported by sea quadrupled between 1960 and 1980. Coal, which historically was *par excellence* a resource processed and consumed near to its place of extraction, experienced a tenfold increase in its maritime transport between 1960 and 1990 (Bunker and Ciccantell, 2007: 1–5).

Japan's strategy was based on three pillars:

- Massive investments in logistics, in particular the construction of industrial port facilities, on its own soil.
- Establishment of long-term contracts with distant suppliers, with investments also made in those supplier countries. In 1960, 50 percent of Japanese foreign direct investment targeted the natural resource sector (agriculture, forestry, fishery, and mines).
- An aggressive policy of manufactured goods exports, in order to pay for the rest.[4]

From the 1950s, Japan bet on a globalization strategy; when the viability of the inward-looking economic model started being questioned, Japan already had a head-start on the new model. Bunker and Ciccantell thus consider that it was Japan, and not the United States that invented the second wave of globalization.

In the 1980s, when Japan was the aspirational model, at a time when Europe and the United States were both mired in a crisis that they did not appear capable of overcoming, it was fashionable to point out that the Japanese ideogram for the word "crisis" was the combination of two ideograms, "danger" and "opportunity," a sign  that what was perceived as a problem for Europe was seen as an opportunity at the other end of Eurasia (Albert and Boissonnat, 1988).

But around the mid-1990s, it was Japan's turn to enter a long recession, in which it is still mired today. All indicators are flashing red: (stagnated) GDP, debt burden, deflation, demographic decline, etc.

The ideogram "crisis," however, has been reincarnated. This time it is used to speak of the incredible performance of China,[5] and this shift neatly sums up the recent internal swings that have occurred in East Asia.

The awakening of China

Between 1980 and 2017, China's share in global income grew from 3 to 15 percent (Alvaredo et al., 2018: 60) (Figure 20.1). There has been no equivalent development in

---

[4] Moreover, Japan's resource weakness pushed the country to adopt technologies that were efficient in raw material use. From the 1970s, Japan started developing its nuclear sector, as well as liquefied natural gas, and its energy/GDP ratio fell. The steel, chemical, cement, aluminum industries declined while electronics and precision mechanics sectors developed. Japan still manufactures cars, but cars that are lighter and more fuel-efficient that its competitors (see Warr et al., 2010, on energy).
[5] See for example, Viveret 2010: 17.

human history. But at the same time this development in many ways simply represents a return to the normal state of human affairs.

During the twelfth and thirteenth centuries, China experienced a period of very rapid growth, accompanied by strong expansion of foreign trade. Mark Elvin describes this period as a medieval revolution, that is the combination of an agricultural revolution, a transport revolution, a credit revolution, and a revolution of techniques (Elvin, 1973).

This period of strong growth was abruptly interrupted due to, among other reasons, a turnabout in imperial policy. A phase of voluntary isolation followed, characterized by the moving of the capital to Beijing, in the interior lands and more to the north, and the end of maritime expeditions (which in the early fifteenth century had reached the coasts of East Africa). Historians have long described China as a stagnant country, stuck between involution and tradition, at a time Europe was birthing capitalism and launching its conquest of the world.

A range of more recent studies, however, prove that the situation in seventeenth- and eighteenth-century China was neither particularly backward, nor particularly different from that of Northwestern Europe, and especially so in China's coastal regions, such as the Yangzi delta (Wong, 1997; Pomeranz, 2000; Hung, 2015). These studies highlight two essential characteristics of China in the late eighteenth century: the country had a solar metabolic regime that was intensive in human labor, as well as very active trade activity, including in its countryside.

From the first Opium War[6] (1839) until the arrival of the communists in power, China went through a period of great social and political instability. The period was marked by "military interventions," or rather outright invasions, undertaken by European powers (the Opium Wars of 1839–42 and of 1856–60, and the Boxer Uprising (1899–1901)), and then by Japan (1894, 1931, and 1935), as well as large-scale insurrections (the Taiping Rebellion in 1851–64) and civil wars (1927–37, then 1945–9). The "last emperor" was deposed in 1912, and the country for long remained fragmented by war lords. Throughout this period, the sovereignty and the unity of China were contested. Not surprisingly, its prosperity suffered.

Its population, which had grown from 381 to 412 million between 1820 and 1840, stagnated for two decades, and then fell to 370 million in 1870. Thereafter it grew slowly to reach 544 million inhabitants in 1949. GDP per capita at the best remained unchanged during this period, whereas it tripled in Japan, quadrupled in the UK and Germany, and grew eightfold in the United States (Table 20.1). Between 1820 and 1952, China's share in global GDP collapsed from 33 to 5 percent (Maddison, 2007: 44)!

To say that China was unable, for almost a whole century, to find its place in the new global configuration engendered by industrialization and the success of the mining metabolic regime, is to put it lightly. And yet, successive governments, whether imperial or republican, attempted to push industrialization to enable the country to replicate Japan's trajectory. Labor-intensive technologies developed by Japan at the end of the

---

[6] The English promoted opium imports (from India) to finance their purchases from China. The "opium wars" were set off in reaction to the Chinese state, determined to fight against the devastating effects of the drug on its populace, destroying opium stocks.

Table 20.1 China, Japan, United Kingdom, United States, and Germany: Per capita GDP (in 1990 dollars) in 1820 and 1950

	1820	1950
China	600	614
Japan	704	1,921
United Kingdom	1,706	6,939
Germany	1,077	3,881
United States	1,257	9,561

Source: Maddison, 2007.

nineteenth century were adopted. During the 1930s, China's textile industry, which was rural-based for the large part, competed with the English industry on South and Southeast Asian markets. The Kuomintang nationalist government had the ambition to implement a veritable industrial policy (promoting inventions and exports, banks, professional associations, mechanisms for labor conflict resolutions, etc.) but most action was taken by local governments without much coordination of the whole.

In 1949, Mao Zedong's arrival in power stabilized the political and military situation of the country, but did not put an end to calamity or upheaval. The first thirty years of Communist China were focused on the ambition to build a self-reliant economy, based on a somewhat amended Soviet model, founded on the financing of industrialization—with special attention for heavy industry—through massive taxation of the agricultural sector. Collectivization of agricultural production and obligatory delivery quotas were the main means employed. In the cities, state enterprises controlled most economic activity.

The agrarian reform program that had already been implemented in the 1940s in the areas controlled by the Communist Party was extended to the entire country until 1952. The reform redistributed land and means of production from large landowners to their farmers or sharecroppers.

In 1955, the faction within the party that favored the creation of agricultural producer cooperatives triumphed. In 1957, 753,000 cooperatives had a total membership of 120 million individuals. The first phase of collectivization appeared to have mostly positive effects, at least as far as production was concerned, as this rose by almost 30 percent between 1952 and 1957; taking into account population growth, this translated into a 10 percent per capita increase.

In 1958, the desire to accelerate the transition towards Communism gave rise to the "Great Leap Forward" policy, which was supposed to increase the country's industrial output and enable China "to catch up with England within five years." For that it was necessary to feed workers and factories. The pressure on the agricultural sector increased. Within three months, the cooperatives were grouped into 24,000 popular communes, which covered on average 5,000 households each, for a total of 120 million households and 90 percent of the rural population. Participation in a popular commune became compulsory, and decision-making in these communes initially was highly centralized, as was the feeding of households, organized in canteens. It was also in 1958 that the law instituting the Communist version of *hukou* was passed. This population registration system established a strict separation between rural and urban dwellers (agricultural and non-agricultural), and assigned each Chinese person to a specified location. The goal was clearly to control and curb migration from the countryside towards towns. Only urban residents could access the social benefits that towns offered under the accelerated industrialization policy.

In the two years that followed, agricultural output collapsed due to the disorganization of labor that the creation of the communes engendered. In effect, one of the tasks of the communes was to mobilize peasants to build and operate mini blast furnaces throughout the country. Despite the fall in harvest, the compulsory production quotas used to feed towns were not reduced. Famine gripped the countryside and, depending on the estimates, killed between 30 and 36 million people, almost all rural, between 1959 and 1961 (Jisheng, 2012).

The Cultural Revolution, followed by Mao's succession, extended the chaos until the end of the 1970s. But massive investment in health and hygiene also gave rise to a veritable population explosion: from 546 million in 1950, the population grew to 667 million in 1960, 818 million in 1970, and 956 million in 1978! Life expectancy rose from forty-three years in 1960 to sixty-five years in 1978.

In 1978, after two years filled with uncertainty following Mao's death, Deng Xiaoping came to power. He had had a political career full of ups and downs—former First Secretary of the Chinese Communist Party (CCP), he was demoted during the Cultural Revolution, and then later rehabilitated. Deng quickly announced that he intended to

Figure 20.1 China's share in global income, 1950–2018

Source: data from the World Inequalities Database, https://wid.world/ (accessed August 16, 2024).

establish "socialism with Chinese characteristics." This was undertaken through a very gradual—compared with what would happen in Soviet bloc countries after the fall of the Berlin Wall—reduction of state intervention in the economy, and the growing reliance on the market and economic incentives. However, political liberalization was not part of the agenda, as the crushing of demonstrators in Tiananmen Square in 1989 clearly demonstrated.

The de-collectivization of agriculture was one of the first measures adopted. It was followed by the privatization or extensive reform of state enterprises from the mid-1980s, gradual elimination of price controls, reduction in trade barriers, and lastly by the adoption of a very proactive policy of export promotion. Special export zones (or special economic zones), specialized in intensive and low-cost manufacturing for the export market, started being tested from 1979 on. In 1986, China submitted an application to join the World Trade Organization (WTO) (GATT at the time), and in 2001 became a member. The normalization of international economic relations, which had started in 1972 with the visit by American president Richard Nixon, was now consolidated.

The one-child policy was adopted in 1979, and thanks to this policy China benefited from a "demographic dividend" for a thirty-five-year period (Cai et al., 2018). The term demographic dividend refers to a period when in a given country its active population (aged 15 to 64 years) rises faster than its dependent population (children and the elderly). In China, this period lasted roughly from 1980 to 2015. In that period, the active population rose from 400 million to 950 million, while the number of dependents remained more or less stable, around 400 million. The labor market thus benefited from a massive influx of healthy and educated individuals, without rising social costs linked to youth and old age.

This sharp policy turn, most certainly in addition to the well-established heavy industry base and investments in education and health achieved during the Maoist period, enabled China to pull off stupendous economic feats over the next forty years: double-digit growth, breakthrough into the industrial goods global export market, extremely rapid urbanization, elimination of poverty, etc.

For Christopher McNally (2012), Sino-capitalism, to use his expression, has three institutional characteristics, which explain the rapidity and the modalities of Chinese growth:

- The use of interpersonal relations, as in the overseas Chinese capitalism model. These relations are based on common cultural norms that emphasize reciprocity (*guanxi* in Chinese) and nurture informal business networks.
- A central role played by the state in the coordination and definition of general strategic orientations. China, on this level, was the perfect illustration of a late-comer strategy under global competition as described by Alexander Gerschenkron (1962), speaking of the late nineteenth century.
- Rapid and strong insertion in the global economy, which at the time was highly globalized in nature. This insertion was formalized by China joining the WTO in 2000, and based on an economic policy that, like its East Asian predecessors, focused on exports, savings, and investments at the expense of household consumption.

China's remarkable economic growth enabled spectacular poverty reduction, much to the pleasure of international organizations supposed to realize the grand commitments of this world—the Millennium Development Goals, which later became the Sustainable Development Goals. According to Chinese government data, the number of people living in poverty fell from 770 million to 300,000 between 1978 and 2017, that is from 97 percent to 3 percent of the total population (Cai et al., 2018: 12)!

The elimination of poverty did not, however, entail reduction of inequality. In 1978, the richest 10 percent Chinese and the least rich 50 percent possessed the same share of national income (27 percent), and the intermediary 40 percent shared between them the rest, that is 47 percent. In 2006, the share of the richest 10 percent grew to 42 percent, and that of the least rich 50 percent fell to 15 percent. The trajectories diverged for the most part between 1998 and 2006; since then, the distribution seems to have stabilized. Discrimination against the rural population compared to urban dwellers persisted, with highly unequal access to education and healthcare. It has even increased, as the average urban income in 1978 was two and half times that of the average rural income, but in 2010, it was three and a half times higher (Alvaredo et al., 2018: 106–22).[7]

The unequal distribution of the gains from growth, when considering macroeconomic variables, is to be put in relation with the enormous and growing share of fixed capital investments and exports in GDP, compared with household consumption until 2006 (Figure 20.2). Ho-Fung Hung describes the situation well:

> The Chinese economic imbalance, which is a main source of imbalances in the U.S. economy and in the global economy at large, is the result of China's excessive dependence on exports and investment, coupled with the relatively low household consumption that this dependence entails. This model of development, as we have seen, stems from a set of government policies that repress the laboring classes' interests and favor the oligarchic party-state elite. This elite is made up of the costal officials fed by rents from the export sector as well as the neo-feudal CCP families that control state companies and siphon benefits from unprofitable investment projects funded by state banks' lax lending. These imbalance-inducing policies include low interest rates and repression of currency appreciation, which force household savers to subsidize the state companies and export manufacturers. They also include the destruction of the rural-agricultural sector that created a large reserve army of labor in the countryside and kept increases in manufacturing wages lagging behind the expansion of the economy at large.
>
> (Hung, 2015: 167)

---

[7] China's growth thus may follow the dynamic of the "wild geese" trajectory of other Southeast Asian countries, but it has not had the redistributive effects seen in the four Asian dragons. The dragons may have had authoritarian regimes, but they implemented relatively egalitarian policies during the Cold War, in particular with regard to rural areas. Their growth can be qualified as economically inclusive, even if it came with political exclusion.

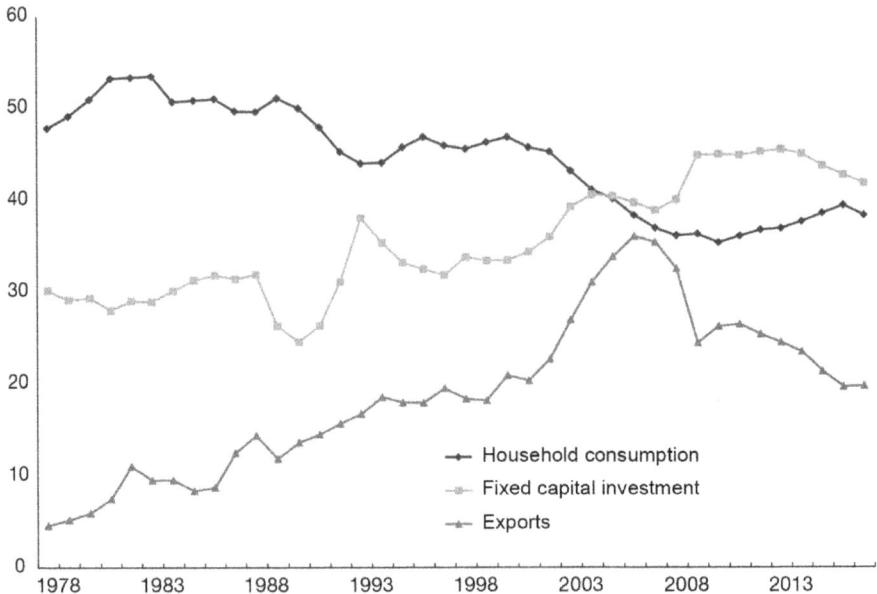

Figure 20.2 China: Consumption, investment, and exports as a % of GDP, 1978–2017
Source: World Bank.

Nonetheless after the 2007–8 financial crisis, China's economic policy changed, with the government now showing interest in generating growth based on domestic consumption. The share of such consumption in GDP rose slightly, at the expense of exports, while the share of investments in GDP remained stable. The shift also stabilized the distribution of income, which stopped its deteriorating trend. Between 2010 and 2015, the share of the richest 10 percent only changed from 42 to 41 percent to the benefit of the middle class, while the share of the poorest 50 percent remained stable at 15 percent.

Converted to capitalism, China now unreservedly adopted the logic of the mining metabolic regime. Becoming the world's workshop obviously involved a dramatic increase in the consumption of underground resources (Figure 20.3), although it should be noted that a part of these resources are re-exported after processing. The increase was particularly marked between 2000 and 2017, with China literally leaving the United States behind in the dust. Chinese consumption of copper and nickel in this period increased sixteenfold, and aluminum and lead consumption eightfold and tenfold respectively. China henceforth occupied a central position in the consumption of a range of raw materials. Today, China accounts for more or less half of global consumption of aluminum, coal, copper, iron ore (China is by far the leading steel producer today, Figure 20.3), nickel, tin, and zinc. Its share is lower for lead (41 percent), phosphate (34 percent), and especially oil (13 percent) due to its use of coal (51 percent of global consumption).

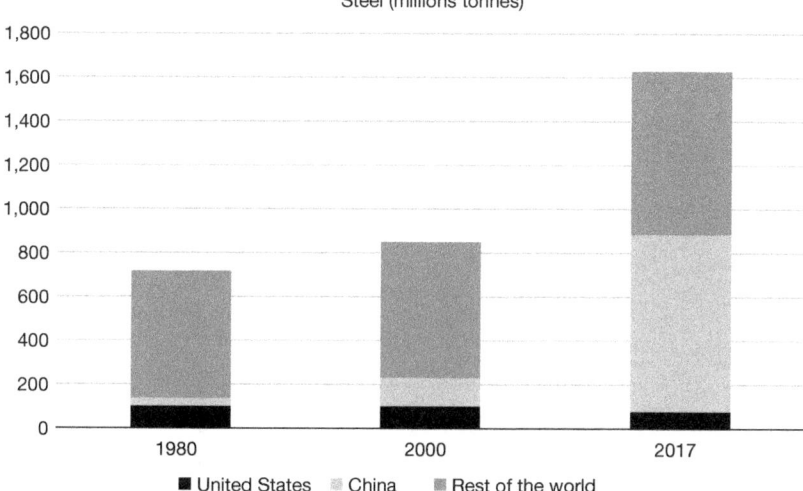

Figure 20.3 China, United States, and the rest of the world: Steel production, 1980–2017
Sources: adapted from the World Bank, 2018: 47 and following.

The country's own resources are far from sufficient to feed this raw material bulimia. China thus relies increasingly on imports of particularly heavy goods, of which fossil fuels are of highest strategic interest. Alongside its own significant coal resources (44 percent of global production), China possesses some oil reserves that it has exploited since the 1970s, when the country even exported oil to Japan. But these reserves are limited. Exploration efforts undertaken in succession in various regions (South China Sea, Xinjiang desert, etc.) have failed to realize the dream of China becoming a second Saudi Arabia. Until 2002, despite Chinese growth, the energy balance of the country remained stable, and sometimes even ran a surplus. Thereafter it shifted to a deficit, including for coal, and there is no end in sight for this deficit, given the sharp rise in imports (Figure 20.4).

The United States[8] and China are currently on diverging trajectories with regard to their energy dependence, reflecting their divergences in the domains of strategy and geopolitics.

Between 1990 and 2017, the share of imports in fossil fuels and metal ores used grew from 1 to 15 percent and from 6 to 35 percent respectively (data from the UN Environment International Resource Panel).[9]

---

[8] Data for the whole of North America, moreover, shows that the region has become a net exporter of energy, thanks to Canada's significant exports. This only serves to reinforce America's energy security.
[9] Website: http://www.resourcepanel.org/global-material-flows-database (accessed August 16, 2024).

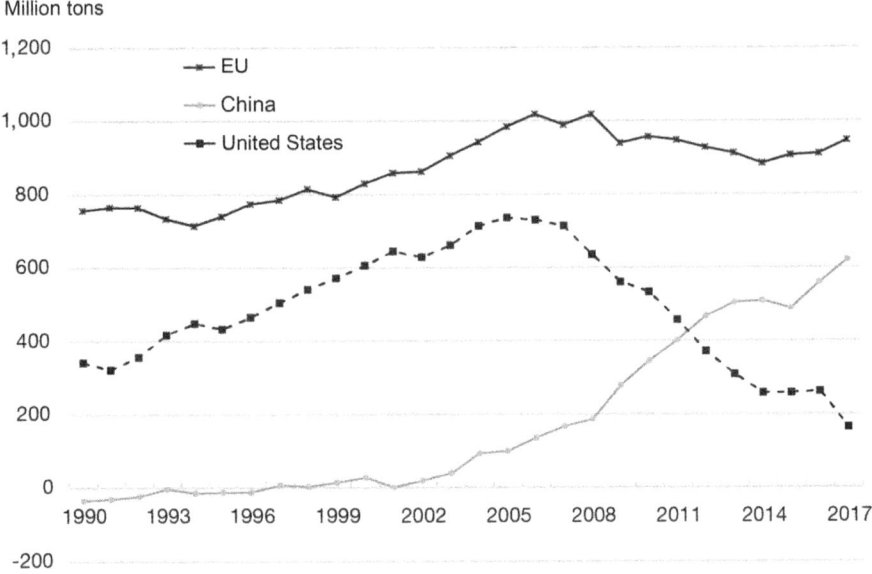

Figure 20.4 China, United States, European Union: Energy trade balance (imports–exports) (in millions of oil equivalent tons)
Source: Enerdata, 2018.

Stephen Bunker and Paul Ciccantell show how, in many regards, China followed in the steps of Japan's supply strategy, copying a number of elements of the highly internationalized model (Bunker and Ciccantell, 2007: 190). Thus, China attempted to secure its supply chains both through negotiating interstate agreements and through foreign investment by state or private enterprises.

The "Going Out" (*zou chuqu*) policy that was formally announced by the Chinese government in 2008—but had been implicitly implemented since 1995—provided a framework for this strategy of securing external supply chains for raw materials and energy by encouraging firms and banks to participate in the supply chains and in developing infrastructure abroad. In 2013, President Xi announced the launch of two complementary projects: the "21st Century Maritime Silk Road" and the "New Silk Road Economic Belt," focused on Eurasia. The two projects were later merged under the title "One Belt, One Road" (also known as the Belt and Road Initiative). These initiatives are a colossal plan for infrastructure investment, mainly in the realm of transport, aimed at facilitating international trade, in particular within the Eurasian continent. Six transnational corridors were identified; for instance, the China Indochina Peninsula Corridor (CICPEC) which stretches from the Pearl River delta and covers six Southeast Asian countries (Thailand, Laos, Vietnam, Cambodia, Myanmar, and Malaysia), and the China Pakistan Economic Corridor, a $46 billion project to connect the western province of Xinjiang to the Gwadar port in southern

Pakistan.[10] These projects have also given rise to investments in port infrastructure in Hambantota, Sri Lanka, and Piraeus, Greece.

The great convergence or the spread of the mining metabolic regime

Inequality may be widening within OECD countries, Russia, and China, but between countries globally inequalities are narrowing. While this tendency is increasingly evident today, it was for long, and still is somewhat, masked by the continued use of vocabulary that opposes the Global North and South, developed and developing countries, and other similar terms. Many international and national organizations, whether state-based or associative, continue to found their visions and actions on this distinction, even at the end of this second decade of the twenty-first century.

But the third millennium is one of indistinct paths and boundaries. I have already addressed the subject of the rapid deepening of intra-national inequality (in relation to "developed" countries, but the phenomenon is generalized). By contrast, the economic and metabolic trajectories of regions of the globe, hastily categorized in distinct, if not opposed, groups, are converging in dramatic fashion. The evolution of two variables since 1950 elucidates this development:

- The distribution of global income across the main regions of the world as estimated by the World Inequality Database team.[11]
- Material consumption by main region, as measured by material flow accounting (see Schaffartzik et al., 2014 for a comparative global analysis, data until 2015 are available on http://www.resourcepanel.org/global-material-flows-database).

The evolution in the distribution of global income is presented in Figure 20.5 which shows the share of OECD countries, "the developed countries," between 1950 and 2017, in global income.

The year 2000 marked the passage to a new period with a clearly distinct trajectory. The earlier period, from 1950 to 2000, was characterized by a relatively stable share of OECD countries in global income, standing at a little more than 50 percent. There was a slight fall in this share in the early 1970s, with the first oil shock, but it rose again

---

[10] The project, which covers a distance of 3,000 km, includes railroads, communication infrastructure, electricity plants, and the construction of an airport in the town of Gwadar (Rahman and Shurong, 2017).

[11] This database uses national income rather than GDP to measure global intra-national inequality. The authors explain: "The concept of gross domestic product (GDP) that is commonly used to compare levels of economic welfare across countries is not satisfactory. We prefer the concept of national income (NI), i.e., GDP minus consumption of fixed capital (capital depreciation) plus net foreign income. National income is more meaningful because it takes into account the depreciation of the capital stock (including in principle natural capital), which is not an income to anyone, as well as the fraction of domestic output that is transferred to foreign capital owners (including in principle offshore wealth)."https://wid.world/methodology/ (accessed August 16, 2024).

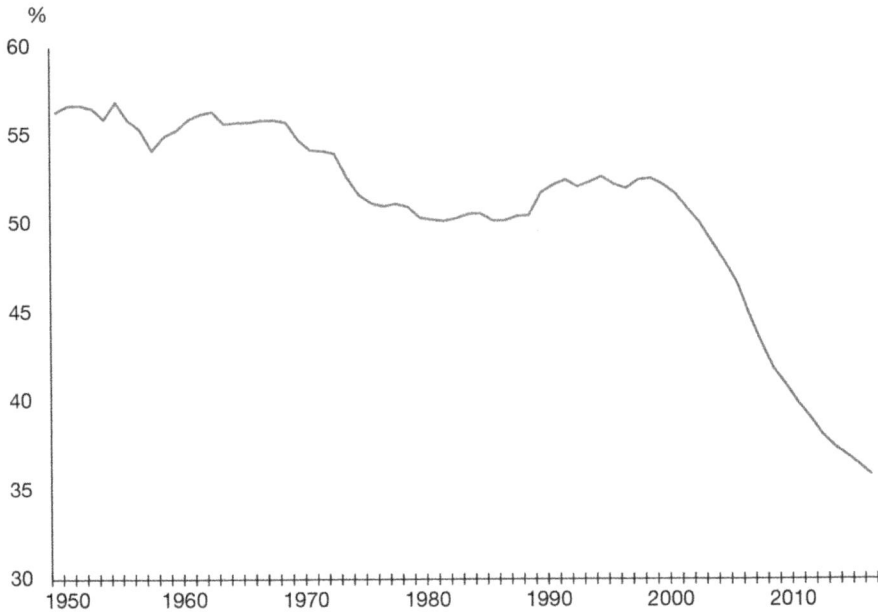

Figure 20.5 Share of OECD in global income, 1950–2017
Source: adapted from Alvaredo et al., 2018.

Table 20.2 Distribution of global income by main world region, 1950–2017 (in %, three-year averages)

	1950	1970	1990	2000	2010	2017
European and neo-European*	71	66	56	51	43	38
East Asia, Japan included	7	9	15	16	22	26

Source: adapted from Alvaredo et al., 2018.

*Expression borrowed from Alfred Crosby to refer to Western Europe, Eastern Europe, North America, Australia, and New Zealand.

at the end of the 1980s following the collapse of the Soviet bloc. In accordance with the Third World thesis, a minority of countries did indeed concentrate the lion's share of global income for fifty years, or almost two generations: an eternity on the policy timescale! The shift that occurred at the turn of the millennium thus could not have been more spectacular. In a little more than 15 years (2000–17), the OECD stumbled and its share of global income fell to 35 percent. The reshuffling of cards benefited only "developing" Asia, whose share rose from 27 percent to 44 percent, thanks to two highly contrasting processes—maximal optimization of the oil windfall by the Middle East, and accelerated industrialization in East Asia.

Another way to understand the shift in the distribution of global wealth (Table 20.2) is to compare the respective shares of East Asia (Japan included) with those of European (East included) and neo-European countries. The ratio, which was 1 to 10 in 1950, stood at only 1 to 1.5 in 2017.

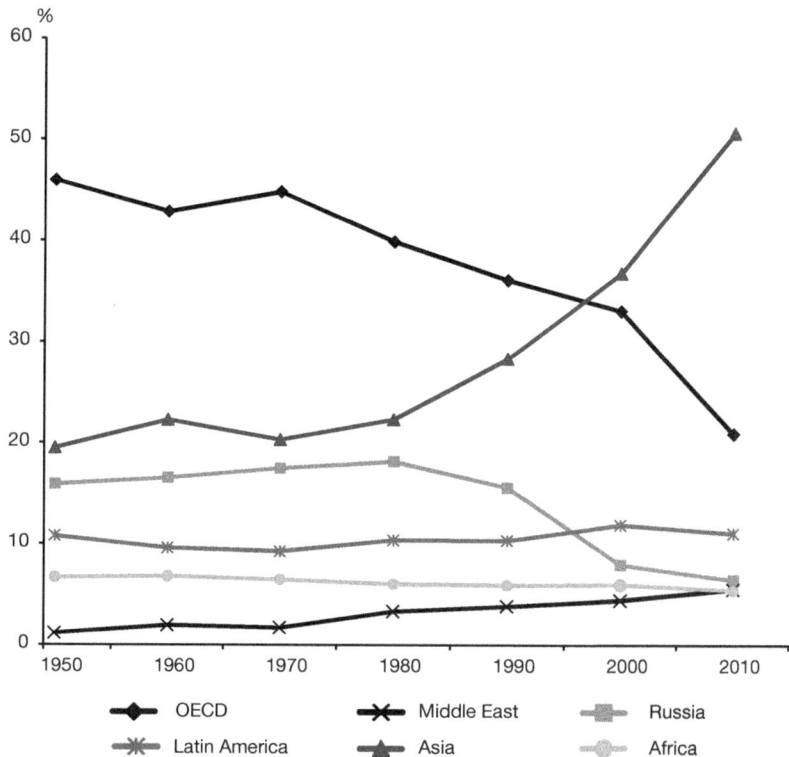

Figure 20.6 Share of various regions in global material consumption, 1950–2010 (in %)
Source: adapted from Schaffartzik et al., 2014.

The evolution of material consumption by region is represented in two figures below covering the period 1950 to 2010. Figure 20.6 shows per capita material consumption while Figure 20.7 shows the share of each region in global material consumption.

The distribution of global material consumption shifted more rapidly towards Asia than did the distribution of income. The shift occurred a bit earlier: the distribution of material consumption was relatively stable until the 1970s, when Asia's consumption rose in mirror image of the OECD's falling share, and in the 1980s of the falling share of the Soviet bloc. By 2000, Asia's share in global material consumption had already overtaken that of the OECD. Since then, the trend has accelerated, and in 2010 "developing Asia," the Middle East excluded, was responsible for 50 percent of global material consumption compared to 20 percent for the OECD.

This evolution of the global geography of material consumption reflects the geography of demography, but is above all, a sign of the great convergence in per capita material consumption, around 12 tons per year per inhabitant (36 kg per day!), of all regions in the world, except Africa. This remarkable convergence is due in part to a slight moderation of consumption in OECD countries, and to the collapse of Russian consumption between 1980 and 2000, but above all to the dazzling rise of Asia and the Middle East. The consumption standard of the mining metabolic regime was without contest imposing itself on a global scale.

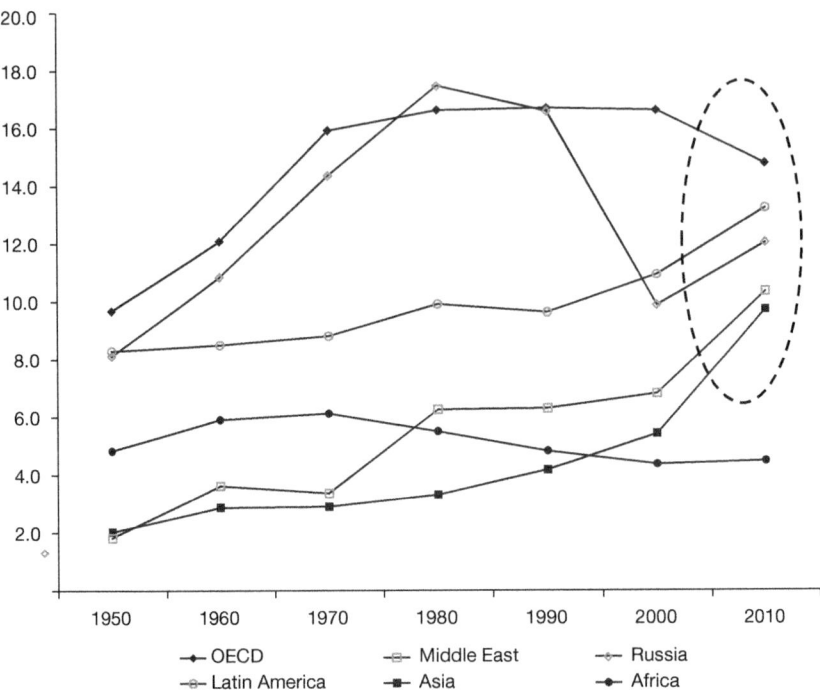

Figure 20.7 Per capita material consumption, 1950–2010 (ton/year)
Source: adapted from Schaffartzik et al., 2014.

21

The "oil-based model" of biomass production and consumption pursues its global conquest

As already mentioned, neither the change in the American growth model during the hegemon's second age, nor the global redistribution of wealth, involved true transformation of the metabolic regime, which remained fundamentally based on extraction. Biomass production and use, and even more specifically for agriculture and agricultural products, also conserved most of their essential characteristics. In an increasing number of countries, chemical farming and the almost exclusive use of agricultural production for human food (with the notable exception of biofuels) became the norm. Consumption of increasing quantities of animal products was a central part of new human diets.

Chemical farming doing well

The chemical frontier advances

The use of chemical inputs, mainly in the form of synthetic fertilizers and pesticides, indispensable ingredients of the Green Revolution, has grown at dizzying rates in the past fifty years. The consumption of nitrogen fertilizer for instance increased tenfold in South Asia, sixfold in East Asia, fivefold in Latin America, fourfold in Africa, and twofold in North America (Table 21.1).[1]

The regional data masks growth that was much faster in some countries: I will limit myself to the two examples of Brazil and India. In Brazil, nitrogen fertilizer consumption has increased at a regular rate (Figure 21.1). Fertilizer consumption per hectare has doubled since the early 2000s, to reach 50 kilograms per hectare today. In India, consumption per hectare has grown by 50 percent during the same

---

[1] Europe and former Soviet countries are exceptions due to two quite distinct processes. The fall in support for agriculture, resulting from the reform of the European Union's Common Agricultural Policy, led to a stabilization and later a fall in fertilizer consumption in Western Europe after 1984 (the case for France and the Netherlands in Figure 21.1). In former socialist countries of the East, reforms undertaken after 1989 led to a sharp collapse in use of agricultural inputs that lasted until 2005. Fertilizer consumption, measured in units of nitrogen, in the Russian Federation fell from 4.3 million tons in 1990 to 830,000 tons in 1998. It bounced back up to 2 million tons in 2017.

Table 21.1 Nitrogen fertilizer consumption by main global region (in millions of tons)

	1971–3	2015–17
Europe and ex-USSR	16.6	17.5
North America	8.1	15.1
Latin America	1.6	8.8
East Asia	5.9	35.3
South Asia	2.2	21.8
Africa	1.0	3.7

Source: International Fertilizer Association, http://www.fertilizer.org/ (accessed August 16, 2024).

period, and now stands at 100 kilograms per hectare, as much as in France, and more than in the United States (80 kg/ha).

It is more difficult to get a picture of how global consumption of pesticides has progressed, as there is no reliable monitoring of pesticide use on a global scale. The FAO provides some data, but only for a short period (1990–16) and, moreover, the data is incomplete and questionable (for example, the same values are given for several years). This dearth of data belies the importance of issues related to pesticide use and the impassioned societal debates around these. Despite health and citizen alerts, the pesticide market seems to be booming (Figure 21.2). Some authors speak of the "herbicide revolution" (Haggblade et al., 2017), highlighting the enthusiasm since the mid-2000s for pesticide use in several countries. Increased pesticide uptake coincides with the period in which certain molecules fell into the public domain (glyphosate in 2000 for instance) and when Asian suppliers capable of producing pesticides at very low cost conquered the market. Pesticide consumption has also been driven by rising rural wages in many countries as weedkillers enable the elimination of arduous tasks like weeding.

Brazil is today the leading market for pesticides, accounting for roughly 20 percent of the global market. Consumption there, measured in active units per hectare, increased fivefold between 1990 and 2018, and today stands at 4 to 5 kilograms per hectare (a little more than in France according to FAO data). Soybean is the main target crop (63 percent of pesticides used), and herbicides are by far the leading type of pesticide used (62 percent of pesticides used).[2] The number of permitted pesticides has greatly increased since Dilma Roussef was ousted, under the administrations of Michel Termer and then Jair Bolsonaro, two presidents with strong links to agroindustry.

The consumption of pesticides in India, on the other hand, is low and not growing much. According to data from the Indian Ministry of Chemicals and Fertilizers, use is estimated at between 0.5 and 0.3 kilograms of active units per hectare, and concerns

---

[2] http://ibama.gov.br/agrotoxicos/relatorios-de-comercializacao-de-agrotoxicos#boletinsanuais (accessed August 16, 2024).

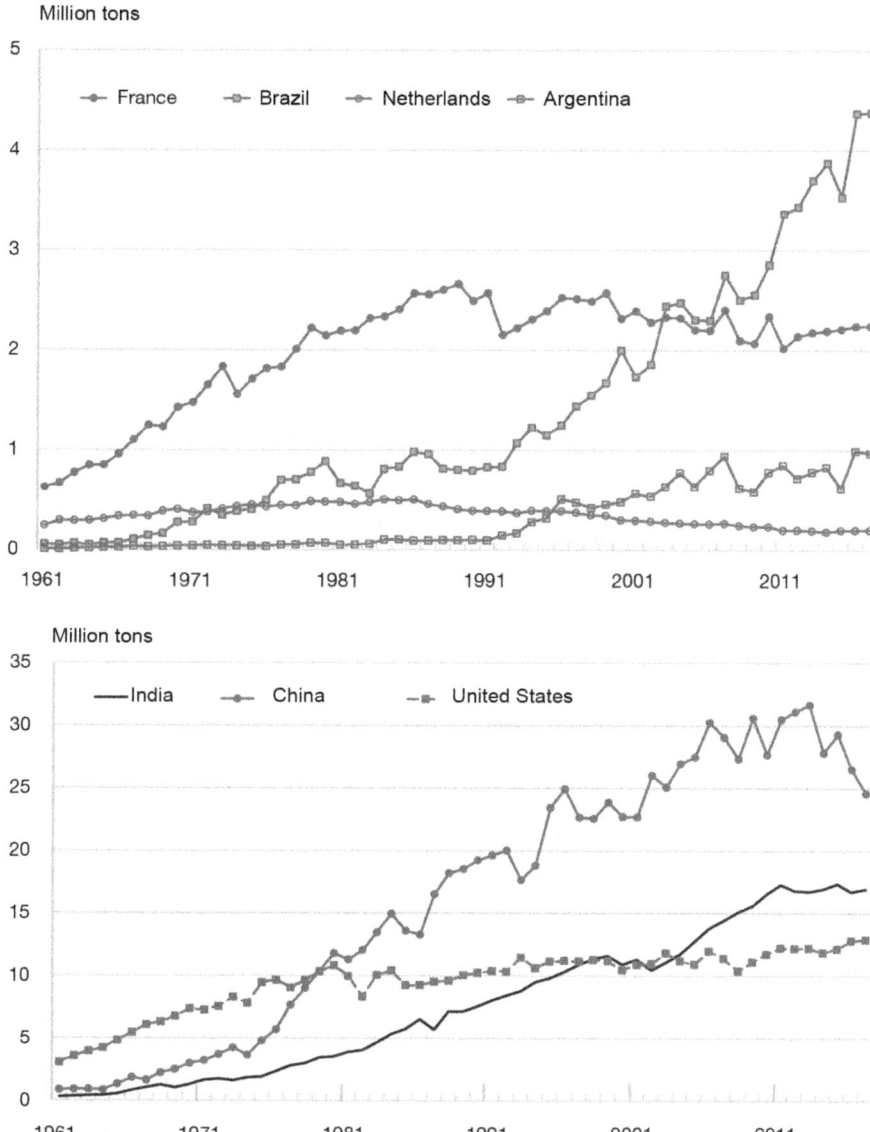

Figure 21.1 Nitrogen fertilizer consumption, 1961–2017 (in millions of tons of nutrients)
Source: International Fertilizer Association.

mainly insecticides (Subash et al., 2017). This is significantly lower than levels in Brazil and France. More recently, however, the "herbicide revolution" seems to be sweeping over the country, and India's herbicide consumption, in terms of quantities used, appears ready to overtake insecticide use (Gupta et al., 2017).

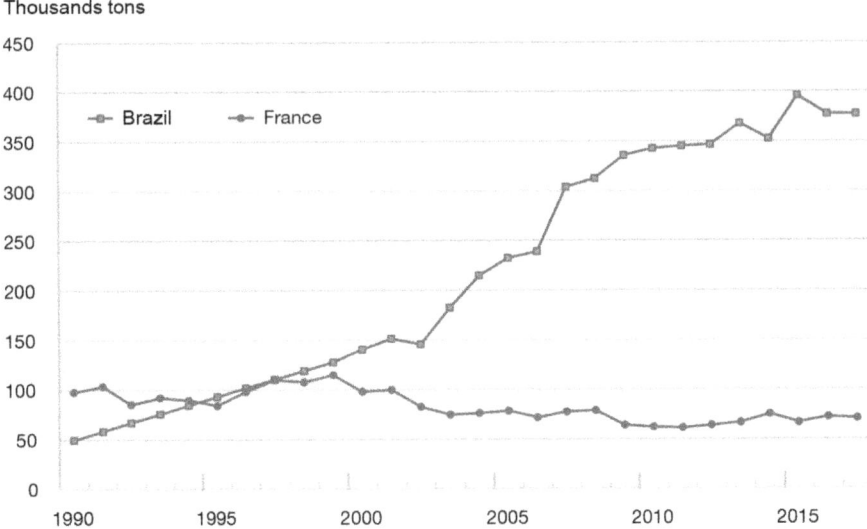

Figure 21.2 Quantity of pesticides used in agriculture in France and in Brazil, 1990–2017 (1,000 tons of active units)

Source: FAOSTAT, https://www.fao.org/ (accessed August 16, 2024).

This brief overview shows the omnipotence, as well as the malleability of chemical farming. Countries with as divergent situations in terms of availability of land or agricultural history as India and Brazil have both surrendered to the logic of chemical farming. The possibility of choosing whether or not to combine chemical farming with motorization–mechanization is one of the mainsprings of its malleability.

Growth in Brazilian agriculture today still relies in large part on the conversion of new land to farmland. However, the purely extractive exploitation of land fertility, followed by subsequent abandonment, has disappeared, replaced by the use of chemical additives. New and old land now "benefit" from a rapidly rising level of fertilization and massive use of herbicides.

In India, as Bruno Dorin and Claire Aubron (2016) underscore, growth in production has been labor-intensive as well as chemical-fertilizer intensive. Farms on average measure 1.16 hectares, with 0.65 hectares available per farm worker, of which a growing number are wage workers. The lower the size of the farm, the higher the quantity of fertilizer per hectare used: farms less than 1 hectare in size use three times more fertilizer than farms larger than 10 hectares, and this gap appears to be increasing (Chand et al., 2011: 8).

The chemical sector takes over the seed sector

The last forty years have seen the creation of a range of genetically modified organisms (GMOs), or transgenic organisms, in the fields of both human health and agriculture: bacteria that can synthetize insulin thanks to a human gene introduced in its genome, or the renowned RoundupReady soybean that is resistant to glyphosate (thanks this time to the introduction of a gene from a bacteria) are examples.

Innovations in genetic engineering aided by computer technology grew, and the costs of decoding and synthetizing DNA have dropped significantly. In the mid-2010s, the development of a technique called CRISPR-Cas9 transformed genome modification. The technique permitted intervention on a single specific gene, the deletion of the gene (by cutting its DNA strand on both sides) and, if desired, the replacement of the gene (that is, gene editing) (Bartkowski et al., 2018).

Chemistry was at the heart of this new episode in the "colonization of nature," at the microscopic level this time. Chemistry played a role not just as a scientific discipline but also as an industrial sector: firms from the chemical sector were decisive for developments.

In Part 4, we saw how during the First World War, a large part of the techniques and accumulated experience of German chemical firms was transferred to the United States. From this transfer were born a series of large firms—Dow, DuPont, American Cyanomin, Union Carbide, Monsanto, etc.—who, from the Second World War, experienced a new phase of rapid growth. According to Alfred Chandler, American government programs during the Second World War amplified "the most significant wave of new products and processes since the formation of the modern chemical industry in the 1880s and 1890s … and then to a postwar boom still unsurpassed in the industry's history" (Chandler, 2009: 23). From 1940 to 1970, the chemical industry grew 2.5 times faster than GNP.

This was the golden age of the petrochemical sector, driven by the creation and production of new polymers. The case of synthetic fibers is a dramatic illustration.[3] By the end of the 1960s, polymers had captured 70 percent of the textile fibers market in the United States, despite the country's status as a major cotton producer.[4] Polymers were the entry door for oil firms into the chemical industry—initially to fabricate base compounds necessary for producing polymers, and later producing standard polymers themselves (polyamide, polystyrene, polyethylene, etc.). Conversely, some chemical firms themselves invested in the oil sector, so as to secure their downstream supply chain. Agrochemicals (pesticides) was another fast-growing sector for investment by oil firms.

The 1970s, however, put an end to this phase of insouciant growth. The rise of oil prices, the emergence of legislation protecting the environment, the recession of the early 1980s, and overproduction capacities led the sector to a deep crisis. Firms tried to recenter on activities with high value addition. Some firms were dismantled through stock market raids (such as Union Carbide). The survival strategy for some firms, the most famous of which, Monsanto, was to opt for investment in living organisms.

---

[3] In chemistry and biology, a polymer is a macromolecule made up of a chain of similar molecules, called monomers. Starch, cellulose, silk, and DNA are natural polymers; nylon, polyethylene (all the "poly's") and Bakelite are examples of synthetic polymers.

[4] I could make readers' heads spin if I had data on the extent to which wood, leather, scales, bones, pearls, fur, and feathers were replaced by plastic materials. Unfortunately, due to the ingratitude of the twentieth century, this data do not exist.

The transformation that molecular biology and genetic engineering engendered was as significant for the chemical industry as had been the transformation induced by petrochemicals in the 1940s and 1950s. Pharmaceuticals and seeds became the key sectors for investment. The development of GMOs in the field of cultivated crops attests to this.

Between 1996 and 2013, 200 seed firms were bought up by chemical industry giants (Howard, 2015). The massive entry of the chemical industry in the seed sector resulted in a spectacular level of concentration. The market share of the first five seed firms grew from 10 percent in 1985 to 47 percent in 2015. In 2015, four of the five leading seed firms had origins in the chemical sector (Monsanto, DuPont, Syngenta, and Dow); Limagrain was the only exception (Bonny, 2017). The agrochemical sector saw a similar drive towards concentration: the market share of the four aforementioned giants grew from 29 percent to 62 percent (Clapp, 2017: 7).

The growing concentration in the seed industry occurred as GMO use spread. Between 1996 and 2017, acreage planted with GMO crops rose from 2 million to 190 million hectares, with the leading countries being the United States, Brazil, Argentina, and Canada. In 2017, the share of global acreage planted with GMO crops had reached 80 percent for cotton, 77 percent for soybean, 32 percent for corn, and 30 percent for rapeseed.[5]

Today, however, GMOs have stopped gaining ground. Stagnation in GMO acreage may explain the current enthusiasm for gene editing techniques, and the spectacular activity of acquisitions and mergers ongoing in the seed sector since 2015. The end of 2015 was marked by the merger between Dow and DuPont.[6] In 2018, after several failed attempts, Bayer succeeded in finalizing the acquisition of Monsanto, while in the meantime ChemChina (China National Chemical Corp) announced its acquisition

Table 21.2 The six large global agrochemical firms in 2015 and their recomposition

Firms	Country	2015 sales of seeds and biotechnology (in $ millions)	2015 sales of agrochemical products (in $ millions)	Firms acquiring them or merging with
BASF	Germany	Low	6,211	None
Bayer	Germany	819	9,548	Monsanto
Dow Chemical	United States	1,409	4,977	DuPont
DuPont	United States	6,785	3,013	Dow Chemical
Monsanto	United States	10,243	4,758	Bayer
Syngenta	Switzerland	2,838	10,005	ChemChina

Source: MacDonald, 2018.

[5] http://www.isaaa.org/resources/publications/pocketk/16/default.asp (accessed August 16, 2024).
[6] The firm that resulted from this merger was organized into three divisions, of which Corteva Agriscience specialized in agrochemicals and seeds.

of Syngenta. This acquisition made ChemChina the second largest global firm in the agrochemicals/seed sector, after Bayer-Monsanto, and far ahead of DuPont and BASF (Table 21.2).

China's unconditional uptake of chemical farming

Collectivization, mandatory delivery quotas, rationing, the quest for self-sufficiency: when China, under Deng Xiaoping, started its economic policy shift towards greater liberalism (in 1978), Chinese agriculture presented characteristics of a true "real socialist" country. The four decades that followed saw the establishment of agricultural policy oriented towards the market and the promotion of the model of the family farmer responsible for their own production choices.

The de-collectivization of agriculture was the first measure for building "socialism with Chinese characteristics." From the first months of 1979, collective labor brigades (communes) were gradually replaced by a system of leasing between farm households and villages, with the latter remaining the owners of the land. Called the "household responsibility system" (*baogan daohu*), these kinds of contracts spread throughout the country within a few years, and communes were eliminated in 1984. The reform gave households back the management of their farms. Collective farms were replaced by a multitude of very small farms (on average 0.5 hectares in size) that were spatially dispersed (each farm was divided in 5.7 plots on average). In terms of output, success was immediate.

The Chinese government also implemented a policy of supporting agricultural intensification, which was very similar to Green Revolution policies implemented in other Asian countries, and also presented continuity with Maoist period policies. The government pursued the very ancient policy of expanding irrigated perimeters. These today cover more than a half of planted acreage in the country. Still in the field of infrastructure development, massive investments were made into rural road networks.

Monsanto, a success story with an unhappy ending

The history of the famed firm Monsanto perfectly illustrates the evolution of agrochemical investments (Elmore, 2018). John Francis Queeny, an ex-employee of a firm distributing saccharine* produced in Germany by Merck, founded Monsanto in 1901. It had its own factory making saccharine, initially using compounds imported from Europe, and then after 1918 using coal tar as a raw material. Monsanto's success at the time was closely linked to the rise of Coca Cola. The Coca Cola Company bought up almost all of Monsanto's saccharine production, and from 1903 its caffeine, which was extracted from used tea leaves (ibid.: 159), as well as synthetic vanilla, which was the third main ingredient of the drink.

Monsanto shifted toward petroleum products as early as 1930, taking advantage, as did its competitors Dow and DuPont, of the abundant supply of by-products from oil refineries, which were booming thanks to the rising consumption of petrol. After the war, Monsanto even attempted vertical integration by acquiring an oil firm, the Lion Oil Company. During that period, Monsanto produced products as diverse as the infamous "agent orange" defoliant, and equally sadly famous pyralen (PCB) used in electrical transformers.

Hit by the 1970s chemical crisis, as others were, Monsanto faced increasing competition from oil firms that moved downstream of the value chain, as well as backlash from a number of environmental scandals, such as the PCB pollution scandal in production sites. The company thus turned towards biotechnology, divesting from its oil activities, and investing massively from 1984 in its own research and development arm, and in the acquisition of numerous biotechnology firms. The rest of the story is known. In 1996, RoundupReady soybean was put on the market; these beans were resistant to glyphosate, a weed-killer produced by Monsanto under the brand name Roundup. Bt cotton was also released; this was a type of cotton which thanks to bacterial gene produced a toxin that repulsed insects.

In June 2018, the German firm Bayer acquired Monsanto. In August 2018, Monsanto was sentenced by a San Francisco court to pay out $289 million to a professional gardener suffering from cancer. In March 2019, Monsanto was once again sentenced this time by the American Federal courts to pay $80 million to an amateur gardener with lymphoma.

*Saccharine was "discovered" accidentally in 1879, apparently while Constantin Fahlberg was experimenting how to produce preservatives from coal tar. It is a very powerful sweetener without any calories. Saccharine rapidly found a market in the food industry, and in particular in soda production (easier to dissolve and cheaper) (De la Peña, 2010: 19).

Research on hybrid rice varieties was undertaken from the early 1960s. By 1978, 60 percent of maize acreage, 13 percent of rice acreage, and 40 percent of sorghum acreage were already planted with hybrids. In that same year, the share of acreage planted with dwarf or semi-dwarf varieties stood at 80 percent for rice, and 40 percent for wheat (Stone, 1988: 795). The International Rice Research Institute (IRRI) and Cimmyt (Centro de Investigacion para el Mejoramiento del Mais y Trigo—Center for Research for the Improvement of Corn and Wheat) (two flagship institutions of the Green Revolution) directly supplied a part of the improved varieties, but also and above all, the strains needed to create new varieties adapted to Chinese conditions.

Agronomic research policy, after several shifts in direction, from 2007 benefited from a considerable increase in public funding: 96,300 researchers now worked in government agronomic research organizations. A technological innovation system was initiated, with fifty sub-systems specialized by plant, and a National Special Program for the Development of Genetically Modified Varieties (Huang and Rozelle, 2018: 494). China, moreover, has the largest technical extension system in the world. The National Special Program for the Development of Genetically Modified Varieties, with a budget of $3.8 billion over 2008–20, enabled China to became the second leading country, after the United States, in terms of number of patents filed for GMO technologies. But GMOs do not have everyone's support. Only Bt cotton and a papaya variety are used in Chinese agriculture. GMO planted acreage is no longer increasing in China. The country, which used to be the second highest GMO user after the United States, now ranks eighth after Paraguay. In 2016, the use of GMO seeds was forbidden in

Heilongjiang province, from where 50 percent of national soybean production comes (Cao, 2018).

The supply of nitrogen fertilizer is a complementary and indispensable element for improved varieties. Before 1948, two factories producing synthetic ammonia existed; with Soviet aid, five new factories were built during the first Five-Year Plan (1953–7). After relations with the USSR were broken, a new factory was built entirely by Chinese know-how in Shanghai, and three were bought, from the UK, the Netherlands, and Italy (Liu, 1965). The first contracts signed with American firms after Nixon's trip in 1972 led to fifteen more factories being added to the existing stock (Smil, 2004).

This set of measures met with success. The value of per capita agricultural production in China started an upward swing from 1979, that has not yet turned today. For Philip Huang (2016), one could speak of a true hidden agricultural revolution! The rate of growth of agricultural GDP grew from 2.2 percent for the 1952–78 period to 4.5 percent for 1979–2016, while the rate of population growth fell from 2 to 1 percent. The years immediately after the launch of the household responsibility system were years of particularly rapid growth: in the space of five years, agricultural GDP grew by 53 percent (Cai et al., 2018: 11).

Industrial production of chemical fertilizers led to a dramatic rise in their use. Chinese agriculture today has one of the highest rates of chemical fertilizer consumption per hectare in the world today. According to estimates based on FAO data, nitrogen addition per hectare in China is two times higher than in France, and three times higher than in the United States. The ratio is even higher for phosphorous and potassium (Table 21.3). China is thus facing grave problems of nitrate pollution of water tables and rivers.

It is also facing several other problems of pollution and contamination linked to its agriculture. China is estimated to use 43 percent of pesticides consumed in the world (Zhang, 2018: 78), with serious consequences for soil, water, air, as well as safety of food products. In addition, 19 percent of arable land is polluted by heavy metals, which are then found in food products. It is estimated, for instance, that 10 percent of rice production is affected by such contamination.

Water is not only polluted; it is also increasingly scarce. The availability of water resources is a particularly sensitive issue (Pomeranz, 2017). The displacement of grain farming towards northern regions of the country has made production increasingly

Table 21.3 Fertilizer consumption per hectare of cultivated* land, 2014–16 average (in kg/ha)

	N	P	K
China	236	121	105
France	100	22	23
United States	77	27	30

Source: FAOSTAT, https://www.fao.org/ (accessed August 16, 2024).

*Cultivated surface area was calculated by adding the arable land area to land under permanent crops.

dependent on pumped irrigation, leading to water-table depletion at dramatic rates. Agriculture's access to water, moreover, has to compete with other uses—urban, industrial, or from the mining sector, such as for example the coal mines, so strategic in China's energy supply.

> ## Splendor and decadence of Chinese pigs
>
> A 1969 text on Chinese agriculture, therefore a text that is not very old, allows us to grasp the scale of the transformations that have occurred in China due to the spread of the mining metabolic regime:
>
> > Hogs have generally been scavengers feeding off garbage in the streets, or have received the husk of rice, pulverized stalks, beans and the like. When they are fed grain, it is only the cheaper varieties such as barley. Even when the fodder is made up of such low-priced items, cost data in a number of sources indicate that the price of pork in China has apparently never been high enough to make raising hogs for pork alone profitable. This was the case in the latter part of the Ming dynasty and it is still true today. What makes hogs profitable is that they are not only a source of pork, but a fertilizer as well. The amount of fertilizer they produce is just enough to make them profitable.
> >
> > (Perkins, 1969: 72)
>
> Today, 63 percent of barley, 71 percent of corn, and almost all the soybean consumed in the country are fed to livestock. And in China, as in France today, hog manure is no longer a resource, but dangerous waste.

Agricultural production has also diversified, in response to food demand generated by rising incomes. The highest increase has been for fruits (+11 percent per year between 1978 and 2016), dairy products (+9 percent), poultry meat (+9 percent), fish (+7.3 percent), and vegetables (+5 percent). Cereal production, on the other hand, has only grown by 2 percent per year (Huang and Rozelle, 2018: 489). The share of cultivated land areas for plants other than basic plant crops (cereals and tubers) grew from 20 to 32 percent between 1978 and 2016, while the share of animal products in agricultural production grew from 20 to 47 percent over the same period (ibid., 2018).

Pork meat production is without doubt the star product of China's agricultural growth. It has increased eightfold since 1978, and is causing increasing pollution challenges despite state-subsidized programs for the creation of biogas plants (Chen et al., 2016).

Consumption: Continuity and change

Spread of the American norm of animal protein consumption

Nutritionists have been ringing the alarm bells for a while now (Popkin et al., 2012; Popkin, 2015; Ronto et al., 2018): the world is facing an epidemic of non-communicable diseases—cardiovascular diseases and diabetes—that are closely associated with overweight and obesity. And this is due to the poor diets of a growing share of humanity, including people in low and middle-income countries (in addition to the lack of physical activity thanks to fossil fuels). In some countries, under-nutrition and over-nutrition exist side-by-side, creating what has been called a double burden of malnutrition.

The shift in diets today with respect to diets of the past in several countries can be summed up as follows: increasing quantities of processed carbohydrates, added sugar, fats, and animal products, and decreasing quantities of fruits and vegetables. The term used to designate this shift is "nutritional transition,"[7] a transition that countries are expected to experience as they become more "developed" (see box below). Food models are converging on a global scale towards a model that strongly resembles American diets (Combris et al., 2011). In some ways, this is an echo of the convergence of metabolic regimes discussed earlier.

The nutritional transition and the mining metabolic regime

The concept of nutritional transition came to the fore in the late 1990s following observation of similarities in the dietary transformations prompted by rising incomes. Summed up in a few words, and taking the example of France (Combris et al., 2011), the thesis is that since the end of the eighteenth century and the Industrial Revolution until the 1990s, human diets have shifted in two phases:

- During the first phase, increased income leads to an increase in the number of calories consumed, or as Pierre Combris and colleagues put it, "a very significant rise in calorie rations per person throughout the nineteenth century." Consumption of all foods increases, without any notable shift in the composition of diets. This first phase lasts until calorie needs are saturated, which effectively occurred around the First World War (Toutain, 1971).

---

[7] The apparently fashionable word "transition" is borrowed from demographers. The demographic transition designates the population trajectory that each country is expected to follow as incomes rise. A first phase involves rapid growth in population size due to the delay between shifts in mortality, which falls rapidly, and birth rates which initially remain stable. In a second phase, birth rates also start falling, and by consequence the population growth rate slows down, or stops completely.

- Then starts a second phase, the actual nutritional transition, strictly speaking (Combris et al., 2011: 40), which involves a profound transformation of diets. The share of basic foods (cereals, starches, dried legumes) in calorie intake falls, while the share of animal products, fatty matter, sugar, and fruits and vegetables rises. The share of carbohydrates in calorie rations went from 70 percent to 45 percent (50 percent in the early 1970s), while that of fats from 16 percent to 42 percent (35 percent in the early 1970s).

This nutritional transition was observed in all European countries during the second half of the twentieth century: stabilization of total calorie intake, reduction of calorie intake from carbohydrates, rise in fatty calories, and unchanged intake of protein calories (Blandford, 1984; Grigg, 1995). The main driver of these transformations was the consumption of animal products (meat and dairy products). The same foods are not consumed in all countries. The share of meat and of dairy products, the type of meat or fatty matter consumed continue to vary from country to country, without however invalidating the overall trend in terms of calories. This leads David Blandford to affirm that: "Despite differences in the level of income across countries and in relative prices, the total volume of food consumption and its composition by major food groups tends to display considerable similarity" (Blandford, 1984: 60).

The concept of nutritional transition, which tends to be used mainly in discussions about the rise of food-related pathologies, however, appears ambiguous and strongly ahistorical to me. It presents man as "naturally omnivorous," and suggests that physiological factors, such as human capacity for satiety, the density of taste buds, etc., are key drivers of human attraction to animal products, an attraction held in check only by the scarcity of supply or an individual's own low income.

We saw, however, the considerable efforts deployed in the United States to promote such a dietary transition, and how it was closely linked to the energy overabundance engendered by the mining metabolic regime. At the least, we can conclude that energy abundance and the agricultural overproduction it causes made necessary the shift from a plant-based diet to an animal-product rich diet, the latter diet not bringing more calories to the plate but consuming many more calories upstream.

Consumption of pork and chicken (Figure 21.3), to take just two examples, has grown at a dazzling rate. In Brazil, Mexico, Russia, Turkey, Saudi Arabia, South Korea, Indonesia, Vietnam, and even India, all countries with very different culinary traditions, the trend is towards more meat. There are, however, some cultural specificities. For a same level of income, volumes consumed vary of course, as does the type of meat consumed. India eats less meat than it "should." Non-Muslim or non-Hindu Asian countries have a strong weakness for pork meat. Latin American countries and Muslim countries lean clearly towards chicken. Russia, for its part, has increased consumption of both pork and chicken.

The rise in meat consumption has provoked increasing consumption of corn and soymeal, needed for feeding livestock. The correlation is not perfect, as some countries,

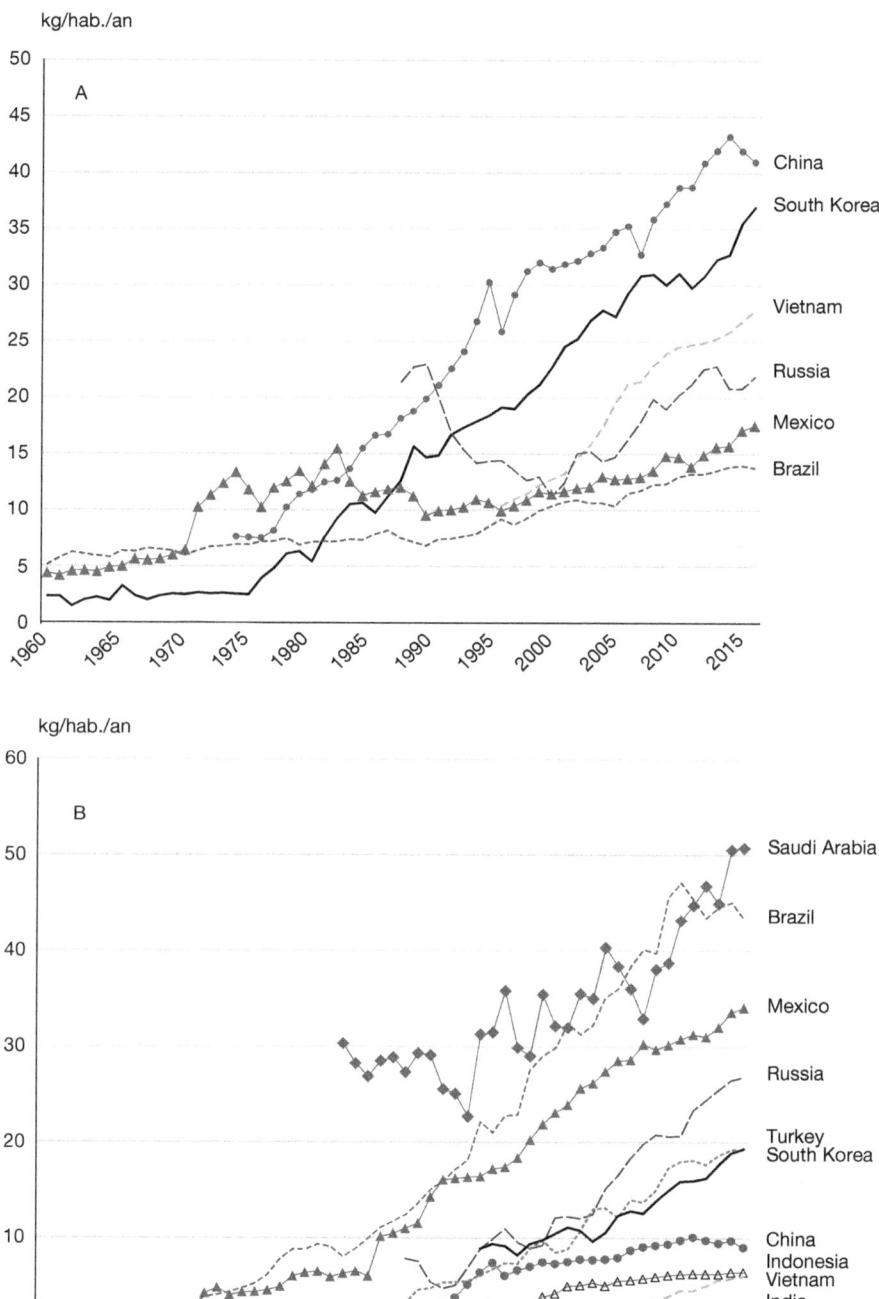

Figure 21.3 Per capita consumption of pork meat (A) and chicken (B) (in kg/person/year)

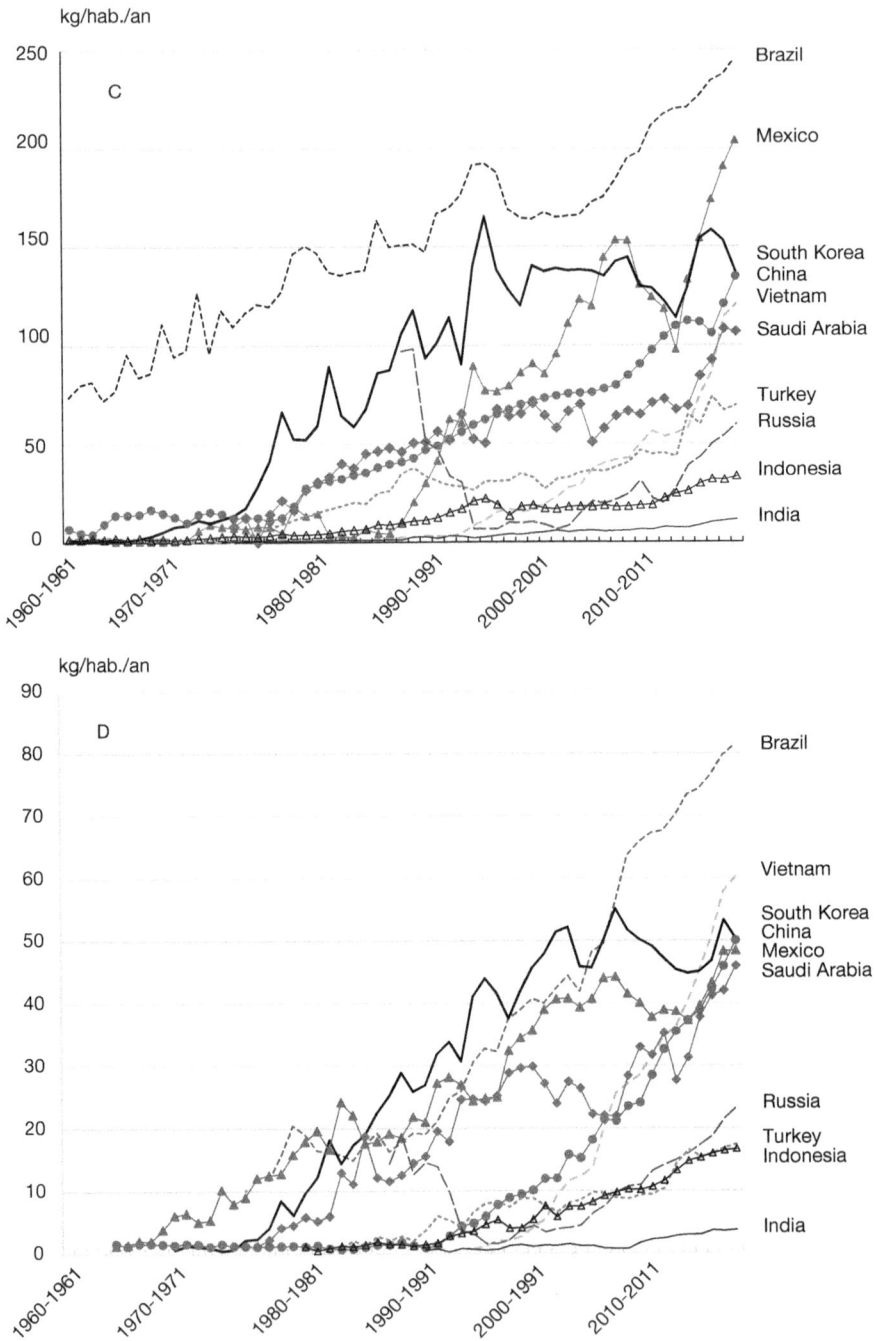

Figure 21.3 *continued* Per capita consumption of corn (C) and soymeal (D) for animal feed (in kg/person/year)

Sources: national consumption adapted from USDA PSD data, https://apps.fas.usda.gov/psdonline/app/index.html#/app/advQuery (accessed August 16, 2024) and Maddison Project Database 2018 for population, https://www.rug.nl/ggdc/historicaldevelopment/maddison/releases/maddison-project-database-2018 (accessed August 16, 2024).

such as Brazil, export meat and thus have a disproportionately high consumption of corn and soybean. Other countries, such as South Korea, import meat and therefore have disproportionately low consumption of the latter. A sort of "meat nationalism" nonetheless has led several countries to actively support development of their own animal production, even if it requires using growing quantities of imported animal feed.

On a global scale, at any rate, the relationship between meat consumption and soymeal consumption is almost arithmetic. For the past fifty years, global consumption of soybeans has grown at an annual rate of 4.5 percent without showing any signs of slowing down. The relationship between meat and corn, however, is less simple today. Because corn is used to produce ethanol as a biofuel, corn for animal feed today "only" accounts for 59 percent of its global consumption.

China: From subsistence to abundance

Dietary intake in China increased considerably after the policy shift of 1978. The end of food rationing in towns, after thirty years (1953–84), as well as the sharp rise in income, albeit unevenly distributed, are obvious explanations. According to United Nations Environmental Programme (UNEP) estimations, in total China's consumption of biomass, both food and non-food, grew from 1.4 tons per capita per year in 1978 to 3 tons in 2017.

Diets in China have also undergone a "nutritional transition," which has deformed the structure of the country's consumption—and the cherry on the cake, now even rural diets are catching up with urban diets. Rising standards of living in China, as elsewhere, were accompanied by a reduction in the direct consumption of cereals, and an increase in consumption of fatty matter (mainly plant-based) and animal proteins. Comparing the quantities of main food products consumed by urban and rural populations between 1985 and 2015, gives an idea of the scale and speed of the transformations: doubling of consumption of fatty matter for both population categories, poultry meat consumption increased threefold (from 3 to 9 kg) for urban populations, and sevenfold (from 1 to 7 kg) for rural populations (Table 21.4). Obesity, and especially childhood and adolescent obesity, has sensationally become a topic for Chinese press coverage.

These dietary changes have contributed to redefining the place that China occupies in global consumption. Its share in human food cereal consumption (rice and wheat) has been falling, while the share of animal products and vegetable oils has been rising. The absolute record is for pork meat: China today, with just 19 percent of the global population consumes 50 percent of all pork. Pork is followed by powdered milk, and then three products used for feeding animals (including fish farming): corn, soybean, and fishmeal.[8] China's share in beef consumption has also risen dramatically, but has fallen for poultry meat, due to repeated avian flu epidemics which reduced production

---

[8] The USDA estimated that around 70 percent of corn consumption is used for animal feed.

Table 21.4 Consumption of various food products by urban and rural populations in China, 1985–2015 (in kg/person/year)

	1985		2015	
	Urban	Rural	Urban	Rural
Grain	135	257	112	159
Vegetables	144	131	104	90
Oils	6	4	11	9
Pork, beef, mutton	18	11	29	23
Poultry	3	1	9	7
Eggs	7	2	10	8
Aquatic products	7	1.6	15	7

Sources: China Statistical Year Book, 1999 and 2016, http://data.stats.gov.cn/ (accessed August 16, 2024).

and eroded consumer trust. China's dominant share in global consumption of aquaculture products, around 90 percent, should also be highlighted.

In the realm of non-food biomass, China today also accounts for a signification share of global consumption, linked directly to the dramatic expansion of the country's industrial sector. China's share in global consumption reached 48 percent for chipboard panels, 27 percent for paper and carton, 40 percent for natural rubber, and 33 percent for cotton (Table 21.5).

Biofuels: A supplementary market for agricultural surpluses or the harbinger of a radical shift in biomass use?

This chapter, which has emphasized continuities in biomass usage resulting from distinct characteristics of the mining metabolic regime, must also address biofuels, which represented, in terms of volume, a novelty of the 1990s.

The biggest biofuel producers and users are the European Union, the United States, and Brazil, followed by China, Indonesia, and India. Brazil has had a policy supporting ethanol production for fuel on a large scale since the 1970s, as a response to rising oil prices at the time. The real boom in ethanol and biodiesel production, however, did not take place until the end of the 1990s and lasted until the 2007–8 surge in global food prices (Table 21.6). Such dramatic development of the biofuel industry was only made possible through massive public support: subsidies, tax exemptions, and measures making biofuel addition to fuels obligatory. In 2009, government support to biofuels reached around $8 billion in total in the European Union, and a similar amount in the United States (International Energy Agency, 2010).

American and European policy support for biofuels, in the initial design at least, was not linked to any ambition to shift away from a mining metabolism. The policies should rather be interpreted as the last avatar—after meat consumption, food aid, or

Table 21.5 Population and consumption of various biomass in China, as % of global total, 1978–2018

	1978–80	1998–2000	2016–18
Share in global population	22	21	19
Agricultural food biomass			
Rice	37	34	30
Wheat	15	19	16
Vegetable oils	5	15	19
Palm oil	1	8	8
Whole milk powder	0	22	49
Beef	1	9	14
Chicken meat	-	18	13
Pork meat	21	47	50
Corn	14	20	24
Soybeans	10	14	31
Agricultural non-food biomass			
Cotton	23	24	33
Rubber	9	15	40
Water-based biomass			
Fishmeal (USDA/PSD)	1	23	34
Fish and sea products[a]	11	32	36
Aquaculture products[2]	65	87	90
Forest biomass			
Paper and carton[b]	4	13	27
Chipboard panels[1]	1	11	48

Sources: agricultural food biomass: USDA/PSD, https://apps.fas.usda.gov/psdonline/app/index.html#/app/advQuery, cotton: ICAC, https://icac.org/About/AboutICAC?MenuId=2, rubber: IRSG, https://www.rubberstudy.org/welcome, forest biomass: FAOSTAT, https://www.fao.org/faostat/en/#home, aquatic biomass: FAO Food Balance Sheet, https://www.fao.org/statistics/highlights-archive/highlights-detail/food-balance-sheets-2010-2022-global-regional-and-country-trends/en (all accessed September 19, 2024). [a] 2011–13 average for the last column; [b] Availability (production—exports + imports), 2015–17 average for the last column.

high-fructose corn syrup[9]—of the creation of new markets for agricultural production perceived as structurally inclined to overproduction. They should also be viewed against a backdrop of a quest for new farm income support mechanisms, at a time when former mechanisms were being dismantled.

The boom in biofuel production that resulted from such policy support had a major impact on global demand for cereals and vegetable oils. Biofuels thus certainly played a role in the international food price surge of 2007–8 (HLPE, 2011; Daviron and Douillet, 2013). Since then, growth in production has considerably slowed,

---

[9] High-fructose corn syrup (HFCS) is a sweetener developed from corn. This new use of corn was strongly encouraged by the American government from the 1970s as a way of replacing cane sugar imports. HFCS thus came to be used in most sodas. It is considered a significant cause of the obesity epidemic in the United States.

Table 21.6 Biofuel production, various countries, 1995–2017 (1,000)

	1995–7	2007–9	2015–17
United States	4,542	34,887	60,946
Ethanol, biodiesel	0	2,037	6,863
European Union	102	4,025	6,639
Ethanol, biodiesel	450	8,877	13,238
Brazil	14,177	25,257	29,340
Ethanol, biodiesel	0	1,060	4,520
China	–	7,072	9,633
Ethanol, biodiesel	–	492	1,030
India	–	1,489	2,397
Ethanol, biodiesel	–	10	165
Indonesia	–	205	216
Ethanol, biodiesel	–	407	3,747
Malaysia	–	0	0
Ethanol, biodiesel	–	189	459

Sources: OECD, 2011 and site https://stats.oecd.org/ (accessed August 16, 2024).

Table 21.7 Share of biofuels in consumption of products in various countries, 2015–17

Country	Products
United States	Corn: 47%
	Vegetable oils: 23%
European Union	Wheat: 4%
	Corn: 8%
	Sugar beet: 11%
	Vegetable oils: 45%
Brazil	Sugarcane: 49%
	Vegetable oils: 31%
World	Wheat: 2%
	Corn: 16%
	Vegetable oils: 13%

Source: OECD https://stats.oecd.org/ (accessed August 16, 2024).

particularly in Europe (Table 21.7). Biofuels, nonetheless, represent a significant case of non-food usage of agricultural biomass. This is a major break with twentieth-century trends. Over the 2015–17 period, 47 percent of corn production in the United States (compared to 43 percent for animal feed), 45 percent of vegetable oil production in the European Union, and 49 percent of Brazilian sugar cane were used for biofuel production. On a global scale, that represented 16 percent of corn consumption and 11 percent of vegetable oil consumption.

For institutional partisans of the bio-economy (European Commission, 2012; OECD, 2008.), the development of biofuels is just a first step. The term "bio-economy" emerged at the end of the 1990s in the discourse of international organizations and national administrations.[10] The expression designates the use, within industry, of biomass as a source of both energy and matter as a replacement for fossil fuels, as well as use of the processes of living organisms as a replacement for chemical or mechanical procedures.

> In terms of science and technology, the bio-economy is based on the combination of increased knowledge about genomes, which makes it possible to obtain more efficient and effective processing agents and facilitates increased use of biotechnological processes, and of increased use of biomass in industrial processes.
> (Colonna and Valceschini, 2017: 157)

European chemical industry giants are at the forefront of this economy. These firms, which historically were built around the quest for biomass substitutes synthetized from coal, and later petrol, are today "chasing their tails" in a quest to synthetize, with the aid of living organisms[11] (thus biomass), substitutes to products created through chemical synthesis. These firms nonetheless continue to ride the wave of the mining metabolic logic, which has not been in any way challenged by this shift in direction. Their discourse is filled with affirmations of the existence of unexploited biomass deposits, sufficient to replace fossil fuels while maintaining our current level of consumption. This position is however completely disconnected from reality, as the agricultural surpluses of yesterday, the current abundance of land in fallow, and rising forest cover in countries like France, are a direct consequence, as we have seen, of the use of fossil fuels, including in agriculture.

---

[10] The term bio-economy was initially proposed by economists such as Georgescu-Roegen and René Passet, who emphasized the need to consider the biological and physical limits, as well as the consequences of economic processes, and were originators of the degrowth political movement. Today, in my opinion, the term has been turned inside out like a glove in discourse promoting the new generation of chemical industries (Georgescu, 1971; Passet, 1979).

[11] Innovations in the field of genome science should enable synthetic biology (or bio-engineering, or metabolic engineering) to use microorganisms to produce compounds that the chemical industry knows how to make, but which do not exist "in nature" (new-to-nature products). For instance, no living organism is capable of creating carbon-fluorine bonds, or carbon-silicon bonds, something that industrial chemistry knows how to do very well (Martinelli and Nikel, 2019). In this case, the genome of a micro-organism would be modified so that it creates new enzymes capable of catalyzing the desired chemical reaction. The micro-organism can thus be characterized a cellular factory, or a chassis, whose capacity for synthesis can be measured (Calero and Nikel, 2019).

22

The incomplete globalization of agricultural markets

The first oil shock in 1973 heralded the start of a slow process of destabilization of the organization of agricultural markets that had prevailed since 1945. Rising incomes, enabled by the raw material boom (including oil of course) and access to cheap loans, generated new import demand from so-called "developing" countries and those from the so-called "East." This incentivized the European Union and the United States to increase even further their production and hence their surpluses. As the two reasserted their exporting vocation,[1] some developing countries also opted to return to proactive agro-exporting strategies (Argentina, Brazil, Malaysia, Indonesia, Thailand, etc.).

When the USSR became the leading wheat importer, 1972–90

The rapid rise in Soviet imports was one of the shocks that destabilized international trade in food products from 1972 onwards. It was also a symptom of the Soviets taking up the American model of consumption.

In 1980, food products accounted for a quarter of total USSR imports—a ratio much higher than that of OECD countries—and the country spent a third of its Western foreign currency export revenues on these imports. Cereals (and sugar which we will not discuss here) made up the bulk of the deficit.

A net exporter of wheat and secondary cereals in the 1960s, the USSR became the leading importer of these products in the 1970s. Its share in global imports of wheat and secondary cereals reached respectively 20 percent and 12 percent in 1973, and grew to 25 percent and 21 percent by 1984.

It all started with an agreement negotiated with the United States in 1972 for the purchase of 10 million tons of cereals (wheat and corn) subsidized by the USDA that was accompanied by a large loan from the Commodity Credit Corporation (Brada, 1983). The announcement of the agreement led to a sharp rise in prices on the international cereal markets, and marked the beginning of a phase of great price instability.

In 1976, a new agreement was signed, with the ambition now to avoid the destabilizing effects of the first agreement. Under the new terms, the USSR

---

[1] "Agriculture must be our oil," proclaimed French president Valéry Giscard d'Estaing in December 1977.

Table 22.1 Composition of USSR food imports (in millions of rubles)

	1972	1980	1989
Cereals	766	3,347	3,271
Raw sugar	196	2,166	2,813
Oilseeds	48	239	165
Meat	80	883	728
Butter	5	267	261
Wheat flour	22	193	27
Vegetable oils	14	169	323
Total	1,131	7,264	7,588

Source: Sizov, 1991.

committed to purchasing between a minimum of 6 million tons of wheat and corn in total, and a maximum of 8 million tons; beyond these quantities a supplementary agreement had to be negotiated with the American government. The agreement only committed the United States for years in which the cereal harvest exceeded 225 million tons.

But this mechanism was not sufficient to stabilize markets. In January 1980, in response to the invasion of Afghanistan, the United States decreed an embargo on cereal exports exceeding a cap of 8 million tons. This embargo, however, was a total failure, and is often cited as a model of failed embargos. In effect, the USSR simply changed supplier and bought large quantities of cereal from Argentina, at the time under a military government (which was nonetheless a US "ally").

The sudden entrance of the USSR in the arena as a cereal importer gave rise to multiple interpretations. The goal of the imports was initially perceived to be about satisfying demand for bread from hungry Soviet citizens. But it turned out to be more about increasing the availability of meat for consumers. Access to cheap food, and in particular meat, had been an important concern of Soviet authorities during the postwar decades. Following the same track as the nutritional transitions in the capitalist world, meat consumption in the USSR had grown from 40 kilograms per inhabitant per year in 1960 to 57 kilograms in 1975. After that date, supply chain constraints stopped further increase, and the level was still far from the "ideal" standard of 78 kilograms determined by the Soviet Academy of Sciences. A food plan was adopted in 1982 which set a target of 70 kilograms for 1990 (Cook, 1985). The events that unfolded afterwards made it difficult to know if the plan had been realistic.

The increase in cereal and food imports also corresponded with an increased availability of foreign currency thanks to rising oil revenues, and in the 1970s, with access to cheap international loans. From this perspective, the USSR's trajectory and its position in international trade in food products resembled that of many countries called "developing." The modalities of its insertion in agricultural markets were not radically different from the dominant postwar logic, characterized by trade of deficits and surpluses administered by states (see Part 5). It was the unprecedented scale of the volumes traded, mainly on the wheat market, which was the novelty with the case of the USSR in 1972.

From 1982, the Latin American debt crisis, and the counter-oil shock led to a contraction of demand and a fall in international food prices. The United States and Europe, carried away by their momentum from the 1970s, now competed directly with each other on markets that were depressed. Having become dependent on foreign markets to manage their agricultural surpluses, they now defended their market shares with massive subsidies, and thus accelerated the fall of prices further. Guaranteed producer price mechanisms, as they existed still at the time in the United States and in Europe, implied increasing subsidies when international prices fell. That proved ruinous in a time of depressed markets, and contributed to depressing the markets even further. Expenditure on support measures went through the roof to fund a trade war that was disastrous for European and American budgets, as well as for farmers in countries with lower budgetary resources.

Discontent mounted amongst competitors with less money, who accused the United States and Europe of unfair practices. The competitors soon came together under the Cairns Group, and called for a moratorium (Daviron and Voituriez, 2006). The Cairns Group is one of the international initiatives that challenged the grand postwar divisions, as its members came from the Global North, South, and the East.[2]

Negotiations on agriculture were opened under GATT in 1985, the first since the organization was created, as an attempt to put an end to the trade war on agricultural markets. The negotiations addressed three issues: market access, export subsidies, and domestic support measures (Bureau et al., 1999: 248).[3] In 1994, they gave rise to the Marrakech Agreement which established a set of rules for agricultural policies, and instituted the principle of decoupling (support was permitted on the condition that it was not proportional to volumes produced) and of tariffs (all import barriers were to be replaced by ad valorem import duties).

After a long slump, international trade in agricultural products grew once more, and accelerated anew after 2000 (Figure 22.1). It is this new phase of growth that truly gave birth to the process of globalization of agricultural markets.[4] But the ideal of self-sufficiency did not disappear, and a truly global food market in which all humans, both

---

[2] The founding members of the Cairns Group in 1986 were Argentina, Australia, Brazil, Canada, Chile, Colombia, Fiji, Hungary, Indonesia, Malaysia, New Zealand, Philippines, Thailand, and Uruguay.

[3] i. For market access, ad valorem tariffs became the norm. All non-tariff barriers were to be eliminated. Sealed domestic markets and disconnection of domestic prices from international prices were thus officially abandoned, because even if domestic prices remained higher than international prices, the application of ad valorem custom duty was supposed to now make them shift with international prices. ii. Export subsidies were capped and to be eliminated progressively. iii. Domestic support measures to farmers were categorized according to the level of distortion that they could cause to international trade. In addition, the amounts that could be spent were capped.

[4] The growth of agricultural trade in the 1970s must be considered the result of highly contrasting policies from "countries of the North" and "countries of the South": support measures for the former, and taxation for the latter. Import demand for food products from oil and mineral exporting countries, and from those who benefited from the "circulation of petrodollars" resulted in large part in these countries having overvalued currencies, which in actuality entailed taxation of their agricultural sectors (what is called implicit taxation). Agricultural product exports from the EEC or the United States—even when they accounted for a significant share of production as was the case for some products—were always linked to surpluses and not to a strategy of international specialization as had been the case with suppliers to the UK in the nineteenth century.

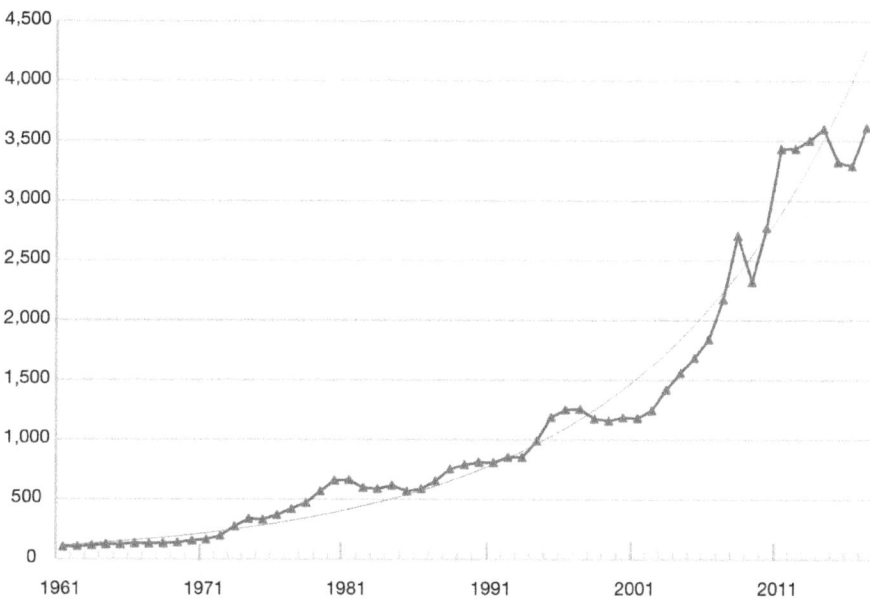

Figure 22.1 Index of international biomass trade volumes, 1961–2017 (1961=100)

Sources: based on UNCTAD data, various years, https://unctadstat.unctad.org/FR/Index.html, and World Bank data, http://www.worldbank.org/en/research/commodity-markets (accessed August 16, 2024). The index was calculated by deflating the value of global biomass (food and non-food) imports, intra-EU trade excluded, by the World Bank's international price index for agricultural products.

producers and consumers, partook and were subjected to the same price changes, was not established.

Agricultural markets not only followed the same general and unified movement towards liberalization and unification, they were also subjected to four developments: a convergence of agricultural policies on a global scale, a spectacular shift of import demand towards Asia, the return of certain historic biomass exporters, as well as in several cases resistance from domestic markets against the influence of international markets.

The convergence of agricultural policies

The Marrakech Agreement provided an outline for moving towards the reunification of agricultural markets at a global level, and in principle, for all GATT (which had become the World Trade Organization, WTO) members, a reconnection of prices that prevailed domestically with international prices. In short, it was the reemergence of a global price as had existed at the end of the nineteenth century. The most radical effect of the agreement was on export subsidies. The EU budget dedicated to such expenditure thus fell from a level of 10 billion euros per year in the 1990s to less than

140 million in 2012. WTO member countries were still permitted to support incomes of their farmers, but only through direct assistance, and on the condition that support was independent (decoupled) from volumes produced (Bureau and Jean, 2012).

In countries that were "under structural adjustment," the rules of the Washington Consensus—jointly defended by the World Bank, the International Monetary Fund (IMF) and the American executive—imposed accelerated liberalization on all sectors of the economy.

These policies, which had disastrous effects in many fields, did manage to reduce the taxation of agriculture (Jensen et al., 2010) and enabled, even with the unfavorable condition of international markets, a gradual improvement in some producer prices between the end of the 1970s and 2004.

Lastly, while OECD countries reduced the forms of agricultural support most disruptive to international trade, some "developing" countries quickly increased their production subsidies. Agricultural policies, and more widely, economic policies, as well as the transfers that they organized between agriculture and the rest of the economy, were modified (Figures 22.2 and 22.3). The level of transfers towards the agricultural sector through price support now tended to converge on a global scale, and in this realm too, the clear distinction that separated so-called "developing countries" from "developed countries" became blurred.

The evolution of the relative rate of assistance (RRA) indicator developed by Kim Anderson (2009) provides a first inkling of the scale of convergence (Figure 22.2) (see also Part 5). The value of RRA in the European Union, the United States, Brazil,

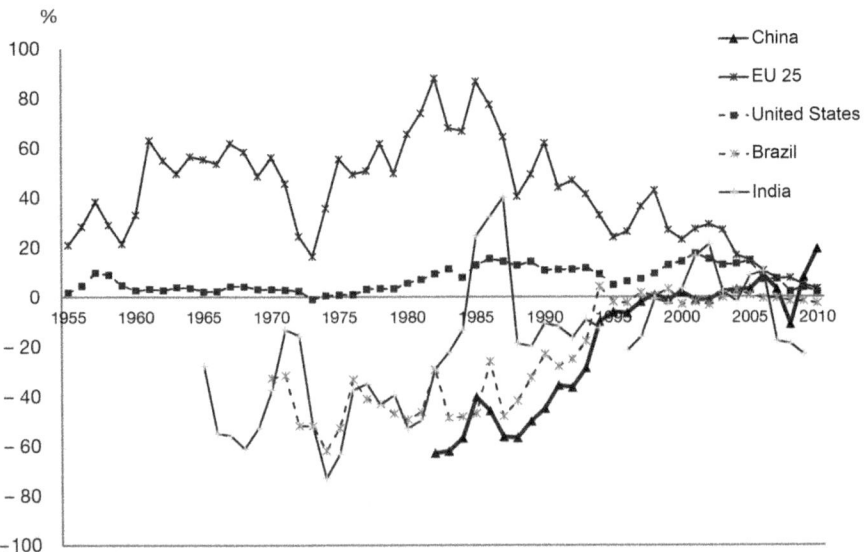

Figure 22.2 Relative rate of assistance (RRA) to agriculture in various countries, 1955–2010

Sources: Anderson and Nelgen, 2012, 2013.

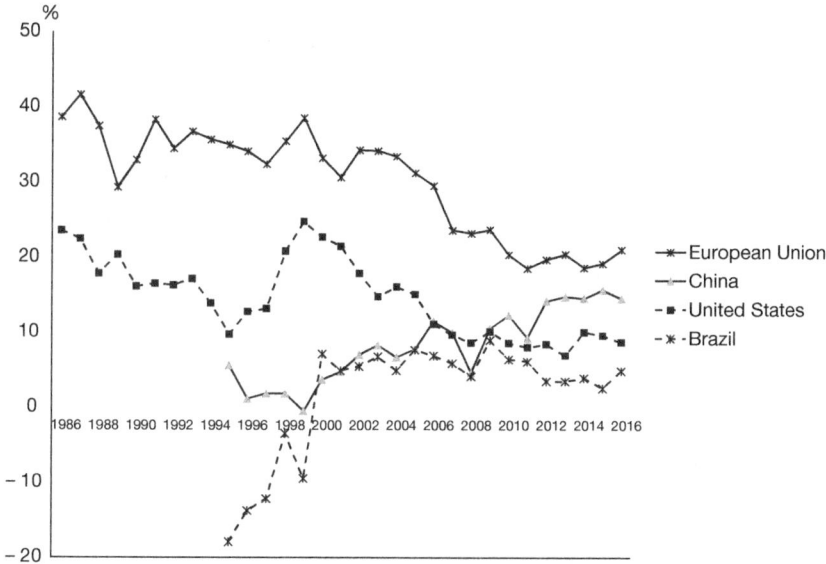

Figure 22.3 Agricultural production support in the European Union, China, United States, and Brazil (PSE), in % of gross agricultural income, 1996–2016

Source: OECD database, https://data-explorer.oecd.org/ (accessed September 19, 2024).

India, and China—which previously illustrated so well the division of the world into "developed countries" supporting their agriculture and "developing countries" taxing their agriculture and protecting industry—clearly converged from the mid-1980s.

The OECD's producer subsidy equivalent indicator (PSE), for its part, considers all forms of intervention that may influence farmers' incomes (OECD, 2017). It is presented as a percentage of agricultural income. The indicator confirms the convergence between "developed" (United States and European Union) and "developing" countries (Brazil and China) (Figure 22.3). Support fell in the former and increased in the latter. Chinese support even exceeded the level of support in the United States. Beyond an overall convergence, there was also a rapprochement in the situations of the EU and of China, countries with biomass deficits, and that became quite distinct from the situations of Brazil and the United States, both rich in arable land.[5] In short, an entirely different agricultural geopolitical arena than that which had characterized the first phase of the American hegemony (Hopewell, 2019) came to be.

The shift of import demand towards Asia

The last six decades have seen the destination of long-distance biomass trade shift from Europe towards Asia. For centuries, Europe was the center of trade. This was still the

---

[5] It goes without saying that the poorest countries are excluded from this convergence of agricultural support.

case after the Second World War. But in the mid-1980s, Asia came to the fore in a shift that is still ongoing. In 2017, Asia accounted for about half of global biomass imports, compared to 20 percent for Europe (Figure 22.4).

Distinction should be made between two regions within Asia. To the west, oil-exporting countries saw their wealth multiplied from 1973 on, and OPEC activity gave rise to a spike in food imports, driven both by rising household incomes, and by the ineluctable sacrifice of agriculture that characterized rentier economies.[6] To the east, there was a completely different dynamic as wealth was founded on the transfer of the global industrial center towards the region, which had become, or almost become, the new heart of the global economy. It is this latter region that I analyze in greater detail here.

Japan's ephemeral breakthrough

In the 1950s, Japan too became a large biomass importer. It was America's biggest client for agricultural products, importing mainly fibers (cotton and wool) needed for its booming textile industry, as well as wood and cereals. In the early 1960s, Japan's biomass imports were still predominantly non-food products. But in the years that followed, while still continuing to protect its rice sector, linked to Japan's identity (but the share of rice in Japanese diets was falling), Japan started to import increasing quantities of corn and soy to be used in animal feed. From the early 1970s, Japan imported almost all its wheat, corn, and soybean consumption.

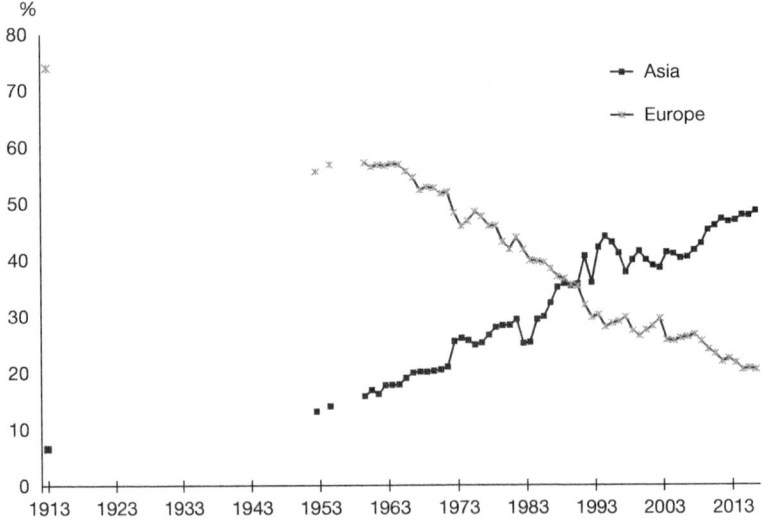

Figure 22.4 Share of Europe and Asia in global biomass imports (intra-EU trade excluded), 1913–2017

Sources: Lamartine Yates, 1959 and Comtrade, https://comtradeplus.un.org/ (accessed September 19, 2024).

---

[6] On this, see for example Karl, 1997.

Finally, from the 1990s, Japan also became an importer of animal products, meat and fish, and fruits and vegetables. The 1986–96 decade saw a tripling in the value of food product imports—from $18 billion to $54 billion. Meat imports in particular rose very sharply: the share of meat consumption that was imported rose from 30 percent to 60 percent for beef, from 15 percent to 40 percent for pork, and from 10 percent to 30 percent for poultry meat over the decade. The rising imports were a reflection of doubts about modern agriculture, whose environmental externalities were difficult for the small Japanese territory to absorb.[7] Meat imports directly substituted the imports of "grain" that had gone to animal feed. As for non-food biomass imports, they gradually came to be limited to just wood and paper pulp (Table 22.2).

But from 2000, Japan experienced a crisis. Economic difficulties were compounded by an aging and falling population, and consumption of certain products stagnated, or even contracted. The growth in biomass imports stopped suddenly: the share of global biomass imports, which had climbed strongly from 5 percent to 17 percent between 1955 to 1996, slid down to 6 percent in 2017 (Figure 22.5). It is rare in international trade to see such reversal in curves. Everything had seemed to call on Japan to become in the twenty-first century what England had been in the nineteenth century, the heart of global food trade, but now Japan was exiting from the arena. And China stepped in.

Table 22.2 Japan: Composition of biomass imports, 1962–2017 (in % of total imports)

	1962–4	1982–4	1998–2000	2015–17
Meat	1	6	13	17
Fish	1	13	25	19
Cereals	17	16	8	10
Oilseeds	9	7	4	4
Seed meal	2	2	4	4
Fruits and vegetables	3	6	10	11
Sugar	8	4	1	1
Coffee, cocoa, tea	2	4	3	4
Drinks and tobacco	2	3	8	10
Food biomass	**47**	**63**	**81**	**88**
Skins and leather	2	2	0	0
Natural rubber	4	2	1	2
Wood and pulp	16	23	13	12
Fibers	29	9	2	0
Non-food biomass	**53**	**37**	**19**	**12**

Source: Comtrade.

[7] Coinciding with the Uruguay Round negotiations, imports rose also due to US pressure.

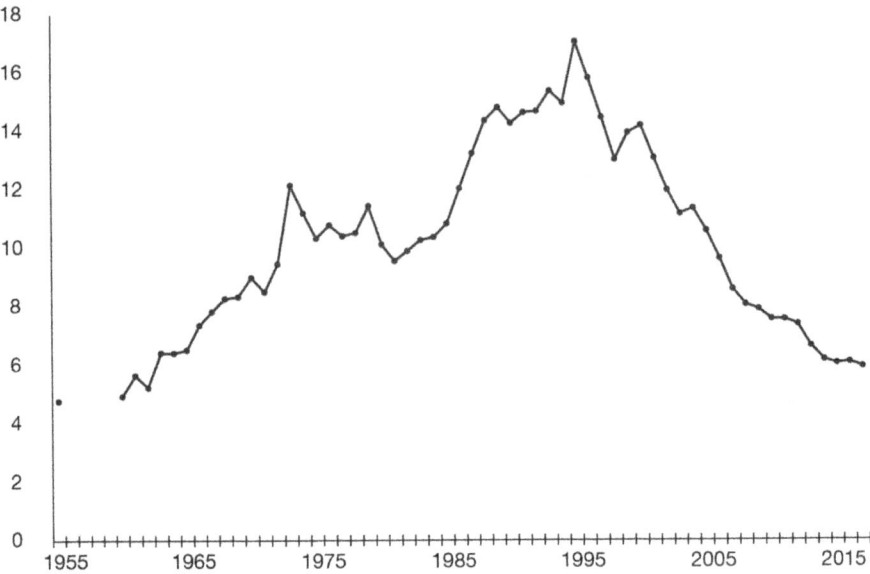

Figure 22.5 Japan's share in global biomass imports
Sources: UNCTAD, various years.

China and the unfeasibility of food self-sufficiency

Self-sufficiency had always been a key objective of the Chinese government, but it was only in 1996 that it publicly affirmed this through the publication of a White Paper on grains (Zhang, 2018: 2) which set a 95 percent self-sufficiency target for wheat, corn, rice, soybean, and tubers. The target was reaffirmed in 2008, when international food prices surged, with the publication of the Medium and Long-Term Plan for National Food Security, 2008–20, which set a 100 percent self-sufficiency target for cereals and maintained the 95 percent target for all grains.

But the remarkable performances of agriculture did not suffice. Even if the watchword remained self-sufficiency, from 2000 on, China imported increasing quantities of biomass. In fact, from 2012, the scale of soy imports made the self-sufficiency ratio for grains fall to 88 percent. The difficulty in responding to rising consumer demand through farming output was of course compounded by the rising pressure on Chinese resources, as already mentioned. The goal of self-sufficiency, and thus of continuously increasing production, was moreover challenged by growing opposition from local governments over land use. A minimum of 120 million hectares of land to be "sanctuarized" for agriculture had been set as a national goal in 2006. But this target was increasingly contested at the local level because, due to fiscal reforms, agriculture no longer contributed to local government revenues, but on the contrary came with increasing costs, without generating as much employment or GDP growth as sectors like industry or construction.

Faced with these constraints and opposition, the official position on self-sufficiency has over the past years been watered down. The Central Economic Working

Conference in early 2014 adopted a new strategy for food security, still founded on domestic production, but now also making reference to "moderate imports"(Zhang and Cheng, 2017). For the supporters of the new policy, increasing imports would make it possible to mobilize lands outside of China, thus lightening pressures that had become unbearable on the country's land, atmospheric, and water resources. The goal for domestic production was no longer to achieve constant self-sufficiency, but rather to maintain a production capacity that, when needed, could assure self-sufficiency.

China's formidable economic growth was as expected accompanied by a similar growth in biomass trade, and a growing role of this trade in the social metabolism of the country. This development represents a radical novelty in the long history of China, and even its more recent history,[8] characterized by the slogan so dear to Mao Zedong: "rely on your own resources." It should be noted nonetheless that between 1960 and 1995, China ran structural deficits in wheat: net imports (imports–exports) in some years were as high as the equivalent of 15 percent of wheat consumption, or even 25 percent in the years that followed the Great Leap Forward. By contrast, after 1995 when the effects of liberalization policies on agricultural production and markets were fully felt, China temporarily became a net corn exporter (Figure 22.6).

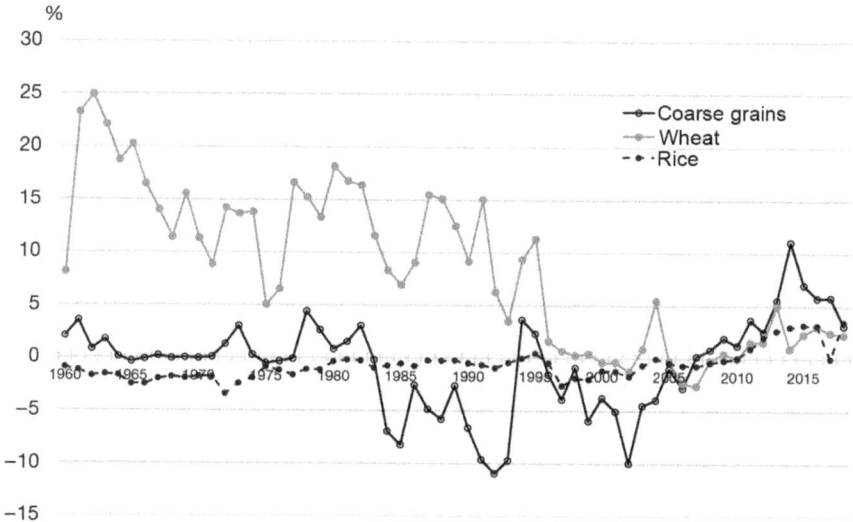

Figure 22.6 China: Ratio of net imports over consumption for wheat, rice, and corn (secondary cereals)

Source: USDA PSD.

---

[8] Dwight Perkins estimates that exports accounted for 1 percent or less of agricultural production value in the 1880s, 2 percent in the 1900s (Perkins, 1969: 132), with tea being the leading product, followed by silk. But the establishment of tea plantations in India and Ceylon by the English, supported by English colonial power, led to a decline in Chinese production. During the first half of the twentieth century, silk by far became the leading export product, while exports of soybean and cereals also emerged. Later, the loss of Manchuria, where a third of exports had been produced, followed by the civil war, and the Japanese invasion led to further reductions in exports. As for imports, in the early twentieth century, China imported small quantities of rice from Siam, Cochinchina, Indochina, and India, mainly for the Shanghai and Canton markets (Brandt, 1985).

The turn of the millennium, and above all, China's accession to the WTO gave a whole new impetus to biomass trade. Between 1999 and 2017, the value of imports grew from $14 billion to $173 billion. The stagnation, or even slight falls, in value of imports between 2013 and 2016, mainly due to falling international biomass prices, was just temporary. In 2017, biomass imports rose vigorously once more (Figure 22.7).

Food biomass imports, which represented the same value and grew at the same rate as non-food biomass until 2012, now greatly superseded the latter. Between 2000 and 2017, the share of food products in biomass imports thus grew from 45 percent to 62 percent. It would appear that the Chinese government had adopted a gradual strategy for biomass imports, initially opening the domestic market only to products that had low strategic interest for the country's food security.

Markets were thus first opened to non-food biomass, which, despite a relative drop in importance, continued to play a more important role in Chinese imports than they played in global biomass trade. In China, 38 percent of biomass imports were for non-food uses in 2017 (50 percent in 2006), compared to just 16 percent on the global scale (Table 22.3). Forest products, wood, and paper pulp were the leading non-food imports followed by rubber, natural fibers (cotton and wool), and lastly, skins and leather. One of the observable tendencies was the shift over time towards imports of less processed and increasingly raw products. The papermaking sector is an instructive case. From the end of the 1990s, paper imports, which at the time were rising vigorously, were replaced with pulp imports which literally shot through the roof in 2009. In more recent years, it appears that wood chips for paper pulp factories, are now replacing pulp imports.

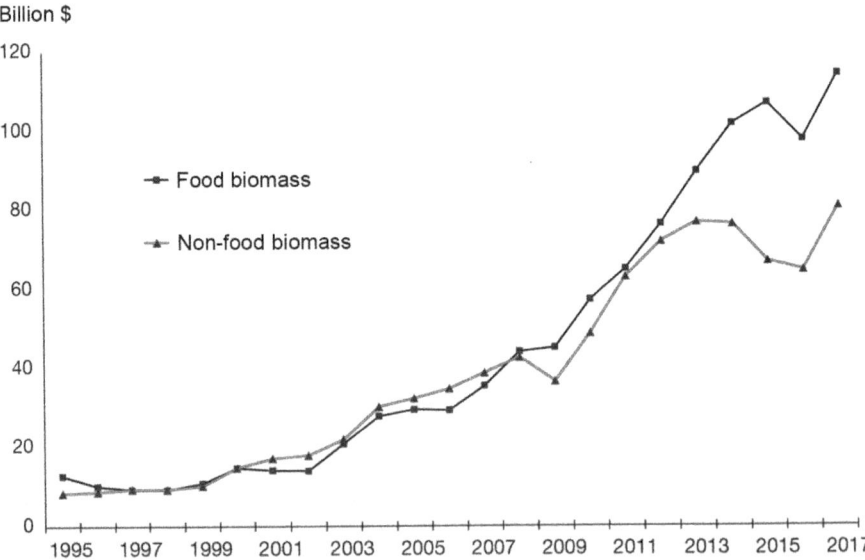

Figure 22.7 Volume of China's biomass imports, 1995–2017 (value in dollars deflated using the World Bank price index)

Sources: UNCTAD STAT and World Bank.

Table 22.3 China: Main biomass imports (as % of total biomass imports)

	1995–7	2015–17
Food biomass	45	62
Oilseeds	15	25
Fruits and vegetables	3	6
Meat	3	6
Cereals	3	5
Fish, crustaceans, mollusks	7	5
Vegetable oils	5	4
Non-food biomass	55	38
Wood	14	12
Wood pulp (paper pulp)	14	12
Natural rubber	7	6
Textile fibers	14	5
Skins and leather	4	2

Source: UNCTAD STAT, https://unctadstat.unctad.org/datacentre/ (accessed September 19, 2024).

Oilseeds, essentially soybean, strongly dominated food biomass imports. The share of cereals was still very limited. But from 2010, China became a net importer of three main cereals: rice, wheat, and corn. To these must be added cereals that are used for animal feed, such as barley and sorghum, whose imports have risen greatly recently. In addition, significant quantities of produce smuggled through the southern border of the country are to be added to the official figures: an estimated 3 tons of rice are currently imported illegally from Vietnam and Burma, that is equivalent to 50 percent, or even 100 percent of legal imports. According to the USDA, from 2013 China became the biggest importer of rice, with 5.3 million tons, or about 11 percent of global imports, but put another way, barely 7 percent of Chinese rice consumption.

Other products are also smuggled into China, such as sugar (2 million tons), or beef, of which an estimated 2 million tons in frozen form, or around 20 percent of the country's consumption (Zhang, 2018: 169). Natural rubber is also part of the smuggled trade, or at least was until 2015: Vietnam declares exporting to China double the quantity that China reports as imports from Vietnam.

The few biomass products for which China still maintains a positive trade balance are: fruits and vegetables, fish, crustaceans and mollusks (either of marine or aquaculture origin) (Figure 22.8), and tropical drinks. The last category, however, plays a minimal role in the country.

The prodigious rise in imports has obviously conferred to China a decisive position in international biomass trade. Until the mid-1990s, Japan was the main engine of Asian biomass import growth. Since then, it has been overtaken by China in spectacular fashion (Figure 22.9). The abruptness of the loss of Japan's standing is in exact symmetry with the rapidity of China's rise (measured in percentage of

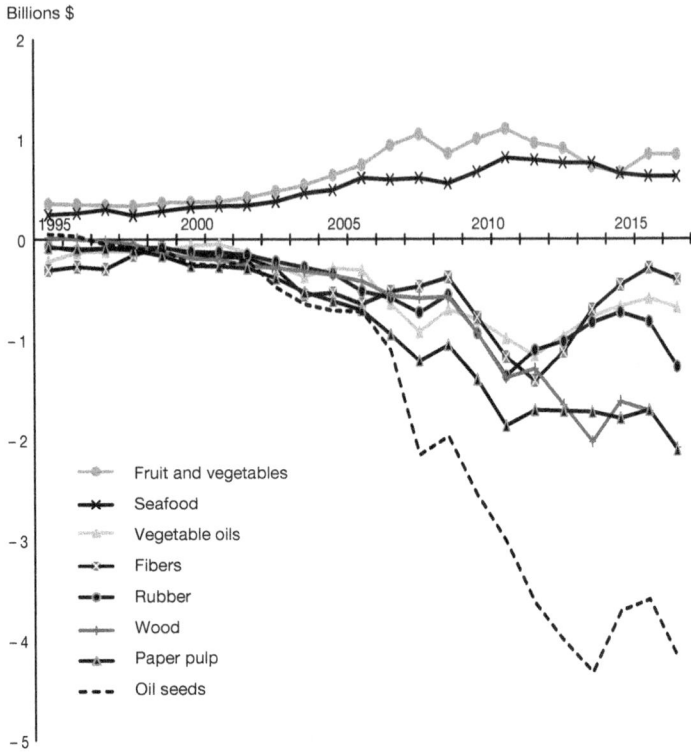

Figure 22.8 China, trade balance for biomass in value (exports–imports), 1995–2017 (in $ billions)

Source: UNCTAD STAT, https://unctadstat.unctad.org/datacentre/ (accessed September 19, 2024).

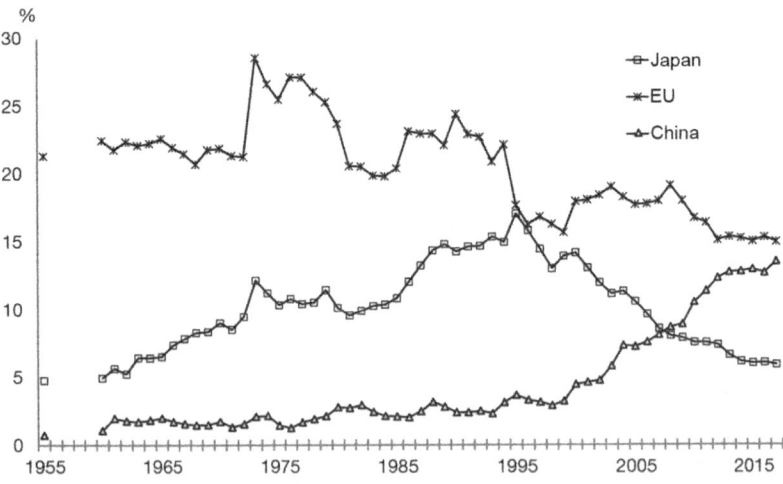

Figure 22.9 Share of Japan and of China in global biomass imports (intra-EU trade excluded), 1962–2015

Sources: based on UNCTAD, various years.

global imports). Japan has returned to the position it occupied in the 1960s, while the share of just China's imports in global biomass imports is now comparable to that of the entire European Union. For some products (oilseeds, pulp, skins, and leathers), China accounts for almost half of global purchases (Table 22.4).

The revenge of historic exporters

The convergence of agricultural policies strongly modified the geography of export supply of food products. One of the most immediate consequences of the reduction in domestic support was a significant slowing of agricultural production growth in the United States, and end of such growth in Europe (Figure 22.10).

Table 22.4 Share of China in % of global biomass imports (intra-EU trade excluded), 1995–2017

	1995–7	2015–17
Oilseeds	3	53
Paper pulp	5	45
Leather and skins	7	40
Wood and cork	2	33
Rubber	7	29
Textile fibers	15	20
Vegetable oils	11	11
Meat	0	10

Source: UNCTAD STAT, https://unctadstat.unctad.org/datacentre/ (accessed September 19, 2024).

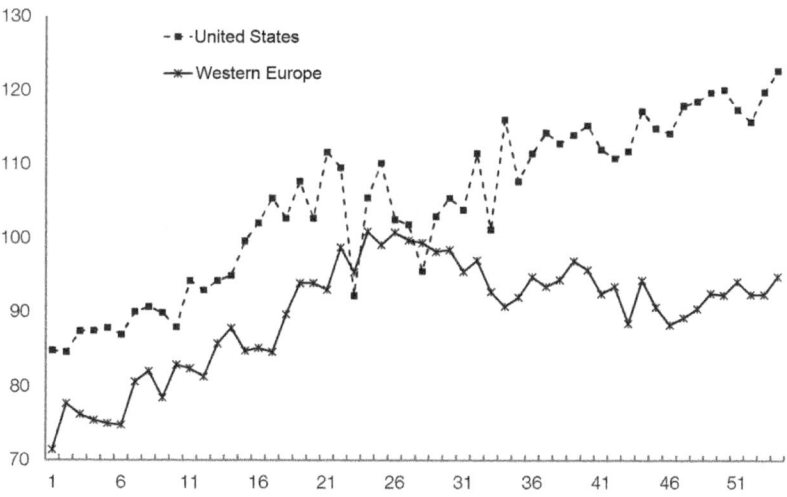

Figure 22.10 Index of per capita agricultural production, 1961–2014 (100 = 1986–9)

Source: FAOSTAT, http://www.fao.org/ (accessed August 16, 2024).

We are not, however, as some claim, in the terminal phase of an ailing model of chemical farming; the model is not being universally challenged. The difficulties that French farmers face (pork farmers for instance) stem chiefly from an issue of competitiveness, linked to the fact that the chemical farming model spread to countries, or to regions, where it has particularly prospered, such as Argentina, Brazil, Ukraine, and Russia where land is (still) relatively abundant. In short, we are witnessing today the reemergence of several nineteenth-century biomass exporters.

The evolution of the respective shares of the United States, the European Union, and Cairns Group countries in exports of non-tropical food products shows how the launch of the Uruguay Round coincided with the EU catching up with the United States (Figure 22.11), and how, since 1994, the US and EU shares in global food exports has fallen, their market shares captured by the Cairns Group.

The differentiated liberalization of policies led to a dispersion of export supply, without (this merits repetition) chemical farming really being challenged as a model. Alongside the large "liberal" or historic exporters like Argentina and Brazil, emerged countries whose exports were a way of disposing of surpluses. India thus arose on markets for rice and beef, for which the country became the world's leading exporter, as well as butter. Far from having liberalized its agricultural policy, India, like the EEC before, had implemented an active self-sufficiency policy which resulted in overproduction, which then had to be exported to avoid falling domestic prices.

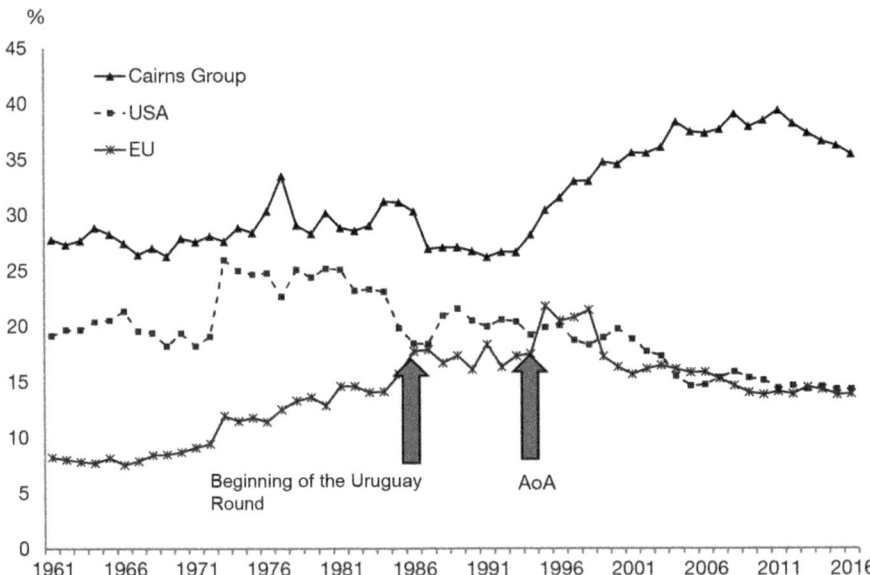

Figure 22.11 Share of the United States, the European Union, and Cairns Group countries in global food exports (intra-EU and tropical products excluded), 1961–2016

Sources: Based on UNCTAD, various years. AoA: Agreement on Agriculture.

The partial reunification of agricultural markets revealed by the 2007-8 "food crisis"

While reforms of agricultural policies did indeed result in convergence in levels of support countries provided, they did not result in a unification of global markets. The price surges which shook international food markets in 2007 and 2008 revealed the continued fragmentation of domestic price formation mechanisms.

From January 2007 to March 2008, the international price of rice increased by 220 percent, and wheat by 120 percent; and those are just two examples. Very quickly, international organizations raised the alarm for the risk of increased global food insecurity. The reference annual report *State of Food Insecurity in the World*, published jointly by the FAO and WFP in 2009, announced an upsurge in the number of malnourished people. For months there was hallowed consensus among political leaders and academics from all sides on the premise that a major global food crisis was to hit—for example, in academia, von Braun (2008) and McMichael (2009), the former a mainstream economist, the latter a Marxist sociologist.

However, quite quickly some voices raised doubts about the FAO's estimation[9] (Headey, 2011). The FAO itself radically changed its discourse in 2013. Figure 22.12 puts together the graphs of the number of undernourished people in the world published in the 2009 and 2013 editions of the report *The State of Food Insecurity in the World*. While the first, in 2009, indeed announced catastrophic hunger, the second, without qualms, in 2013 contradicted this and showed instead a continuous trend of declining under-nutrition. Many parties evidently "played the crisis" for various tactical reasons. But the convergence of positions was also a result of a consensual but erroneous representation of agricultural markets as being unified on a global level.

Why did soaring food prices on the international markets not result in a global food crisis? Firstly, because in many countries, local prices of agricultural products are not linked to fluctuations in international prices. Figure 22.13 presents the evolution of prices from January 2000 until April 2018 in four markets: the international price of wheat (price for Hard Red Winter on the US west coast), the price of wheat in China (wholesale market in Hebei), the price of wheat in India (wholesale market in New Delhi), and lastly the price of millet, the main cereal consumed, in Niger (wholesale market in Maradi).

The three national prices selected mirror neither the 2007–8 spike in international prices, nor the 2011 spike, which incidentally was of the same scale as the earlier 2007–8 one, but did not elicit much international outcry. However, what went on in India and China was quite distinct from the dynamic in Niger. Prices in China and India were overall stable, with China showing also a trend of rising prices; in Niger, on the other hand, prices were structurally very unstable.

---

[9] Derek Headey of IFPRI was among the first to point out that the insufficient data on the largest developing countries, India and China in particular, meant there was an element of uncertainty in the FAO calculations. He moreover compared those calculations with results from global surveys and opinion polls undertaken by the polling institute Gallup, which found that the number of food-insecure people between 2005 and 2008 had not risen, but fallen.

2009

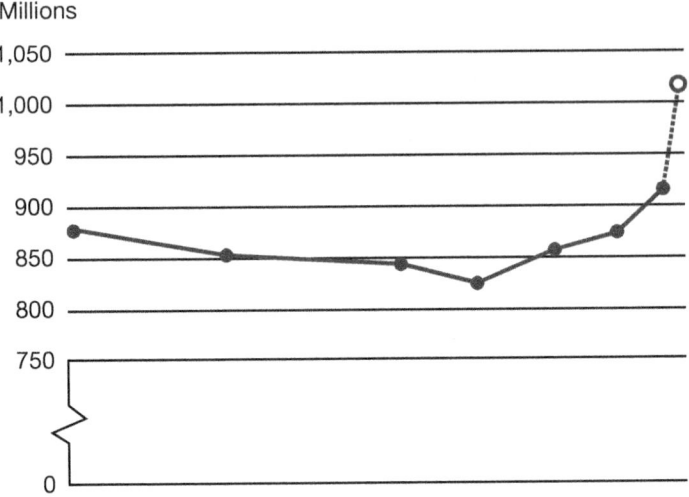

2013

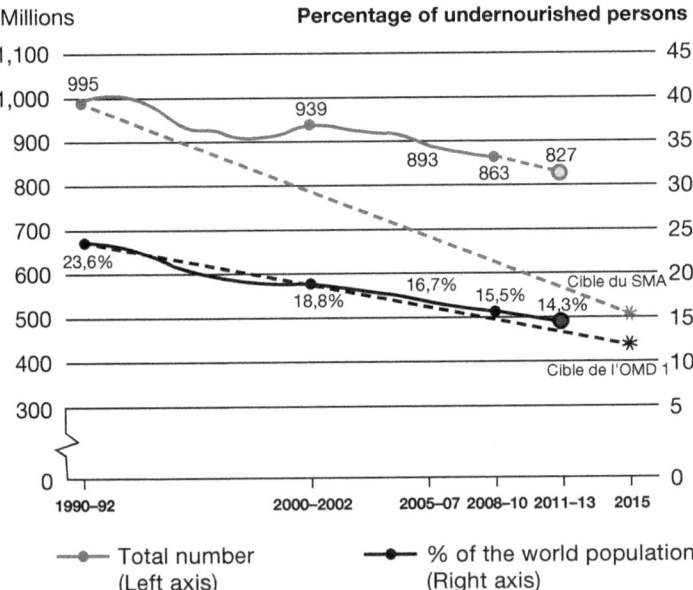

Figure 22.12 Evolution of number of undernourished persons in the world according to the FAO, in 2009 and in 2013, in the annual report *The State of Food Insecurity in the World*

Sources: FAO and WFP, 2009: 11; FAO and WFP, 2013: 9. WFS: World Food Summit; MDG: Millennium Development Goals

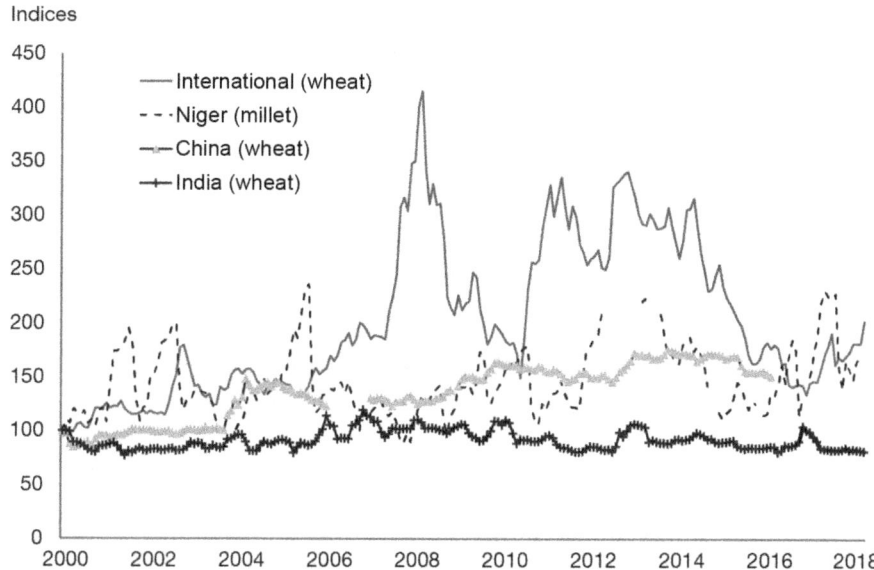

Figure 22.13 Index of the international price and of real national prices of cereals, monthly data 2000–18 (100 = January 2000)

Sources: FAO, SMIAR, http://www.fao.org/giews/fr/ (accessed August 16, 2024 for national prices); FAO, Food Price Monitoring and Analysis Tool, http://www.fao.org/giews/food-prices/price-tool/fr/ (accessed August 16, 2024 for national prices); World Bank, Commodity Markets, http://www.worldbank.org/commodities (accessed August 16, 2024 for the international wheat price).

This is because India and China, following the model of postwar agricultural policies, are still implementing proactive policies to isolate their domestic markets from international price fluctuations, with the aid of taxes, export quotas or outright embargos, stock drawdowns, and consumer subsidies. Acharya and colleagues thus note that in India, where the largest number of malnourished people live, that: "During 2007 to 2009, the movement in global prices and domestic prices of rice and wheat was almost in contrast to each other" (Acharya et al., 2012: 31). Namrata Ghosh, who studied price transmission for five products (rice, wheat, soybean, sugar, and peanut oil), concluded "that out of the five commodities that we have undertaken for our study only one, that is soybean, shows integration between domestic and international prices" (Ghosh, 2012: 21).

China, the country with the second highest number of malnourished people in 2008, also shows the same national capacity to limit the repercussions of global prices on domestic prices. The Chinese state, which at the time imported low quantities of cereals and had significant financial resources available, took measures to protect its population from international fluctuations (Jensen and Miller, 2008; Lu and Yu, 2011).

In Niger, however, the isolation of domestic prices from global fluctuations arises from an entirely different set of reasons, such as:

- The "non-tradeable"[10] nature of local cereals (millet, sorghum, and even corn).
- The low degree of substitutability in consumption of local cereals by imported cereals.

We find a similar situation in several African countries, where yellow corn, fonio, tubers (cassava and yams), and plantains which play an essential role in food security, are not "tradeable" (Minot, 2012).

In the end, the price shocks experienced on the international food markets were transmitted only to a limited number of food-insecure countries. These included some very poor countries, like Bangladesh, and countries highly dependent on imports, like Iran, Yemen, and Iraq, which import respectively 132, 148, and 158 kilograms of cereals per inhabitant per year. In these countries, despite considerable state subsidies, the price of basic foods rose dramatically. Likewise, most countries in the Middle East and North Africa suffer "some degree of vulnerability to international food price increases for virtually most of the MENA countries" (Ianchovochina et al., 2012: 18). Nonetheless, within this group, there are countries, like Algeria for instance, which, thanks to oil revenues, were capable of limiting price transmission owing to massive consumer subsidies.

Given the variety of obstacles to transmission of the volatility of international prices, only 1 percent of the global food-insecure population was directly exposed to the 2007–8 international price surge (Daviron and Douillet, 2013). This ghost "global food crisis" was thus a clear demonstration, and fortunately so in this case, that the reunification of global agricultural markets is far from effective.

Sustainability standards, or reconciling the irreconcilable

Sustainability: develop and sustain, sustain and develop—such is the new mantra of political and economic elites. The unanimous adoption of the Sustainable Development Goals (SDGs)[11] by the United Nations General Assembly in 2015 attests to the level of consensus around this oxymoronic formula. If sustainability is on the agenda, it is in effect because for the world as we[12] know it, sustainability cannot be taken for granted, as scientists have been explaining to us for five decades now, and that even the rich and powerful may find their survival threatened.

---

[10] The term non-tradable, used by economists, means that there is no international market for the product in question. In Africa, the share of tradable food products, for which international markets exist, once corn is excluded, ranges from a low of 4 percent in Burundi and Malawi, to a high of 53 percent in Madagascar. The second highest share after Madagascar is in Côte d'Ivoire, with only 27 percent.

[11] The contradiction is even more evident in the French term "développement durable"—*durable* development. How long can development last and still be sustainable for the planet?

[12] European middle classes, or assimilated.

How can you actually reconcile sustainable development and globalization? How can you "internalize negative externalities" (as economists put it; that is, pollution, biodiversity loss, and other degradation of common goods that are not accounted for in costs) of biomass production, when those negative externalities are made invisible by distance for a whole range of players and for consumers (Princen, 1997)?

One response: sustainability standards. That is, private mechanisms aimed at guaranteeing that internationally traded biomass is produced in a manner that respects the SDGs (Cheyns et al., 2016), without undermining the main concern of historic standards (Part 3) which was to facilitate the substitutability between different batches and different sources.

Sustainability standards are the products of an alliance between large firms (agrifood firms such as Danone and Unilever, banks such as Rabobank, and wholesalers such as Olam) and the BINGOs (Big International Non-Governmental Organizations, such as the WWF and the Rainforest Alliance) to correct the most visible negative impacts of the mining metabolic regime on the living planet.

These mechanisms are all based on requirements for producers on a number of social and environmental criteria, and the respect of these is verified by specialized firms which then provide certificates authorizing the sale of the product with a specific label. Some of these labels are well known: Max Havelaar, Rainforest Alliance, and so on. Historically designed and presented as an alternative to a dominant system, sustainability labels have become the little helpers of joyful globalization.

The definition of sustainability standards under multipartite frameworks started in the mid-1990s, with the Forest Stewardship Council (1993) and the Marine Stewardship Council (1997). The movement accelerated in the 2000s with the emergence of several initiatives—often called "roundtables"—for specific crops from tropical zones (soybean, palm oil, cotton, cane sugar, coffee, tobacco, etc.) (Pattberg, 2005; Fransen and Kolk, 2007).

In just a few years, these mechanisms became arenas for debates about the links between international agricultural product markets and development. Contrary to the international agreements on specific products (which have all faded away) that were negotiated by states, or groupings of producer and consumer states within international organizations with the main goal being price stabilization, the sustainability mechanisms are focused on what supposedly informed consumers expect as behavior from producers, and their organizations. The new initiatives focus on a product (palm oil) or group of products (sea products), and most often result from an alliance between NGOs, firms, and international organizations. From this perspective, they may be interpreted as an attempt at creating a form of sovereignty that competes with that of producer states, a condemnation of the failure of those states to implement sustainable development.

Conclusion

After a decade of stagflation (unemployment and high inflation) in OECD countries, the 1980s brought a clear change in the logic of economic policies, but not of the metabolic regime. Openness to trade and to competition, and therefore to competitiveness, became the new norm for OECD countries, even in their agriculture sectors. East Asian countries, however, were the main beneficiaries in terms of economic growth.

From 2000, China vigorously marched to the tune of the mining metabolic regime to become the workshop of the world. Industrial growth and income growth brought with them sharp increases in biomass imports, with China's agriculture, already input-intensive, no longer able to keep up with rising consumption. In little less than fifteen years, China became the main market for several agricultural, forest, and marine products, providing a renewed impetus, as in the case of soybean, to chemical farming and its conquest of new spaces (Latin America, Southeast Asia, Ukraine, etc.). The frequent use of the word "crisis" to characterize the current status of chemical farming or "conventional" agriculture, therefore, appears to my eyes as premature—much to my dismay.

The bio-economy, which may appear like the great novelty in biomass use, is still at an embryonic stage. The French Minister of Agriculture, Stéphane Le Foll, may have declared in January 2017 during the presentation of the national bio-economy strategy, that the goal is to "put photosynthesis back at the heart of our economy," but the bio-economy remains strongly imprinted with the mining metabolism logic (which lies at the heart of the chemical industry).

This "mining" logic implies the existence of "biomass deposits," dormant as oil deposits had been for long. It is true that the spectacle of expanding fallow land and forest in a country such as France enables that illusion. Yet, the abandonment of agriculture would not have been possible without oil, which has enabled higher yields, and therefore the reduction of cultivated acreage, and moreover, has provided several substitutes for non-food biomass products. In a metabolism entirely based on "photosynthesis," the supply of biomass would certainly be lower, and uses of this supply would be multiple and competing with each other. The issue of biomass production therefore cannot be neglected.

There is also the concomitant issue of the hierarchy of biomass uses. On this issue, the biofuels venture does not presage well. The high level of support that biofuels garnered gives an idea of the risks of problematic slippage. Biofuels, both in Europe and in the United States, were first thought of as a means to support an agriculture characterized by structural surpluses and not subject to WTO rules, and not for the virtue of their bio-economic relevance.[1] They very quickly proved destabilizing for food markets.

---

[1] Rapeseed and corn, the crops most planted for biofuel use in Europe and the United States, have energy yields in the range of 0.8 and 1.7 calories produced per calorie invested (Gasparatos and Stromberg, 2012).

General conclusion

Conventional agriculture, which we have frequently referred to as "chemical farming" in this book, while still gaining ground across the world today, is also being strongly contested, mainly due to the pollution it generates (such as greenhouse gases, pesticides, active nitrogen) and its effects on ecosystems and human health. It is thus time for a "transition," for a new model of agriculture to prevail; this model is often called agro-ecological.

Is it still possible to remain indifferent to the ecological critique of conventional agriculture? Such criticism is widely informed by a multitude of recognized scientific research. The imperative to move towards a "transition," on the other hand, seems more problematic, and not just for the agricultural sector. The energy transition is also a current public policy watchword. In France, for example, this transition was signed into law in 2015.

On the policy level, the concept of "transition" implies change that is both radically proactive, even to the point of being demiurgic, and inherently reformist. In practice, profound transformation of our world may be the aim (reduce greenhouse gas emissions by a quarter by 2050!), but certainly not through a revolution; even if the set timelines are tight, the means deployed are about changing the world softly, without great constraints, without redistribution of property rights, and certainly without renouncing on sacred growth. Responsibility for achieving the salvative transition has been given to markets for pollution rights, citizen initiatives and citizen responsibility, and above all, new technologies.

This book, which aimed to provide an analysis of the origins of conventional agriculture by examining the history of the relations between biomass, wealth, and power, hopes to contribute to shifting this vision of change.

Summing up

Let us remind ourselves of the main ideas: starting from the sixteenth century, the relation between biomass, wealth, and power was "shaped" by two temporalities: the temporality of social metabolism and that of hegemonies.

There was a major break in social metabolism during the course of the eighteenth century with the passage—one could say transition—from a solar metabolic regime to an mining metabolic regime. Under the first regime, biomass was the main source of energy and matter for practically all human needs: food, clothing, heating, soil fertility, etc. As for mechanical energy, only wind and water bodies offered assistance which gave maritime and river transport a distinct advantage. For the rest, and notably for land transport, energy depended entirely on the labor of humans or animals, themselves biomass, fed on biomass.

The second regime, a child of the "industrial revolution," was characterized first and foremost by its intensive exploitation of fossil fuel deposits of coal, oil, and natural gas. The mining metabolic regime involved high energy availability, initially thermic and later mechanic, at a level unmatched by that of the solar metabolic regime. This abundance of energy caused a sharp reduction in the costs of land transport. It also enabled the development of the second component of this metabolic regime—the large-scale extraction and processing of various mineral resources and their employment for multiple purposes. Lastly, it enabled the chemical industry to progressively develop a vast activity of production of synthetic materials. With time, biomass usage was reduced, as development of synthetic products progressed. Feeding humans then became the almost exclusive way that agricultural products were used.

Upon the social metabolic temporality was superposed the temporality of hegemons. One should perhaps speak of codetermination rather than superposition: international rivalries in the quest for wealth and power incited exploitation of new sources of energy and matter, or new ways of exploiting these. The capacity of innovation in these two fields determined access to hegemony.

In the seventeenth century, the United Provinces were defined by two characteristics: they were operating under a solar metabolic regime, and therefore dependent on biomass as an almost exclusive source of energy and matter, and they had only limited space available, which obliged them in their rise to power to mobilize biomass of foreign origins. Fishing and trade were two means to organize such flows of external biomass. The agriculture of the United Provinces, which was very efficient, benefited doubly from its proximity to towns, which provided a market for both food and non-food products, and which supplied, through their organic waste, the fertilizer agriculture needed. This positive relationship between town and countryside itself depended strongly on the country's insertion in long-distance trade activity. Trading provided both income and a large part of the food provisions for towns, and thus indirectly ensured the continuous transfer of fertility towards the countryside.

The two eighteenth-century rivals, France and England, had much larger territories (both in terms of metropoles and colonies). The mercantilist policies deployed by the two countries expressed their determination to make the most out of the resources of their territories to climb above their status of being on the "semi-periphery" of the Dutch hegemon.

The creation of a national market was one of the means that the two countries put into effect to achieve this. The construction of roads and, even more significantly, canals enabled the physical unification of their territories, and progressively eliminated domestic custom duties, while policies of protection at their national borders ensured their economic unification. The quest for more efficient agriculture was another component of mercantilism. Here England won the game with its "agricultural revolution" founded on the adoption of Dutch techniques.

The wealth and power of France and England, however, were not based entirely on their own territory. Their distant colonies, which occupied a central position in their trade under the colonial exclusivity principle, supplemented supplies of energy and matter, albeit marginally, but this was nonetheless an essential element from the point of view of the dynamics of capitalism. From these limited spaces were drained resources that were external to both the colony and the metropole. In their Caribbean colonies and American flagships, the "exterior" provided labor (African slave labor), food and wood (continental American), and genetic resources (sugar cane, coffee, indigo were all of Asian or African origin). The settlements in Canada provided furs and codfish captured in vast oceanic and continental spaces beyond their control. In India, European presence for long was limited to trading posts, points of collection of the abundant and preexisting production of cotton cloth (among other things).

Last but not least, early exploitation of coal in England did more than just resolve the energy crisis that was the certain destiny of the fast-deforesting country. Agricultural revolution, victory in India, and early coal exploitation combined to give England the edge.

Established as the hegemon and fully converted to the mining metabolic regime, England continued to use biomass, for food of course, but also as a raw material for industry. But it was coal, which had become its almost exclusive source of energy, that enabled England to both process increasing quantities of biomass, in particular textiles, and to go and seek biomass in the periphery which progressively extended to cover all corners of the globe. England replicated the Dutch model of external supply of biomass, but on a larger scale in terms of volumes and space. The nineteenth century was thus marked by a series of technical innovations (steam engine, telegraph, undersea cables, etc.) and institutional innovations (standards and futures markets) which facilitated long-distance exchange on the basis of trade relations established mainly outside the empire.

English demand, and soon that of other European countries, stimulated mass migration and sizable flows of capital towards investments in transport infrastructure, instruments for opening up and advancing multiple frontiers on all continents of the planet. In many of these new farm lands, migrants, who discovered land reserves that appeared inexhaustible, adopted extractive practices towards the fertility of the soils.

In England, and soon after in some Northwestern European countries, agriculture became specialized in animal production using imported feed, thus initiating a production model that would triumph in the twentieth century.

In the early twentieth century, Germany and the United States, both historic biomass suppliers to Great Britain, became the latter's challengers. As had done France and England in the seventeenth and eighteenth century before them, the two countries, recentered their economies on their own territories. They exploited fossil fuel deposits to produce synthetic biomass substitutes, and to increase the performance of their agriculture. Germany led on both these fronts thanks to its dynamic chemical industry. German achievements in synthetizing ammonia are the best demonstration of that preeminence.

But the United States had a much larger territory that, moreover, was protected by two oceans. During the second Thirty-Year War, Germany consumed itself in its quest for space, and after its defeat, the United States appropriated the know-how of its rival in the field of chemistry.

Victorious America did not change course away from its domestic refocus. The model of "conventional" agricultural was perfected in the United States. This type of agriculture was doubly stamped with the seal of chemistry as both a scientific discipline and an industrial sector. Chemistry is what pushed agriculture to specialize in food production. The popularity of yesterday's concept of agrifood, and today's concept of "food system" in academia and public debate, makes this state of affairs appear natural. These concepts more or less openly affirm that choices regarding agriculture should first and foremost be taken in response to the requirements of "eaters," who for the most part are urban.

Chemistry was also the foundation of the "modernization" of agriculture as it provided fertilizer, especially nitrogen fertilizer, pesticides, as well as fuel for spark engines. Without techniques for fixing atmospheric nitrogen, in particular the Haber–Bosch process, the remarkable growth in yields during the twentieth century would not have been possible. And it was this growth in yields that enabled rapid population growth, as well as the implementation of national (or regional in the case of Europe) food self-sufficiency strategies which characterized the century.

The transfer of German chemical know-how to the United States during the First World War was critical for America's rise to hegemony. It enabled the United States to find a way out of its long farm crisis that had followed the end of the American frontier, thanks to a combination of the German logic of substitution with an American logic of mechanization. As Edward Melillo so aptly points out:

> On a finite planet, ideologies of limitless growth require corresponding theories of substitution. In an earlier era, colonialism offered a geographical fix for such constraints to capitalist accumulation. By employing "ghost acreage", imperialist nations relied on spaces beyond their own *terra firma*, such as oceans and foreign lands, to supplement their harvests and augment their resource stocks. [...] The promoters of the Synthetic Age promised that the laboratory would provide a post-colonial escape from such confrontations with the "limits to growth."
> (Melillo, 2013: 254)

I would add, on the condition of being able to access a fossilized carbon source of energy.

Another dimension of conventional agriculture, the relationship between humans and animals, which we have not addressed much, is revealing of the particular relationship the mining metabolic regime has with biomass. Animals, which in the past lived off the waste of humans, or in uncultivated spaces, and provided a range of non-food resources (leather, bone, hairs, feathers, fats, heat, labor, manure,[1] etc.), now became the vital market for plethoric plant production (and "clients" of strategic importance for the pharmaceutical sector). And the main part of what animals produced, proteins aside, now became waste (heat, manure, etc.).

---

[1] The Millau Museum of Gloves teaches us that dog poop was an indispensable ingredient for the tanning process in the early twentieth century, and industrialists from the town had to import such waste from Istanbul.

No doubt, it is chicken that best embodies the "new animal" that laboratories of the minng metabolic regime engendered:

> Modern broiler chickens are morphologically, genetically and isotopically distinct from domestic chickens prior to the mid-twentieth century. The global range of modern broilers and biomass dominance over all other bird species is a product of human intervention. As such, broiler chickens vividly symbolize the transformation of the biosphere to fit evolving human consumption patterns, and show clear potential to be a biostratigraphic marker species of the Anthropocene.
> (Bennett et al., 2018: 9)

It is likely that kitty kondos covered in fake fur will also be a good geological marker in the future, for while distance was being put between animals reared for meat, a very new type of animal-rearing emerged, the rearing of pet animals characterized by a fusional relationship.

And what now?

The main conclusion that we can logically draw from the narrative presented in this book is that a shift in agricultural model (some would even call it a paradigm shift) will certainly not come from agriculture alone, nor from its eaters. It is true that many local initiatives have flourished, and there are many individuals who choose to "consume differently." But the perspective adopted in this book, shows agricultural models as expressions of a relationship with biomass which is one of the components of the metabolic regime, as well as one of the characteristics of hegemonic power. The questions that must be asked therefore relate to the future of the United States as a hegemon, the probability of a Chinese succession, and the emergence or lack of emergence of signs of a change in metabolic regime.

Despite repeated failures since 2001, the United States still maintains uncontested military superiority,[2] but they have lost their position as leader in a number of economic fields. Paradoxically, however, on the cultural level they have maintained their capacity to create new consumer goods (both tangible and intangible) that are desired by all.

But American society has seen transformations during the past thirty years which challenge their capacity to continue embodying the model that other countries want to copy. The most striking development is the rise in inequalities and the spread of extreme poverty.[3] One of the consequences has been a fall in life expectancy for certain social categories ("white men without a college degree"), a radically new phenomenon in more than a century of history.

---

[2] According to the Stockholm International Peace Research Institute, US military expenditure totaled $610 billion in 2017, three times the amount spent by China, and ten times the amount spent by Russia: http://www.sipri.org/databases/milex (accessed August 16, 2024).

[3] See Alvaredo et al. (2018) as well as the December 2017 United National Special Rapporteur on Extreme Poverty and Human Rights on this point: https://www.ohchr.org/en/statements/2017/12/statement-visit-usa-professor-philip-alston-united-nations special-rapporteur (accessed September 16, 2024).

Life expectancy, perhaps alongside birth rate, is the star indicator of "development," a marker that indicated progress and that enabled "developing countries" to be distinguished from "developed countries."

In a world where the fight against poverty had become the mantra of aid agencies and of the illustrious Sustainable Development Goals, the "development" compass undoubtedly has lost its bearings and its North; if developmentalists continue running, they do so like headless chickens, by mere reflex.

The election of Donald Trump can also be viewed as a consequence of rising inequality and the marginalization of the working classes, even if the policies he implements are highly likely to aggravate, rather than solve, these problems. The nationalist slogan "America First," on the other hand sits poorly with the position of global hegemon, which by its position is expected to take on the costs of maintaining international order.

As for China, it is still much too early to judge its capacity to become the next hegemon. For the moment, China has not challenged the American international order. One of the specific problems China presents, to the world and to itself, is that of its size. The impact of China's growth on the global economy, and the speed at which it is occurring, has no historic precedent. Maintaining an open global economy would suppose that China takes the reins of, and/or imposes, some (new) international institutions, and does this much faster than the United States did during their phase of emergence. This would imply a radical break with history, as it would mark the end of two centuries of global domination by Europe and its neo-European extensions.

But is China really on a trajectory towards hegemony? Is China in the position that the United Kingdom was in the mid-nineteenth century, propelling the first wave of globalization, or is it in the position of Japan in the 1990s, in the antechamber of paralysis?

Demography certainly invites the comparison with Japan. China in the past may have constituted a population bomb, but today it is its aging population that makes headlines. The demographic dividend is now behind China: since 2015, the size of the active population has fallen while that of dependents is rising. According to some projections, the active/dependent ratio, which today stands around 2 to 1, will be 1 to 1 in 2050. If China is in the position that Japan was in the 1990s, it should also sooner or later, experience a financial crisis and competition from a rival (India?) who will snatch away its export markets and put an end to two decades of accelerated growth.

If China is in the position of the UK in 1840, a plausible scenario would be that it adopts a biomass importing strategy on a much larger scale. This possibility was raised in the last chapter. The environmental cost of food self-sufficiency has become untenable for China. Conversely, the current investments in transport infrastructure under the Belt and Road Initiative could tomorrow constitute the backbone for such an import strategy. As for biomass supply, vast spaces are still available in Ukraine, in Russia, in Latin America, and in Africa, to increase biomass production and export. Heavy environmental and social consequences are to be feared for these territories, if one recalls the global fallout of the United Kingdom's supply policy in the nineteenth century, when that country only had a population of 40 million.[4]

---

[4] For a classic on this topic, see Brown (1995).

What can we say about the future of the mining metabolic regime? Oil is still king today. Despite all the calls to decarbonize our economies, and dreams of "zero-carbon" capital cities, oil remains the main source of energy. The mining metabolic regime reigns over almost the whole planet, and those who have not yet accessed the regime, want in.

Most experts agree that fossil fuel reserves are still considerable. The costs of exploiting these reserves may, and probably will, rise, but it will not be lack of reserves that will put an end to the mining metabolic regime. Everyone today is aware that the pursuit of the mining metabolic regime involves generating profuse amounts of waste, of which first and foremost greenhouse gases. Is it possible to hope that the thunderous declarations and sweeping commitments made these past few years actually result in fossil fuels being abandoned? I have difficulty believing so, for the simple reason of the ongoing quest for wealth and power which animates a whole range of players in a world in which rivalry is not ready to disappear yet.

But, if we leave aside this objection and suppose that true alternatives to fossil fuel economies will be implemented, it appears obvious that then non-food uses of biomass shall need to regain the prominence they held under the solar metabolic regime. Yet, the quantity of biomass available is limited. The impression that biomass is abundant and under-utilized (declining farm activity, fallow land, food waste, etc.), at least in Europe and North America, results from nothing else than the massive use of oil in all branches of human activity, as a source of energy and matter, including, as we have seen, in agriculture itself. The abundance of urban organic waste is thus also indirectly, produced, thanks to massive injections of fossil fuel. The re-utilization of this waste, as virtuous as that may be, is just a loop in the circuit.

The massive reliance on "subterranean forests," however, has not shielded the planet from deforestation and the accompanying biodiversity depletion, or from depletion of fish stocks. There can be no doubt: in a post-oil economy, biomass would be rare, and its uses would be multiple and in competition with each other. It would thus become necessary to hierarchize uses: what part should be dedicated to food? What part to transport? What part to maintaining soil fertility, and so on? This would suppose debate within our democratic societies over the distribution of this limited resource when making public policy decisions and setting the direction desired for agricultural production. This is a vast ambition that goes well beyond the goal of orienting agriculture in function of expectations of urban eaters.

But alas, this alarming conclusion is perhaps a vain one. On that terrain, I willingly leave the last word to chief pessimist Nicolas Bouvier:

> A village chief in the district the other day told me: "I no longer make scarecrows, they have become useless; birds today are too intelligent." When you consider those Japanese scarecrows which are curses in the form of straw, wrath in the form of wood, the most mortal maledictions in the form of sack jute and tar, you wonder whether the birds are instead, just like us, becoming slowly dumber, blind to all omens and signs.
>
> (Bouvier, 2004: 226)

Bibliography

Abu-Lughod J.L., 1991. *Before European Hegemony: The World System A.D. 1250-1350*. New York/Oxford, Oxford University Press.

Acharya S.S., Chand R., Birthal P.S., Kumar S., Negi D.S., 2012. *Market Integration and Price Transmission in India: A Case of Rice and Wheat with Special Reference to the World Food Crisis of 2007/08*. Rome, FAO.

Adas M., 2009. Continuity and transformation: Colonial rice frontiers and their environmental impact on the great river deltas of mainland Southeast Asia. *In: The Environment and World History* (Burke E., Pomeranz K., dir.). Berkeley, University of California Press, 191-207.

Adelman J., 1994. *Frontier Development: Land, Labour, and Capital on the Wheatlands of Argentina and Canada, 1890-1914*. Oxford, Clarendon Press.

Aglietta M., 1976. *Régulation et crise du capitalisme. L'expérience des États-Unis*. Paris, Calmann-Lévy.

Ahlberg K.L., 2007. "Machiavelli with a heart": The Johnson administration's Food for Peace Program in India, 1965-1966. *Diplomatic History*, 31 (4), 665-701.

Akamatsu K., 1962. A historical pattern of economic growth in developing countries. *The Developing Economies*, 1 (s1), 3-25.

Alavi H., Shanin T., 1988. Introduction to the English edition: Peasantry and capitalism. *In: The Agrarian Question* (Kautsky K.). London, Zwan Publications, xi–xxxix.

Albert M., Boissonnat J., 1988. *Crise, krach, boom*. Paris, Seuil.

Allaire G., 1995. De la productivité à la qualité: transformation des conventions et régulations dans l'agriculture et l'agro-alimentaire. *In: La grande transformation de l'agriculture* (Allaire G., Boyer R., dir.). Versailles/Paris, Inra éditions/Economica, 381-411.

Allen G.C., 1981. *Short Economic History of Modern Japan*. London, Palgrave Macmillan.

Allen R.C., 2005. Real wages in Europe and Asia: A first look at long-term patterns. *In: Living Standards in the Past: New Perspectives on Well-Being in Asia and Europe* (Allen R.C., Bengtsson T., Dribe M., dir.). Oxford, Oxford University Press, 111-30.

Allen R.C., 2008a. The nitrogen hypothesis and the English agricultural revolution: A biological analysis. *The Journal of Economic History*, 68 (1), 182-210.

Allen R.C., 2008b. Agriculture during the industrial revolution, 1700-1850. *In: The Cambridge Economic History of Modern Britain. Volume 1: Industrialisation, 1700-1860* (Floud R., Johnson P., dir.). Cambridge, Cambridge University Press, 96-116.

Alphandéry P., Bitoun P., Dupont Y., 1989. *Les champs du départ. Une France rurale sans paysans?* Paris, La Découverte.

Altschul E., Strauss F., 1937. *Technical Progress and Agricultural Depression*. New York, NBER.

Alvaredo F., Chancel L., Piketty T., Saez E., Zucman G. (dir.), 2018. *World Inequality Report 2018*. Cambridge, MA, Belknap Press of Harvard University Press.

Ambrosoli M., 1997. *The Wild and the Sown: Botany and Agriculture in Western Europe, 1350-1850*. Cambridge/New York, Cambridge University Press/Past and Present Publications.

Anderson K. (dir.), 2009. *Distorsions to Agricultural Incentives: A Global Perspective, 1955-2007*. Washington D.C., Palgrave Macmillan/The World Bank.

Anderson K., 2018. From taxing to subsidizing farmers in China post-1978. *China Agricultural Economic Review*, 10 (1), 36-47.

Anderson K., Nelgen S., 2012. *Updated national and global estimates of distortions to agricultural incentives, 1955 to 2010*. Washington D.C., The World Bank.

Anderson K., Nelgen S., 2013. *Updated national and global estimates of distortions to agricultural incentives, 1955 to 2011*. Washington D.C., The World Bank.

Anghie A., 2002. Colonialism and the birth of international institutions: Sovereignty, economy and the mandade system of the League of Nations. *Journal of International Law and Politics*, 34 (3), 513-632.

Apostolides A., Broadberry S., Campbell B., Overton M., van Leeuwen B., 2008. *English agricultural output and labour productivity, 1250-1850*. Working Paper. Warwick, Warwick University.

Arndt H.W., 1973. Development economics before 1945. In: *Development and Planning: Essays in Honour of Paul Rosenstein Rodan* (Bhagwati J., Eckaus R.S., dir.). Cambridge, MA, The MIT Press, 13-29.

Arnould A.M., 1791. *De la balance du commerce et des relations commerciales extérieures de la France: dans toutes les parties du globe, particulièrement à la fin du règne de Louis XIV, et au moment de la révolution; ... avec la valeur de ses importations et exportations progressives depuis 1716 jusqu'en 1788 inclusivement*. Paris, Buisson.

Arrighi G., 1994. *The Long Twentieth Century: Money, Power and the Origins of our Times*. London, Verso.

Arrighi G., 2005. Global governance and hegemony in the modern world system. In: *Contending Perspective on Global Governance: Coherence, Contestation and World Order* (Ba A.D., Hoffmann M.J., dir.). London, Routledge, 57-71.

Arrighi G., 2007. *Adam Smith in Beijing: Lineages of the Twenty-First Century*. London, Verso Books.

Arrighi G., Hamashita T., Selden M. (dir.), 2003a. *The Resurgence of East Asia: 500, 150 and 50 Year Perspectives*. New York, Routledge.

Atkinson A.B., Piketty T. (dir.), 2007. *Top Incomes over the 20th Century: A Contrast between Continental European and English-Speaking Countries*. Oxford, Oxford University Press.

Attman A., 1981. The Russian market in world trade, 1500-1860. *Scandinavian Economic History Review*, 29 (3), 177-202.

Aubert C., 2005. Politiques agricoles chinoises: la porte étroite. In: *L'économie mondiale 2006* (Cepii). Paris, La Découverte, 69-83.

Avalle C., 1798. *Tableau comparatif des productions des colonies françaises aux Antilles avec celle des colonies anglaises, espagnoles et hollandaises de l'année 1787 à 1788*. Paris, Goujon/Debray/Fuschs.

Backman J., 1938. *Government Price-Fixing*. New York/Chicago, Pitman Publishing Corporation.

Bairoch P., 1973. Agriculture and the Industrial Revolution 1700-1914. In: *The Fontana Economic History of Europe: The Industrial Revolution* (Cipolla C.M., dir.). London, Collins/Fontana Books, 452-501.

Bairoch P., 1989. European trade policy, 1815-1914. In: *The Cambridge Economic History of Europe. Volume 8: The Industrial Economies: The Development of Economic and Social Policies* (Mathias P., Pollard S., dir.). Cambridge, Cambridge University Press, 1-160.

Bairoch P., 1993. *Mythes et paradoxes de l'histoire économique*. Paris, La Découverte.

Bairoch P., 1999. *L'agriculture des pays développés: 1800 à nos jours*. Paris, Economica.

Bank for International Settlements, 1960. *Thirthieth Anual Report*. Basel, BIS.

Barlow C., 1986. *Changes in the economic position of workers on rubber estates and smallholdings in peninsular Malaysia, 1910-1985*. Working Papers in Trade and Development. Canberra, Australia National University.

Barnhart M.A., 2013. *Japan Prepares for Total War: The Search for Economic Security, 1919-1941*. Ithaca, Cornell University Press, coll. Cornell Studies in Security Affairs.

Barrett C.B., Carter M.R., Timmer C.P., 2010. A century-long perspective on agricultural development. *American Journal of Agricultural Economics*, 92 (2), 447-468.

Bartkowski B., Theesfeld I., Pirscher F., Timaeus J., 2018. Snipping around for food: Economic, ethical and policy implications of CRISPR/Cas genome editing. *Geoforum*, 96, 172-80.

Bataille G., 1967. *La part maudite: précédé de La notion de dépense*. Paris, Éditions de Minuit.

Bates R.H., 1984. Governments and agricultural markets in Africa. In: *The Role of Markets in the World Food Economy* (Johnson G.D., Schuh G.E., dir.). Boulder, Westview Press, 153-85.

Bayliss-Smith T., 1982. *The Ecology of Agricultural Systems*. Cambridge, Cambridge University Press.

Bean R.N., 1977. Food imports in the British West Indies: 1680-1845. *Annals of the New York Academy of Sciences*, 292 (1), 581-90.

Belich J., 2009. *Replenishing the Earth: The Settler Revolution and the Rise of the Anglo-World, 1783-1939*. Oxford/New York, Oxford University Press.

Bennet M.K., 1936. *World wheat utilization since 1885-1886*. Wheat Studies of the Food Research Institute. Stanford, Food Research Institute.

Bennett C.E., Thomas R., Williams M., Zalasiewicz J., Edgeworth M., Miller H., Coles B., Foster A., Burton E.J., Marume U., 2018. The broiler chicken as a signal of a human reconfigured biosphere. *Royal Society Open Science*, 5 (12), 180325.

Bensaude-Vincent B., Stengers I., 2001. *Histoire de la chimie*. Paris, La Découverte.

Benz H., Mendez Del Villar P., 1994. *Le marché international du riz, facteurs d'instabilité et politiques des exportations*. Document de travail. Montpellier, Cirad.

Berry S., 1992. Hegemony on a shoestring: Indirect rule and access to agricultural land. *Africa*, 62 (3), 327-55.

Bertrand J.-P., Laurent C., Leclercq V., 1985. *Le monde du soja*. Paris, La Découverte.

Besnier R., Meignen L., 1978. Le commerce extérieur de la France à la fin de l'Ancien Régime: déficit apparent, prospérité réelle mais fragile. *Revue historique de droit français et étranger*, 56 (4), 583-614.

Bessis S., 1979. *L'arme alimentaire*. Paris, François Maspero.

Bivens J., Gould E., Mishel L.R., Shierholz H., 2014. *Raising America's Pay: Why It's Our Central Economic Policy Challenge*. Washington D.C., Economic Policy Institute.

Blainey G., 1966. *The Tyranny of Distance: How Distance Shaped Australia's History*. Melbourne, Sun Books.

Blandford D., 1984. Changes in food consumption patterns in the OECD area. *European Review of Agricultural Economics*, 11 (1), 43-64.

Blau G., 1946. Wool in the world economy. *Journal of the Textile Institute Proceedings*, 37 (9), 454-6.

Bloch M., 1930. La lutte pour l'individualisme agraire dans la France du xviiie siècle. Première partie: l'œuvre des pouvoirs d'Ancien Régime. *Annales d'histoire économique et sociale*, 2 (7), 329-83.

Bloch M., 1952. *Les caractères originaux de l'histoire rurale française*. Paris, Armand Colin.
Block M., 1860. *Statistique de la France comparée avec les autres États de l'Europe*. Paris, Librairie d'Amyot.
Block F.L., 1977. *The Origins of International Economic Disorder: A Study of United States International Monetary Policy from World War II to the Present*. Berkeley, University of California Press.
Blum J., 1978. *The End of the Old Order in Rural Europe*. Princeton, Princeton University Press.
Board of Trade, 1917. *The Food Supply of the United Kingdom*. London, His Majesty's Stationery Office.
Boatcă M., 2013. Coloniality of labor in the global periphery: Latin America and Eastern Europe in the world-system. *Review (Fernand Braudel Center)*, 36 (3-4), 287-314.
Bogue A.G., 1983. Changes in mechanical and plant technology: The Corn Belt, 1910-1940. *The Journal of Economic History*, 43 (1), 1-25.
Boizard E., Tardieu H., 1891. *Histoire de la législation des sucres (1664-1891)*. Paris, Bureaux de la "Sucrerie indigène et coloniale."
Bonneuil C., 1999. "Pénétrer l'indigène": arachide, paysans, agronomes et administrateurs coloniaux au Sénégal (1897-1950). *Études rurales*, 151-2, 199-223.
Bonneuil C., Fressoz J.-B., 2013. *L'événement anthropocène: la Terre, l'histoire et nous*. Paris, Seuil.
Bonny S., 2017. Corporate concentration and technological change in the global seed industry. *Sustainability*, 9 (9), 1632.
Borkin J., Welsh C., 1943. *Germany's Master Plan: The Story of an Industrial Offensive*. New York, Duell, Sloan and Pearce.
Boserup E., 1965. *The Condition of Agricultural Growth: The Economics of Agrarian Change under Population Pressure*. London, G. Allen & Urwin.
Bouvier N., 2004. *Le vide et le plein: carnets du Japon 1964-1970*. Paris, Hoëbeke.
Boyer R., 1979. Wage formation in historical perspective: The French experience. *Cambridge Journal of Economics*, 3 (2), 99-118.
Boyer R., 1986. *La théorie de la régulation: une analyse critique*. Paris, La Découverte.
Boyer R., 1995. Du fordisme canonique à une variété de modes de développement. In: *Théorie de la régulation, l'état des savoirs* (Boyer R., Saillard Y., dir.). Paris, La Découverte, 369-77.
Boyer R., 2015. *Économie politique des capitalismes: théorie de la régulation et des crises*. Paris, La Découverte.
Brada J.C., 1983. The Soviet-american grain agreement and the national interest. *American Journal of Agricultural Economics*, 65 (4), 651-6.
Brandt K., 1945. *The Reconstruction of World Agriculture*. London, George Allen & Unwin.
Brandt K., 1953. *Germany's Agricultural and Food Policies in World War II*. Stanford, Stanford University Press.
Brandt W., 1980. *Nord Sud: un programme de survie. Rapport de la Commission indépandante sur les problèmes de développement international*. Paris, Gallimard.
Brandt L., 1985. Chinese agriculture and the international economy, 1870-1930s: A reassessment. *Explorations in Economic History*, 22, 168-93.
Braudel F., 1979a. *Civilisation matérielle, économie et capitalisme, xve-xviiie siècle. 1. Les structures du quotidien: le possible et l'impossible*. Paris, Armand Colin.
Braudel F., 1979b. *Civilisation matérielle, économie et capitalisme, xve-xviiie siècle. 2. Les jeux de l'échange*. Paris, Armand Colin.

Braudel F., 1979c. *Civilisation matérielle, économie et capitalisme, xve-xviiie siècle. 3. Le temps du monde.* Paris, Armand Colin.
Braudel F., 1981. *Civilization and Capitalism, 15th-18th century. Volume 1: The Structures of Everyday Life.* London, Collins.
Braudel F., 1983. *Civilization and Capitalism, 15th-18th century. Volume 2: The Wheel of Commerce.* London, Collins.
Braudel F., 1984. *Civilization and Capitalism, 15th-18th century. Volume 3: The Perspective of the World.* London, Collins.
Braudel F., 1986. *L'identité de la France: les hommes et les choses.* Paris, Arthaud/Flammarion.
Braun N., 2017. Portée et limites des nouvelles techniques d'obtention végétale, les New Plant Breeding Techniques (NPBT). *Annales des Mines. Réalités industrielles*, 1, 90-3.
Bredahl M.E., Green L., 1983. Residual supplier model of coarse grains trade. *American Journal of Agricultural Economics*, 65 (4), 785-90.
Brenner R.P., 1976. Agrarian class structure and economic development in pre-industrial Europe. *Past & Present*, 70, 30-75.
Bricas N., Daviron B., 2012. La crise alimentaire: une recomposition du jeu d'acteurs. *In: Regards sur la Terre 2012* (Jacquet P., Pachauri R.K., Tubiana L., dir.). Paris, Armand Colin.
Briggs H.E., 1932. Early bonanza farming in the Red River valley of the north. *Agricultural History*, 6 (1), 26-37.
Brook T., 2010. *Le chapeau de Vermeer. Le xviie siècle à l'aube de la mondialisation.* Paris, Payot.
Brown L.R., 1995. *Who Will Feed China? Wake-up Call for a Small Planet.* New York, W. W. Norton & Company.
Brown W., 2007. *Les habits neufs de la politique mondiale: néolibéralisme et néo-conservatisme.* Paris, Les prairies ordinaires.
Brunier S., 2012. *Conseillers et conseillères agricoles. L'amour du progrès aux temps de la "révolution silencieuse" (1945-1983).* Thèse de doctorat, Grenoble, Université de Grenoble.
Brunt L., 2007. Where there's muck, there's brass: The market for manure in the Industrial Revolution. *The Economic History Review*, 60 (2), 333-72.
Bulbeck D., Reid A., Tan L.C., Wu Y. (dir.), 1998. *Southeast Asian Exports since the 14th Century: Cloves, Pepper, Coffee, and Sugar.* Data paper series: sources for the economic history of Southeast Asia. Singapore/Leiden, Institute of Southeast Asian Studies/KITLV Press.
Bunker S.G., Ciccantell P.S., 2005. *Globalization and the Race for Resources.* Baltimore, Johns Hopkins University Press.
Bunker S.G., Ciccantell P.S., 2007. *East Asia and the Global Economy: Japan's Ascent, with Implications for China's Future.* Baltimore, Johns Hopkins University Press.
Burch D., Lawrence G., 2009. Towards a third food regime: Behind the transformation. *Agriculture and Human Values*, 26 (4), 267-79.
Bureau D., Bureau J.-C., Champsaur P., 1999. *Agriculture et négociations commerciales.* Paris, La documentation française/Conseil d'analyse économique.
Bureau J.-C., Jean S., 2012. Trade liberalization in the bio-economy: Coping with a new landscape. *In: 28th Triennal Conference of the International Association of Agricultural Economists.* Foz de Iguaçu (Brésil), IAAE, 18-24 août.
Bureau J.-C., Thoyer S., 2014. *La Politique agricole commune.* Paris, La Découverte, coll. Repères.

Bureau of the Census, 1902. *Statistical Abstract of the United States 1901*. Washington D.C., Government Printing Office.
Byerlee D., 2014. The fall and rise again of plantations in tropical Asia: History repeated? *Land*, 3 (3), 574-97.
Cai F., Garnaut R., Song L., 2018. 40 years of China's reform and development: How reform captured China's demographic dividend. In: *China's 40 Years of Reform and Development: 1978-2018* (Garnaut R., Song L. Cai. F., dir.). Moorebank, ANU Press, 5-25.
Caldwell J., Missingham B., Marck J., 2001. *The population of Oceania in the second millennium*. Canberra, Australian National University.
Calero P., Nikel P.I., 2019. Chasing bacterial chassis for metabolic engineering: A perspective review from classical to non-traditional microorganisms. *Microbial Biotechnology*, 12 (1), 98-124.
Calvet R., 2002. La réforme agraire japonaise de 1946. *Histoire & sociétés rurales*, 18 (2), 65-89.
Cao C., 2018. *GMO China: How Global Debates Transformed China's Agricultural Biotechnology Policies*. New York, Columbia University Press.
Cardoso F.H., Faletto E., 1979. *Dependency and Development in Latin America*. Berkeley, University of California Press.
Carroll P., 2017. Shall we or shall we not? The Japanese, Australian, and New Zealand decisions to apply for membership in the OECD, 1960-1973. In: *The OECD and the International Political Economy since 1948* (Leimgruber M., Schmelzer M., dir.). Dordrecht, Springer, 113-36.
Carson R., 1962. *Silent Spring*. Boston, Houghton Mifflin Company.
Carson R., 1963. *Printemps silencieux*. Paris, Plon.
Carsten F.L., 1947. The origins of the junkers. *The English Historical Review*, 62 (243), 145-78.
Carter S.B., Gartner S.S., Haines M.R., Olmstead A.L., Sutch R., Wright G. (dir.), 2006. *Historical Statistics of the United States: Millennial Edition*. Volume 4. Cambridge, Cambridge University Press.
Chand R., Prasanna P.L., Singh A., 2011. Farm size and productivity: Understanding the strengths of smallholders and improving their livelihoods. *Economic and Political Weekly*, 46 (26), 5-11.
Chandler A.D., 1977. *The Visible Hand: The Managerial Revolution in American Business*. Cambridge/London, The Belknap Press of Harvard University Press.
Chandler A.D., 2009. *Shaping the Industrial Century: The Remarkable Story of the Evolution of the Modern Chemical and Pharmaceutical Industries*. Cambridge, MA, Harvard University Press.
Chandler T., Fox G., 1987. *3000 Years of Urban Growth*. Lewinston, Edwin Mellen Press.
Chaptal J.-A., 1819. *De l'industrie française*. Paris, Antoine-Augustin Renouard.
Chase-Dunn C., Jorgenson A.K., Reifer T.E., Lio S., 2005. The trajectory of the United States in the world-system: A quantitative reflection. *Sociological Perspectives*, 48 (2), 233-54.
Chaudhuri K.N., 1985. *Trade and Civilisation in the Indian Ocean: An Economic History from the Rise of Islam to 1750*. Cambridge/New York, Cambridge University Press.
Chaumet J.-M., 2018. Le secteur laitier chinois. Entre pression des importations et reprise en main interne. *Économie rurale*, 364, 91-108.
Chaunu P., 1969. *Conquête et exploitation des nouveaux mondes*. Paris, Presses universitaires de France, coll. Nouvelle Clio.

Chauveau J.-P., 1994. Participation paysanne et populisme bureaucratique: essai d'histoire et de sociologie de la culture du développement. In: *Les associations paysannes en Afrique: organisation et dynamiques* (Jacob J.-P., Delville P., dir.). Paris, Apad/Karthala/IUED.
Chen Y., Wang S.-J., Tsai C.-C., Zhang C.-J. 2016. Assessment of subsidies to minimize environmental pollution by Intensive Hog Feeding Operation (IHFO). *Journal of Cleaner Production*, 112 (4), 2529-35.
Chevalier A., 1908. *Le cacaoyer dans l'Ouest africain*. Paris, A. Challamel.
Chew S.C., 1992. *Logs for Capital: The Timber Industry and Capitalist Enterprise in the Nineteenth Century*. Westport, Greenwood Press, coll. Contributions in Economics and Economic History, 138.
Cheyns E., Daviron B., Djama M., Fouilleux E., Guéneau S., 2016. La normalisation du développement durable par les filières agricoles insérées dans les marchés internationaux. In: *Développement durable et filières tropicales* (Biénabe E., Rival A., Loeillet D., dir.). Versailles, Éditions Quæ, 275-94.
Chou S.-H., 1971. Railway development and economic growth in Manchuria. *The China Quarterly*, 45, 57-84.
Ciriacy-Wantrup S.V., 1946. Resource conservation and economic stability. *The Quarterly Journal of Economics*, 60 (3), 412-52.
Clapp J., 2017. *Bigger is not always Better: The Drivers and Implications of the Recent Agribusiness Megamergers*. Waterloo (Canada), University of Waterloo.
Clarence-Smith W.G., 2000. *Cocoa and Chocolate, 1765-1914*. London/New York, Routledge.
Clark B., Foster J.B., 2009. Ecological imperialism and the Global Metabolic Rift: Unequal exchange and the guano/nitrates trade. *International Journal of Comparative Sociology*, 50, 311-34.
Clark G., 1999. Too much revolution: Agriculture in the Industrial Revolution, 1700-1860. In: *The British Industrial Revolution: An Economic Perspective* (Mokyr J., dir.). Boulder, Westview Press, 206-39.
Clark G., 2007. *A Farewell to Alms: A Brief Economic History of the World*. Princeton/Oxford, Princeton University Press.
Cleveland C.J., 1995. The direct and indirect use of fossil fuels and electricity in USA agriculture, 1910-1990. *Agriculture, Ecosystems and Environment*, 55 (2), 111-21.
Cnuced, 1976. *Manuel de statistiques du commerce international et du développement*. Genève, Cnuced.
Cochet H., 2011. *L'agriculture comparée*. Versailles, Éditions Quæ.
Cochrane W., 1979. *The Development of American Agriculture: A Historical Analysis*. Minneapolis, University of Minnesota Press.
Coclanis P.A., 1993. Distant thunder: The creation of a world market in rice and the transformations it wrought. *The American Historical Review*, 98 (4), 1050-78.
Cohn T.H., 1993. The changing role of the United States in the global agricultural trade regime. In: *World Agriculture and the GATT* (Avery W.P., dir.). London, Lynne Rienner Publishers, 17-39.
Colonna P., Valceschini E., 2017. La bioéconomie: vers une nouvelle organisation des systèmes agricoles et industriels? In: *Transformations agricoles et agroalimentaires. Entre écologie et capitalisme* (Allaire G., Daviron B., dir.). Versailles, Éditions Quæ, 153-65.
Combris P., Maire B., Réquillart V., Caillavet F., Champenois A., Dury S., Gojard S., 2011. Consommation et consommateurs. In: *Pour une alimentation durable. Réflexion stratégique duALIne* (Esnouf C., Russel M., Bricas N., dir.). Versailles, Éditions Quæ, 37-60.

Comité national de réforme et développement, 2008. *Plan de moyen et long terme pour la sécurité alimentaire nationale* 国家粮食安全中长期规划纲要 *(2008-2020)*. Beijing, Bureau d'information du Conseil d'État.

Commission de modernisation rurale, 1946. *Premier rapport de la Commission de modernisation de l'équipement rural*. Paris, Commissariat général du Plan.

Commission européenne, 2012. *L'innovation au service d'une croissance durable: une bioéconomie pour l'Europe*. Communication au Parlement européen, au Conseil, au Comité économique et social européen et au Comité des régions.

Conseil D'État, 1994. *Note sur l'approfondissement des réformes de la structure d'approvisionnement et de commercialisation des grains*. Beijing, Conseil d'État.

Cook E., 1985. Soviet agricultural policies and the feed-livestock sector. *American Journal of Agricultural Economics*, 67 (5), 1049-54.

Cooper F., 1977. *Plantation Slavery on the East Coast of Africa*. New Haven, Yale University Press.

Cooper F., 1996. *Decolonization and African Society: The Labor Question in French and British Africa*. Cambridge, Cambridge University Press, coll. African Studies Series.

Cooper M.R., Barton G.T., Brodell A.P., 1947. *Progress of Farm Mechanization*. Washington D.C., US Department of Agriculture.

Coquery-Vidrovitch C., 1970. De l'impérialisme britannique à l'impérialisme contemporain: l'avatar colonial. *L'homme et la société*, 18, 61-90.

Cottrell W.F., 1970. *Energy and Society: The Relation between Energy, Social Change, and Economic Development*. Westport, Greenwood Press.

Crafts N., Toniolo G. (dir.), 1996. *Economic Growth in Europe since 1945*. Cambridge, Cambridge University Press.

Crammond E., 1914. The economic relations of the British and German Empires. *Journal of the Royal Statistical Society*, 77 (8), 777-824.

Cronon W., 1991. *Nature's Metropolis: Chicago and the Great West*. New York, W. W. Norton.

Cronon W., 2011. *Changes in the Land: Indians, Colonists, and the Ecology of New England*. New York, Farrar, Straus and Giroux.

Crosby A.W., 1973. *The Columbian Exchange: Biological and Cultural Consequences of 1492*. Westport, Greenwood Press.

Crosby A.W., 1986. *Ecological Imperialism: The Biological Expansion of Europe, 900-1900*. Cambridge, Cambridge University Press.

Crossley J.C., Greenhill R., 1977. The river plate beef trade. In: *Business Imperialism, 1840-1930: An Inquiry Based on the British Experience in Latin America* (Platt D.C.M., dir.). Oxford, Clarendon Press, 284-334.

Crouzet F., 1966. Angleterre et France au xviiie siècle: essai d'analyse comparée de deux croissances économiques. *Annales. Économies, sociétés, civilisations*, 21 (2), 254-91.

Cullather N., 2004. Miracles of modernization: The Green Revolution and the apotheosis of technology. *Diplomatic History*, 28 (2), 227-54.

Cullather N., 2010. *The Hungry World: America's Cold War Battle against Poverty in Asia*. Cambridge/London, Harvard University Press.

Cunfer G., 2004. Manure matters on the Great Plains frontier. *Journal of Interdisciplinary History*, 34 (4), 539-67.

Cunfer G., Krausmann F., 2009. Sustaining soil fertility: Agricultural practice in the Old and New Worlds. *Global Environment*, 4, 8-47.

Curry-Machado J., Bosma U., 2012. Two islands, one commodity: Cuba, Java, and the global sugar trade (1790-1930). *New West Indian Guide/Nieuwe West-Indische Gids*, 86 (3-4), 237-62.

Curtin P.D., 1984. *Cross-Cultural Trade in World History*. Cambridge, Cambridge University Press.

Curtin P.D., 1990. *The Rise and Fall of the Plantation Complex: Essays in Atlantic History*. Cambridge/New York, Cambridge University Press, coll. Studies in Comparative World History.

Danbom D., 1995. *Born in the Country: A History of Rural America*. Baltimore, Johns Hopkins University Press.

Dardot P., Laval C., 2009. *La nouvelle raison du monde: essai sur la société néolibérale*. Paris, La Découverte.

Daumas M., 1968. *Histoire générale des techniques. Tome 3: L'expansion du machinisme*. Paris, Presses universitaires de France.

Davidson E.A., 2009. The contribution of manure and fertilizer nitrogen to atmospheric nitrous oxide since 1860. *Nature Geoscience*, 2, 659-62.

Daviron B., 1993. *Conflit et coopération sur le marché international du café: une analyse de longue période*. Thèse de doctorat, Montpellier, École nationale supérieure agronomique.

Daviron B., 1994. La crisis del mercado cafetalero internacional en una perspectiva de largo plazo. *In: Crisis y perspectiveas del café latinoamericano* (Samper M., dir.). San José, Icafe-Una, 37-78.

Daviron B., 2002. Small farm production and the standardization of tropical products. *Journal of Agrarian Change*, 2 (2), 162-84.

Daviron B., 2008. The historical integration of Africa in international food trade: A food regime perspective. *Globalization and Restructuring of African Commodity Flows* (Fold N., Larson M., dir.). Uppsala, Nordika Afrikain Institutet, 44-79.

Daviron B., 2010. Mobilizing labour in colonial African agriculture: The role of the International Colonial Institute in the elaboration of a standard of colonial government. *Journal of Global History*, 5 (3), 479-501.

Daviron B., 2014. Turning organic economies into mineral economies: Two centuries of oils and fats use and supply in France. *In: European Social Science History Conference*. Vienne, 23-26 avril.

Daviron B., 2016. Agriculture et économie: du solaire au minier ... et retour? *Agronomie, environnement et société*, 6 (1), 23-32.

Daviron B., Doré T., Fort J.-L., Jeuffroy M.-H., Nesme T., 2016. Regards agronomiques sur les relations entre agriculture et ressources naturelles: éditorial. *Agronomie, environnement et sociétés*, 6 (1), 9-10.

Daviron B., Douillet M., 2013. *Major Players of the International Food Trade and the World Food Security*. Wageningue, LEI Wageningen UR.

Daviron B., Ponte S., 2005. *The Coffee Paradox: Global Markets, Commodity Trade and the Elusive Promise of Development*. London, Zed Books.

Daviron B., Vagneron I., 2008. Market access for small farmers: The new standard challenge. *In: Agriculture and Development* (Kochendörfer-Lucius G., Pleskovic B., dir.). Washington D.C., The World Bank/Inwent, 41-8.

Daviron B., Voituriez T., 2003. Les paradoxes de la longévité du projet de stabilisation des marchés agricoles au xxe siècle: quelques enseignements de la pensée anglo-saxonne. *Économies et sociétés*, 37, 1579-1609.

Daviron B., Voituriez T., 2006. Quelle régulation des échanges agricoles internationaux? Un éclairage par la théorie des régimes. In: *La question politique en économie internationale* (Berthaud P., Kébadjian G., dir.). Paris, La Découverte, 110–23.

Davis K.G., 1952. The origines of the commission system in the West India trade. *Transactions of the Royal Historical Society*, 5 (2), 89–107.

Davis R., 1954. English foreign trade, 1660–1700. *The Economic History Review*, 7 (2), 150–66.

Davis R., 1962. English foreign trade, 1700–1774. *The Economic History Review*, 15 (2), 285–303.

Davis R., 1979. *The Industrial Revolution and British Overseas Trade*. Leicester, Leicester University Press.

Davis M., 2002. *Late Victorian Holocausts: El Niño Famines and the Making of the Third World*. London/New York, Verso.

Davis L., Huttenback R.A., 1985. The export of British finance, 1865–1914. *The Journal of Imperial and Commonwealth History*, 13 (3), 28–76.

Davis Bowman S., 1993. *Masters & Lords: Mid-19th Century U.S. Planters and Prussian Junkers*. Oxford, Oxford University Press.

de Bromhead A., Fernihough A., Lampe M., O'Rourke K.H., 2017. *When Britain turned inward: Protection and the shift towards Empire in interwar Britain*. NBER Working Paper 23164. Cambridge, National Bureau of Economic Research.

De Decker K., 2015. Medieval smokestacks: Fossil fuels in pre-industrial times. *Low-Tech Magazine*, February 1, 2015, available online: http://www.lowtechmagazine.com/2011/09/peat-and-coal-fossil-fuels-in-pre-industrial-times.html (accessed July 13, 2019).

De Graef P., 2014. The sprawl of urban manure: A micro-perspecitve on the allocation and recycling of urban waste in rural economy of early modern Flanders. In: *European Social Science History Conference*. Vienne, 23–26 avril.

De Janvry A., 1981. *The Agrarian Question and Reformism in Latin America*. Baltimore, Johns Hopkins University Press.

De La Peña C.T., 2010. *Empty Pleasures: The Story of Artificial Sweeteners from Saccharin to Splenda*. Chapel Hill, The University of North Carolina Press.

De Patoul B., van Schoute R. (dir.), 1994. *Les primitifs flamands et leur temps*. Louvain-la-Neuve, La renaissance du livre.

De Vries J., 1974. *The Dutch Rural Economy in the Golden Age, 1500–1700*. New Haven, Yale University Press.

De Vries J., 1994. The Industrial Revolution and the industrious revolution. *The Journal of Economic History*, 54 (2), 249–70.

De Vries J., 2008. *The Industrious Revolution: Consumer Behavior and the Household Economy, 1650 to the Present*. Cambridge, Cambridge University Press.

De Vries J., van der Woude A., 1997. *The First Modern Economy: Success, Failure, and Perseverance of the Dutch Economy, 1500–1815*. Cambridge, Cambridge University Press.

De Zeeuw J.W., 1978. Peat and the Dutch golden age: The historical meaning of energy-attainability. *A.A.G. Budragen*, 21, 3–31.

Dean W., 1976. *Rio Claro: A Brazilian Plantation System, 1820–1920*. Stanford, Stanford University Press.

Dean W., 1997. *With Broadax and Firebrand: The Destruction of the Brazilian Atlantic Forest*. Berkeley, University of California Press.

Debatisse M., 1963. *La révolution silencieuse*. Paris, Calmann-Lévy.

Debeir J.-C., Deléage J.-P., Hémery D., 2013. *Une histoire de l'énergie*. Paris, Flammarion.
Debray R., 2017. *Civilisation. Comment nous sommes devenus américains*. Paris, Gallimard.
Delahaye O., 2003. Réforme agraire et marché foncier: la réflexion aux États-Unis et son impact dans les institutions multilatérales de développement. *Revue Tiers Monde*, 174, 449-66.
Deléage J.-P., Julien J., Souchon C., 1979. *Analyse eco-énergétique du système agricole français et son évolution*. Paris, Laboratoire d'écologie générale et appliquée, Université Paris VII.
Deléage J.-P., Julien J., Sauget-Naudin N., Souchon C., 1979. Eco-energetics analysis of an agricultural system: The French case in 1970. *Agro-ecosystems*, 5 (4), 345-65.
Denys O., 1918. L'agriculture indigène dans les colonies françaises. In: *Congrès d'agriculture coloniale de l'Union coloniale française*. Paris, Augustin Challamel.
Deutsch K.W., Eckstein A., 1961. National industrialization and the declining share of the international economic sector, 1890-1959. *World Politics*, 13 (2), 267-99.
Dewhurst J.F. (dir.), 1947. *America's Needs and Resources*. New York, The Twentieth Century Fund.
Deyon P., 1969. *Le mercantilisme*. Paris, Flammarion.
Didry C., Wagner P., 1999. La nation comme cadre de l'action économique. La Première Guerre mondiale et l'émergence d'une économie nationale en France et en Allemagne. In: *Le travail et la nation. Histoire croisée de la France et de l'Allemagne* (Zimmerman B., Didry C., Wagner P., dir.). Paris, Éditions de la Maison des sciences de l'homme, 29-55.
Dies E.J., 1942. *Soybeans: Gold from the Soil*. New York, The Macmillan Co.
Di Fulvio, 1947. *Le café dans le monde*. Rome, Institut internationale d'agriculture.
Dorin B., Aubron C., 2016. Croissance et revenu du travail agricole en Inde. Une économie politique de la divergence (1950-2014). *Économie rurale*, 352, 41-65.
Downey E., 1906. *Charles Lever, His Life in His Letters*. Edinburgh, William Blackwood & Sons.
Downey E., 2008. *Charles Lever, His Life in His Letters*. Lakewood, Church Press.
Doyle A.C., 1909. *The Crime of the Congo*. London, Hutchinson & Co.
Drake P., 1972. Natural resources versus foreign borrowing in economic development. *The Economic Journal*, 82 (327), 951-62.
Duara P., 2006. The new imperialism and the post-colonial developmental State: Manchukuo in comparative perspective. *Japan Focus*, 4 (1), 1-18.
Duffy J., 1967. *A Question of Slavery*. Oxford, Clarendon Press.
Dumont R., 1946. *Le problème agricole français: esquisse d'un plan d'orientation et d'équipement*. Paris, Les éditions nouvelles.
Dumont R., 1949. *Les leçons de l'agriculture américaine*. Paris, Flammarion.
Earle C., 1992. The price of precocity: Technical choice and ecological constraint in the Cotton South, 1840-1890. *Agricultural History*, 66 (3), 25-60.
Eckstein A., Chao K., Chang J., 1974. The economic development of Manchuria: The rise of a frontier economy. *The Journal of Economic History*, 34 (1), 239-64.
Economic Committee, 1931. *The Agricultural Crisis*. Genève, League of Nations.
Economy E.C., Levi M., 2014. *By all Means Necessary: How China's Resource Quest is Changing the World*. Oxford, Oxford University Press.
Edwards B., 1819. *The History Civil and Commercial of the British West Indies. Volume 5, Appendix*. London, Printed for John Stockdale.

Edwards M.M., 1967. *The Growth of the British Cotton Trade, 1780-1815*. Manchester, Manchester University Press.

Eicher C.K., Staatz J.M., 1998. *International Agricultural Development*. Baltimore, Johns Hopkins University Press.

Ellison T., 1886. *The Cotton Trade of Great Britain: Including a History of the Liverpool Cotton Market and of the Liverpool Cotton Brokers' Association*. London, Effingham Wilson.

Elmore B.J., 2018. The commercial ecology of scavenger capitalism: Monsanto, fossil fuels, and the remaking of a chemical giant. *Enterprise & Society*, 19 (1), 153–78.

Eltis D., 2001. The volume and structure of the transatlantic slave trade: A reassessment. *The William and Mary Quarterly*, 58 (1), 17–46.

Eltzbacher P. (dir.), 1914. *Die deutsche Volksernährung und der englische Aushungerungsplan*. Dordrecht, Springer.

Elvin M., 1973. *The Pattern of the Chinese Past: A Social and Economic Interpretation*. Stanford, Stanford University Press.

Enerdata, 2018. *Global Statistical Yearbook 2018*. Grenoble, Enerdata.

Engerman S.L., 1986. Servants to slaves to servants: Contract labour and European expansion. *In: Colonialism and Migration: Indentured Labour before and after Slavery* (Emmer P.C., dir.). Dordrecht, Springer, 263–94.

Engerman S.L., 1996. Slavery, serfdom and other forms of coerced labour: Similarities and differences. *In: Serfdom and Slavery: Studies in Legal Bondage* (Bush M.L., dir.). London, Longman, 18–41.

Ericson S.J., 2015. Japonica, Indica: Rice and foreign trade in Meiji Japan. *The Journal of Japanese Studies*, 41 (2), 317–45.

Ernle R.E.P.B., 1888. *The Pioneers and Progress of English Farming*. London, Longmans Green.

Escobar A., 1995. *Encountering Development: The Making and Unmaking of the Third World*. Princeton, Princeton University Press.

Etemad B., 2000. *La possession du monde: poids et mesures de la colonisation (xviiie-xixe siècles)*. Bruxelles, Éditions Complexe.

European Commission, 2012. *Innovating for Sustainable Growth: A Bioeconomy for Europe: Communication from the Commission to the European Parliament, the Council and the European Economic and Social Committee and the Committee of the Regions*. Brussels, Publications Office of the European Union.

Eurostat, 1973. *Commerce extérieur: statistique mensuelle, 2/1973*. Luxembourg, Eurostat.

Eurostat, 2008. *External and Intra-European Union Trade: Statistical Yearbook: Data 1958-2006*. Luxembourg, European Commission.

Evans J.W., 1968. The General Agreement on Tariffs and Trade. *International Organization*, 22 (1), 72–98.

Fairlie S., 1965. Dyestuffs in the eighteenth century. *The Economic History Review*, 17 (3), 488–510.

Falkus M.E., 1966. Russia and the international wheat trade, 1861-1914. *Economica*, 33 (132), 416–29.

FAO, 1947. *World Fiber Survey*. Washington D.C., FAO.

FAO, PAM, 2009. *L'état de l'insécurité alimentaire dans le monde 2009. Crises économiques: répercussions et enseignements*. Rome, FAO.

FAO, PAM, 2013. *L'état de l'insécurité alimentaire dans le monde 2013: les multiples dimensions de la sécurité alimentaire*. Rome, FAO.

Fasseur C., 1991. Purse or principle: Dutch colonial policy in the 1860s and the decline of the cultivation system. *Modern Asian Studies*, 25 (1), 33-52.

Federico G., 2005. *Feeding the World: An Economic History of Agriculture, 1800-2000*. Princeton, Princeton University Press.

Feis H., 1930. *Europe, the World's Banker, 1870-1914: An Account of European Foreign Investment and the Connection of World Finance with Diplomacy before the War*. New Haven, Yale University Press.

Ferguson D.T., 2014. Nightsoil and the "Great Divergence": Human waste, the urban economy and economic productivity, 1500-1900. *Journal of Global History*, 9 (3), 379-402.

Ferrie J., Hatton T., 2013. *Two Centuries of International Migration*, IZA Discussion Papers, No. 7866, Institute for the Study of Labor, Bonn.

Findlay R., O'Rourke K.H., 2007. *Power and Plenty: Trade, War, and the World Economy in the Second Millennium*. Princeton, Princeton University Press.

Finlay M.R., 2003. Old efforts at new uses: A brief history of chemurgy and the American search for biobased materials. *Journal of Industrial Ecology*, 7 (3-4), 33-46.

Fischer-Kowalski M., Erb K.-H., 2016. Core concepts and heuristics. In: *Social Ecology* (Haberl H., Fischer-Kowalski M., Krausmann F., Winiwarter V., dir.). Dordrecht, Springer, 29-61.

Fischer-Kowalski M., Haberl H., 1993. Metabolism and colonization: Modes of production and the physical exchange between societies and nature. *Innovation: The European Journal of Social Science Research*, 6 (4), 415-42.

Fischer-Kowalski M., Haberl H., 1998. Sustainable development: Socio-economic metabolism and colonization of nature. *International Social Science Journal*, 50 (158), 573-87.

Fischer-Kowalski M., Haberl H. (dir.), 2007. *Socioecological Transitions and Global Change: Trajectories of Social Metabolism and Land Use*. Cheltenham, Edward Elgar Publishing

Fischer-Kowalski M., Haberl H., 2015. Social metabolism: A metric for biophysical growth and degrowth. In: *Handbook of Ecological Economics* (Martínez-Alier J., Muradian R., dir.). Cheltenham, Edward Elgar Publishing, 100-38.

Fischer-Kowalski M., Weisz H., 1999. Society as hybrid between material and symbolic realms: Toward a theoretical framework of society-nature interaction. *Advances in Human Ecology*, 8, 215-51.

Fishlow A., 2000. Internal transportation in the nineteenth and early twentieth centuries. In: *The Cambridge Economic History of the United States. Volume 2: The Long Nineteenth Century* (Engerman S.L., Gallman R.E., dir.). Cambridge, Cambridge University Press, 543-642.

Fitzgerald D., 1986. Exporting American agriculture: The Rockefeller Foundation in Mexico, 1943-53. *Social Studies of Science*, 16 (3), 457-83.

Fletcher, M.E., 1958. The Suez Canal and world shipping, 1869-1914. *The Journal of Economic History*, 18 (04), 556-73.

Fogel R.W., 1989. *Without Consent or Contract: The Rise and Fall of American Slavery*. New York, W. W. Norton & Company.

Fogel R.W., Engerman S.L., 1995. *Time on the Cross: The Economics of American Negro Slavery*. New York/London, W. W. Norton & Company.

Fornari H.D., 1979. The big change: Cotton to soybeans. *Agricultural History*, 53 (1), 245-53.

Foster J.B., 1999. Marx's theory of metabolic rift: Classical foundations for environmental sociology. *The American Journal of Sociology*, 105 (2), 366-405.

Foster J.B., Clarck B., 2009. Ecological imperialism and the global metabolic rift: Unequal exchange and the guano/nitrates trade. *International Journal of Comparative Sociology*, 50 (3–4), 311–34.

Fourastié J., 1979. *Les Trente Glorieuses*. Paris, Fayard.

Francks P., 2016. *Japan and the Great Divergence: A Short Guide*. Dordrecht, Springer.

Frank A.G., 1966. *The Development of Underdevelopment*. Boston, New England Free Press.

Frank A.G., 1998. *ReOrient: Global Economy in the Asian Age*. Berkeley/London, University of California Press.

Fransen L.W., Kolk A., 2007. Global rule-setting for business: A critical analysis of multi-stakeholder standards. *Organization*, 14 (5), 667–84.

Friedmann H., 1978. World market, State, and family farm: Social bases of household production in the era of wage labour. *Comparative Studies in Society and History*, 20 (4), 545–86.

Friedmann H., 1982. The political economy of food: The rise and fall of the postwar international food order. *American Journal of Sociology*, 88, 248–86.

Friedmann H., 1991. Changes in the international division of labor: Agri-food complexes and export agriculture. *In: Towards a New Political Economy of Agriculture* (Fridland W.H., Busch L., Buttel F.H., Rudy A.P., dir.). Boulder, Westview Press, 65–94.

Friedmann H., 1992. Distance and durability: Shaky foundations of the World food economy. *Third World Quarterly*, 13 (2), 371–83.

Friedmann H., 1993. The political economy of food: A global crisis. *New Left Review*, 197, 29–57.

Friedmann H., McMichael P., 1989. Agriculture and the state system: The rise and decline of national agricultures, 1870 to the present. *Sociologia Ruralis*, 29 (2), 93–117.

Frödin O., 2013. Modernization, neo-liberal globalization, or variegated development: The Indian food system transformation in comparative perspective. *International Review of Sociology*, 23 (1), 221–42.

Furtado C., 1970. *Economic Development of Latin America: A Survey from Colonial Times to the Cuban Revolution*. Cambridge, Cambridge University Press.

Galbraith J.K., 1958. *The Affluent Society*. Boston, Houghton Mifflin.

Gallagher J., Robinson R., 1953. The imperialism of free trade. *The Economic History Review*, 6 (1), 1–15.

Galloway J.H., 1989. *The Sugar Cane Industry: An Historical Geography from its Origins to 1914*. Cambridge, Cambridge University Press.

Gammer M., 2005. Russia and Eurasian steppe nomads: An overview. *In: Mongols, Turks, and Others: Eurasian Nomads and the Sedentary World* (Amitai R., Biran M., dir.). Leiden/Boston, Brill, 483–502.

Gasparatos A., Stromberg P., 2012. *Socioeconomic and Environmental Impacts of Biofuels: Evidence from Developing Nations*. Cambridge, Cambridge University Press.

Geiger D., 2009. *Turner in the Tropics: The Frontier Concept Revisited*. Thèse de doctorat, Lucerne, Sozialwissenschaftlichen Fakultät der Universität Luzern.

Georgescu-Roegen N., 1971. *The Entropy Law and the Economic Process*. Cambridge, MA, Harvard University Press.

Georgescu-Roegen N., Mayumi K., Gowdy J.M., 1999. *Bioeconomics and Sustainability: Essays in Honor of Nicholas Georgescu-Roegen*. Cheltenham/Northampton, Edward Elgar Publishing.

Gerhard G., 2009. Food and genocide: Nazi agrarian politics in the occupied territories of the Soviet Union. *Contemporary European History*, 18 (1), 45–65.

Gerhard G., 2015. *Nazi Hunger Politics: A History of Food in the Third Reich*. Lanham, Rowman & Littlefield.
Gerrior S., Bente L., Hiza H., 2004. *Nutrient Content of the US Food Supply, 1909-2000*. Washington D.C., USDA.
Gerschenkron A., 1962. *Economic Backwardness in Historical Perspective: A Book of Essays*. Cambridge, MA, Belknap Press of Harvard University Press.
Gerschenkron A., 1966. *Bread and Democracy in Germany*. Ithaca, Cornell University Press.
Gervais M., Jollivet M., Tavernier Y., 1978. *Histoire de la France rurale. 4. La fin de la France paysanne de 1914 à nos jours*. Paris, Seuil.
Ghosh N., 2012. *Market integration in agricultural commodities in India: A study on impact of movement in international prices on household welfare*. Sanei Working Paper Series. Dacca, Sanei.
Gierlinger S., Krausmann F., 2012. The physical economy of the United States of America. *Journal of Industrial Ecology*, 16 (3), 365-77.
Gini C., Vinci F., Sloutski N., 1921. *Report on the Problem of Raw Materials and Foodstuffs*. Genève, League of Nations.
Giraud P.-N., 1996. *L'inégalité du monde: économie du monde contemporain*. Paris, Folio.
Gittinger J.P., 1961. United States policy toward agrarian reform in underdeveloped nations. *Land Economics*, 37 (3), 195-205.
Glamann K., 1977. The changing patterns of trade. In: *The Cambridge Economic History of Europe. Volume 5: The Economic Organization of Early Modern Europe* (Rich E.E., Wilson C.H., dir.). Cambridge, Cambridge University Press, 185-289.
Glickman L., 2004. "Acheter par amour de l'esclavage": l'abolitionnisme et les origines du mouvement consumériste américain. In: *Au nom du consommateur: Consommation et politique en Europe et aux États-Unis au xxe siècle* (Chatriot A., Chessel M.-E., Hilton M., dir.). Paris, La Découverte, 213-30.
Goldsmith J.L., 1984. The agrarian history of preindustrial France. Where do we go from here? *Journal of European Economic History*, 13 (1), 175.
Goody J., 2006. Gordon Childe, the urban revolution, and the haute cuisine: An anthropo-archaeological view of modern history. *Comparative Studies in Society and History*, 48 (3), 503-19.
Gorman H.S., 2013. *The Story of N: A Social History of the Nitrogen Cycle and the Challenge of Sustainability*. New Brunswick, Rutgers University Press.
Grant O., 2009. Agriculture and economic development in Germany 1870-1939. In: *Agriculture and Economic Development in Europe since 1870* (Lains P., Pinilla V., dir.). London, Routledge, 178-209.
Gray L.C., Thompson E.K., 1933. *History of Agriculture in the Southern United States to 1860*. Washington D.C., The Carnegie Institution of Washington.
Greif A., 2002. Institutions and impersonal exchange: From communal to individual responsibility. *The Journal of Institutional and Theoreritical Economics*, 158 (1), 168-204.
Grigg D.B., 1974. *The Agricultural Systems of the World: An Evolutionary Approach*. Cambridge, Cambridge University Press.
Grigg D.B., 1992. *The Transformation of Agriculture in the West*. Oxford, Blackwell Publishing.
Grigg D., 1995. The nutritional transition in Western Europe. *Journal of Historical Geography*, 21 (3), 247-61.

Grjebine A., 1980. *La nouvelle économie internationale: de la crise mondiale au développement autocentré*. Paris, Presses universitaires de France.
Grove R., 1995. *Green Imperialism: Colonial Expansion, Tropical Island Edens and the Origins of Environmentalism, 1600-1860*. Cambridge, Cambridge University Press.
Gruber C., 2014. Escaping Malthus: A comparative look at Japan and the "Great Divergence." *Journal of Global History*, 9 (3), 403-24.
Guerreau A., 1988. Mesures du blé et du pain à Mâcon (xive-xviiie siècles). *Histoire & Mesure*, 3 (2), 163-219.
Gupta S.D., Minten B., Rao N.C., Reardon T., 2017. The rapid diffusion of herbicides in farming in India: Patterns, determinants, and effects on labor productivity. *The European Journal of Development Research*, 29 (3), 596-613.
Haggblade S., Minten B., Pray C., Reardon T., Zilberman D., 2017. The herbicide revolution in developing countries: Patterns, causes, and implications. *The European Journal of Development Research*, 29 (3), 533-59.
Hamilton A., Balogh S.B., Maxwell A., Hall C.A., 2013. Efficiency of edible agriculture in Canada and the US over the past three and four decades. *Energies*, 6 (3), 1764-93.
Harris C.D., 1957. Agricultural production in the United States: The past fifty years and the next. *Geographical Review*, 47 (2), 175-93.
Harris M., 1977. *Cannibals and Kings*. New York, Random House.
Harris C.K., Macheski G.E., 1992. Social dimensions of energy use in agriculture. In: *Energy in Farm Production* (Fluck R.C., dir.). Amsterdam, Elsevier, 311-32.
Hayami H., 1988. *Japanese Agriculture under Siege*. Berlin, Springer.
Hayami Y., 1971. *An International Comparison of Agricultural Production and Productivities*. Minneapolis, University of Minnesota.
Hayami Y., 2001. Industrial Revolution versus industrious revolution. *Journal of Japanese Trade and Industry*, 20 (6), 48-52.
Hayami Y., 2003. Family farms and plantations in tropical development. *Asian Development Review*, 19 (2), 67-89.
Hayami Y., Ruttan V.W., 1985. *Agricultural Development: An International Perspective*. Baltimore, Johns Hopkins University Press.
Hayami Y., Ruttan V.W., 1998. *Agriculture et développement, une approche internationale*. Versailles, Éditions Quæ.
Hayes P., 2000. IG Farben revisited: Industry and ideology ten years later. In: *The German Chemical Industry in the Twentieth Century* (Lesch J.E., dir.). Dordrecht, Springer, 7-14.
Headey D., 2011. Was the global food crisis really a crisis? Simulations versus self-reporting. *East Asia*, 16, 18-15.
Heckscher E.F., Shapiro M., 1935. *Mercantilism*. London, George Allen & Unwin.
Heim S., 2008. *Plant Breeding and Agrarian Research in Kaiser-Wilhelm-Institutes 1933-1945: Calories, Caoutchouc, Careers*. Dordrecht, Springer Science & Business Media.
Henriksen I., 2009. The contribution of agriculture to economic growth in Denmark, 1870-1939. In: *Agriculture and Economic Development in Europe since 1870* (Lains P., Pinilla V., dir.). London, Routledge, 118-47.
Henriksen I., O'Rourke K.H., 2005. Incentives, technology and the shift to year-round dairying in late nineteenth-century Denmark. *Economic History Review*, 58 (3), 520-54.
Henshall K.G., 1999. *A History of Japan: From Stone Age to Superpower*. New York, St. Martin's Press.

Herbert V., Bisio A., 1985. *Synthetic Rubber: A Project that Had to Succeed*. Westport, Greenwood Press.
Higman B.W., 2000. The sugar revolution. *The Economic History Review*, 53 (2), 213-36.
Hilliard d'Aubertueil M.-R., 1776. *Considérations sur l'état présent de la colonie française de Saint-Domingue. Ouvrage politique et législatif présenté au Ministre de la Marine*. Paris, Grangé.
Hirano K., 2015. Thanatopolitics in the making of Japan's Hokkaido: Settler colonialism and primitive accumulation. *Critical Historical Studies*, 2 (2), 191-218.
Hirschman A.O., 1945. *National Power and the Structure of Foreign Trade*. Berkeley, University of California Press.
Hirschman A.O., 1968. The political economy of import-substituting industrialization in Latin America. *Quarterly Journal of Economics*, 82 (1), 1-32.
Hirst E., 1974. Food-related energy requirements. *Science*, 184 (4133), 134-8.
HLPE, 2011. *Price Volatility and Food Security. A Report by the High Level Panel of Experts on Food Security and Nutrition of the Commitee on World Food Security*. Rome, HLPE.
Hobsbawm E.J., 2003. *L'âge des extrêmes. Histoire du court vingtième siècle, 1914-1991*. Bruxelles, Éditions Complexe.
Hochschild A., 1998. *King Leopold's Ghost: A Story of Greed, Terror, and Heroism in Colonial Africa*. Boston, Houghton Mifflin.
Hoda A., Gulati A., 2013. *India's agricultural trade policy and sustainable developments goals*. Issue Paper No. 49. Genève, ICTSD.
Hoffmann R.C., 2000. Frontier foods for late medieval consumers: Culture, economy, ecology. *Environment and History*, 7 (2) 131-67.
Hohenberg P.M., 1967. *Chemicals in Western Europe, 1850-1914*. Chicago, Rand McNally & Company.
Holloway T.H., 1978. Creating the reserve army? The Immigration Program of Sao Paolo 1886-1930. *International Migration Review*, 12 (2), 187-209.
Holt Giménez E., Shattuck A., 2011. Food crises, food regimes and food movements: Rumbling of reform or tides of transformation. *The Journal of Peasant Studies*, 38 (1), 109-44.
Holt Stone A., 1915. The cotton factorage system of the Southern States. *The American Historical Review*, 20 (3), 557-65.
Hongler P., 2017. The construction of a Western voice: OECD and the first UNCTAD of 1964. In: *The OECD and the International Political Economy since 1948* (Leimgruber M., Schmelzer M., dir.). Dordrecht, Springer, 137-58.
Hopewell K., 2019. US-China conflict in global trade governance: The new politics of agricultural subsidies at the WTO. *Review of International Political Economy*, 26 (2), 207-31.
Hopkins R.F., Puchala D.J., 1980. *Global Food Interdependance: Challenge to American Foreign Policy*. New York, Columbia University Press.
Hornborg A., 1998. Towards an ecological theory of unequal exchange: Articulating world system theory and ecological economics. *Ecological Economics*, 25 (1), 127-36.
Hornborg A., 2006. Footprints in the cotton fields: The Industrial Revolution as time-space appropriation and environmental load displacement. *Ecological Economics*, 59 (1), 74-81.
Horowitz R., 2006. *Putting Meat on the American Table: Taste, Technology, Transformation*. Baltimore, Johns Hopkins University Press.

Horrell S., Humphries J., 1995. Women's labour force participation and the transition to the male-breadwinner family, 1790–1865. *The Economic History Review*, 48 (1), 89–117.

Howard P.H., 2015. Intellectual property and consolidation in the seed industry. *Crop Science*, 55 (6), 2489–2495.

Huang P.C.C., 2016. China's hidden agricultural revolution, 1980–2010, in historical and comparative perspective. *Modern China*, 42 (4), 339–376.

Huang J., Rozelle S., 2018. China's 40 years of agricultural development and reform. In: *China's 40 Years of Reform and Development: 1978–2018* (Garnaut R., Song L., Cai F., dir.). Canberra, ANU Press, 487–506.

Huff G., 2007. Globalization, natural resources, and foreign investment: A view from the resource-rich tropics. Oxford Economic Papers, 59 (suppl. 1), i127–i155.

Huff G., Caggiano G., 2007. Globalization, immigration, and lewisian elastic labor in pre-World War II Southeast Asia. *The Journal of Economic History*, 67 (1), 33–68.

Huff G., Caggiano G., 2008. Globalization and labor market integration in late nineteenth- and early twentieth-century Asia. *Research in Economic History*, 25, 285–347.

Hugill P.J., Bachmann V., 2005. The route to the techno-industrial world economy and the transfer of German organic chemistry to America before, during, and immediately after World War I. *Comparative Technology Transfer and Society*, 3 (2), 158–86.

Hung H.-F., 2015. *The China Boom: Why China Will not Rule the World*. New York, Columbia University Press.

Hunt S., 1973. *Growth and Guano in the Nineteenth Century Peru*. Princeton, Woodrow Wilson School/Princeton University, 123.

Huriot J.-M., 1994. *Von Thünen: économie et espace*. Paris, Economica.

Hybel N., 2002. The grain trade in northern Europe before 1350. *The Economic History Review*, 55 (2), 219–47.

Ianchovochina E., Loening J., Wood C., 2012. *How vulnerable are Arab countries to global food price shocks?* Policy Research Working Paper 6018. Washington D.C., World Bank.

Infante-Amate J., Soto D., Aguilera E., García-Ruiz R., Guzmán G., Cid A., González de Molina M., 2015. The Spanish transition to industrial metabolism: Long-term material flow analysis (1860–2010). *Journal of Industrial Ecology*, 19 (5), 866–76.

Insee, 1952. *Annuaire statistique 1951*. Paris, Imprimerie nationale.

Institut international de l'agriculture, 1914. *Production et consommation des engrais chimiques dans le monde*. Rome, IIA.

Institut international de l'agriculture, 1939. *La production et le commerce international des huiles et graisses. Iere partie*. Rome, IIA.

International Cotton Advisory Committee Cotton, 1993. *World Statistics*. Washington D.C., ICAC.

International Energy Agency, 2010. *World Energy Oultook 2010*. Paris, IEA.

International Rubber Study. *Group Rubber Statistical Bulletin*. Wembley, IRSG.

International Sugar Council, 1963. *The World Sugar Economy, Structure and Policies*. London, ISC.

Iriarte-Goñi I., Ayuda M.-I., 2012. Not only subterranean forests: Wood consumption and economic development in Britain (1850–1938). *Ecological Economics*, 77, 176–84.

Israel J.I., 1989. *Dutch Primacy in World Trade, 1585–1740*. Oxford, Oxford University Press.

Jachertz R., Nützenadel A., 2011. Coping with hunger? Visions of a global food system, 1930–1960. *Journal of Global History*, 6 (1), 99–119.

Jacks D., 2006. What drove nineteenth century commodity market integration? *Explorations in Economic History*, 43 (3), 383–412.

Janiçon F.M., 1729. *État présent de la République des Provinces Unies et des païs qui en dépendent*. La Haye, Jean van Duren.

Jensen R.T., Miller N.H., 2008. The impact of food price increases on caloric intake in China. *Agricultural Economics*, 39 (1), 465–76.

Jensen H., Robinson S., Tarp F., 2010. Measuring agricultural policy bias: General equilibrium analysis of fifteen developing countries. *American Journal of Agricultural Economics*, 92 (4), 1136–1148.

Jisheng Y., 2012. *Tombstone: The Great Chinese Famine, 1958–1962*. London, Macmillan.

Johnson D.G., 1973. *World Agriculture in Disarray*. London, Macmillan.

Johnson C., 1982. *MITI and the Japanese Miracle: The Growth of Industrial Policy: 1925–1975*. Stanford, Stanford University Press.

Johnson T., 2016. Nitrogen nation: The legacy of World War I and the politics of chemical agriculture in the United States, 1916–1933. *Agricultural History*, 90 (2), 209–29.

Jones E., 1981. *The European Miracle: Environments, Economies and Geopolitics in the History of Europe and Asia*. Cambridge, Cambridge University Press.

Jordan A.J., 2016. *The Price of Spice: Archaeological Investigations of Colonial Era Nutmeg Plantations on the Banda Islands, Maluku Province, Indonesia*. Thèse de doctorat, Seattle, University of Washington.

Jorgensen S.E., Svirezhev Y.M., 2004. *Towards a Thermodynamic Theory for Ecological Systems*. Amsterdam, Elsevier.

Kagarlitsky B., 2008. *Empire of the Periphery: Russia and the World System*. London, Pluto Press.

Kaldor M., 1999. *New and Old Wars: Organized Violence in a Global Era*. Stanford, Stanford University Press.

Kander A., Warde P., 2011. Energy availability from livestock and agricultural productivity in Europe, 1815–1913: A new comparison. *The Economic History Review*, 64 (1), 1–29.

Kander A., Malanima P., Warde P., 2014. *Power to the People: Energy in Europe over the Last Five Centuries*. Princeton, Princeton University Press.

Karl T.L., 1997. *The Paradox of Plenty: Oil Booms and Petro-States*. Berkeley, University of California Press.

Kaukiainen Y., 1993. Finland and the core: Stages of integration (ca. 1600–1850). *Review (Fernand Braudel Center)*, 16 (3), 341–55.

Kaukiainen Y., 2001. Shrinking the world: Improvement in the speed of information transmission, c. 1820–1870. *European Review of Economic History*, 5 (1), 1–28.

Kautsky K., 1900. *La question agraire: étude sur les tendances de l'agriculture moderne*. Paris, V. Giard & E. Brière.

Kawagoe T., 1999. *Agricultural land reform in postwar Japan: Experiences and issues*. World Bank Policy Research Working Paper 2111. Washington D.C., World Bank Publications.

Keck M.E., Sikkink K., 1998. *Activists beyond Borders: Advocacy Networks in International Politics*. Ithaca, Cornell University Press.

Kelly T.D., Matos G.R., 2013. *Historical statistics for mineral and material commodities in the United States. 2013 Version*. U.S. Geological Survey Data Series 140, available online at: http://minerals.usgs.gov/minerals/pubs/historical-statistics (accessed June 8, 2014).

Kenney M., Lobao L.M., Curry J., Goe W.R., 1989. Midwestern agriculture in US fordism: From the New Deal to economic restructuring. *Sociologia Ruralis*, 29 (2), 131–48.

Keohane R.O., 1984. *After Hegemony: Cooperation and Discord in the World Political Economy*. Princeton, Princeton University Press.

Keynes J.M., 1920. *The Economic Consequences of the Peace*. New York, Harcourt, Brace and Howe.

Kim C.K., Curry J., 1993. Fordism, flexible specialization and agri-industrial restructuring: The case of the US broiler industry. *Sociologia Ruralis*, 33 (1), 61–80.

Kindleberger C.P., 1973. *The World in Depression, 1929–1939*. Berkeley, University of California Press.

Kindleberger C.P., 1975. The rise of free trade in Western Europe, 1820–1875. *The Journal of Economic History*, 35 (1), 20–55.

Kindleberger C.P., 1981. Dominance leadership in international economy: Exploitation, public goods and free rides. *International Studies Quarterly*, 25 (2), 242–254.

Kingsman J., Gafner C., 2000. *Sugar Trading Manual*. London, Woodhead Publishing.

Kirby J., Nash S., Cannon J. (dir.), 2010. *Trade in Artists' Materials: Markets and Commerce in Europe to 1700*. London, Archetype Publications.

Kloppenburg J., 2005. *First the Seed: The Political Economy of Plant Biotechnology*. Madison, University of Wisconsin Press.

Kolchin P., 1998. *Une institution très particulière: l'esclavage aux États-Unis, 1619–1877*. Paris, Belin.

Kolchin P., 2009. *Unfree Labor: American Slavery and Russian Serfdom*. Cambridge, MA, Harvard University Press.

Koning N., 1994. *The Failure of Agrarian Capitalism: Agrarian Politics in the UK, Germany, the Netherlands and the USA, 1846–1919*. London, Routledge.

Krasner S.D., 1976. State power and the structure of international trade. *World Politics*, 28 (3), 317–47.

Krausmann F., 2004. Milk, manure and muscular power: Livestock and the industrialization of agriculture. *Human Ecology*, 32 (6), 735–73.

Krausmann F., Fischer-Kowalski M., 2013. Global socio-metabolic transitions. *In: Long Term Socio-Ecological Research: Studies in Society/Nature Interactions across Spatial and Temporal Scales* (Singh S.J., Haberl H., Chertow M., Mirtl M., Schmid M., dir.). Dordrecht, Springer, 339–65.

Krausmann F., Fischer-Kowalski M., 2017. Transitions socio-métaboliques globales. *In: Transformations agricoles et agroalimentaires. Entre écologie et capitalisme* (Allaire G., Daviron B., dir.). Versailles, Éditions Quæ, 23–40.

Krausmann F., Schandl H., Sieferle R.P., 2008. Socio-ecological regime transitions in Austria and the United Kingdom. *Ecological Economics*, 65 (1), 187–201.

Krausmann F., Gingrich S., Nourbakhch-Sabet R., 2011. The metabolic transition in Japan. *Journal of Industrial Ecology*, 15 (6), 877–92.

Krausmann F., Schaffartzik A., Mayer A., Eisenmenger N., Gingrich S., Haberl H., Fischer-Kowalski M., 2016a. Long-term trends in global material and energy use. *In: Social Ecology* (Haberl H., Fischer-Kowalski M., Krausmann F., Winiwarter V., dir.). Dordrecht, Springer, 199–216.

Krausmann F., Gaugl B., West J., Schandl H., 2016b. The metabolic transition of a planned economy: Material flows in the USSR and the Russian Federation 1900 to 2010. *Ecological Economics*, 124, 76–85.

Krueger A.O., 1992. *The Political Economy of Agricultural Pricing Policy: A Synthesis of the Political Economy in Developing Countries*. Baltimore, Johns Hopkins University Press.

Krueger A.O., Schiff M.W., Valdés A., 1991. *The Political Economy of Agricultural Pricing Policy: A Synthesis of the Political Economy in Developing Countries*. Washington D.C., World Bank.
Kunnas J., 2007. Potash, saltpeter and tar: Production, exports and use of wood in Finland in the 19th century. *Scandinavian Journal of History*, 32 (3), 281-311.
Laborde D., Tokgoz S., Torero M., 2013. *Long term drivers of food and nutrition security*. Foodsecure Working Paper 06. La Haye, Foodsecure.
Laborie P.J., 1798. *The Coffee Planter of Saint Domingo*. London, T. Cadell and W. Davis.
Lacoste Y., 1976. *La géographie, ça sert, d'abord, à faire la guerre*. Paris, Maspero.
Lamartine Yates P., 1959. *Forty Years of Foreign Trade: A Statistical Handbook with Special Reference to Primary Products and Under-Developed Countries*. London, George Allen & Unwin.
Landy P., 1938. Le commerce et l'industrie du soja. *Annales de géographie*, 265, 9-24.
Larsen C.S., 2006. The agricultural revolution as environmental catastrophe: Implications for health and lifestyle in the Holocene. *Quaternary International*, 150 (1), 12-20.
Lasch C., 1996. *La révolte des élites*. Castelnau-le-Lez, Éditions Climats.
Lasley F.A., 1983. The US poultry industry: Changing economics and structure. *Agricultural Economic Report*, 502. Washington D.C., USDA.
Latham A.J.H., 1988. From competition to constraint: The international rice trade in the nineteenth and twentieth centuries. *Business and Economic History*, 17, 91-102.
Latour B., 1995. *La science en action*. Paris, Gallimard.
Lavit F., 1937. La production cotonnière dans la France d'outre-mer. *In: VIIe Congrès international d'agriculture tropical et subtropicale*. Paris, Secrétariat général de l'Association scientifique internationale d'agriculture des pays chauds et de son comité français.
Law R. (dir.), 1995. *From Slave Trade to "Legitimate" Commerce: The Commercial Transition in Nineteenth-Century West Africa*. Cambridge, Cambridge University Press.
Lazarus E.D., 2014. Land grabbing as a driver of environmental change. *Area*, 46 (1), 74-82.
Le Roy Ladurie E., 1975. *Histoire de la France rurale. 2. De 1340 à 1789*. Paris, Seuil.
League of Nations, 1939. *Review of World Trade 1938*. League of Nations, Genève.
Lee T.J., 2010. *Economic Policies of Japan in the Colonial Korea and Taiwan*. Séoul, Yonsei Economic Research Institute Workshop, 18 décembre.
Leigh G.J., 2004. *The World's Greatest Fix: A History of Nitrogen and Agriculture*. Oxford/New York, Oxford University Press.
Leimgruber M., Schmelzer M., 2017. From the Marshall Plan to global governance: Historical transformations of the OEEC/OECD, 1948 to present. *In: The OECD and the International Political Economy since 1948* (Leimgruber M., Schmelzer M., dir.). Dordrecht, Springer, 23-61.
Leslie E., 2005. *Synthetic Worlds: Nature, Art and the Chemical Industry*. London, Reaktion Books.
Levasseur É., 1911. *Histoire du commerce de la France*. Paris, Arthur Rousseau.
Lewis W.A., 1978. *Growth and Fluctuations, 1870-1913*. London, George Allen & Unwin.
Liebig J., 1844. *Chimie appliquée à la physiologie végétale et à l'agriculture*. Paris, Librairie de Fortin, Masson et Cie.
Liebig J., 1840. *Organic Chemistry in its Application to Agriculture and Physiology*. London, Taylor & Walton.
Liebig J., 1862. *Lettres sur l'agriculture moderne*. Bruxelles, Émile Tarlier éditeur.

Lindert P.H., Williamson J.G., 2001. *Does globalization make the world more unequal?* NBER Working Paper No. 8228. Cambridge, National Bureau of Economic Research.

Lindqvist S., 1999. *Exterminez toutes ces brutes: l'odyssée d'un homme au cœur de la nuit et les origines du génocide européen*. Paris, Le serpent à plumes.

Lindqvist S., 2007. *Terra Nullius: A Journey through No One's Land*. London, Granta Books.

Lipsey R.E., 1963. *Price and Quantity Trends in the Foreign Trade of the United States*. Princeton, Princeton University Press, coll. Studies in International Economic Relations.

Littell J., 2006. *Les Bienveillantes*. Paris, Gallimard.

Liu J.-C., 1965. Fertilizer supply and grain production in communist China. *American Journal of Agricultural Economy*, 47 (4), 915–32.

Llano G.A., 1948. Economic uses of lichens. *Economic Botany*, 2 (1), 15–45.

Lloyd C., Metzer J., 2013. Settler colonization and societies in world history: Patterns and concepts. In: *Settler Economies in World History* (Lloyd C., Metzer J., Sutch R., dir.). Leiden, Brill, 1–35.

Loth V.C., 1995. Pioneers and perkeniers: The Banda Islands in the 18th century. *Cakalele*, 6, 13–35.

Lu S.X., 2016. Colonizing Hokkaido and the origin of Japanese trans-Pacific expansion, 1869–1894. *Japanese Studies*, 36 (2), 251–74.

Lu K., Yu B., 2011. The impact of high food prices on poverty in China. *Development in Practice*, 21 (4–5), 676–90.

Lucassen J., 2004. A multinational and its labor force: The Dutch East India Company, 1595–1795. *International Labor and Working-Class History*, 66, 12–39.

Lustig R.H., 2013. *Fat Chance: Beating the Odds Against Sugar, Processed Food, Obesity, and Disease*. New York, Penguin Group.

MacDonald J.M., 2018. Mergers and competition in seed and agricultural chemical markets. *Amber Waves*, available online at: https://www.ers.usda.gov/amber-waves/2017/april/mergers-and-competition-in-seed-and-agricultural-chemical-markets/ (accessed September 19, 2024).

MacMillan M., 2013. *The War that Ended Peace: The Road to 1914*. Toronto, Penguin Canada.

Maddison A., 2001. *The World Economy: A Millennial Perspective*. Paris, OECD.

Maddison A., 2007. *Chinese Economic Performance in the Long Run*. Paris, OECD.

Madley B., 2004. Patterns of frontier genocide 1803–1910: The Aboriginal Tasmanians, the Yuki of California, and the Herero of Namibia. *Journal of Genocide Research*, 6 (2), 167–92.

Maier C.S., 1987. *In Search of Stability: Explorations in Historical Political Economy*. Cambridge, Cambridge University Press.

Maier C.S., 2009. *Among Empires*. Cambridge, MA, Harvard University Press.

Malassis L., 1997. *Les trois âges de l'alimentaire*. Paris, Cujas.

Malowist M., 1959. The economic and social development of the Baltic countries from the fifteenth to the seventeenth centuries. *The Economic History Review*, 12 (2), 177–89.

Malowist M., 2010. Commercial capitalism and agriculture. In: *Western Europe, Eastern Europa and World Development, 13th–18th Centuries: Collection of Essays of Marian Malowist* (Batou J., Szlajfer H., dir.). Leiden, Brill, 15–73.

Malthus T.R., 1798. *An Essay on the Principle of Population*. London, J. Johnson.

Mann M., 1988. *States, War, and Capitalism: Studies in Political Sociology*. Oxford/New York, Blackwell Publishers.

Mantero F., 1910. *A mao d'obra em S. Thome e Principe*. Lisbonne, Typ. do annuario commercial.
Marks R., 1998. *Tigers, Rice, Silk, and Silt: Environment and Economy in Late Imperial South China*. Cambridge, Cambridge University Press.
Marloie M., 1984. *L'internationalisation de l'agriculture française*. Paris, Éditions de l'Atelier.
Marseille J., 1984. *Empire colonial et capitalisme français: histoire d'un divorce*. Paris, Albin Michel.
Martinelli L., Nikel P.I., 2019. Breaking the state-of-the-art in the chemical industry with new-to-nature products via synthetic microbiology. *Microbial Biotechnology*, 12 (2), 187-90.
Martinez S.W., 1999. *Vertical Coordination in the Pork and Broiler Industries: Implications for Pork and Chicken Products*. Washington D.C., United States Department of Agriculture, Economic Research Service.
Masselman G., 1961. Dutch colonial policy in the seventeenth century. *The Journal of Economic History*, 21 (4), 455-68.
Mauro F., 1979. Le Brésil de 1919 a 1945. *Europe*, 599, 6.
Mazoyer M., Roudart L., 1998. *Histoire des agricultures du monde. Du néolithique à la crise contemporaine*. Paris, Seuil.
Mazoyer M., Roudart L., 2002. Mondialisation, crise et conditions de développement durable des agricultures paysannes. *In: Une alternative paysanne à la mondialisation néolibérale* (Vía Campesina, dir.). Genève, Cetim, 7-41.
McCalla A.F., 1966. A duopoly model of world wheat pricing. *Journal of Farm Economics*, 48 (3), 711-27.
McCusker J.J., Menard R.R., 1985. *The Economy of British America, 1607-1789*. Chapel Hill, The University of North Carolina Press.
McKeown A., 2004. Global migration, 1846-1940. *Journal of World History*, 15 (2), 155-89.
McKinnon Wood H., 1918. Methods of food control in war-time. *Journal of Comparatvie Legislation and International Law*, 18 (1), 100-10.
McMichael P., 1996. *Development and Social Change: A Global Perspective*. Thousand Oaks, Pine Forge Press.
McMichael P., 2005. Global development and the corporate food regime. *In: New Directions in the Sociology of Global Development: Research in Rural Sociology and Development*. Volume 11 (Buttel F.H., McMichael P., dir.). Amsterdam, Elsevier, 265-99.
McMichael P., 2009. A food regime analysis of the "world food crisis." *Agriculture and Human Values*, 26 (4), 281-95.
McMichael P., 2013. A food regime genealogy. *Critical Perspectives in Rural Development Studies*. London, Routledge, 129-58.
McMichael P., 2016. Commentary: Food regime for thought. *The Journal of Peasant Studies*, 43 (3), 648-70.
McNally C.A., 2012. Sino-capitalism: China's reemergence and the international political economy. *World Politics*, 64 (4), 741-76.
McNeill W.H., 1982. *The Pursuit of Power: Technology, Armed Force, and Society since A.D. 1000*. Chicago, University of Chicago Press.
McNeill W.H., 1989. *Plagues and Peoples*. New York, Anchor Books.
McNeill W.H., 1992. *The Global Condition: Conquerors, Catastrophes and Community*. Princeton, Princeton University Press.

McNeill J.R., 2000. *Something New under the Sun: An Environmental History of the Twentieth Century*. London, Allen Lane.

McNeill J.R., 2010. *Mosquito Empires: Ecology and War in the Greater Caribbean, 1620-1914*. New York, Cambridge University Press.

Mehring A.L., Richard Adams J., Jacob K.D., 1957. *Statistics on Ferilizers and Liming Materials in the United States*. Washington D.C., USDA, Statistical Bulletin.

Melillo E.D., 2012. The first Green Revolution: Debt peonage and the making of the nitrogen fertilizer trade, 1840-1930. *American Historical Review*, 117 (4), 1028-60.

Melillo E.D., 2013. Global entomologies: Insects, empires, and the "synthetic age" in world history. *Past & Present*, 223 (1), 233-70.

Merivale H., 1861. *Lectures on Colonization and Colonies*. London, Longman, Green, Longman, and Roberts.

Meuriot V., Temple L., Madi A., 2011. Faible transmission des prix internationaux aux marchés domestiques: le poids des habitudes alimentaires au Cameroun. *Économie appliquée*, 64 (3), 59-84.

Meyer-Thurow G., 1982. The industrialization of invention: A case study from the German chemical industry. *Isis*, 73 (3), 363-81.

Middleton T.H., 1916. *The Recent Development of German Agriculture*. London, Board of Agriculture and Fisherires.

Miers S., 1975. *Britain and the Ending of the Slave Trade*. London, Longman Group.

Miers S., Roberts R.L., 1988. *The End of Slavery in Africa*. Madison, The University of Wisconsin Press.

Ministre des Travaux Publics D.L.a.E.D.C., 1838. *Statistique de la France. Volume 7: Commerce extérieur*. Paris, Imprimerie royale.

Minot N., 2012. Food price volatility in sub-Saharan Africa: Has it really increased? *In: International Association of Agricultural Economists (IIAE) 2012 Triennial Conference*. Foz de Iguaçu (Brésil), IIAE, 18-24 août.

Mintz S.W., 1986. *Sweetness and Power: The Place of Sugar in Modern History*. London, Penguin Books.

Mitchell B.R., 1962. *Abstract of British Historical Statistics (Cambridge, 1962)*. Cambridge, Cambridge University Press.

Mitchell B.R., 1975. *European Historical Statistics 1750-1970*. London, The Macmillan Press.

Mitchell B.R., 1992. *International Historical Statistics Europe 1750-1988*. Dordrecht, Springer.

Mitchell T., 2013. *Carbon Democracy. Le pouvoir politique à l'ère du pétrole*. Paris, La Découverte.

Mixed Commitee of the League of Nations on the relation of nutrition to health, agriculture and economic policy, 1937. *Final Report*. Genève, League of Nations.

Mollard É., Walter A., 2008. *Agricultures singulières*. Bondy, IRD éditions.

Moon D., 2005. The environmental history of the Russian steppes: Vasili Dokuchaev and the harvest failure of 1891. *Transactions of the Royal Historical Society*, 15, 149-74.

Moore J.W., 2000. Sugar and the expansion of the early modern World-economy: Commodity frontiers, ecological transformation, and industrialization. *Review (Fernand Braudel Center)*, 23 (3), 409-33.

Moore J.W., 2010. "Amsterdam is standing on Norway." Part I: The alchemy of capital, empire and nature in the diaspora of silver, 1545-1648. *Journal of Agrarian Change*, 10 (1), 33-68.

Moore J.W., 2011. Transcending the metabolic rift: A theory of crises in the capitalist world-ecology. *The Journal of Peasant Studies*, 38 (1), 1-46.
Moreno Fraginals M., 1978. *El ingenio. Complejo económico social cubano del azúcar*. La Havane, Editorial de ciencias sociales.
Moriceau J.-M., 1994. Au rendez-vous de la "Révolution agricole" dans la France du xviiie siècle. À propos des régions de grande culture. *Annales. Histoire, sciences sociales*, 49 (1), 27-63.
Morineau M., 1968. Y a-t-il eu une révolution agricole en France au xviiie siècle? *Revue historique*, 239 (2), 299-326.
Morris P., Travis A.S., 1992. A history of the international dyestuff industry. *American Dyestuff Reporter*, 81, 59-59.
Muldrew C., 2011. *Food, Energy and the Creation of Industriousness: Work and Material Culture in Agrarian England, 1550-1780*. Cambridge, Cambridge University Press.
Muller P., 1984. *Le technocrate et le paysan*. Paris, Les éditions ouvrières.
Multatuli, 1860. *Max Havelaar, of De koffie-veilingen der Nederlandsche handelsmaatschappij*. Amsterdam, De Ruyter.
Mumford L., 2011. *La cité à travers l'histoire*. Marseille, Agone.
Mumford L., 2016. *Technique et civilisation*. Marseille, Éditions parenthèses.
Mummert A., Esche E., Robinson J., Armelagos G.J., 2011. Stature and robusticity during the agricultural transition: Evidence from the bioarchaeological record. *Economics & Human Biology*, 9 (3), 284-301.
Myers R.H., Peattie M.R., 1984. *The Japanese Colonial Empire, 1895-1945*. Princeton, Princeton University Press.
Myint H., 1966. *Les politiques de développement*. Paris, Éditions ouvrières.
Myrdal G., 1960. *Beyond the Welfare State: Economic Planning and its International Implications*. New Haven, Yale University Press.
Navarro I.B., 2000. *Los brazos necesarios: inmigración, colonización y trabajo libre en Cuba, 1878-1898*. Valence, Centro Francisco Tomás y Valiente UNED Alzira-Valencia.
Nef J.U., 1932. *The Rise of the British Coal Industry*. London, Routledge.
Netting R.M., 1993. *Smallholders, Householders: Farm Families and the Ecology of Intensive, Sustainable Agriculture*. Stanford, Stanford University Press.
Nicourt C., 2013. *Être agriculteur aujourd'hui: l'individualisation du travail des agriculteurs*. Versailles, Éditions Quæ.
Nieto-Galan A., 2001. *Colouring Textiles: A History of Natural Dyestuffs in Industrial Europe*. Dordrecht, Springer Science & Business Media.
North D., 1958. Ocean freight rates and economic development. *The Journal of Economic History*, 18 (4), 537-55.
Northrup D., 1995. *Indentured Labor in the Age of Imperialism, 1834-1922*. Cambridge, Cambridge University Press.
Nugent W., 1989. Frontiers and empires in the late nineteenth century. *The Western Historical Quarterly*, 20 (4), 393-408.
O'Brien P., 1982. European economic development: The contribution of the periphery. *The Economic History Review*, 35 (1), 1-18.
O'Brien P., Griffiths T., Hunt P., 1991. Political components of the industrial revolution: Parliament and the English cotton textile industry, 1660-1774. *The Economic History Review*, 44 (3), 395-423.
O'Connor P.A., Cleveland C.J., 2014. US energy transitions 1780-2010. *Energies*, 7 (12), 7955-93.

O'Rourke K.H., 1997. The European grain invasion, 1870–1913. *The Journal of Economic History*, 57 (4), 775–801.
O'Rourke K.H., de la Escosura L.P., Daudin G., 2010. Trade and empire. In: *The Cambridge Economic History of Modern Europe. Volume 1: 1700–1870* (Broadberry S., O'Rourke K.H., dir.). Cambridge, Cambridge University Press, 96–121.
O'Rourke K.H., Williamson J.G., 1999. *Globalization and History: The Evolution of a Nineteenth-Century Atlantic Economy*. Cambridge, MA, MIT Press.
OECD, 2006. La bioéconomie en 2030: définition d'un programme d'action. Document exploratoire. Paris, OECD.
OECD, 2008. *Biofuel Support Policies: An economic assesement*. Paris, OECD Publishing.
OECD, 2017. *Agricultural Policy Monitoring and Evaluation 2017*. Paris, OECD Publishing.
Offer A., 1989. *The First World War: An Agrarian Interpretation*. Oxford, Clarendon Press.
Olmstead A., Rhode P., 2000. The transformation of Northern agriculture, 1910–1990. In: *The Cambridge Economic History of the United States* (Engerman S.L., Gallman R.E., dir.). Cambridge, Cambridge University Press, 693–742.
Olmstead A.L., Rhode P.W., 2001. Reshaping the landscape: The impact and diffusion of the tractor in American agriculture, 1910–1960. *The Journal of Economic History*, 61 (3), 663–698.
Ormrod D., 2003. *The Rise of Commercial Empires: England and the Netherlands in the Age of Mercantilism, 1650–1770*. Cambridge/New York, Cambridge University Press.
Orsenigo L., 1989. *The Emergence of Biotechnology: Institutions and Markets in Industrial Innovation*. London, Pinter Publishers.
Osterhammel J., 2014. *The Transformation of the World: A Global History of the Nineteenth Century*. Princeton, Princeton University Press.
Overton M., 1996. *Agricutural Revolution in England: The Transformation of the Agrarian Economy, 1500–1850*. Cambridge, Cambridge University Press.
Overton M., Campbell B., 1996. Production et productivité dans l'agriculture anglaises, 1086–1871. *Histoire & Mesure*, 11, 255–97.
Owen N.G., 1971. The rice industry of mainland SouthEast Asia 1850–1914. *Journal of the Siam Society*, 59, 75–143.
Özveren Y.E., 2000. Shipbuilding, 1590–1790. *Review (Fernand Braudel Center)*, 15–86.
Paarlberg D., 1954. Production and consumption of food: Toward a better balance. In: *Increasing Understanding of Public Problem and Policies*. Chicago, Farm Foundation, 46–51.
Pares R., 1970. *Merchants and Planters*. Cambridge, Cambridge University Press.
Passet R., 1979. *L'économique et le vivant*. Paris, Payot.
Passet R., 2012. La bioéconomie, un monde à réinventer. *Écologie & politique*, 45, 83–91.
Pattberg P.H., 2005. The forest stewardship council: Risk and potential of private forest governance. *The Journal of Environment & Development*, 14 (3), 356–74.
Peattie M.R., 1988. The Japanese colonial empire, 1895–1945. In: *The Cambridge History of Japan. Volume 6: The Twentieth Century* (Duus P., dir.). Cambridge, Cambridge University Press, 215–70.
Pechlaner G., Otero G., 2008. The third food regime: Neoliberal globalism and agricultural biotechnology in North America. *Sociologia Ruralis*, 48 (4), 351–371.
Peet R., 1969. The spatial expansion of commercial agriculture in the nineteenth century: A Von Thunen interpretation. *Economic Geography*, 45 (4), 283–301.

Peet R., 1972. Influences of the British market on agriculture and related economic development in Europe before 1860. *Transactions of the Institute of British Geographers*, 56, 1–20.

Perkins D.H., 1969. *Agricultural Development in China, 1368–1968*. Chicago, Aldine Publishing House.

Perkins J.A., 1981. The agricultural revolution in Germany, 1850–1914. *Journal of European Economic History*, 10 (1), 71–118.

Perkins J.H., 1982. *Insects, Experts, and the Insecticide Crisis: The Quest for New Pest Management Strategies*. New York, Plenum Press.

Perkins J., 1990. Nazi autarchic aspirations and the beet-sugar industry, 1933–9. *European History Quarterly*, 20 (4), 497–518.

Perren R., 1978. *The Meat Trade in Britain, 1840–1914*. London/Boston, Routledge/Kegan Paul.

Peyrefitte A., 1973. *Quand la Chine s'éveillera ... Le monde tremblera*. Paris, Fayard.

Pickering A., 2005. Decentering sociology: Synthetic dyes and social theory. *Perspective on Science*, 13 (3), 352–405.

Pigman G.A., 1997. Hegemony and trade liberalization policy: Britain and the Brussels Sugar Convention of 1902. *Review of International Studies*, 23 (2), 185–210.

Piketty T., 2003. Income inequality in France, 1901–1998. *Journal of Political Economy*, 111 (5), 1004–42.

Piketty T., Saez E., *National Bureau of Economic Research, 2001. Income inequality in the United States, 1913–1998*. NBER Working Paper No. 8467. Cambridge, National Bureau of Economic Research.

Pinilla V., Willebald H., 2018. *Agricultural Development in the World Periphery: A Global Economic History Approach*. Dordrecht, Springer.

Poitrineau A., 1965. *La vie rurale en Basse-Auvergne au XVIIIe siècle (1726–1789)*. Paris, Presse Universitaire de France.

Polanyi K., 1983 [1944]. *La grande transformation: aux origines politiques et économiques de notre temps*. Paris, Gallimard.

Pollard S., 1980. A new estimate of British coal production, 1750–1850. *The Economic History Review*, 33 (2), 212–34.

Pomeranz K., 2000. *The Great Divergence: China, Europe and the Making of the Modern World Economy*. Princeton, Princeton University Press.

Pomeranz K., 2012. Contemporary development and economic history: How do we know what matters? *Economic History of Developing Regions*, 27 (sup. 1), S136–48.

Pomeranz K., 2017. Water, energy, and politics: Chinese industrial revolutions in global environmental perspective. In: *Economic Development and Environmental History in the Anthropocene: Perspectives on Asia and Africa* (Austin G., dir.). London/New York, Bloomsbury Academic, 271–90.

Pope P., 2008. Transformation of the maritime cultural landscape of Atlantic Canada by migratory European fishermen, 1500–1800. In: *Beyond the Catch: Fisheries of the North Atlantic, the North Sea and the Baltic, 900–1850* (Sicking L., Abreu-Ferreira D., dir.). Leiden, Brill, 123–54.

Popkin B.M., 2015. Nutrition transition and the global diabetes epidemic. *Current Diabetes Reports*, 15 (9), 64.

Popkin B.M., Adair L.A., Ng S.W., 2012. Now and then. The global nutrition transition: The pandemic of obesity in developing countries. *Nutritions Reviews*, 70 (1), 3–21.

Poussou J.-P., 1999. *La terre et les paysans en France et en Grande-Bretagne aux xviie et xviiie siècles*. Paris, Éditions Cned-Sedes.

Prebisch R., 1949. El desarrollo economico de la American Latina y algunos de sus principales problemas. *In: Estudio Economico de la America Latina 1948* (Cepal, dir.). Santiago, Cepal.

Prebisch R., 1964. *Nueva política comercial para el desarrollo*. Mexico, Fondo de cultura económica.

Prigogine I., Stengers I., 1979. *La nouvelle alliance: métamorphose de la science*. Paris, Gallimard.

Princen T., 1997. The shading and distancing of commerce: When internalization is not enough. *Ecological Economics*, 20 (3), 235-53.

Prinsen-Geerligs H.C., 1912. *The World's Cane Sugar Industry: Past and Present*. Altrincham, Norman Rodger.

Pritchard W.N., 1998. The emerging contours of the third food regime: Evidence from Australian dairy and wheat sectors. *Economic Geography*, 74 (1), 64-74.

Prodöhl I., 2013. Versatile and cheap: A global history of soy in the first half of the twentieth century. *Journal of Global History*, 8 (3), 461-82.

Rahman S.U., Shurong Z., 2017. Analysis of Chinese economic and national security interests in China Pakistan Economic Corridor (CPEC) under the framework of One Belt One Road (OBOR) Initiative. *Arts Social Sciences Journal*, 8 (4), 1-7.

Rahnema M., Bawtree V. (dir.), 1997. *The Post-Development Reader*. London, Zed Books.

Raschka A., Carus M., 2012. *Industrial Material Use of Biomass Basic Data for Germany, Europe and the World*. Hürth, Nova-Institut.

Rasmussen W.D., 1962. The impact of technological change on American agriculture, 1862-1962. *The Journal of Economic History*, 22 (4), 578-91.

Rasmussen M.B., Lund C., 2018. Reconfiguring frontier spaces: Territorialization and resource control. *World Development*, 101, 388-99.

Rastoin J.-L., Ghersi G., 2010. *Le système alimentaire mondial: concepts et méthodes, analyses et dynamiques*. Versailles, Éditions Quæ.

Razac O., 2000. *Histoire politique du barbelé: la prairie, la tranchée, le camp*. Paris, La fabrique éditions.

Rees G.L., 1972. *Britain's Commodity Markets*. London, Elek.

Reimund, D.A. Martin J.R., Moore C.V., 1981. *Structural change in agriculture: The experience for broilers, fed cattle, and processing vegetables*. Technical Bulletins 157701, Washington D.C., United States Department of Agriculture, Economics and Statistics Service.

Richards J.F., 1990. Land transformation. *In: The Earth as Transformed by Human Action: Global and Regional Changes in the Biosphere over the Past 300 Years* (Turner B.L., Clark W.C., Kates R.W., Richards J.F., Mathews J.T., Meyer W.B., dir.). Cambridge, Cambridge University Press, 163-178.

Richards J.F., 2002. Toward a global system of property rights in land. *In: The Environment and World History* (Burke III E., Pomeranz K., dir.). Berkeley, University of California Press, 54-78.

Richards J.F., 2003. *The Unending Frontier: An Environmental History of the Early Modern World*. Berkeley, University of California Press.

Richardson B., 2009. *Sugar: Refined Power in a Global Regime*. London, Palgrave Macmillan.

Riello G., 2009. The making of a global commodity: Indian cottons and European trade, 1450-1850. *In: First Congress of the Asian Association of World Historians*, 28-31 May, Osaka, AAWH.

Riello G., 2013. *Cotton: The Fabric that Made the Modern World*. Cambridge, Cambridge University Press.

Rist G., 1996. *Le développement: histoire d'une croyance occidentale*. Paris, Les presses de Science Po.

Roberts R.L., Miers S., 1988. The end of slavery in Africa. In: *The End of Slavery in Africa* (Miers S., Roberts R.L., dir.). Madison, The University of Wisconsin Press, 3–68.

Ronto R., Wu J.H., Singh G.M., 2018. The global nutrition transition: Trends, disease burdens and policy interventions. *Public Health Nutrition*, 21 (12), 2267–70.

Rosenstein-Rodan P.N., 1944. The international development of economically backward areas. *International Affairs*, 20 (2), 157–65.

Rothstein M., 1983. The rejection and acceptance of a market innovation: Hedging in the late 19th century. *Review of Research in Futures Markets*, 2 (2), 201–14.

Rubner M., 1913. *Wandlungen in der Volksernährung*. Leipzig, Akad. Verlagsgesellsch.

Rudel T.K., Hernandez M., 2017. Land tenure transitions in the global south: Trends, drivers, and policy implications. *Annual Review of Environment and Resources*, 42, 489–507.

Ruf F., 1995. From forest rent to tree-capital: Basics "law" of cocoa supply. In: *Cocoa Cycle: The Economics of Cocoa Supply* (Ruf F., Siswoputranto P.S., dir.). Oxford, Woodhead Publishing Limited, 1–53.

Ruggie J.G., 1982. International trade, transactions, and change: Embedded liberalism in the postwar economic order. *International Organization*, 36 (2), 379–415.

Ruggie J.G., 1998. *Constructing the World Polity: Essays on International Institutionalization*. London, Routledge.

Russell E., 2001. *War and Nature: Fighting Humans and Insects with Chemicals from World War I to Silent Spring*. Cambridge, Cambridge University Press.

Ruttan V.W., 1977. Induced innovation and agricultural development. *Food Policy*, 2 (3), 196–216.

Ruttan V.W., 1978. Structural retardation and the modernization of French agriculture: A skeptical view. *The Journal of Economic History*, 38 (3), 714–28.

Saez E., Zucman G., 2019. *The Triumph of Injustice: How the Rich Dodge Taxes and How to Make them Pay*. New York, W. W. Norton & Company.

Sahlins M.D., 1976. *Âge de pierre, âge d'abondance: l'économie des sociétés primitives*. Paris, Gallimard.

Sapir J., 1990. *L'économie mobilisée: essai sur les économies de type soviétique*. Paris, La Découverte.

Sarraut A., 1923. *La mise en valeur des colonies françaises*. Paris, Payot.

Sato K., 1991. Japan's resource imports. *The Annals of the American Academy of Political and Social Science*, 513, 76–89.

Satre L.J., 2005. *Chocolate on Trial: Slavery, Politics, and the Ethics of Business*. Athens, Ohio University Press.

Saul S.B., 1960. *Studies in British Overseas Trade, 1870–1914*. Liverpool, Liverpool University Press.

Scarborough W.K., 1966. *The Overseer: Plantation Management in the Old South*. Baton Rouge, Louisianna State University Press.

Schaffartzik A., Mayer A., Gingrich S., Eisenmenger N., Loy C., Krausmann F., 2014. The global metabolic transition: Regional patterns and trends of global material flows, 1950–2010. *Global Environmental Change*, 26, 87–97.

Scherner J., 2008. The beginnings of Nazi autarky policy: The "National Pulp Programme" and the origin of regional staple fibre plants. *The Economic History Review*, 61 (4), 867–95.
Schlote W., 1976. *British Overseas Trade from 1700 to the 1930s*. Westport, Greenwood Press.
Schneider M., McMichael P., 2010. Deepening, and repairing, the metabolic rift. *The Journal of Peasant Studies*, 37 (3), 461–84.
Schumpeter E.B., 1961. *English Overseas Trade Statistics, 1697–1808*. Oxford, Clarendon Press.
Schurr S.H., Netschert B.C., Eliasberg V., Lerner J., Landsberg H., 1960. *Energy in the American Economy, 1850–1975*. Baltimore, Johns Hopkins University Press.
Scott J.C., 2017. *Against the Grain: A Deep History of the Earliest States*. New Haven, Yale University Press.
SDN, 1938. *Étude de l'économie mondiale*. Genève, SDN.
Servolin C., 1985. Les politiques agricoles. In: *Traité de science politique*. Volume 4 (Grawitz M., Leca J., dir.). Paris, Presses universitaires de France, 155–260.
Shanahan E.W., 1920. *Animal Foodstuffs: Their Production and Consumption, with a Special Reference to the British Empire. A Study in Economic Geography and Agricultural Economics*. London, Routledge.
Sharron A.O., 1957. *An Analysis of Japan's External Disequilibrium Ten Years after the End of World War II*. PhD thesis, American University, Washington D.C.
Shaw N., 1911. *The Soya Bean of Manchuria*. Shanghai, Statistical Department of the Inspectorate General of Customs.
Shaw M., 1988. *Dialectics of War: An Essay in the Social Theory of Total War and Peace*. London, Pluto.
Sheingate A.D., 2001. *The Rise of the Agricultural Welfare State: Institutions and Interest Group Power in the United States, France and Japan*. Princeton, Princeton University Press.
Shiel R.S., 1991. Improving soil productivity in the pre-fertiliser era. In: *Land, Labour and Livestock: Historical Studies in European Agricultural Productivity* (Campbell B.M.S., Overton M., dir.). Manchester, Manchester University Press, 51–77.
Shiel R.S., 2006. Nutrient flows in pre-modern agriculture in Europe. In: *Soils and Societies: Perspectives from Environmental History* (McNeill J.R., Winiwarter V., dir.). Cambridge, The White Horse Press, 216–242.
Sieferle R.P., 2001. *The Subterranean Forest: Energy Systems and the Industrial Revolution*. Cambridge, The White Horse Press.
Siguret R., 1968. Esclaves d'indigoteries et de caféières au quartier de Jacmel (1757–1791). *Revue française d'histoire d'outre-mer*, 199, 190–230.
Sizov A.E., 1991. Soviet food imports: The growing necessity for change. *Food Policy*, 16 (4), 291–98.
Skene Keith G., 1802. A general view of the corn trade and Corn Laws of Great Britain. *The Farmer's Magazine*, 3 (11), 277–96.
Slatta R.W., 1992. *Gauchos and the Vanishing Frontier*. Lincoln/London, University of Nebraska Press.
Slicher van Bath N.H., 1963. *The Agrarian History of Western Europe, A.D. 500–1850*. New York, St Martin's Press.
Smil V., 2001. *Enriching the Earth: Fritz Haber, Carl Bosch, and the Transformation of World Food Production*. Cambridge/London, MIT Press.

Smil V., 2004. *China's Past, China's Future: Energy, Food, Environment.* New York/London, Routledge.
Smil V., 2010. *Prime Movers of Globalization: The History and Impact of Diesel Engines and Gas Turbines.* Cambridge, The MIT Press.
Smith A., 1776. *The Wealth of Nations.* New York, The Modern Library.
Solow B.L., 1987. Capitalism and slavery in the exceedingly long run. *The Journal of Interdisciplinary History*, 17 (4), 711–37.
Spector C., 2003. Le concept de mercantilisme. *Revue de métaphysique et morale*, 39, 289–309.
Spencer V.E., 1980. *Raw Materials in the United States Economy: 1900–1977.* Washington D.C., United States Department of Commerce, Bureau of the Census.
Stanhill G. (dir.), 1984a. *Energy and Agriculture.* Dordrecht, Springer.
Stanhill G., 1984b. Agricultural labour: From energy source to sink. In: *Energy and Agriculture* (Stanhill G., dir.). Dordrecht, Springer, 113–30.
Stanziani A., 2013. Introduction. In: *Labour, Coercion, and Economic Growth in Eurasia, 17th–20th Centuries* (Stanziani A., dir.). Leiden, Brill, 1–26.
Starling E.H., 1920. The food supply of Germany during the war. *Journal of the Royal Statistical Society*, 83 (2), 225–54.
Steen K., 2000. German chemicals and American politics, 1919–1922. In: *The German Chemical Industry in the Twentieth Century* (Lesch J.E., dir.). Dordrecht, Springer, 323–46.
Steinhart J.S., Steinhart C.E., 1974. Energy use in the US food system. *Science*, 184 (4134), 307–16.
Stokes R.G., 1994. *Opting for Oil: The Political Economy of Technological Change in the West German Chemical Industry, 1945–1961.* Cambridge/New York, Cambridge University Press.
Stone B., 1988. Developments in agricultural technology. *The China Quarterly*, 116, 767–822.
Strauss F., 1941. The food problem in the German war economy. *The Quarterly Journal of Economics*, 55 (3), 364–412.
Subash S., Chand P., Pavithra S., Balaji S., Pal S., 2017. *Pesticide Use in Indian Agriculture: Trends, Market Structure and Policy Issues.* New Delhi, ICAR Policy Brief, n° 43.
Sugihara K., 2003. East Asian economic development. In: *The Resurgence of East Asia: 500, 150 and 50 Year Perspectives* (Arrighi G., Tamashita T., Selden M., dir.). New York, Routledge, 78–123.
Sugihara K., 2013. Labour-intensive industrialization in global history: An interpretation of East Asia experience. In: *Labour-Intensive Industrialization in Global History* (Austin G., Sugihara K., dir.). London, Routledge, 20–64.
Sussman C., 2000. *Consuming Anxieties: Consumer Protest, Gender, and British Slavery, 1713–1833.* Stanford, Stanford University Press.
Sutch R.C., 2008. Henry Agard Wallace, the Iowa corn yield tests, and the adoption of hybrid corn. *NBER Working Paper No. 14141.* Cambridge, National Bureau of Economic Research.
Takigawa T., 1972. Historical background of agricultural land reform in Japan. *The Developing Economies*, 10 (3), 290–310.
Tarrade J., 1972. *Le commerce colonial de la France à la fin de l'Ancien Régime: l'évolution du régime de "l'Exclusif" de 1763 à 1789.* Paris, Presses universitaires de France.
Taylor A.E., 1932. *Corn and Hog Surplus of the Corn Belt.* Stanford, Food Research Institute.

Taylor F.S., 1957. *A History of Industrial Chemistry*. London, Heinemann.
Taylor A.M., 1992. External dependence, demographic burdens, and Argentine economic decline after the Belle Epoque. *The Journal of Economic History*, 52 (4), 907-36.
Teives Henriques, S. Sharp P., 2014. The Danish Agricultural Revolution in an energy perspective: A case of development with few domestic energy sources. *Discussion Papers on Business and Economics No. 9/2014*. Odense, University of Southern Denmark.
Tena-Junguito A., Willebald H., 2013. On the accuracy of export growth in Argentina, 1870-1913. *Economic History of Developing Regions*, 28 (1), 28-68.
Thomas B., 1982. Feeding England during the Industrial Revolution: A view from the Celtic fringe. *Agricultural History*, 56 (1), 328-42.
Thomas B., 1985. Food supply in the United Kingdom during the industrial revolution. In: *The Economics of the Industrial Revolution* (Mokyr J., dir.). London, George Allen & Unwin, 137-50.
Thompson F.M.L., 1968. The second agricultural revolution, 1815-1880. *The Economic History Review*, 21 (1), 62-77.
Thomsen F.L., 1951. *Agricultural Marketing*. New York, McGraw Hill.
Thornton R., 1987. *American Indian Holocaust and Survival: A Population History since 1492*. Norman, University of Oklahoma Press.
Tilly C., 1985. War making and State making as organized crime. In: *Bringing the State Back* (Evans P., Rueschemeyer D., Skocpol T., dir.). Cambridge, Cambridge University Press, 1985, 169-91.
Tilly C., 1998. *Work under Capitalism*. Boulder, Westview Press.
Timmer C.P., 1988. The agricultural transformation. In: *The Handbook of Development Economics* (Chenery H.B., Srinivasan T.N., dir.). Amsterdam, Elsevier, 275-332.
Timmer C.P., 2009. *A World without Agriculture: The Structural Transformation in Historical Perspective*. Washington D.C., AEI Press.
Tinker H., 1993. *A New System of Slavery: The Export of Indian Labour Overseas, 1830-1920*. London, Hansib Publications.
Tits-Dieuaide M.-J., 1981. L'évolution des techniques agricoles en Flandre et en Brabant: xive-xvie siècle. *Annales. Économies, société, civilisation*, 36 (3), 362-81.
Todhunter E.N., 1959. The story of nutrition. In: *Food: The Yearbook of Agriculture* (United States Department of Agriculture). Washington D.C., United States Government Printing Office, 7-22.
Tolstoï L., 1928, *Anna Karénine*, tome II. Paris, Hachette.
Tomich D., 1991. World slavery and Caribbean capitalism. *Theory and Society*, 20 (3), 297-319.
Tomich D., Zeuske M., 2008. Introduction, the second slavery: Mass slavery, World-economy, and comparative microhistories. *Review (Fernand Braudel Center)*, 31 (2), 91-100.
Tooze A., 2006. *The Wages of Destruction: The Making and Breaking of the Nazi Economy*. London, Allan Lane.
Tooze A., 2008. The economic history of the Nazi regime. In: *Nazi Germany* (Caplan J., dir.). Oxford, Oxford University Press, 168-95.
Topik S., Clarence-Smith W. (dir.), 2003. *The Global Coffee Economy in Africa, Asia and Latin America, 1500-1989*. Cambridge, Cambridge University Press.
Torp C., 2010. The "Coalition of 'Rye and Iron'" under the pressure of globalization: A reinterpretation of Germany's political economy before 1914. *Central European History*, 43 (3), 401-27.

Toutain J.-C., 1961. *Le produit de l'agriculture française de 1700 à 1958*. Paris, Institut de science économique appliquée, coll. Cahiers de l'Institut de science économique appliquée, 115.

Toutain J.-C., 1971. La consommation alimentaire en France de 1789 à 1964. *Économies et sociétés. Cahiers de l'Isea*, 5 (11), 1909-2049.

Towne M., Rasmussen W., 1960. Farm gross product and gross investment in the nineteenth century. *In: Trends in the American Economy in the Nineteenth Century* (National Bureau of Economic Research). Princeton, Princeton University Press, 255-316.

Toye J., Toye R., 2004. *The UN and Global Political Economy: Trade, Finance and Development*. Bloomington, Indiana University Press.

Toynbee A., 1887. *Lectures on the Industrial Revolution in England: Popular Addresses, Notes and other Fragments*. London, Rivingtons.

Toynbee A.J., 1977. *La grande aventure de l'humanité*. Paris, Bordas.

Tracy M., 1986. *L'État et l'agriculture en Europe occidentale. Crises et réponses au cours d'un siècle*. Paris, Economica.

Tracy J.D. (dir.), 1990. *The Rise of Merchant Empires, 1500-1800*. Cambridge, Cambridge University Press.

Traverso E., 2007. *À feu et à sang: de la guerre civile européenne 1914-1945*. Paris, Stock.

Travis A.S., 2015. *The Synthetic Nitrogen Industry in World War I: Its Emergence and Expansion*. Dordrecht, Springer.

Tucker R.P., Richards J.F. (dir.), 1983. *Global Deforestation and the Nineteenth-century World Economy*. Durham, Duke University Press.

Tucker R.P., Russell E., 2004. *Natural Enemy, Natural Ally: Toward an Environmental History of Warfare*. Corvallis, Oregon State University Press.

Tully J., 2009. A victorian ecological disaster: Imperialism, the telegraph, and gutta-percha. *Journal of World History*, 20 (4), 559-79.

Turner F.J., 1986 [1893]. The significance of the frontier in American history. *In: Frederick Jackson Turner: Wisconsin's Historian of the Frontier* (Ridge M., dir.). Madison, State Historical Society of Wisconsin.

Unger R.W., 1980. Dutch herring, technology, and international trade in the seventeenth century. *The Journal of Economic History*, 40 (2), 253-79.

Unger R.W., 1999. Feeding low countries towns: The grain trade in the fifteenth century. *Revue belge de philologie et d'histoire*, 77 (2), 329-58.

United States Department of Agriculture (USDA), 1962. *Agricultural Statistics*. Washington D.C., USDA.

United States Department of Agriculture (USDA), 1970. *Wool Statistics and Related Data 1930-1969*. Washington D.C., USDA.

United States Department of Commerce (USDC), Bureau of the Census, 1976. *The Statistical History of the United States, from Colonial Times to the Present/Historical Statistics of the United States, Colonial Times to 1970*. New York, Basic Books.

United States Department of Commerce (USDC), Bureau of the Census, 1977 *1974 Census of Agriculture, Volume 1, Part 51, United States Summary and State Data*. Washington D.C., USDC.

United States Department of Commerce, National Production Authority, 1952. *Material Survey: Rubber*. Washington D.C., National Security Resources Board.

Urwin D.W., 2014. *The Community of Europe: A History of European Integration since 1945*. London, Routledge.

Valéry P., 1931. *Regards sur le monde actuel*. Paris, Librairie Stock, Delamain et Boutelleau.

van Beusekom M., 1997. Colonisation indigene: French rural development ideology at the Office du Niger. *The International Journal of African Historical Studies*, 30 (2), 299–323.

Van Creveld M., 1998. *La transformation de la guerre*. Paris, Éditions du Rocher.

Van Driel J., 2014. Ashes to ashes: The stewardship of waste and oeconomic cycles of agricultural and industrial improvement, 1750–1800. *History and Technology*, 30 (3), 177–206.

Van Tielhof M., 2002. *The "Mother of all Trades": The Baltic Grain Trade in Amsterdam from the Late 16th to the Early 19th Century*. Boston, Brill.

Van Welie R., 2008. Slave trading and slavery in the Dutch colonial empire: A global comparison. *New West Indian Guide/Nieuwe West-Indische Gids*, 82 (1–2), 47–96.

Varshney A., 1989. Ideas, interest and institutions in policy change: Transformation of India's agricultural strategy in the mid-1960's. *Policy Sciences*, 22 (3–4), 289–323.

Vermeylen F., 2010. The colour of money: Dealing in pigments in sixteenth-century Antwerp. In: *Trade in Artists' Materials: Markets and Commerce in Europe to 1700* (Kirby J., Nash S., Cannon J., dir.). London, Archetype Publications, 356–65.

Viard A., Hénault C., Rochette P., Kuikman P., Flénet F., Cellier P., 2013. Le protoxyde d'azote (N2O), puissant gaz à effet de serre émis par les sols agricoles: méthodes d'inventaire et leviers de réduction. *Oléagineux, corps gras, lipides*, 20 (2), 108–18.

Viner J., 1948. Power versus plenty as objectives of foreign policy in the seventeenth and eighteenth centuries. *World Politics*, 1 (1), 1–29.

Vink M., 2003. "The world's oldest trade": Dutch slavery and slave trade in the Indian Ocean in the seventeenth century. *Journal of World History*, 14 (2), 131–77.

Viveret, Patrick. "Sortir de la démesure." Projet 1 (2010): 13–19.

Von Braun J., 2008. *Responding to the World Food Crisis: Getting on the Right Track*. Washington D.C., International Food Policy Research Institute.

Von Thünen J.H., 1851. *Recherches sur l'influence que le prix des grains, la richesse du sol et les impôts exercent sur les systèmes de culture*. Paris, Guillaumin.

Wade R., 1990. *Governing the Market: Economic Theory and the Role of Government in East Asian Industrialization*. Princeton, Princeton University Press.

Wakeman R., 2003. The golden age of prosperity, 1953–73. In: *Themes in Modern European History since 1945* (Wakeman R., dir). London, Routledge, 59–85.

Wall I.M., 1991. *The United States and the Making of Postwar France, 1945–1954*. Cambridge, Cambridge University Press.

Wallace H.A., 1934. *New Frontiers*. New York, Reynal & Hitchcock.

Wallerstein I., 1974. *The Modern World-System I: Capitalist Agriculture and the Origins of the European World-Economy in the Sixteenth Century*. New York, Academic Press.

Wallerstein I., 1983. The three instances of hegemony in the history of the capitalist world economy. *International Journal of Comparative Sociology*, 24 (1–2), 100–8.

Wallerstein I.M., 1989. *The Modern World-System III: The Second Era of Great Expansion of the Capitalist World-Economy, 1730–1840s*. San Diego, Academic Press.

Wallerstein I., Collins R., Mann M., Derleugian G., Calhoun C., 2013. *Does capitalism have a future?* Oxford, Oxford University Press.

Waltz K.N., 1999. Globalization and governance. *PS: Political Science & Politics*, 32 (4), 693–700.

Warde P., 2007. *Energy Consumption in England & Wales, 1560–2000*. Naples, Consiglio nazionale delle ricerche.

Warde P., 2009. Energy and natural resource dependency in Europe, 1600–1900. *Brooks World Poverty Institute Working Paper 77*. Manchester, The University of Manchester, Brooks World Poverty Institute.

Warr B., Ayres R., Eisenmenger N., Krausmann F., Schandl H., 2010. Energy use and economic development: A comparative analysis of useful work supply in Austria, Japan, the United Kingdom and the US during 100 years of economic growth. *Ecological Economics*, 69 (10), 1904-17.
Watson A.M., 1974. The Arab Agricultural Revolution and its diffusion, 700-1100. *The Journal of Economic History*, 34 (1), 8-35.
Webb W.P., 1964. *The Great Frontier*. Austin, University of Texas Press.
Webb S.B., 1982. Agricultural protection in Wilhelminian Germany: Forging an empire with pork and rye. *The Journal of Economic History*, 42 (2), 309-26.
Webb M.C., Krasner S.D., 1989. Hegemonic stability theory: An empirical assessment. *Review of International Studies*, 15 (2), 183-98.
Weber M., 1927. *General Economic History*. New York, Greenberg.
Weber M., 1963 [1919]. *Le savant et le politique*. trad. de l'allemand par J. Freund, Paris, Plon.
Wenzlhuemer R., 2013. *Connecting the Nineteenth-Century World: The Telegraph and Globalization*. Cambridge, Cambridge University Press.
Wilcox W.W., 1954. Methods of increasing domestic consumption of farm products. *Journal of Farm Economics*, 36 (3), 509-12.
Wilkins M., 2000. German chemical firms in the United States from the late 19th century to post-World War II. In: *The German Chemical Industry in the Twentieth Century* (Lesch J.E., dir.). Dordrecht, Springer, 285-321.
Williams M., 2006. *Deforesting the Earth. From Prehistory to Global Crisis: An Abridgment*. Chicago, University of Chicago Press.
Williams E.E., Brogan D.W., 1968. *Capitalisme et esclavage*. Paris, Présence africaine.
Williamson J., 2009. A short history of the Washington Consensus. *Law and Business Review of the Americas*, 15 (1), 7-23.
Wilson C., 1973. Transport as a factor in the history of economic development. *Journal of European Economic History*, 2 (2), 320.
Winders B., Nibert D., 2004. Consuming the surplus: Expanding "meat" consumption and animal oppression. *International Journal of Sociology and Social Policy*, 24 (9), 76-96.
Wolff D., 2000. Bean there: Toward a soy-based history of Northeast Asia. *South Atlantic Quarterly*, 99 (1), 241-52.
Wolman L., 1929. Consumption and standard of living. In: *Recent Economic Changes in the United States* (Committee on Recent Economic Changes of the President's Conference on Unemployment). Washington D.C., NBER, 13-78.
Wong R.B., 1997. *China Transformed: Historical Change and the Limits of European Experience*. Ithaca/London, Cornell University Press.
Wood T.B., 1917. *The National Food Supply in Peace and War*. Cambridge, Cambridge University Press.
World Bank, 1986. *World Development Report 1986*. New York, Oxford University Press.
World Bank, 2018. *Commodity Markets Outlook. The Changing of the Guard: Shifts in Commodity Demand*. Washington D.C., The World Bank.
Wrigley E.A., 1985. Urban growth and agricultural change: England and the continent in early modern period. *Journal of Interdisciplinary History*, XV, 683-728.
Wrigley E.A., 1987. *People, Cities, and Wealth: The Transformation of Traditional Society*. Oxford, Blackwell.
Wrigley E.A., 1988. *Continuity, Chance & Change: The Character of the Industrial Revolution in England*. Cambridge, Cambridge University Press.

Wrigley E.A., 1991. Energy availability and agricultural productivity. *In: Land, Labour and Livestock: Historical Studies in European Agricultural Productivity* (Campbell B., Overton M., dir.). Manchester, Manchester University Press, 323–39.

Wrigley E.A., 2004. *Poverty, Progress, and Population.* Cambridge, Cambridge University Press.

Wrigley E.A., 2006. The transition to an advanced organic economy: Half a millennium of English agriculture. *Economic History Review*, LIX (3), 435–80.

Wrigley E.A., 2010. *Energy and the English Industrial Revolution.* Cambridge, Cambridge University Press.

Yasuba Y., 1996. Did Japan ever suffer from a shortage of natural resources before World War II? *The Journal of Economic History*, 56 (3), 543–60.

Young D.B., 1976. A wood famine? The question of deforestation in Old Regime France. *Forestry: An International Journal of Forest Research*, 49 (1), 45–56.

Zapoleon L.B., 1931. International and domestic commodities and the theory of prices. *The Quarterly Journal of Economics*, 45 (3), 409–59.

Zemyatchenskii P., 1894. Velikoanadolskii uchastok. Trudy Ekspeditsii, snaryazhennoi Lesnym Departmentom, pod rukovodstvom professora Dokuchaeva. *Nauchnii otdel*, 1, 3.

Zhang H., 2018. *Securing the "Rice Bowl": China and Global Food Security.* London, Palgrave Macmillan.

Zhang H., Cheng G., 2017. China's food security strategy reform: An emerging global agricultural policy. *In: China's Global Quest for Resources: Energy, Food and Water* (Wu F., Zhang H., dir.). London, Routledge, 23–40.

Zimmerer J., 2008. Colonialism and the holocaust: Towards an archeology of genocide. *Development Dialogue*, 50, 95–124.

Zimmerman E.W., 1951. *World Resources and Industries: A Functional Appraisal of Availability of Agricultural and Industrial Resources.* New York, Harper and Brothers.

Index

A

Africa 13, 16, 55, 65, 98, 103, 110, 114, 118, 124–30, 139, 141, 150–1, 155–6, 158–9, 186, 194–6, 231, 265, 267, 275, 281, 286, 293, 301–2, 305, 315, 317, 354, 363

Agricultural policy 4, 168, 185, 251, 317, 323, 350

Agricultural revolution 15, 30, 49, 71–2, 74, 78–80, 174, 176, 245, 305, 325, 359–60

Agriculture 1–4, 6–11, 14–16, 27, 29, 39, 43–4, 64–5, 71, 74–83, 86, 92, 95–9, 122, 133, 136, 138, 152–3, 156, 158, 166, 168, 170, 173–4, 176–7, 179, 182–3, 185–6, 188, 194, 196, 198, 200, 208, 211, 213–19, 221–9, 232–4, 241, 243, 245, 248–50, 258–63, 266–7, 269, 278, 280, 304, 308, 317, 320, 323–5, 335, 340–4, 356, 358–64

Argentina 9, 15, 98, 110, 111, 115, 119, 125, 127–31, 140, 155, 166, 186, 194, 198, 216–17, 265, 275–6, 282, 322, 336–8, 350

Asia 10, 13, 16, 21, 29, 39–45, 49, 55, 57, 61, 95–6, 98–100, 103, 110, 120, 125–128, 131, 138, 150–1, 158–9, 190, 194, 198–9, 201, 207, 248, 231, 267, 269–70, 274, 276, 281, 286, 291, 293, 301–4, 314–18, 339, 341–2, 356

B

Baltic 21, 24–5, 27–9, 31–3, 35–8, 44, 49, 91–2, 96, 110, 188

Biofuel 16, 292, 317, 331, 333–4, 356

Biomass 1, 4–17, 21–2, 26–9, 31, 37, 44–5, 49–50, 54, 67, 69, 73–4, 86–100, 103–16, 122, 124, 126, 129–30, 132–6, 142, 155, 159–60, 165–94, 201, 208–9, 216, 227–8, 235, 238–44, 252–3, 264, 278, 281, 285, 288, 292, 317–35, 339, 342–50, 355–6, 359–64

Burma 15, 114, 125, 129, 132, 204, 207, 347

C

Capital 2–4, 37, 40, 51, 62, 64–5, 100, 114, 139, 145, 154–60, 194, 201, 203–4, 231, 236, 248–9, 275, 297, 364

Capitalism 2–4, 22, 33–4, 51, 114, 138–9, 153, 253, 305, 308, 310, 360

Center 3, 21, 41, 253, 271, 276, 288, 301, 324, 341–2

Cereal 29, 31–4, 45, 74, 80, 92–3, 95, 103, 122, 132, 136, 168–9, 184–8, 196, 212, 214, 242, 263, 267, 326, 331, 337, 351

Chemical farming 1, 232, 244, 249, 259, 288, 292, 317, 320, 350, 356, 358

Chemical industry 165, 170, 220–3, 227, 240, 248, 285, 321–2, 335, 356, 359

China 4, 16–17, 22, 50, 58, 124–5, 127–8, 147, 151, 171, 201, 203–7, 269, 277, 292, 301, 303–8, 310–13, 323–5, 326, 331–3, 341, 343–9, 351, 353, 363

Coal 2, 5, 6–7, 15, 30, 50, 71, 74, 81–5, 99, 105, 108, 119, 164–5, 171–5, 189, 191–2, 201–2, 220, 227–8, 235, 238–40, 252, 256, 285, 304, 310–11, 323–4, 326, 335, 360

Coercion 11, 13, 22, 40, 45, 59, 138, 151, 153, 181

Colonial 15, 42, 49, 53–8, 66, 69, 87, 92, 99–100, 103, 109, 114, 118, 129, 140–1, 147–8, 151, 155, 158–60, 178, 186, 193–8, 203, 208, 253, 274–5, 286, 303, 345, 360–1

Colonization 8, 10, 49–50, 59, 62, 64–6, 103, 128, 130–2, 151, 153, 164, 184, 188–9, 194, 196–7, 201–3, 205, 208, 211, 253, 270, 301, 321

Competition 3, 10, 13, 33, 38, 40–1, 45, 49, 52, 64, 100, 133, 139, 153, 166–7, 170, 192, 194–5, 197, 216, 218, 220, 234, 244, 248, 285, 294, 296–7, 299, 308, 324, 356, 363

Corn 10, 50, 54, 79–80, 87, 100, 103, 105, 133, 178, 185, 192, 209, 212, 216–20,

224–6, 240, 244–5, 248, 263, 283, 322, 324, 326, 328, 330–4, 336, 342, 344, 345, 347, 354
Cotton 28, 49, 54–5, 58, 74, 89–90, 94–8, 100, 105, 108, 110, 120, 143–5, 165, 190–1, 196–9, 201, 202, 209, 211–13, 218, 220–1, 223, 232, 238, 240, 250, 282, 285–6, 324, 332–3, 342, 346, 355, 360
Currency 15, 23, 49, 56, 100, 234, 297, 309, 336–7

D

Division of labor 15, 24–5, 69, 77, 104, 135, 160, 165, 188, 232, 248, 253, 264, 288, 297
Dye 29, 74, 95, 170–2, 220–1

E

East Asia 199, 201, 207, 291, 301–4, 314, 317–18
Empire 9, 21, 23, 62, 81, 112–15, 131, 140, 155–6, 167–9, 178, 188, 193–5, 197–9, 203, 259, 293, 360
Energy 1, 4–8, 11, 15–16, 30, 44, 56, 73–4, 76, 81–4, 99, 100, 105, 159, 164, 167, 172, 173, 175–6, 183, 194, 214, 216–20, 228, 231, 235, 238–40, 247, 249–50, 261, 288, 297, 311–12, 328, 358–9, 360, 364
Europe 1–5, 10, 12, 15–16, 21–9, 33–4, 39–41, 45, 54, 58, 62, 65, 67–8, 73, 76, 78, 86–7, 89–90, 92, 103–60, 163, 168, 173, 181, 186, 220, 222, 228, 235, 242, 244–5, 255–7, 259, 262, 264, 275, 280, 283, 285–6, 293, 299, 301–5, 317, 334, 338, 341–2, 356, 361–4

F

Fertilizer 30, 80, 132, 165, 173–4, 176–7, 185, 200, 204, 206, 213, 222, 225, 227–8, 244–5, 258, 260, 317–20, 325–6, 359, 361
Fishing 9, 36–8, 45, 91, 203, 359
Food 1–8, 12, 15–16, 22, 29, 31, 36, 38, 49, 50–3, 60, 68–9, 73–4, 80, 86–7, 88, 90–100, 103, 105–10, 112, 122, 146, 158, 160, 167, 170–3, 178, 179–89, 198, 206, 209, 217, 231–88, 317, 325, 328, 331–3, 336–7, 342–7, 350–4, 357, 359–64

Food regime 2–7, 15
Forest 4, 35–6, 44, 64–5, 83–4, 86, 106, 125–6, 132, 145, 151, 158, 174, 209, 228, 238, 335, 346, 355–6
Fossil fuel 16, 165, 201, 213, 218, 235, 261, 292, 359, 360, 364
France 4, 13, 15, 24, 26–9, 36–8, 40, 45, 49–100, 103, 117, 132, 140, 149, 153, 155, 169, 171, 181, 188, 193–207, 211, 250, 254–60, 265, 273, 299, 318, 320, 325, 327, 335–6, 358–60
Frontier 9, 12, 16–17, 34–5, 64, 119, 124–5, 127, 129–32, 144–5, 147, 158, 166, 168, 172, 206, 208–28, 235, 245, 317, 361

G

Germany 4, 15, 24, 27, 29, 117, 131, 140, 149, 163–228, 234, 240, 254, 258–60, 268, 283, 286, 306, 322, 360
Globalization 16, 109–12, 116, 154, 179, 194, 228, 231, 237, 255, 257, 264–5, 291–357, 363
Great Britain 49–50, 54, 82–8, 92, 94, 96, 100, 103, 105, 108, 113, 117, 159, 166, 172, 206, 220, 360

H

Hegemon 1, 3–4, 6, 15, 45, 101, 105, 133, 138, 159–60, 164–5, 232, 234, 237, 248, 252, 292, 360, 363
Hegemony 3–4, 6–7, 15–16, 103, 135, 159–60, 163–6, 168–9, 186, 193, 197, 204, 231–87, 264

I

Import substitution 50, 95, 99, 165, 178, 264–6, 276, 291
Indentured labor 11–12, 60, 100, 119, 138, 141
Industrial revolution 1, 6, 11, 15, 50, 71, 74, 78, 81, 83, 85, 89, 94–5, 103, 147, 163, 165, 209, 327, 359
Industrialization 2, 16, 27–8, 94, 160, 166–92, 201, 216, 238, 248, 264–7, 276, 283, 291, 299, 303, 305–7, 314
Inequality 297–9, 309, 313, 363
International organization 273, 234, 253, 272, 278, 283, 288, 309, 335, 351, 355

International trade 2, 16, 96, 99–100, 103, 136, 143, 158, 177, 202, 228, 232, 234, 237, 257, 264, 276–9, 282–8, 291, 296, 312, 336–8, 340, 343

Island 40, 42, 55, 58, 61–2, 64–5, 67, 69, 91, 100, 139, 140–2, 144, 146–8, 152, 159, 172, 200–4

J

Japan 44, 126, 155, 171, 191, 193, 199–201, 203–7, 225, 234, 254–5, 257–8, 260, 268, 282–3, 291, 293–4, 302–6, 314, 342–3, 363

L

Labour 249, 274

Land 9–10, 12, 22, 24–5, 29–30, 34, 53, 59, 62, 64–5, 74, 77–80, 84, 86, 89, 99–100, 116, 122, 124–6, 128, 130–2, 140, 145–7, 149–50, 58, 174, 187–8, 198, 202–4, 211–18, 220, 224–6, 231–2, 235, 244, 260, 263, 268–70, 306, 320, 325–6, 341, 344–5, 350, 356, 359–60, 364

Latin America 16, 34, 115, 125, 129, 147, 154, 231, 264–6, 269–70, 274, 276, 281, 293, 317–18, 356, 363

Long-distance trade 14, 33, 37, 39, 87, 104, 121, 138, 142, 149, 152, 158, 168, 170, 172, 181, 201, 209, 282, 285, 359

M

Manufacture 34, 82, 96, 132, 189, 190, 194, 197, 222–3, 240, 293, 304

Mediterranean 21, 24–5, 29, 31, 39, 49, 61, 98, 110, 131, 144, 301

Mercantilism 45, 51–70, 103, 105, 114, 167, 237, 359

Metabolic regime 5–6, 8, 15–16, 22, 30, 86, 99, 103, 105, 159, 176, 231, 235–6, 249, 265, 285, 288, 292, 297–8, 305, 310, 313, 315, 317, 326–8, 332, 356, 358–64

Metropole 54, 56, 58, 67–8, 100, 112, 114, 120, 193, 196, 198, 275, 359–60

Migration 2, 9, 12, 38, 60, 86, 115, 119, 124–7, 129–30, 145–60, 176, 196, 201, 204, 206, 270, 307, 360

N

Nation-state 2, 21, 51, 167

Neo-European countries 98, 127, 155, 163, 169, 301, 314

Neoliberalism 16, 291, 296, 298–300

Nitrogen 74–5, 172–4, 177, 185, 188–90, 214, 220–3, 225, 227, 245, 317, 319, 325, 358, 361

North-South 233, 253–77

O

Oil 5–7, 16, 27, 29, 31, 38, 44, 70, 89, 91, 105, 150, 165, 179, 188, 190, 194, 206, 208, 216, 228, 232, 239, 242, 249, 252, 256, 269, 280–1, 284, 288, 291–5, 300, 303, 310–14, 321, 323, 332–3, 336–8, 347, 353, 355–6, 364

Organic chemistry 6, 170–3, 220, 223

P

Periphery 21, 23, 25, 80, 253, 264, 276, 280, 288, 359–60

Pesticide 16, 166, 220, 223, 232, 244, 267, 317–18, 320–1, 325, 358, 361

Plantation 11–13, 15, 21, 41–2, 49–50, 56, 58–62, 65–7, 119, 132, 138, 140–3, 145, 150–2–156–8, 208–9

Population 8–9, 12–13, 25, 27–8, 34, 42, 44, 54, 59, 63, 65, 71–3, 75, 76–7, 79, 81, 85, 87, 112, 114, 127–31, 135, 138, 144, 147–50, 159–60, 163–4, 166–7, 181, 184–7, 189, 193, 196, 201–3, 206–8, 212, 214–15, 244, 262, 264, 268, 275, 296, 297, 302, 305–6, 308–9, 327, 331–2, 343, 353, 354, 361, 363

Power 1–4, 6, 8–9, 12, 15–16, 21–45, 51–2, 56, 65, 68, 72, 74, 76, 78, 81, 87, 96, 99–100, 103, 105, 114, 118, 124, 138, 140, 142, 149–50, 163, 165, 176, 179, 181, 183–4, 187, 194, 201, 206, 219–20, 228, 231, 244, 254, 269–70, 282, 288, 291, 294, 298, 300, 305–6, 345, 358–60, 364

Price risk 14, 33, 67

Protection 12, 14, 132, 139, 167, 170, 176, 195, 203, 220–1, 223–4, 257–9, 264, 267, 275, 278, 281, 283–4, 291, 299, 359

R

Railway, railroad 14, 83, 103, 109, 116–18, 147, 155, 204–5, 208–9, 217

Resources 2, 4–6, 9, 15, 22, 24–5, 30, 36, 44–5, 52, 64–5, 71–86, 95, 99–100, 105, 127, 131, 159–60, 165, 168, 172, 181, 187–8, 196, 200–1, 203–4, 206–7, 217–18, 228, 235, 241, 266, 271, 274, 285, 288, 291, 297–8, 303, 310–11, 322, 338, 344–5, 353, 360–1

Rivalry 1, 4, 15, 86, 99, 163–228, 234, 359, 364

Russia 9, 15, 21, 83, 96, 104, 110, 116, 125–7, 129, 131–2, 138, 140, 149, 150, 155, 159, 169, 178, 182, 186–7, 199, 201, 204–5, 231, 299, 313, 315, 328, 350, 363

S

Sea 4, 21, 24–5, 27, 28, 30–8, 45, 61, 75, 91, 94, 110, 116, 118, 125, 131, 132, 154, 201, 209, 301, 304, 311, 355

Seeds 8, 16, 145, 158, 166, 196, 198, 203, 223–6, 228, 232, 241, 244, 245, 271, 320–4

Self-sufficiency 16, 49, 50, 95, 168, 174, 181, 183–5, 188–90, 203, 227, 232, 258, 271, 278, 283, 292, 323, 344–9, 350, 361, 363

Serfdom 11, 12, 33–4, 138, 142, 149–50, 168

Slave 12, 42–3, 50, 55, 58–70, 91, 98, 130, 139, 140–9, 151–2, 160, 166, 170, 208–9, 302, 360

Slavery 11, 13, 42, 65, 103, 119, 138–44, 146–7, 151, 178, 209

Social metabolism 1, 5, 7, 15, 31–2, 86–98, 100, 252, 288, 345, 358–9

Soybean 17, 184, 201, 205, 206, 224–6, 245, 258–9, 283, 318, 321–2, 324–6, 331, 342, 344, 347, 353, 355–6

Spices 13, 21, 23, 25, 39–43, 45, 49, 87, 90–1, 100, 170

State intervention 166, 178, 181, 208, 217, 224, 231–2, 244–5, 254, 297, 308

Steam engine, steam machine 15, 50, 83, 84, 98, 105, 116–19, 137, 142, 147, 159, 176, 209, 218, 360

Substitute 6, 15, 16, 50, 84, 123, 181, 189–92, 195, 200, 223, 227, 278, 285, 335, 343, 356, 360

Sugar 25, 28, 31, 45, 49, 50, 54, 56–65, 67–9, 78, 87, 88, 90, 92, 100, 108, 110, 112–13, 140–147, 150, 169, 170, 173–9, 187, 192, 200–1, 204, 209, 216, 243, 280, 285, 327–8, 334, 336–7, 353, 355, 360

Supply chain 54–5, 92, 103, 109–12, 116, 159, 165, 168, 179–81, 182, 193–4, 197, 198, 204, 206, 227, 312, 321, 337

Synthetic products 15, 165–6, 171, 189–90, 92, 227, 232, 240, 359

T

Territory 5–6, 8–9, 12, 15–16, 21–2, 24–30, 33–4, 37, 39–40, 44–5, 49–100, 112–15, 118, 125, 127, 140, 142–3, 149, 164–6, 174–82, 186–9, 198, 200–2, 204, 206, 208, 216–17, 228, 244, 268, 274–5, 343, 359, 360, 363

Textile 28–9, 38, 45, 56–7, 85, 86, 95–7, 106, 108, 144, 164, 170, 172, 184, 189–192, 194, 198, 201, 220, 240, 264, 285–6, 291, 303, 306, 321, 342, 360

Tractor 16, 166, 176, 218–20, 228, 232, 244–5, 263

Transportation 22, 53, 66, 92, 116, 118–20, 142, 182, 209, 239

U

United Kingdom 1–4, 15, 49, 54, 106, 108–14, 118, 120, 122–3, 133–5, 154–7, 160, 163–5, 167–71, 173, 177, 178–9, 181, 186, 193, 201, 203, 211, 234–8, 258, 273, 285, 299, 306, 363

United Provinces 3, 7, 15, 21–32, 35–8, 40, 42, 44–5, 49, 51–3, 72–3, 86, 96, 99–100, 124, 159, 167, 170, 200, 303, 359

United States of America 2–4, 15–16, 55, 61, 69, 98, 100, 108, 110–11, 116–20, 123, 126–30, 135, 139, 142–5, 152–6, 160, 163–6, 169, 171, 177, 181, 186–7, 190–2, 194, 206–26, 228, 231–44, 246–9, 252–61, 263–4, 269–71, 273–5, 279–81, 283, 285–8, 292–6, 298–300, 303–6, 310–12, 318, 321–2, 324–5, 328, 333–4, 336–8, 341, 349–50, 357, 360–3

Urbanization 16, 25–7, 29, 32, 44, 71–3, 75, 94, 124

V

Violence 10–11, 39–42, 60, 144, 159–60, 180

W

War 2, 4, 11, 16, 28, 40, 56, 83, 100, 106, 108, 110, 112, 118, 123, 126–9, 133, 144–5, 151, 154, 156, 163–6, 168, 173, 177–87, 189–97, 203, 205–9, 211–12, 216–18, 220–5, 227–8, 231–2, 234–5, 237, 241–3, 245, 247, 251, 253–5, 257–8, 260, 262–5, 268, 270–5, 278–80, 282–3, 285–6, 291, 295, 299, 302–3, 305, 321, 323, 327, 338, 342, 345, 360–1

Wealth 1, 3–4, 16, 22, 44–5, 51–4, 58, 71, 99–100, 116, 228, 264, 276, 288, 291, 294, 314, 317, 342, 359–60, 364

Wheat 22, 73, 75, 88, 92, 94, 106, 110–13, 118, 122–3, 132, 134, 209, 212–13, 215, 242–4, 260, 271, 282–4, 324, 336–7, 345, 351, 353

World-economy 3, 6, 9, 21–3, 39–43, 49, 138, 234, 301

Y

Yield 11, 16, 74–5, 83, 174, 176–7, 204, 212–14, 225–6, 245, 248–9, 260–3, 270, 361